PURCHASING

PURCHASING

SIXTH EDITION

Selection and Procurement

for the Hospitality Industry

Andrew Hale Feinstein

John M. Stefanelli

WILEY

JOHN WILEY & SONS, INC.

Published by John Wiley & Sons, Inc., Hoboken, New Jersey
Published simultaneously in Canada

For general information on our other products and services or for technical support, please contact our Customer Care Department within the United States at (800) 762-2974, outside the United States at (317) 572-3993 or fax (317) 572-4002.

Wiley also publishes its books in a variety of electronic formats. Some content that appears in print may not be available in electronic books. For more information about Wiley products, visit our web site at www.wiley.com.

Library of Congress Cataloging-in-Publication Data:
Feinstein, Andrew Hale.
    Purchasing : selection and procurement for the hospitality industry / Andrew
Hale Feinstein, John M. Stefanelli. — 6th ed.
        p. cm.
    Published simultaneously in Canada.
    Includes index.
    ISBN 0-471-46005-2 (cloth)
  1. Hospitality industry—Purchasing. 2. Hospitality industry—Purchasing.
I. Stefanelli, John M. II. Title.
    TX911.3.P8F45 2005
    647.95′068′7—dc22

Printed in the United States of America
10 9 8 7 6 5 4 3 2 1

CONTENTS

PREFACE

IN 1976, AFTER CONSULTING WITH Dr. Tom Powers, Consulting Editor for the Wiley Service Management Series, John Stefanelli undertook the tremendous task of writing a purchasing textbook that combines generally accepted purchasing principles and procedures with some description of the products and services the typical hospitality enterprise normally purchased. Critics lauded Purchasing: Selection and Procurement for the Hospitality Industry as an excellent investment and resource for hospitality managers and students who would like a hands-on approach to understanding the purchasing function.

Since this first edition of the book, many hospitality educators have adopted this approach to purchasing instruction. Many colleagues, both in education and industry, continue to find that it is valuable for their students, most of whom will not become purchasing agents but who will be involved with some phase of purchasing throughout their careers. As one colleague put it, this book is a purchasing book for nonpurchasing agents. The book provides a comprehensive and understandable view of the activity, as well as its relationship to the management of a successful operation.

The sixth edition of Purchasing: Selection and Procurement for the Hospitality Industry maintains the original objectives: It includes discussions of the purchasing activity and product information from a management perspective. Each chapter has been revised to include the most current concepts available and to explore new topics and provide more in-depth coverage of hospitality purchasing. In essence, great care has been taken to maintain the integrity and readability of the original text while modernizing the discussions of purchasing techniques and practices currently being employed in the hospitality industry. Although many of the theoretical underpinnings of the purchasing function have not changed in decades—product distribution channels and forces that affect the price of goods remain relatively unchanged, and specifications and purchase orders are still required to order these goods—the use of technology in implementing and maintaining effective purchasing policies and procedures has changed drastically. To inform readers about these changes, technology applications in the purchasing function are now discussed throughout the majority of the first 16 chapters that encompass purchasing principles.

WHAT'S NEW FOR THE SIXTH EDITION

Many important changes and additions have been made to Purchasing: Selection and Procurement for the Hospitality Industry to make the text even more useful. Among the most significant changes are:

- The sixth edition again pays careful attention to the rapid evolvement of the hospitality purchasing field, particularly in the area of technology. The latest technology and techniques are discussed in detail. This discussion is not only housed in a separate chapter (Chapter 2) but also has been included in each of the first 16 chapters.

- New to this edition, Industry Insights are available at the end of select chapters. These insights provide insider information on current and future trends related to purchasing.

- Sidebars have been included in several chapters to discuss technology companies and their applications to the purchasing function, the perspectives of industry experts on the future of purchasing, and new techniques for calculating the amount of products to purchase.

- Detailed references at the end of each chapter have been increased and updated to provide readers with current materials to supplement their readings.

- Throughout the text, dozens of links to key Websites provide readers with access to current information.

- Dozens of completely revised figures provide clear illustrations and photographs of concepts, companies, and products relating to the purchasing function.

- Revised Questions and Problems sections provide discussion topics and exercises to increase participation. Further, the first 16 chapters have several experiential exercises to assist readers in actively learning about the function of purchasing.

- A completely revised Instructor's Manual (0-471-69315-4) that provides several syllabi examples, teaching suggestions, test questions, PowerPoint slides, and term projects is available to qualified instructors through their Wiley sales representative or wiley.com/college/feinstein.

- A companion Website provides readers with further information on dozens of topics affecting the purchasing function.

- The National Restaurant Association (NRA) Educational Foundation, in consultation with the authors, has developed a Student Workbook for its ProMgmt certificate program. The workbook contains exercises and a study outline for each chapter, and a practice test of 80 multiple-choice questions. This practice test will assist students in preparing for the certificate examination.

- In addition, an Instructor's Guide (0-471-69313-8) is available to qualified instructors to complement and highlight the information in the textbook and Student Workbook.

ACKNOWLEDGMENTS

The authors would like to thank the following individuals for their continued assistance in developing and refining this text:

Connie Cahill and Alice Heinz of The American Egg Board

Dave and Doug Coon at Anderson Dairy

Mark Watkins at http://www.sheffieldplaters.com/

Ty Buel and Bill Cockroft at Mammoth Mountain Ski Area

Greg Koontz at the Foodservice Symposium

Danny Campbell at the MGM Grand

Rachael Buzzetti at the Nevada Beef Council

(Butcher) Bob Butler at Wolf Pack Meats

Jim Caldwell at Domino's Pizza

Karyl Toms at Eatec

George Baggott, formerly at Cres Cor

Michael Ferguson at Barley's Casino and Brewing Company

Adam Carmer at the Freakin' Frog

Janet Westfall at the National Restaurant Association Educational Foundation

Paul McGinnis at DayDots

Jean Hertzman at UNLV

Judy Feliz at UNLV

Barry McCool at UNLV

Ervine Crawford at UNLV

Mark Hamilton at Aloha

Diane Bush of Kendall College

Ezat Moradi of Houston Community College

William Niemer of The Art Institutes International Minnesota

Greg Forte of Utah Valley State College

Nigar Hale, JoAnna Turtletaub, Julie Kerr, and Tzviya Siegman at John Wiley & Sons.

THE CONCEPTS OF SELECTION AND PROCUREMENT

The Purpose of this Chapter

After reading this chapter, you should be able to:

- Define the terms "purchasing," "selection," and "procurement."
- Identify commercial and noncommercial hospitality operations.
- Explain how technology and e-commerce applications are changing in the hospitality industry.

INTRODUCTION

To most hospitality students, the term "purchasing" means paying for an item or service. This conveys a far too restrictive meaning because it fails to suggest the complete scope of the buying function. Perhaps the terms "selection" and "procurement" are better.

"Selection" can be defined as choosing from among various alternatives on various levels. For example, a buyer can select from among several competing brands of beef, a specific quality of beef, a particular beef supplier, and a fresh or processed beef product. One buyer may not perform all these activities—make all these choices—at one time. But he or she will be involved in most of them at some level.

"Procurement," as opposed to "selection," can be defined as an orderly, systematic exchange between a seller and a buyer. It is the process of obtaining goods and services, including all of the activities associated with determining the types of products needed, making purchases, receiving and storing shipments, and administering purchase contracts.

Most people see procurement as the nuts and bolts of the buyer's job. Once buyers know what they want, they set about locating the suppliers who can best fulfill their needs. Buyers then attempt to order the correct amounts of products or services at the appropriate times and best prices, see to it that shipments are timely, and ensure that the delivered items meet company requirements. A host of related duties surround these activities: being on the lookout for new items and new ideas, learning the production needs of other departments, appraising the reliability of suppliers, identifying new technologies for procurement, and so on.

Few operations have full-time buyers; most have managers and supervisors who do the buying in addition to their other duties. To these employees, buying means more than the term "procurement" by itself implies. These employees must also be aware of the relationship between purchasing and the other activities in the hospitality operation.

Because there are so few full-time purchasing agents in our field, a textbook that focuses solely on hospitality buying principles and procedures or product identification, although useful to some, would unnecessarily restrict operating managers and supervisors in hospitality. In other words, it is not enough to know how to procure beef. The typical operating manager must also consider what form of beef to purchase, as well as whether or not beef should even be on the menu.

Today, operating managers must also deal with technology that has revolutionized how buyers and suppliers procure products and services. This technology enables purchasing managers to complete complex procurement functions with a few clicks of the mouse. Most of these types of functions are taking place over the Internet.

Transactions done electronically are commonly referred to as "e-commerce" (electronic commerce). "B2B e-commerce" is the term used for business-to-business electronic transactions and "B2C e-commerce" refers to business to consumer e-commerce. Amazon.com, for example, relies on B2C e-commerce to sell its products to consumers. B2B e-commerce that focuses specifically on procurement activities is referred to as "e-procurement" (electronic procurement). Examples of companies that provide e-procurement applications to a wide variety of industry segments include:

Perfect Commerce (www.perfect.com)
CommerceOne (www.commerceone.com)

SAP (www.sap.com/solutions/marketplace/)

Ariba (www.ariba.com)

VerticalNet (www.verticalnet.com)

Sterling Commerce (www.sterlingcommerce.com/)

These companies have successfully revolutionized the way procurement is conducted by harnessing the power of the Internet. One major company that focuses on the development of e-procurement applications in the foodservice industry is Instill (www.instill.com). Companies such as Applebee's, Sodexho, Hilton, and the purchasing arm for Yum! Brands rely on Instill's e-procurement applications to streamline their selection and procurement functions. Avendra (www.avendra.com) has primarily focused on building e-procurement applications for hotels. The company was formed by ClubCorp USA, Inc., Fairmont Hotels & Resorts, Hyatt Hotels Corporation, Marriott International, Inc., and Six Continents Hotels.

We discuss technology applications as they relate to purchasing in more detail in Chapter 2. Further, to better explain how technology has radically changed selection and procurement in the hospitality industry, we explore new software, hardware, and e-procurement applications throughout this textbook. We also examine the effect and ramifications this technology has had on operating managers who are directly involved in hospitality selection and procurement functions.

TYPES OF HOSPITALITY OPERATIONS

The hospitality industry includes three major segments. The first is the commercial segment—the profit-oriented companies. The second is the institutional segment—those facilities that are operated on a break-even basis. The third is the military segment—those operations that include troop feeding and housing, as well as the various military clubs and military exchanges that exist within military installations. The second and third segments are collectively referred to as "noncommercial" hospitality operations (see Figure 1.1).

The following types of operations are generally considered part of the commercial segment:

1. Hotels
2. Motels
3. Casinos
4. Resorts

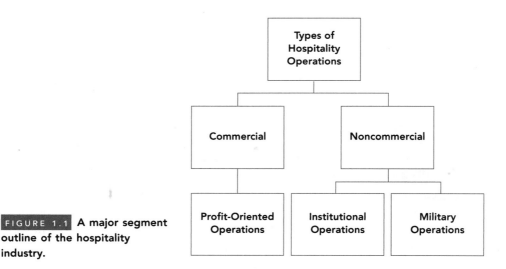

FIGURE 1.1 A major segment outline of the hospitality industry.

5. Lodges

6. Spas

7. Quick-service (limited-service) restaurants

8. Table-service (full-service) restaurants

9. Snack bars

10. Food courts

11. Taverns, lounges, and bars

12. Cafeterias

13. Buffets

14. On-premises caterers

15. Off-premises caterers

16. Vending-machine companies

17. Ice cream parlors and stands

18. In-transit food services (e.g., cruise ships and airlines)

19. Contract foodservice companies, which typically operate in plants, office buildings, day care facilities, assisted care facilities, senior care facilities, schools, recreation centers, hospitals, and sports centers

20. Convenience stores with food services

21. Supermarkets with food services
22. Department stores and discount stores with food services

The following types of operations are generally considered part of the non-commercial division of the hospitality industry:

1. Employee-feeding operations
2. Public and parochial elementary- and secondary-school food services
3. College and university dormitories and food services
4. Transportation food services, such as the Meals on Wheels program
5. Hospitals
6. Extended-care facilities
7. Clubs
8. Self-operated community centers, such as senior centers and day care centers
9. Military installations
10. Camps
11. Public institutions, such as the food services in some government facilities
12. Adult communities
13. Correctional facilities
14. Religious facilities
15. Shelters

MAJOR PURCHASING DISTINCTIONS IN HOSPITALITY-OPERATION TYPES

In Chapter 6, we offer a more detailed discussion of the distinctions in the purchasing function that the industry makes among the various types of hospitality operations. Here in this introductory chapter, however, we attempt only to provide you with sufficient understanding to carry you through to Chapter 6. When we discuss hospitality operations in their traditional mode, we think first of the independent operation. In addition, those in the trade usually arrange the independent operations according to size: the small, medium, and large independents. The other major type of hospitality operation includes the multiunits and the franchises, which we discuss second.

The Independent Operation

The small independent is typically run by an owner-manager who usually does all of the buying for the business. He or she also oversees the other related purchasing activities, such as receiving deliveries and paying the bills.

The medium independent generally involves more than one person in the purchasing function. Usually, the general manager coordinates the various activities that other management personnel perform. For instance, he or she typically coordinates the purchases of department heads, such as the dining room manager who needs ashtrays, the bartender who requires liquor, and the chef who needs food. The general manager also oversees other related purchasing activities.

The large independent, such as a hotel, follows the purchasing function in much the same way the medium independent does, except that it may employ a full-time buyer. This buyer purchases for the various production departments, such as housekeeping, maintenance, engineering, and food service. Alternately, a designated employee from each of these departments may be doing the purchasing: for example, a hotel may employ an executive steward to order supplies and to supervise the sanitation crew. Most familiar is the large independent operation that has a full-time food buyer, a beverage buyer, and an equipment and other nonfood supplies buyer. A purchasing vice president or an equivalent official may or may not supervise these three buyers. The buyers are, almost certainly, supervised by a management person.

In the past, small- and medium-sized businesses may have had a tough time competing in the same markets as larger companies. This was mainly because these smaller businesses had to pay higher prices for many of the products that they procured because they were not afforded the same discounts as large companies (we talk more about these types of discounts in Chapter 7). However, e-procurement technology has leveled the playing field in many instances by enabling these smaller companies to procure products at more competitive prices, and therefore to compete with larger hospitality operations.

Today, hospitality buyers can select and procure many quality goods and services from suppliers and distributors all over the world. These buyers and sellers can come together in virtual marketplaces online (commonly referred to as "e-marketplaces"), which allow suppliers the opportunity to sell their wares to a variety of hospitality operations. Examples of these marketplaces include Foodservice Central (www.foodservicecentral.com) and Restaurants and Institutions Marketplace (www.rimarketplace.com).

An idea addressed more completely in Chapter 6 is co-op buying, a concept that enjoys popularity among some independent hospitality operations, particularly some foodservice operations. As the phrase implies, co-op buying is a system whereby hospitality operations come together to achieve savings through the purchase of food and supplies in bulk. Either the operations rotate the purchasing duties among themselves, or they hire someone (or a company) to coordinate all of the purchasing for them. For instance, some lodging properties belong to referral groups that provide, among other things, some central purchasing activities.

E-commerce has significantly affected co-op buying. Companies are currently aggregating purchasing processes for similar hospitality organizations throughout the country. These companies are commonly referred to as "aggregate purchasing companies" or "group purchasing organizations" (GPOs).

These aggregate purchasing companies do not buy or sell products. Instead, they negotiate contracts on behalf of restaurants, hotels, management companies, resorts, and Real Estate Investment Trusts (REITs). Each company enrolling in this "electronic co-op" might receive a purchasing guide that includes the names, e-mail addresses, and telephone numbers of suppliers, along with a brief description of the programs negotiated on purchasing companies' behalf. Buyers can then access a private e-commerce marketplace—or portal—to conduct business with approved distributors or suppliers. As more buyers become members of the GPO, purchasing power increases and so do savings. Typically, either buyers pay a participation fee that provides access to the aggregate purchasing companies' pricing or the GPO takes a percentage of the savings achieved.

The Multiunits and Franchises

The second major category of hospitality operations in the purchasing function includes the multiunit companies and franchises. These interlocking operations organize their purchasing somewhat differently from independent organizations. One usually finds, when examining a chain of hospitals, for example, a centrally located vice president of purchasing. Moreover, the company may maintain one or more central commissaries or distribution warehouses. The managers of the company-owned outlets receive supplies from the central distribution points under the authority of the vice president of purchasing. But these managers may also do a minimal amount of purchasing from local or national suppliers that this vice president approves; in some cases the managers may order from approved suppliers without consulting the vice president of purchasing, or they may order everything from a central commissary.

In company-owned unit outlets, the internal organization for buying, particularly for restaurants, stipulates that the unit manager order most products from the central commissary or approved suppliers. The unit managers may, however, have the authority to make a few purchases on their own, such as a cleaning service or a locally produced beer. But when the unit managers do this sort of purchasing, they nevertheless need to follow company policies and procedures.

In company-owned, large-hotel properties, a system similar to that of the large independents generally exists. That is, the vice president of purchasing at corporate headquarters may draw up some national contracts, establish purchase specifications, and set general purchasing policy. He or she may also purchase the stock for the central distribution warehouses and/or the central commissaries that the company owns. But by and large, vice presidents of purchasing handle overall policy, while the individual hotel units, although they do not have complete freedom, exercise a great deal of purchasing discretion within established limitations.

The typical franchise receives many supplies from a central commissary, but many of these non-company-owned units try to do some purchasing locally—to maintain good relations in the community, if nothing else. However, they quickly discover that they save considerable time, money, and energy by using the central commissary and/or central distribution center as much as possible. If no central commissaries and distribution centers are available, the franchises usually order their needed stock from suppliers that the vice president of purchasing has prescreened and approved. The franchises are, however, usually free to buy from anyone as long as that supplier meets the company's requirements.

THE USE OF THIS BOOK

This book has been designed for those students who expect to have careers in the hospitality industry. Because we seek to address all of those individuals, not merely the readers who expect to specialize in hospitality purchasing, we have added several areas of discussion not usually found in a book aimed specifically at the professional purchasing agent.

We emphasize the managerial principles of the purchasing function and intertwine the purchasing function with the other related management activities that the hospitality operator faces on a day-to-day basis. We also de-emphasize product characteristics.

The typical way to instruct hospitality purchasing agents is to teach them all about the various products that will be purchased—that is, to focus on the development of product knowledge, since an item cannot be purchased effectively without the purchaser's knowing a great deal about it. We have not eschewed the product knowledge approach in this volume. But we have presented this approach in such a way that the typical hospitality operator will learn just enough about the major product categories so that he or she can easily take on the burden, if necessary, of preparing the appropriate product specification required to select and procure an item adequately.

This book includes product information, but it also includes several related purchasing activities, such as bill paying, that most purchasing agents do not perform. However, the typical hospitality manager eventually becomes involved with many of these related activities.

We also incorporate a great deal of information on technology applications related to the purchasing function that will enable a hospitality student to learn the technological aspects of procurement. With this person in mind, we begin our discussion of selection and procurement for the hospitality industry.

KEY WORDS AND CONCEPTS

A broad view of purchasing

Aggregate purchasing companies

Business-to-business (B2B)

Business-to-consumer (B2C)

Central distribution center

Commercial hospitality operations

Commissary

Co-op buying

Electronic commerce (e-commerce)

Electronic marketplace (e-marketplace)

Electronic procurement (e-procurement)

Executive steward

Franchise

Group purchasing organization (GPO)

Noncommercial hospitality operations

Portal

Procurement

Purchasing

Real Estate Investment Trust (REIT)

Referral groups

Selection

Varying purchasing organizations

QUESTIONS AND PROBLEMS

1. Define the term "selection."
2. Define the term "procurement."
3. Explain the advantages of studying the broad view of the purchasing function.
4. What is an e-procurement application?
5. Briefly describe the major segments of the hospitality industry.
6. Briefly differentiate between the ways in which the small and the large independents generally do their purchasing.
7. Briefly describe co-op buying.

8. How has e-commerce affected co-op buying?

9. Briefly describe two typical purchasing procedures found in multiunits and franchises.

10. Briefly describe how a local restaurant that is part of a large restaurant chain probably does its purchasing.

11. Name one reason why a franchise might do some local buying.

12. Describe three duties of a vice president of purchasing in a large hotel or restaurant chain.

13. Why might a small, independent hospitality operation be interested in co-op buying?

14. Under what conditions do you think a franchise operation might be interested in co-op buying?

15. Define the term "purchasing."

16. Define the term "e-marketplace."

17. What is a referral group?

18. Briefly describe the benefits of e-commerce.

19. How do you think e-commerce has changed the hospitality industry?

EXPERIENTIAL EXERCISES

1. Ask a manager of a local franchise operation the following questions.
   a. Do you currently purchase items from a commissary?
      i. *If so: What items are you required to purchase from the commissary?*
      ii. *Do you have to follow specific guidelines on the other products you purchase outside of the commissary?*
   b. What are the benefits of purchasing from a commissary?
   c. What are the drawbacks of purchasing from a commissary?

   Write a report detailing your findings.

2. Interview a noncommercial hospitality operator. Ask him or her to describe the job and explain how the responsibilities differ from those of a commercial hospitality operator. Write a report detailing your discussion with the operator.

3. Shadow (follow around) the owner of a small independent operation for a day. Prepare a diary of all activities performed by the owner.

TECHNOLOGY APPLICATIONS
IN PURCHASING

The Purpose of this Chapter

After reading this chapter, you should be able to:

■ **Explain how technologies are used by hospitality operators in the selection, procurement, and inventory processes.**

INTRODUCTION

Technological applications in the selection and procurement function are evolving rapidly. Today, many forms of technology are available to help distributors and buyers to transact effectively with each other. Those who decide to use these tools can considerably streamline the cycle of purchasing, distribution, receiving, storage, issuing, and product usage. Many of these tools are becoming a vital part of the procurement process.

TECHNOLOGIES THAT DISTRIBUTORS USE

Distributors can use computer software applications to track and analyze many business functions. Typically, distributors use specialized software to build customer databases that can help to predict customer behavior. In addition, this type of software can also be used to estimate, or forecast, the number and types of hospitality operations that might, or should, open in a particular area.

Distributors also utilize software applications to facilitate the sales process. For instance, some distributors have all inventories counted, costed, organized, and stored on computerized product databases. This detailed information enables the distributors to manage and price their products quickly and easily. It is much more convenient for everyone than the traditional method, whereby buyers receive printed product lists from distributors that note product names, manufacturers, identification numbers, and other descriptive information. To obtain product status, buyers must call either the sales representative or the distributor directly. The buyer then must call in the order or place it with the sales representative. This traditional method is still widely used, though many buyers use the fax machine or e-mail instead of the telephone to communicate.

Some distributors have further streamlined the sales process and taken it to the technological forefront by developing extensive online ordering systems, sometimes referred to as "Web order entry systems." Through this type of system, buyers and large distributors communicate directly with each other over the Internet. This method of communication permits buyers to order products directly and receive instant feedback on pricing and availability. Such systems also minimize the ordering function and the paper trail for both buyers and distributors. Distributors typically provide these services free of charge. Examples of these types of online ordering systems include usfood.com (www.usfood.com)—US Foodservice's Web order entry system—and esysco (www.esysco.net)—Sysco's Web order entry system. These companies are two of the largest broadline foodservice distributors in the United States.

With the rapid development of inexpensive global positioning systems (GPS), many distributors use logistics and mapping software to outline the routing sequences their delivery drivers must follow when delivering products. A distributor can enter into the GPS all of the locations drivers need to visit the following day simply by typing an address or placing a marker on a digital map. Using a routing model, the computer determines the most efficient route to take and indicates the optimal number of delivery trucks to use.

Logistics software is often integrated with time efficiency programs. A time efficiency program estimates both driver downtime and the amount of product that should be delivered per hour by taking into account street traffic flow, various times of day, and the expected time spent loading and unloading shipments. This kind of program can also compare these estimates with actual results. In addition the software can provide further feedback, such as which streets to take and what time of day to avoid them in order to reduce delays caused by traffic or highway construction. Related software can be integrated with a time efficiency program to track delivery errors, discrepancies, and complaints or comments by customers, receiving agents, and/or salespersons.

All of these software programs are usually integrated to form one cohesive process. This process enables the distributor to minimize order-placing and delivery costs, as well as to resolve problems quickly, ultimately increasing margins and profitability.

TECHNOLOGIES THAT BUYERS USE

Recently, many technological products have been developed to streamline the selection and procurement process and make life easier. Hospitality operators have generally been eager to adopt labor- and time-saving electronic equipment to enhance the purchasing function and the overall inventory control process.

Fax Machine

The introduction of a cost-effective fax (facsimile) machine in the 1980s revolutionized the order-taking and -receiving process in hospitality operations. It permitted buyers to check off on a piece of paper those items they wanted to purchase and then to submit this information instantaneously over the telephone lines. This process significantly reduced the confusion and mistakes sometimes associated with verbal orders. Furthermore, since a fax machine's printed output could be stored for historical records, it was used to verify orders, prove they were sent, and establish usage patterns. However, as many managers soon realized, the thermal paper that fax machines originally used had a limited life span. The 1990s saw the introduction of fax machines that used plain paper, could store numerous faxes for distribution at off-peak hours, and could even use the Internet to send and receive documents (see Figure 2.1).

Although fax machines are still a very common tool that hospitality operations use to order products and services, personal computers (PCs) are quickly overtaking the duties of this office workhorse. Today, most hospitality operators now embrace the digital world.

Personal Computers

The PC is by far the most powerful and useful tool that a hospitality owner-manager can have, even if it is a stand-alone machine not connected to other com-

FIGURE 2.1 A fax machine. Courtesy of PhotoDisc, Inc.

puters or the Internet. With the invention of the first spreadsheet software program for PCs in 1979 (VisiCalc [http://www.bricklin.com/visicalc.htm]), hospitality operators were given the ability to analyze huge amounts of data and to manage inventories more effectively. Previously, the majority of inventory costing and counting had been done by individuals armed with calculators, paper, and pencils. PCs have also made it possible for hospitality operators to base their purchasing decisions on current data, thus minimizing the need to estimate such items as current food costs and menu item popularity.

Computerized Point-of-Sale Systems

Before the introduction of the computerized point-of-sale (POS) system, it was very difficult to track sold menu items. The gear-driven cash register merely stores cash and provides some limited sales information on printed receipts. Today, POS systems use PCs and are highly integrated in the daily functions of operations (see Figure 2.2). These systems can tabulate and organize tremendous amounts of sales data very quickly.

Most POS systems now feature touch-screen technology. They also permit users to delete menu items, track employee activity, analyze worker productivity, and force order modifiers (e.g., when a food server enters a steak order, the computer asks, "What temperature?" or when the food server enters a baked potato order, the computer asks, "Butter and sour cream with that?"). Some advanced POS systems even allow a server to carry a wireless ordering system to the table; orders entered this way are automatically sent to the display screen in the bar and/or kitchen.

In most hospitality operations, POS systems are networked and communicate with a central computer, referred to as a "server." This server can track sales from the connected computers in all departments or areas within the hospitality operation and instantly provide vital information to managers. Advanced POS systems integrate with inventory-tracking systems that automatically delete from inventory the standard amount of each ingredient that is used to make each menu item. The integration of POS and inventory systems provides the manager with a theoretical inventory usage figure that can later be compared with actual physical counts. Furthermore, some POS systems facilitate the ability to permit purchase orders to be drafted directly to the distributors, based on sales and inventory reduction information.

Bar Code Reader

Some hospitality operations place bar code labels on their inventory items (or use those the distributors applied) to streamline the inventory-control process (see Figure 2.3). Bar code labels are vertical lines of varying thicknesses separated by blank spaces. These lines and spaces, or "elements," are used to provide a bar code reader with an identification code (ID). This ID is then used to look up the product on a database. Bar code elements, IDs, and corresponding product information are based on a standard that associates these pieces of information. The most

FIGURE 2.2 A sample screen of one available POS system, Revelation. Courtesy of InfoGenesis.

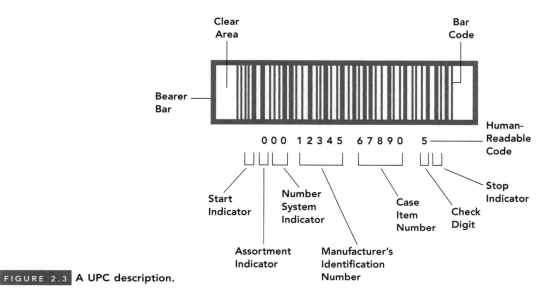

A UPC description.

commonly used standard is the Universal Product Code (UPC). However, other standards, such as EAN, Codabar, and Code 128, are also in use.

When a bar code system is used, the physical inventory count of a hospitality operation usually consists of scanning each product in the storeroom with a portable bar code reader. There is no need to spend large amounts of time locating a product on a lengthy printed inventory list and recording, by hand, the total number of units in inventory at the end of the month. Instead, the data are gathered quickly with the portable bar code reader and downloaded to the computer for instant analysis. Many bar code readers now provide wireless communication to a computer and can instantaneously download and upload information over radio frequencies (RFs) (see Figure 2.4).

The portable bar code reader can also be used to count in-process inventories. For instance, each type of alcohol in a lounge can be bar coded to streamline the beverage inventory procedure. Without bar codes, the typical procedure in beverage operations is to estimate, by sight, the amount of beverage remaining in a container to the nearest tenth. This is a very tedious, time-consuming process that often yields inaccurate results. Using a handheld bar code reader and a programmable small scale (see Figure 2.5), the operator simply reads the bar code and then places the container on the scale. By reading the code, the computerized scale associates the product ID with the type and container size of the beverage, computes the total weight, and subtracts the container weight and, if necessary, the weight

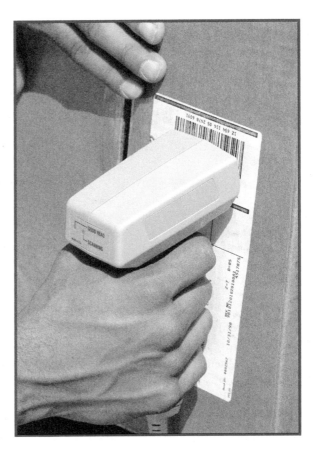

FIGURE 2.4 (a) A bar code reader. Courtesy of Corbis Digital Stock.

of the attached pourer. Next, the scale calculates the residual weight and converts it to fluid ounces or milliliters. This precise measurement system provides an incredible amount of cost control in the beverage area because it immediately highlights discrepancies between the amount of beverage the POS system indicates should have been used and the actual usage computed with the bar code reader.

Product Identification and Specifications

Buyers have many options available to "spec out" products for their hospitality operations. Traditional forms include buyers' guides, such as the North American Meat Processors Association (NAMP [www.namp.com]) *The Meat Buyers Guide* (*MBG*), originally published in 1963. This printed guidebook notes specific product information and is illustrated with many full-color photographs. Computer tech-

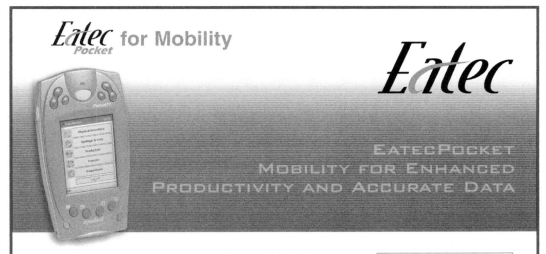

Eatec for Mobility

Eatec

EATECPOCKET
MOBILITY FOR ENHANCED
PRODUCTIVITY AND ACCURATE DATA

EatecPocket is a wireless pocket PC accessory of EatecNetX, the leading enterprise back-office solution for the foodservice and hospitality industries.

EatecPocket is a mobile tool that allows you to perform EatecNetX functions on a wireless local area network (WLAN) pocket PC device. With EatecPocket, you can perform transactions where and when needed. EatecPocket gives users more flexibility on the job, resulting in significant productivity gains.

EatecPocket offers:

Quick and Easy Functions

EatecPocket can be used to perform a variety of EatecNetX functions. You can:

- Record physical inventory – bring up a pre-determined list for data entry, or scan an item and then record the count. Ability to input multiple pack sizes for each item.

- Input spoilage and loss quantities by inventory location.

- Create requisitions and enter transfer activity between outlets.

- Post production on finished good items.

Bar Code Labels and Scanning

- Scanner-equipped pocket PCs can take advantage of bar code labels generated from EatecNetX.

- Scanning items will facilitate data entry for all EatecPocket transactions.

- Labels can be printed automatically upon merchandise arrival, according to the quantity of each item received.

Instant Data Availability

- Data entry into EatecPocket results in real-time updates of the central EatecNetX database.

- Updating EatecNetX with EatecPocket is a quick and easy process—no uploading… no downloading…no synchronization… just up to-the-minute reports.

Using EatecPocket, users do not have to jot down information that has to be entered again at a workstation. The result is an easier and faster workflow. The process is not only more efficient, it can reduce errors because the data can be entered at the source.

Markets Supported by EatecPocket:

- Restaurant Chains
- Hotels, Resorts & Casinos
- Stadium/Arenas,
- Convention Centers,
- Airports & Racetracks
- Universities
- Supermarket Foodservice
- Theme Parks & Attractions
- Foodservice Management
- Cruise Lines

FIGURE 2.4 (*b*) **An example of a wireless inventory management system. Courtesy of Eatec Corporation.**

EatecPocket Software Requirements
EatecPocket is an accessory of EatecNetX. Please refer to http://www.eatec.com/techinfo.htm for EatecNetX technical requirements.

EatecPocket Hardware Requirements
EatecPocket works with pocket PC devices utilizing the Windows CE platform. Currently, EatecPocket runs on the Symbol Portable Pen Terminal (PPT) 2800 Series, which is available from Eatec. This Symbol device is equipped with a scanner.

EatecPocket requires a wireless local area network (WLAN) environment consistent with IEEE 802.11 or 802.11b standards.

EatecPocket Availability
EatecPocket is available immediately for all EatecNetX clients. For more information about EatecPocket and EatecNetX, visit our web site at www.eatec.com, contact an Eatec sales representative at 510-594-9011, ext. 2 or e-mail sales@eatec.com

About EatecNetX
EatecNetX, Eatec's proven software solution, is recognized as a state-of-the-art foodservice management system that is centralized, scalable, web-centric and user-friendly for food and beverage operators of every variety. EatecNetX helps reduce costs and improve operational efficiencies, resulting in a quick return on investment. EatecNetX makes it easy to manage both multi-site and multi-outlet operations.

Robust features of EatecNetX include forecasting, purchasing and receiving, inventory management, production management, recipes and menu engineering, requisitions and transfers. Optional add-on modules are banquet catering, in-suites catering, airline catering, concessions, manufacturing and retail merchandise. EatecNetX accessories include EatecPocket, a mobile tool, and EatecTouch, a touch screen inventory reporting tool.

EatecNetX interfaces to most point-of-sale (POS) and financial systems and utilizes XML technology for B2B transactions and real-time interfaces to other systems.

EatecPocket Menu Screen — Posting Physical Inventory

Eatec Corporation
1350 Ocean Avenue
Emeryville, CA 94608
Tel: 510-594-9011
Fax: 510-594-9091
Web: www.eatec.com

FIGURE 2.4 *(b)* (Continued.)

FIGURE 2.5 The Free Pour Bottle Check system. Courtesy of Free Pour Controls, Inc.

nology, though, permits printed guidebooks to be converted to digital formats. For instance, printed publications, such as *MBG*, are also available on a compact disc (CD-ROM, or CD for short) and should be available online in the near future. This digital version enhances the buyer's ability to select meat products very efficiently. The buyer no longer has to flip through hundreds of pages to find a specific cut of meat. He or she is able to search and find a suitable product in a few seconds. Furthermore, this CD allows the buyer to view the exact location on a meat carcass from which a specific retail cut of meat originates. In the future, this retail cut of meat might then be linked to software that will suggest appropriate recipes and cooking techniques.

Other CD products on the market can also streamline the product identification and specification process. These software packages enable users to search database indexes listing thousands of product categories and to locate information about the distributors who sell them. These CDs contain a seemingly endless amount of information. If a product is made somewhere in the world and is distributed, chances are that it can be found on one of these discs.

An example of this is the *Thomas Food and Beverage Market Place* (www.tfir .com). The *Thomas Food and Beverage Market Place* brings buyers and sellers together through a searchable database of more than 40,000 company listings and nearly 6000 product categories. All company listings are cross-indexed, and one may search by product, location, company, or brand name. Originally named the *Thomas Food Industry Register*, the *Thomas Food and Beverage Market Place* has been making a printed version of this document for more than 100 years. The company's digital products, including CD and online versions, make searching even easier. Every day, thousands of food-industry buyers use TFIR to search for new products, comparison shop, and find new distributors.

Product Ordering

As discussed earlier in Chapter 1, several software companies specializing in e-procurement have developed systems that permit buyers to order products online. These e-procurement applications streamline and minimize a buyer's ordering procedure, thereby creating a value-added service for the buyer. At the same time, when a buyer uses this ordering system, he or she could streamline the order-taking process at the distributor's end. Previously, a distributor had to enter a buyer's order from a fax, telephone call, or written purchase order, but with the new system, the inefficiencies of the "multiple-ordering" process are eliminated. Instead, a buyer enters the order on an e-marketplace and sends it directly to the distributor. This process reduces labor costs and time on both the buyer's and the distributor's end. Another distributor benefit of the process is the likelihood that users of this ordering system will become "house" or "prime-vendor" accounts.

These e-marketplaces also allow hospitality purchasing managers and distributors to negotiate contractual pricing agreements on selected products prior to ordering (see Figure 2.6). Buyers and distributors who join an e-marketplace have

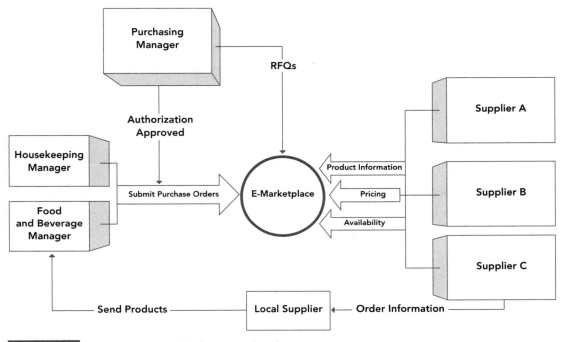

FIGURE 2.6 A conceptual model of an e-marketplace.

an instant line of communication to negotiate products and prices. Buyers begin this process by searching for an item they are interested in purchasing and identifying vendors who offer this product. The buyers then submit a request for quote (RFQ) to these vendors. An RFQ is a request for a formal document stating the purchase price of a product from the vendor. Distributors then make an offer, and the buyer chooses the vendor from whom the buyer will procure the product or service.

After pricing arrangements have been set, purchasing managers can allow departmental managers or staff to order items directly from the vendor through the e-marketplace. This method of ordering minimizes the time between when an order is placed and when it is authorized. Authorized individuals are given an account and can order specific products as long as these orders do not exceed a designated spending limit. For example, a housekeeping manager might be able to order shampoo and soap on the e-marketplace without writing out a purchase requisition as long as the order does not exceed $1000.

Product information on e-marketplaces can typically be retrieved in several ways, unlike the typical printed catalog in which everything is listed alphabetically and/or by product categories. For instance, databases on the e-marketplace enable users to search for and evaluate all of the types of hot dogs a particular vendor sells. Buyers might view hot dogs by size, types of ingredients, and packers' brands. Users can also narrow the search, for example, to 4–1 (four hot dogs per pound), pure-beef, Oscar Mayer® brand hot dogs. From this narrow list, users can then choose the desired product or continue to refine and narrow the search. Once users find the desired product, the hospitality operators can then "tag," or choose, products they want to procure or submit for RFQ.

If an order is acceptable to the buyer, the order can be transmitted right on the computer. The buyer can also attach a note telling the vendor more specific information about an order. Orders are then instantly communicated to the vendor, who might send this information to a local distribution center for processing and delivery.

Inventory-Tracking and Storage Management

If product orders have been made through an online ordering system, this information can also be used in a number of ways. For instance, it can be linked to other software and used in the equations and formulas noted in Chapters 9, 10, and 15.

Today, many hospitality operators use some type of computer application to increase their inventory and cost-control efforts. For example, some operators develop elaborate spreadsheets using generic spreadsheet software, such as Microsoft Excel®, through which they list all of their products in inventory and then develop mathematical formulas to calculate costs and usage. On the last day of each month, they physically count their storeroom and in-process inventories and enter this information on the spreadsheet. They also enter all product costs, which usually come from typing in invoice receipts for the month or from directly downloading the information from an ordering system they are using. The information currently entered is the "ending inventory," and the information entered the previous month is the "beginning inventory." Once the major variables have been entered (beginning inventory, ending inventory, purchases, and other end-of-month adjustments), the computer can easily calculate the monthly cost of goods sold.

Some hospitality operators use off-the-shelf software packages and services that are specifically designed to manage inventory in a hospitality environment. These software packages can streamline the back-of-the-house hospitality operation. Many of these software packages can be linked to an operator's POS system. These packages can also cost recipes, analyze a recipe's nutritional information, calculate food and beverage costs, evaluate a food item's sales history, forecast sales, develop audit trails, allow instant stock level information, and enhance menu planning efforts. In addition, many of these software packages can track employee work schedules, attendance patterns, and work-hour accumulations.

When generic spreadsheet programs or off-the-shelf software do not meet a hospitality operator's needs, he or she might hire a software consulting firm that specializes in the hospitality industry. A specialist can develop customized software applications to satisfy almost any need. Alternately, the developers of some off-the-shelf software products can customize some or all of their software packages.

Internet

As previously discussed, the Internet is rapidly changing the way hospitality operations select and procure products. It can streamline operations and minimize costs for distributors and buyers. The Internet also allows buyers and sellers to communicate information relatively quickly. Furthermore, it enables buyers and distributors to acquire information from a wide variety of worldwide sources.

Although many software companies and forward-looking hospitality and foodservice distributors have already developed Internet applications, content related to the purchasing activity is currently in its infancy. However, a vast amount of information in this area can already be accessed. Over the next few years, the Internet will become more useful and more user-friendly, which, in turn, will cause the selection and procurement process to evolve into a highly technical, mechanical process.

The Internet is a worldwide network of computers. Its name derives from "internetworking," the original description of computers and networks linked together. It all began in the late 1960s at the Advanced Research Projects Agency Network of the U.S. Department of Defense. Its original name was ARPANET, and its original intention was to give scientists a way to communicate directly with one another while simultaneously exchanging information with all of the other individuals who had access to the system.

The first system consisted of computers located at Stanford University, the University of California at Los Angeles (UCLA), the University of California at Santa Barbara (UCSB), and the University of Utah. Computers linked to the Internet typically communicate via telephone line transmission, although cable, wireless, and optical communications are also in use. More information on the history of the Internet can be found at www.historyoftheinternet.com.

This worldwide network offers many benefits to the hospitality buyer. The major ones are described in the following paragraphs.

Electronic Mail   Electronic mail (e-mail) enables hospitality buyers to communicate with primary sources, intermediaries, colleagues, and any other person who has an e-mail address. E-mail allows buyers to send information or documents to other individuals. For instance, a buyer can compose a letter to a distributor, soliciting competitive bid data. However, instead of sending the letter through the postal system, the buyer can send it electronically to the distributor's e-mail address.

An e-mail address consists of a person's user name and the host providing access to the Internet at that location. A buyer can also send the same letter simultaneously to all of the persons on a distribution list. A distribution list is a group of contacts to whom you can send e-mail. For instance, you can request pricing information on lettuce simply by sending one e-mail to a distribution list that includes all of your produce distributors.

E-mail also enables the sender to attach files and documents to the original communication. For those who want the full range of capability, e-mail applications now let senders embed Web pages, photographs, graphics, animation, and sound bytes into the message.

Newsgroups and Mailing Lists   A newsgroup is an electronic bulletin board where many individuals who have a common interest can post messages. In fact, newsgroups are sometimes referred to as "interest groups." Each newsgroup specializes in a particular topic, and groups are organized hierarchically. People with similar interests can post messages to a newsgroup, and other subscribers to the group can read and respond to them. A good starting point to find out more about newsgroups can be found at www.usenet.org.

Similar to newsgroups are mailing lists. Mailing lists use e-mail to send messages to groups of individuals who have the same interests. Individuals can post messages that are in turn sent out to all members of the mailing list. Mailing lists that are moderated are referred to as "manual" lists, whereas those that route messages automatically to all members are referred to as "LISTSERVs."

Newsgroups and mailing lists offer a great way to keep current in the hospitality field. They allow individuals to obtain specific information very quickly. For instance, a buyer can compose a short message soliciting distributor references, the cost of joining a purchasing co-op, or the availability of a unique product; send it to the group; and receive relevant information without the normal time delay inherent in other forms of communication.

World Wide Web   The most active part of the Internet is the World Wide Web (Web or WWW for short). The Web is a graphical interface that allows information to be connected through "hyperlinks." Hyperlinks permit users to select a word or image and connect to more information about that topic. Users who have graphical browser software on their systems can easily locate and view all pertinent information about any topic on the Web.

Information is located on various "Websites." A site, or site "location," is referred to as a Uniform Resource Locator (URL). Information can be found by entering the site URL or by using one of the many search engines that are designed to locate information based on key words or associations.

The Web portion of the Internet has many sites that are useful in terms of the selection and procurement function. Many of these sites provide detailed, current information and can include text, graphics, photographs, sound bytes, animation, full-motion video, and interactivity.

A great deal of information on the Internet can assist the hospitality buyer. For instance, sites range from those providing daily news about the hospitality industry to those specializing in unique cookware and equipment, and just about anything in between. The amount of information, already rather huge, nevertheless continues to grow each day.

An example of the use of this dynamic technology is the U.S. Department of Agriculture's (USDA's) Website (www.usda.gov). A portion of this site is dedicated to information about fresh-produce farming and distribution within the United States. This site allows users to view current information about products currently grown and harvested in certain geographic regions and provides detailed weather information.

Although this information may seem too detailed for the average hospitality operator, it can be useful in certain situations. For instance, this site provides information about the seasonality of specific fresh-produce items and the current weather in their growing regions. While a buyer's printed produce specification guide might note that, for example, the growing season of asparagus is over, data on this Website might indicate that, in fact, the growing season has been extended for several weeks due to unseasonably good weather. Moreover, if a buyer wants to know why lettuce prices have increased, he or she might find that recent flooding in the lettuce-growing region has caused considerable crop damage, thereby inflating prices.

Other Websites can help buyers spec out products. For example, many food-marketing boards in the United States have been organized to provide information about a particular product to interested persons. The California Avocado Commission (www.avocado.org), for instance, is responsible for promoting the sale and purchase of avocados. This board, as well as many others, such as the California

Walnut Commission (www.walnut.org), the Australian Pork Corporation (www. pork.gov.au), and the California Cherry Advisory Board (www.calcherry.com), have Websites that include information about their products. The sites might include recipes, current crop reports, and variety and grade specifications. These sites also enable viewers to engage in question/answer activity with the board administrators.

Information on food Websites can help the buyer make key decisions about the type, variety, and quality of product that should be ordered. The buyer can find recipe suggestions and consult with experts about a particular product. Although the buyer's local distributors are usually very knowledgeable about their products, the food sites, especially those the marketing boards maintain, have the ability to gather immediately vast amounts of current information from growers, processors, and manufacturers. This is primarily because these distributors pay to maintain these associations and their Websites.

Many national premium brands also have Websites. For instance, well-known brands such as Nabisco® (www.nabisco.com), Land O'Lakes® (www.land olakes.com), Ragú® (www.ragu.com), Birds Eye® (www.birdseyefoods.com), McCormick® (www.mccormick.com), Butterball® (www.butterball.com), and Indian Harvest® (www.indianharvest.com) are just a few keystrokes and/or mouse clicks away.

Instant Messaging One of the latest technological advances and most talked about communication applications on the Web is instant messaging. Software such as MSN Messenger® (www.msn.com) and ICQ (web.icq.com) allow users to communicate online instantaneously, either through computers or even personal digital assistants (PDAs) and cell phones. Users can also send a wide variety of files to each other and can either chat in private or discuss topics with the public in assigned areas called "chat rooms." This technology may have substantial implications for hospitality procurement as it can allow buyers to instantaneously communicate with distributors, and vice versa. Using this technology, a buyer could find out immediately the availability of a product from a salesperson without needing to pick up the phone. Distributors could notify their customers that an order should be arriving at their back door in a matter of minutes.

ROADBLOCKS TO ADOPTION OF E-PROCUREMENT

B2B was one of the darling sectors of the explosive Internet-driven stock market surges in the late 1990s. However, this technology has recently come on hard times. Many companies that develop e-procurement solutions are now trading for a fraction of their former heyday prices or are gone entirely. Although much of the drop in stock price in these companies can be correlated with the collapse of the technology-laden NASDAQ Composite at the beginning of the new millennium, a portion of this is due to the unanticipated slowness of hospitality operators to adopt and take advantage of the e-procurement revolution.

Understanding the Hospitality Industry

Most restaurants in the United States are independent operations. These operators—many of whom are owner/operators—have a limited amount of time to spend selecting and procuring products. However, a lack of attention in this area can quickly result in a foodservice operation becoming part of the unbelievably high estimated restaurant failure statistic. It has been said that one in three restaurants fail in the first year of operation.[1] Although location is still considered the number one predictor of success, proper product selection is not far behind.[2] Because of this, foodservice operators must pay particular attention to their selection and procurement procedures.

In particular, considerable time must be taken to select and procure fresh produce and seafood because prices, quality, and availability of these items vary drastically. Perishable items are often acquired after a review of daily bid sheets (we discuss this in more detail in Chapter 12), rather than through a formal bidding process. Several suppliers can fax these sheets to supply managers on a weekly (or sometimes daily) basis, and some now e-mail these documents. For instance, a produce distributor in Las Vegas provides its customers with a choice of sources for pricing information on their products: (1) faxed bid sheets, (2) quotes directly entered into operator provided templates, or (3) information directly distributed through an e-procurement application. More than 90 percent of their customers still prefer to receive their pricing information via fax.

Much of this reliance on the antiquated fax machine can be attributed to the state of technology usage in the foodservice industry. In a recent study by the National Restaurant Association (NRA), only 60 percent of table-service operations and 25 percent of quick-service operations have access to the Internet.

Because independent operators have limited time to select and procure products, many simply give in to the temptation to one-stop shop these products and accept whatever prices are given to them rather than seek bids from other suppliers.

Multiunit foodservice operators do not typically have these procurement problems. The majority of their products are acquired from central distribution warehouses or commissaries. If they do procure items from local suppliers, they are typically restricted to using an approved supplier list or following exacting specifications; many times, price is secondary.

Major multiunit and independent hotel properties, casinos, and resorts—such as those located in Las Vegas—provide a tremendous amount of technological resources to the supply manager to assist in product selection and procurement. It is not uncommon for these managers to supervise the procurement of up to $100 million of products annually, ranging from live specialty seafood to please their international guests to exotic cars for their high rollers. Their challenge has nothing to do with limited time to allocate to these duties; they typically have subordinate buyers and directors specifically devoted to the purchasing function. Their purchasing challenge lies in the management of people and information. These supply managers (with titles ranging from vice president of purchasing to director of materials management) focus their efforts on determining departmental product needs, assisting in the development of specifications, identifying acceptable products, approving requisitions, and managing buyers. Their job revolves around interpersonal relationships and requires effective communication skills. One of their biggest challenges is managing the vast amount of paperwork that revolves around product requisitions. Departments ranging from housekeeping to engineering are continually replenishing shampoo, linen, and light bulbs at astonishing rates. The supply manager not only approves these requisitions and converts them to orders, but must also manage the entry of these new products into their back-of-the-house inventory management system.

These types of operations were some of the first companies to adopt e-procurement models in the hospitality industry. PurchasePro® (an early e-commerce enabler) was founded in Las Vegas and was quickly adopted by MGM Mirage®. However, MGM Mirage and other large hospitality operations soon realized that there were significant challenges in implementing an e-procurement solution and a slowdown occurred. Eventually, PurchasePro's aggressive growth strategy stagnated, and the company was eventually bought in 2003 by Perfect Commerce® (www.perfect.com).

Entities that Affect the Hospitality E-Procurement Process

The main reasons for adoption slowdown in the hospitality industry can be attributed to three entities within the selection and procurement process: employees, suppliers, and organizations. From an employee perspective, there are both classic and "future shock" reasons for resisting change. From a supplier perspective, the slow adoption of e-technology can be attributed to issues such as a fear of "disintermediation" or the unwillingness to let go of proprietary systems in which they have invested heavily. Finally, organizational adoption may be hindered due to internal issues such as problems with product standardization, concerns about using untested third-party dot.com companies, a lack of equipment or time to monitor an e-procurement solution, and a general feeling that e-procurement depersonalizes the relationship between supply managers and vendors (Figure 2.7).

Employees Employee buy-in is critical to the success of an e-procurement strategy. Unfortunately, there are many employees who are reluctant to participate. There are two categories of classic reasons that employees resist changes in an organization: (1) resistance due to situational variables, and (2) resistance due to social-psychological and personality variables.[3] Some of the resistance due to situational variables stems from an employee's fear of losing position power or, more importantly, the position itself. Other variables include reluctance to change habits, issues surrounding inertia, disruption in the organizational culture and climate, experience with prior failed change efforts, peer group pressure, and a lack of participation in the process.

Furthermore, resistance to change is often associated with an employee's social-psychological and personality variables, such as cognitive dissonance, risk aversion, lack of faith or confidence, conservative outlook, or the "what's in it for me" Machiavellian personality characteristic.

Employees

Classic reasons for organizational resistance to change (Anderson Consulting, 2001)

Future Shock—or the fear/resistance to technological advancement (Toffler, 1991)

Suppliers

Fear of middlemen disintermediation (Hartmann, 2000)

Unwillingness to let go of heavily invested proprietary systems (Pye, 1997; Morgan, 2000)

Organizations

Problems with product identification standardization (Porter, 2000)

Concerns with using third-party dot.com companies (Carter et al., 2000; Sheth, 1980; Wenninger, 1999; Purchasing Online, 2000)

Many companies are too small to afford the equipment needed or time required to monitor an e-procurement solution

Issues of depersonalization (Parseghian, 2000)

FIGURE 2.7 **Main reasons for the e-procurement adoption slowdown in the hospitality industry.**

As if the classic reasons for resistance to change were not enough, it has been suggested that many employees also have an inherent fear of or resistance to technological advancement. Alvin Toffler originally discussed this fear in 1970 and termed it "future shock."[4] His belief is that, while a human being's capacity to adjust physically, psychologically, and socially to change is finite and quite limited, the pace of technological change is increasing and expanding into more and more areas of individuals' lives. Moreover, individuals are not asking for these profound and endless changes; they stem from economic impulses of the marketplace rather than from any kind of consumer demand. Future shock happens when people are no longer able to cope with the pace of change. This fear can significantly affect productivity and seriously hinder e-procurement efforts.

Suppliers The diffusion and adoption of e-procurement technology is impossible without the participation and drive of suppliers. Diffusion theory explains "the flow of information, ideas, practices, products, and services within and across cultures and subcultures, or markets and market segments."[5] Adoption is "a component of the diffusion process [and] refers to an evaluation of the results of a trial use of the innovation and a decision to continue using the innovation in the future."[6] Little research exists on the role of hospitality suppliers in the diffusion and adoption process, even though it is common knowledge that they occupy a critical position in the procurement process.[7] Unfortunately, it is also known that suppliers can hinder e-procurement solutions due to their fear of "disintermediation" (the act of shutting out middlemen, who are traditionally involved in the process of selling something),[8] and their unwillingness to let go of proprietary computer systems in which they have invested heavily.

Hartmann[9] raises the question of whether intermediaries are still needed in the purchasing process in the Internet age (we discuss more about intermediaries in Chapter 3). Hospitality intermediaries (primarily food distributors) have traditionally put buyers (operators) and sellers (growers, manufacturers, or processors) together. In today's new markets, buyers and manufacturers alike are looking to cut costs and communicate directly. Given this, intermediaries have a real fear of disintermediation—either that their level of involvement in the procurement function will lessen, or worse, that they will be completely eliminated from the supply chain.

Some suppliers are also reluctant to invest in new technologies. Many have already invested considerable amounts of capital to develop what they thought would be their technological opus and gateway to customers. Networks were constructed to allow supply managers access to supplier inventories in an effort to streamline the procurement process and minimize the double entry of orders and invoices that faxing required. These suppliers are now at the crossroads of deciding whether or not to abandon these proprietary systems and jump on the e-procurement/e-marketplace bandwagon. In a situation analogous to employees' fearing future shock, many suppliers are apprehensive of investing in this technology because they fear its impending obsolescence.

Organizations Adoption may also be hindered due to organizational issues such as problems with product identification standardization, reluctance to work with third-party dot-com companies (Web companies that develop software, such as e-procurement applications), a lack of resources to effectively monitor an e-procurement solution, and possible feelings of depersonalization.

Product identification standardization issues are one of the primary bottlenecks in e-procurement adoption by hospitality operators.[10] For years, the foodservice industry in particular has been pushing for the development of identification standards on commercial foodservice products. In an attempt to address this issue, reduce costs, and improve overall supply chain effectiveness, members of the International Foodservice Manufacturers Association and the International Foodservice Distributors Association, along with ten other large foodservice industry associations, convened in 1994 and developed the Efficient Foodservice Response (EFR) initiative.[11] We discuss the EFR initiative in detail in Chapter 3.

Although this initiative shows great potential for reducing organizational costs associated with the purchasing function, it has been hindered by the inability of the foodservice and hospitality industries to develop common terminology for products and standard bar code identifiers. Because of this, organizations e-procuring a common produce item, such as broccoli, find that it requires considerable effort to ensure that all bidding suppliers can interpret an organization's identifying codes. Even within a hospitality organization, many units may not use the same terminology to identify or categorize broccoli. Some may categorize it under produce, others under vegetables. Further, few operations use bar codes on these types of fresh produce products to track them.

In addition to standardization issues, organizations still harbor concerns about doing business with third-party dot-com companies. Some firms fail to see the real benefits that e-procurement can bring to the organization, while other firms continue to have concerns with the security of transactions, the risks inherent in sharing critical information, and the added costs of switching systems.[12] Further, many hospitality organizations are just too small and lack the necessary time, personnel, and equipment to properly monitor an e-procurement solution.

Finally, organizations also have to deal with the issue of depersonalization in the channel of distribution.[13] Many supply managers believe that online purchasing will depersonalize the process. Part of the relationship with vendors is personal service: Managers are asking themselves, "Who will be there for me after hours when I have an emergency?"

THE FUTURE OF E-PROCURMENT

It is clear that e-procurement models are the future of hospitality purchasing. Although some have argued that reverting back to private networks will eliminate many of the risks associated with public B2B e-marketplaces,[14] the use of the Internet is hard to resist.

The challenge is to not revert back to a system that limits communication and severely impedes the evolution of the procurement process. Rather, hospitality operators and suppliers should embrace a free market where even the smallest operators can realize substantial benefits in product selection, price, and use of their time, while suppliers have access to thousands of potential customers and can take advantage of cost efficiencies associated with electronic transactions.

In order to overcome the roadblocks discussed above, some strategies that might resolve some of the aforementioned issues are outlined below.

Employees: Communication Is Key

Operators should discuss with their employees the impending implementation of an e-procurement model. Care should be taken in identifying concerns regarding e-procurement, and all employees in the purchasing function should be involved in the implementation process through focus groups and committee membership.

Suppliers: Buyers are Driving Supplier Adoption

Understand that buyers are driving suppliers' pace of technological development. Many hospitality operators will no longer do business with suppliers who do not have the ability to connect to their e-marketplace. Simply put, keep up with the technological needs of your customers, or they will go elsewhere. In the future, it is thought that the distinguishing factors between hospitality suppliers will not be so much the products they sell (the major products are already very close in quality and cost), but the services they provide and the technology they use.

Organizations: Standardization Issues Must Be Resolved

Hospitality operators will continue to experience more competitive markets, slimmer profit margins, a shrinking labor force, and less time to make key managerial decisions. E-procurement models will help hospitality operators to overcome these obstacles and ultimately contribute to the success of their business. However, the first step is to develop a system of identification standards where the term "broccoli" and its associated identification code are universally understood. This can be easily accomplished through database synchronization and by following standards such as those provided by the EFR initiative.

WHAT LIES AHEAD?

It is hard to believe that the use of computer technology in the selection and procurement function is only in its infancy. In the future, technology will bring more ideas, tools, and information to hospitality operators. And it cannot come too soon—since hospitality operators will continue to experience more competitive markets, slimmer profit margins, and a shrinking labor force. Technology will help operators to overcome these obstacles and will, ultimately, contribute to the success of their business.

In a competitive environment, hospitality operators have less time to make key managerial decisions. Making the correct decision quickly can be done, but only if operators have access to the necessary technological tools.

In the future, distributors will probably bear more of the burden of providing hospitality operators with the proper technology to suit a more technical, mechanical selection and procurement process, as well as the burden of helping operators control their businesses more efficiently. Since hospitality businesses are the distributors' customers, it is in their best interest to ensure that these companies make the correct purchasing and other key management decisions. Distributors, therefore, will be more actively involved with their customers, helping them to develop and evaluate new menus, substitution possibilities, inventory management procedures, and marketing strategies, as well as assisting them to streamline the business process through the use of electronic commerce.

In the future, the distinguishing factors between distributors most likely will be the services they provide and the technology they use and can share with hospitality operators. In addition, because of time constraints, competition, and economies of scale, many industry experts feel that more hospitality operators will practice one-stop shopping, thereby teaming with prime vendors to enhance their competitive positions.

Empowering Enterprise Technology | alohapos.com | 800.79.ALOHA

PRODUCT **PROFILE**

Do you know your true cost of sales and how to leverage the most operational profits?

The reality today is that the hospitality foodservice market is highly competitive. To stay ahead of your competition as a restaurateur, you have no choice but to keep this kind of data at your fingertips.

Aloha's state-of-the-art Inventory Control package provides the answers that you've been looking for in effectively controlling food, beverage and paper costs – your variable operating costs. By providing simple, but powerful analytical processing tools – including actual vs. theoretical comparisons, variance analysis, choices of FIFO, Average or Standard costing modules, theft and waste control monitoring and simple-to-process accounting principles – Aloha puts complete cost control at your fingertips.

Stop backtracking and duplicating process today! Aloha Inventory Control automates the ordering and receiving process. New purchase orders can easily be created at unit level, and if you routinely submit similar vendor purchase orders, standardized templates can be utilized to save valuable time. In addition, purchase orders can be set to automatically generate based on projected and/or par levels set though the system. Orders can be delivered through an electronic ordering process interfaced to most industry standard suppliers. The system searches vendor files for products needed and vendors that supply the product, then creates the purchase orders with the vendors with the best price for the product that is required. Let the system price comparison shop for you!

Accurate and Easy Receiving

With Aloha Inventory Control, receiving is accurate and easy. When the deliveries hit the back door, your staff can easily and accurately receive goods based on the purchase order being automatically converted to your receiving invoice. Aloha Inventory lets you control what comes in the door by verifying and tracking price, cost, item quantity and vendor substitution, before it's placed on the shelves.

Aloha Inventory

Inventory Forecasting

Keep your cash in the bank and not in your walk-in cooler. Reduce your standing inventory to proper levels for your business and direct it to other areas to grow your hospitality empire. Through the use of sales projections, you will be able to order product when you need it, and stock only what you need. By forecasting sales projections, the system will indicate what to produce for your next production cycle based on previous history.

Simplified Counting

Count and track your inventory easily via any method you prefer. The same product can be counted by the cases in the freezer, boxes in the dry storage, and units on the line. You determine the units of measure, description and stocking location. We give you the tools to count it as you see it, when you see it.

Aloha Inventory Control puts your finger on the true cost of sales…and keeps it there.

Courtesy of Aloha Technologies.

Aloha Technologies **Aloha Inventory**

Multi-unit Management

Aloha Inventory Replication Manager lets the multi-unit restaurateur control top-level inventory management items for their stores such as recipe updates, price changes, menu item additions, and vendor modifications. We also provide you with the needed corporate inventory exception reporting to find out where you can improve your current cost of goods sold.

Behind this cutting-edge technology stands Aloha Technologies: a customer-focused company with the experience, strength and resources to enhance your organization's competitive advantage. That makes Aloha Inventory Control more than just a solid foundation for you to manage your business – *that makes it a smart business decision.*

Features:

- "Sales Wizard" for product forecasting, reporting and purchase order creation
- Vendor price history and product quotes for competitive analysis
- Up to 99 stored periods of transaction history
- Multiple costing methods (FIFO, average and standard)
- Automatic conversion between units of measure for purchase, count, and usage
- Tracking of multiple vendors and stocking locations per item
- Accurate update of general ledger
- Audit trails of sales and inventory edits
- Easy to operate
- Entire Windows™ 32-bit design
- Reporting designed with filter and sort options for user-defined count
- Historical sales comparison
- Par and projected order capabilities

Benefits:

- Reduction in food costs by a minimum of 1-2%
- Reduction in administrative labor
- Improved communications
- Reduction in manager time through exception managing
- Usable responsible information
- Reduced errors in ordering

Intelligent Solutions

The Inventory Control system, as well as the entire suite of Aloha BackOffice and Customer Management Solutions, employs the "Intelligent Restaurant" concept. This means that computerized entries are made one time only. Sales through the POS terminals, vendor transactions, and accounting entries all flow to the correct place in the system. This is critical when inventory is the issue, since there is no room for mistakes. As a restaurateur, you need the most accurate system available to take your business to the next level without worrying about numbers, budgets, ordering or stock. Inventory from Aloha lets you relax and does the computing for you.

Aloha BackOffice solutions were created with the most advanced, open systems technology available today. Whether you want Windows 95™ or Windows NT™, Aloha's 32-bit applications and ODBC compliant design make integration a snap. With Aloha's open architecture, we can easily integrate the applications you need to make your business prosper. In short, Aloha Inventory ensures that your operation will never miss a beat.

For more information on Inventory Control or other Aloha products, partners, customers and services visit our web site at www.alohapos.com or call us at 800.79.ALOHA.

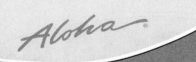

1320 Tennis Drive, Bedford, Texas 76022
800.79.ALOHA • Fax 817.252.9490 • www.alohapos.com
Copyright © Aloha Technologies, LTD., 2002. All rights reserved.

Empowering Enterprise Technology | alohapos.com | 800.79.ALOHA

PRODUCT **PROFILE**

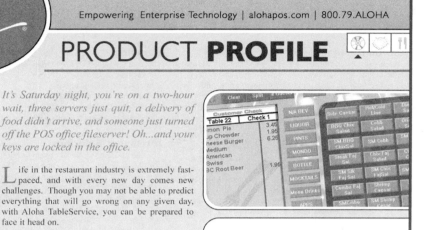

It's Saturday night, you're on a two-hour wait, three servers just quit, a delivery of food didn't arrive, and someone just turned off the POS office fileserver! Oh...and your keys are locked in the office.

Life in the restaurant industry is extremely fast-paced, and with every new day comes new challenges. Though you may not be able to predict everything that will go wrong on any given day, with Aloha TableService, you can be prepared to face it head on.

Aloha TableService

Intuitive and Easy-to-use

TableService's intuitive touchscreens put the user in control with the touch of a finger, making operating and customizing the system a snap, allowing you to decrease training time and increase employee productivity. With Aloha, it's easier than ever to enter orders, manage guest checks, run promotions and process payments. Whether you're printing individual, combined or split checks, modifying orders or transferring tables, Aloha TableService makes it easy. What used to take several days of training now only takes a few hours.

Powerful Management Functionality

Whether you have weekly promotions or daily menu changes, Aloha's built-in Event Scheduler lets you program events that are automatically activated at a specified time. Special messages can be entered to appear on screen, keeping your employees informed and in-the-know.

Aloha's comprehensive reporting package allows you to keep track of real-time sales results and other data. Aloha makes front-of-house operations a breeze without sacrificing security and control. With extensive front-of-house reporting features like real-time sales statistics, product mix reports, employee check-in stats and server sales, you're able to spend more time with your customers and still keep up with the latest profit margins and performance measures.

Virtual Order Processing

With Aloha TableService, communication flows smoothly and seamlessly from your wait staff to the kitchen staff. Voids, order changes and adds can now be handled effortlessly through the Aloha system, eliminating unnecessary trips to and from the kitchen. And with Aloha's menu item availability feature, you're able to count down selected items or specials as they're ordered so servers never order out-of-stock items – which ensures your customers will continue to receive only the best possible service.

The TableService Advantage

Aloha TableService offers advanced point-of-sale functionality, intuitive Windows™-based touchscreens, open architecture, built-in redundancy, extensive front-of-house reporting, and much more to meet the needs of your business. This peerless POS system provides you with the tools to effectively and efficiently manage your operations. No matter how you configure it, the end result is always a smooth-running, seamlessly integrated system.

Aloha TableService is the key to reliability and performance for your hospitality POS needs.

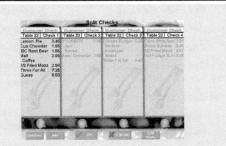

Behind the cutting-edge technology stands Aloha Technologies: a customer-focused company with the experience, strength and resources to provide your organization the competitive advantage it needs to be successful now and into the future. That makes Aloha TableService more than just a solid foundation for you to manage your business – *that makes it a smart business decision.*

Benefits:

- Unmatched performance, functionality and features
- Order processing ease
- Powerful management functions
- Unparalleled menu management capacity
- Built-in security system
- Modular, flexible design that allows the system to meet your current and future needs
- Detailed reporting and audit tracking
- Automated scheduled menu and promotion events
- Fast and easy to train

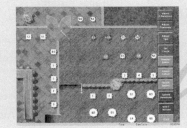

Features:

- Intuitive touchscreen interfaces
- Built-in redundancy
- User-customizable screens and screen flow
- Menu management
- Integrated customized table floorplan
- Comprehensive reporting package
- Microsoft Windows™-based
- Several graphical user interfaces
- Performance measurements for servers
- Open architecture
- Off-the-shelf, non-proprietary hardware
- Enterprise capabilities
- Extensive kitchen chit printing options
- Simple check or item splitting and combining functionality

Optional Packages for Aloha TableService

Aloha Credit Card

Authorize, process and settle credit card transactions easily and efficiently with this full-featured package. Features include IP-based credit card processing, multi-transaction processing, multi-processor support and split dialing capabilities, complete reporting, audit trail functionality, and tip processing.

Aloha Customer Management

Manage a complete customer database to offer loyalty programs and track vital customer information with this profitable delivery/carry-out package. Features include a state-of-the-art frequent buyer program with multiple customizable bonus plans, detailed history of buyer trends and a centralized database.

Aloha PMS Interface

Integrate your hotel, country club or resort restaurant operations with your property management systems using this uniform POS-to-PMS interface. Transactions are posted to the property management system and daily charge reports are created, allowing hotel accounting personnel simple tracking capabilities.

Aloha Kitchen Display System

This package provides you the flexibility that you need to route menu items automatically to video monitors in the kitchen and food preparation areas. This package increases your productivity with features like menu item routing, expedited order processing, order recall verification, paperless routing of orders, split screen, item summary and more.

For more information about TableService or other Aloha products, partners, customers and services, visit our web site at www.alohapos.com or call us at 800.79.ALOHA

Aloha®

KEY WORDS AND CONCEPTS

Bar code element	Logistics software	Server
Bar code reader	Mailing list	Specifications
Chat room	Manual list	Spreadsheet software
Compact disc read-only memory (CD-ROM)	Marketing boards	Theoretical inventory usage
Cost control	Newsgroup	Third-party dot-com companies
Database	North American Meat Processors Association (NAMP)	Thomas Food and Beverage Market Place
Disintermediation		
Distribution list	One-stop shopping	Time efficiency program
Efficient foodservice response (EFR)	Online ordering system	Touch-screen technology
	Order modifier	Uniform resource locator (URL)
Electronic mail (e-mail)	Organizational resistance to change	
Fax machine		Usenet system
Future shock	Point-of-sale system (POS system)	Vendor
House account		Virtual discussion group
Instant messaging	Prime-vendor account	Web order entry system
Interest group	Product identification	Website
Internet	Product status	Wireless ordering system
LISTSERV	Request for quote (RFQ)	World Wide Web (WWW)
	Search engine	

REFERENCES

1. R. C. Mill, *Restaurant Management: Customers, Operations, and Employees* (Upper Saddle River, NJ: Prentice Hall, 1998).

2. Anonymous, "Small Space, Big Performance," *Nation's Restaurant News*, April 24, 2000, pp. 52–54.

3. Anderson Consulting, "261 Reasons Why Employees Resist Change." Anderson Consulting Web page, retrieved 2001 (Available http://www.andersonconsulting.com/org/resist.htm).

4. A. Toffler, *Future Shock*. (New York: Bantam Books, 1991).

5. H. Gatignon and T. S. Robertson, "A Propositional Inventory for New Diffusion Research,"
Journal of Consumer Research, March 1985, (11), pp. 849–867.

6. C. Pye, "Internet-Based EDI: Another Option for Electronic Communication? Is It the Wave of the Future? The Internet May Facilitate Smaller Organizations' Use of EDI," *Purchasing Today*, December 1997, pp. 38–40. See also: J. P. Morgan, "EDI's Very Cloudy Future," *Purchasing*, December 22, 2000 (Available: online Mag at www.manufacturing.net) Weber (1999).

7. R. T. Frambach, "An integrated model of organizational adoption and diffusion," *Industrial Marketing Management*, July 1993, 26(4), pp. 341–353. See also: H. Gatignon and T. S. Robertson, "Technology Diffusion: An Empirical Test of

Competitive Effects," *Journal of Marketing,* January 1989, (53), pp. 35–89.

8. D. Willmott, "Disintermediation: The Buzzword from Hell," *PC Magazine Online,* September 10, 1997 (Available http://www.zdnet.com/pcmag/insites/willmott/dw970910.htm).

9. G. Hartmann, "Pleasures and Pitfalls of E-Procurement," *Lodging Hospitality,* November 2000, 56(15), p. 58.

10. A. M. Porter, "The Hunt for Interoperability," *Puchasing Online,* June 15, 2000. (Available: www.manufacturing.net).

11. H. A. Ryan, "Foodservice 2005 and Efficient Foodservice Response—Tools for Reshaping the Industry," *IFDA Food Distributor,* April/May 1996, p. 8. See also: Anonymous, *Leading Foodservice Companies Align Item, Price Data in First Phase of EFR Project,* retrieved January 2001 (Available: http://www.efr-central.com/newsroom/newsroom.html); K. Malchoff, "The EFR Train is Ready for Departure—Are You Ready to Ride?" *IFDA Food Distributor,* 1996, p. 19; C. W. Witt, "Foodservice Industry Takes Bite Out of Inefficiency." *Material Handling Management,* p. 44.

12. P. L. Carter, J. L. Carter, R. M. Monczka, T. H. Slaight, and A. J. Swan, "The Future of Purchasing and Supply: A Ten Year Forecast," *Journal of Supply Chain Management,* Winter 2000, 36(1), pp. 14–26. See also: J. N. Sheth, "Research in Industrial Buying Behavior—Today's Needs, Tomorrow's Seeds," *Marketing News,* Chicago. April 4, 1980, 13(20), p. 14; J. Wenninger, "Business to Business Electronic Commerce," *Current Issues in Economics and Finance,* 1999, 5(10), pp. 1–6.

13. P. Parseghian, "E-Business Bewilderment, Benefits Top Topics and Food and Wine Classic." *Nation's Restaurant News,* retrieved August 2000 (Available: http://www.nrn.com).

14. N. Harris, "'Private Exchanges' May Allow B-to-B Commerce to Thrive after All." *The Wall Street Journal,* March 16, 2001, p. B1.

QUESTIONS AND PROBLEMS

1. How has a Web order entry system changed the ordering process?

2. What are the primary differences between a gear-driven cash register and a POS system?

3. How can a spreadsheet program, such as Microsoft Excel, assist managers in controlling their inventory?

4. What is an order modifier?

5. How could a wireless ordering system improve customer service in a hospitality operation?

6. What is a computer server?

7. Provide a brief history of the Internet.

8. How can placing bar codes on all products in inventory streamline the order-taking process?

9. What would be the advantages and disadvantages of using an online version of *The Meat Buyers Guide* versus a CD-ROM version?

10. Differentiate e-procurement from e-commerce.

11. What is the difference between instant messaging and e-mail?

12. What is the difference between a newsgroup and a mailing list?

EXPERIENTIAL EXERCISES

1. Visit a local distributor to view his or her computerized ordering, routing, delivering, and invoicing system.

2. Visit a local hospitality operation that uses an e-procurement application.

3. Go online and research a current hospitality-related POS system. Provide a one-page report explaining the capabilities of the system. A good place to start is the National Restaurant Association's Website (www.restaurant.org). Here, you can search their Buyer's Guide (http://www.restaurant.org/business/buyersguide/) for numerous companies that provide POS systems to the foodservice industry.

4. Visit a food marketing board Website described below and provide a one-page report evaluating the site based on the following criteria:

   Graphical design
   Ease of use
   Usability of information
   Effective use of technology

   National Cattlemen's Beef Association (www.beef.org)
   Initiated in 1898, the National Cattlemen's Beef Association is the marketing organization and trade association for America's one million cattle farmers and ranchers. Make sure to check out the R&D ranch.

   National Pork Producers Council (www.nppc.org)
   Everything you need to know about that "other white meat," and the world's largest pork event—the World Pork Expo—including food and nutrition information, industry news, food fun for kids!

   National Bison Association (www.bisoncentral.com)
   The National Bison Association promotes the preservation, production, and marketing of bison. Did you know that the American buffalo is not a true buffalo? Bison is its scientific name and it belongs to the bovine family of mammals, as do domestic cattle. Want more tidbits of bison trivia? Check out this site.

DISCUS (www.discus.org)

The Distilled Spirits Council of the United States (DISCUS) is the national trade association representing the producers and marketers of distilled spirits products sold in the United States.

The Beer Institute (www.beerinstitute.org)

Founded in 1986, the Beer Institute is the official trade association for the American brewing industry, whose 222 members include national, regional, local, and international brewers as well as suppliers of brewing goods, services, and agricultural products. Check out this site to find out how the discovery of beer led to civilization as we know it. Did you know that the oldest written recipe in the world is for beer?

Beertown! (www.aob.org)

A graphically cool site, Beertown was created by the Association of Brewers to provide you with one convenient place to locate all the information you need in the pursuit of quality beer. Whether it is professional brewing or homebrewing, you'll find what you are looking for in Beertown!

Massachusetts Maple Producers (www.massmaple.org)

This is a nonprofit organization dedicated to the preservation and promotion of maple sugaring in Massachusetts. For some "Sweet Talk," check out the glossary of maple sugaring terms.

California Avocado Commission (www.avocado.org)

Created in 1961, the California Avocado Commission (CAC) is the official information source for California avocados and the California avocado industry. Take the California Avocado Commission (CAC) Avocado Quiz for a chance to win a CAC mousepad! You can also stop alien insects or create your own Mr. Avocadohead at this cool site.

National Potato Council (www.npcspud.com)

The National Potato Council mission is to promote the welfare of the potato industry of the United States and to promote increased use of potatoes. Make sure to check out the Spudletter to get your "new potato" information.

Wheat Foods Council (www.wheatfoods.org)

The Wheat Foods Council is a national nonprofit organization formed to help increase awareness of dietary grains as an essential component of a healthy diet. Lots of information here including handouts, newsletters, and presentation materials. Learn the "Grains of Truth About Fad Diets & Obesity."

Texas' Best Beef Recipes and Cooking Tips (www.txbeef.org)
This site from the Texas Beef Council has recipes, beef information, and news on Texas Ranching. "It's What's for Dinner." Also, sign up for "Beef Bytes."

The Penguin Pages (www.peterpenguin.com)
This site is brought to you by the Frozen Food Council of Northern California. Be sure to stop by and say, "Hi" to Peter Penguin, the Frozen Food Council's "spokes-penguin."

National Honey Board (www.nhb.org)
This site is loaded with facts about honey. Be sure to check out their "Honey do" list.

American Egg Board (www.aeb.org)
Here, egg lovers will find recipes, answers to frequently asked questions (FAQs), egg facts, egg nutrition information, and egg industry information.

California Fig Advisory Board (www.californiafigs.com)
While the original figs came from the sunny spots around the Mediterranean, to-day's best figs come from California's great San Joaquin Valley. California ranks number two in the world in fig production, but number one in quality assurance, from growing through harvesting, drying, inspection, and packing. This site is truly your source for information about figs.

The Real California Cheese Page (www.realcaliforniacheese.com)
Brought to you by the California Milk Advisory Board, this is a great site for all you "cheeseheads." There is plenty of information and specifications about cheese here. Make sure to check out the cheesemaking virtual tour.

Dairy Farmers of Ontario (www.milk.org)
This site has information on milk nutrition, education, and dairy farming. Check out their education section and find out how milk goes from "moo to you."

California Cherry Advisory Board (www.calcherry.com)
Check out this site to find out why "when it comes to taste and appearance, you can't beat the Bing!"

The Future of Foodservice Procurement

Reid A. Paul, *Managing Editor*, Hospitality Technology *magazine*

A few years ago, in the heyday of the technology boom, restaurant operators were told that the Internet would change their lives overnight. Experts insisted that the future of procurement had finally arrived, that e-procurement would become as ubiquitous as e-mail.

Times have changed and the hype has vanished. Most of the high-profile Internet-based procurement companies (also known as ASPs: application service providers) have come and gone; others have been purchased or developed a much lower profile. The idea and promise of online procurement did not die—it just grew more complicated.

This conclusion should hardly seem surprising. After all, if procurement were not complex, you undoubtedly would not be reading an entire textbook on the subject. What many of the early advocates for e-procurement forgot was that relationships between restaurants and foodservice distributors were frequently built on personal relationships, and on a host of other factors that are not easily translated to the Internet.

Still, despite the failure of the early e-procurement pioneers, that technology is now in use at many restaurants—typically in the hands of food distributors or the restaurants themselves. The Internet and e-procurement are slowly but steadily taking more significant roles in supply-chain management and procurement.

Especially for multiunit restaurant operators, online tools help standardize procurement, and provide necessary checks on individual restaurant managers. These tools give corporate management greater control over procurement and play a large role in the efforts of restaurant companies to keep costs under control.

In fact, technology will continue to play an increasingly important role in procurement and supply-chain management. Although wireless Internet access in hotels and restaurants may get the most publicity, procurement and supply-chain management technologies will drive a growing number of restaurant companies to adopt wireless networks in the back of the house.

Already, many warehouses, consumer goods firms, and retail establishments have implemented wireless networks to improve inventory and supply-chain management control. These wireless networks allow workers to scan boxes, pallets, or individual items with a handheld device and wirelessly transmit the data to necessary systems.

In the world of retail, the momentum in this direction has been dramatically elevated by Walmart's declaration that all of its suppliers must implement RFID (Radio Frequency Identification) tags on each box or pallet by 2006. RFID tags—the same technology that allows electronic wireless toll payment in many states or the ExxonMobile SpeedPass wireless payment system— transmit data wirelessly to a sensor.

With the technology in place, Walmart will be able to monitor its storage room automatically. As a result, Walmart will be able to automate an increasing part of its procurement process with the data from the RFID-tagged shipments and improve its entire supply-chain management.

Not surprisingly, Walmart and RFID technology have been afforded the same kind of attention and received the same kind of predictions that e-procurement received not long ago. The promise of RFID technology cannot be denied, but the reality of its implementation remains to be seen.

As the nation's largest retailer, Walmart's leadership is significant, but the effect of this particular decision on foodservice procurement will most likely be muted. Retailers have utilized bar codes on their shipments for many years, while restaurant operators have struggled to do the same. For years, organizations like Efficient Foodservice Response (www.efr-central.com) have advocated the inclusion of bar codes on all foodservice shipments, with limited success.

Still, it is hard not to see the potential for restaurant procurement. Automated ordering and less time in the storage room or freezer easily translates into greater efficiency for restaurant operators. And efficiency is a word that all restaurant operators like.

As the experience of e-procurement vendors seems to indicate, restaurant operators are happiest, not in the forward lines of technological innovation, but following closely behind. In the study *Implementation Trends and Strategic Growth of Restaurant IT* (*Hospitality Technology*, University of Delaware and University of Nevada–Las Vegas, 2003), 40 percent of restaurant operators indicated that their company was a "Close Follower" when it comes to information technology. In contrast, only 18 percent considered their company a technology "Innovator or Leader." In the same study, while only 4 percent of the respondents indicated that more than half of their procurement was contracted online in 2002, 15 percent expect to utilize e-procurement at least half the time by 2004.

These may not be the monumental shifts predicted by the early e-procurement vendors, but they do indicate that restaurant operators are willing to closely follow new technology initiatives.

3

DISTRIBUTION SYSTEMS

The Purpose of this Chapter

After reading this chapter, you should be able to:

- Outline the distribution systems in the hospitality industry.

- Explain the economic values added to products and services as they journey through the channel of distribution.

- Evaluate the determination of optimal values and supplier services in the hospitality industry.

INTRODUCTION

Food, beverages, nonfood supplies, furniture, fixtures, equipment, and services follow relatively specific distribution channels. In most instances, an item goes from its primary source through various intermediaries to the retailer, as Figure 3.1 illustrates. As shown, however, the possibility of a retailer's bypassing the intermediaries and dealing directly with the primary source also exists.

DISTRIBUTION SYSTEM FOR FOOD, NONALCOHOLIC BEVERAGES, AND NONFOOD SUPPLIES

This distribution system involves a tremendous number of primary sources, intermediaries, and hospitality retailers. In the United States, thousands of primary sources and intermediaries compete to serve approximately 870,000 food-

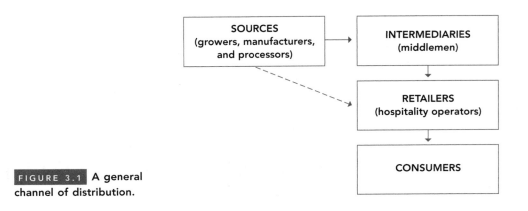

FIGURE 3.1 **A general channel of distribution.**

service operations and 41,393 lodging facilities.[1] The typical nonchain hospitality property uses about 10 to 12 types of suppliers, but chain units generally use only about 6 to 8.[2]

Efficient Foodservice Response

With the rapid growth of foodservice operations in the United States, the foodservice industry has become very competitive, and the need for streamlining costs in the channel of distribution is evident. Because of this, a concerted effort by the foodservice industry to analyze methods of cost reduction arose. Between 1994 and 1996, members of the International Foodservice Manufacturers Association and the International Foodservice Distributors Association, along with ten other large foodservice industry associations, convened and developed the Efficient Foodservice Response (EFR) initiative.[3]

EFR was initially conceived to analyze opportunities for all industry segments to reduce costs and improve overall supply chain effectiveness.[4] It is believed that EFR might be a solution to the ongoing problems of inefficiency in the product distribution channels.[5] A formal report on the initiative documents that $14.3 billion in immediate supply chain savings can be obtained across five strategies:

1. **Equitable Alliances.** A strategy to reduce non-value-added costs so that trading partners and consumers benefit.

2. **Supply-Chain Demand Forecasting.** The concept that the end consumer drives each member in the channel of distribution; this should be taken into consideration during planning.

3.   **E-Commerce.** Refer back to Chapters 1 and 2.

4.   **Logistics Optimization.** Product transportation methods, such as direct ship-ment, slow-mover consolidation, shared distribution, coordinated transport, and cross-docking, should be implemented.

5.   **Foodservice-Category Management.** Product categories should be efficiently managed through balanced variety, product deletions, new product intro-ductions, and centralized conversion strategies.[6]

The EFR initiative grew out of other movements that were taking place in other industries, such as the Efficient Consumer Response (ECR) and Quick Re-sponse (QR) methods that the 120-year-old warehousing industry utilizes. ECR is an initiative that revolutionized the grocery industry and is similar to EFR. QR is a distribution method that combines a just-in-time (JIT) delivery mechanism with a flexible and controllable supply stream that can be changed to meet a retailer's specific needs. Much like EFR, QR relies on several specific technological compo-nents, including forecasting systems, bar code technology, automatic data capture equipment, and e-commerce capabilities.

The use of EFR in the hospitality industry is becoming more evident and will continue to grow. More information on EFR can be found at www.efr-central.com.

Sources

Three major sources supply products to hospitality operations:

1.   **Growers.** Many farmers and ranchers provide fresh food products to the hos-pitality industry (see Figure 3.2).

2.   **Manufacturers.** A manufacturer controls the production of an item from raw materials. For example, a paper products manufacturer can take wood mate-rials and create paper napkins, bags, and placemats.

3.   **Processors.** A processor, sometimes referred to as a "fabricator," takes one or more foods and assembles them into a new end product. For example, a processor could combine flour, water, yeast, tomato sauce, cheese, and seasonings to produce frozen pizzas. The new end product is usually re-ferred to as a "convenience," "efficiency," or "value-added" food. Some processors are also manufacturers, but not all manufacturers are proces-sors. The difference is that processors always work with food products (see Figure 3.3).

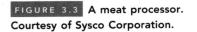 **A farmer. Courtesy of Corbis Digital Stock.**

FIGURE 3.3 **A meat processor. Courtesy of Sysco Corporation.**

Intermediaries

Several intermediaries, or middlemen, can be found in this distribution system:

1. **Distributors.** Distributors, who sometimes are referred to as "merchant-whole-salers," purchase products directly from growers, manufacturers, and/or processors for resale and delivery to customers. It is more than likely that hospitality buyers purchase most of their product requirements from one or more distributors. There are three major types of distributors:

   a. Specialty Distributor. A company that handles only one type or classification of products.

   b. Full-Line Distributor. A company that provides food and nonfood supplies.

   c. Broadline Distributor (see Figure 3.4). A company that provides food, nonfood supplies, and equipment. Broadline distributors are commonly referred to as "broadliners."

2. **Brokers.** Agents who represent one or more primary sources. Brokers neither buy nor resell. Their job is to promote products to potential buyers. Brokers usually represent primary sources that do not employ their own sales forces.

   A broker most often works among hospitality operation buyers, generating enthusiasm for a particular product. If the broker is successful, he or she then convinces a distributor that a good "market" for the product exists and

BROADLINER NAME	COMPANY WEBSITE
Ben E. Keith Foods	www.benekeith.com/pages/food/index.html
Food Services of America	www.fsafood.com/fsacom/default.htm
Gordon Food Service	www.gfs.com
Maines Paper and Food Service, Inc.	www.maines.net
Performance Food Group	www.pfgc.com
Reinhart Foodservice, Inc.	www.reinhartfoodservice.com
Shamrock Foods Co.	www.shamrockfoods.com
Sysco Corporation	www.sysco.com
The IJ Company	www.ijcompany.com
U.S. Foodservice	www.usfoodservice.com

FIGURE 3.4 **Ten of the largest broadline foodservice distributors in the United States.**

that the distributor can easily resell that product. In this example, the broker provides the sales effort, and the distributor provides the "end-user" services, that is, everything but the sales effort. The broker earns a sales commission, and the distributor earns a profit on the resale. The broker's objective is to provide the sales effort. In effect, he or she puts sellers in contact with buyers.[7] An excellent resource for more information on food brokers can be found at www.foodbrokersusa.com.

3. **Manufacturer's Representatives.** These middlemen serve a function similar to that of brokers. One major difference is that they do more than simply get sellers and buyers together. They often provide such additional end-user services as actually carrying items in stock themselves, perhaps delivering items, and possibly even providing additional service to the buyers. Representatives—or "reps" for short—seem to work more frequently with the equipment and furnishings trade, whereas brokers are usually found in the food- and nonfood-supplies trade.

4. **Manufacturer's Agents.** These intermediaries are similar to manufacturer's representatives. The major differences, though, are that primary sources employ agents to represent them in a specific geographic area, and that agents typically work exclusively for one source. Usually, the agent is a manufacturer or processor who agrees to take on another primary source's products and to try to sell them. This other primary source typically is a very small company that cannot afford to market and distribute its own products to a wide market area.

   Recently, the differences in responsibilities between many manufacturer's representatives and manufacturer's agents have become very slight, and many people now use these two terms interchangeably. The Manufacturers' Agents National Association provides an excellent Website (www.manaonline.org) that can provide more detailed information on the responsibilities of a manufacturer's agent.

5. **Commissaries.** A commissary is usually owned and operated by a large food-service company. A commissary processes food products according to exact requirements that the company has determined. It is intended to sell and ship products to company-owned restaurants or those approved franchisees own. Some commissaries, though, may also serve other types of restaurants that are not affiliated with the parent company.

6. **Wholesale Clubs.** Wholesale clubs are "cash-and-carry" operations that are patronized primarily by small businesses who do not order enough products from distributors to qualify for deliveries. Distributors usually cannot make a

profit on small-order deliveries. Some distributors have opened storefronts in their warehouses to provide cash-and-carry service, thereby accommodating the small businessperson, as well as the large.[8]

Costco (www.costco.com) originally started as a wholesale club (formerly named Price Club) where small businesses could go to select and procure products. Over the last decade, Costco has reduced their requirements for becoming a member and now just about anyone willing to pay their annual membership fee can benefit from their low prices.

7. **Buying Clubs.** Buying clubs (sometimes referred to as "price clubs") are a group of independent purchasers who join together to purchase collectively in order to obtain more competitive prices that can save them money in the long run.[9] The most typical kind of buying club is the purchasing co-op, which usually includes several small, independent foodservices and lodging properties. Some buying clubs, such as "contract houses," are operated by third parties that pass on some of the savings obtained through bulk purchasing to those buyers who are permitted to purchase from them. Buying clubs typically purchase directly from primary sources in order to obtain the lowest possible prices. As discussed in Chapter 1, aggregate purchasing companies and group purchasing organizations (GPOs) can be considered buying clubs.

8. **E-Commerce Enablers.** E-commerce enablers (such as those described in Chapter 1 and Chapter 2) provide and facilitate software applications—such as e-procurement applications—that allow sources, intermediaries, and buyers to communicate, thereby allowing them to connect to each other and set up procurement relationships. Although e-commerce enablers are usually not involved in the delivery process, they act as a means to an end in the cycle of selection and procurement.

DISTRIBUTION SYSTEM FOR BEER, WINE, AND DISTILLED SPIRITS

Sources

Three major sources supply beverage alcohol products:

1. **Brewers.** They provide fermented beverages made primarily from grains (see Figure 3.5).

2. **Wine Makers.** They provide fermented beverages made primarily from grapes (see Figure 3.6).

FIGURE 3.5   Michael Ferguson, brewmaster at Barley's Casino and Brewing Company.

3. **Distillers.** They provide beverage alcohol that has undergone a distillation process. They may also supply other similar high-alcohol-content items.

Intermediaries

Three major intermediaries, or middlemen, are part of this distribution system:

1. **Importers-Wholesalers.** These intermediaries are responsible for importing alcoholic beverages into the United States, as well as into each state and local municipality. Most of these intermediaries also act as liquor distributors in that they buy the liquor from primary sources for resale to retail establishments, such as restaurants, hotels, taverns, and supermarkets.

2. **Distributors.** Liquor distributors are specialized wholesalers who operate under a variety of legal sanctions. These distributors purchase from primary

FIGURE 3.6   A winery. Courtesy of Kenwood Vineyards.

sources and sell to retailers, and they are careful not to overstep their legal boundaries because their business is continually examined by regulatory authorities. In most states, so-called "tied-house laws" prohibit these distributors from becoming primary sources or retailers; the laws mandate separate ownership for primary sources, intermediaries, and retailers.

In many states, liquor distributors operate in exclusive territories; that is, they are the only suppliers to carry and offer particular brands to hospitality buyers. As a result, little competition exists in the wholesale liquor trade.[10] In fact, the alcoholic beverage distribution system is defined so precisely that an individual purchaser has very little discretion in buying these items and almost no control over how the channel of distribution operates.

3. **Alcohol Beverage Commissions.** All states have one or more liquor control authorities, often referred to as the Alcohol Beverage Commission (ABC), or some similar title. The ABC rigidly controls the sale and purchase of alcoholic beverages. In some states, control is so tight that the state itself is the only

purveyor of alcoholic beverages. When the state alone can sell alcoholic beverages, it is called a "control state" (as opposed to a "license state," in which the ABC grants licenses to importers-wholesalers, distributors, and retailers, who then handle the distribution of these products). When operating in a control state, purchasers have no discretion. They must adhere exactly to the purchasing, receiving, and bill-paying procedures the governmental authority sets forth.[11]

DISTRIBUTION SYSTEM FOR FURNITURE, FIXTURES, AND EQUIPMENT (FFE)

Source

There is one major source for FFE items: the manufacturer. The number of manufacturers of these items tends to be smaller than the number of sources in the other distribution systems.

Intermediaries

Seven major intermediaries can be found in this distribution system:

1. **Dealers.** An equipment dealer typically functions much like a food distributor. Dealers usually buy equipment items from primary sources, earning their profit when they resell them to hospitality buyers. There are four major types of dealers:[12]

    a. Catalog House. This is typically a very small dealer that carries no inventory, or very little inventory, in stock. Items are selected by customers from one or more catalogs, and the dealer handles the ordering, delivery, setup, and so forth. Some of these catalogs are now available online.

    b. Storefront Dealer. Storefront dealers (sometimes referred to as "discount operations") usually carry a minimum amount of inventory. They typically specialize in handling small, portable types of FFE.

    c. Heavy Equipment Dealer. Heavy equipment dealers specialize in handling large equipment installations. They carry inventory and are usually involved in the layout and design of new hospitality properties or major renovations.

    d. Full-Service Dealer. Full-service dealers typically carry a full line of inventory and are able to provide all end-user services to their customers.

2. **Brokers.** FFE brokers are similar to brokers working in the distribution system for food, nonalcoholic beverages, and nonfood supplies. However, FFE brokers are not as numerous as their counterparts in other distribution systems.

3. **Designers.** These individuals typically work as consultants for hospitality operators. They are hired to design, say, an addition to an existing kitchen. During their work, they see to it that the appropriate FFE are ordered from the primary sources. Designers also make sure that the required end-user services, such as delivery, are provided in a timely manner. Designers earn their income from the hospitality operator who employs them; they work for a fee.

4. **Architects.** They perform a function similar to that of designers.

5. **Construction Contractors.** They also perform a function similar to that of designers.

6. **Distributors.** Many distributors of food, nonalcoholic beverages, and nonfood items often supply several of the most commonly purchased FFE items. They typically sell replacement items and are not normally involved with the design and construction of new hospitality operations.

7. **Leasing Companies.** It is relatively common for retailers to lease FFE. For example, computers, ice machines, and video equipment are frequently leased or purchased on a rent-to-own plan.

DISTRIBUTION SYSTEM FOR SERVICES

Such services as advertising, consulting, and waste removal follow slightly different distribution patterns. Few large national sources exist, and most sources are local and consist of many "mom-and-pop" operations or small partnerships. A few of these may be local offices of a national firm or franchisees of a national firm. For instance, major accounting firms and printing companies have local offices or franchisees.

It is important to make sure that these small companies have actual expertise. Anyone can claim to be an accountant, for example, but a person qualified to provide a complete range of accounting, bookkeeping, and financial services usually is a certified public accountant (CPA).

RETAILERS

You, the hospitality operator, are generally classified as a retailer, or someone who sells a product or service to its ultimate consumer.[13] You deal most often with one or more distributors. You probably make fewer contacts with brokers and manufacturers' representatives. As a rule, small operations rarely deal directly with a primary source. If they do, this happens only when they purchase new equipment. Large corporations may, however, achieve economies of scale by purchasing large quantities of products directly from a primary source.

WHAT HAPPENS THROUGHOUT THE CHANNEL OF DISTRIBUTION?

We often hear that "the middleman makes all the money." It is, for example, suggested that the loaf of bread we buy contains only a few pennies' worth of food ingredients. What accounts for the rest of the price we pay for it? As with most items purchased, the price paid is the sum total of several costs. Some cost is tacked on during the bread's journey through the distribution channel each time someone adds value to the original food ingredients. Four kinds of economic values may be added to a product as it passes from the primary source to the retailer: time, form, place, and information.

Time Value

If you want to buy a product at the time you select, you must be willing to pay for this privilege. If, for instance, you wish to buy canned vegetables a little at a time instead of in bulk, your supplier will have to store these products and wait for you to order them. This is a major problem for the supplier because he or she must assume the risk and cost of storing the items. The supplier also will have money sitting on the shelf.

Whoever pays money for a product, regardless of where it is in the distribution channel, loses the use of that money for a while. For example, a vegetable canner may have to pay cash for raw vegetables and may also have to store the finished products, the canned vegetables, for many weeks. During this time, the canner's money is tied up. And the longer money is tied up, the more the vegetable canner has to charge for the canned vegetables. In other words, the processor adds an interest cost for capital tied up in processing since he or she probably borrows money from a bank to carry inventory.

The time economic value can also include other types of financing. For example, the typical intermediary often provides credit financing to hospitality buyers. It is a generally accepted procedure in the industry for suppliers to grant credit terms to their customers. These terms usually allow buyers about 30 to 45 days after delivery before they must pay the bill. Obviously, these purveyors must earn an interest income for capital tied up in accounts receivable.

Some restaurant operators follow the same practice when they price wines. They usually start with a certain price, and for every year they must keep the wine in their wine cellar waiting for a buyer, they add a percentage markup to the price.

Thus, members of the distribution channel consider financing an investment. If they invest money in products, they cannot invest it elsewhere. Consequently, this investment must offer them a certain return at least equal to the amount of interest they would have to pay to borrow these same funds. And in a productive, profitable business, the expected rate would exceed the cost of borrowed capital.

Form Value

Form is usually the most expensive value added to the products our industry purchases. Form is what turns a raw ingredient into something more user-friendly. For instance, a precut steak is much easier to purchase, store, and use than a large cut of beef that must undergo quite a bit of processing in a restaurant kitchen. Unfortunately, the processed item is much more expensive than the raw, unprocessed product.

The form value is also very expensive because highly processed items are usually packaged in costly containers. In fact, packaging becomes more expensive every day, especially for products that can be reconstituted in their own packages. In addition, buyers pay close attention to frozen-food packaging, particularly if these products are to be stored on their premises for a while. The demand and the need for stronger and more effective packaging have raised the price that retailers must pay.

Another reason packaging and, hence, form value, add so much to an item's final price is that there are numerous package sizes from which to choose. For example, catsup comes in several package types and sizes. You must be ready to pay more for individual servings of catsup than for catsup in large cans.

Place Value

If you want an item delivered to the place of your choice, you must pay for this convenience. For instance, all other things being equal, it costs more to buy a car at your local dealership than if you traveled to Detroit to purchase the car you want. Whoever moves a product from one place to another must recoup these costs in the selling price. This value is very expensive, especially when refrigerated and frozen products must be shipped.

Information Value

This is the least understood and, quite often, the most controversial economic value. An operator may be willing to pay more for a product if some information—for example, directions for use—comes with it. This operator might not mind paying a little more for a dishwashing machine if the company sends an instructor for three or four days to show workers how to use the machine. On the other hand, most hospitality operators would not care to pay anything extra for the recipes on the backs of flour bags.

Supplier Services Value

In addition to the four economic values discussed above, intangible supplier services accompany the items you purchase. When you purchase something, you purchase not only whatever you desire, but also any additional services that come with it. For instance, a salesperson who puts a rush order in his or her car and runs it over to your operation in an emergency is a good friend; an accountant who prepares a special report "overnight" also is valuable to you. But how much more are you willing to pay for such additional supplier services? This is not an easy question to answer. But you can be sure that supplier services (sometimes referred to as "support functions") work their way into an item's final price tag.

ULTIMATE VALUE

In the final analysis, a product's ultimate value consists of its quality and the values added to it. This final analysis does not always apply, especially when a perishable product must be price-discounted before it spoils. But, more often than not, the largest component of a product's final cost to the hospitality buyer can be attributed to the values added to that item as it journeys through the channel of distribution.

THE BUYER'S PLACE IN THE CHANNEL OF DISTRIBUTION

The buyers for most hospitality operations deal with several middlemen, and the typical middleman is the distributor. Larger corporations normally break out of this strict pattern and purchase many of their items directly from the primary source. In effect, they bypass some intermediaries. Large firms feel that buying directly from the primary source offers considerable cost savings. For example, buyers find car prices in Detroit to be generally cheaper than those in San Francisco simply because Detroit buyers can take advantage of the place value; in effect, they are compensated for receiving the car at its place of manufacture.

Consider, too, buyers who pick up food supplies in their own vehicle instead of waiting for the delivery. In this case, the price of the food should be lower because the buyers are providing the transportation value. (Notice, though, that the practice of picking up food yourself uses time and gasoline.) But assuming that the primary sources and middlemen would permit this choice, can you provide the economic values more cheaply yourself? Many large multiunit corporations think so and have moved into what is called "direct buying with central distribution." They buy from the primary sources, take delivery of the products at central-distribution centers, perhaps add some form value to the raw ingredients in their commissaries (e.g., clean, cut, and package raw vegetables), and then deliver the products to their restaurants or hotel properties via their own transportation.

Some hospitality companies claim that buying directly in this manner saves a great deal of money.[14] In addition to benefiting from this cost reduction, these firms feel that they enjoy supply assurances, greater quality control, improved coordination, and an ability to overcome local suppliers' lack of technological capabilities.

Other firms, though, do not agree that eliminating the middlemen necessarily makes their operations easier and less costly.[15] For instance, many of them fear the considerable investment that may be necessary to launch such ventures. Some companies also feel that they may lack the necessary expertise and, thus, could become very inefficient and inflexible over time. Furthermore, these firms are not always eager to cut out local suppliers who may be able to provide unique supplier services, purchase discounts, and offer other competitive advantages.

E-procurement applications, which allow companies to buy and sell products and services online, can provide access to hundreds of thousands of products and services. Businesses that participate can often purchase products without dealing with faxes, copies, or time out of the office. In essence, these applications can be a significant time-saver, allowing customers to order products from their desktops.

Direct or online procurement, central distribution, and the surrounding issues are controversial. The major problem seems to be that everyone has a different view of the importance of variouis aspects of the supply chain. Historically, few companies have been able to increase profitability by "eliminating the middleman."

Disintermediation can divert operators' attention from the major part of their businesses—their core competencies—thereby causing them to lose sight of their customers.[16]

The Optimal Economic Values and Supplier Services

When the hospitality business is doing well, hospitality company officials are not usually eager to provide too many economic values and supplier services themselves. They would rather spend their time, for example, convincing retail customers to purchase hamburgers than concern themselves with the care and feeding of steers. But when business takes a nosedive, hospitality company officials begin to examine, for instance, the as-purchased (AP) price of preportioned steak per pound versus the AP price of a side of beef per pound. In other words, in recessionary periods, management may try to provide some of its own economic values and supplier services with the hope of restoring prerecessionary profits.

This type of thinking has cost many companies quite a bit of money. Middlemen are experts, and, in the long run, they can usually provide these values and services less expensively than the individual hospitality operation.

SELECTING ECONOMIC VALUES

Full-time buyers do not normally have complete control over which economic values their company provides for itself. As with the determination-of-quality issue, the owner-manager must make these decisions. Full-time buyers may, of course, make suggestions and help inform the decision-making process.

Part-time buyers, especially those who have other management responsibilities, often are expected merely to maintain the economic values top management has decided upon. Like full-time buyers, however, part-time buyers may also make relevant suggestions and recommendations.

When managements do consider the feasibility of providing their own economic values, they tend to slant the analyses in the direction they desire. This skewing is easily done since everyone has a particular idea of what it costs, for example, to cut his or her own steaks. Some managers include an extra labor expense; others assume no extra labor expense, thinking existing employees can absorb this extra task.

There is no doubt that it is very costly to provide your own economic values, particularly the form economic value. There are sound reasons that a precut, preportioned New York sirloin steak sells for about 60 percent more per pound than the wholesale cut of beef (the short loin) that contains this type of steak, along with extra fat and trim. To obtain the convenience of prefabrication, a buyer must compensate a primary source and/or a middleman for the cost of payroll, payroll-related administrative expenses, the waste associated with meat processing, and the cost of energy needed to process and store the finished products.

But factors other than the "hard-cost" figures can enter the picture and haunt the manager later. The following are three of them:

1. Does the manager really want to get into the meat packing business? Does he or she really want to buy a truck? Does the manager have the long-term desire, the expertise, and the time to engage in these activities?

2. Will antitrust problems arise? Large companies must consider this possibility. For instance, some supermarket chains have expressed an interest in going way back in the channel of distribution for meat and becoming their own primary source. But no one is quite sure what the U.S. Justice Department would say about this plan. And it does not seem that too many want to find out.

3. What will other company employees, especially hourly employees and supervisors, say about taking on additional burdens? What will the labor unions say about this?

SELECTING SUPPLIER SERVICES

Buyers usually do have something to say about which supplier services their company should be willing to pay for. These supplier services are correlated with AP prices. Since buyers are not normally restricted to exact AP price limitations, they have a bit more discretion in deciding how much they are willing to pay for supplier services.

Generally, the arguments for and against supplier services are the same as those that center on the economic-values issue. On one hand, some owner-managers and buyers are convinced that they can do it all. On the other hand, others regard the supplier as a kind of "employee," and if the "employee" performs additional "service," he or she should be compensated for it. Thus, if the supplier performs additional service, these owner-managers are willing to pay for it—and choose to do so if the supplier's cost for the service is less than the in-house cost.

Many analysts have searched futilely for a middle ground between these extremes. Perhaps there is no middle ground. But it is undoubtedly worthwhile to accept, and pay for, many supplier services. An executive in the hospitality industry once put it this way:

> Let's try to relate purchasing dollars to sales dollars to help us judge how much service is worth. Look at some hypothetical figures.

PURCHASES PER MONTH	
Distributor's cost	$5,000.00
Average distributor markup of 15%	+750.00
	$5,750.00
Monthly sales	$90,000.00
12 hours per day, 30 days per month	12 × 30 = 360 hours
$90,000 ÷ 360 = $250.00 sales per hour	

> Let's say we find a really great distributor who provides all those extras that we like, but who asks for a 17 percent markup on the same $5000 monthly purchases. That's $850.00 or $100.00 more per month, or 28 cents per operating hour. Where should we devote our time and attention? To satisfying our customers and earning $250.00 worth of sales per operating hour? Or riding hard on our distributor to save 28 cents per operating hour? If you choose to cherry pick, have rigid receiving hours, and generally have a one-way relationship, you'll probably wind up paying more for less and spend more time at it.
>
> We believe that if we are to make a profit, we must give something of value to our customers. We know what we give our customers and [what we] must do to satisfy them. We hope that our distributors do also.[17]

In this example, it is assumed that the manager can increase sales if he or she spends more time with the restaurant's customers. Of course, many factors contribute to sales revenue; however, the point is well taken, and this example's approach is an honest attempt to quantify the difficult decision-making factors that surround the supplier-services issue.

KEY WORDS AND CONCEPTS

Alcohol Beverage Commission (ABC)	Brewers	Cash-and-carry
Architects	Broadline distributor	Catalog house
	Brokers	
As-purchased price (AP price)	Buying clubs	Central distribution

Certified public accountant (CPA)	Efficient foodservice response (EFR)	Manufacturer's agents and representatives
Channel of distribution	End-user services	Merchant wholesalers
Commissary	Equipment dealers	Middlemen
Construction contractors	Exclusive territories	Portal
Contract houses	Fabricators	Price club
Control state	Five strategies of EFR	Primary sources
Convenience foods	Full-line distributor	Processors
Co-op purchasing	Full-service dealer	Quick response (QR)
Designers	Furniture, fixtures, and equipment (FFE)	Storefront dealer
Direct buying	Growers	Supplier services
Discount operations	Heavy-equipment dealer	Support functions
Distillers	Importers-wholesalers	Tied-house laws
Distributors	Intermediaries	Value-added foods
Economic values	Leasing companies	Wholesale clubs
Efficiency foods	License state	Wine makers
Efficient consumer response (ECR)	Liquor distributors	

REFERENCES

1. National Restaurant Association (NRA [www.restaurant.org]) and American Hotel and Lodging Association (AH&LA [www.ahma.com]) estimates as of June 2003.

2. Patt Patterson, "Single Source of Supply: Does It Really Work?" *Nation's Restaurant News*, July 19, 1993, p. 109.

3. Clyde W. Witt, "Foodservice Industry Takes Bite Out of Inefficiency," *Material Handling Management*, October 2000, p. 44. See also: Anonymous, "Leading Foodservice Companies Align Item, Price Data in First Phase of EFR Project," retrieved January 2001 (Available http://www.efr-central.com/newsroom/newsroom.html).

4. H. A. Ryan, "Foodservice 2005 and Efficient Foodservice Response—Tools for Reshaping the Industry," *IFDA Food Distributor*, April/May 1996, p. 8.

5. K. Malchoff, "The EFR Train Is Ready for Departure—Are You Ready to Ride?" *IFDA Food Distributor*, April/May 1996, p. 19.

6. Anonymous, "About EFR—A Brief Overview," retrieved June 2003 (Available http://www.efr-central.com/aboutefr.html).

7. Michael Selz, "Independent Sales Reps Are Squeezed by the Recession," *The Wall Street Journal*, December 27, 1991, p. B2.

8. Jack Hayes, "Cash and Carry Wholesalers Pay Off for Small-Order Operators," *Nation's Restaurant News*, July 23, 1990, p. 27.

9. See http://www.cooperative.org/ and http://www.coop.org/.

10. Mort Hochstein, "Questioning the Laws of Beverage Distribution," *Nation's Restaurant News*, May 9, 1994, p. 51. See also: Sharon Gerrie, "Liquor Market: Liquid Gold. Two Companies Dominate Nevada's Lucrative Wholesale Liquor Market," Sunday, June 17, 2001 (Available

http://www.reviewjournal.com/lvrj_home/2001/Jun-17-Sun-2001/business/16219020.html).

11. Marj Charlier, "Existing Distributors Are Being Squeezed by Brewers, Retailers," *The Wall Street Journal*, November 22, 1993, p. 1A. See also: State of Tennessee, "Rules of the Alcohol Beverage Commission," retrieved June 2003 (Available http://www.state.tn.us/sos/rules/0100/0100-01.pdf).

12. Patt Patterson, "Dealer Evolution Gives Rise to Many New Options," *Nation's Restaurant News*, September 21, 1992, p. 128.

13. You could, of course, "sell" products in a not-for-profit organization, such as in most hospitals. Generally, though, both commercial and noncommercial operators adopt similar points of view concerning the management of any type of hospitality operation.

14. See, for example, Foster Frable, Jr., "More for Your Buck: Manufacturers Need to Show Potential Buyers Better Value," *Nation's Restaurant News*, August 7, 2000, p. 26. See also: Ron Ruggless, "Furr's/Bishop's Tackles Food Manufacturing," *Nation's Restaurant News*, January 11, 1993, p. 7; Jack Hayes, "CHPD Cuts Costs, Maintains Quality," *Nation's Restaurant News*, March 29, 1993, p. 74.

15. See, for example, Laurie P. Cohen, "The Man with the Midas Touch Meets His Match in the Nation's Steakhouses," *The Wall Street Journal*, January 3, 1994, p. B1. See also: Richard Martin, "LaSalsa, Green Burrito Gear Up for Showdown," *Nation's Restaurant News*, February 8, 1993, p. 1; Jim Yardley, "A Revolution in the Fish Industry That Hasn't Quite Taken Hold," *New York Times*, June 7, 2000, p. H19.

16. Charles Bernstein, "Catch 22: Should Suppliers Operate Restaurants?" *Nation's Restaurant News*, May 28, 1990, p. 21.

17. George Topor, "What Price Service?" *Restaurant Business*, February 1977, p. 101.

QUESTIONS AND PROBLEMS

1. Define the major primary sources in the hospitality channels of distribution, and explain how they differ from one another.

2. Describe the various intermediaries (the middlemen) with whom hospitality operators deal. How do these middlemen differ from one another?

3. Interview a purchasing manager at a hospitality operation. Determine how this company is using e-commerce enablers to select and procure products.

4. How does the channel of distribution for services differ from the distribution channel for food?

5. Define the four economic values. Why might buyers be reluctant to pay for the information value?

6. Would it be profitable for a small-restaurant owner to buy directly from a primary source? What specific items do you feel lend themselves particularly to this sort of buying?

7. Discuss how the need for financing adds to the ultimate cost of a product.

8. Assume that you are the buyer for a large corporation. Of the four specific values discussed in this chapter, which do you think you can provide more cheaply than the middleman? Why? Which do you think a middleman can provide more cheaply? Why?

9. What is the buyer's normal role in determining which economic values the company should provide for itself?

10. What is the buyer's normal role in determining which supplier services should be "purchased"?

11. What is the difference between a manufacturer's agent and a manufacturer's representative?

12. What is the difference between a price club and a wholesale club?

13. Assume that you are a small restaurateur. You have the opportunity to purchase your precut steaks less expensively from a competing restaurant chain's central commissary. Should you do this? Why?

14. Identify an advantage of purchasing a piece of equipment on the rent-to-own plan.

15. Assume that you have been purchasing your produce from one supplier for several years. You have been satisfied during this time. A new produce supplier seeks your business and offers you a $3^1/_2$ percent discount from what you currently are paying. What would you do?

16. Define the term "end-user services."

17. Give an example of each of the four economic values.

18. Give an example of a supplier service.

19. Briefly describe the typical distribution system for fresh meat.

20. What is the difference between a broker and a food distributor?

21. The food distributor normally earns a larger percentage of profit than the broker. What are some of the reasons you feel might account for this?

22. List three typical intermediaries you will find in the distribution system for FFE.

23. What is the primary function of a commissary?

24. What is the difference between a control state and a license state?

25. What is meant by the term "efficiency foods"?

EXPERIENTIAL EXERCISES

1. Interview a purchasing manager at a hospitality operation. Determine how this company is using EFR to streamline the procurement process. Write a report that discusses the company's implementation of the five EFR strategies.

2. Find one or two chain companies that provide many of their own economic values. Try to arrange a visit to their facilities. Also, try to get the managers talking about the costs and benefits of providing many of their own economic values. Before you go, see whether you can determine beforehand what they will say. (*Hint:* Even though many companies have lost money at this, they all seem to argue that their quality control has improved immensely. In addition, some firms are so insistent about certain types of services—usually those that suppliers are reluctant to provide, such as daily deliveries—that they embark on this difficult activity just to get exactly what they want, regardless of the cost!)

3. Interview two sales representatives of different local liquor distributors. Ask each sales representative for a list of distilled spirit brands that they sell. Determine if there is any crossover of distilled spirit brands between the distributors; there should be none. Ask one sales representative if they can provide you a particular brand that another distributor sells. If he or she says no—which most certainly will be the case—ask that representative for suggestions of an alternative brand. Write a two-page report detailing how you would purchase distilled spirits for a bar in your local area.

FORCES AFFECTING THE DISTRIBUTION SYSTEMS

The Purpose of this Chapter

After reading this chapter, you should be able to:

- Identify the economic forces that affect the channel of distribution.
- Identify the political forces that affect the channel of distribution.
- Identify the legal restrictions that affect the channel of distribution.
- Identify the technological advances that affect the channel of distribution.

INTRODUCTION

In Chapter 3, we discussed the overall pattern of distribution in the hospitality business, as well as the values added throughout the distribution channel. That discussion did not take into consideration the forces that might interfere with the flow of products and services or with the final purchase price retailers must pay. In other words, several forces in the environment can have some effect on the price and availability of the products a hospitality operation needs. Figure 4.1 shows the major forces that affect the distribution channel, and the next sections discuss these forces.

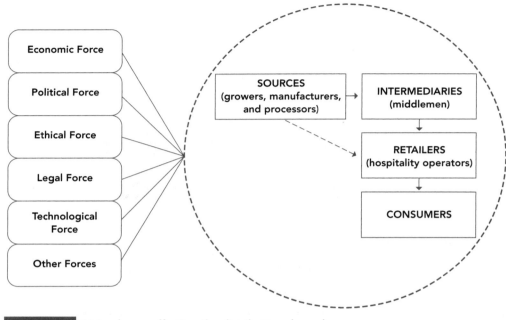

FIGURE 4.1 Major forces affecting the distribution channels.

ECONOMIC FORCE

Supply-and-demand considerations have a powerful effect on purchase prices, particularly the prices of perishable items. At the beginning of the channel of distribution, at the primary source level, supply and demand can be extremely important. Generally, at this level, the products are in their initial stages of production and are not readily distinguishable, regardless of the producer who has them. Little value has been added to these products; as a result, the prices at this stage are often set through a bidding procedure.

For example, many of the food products that eventually reach the retailer start out as such basic commodities as wheat, corn, cattle, and poultry. Within the same product quality class, small or no differences may exist between Farmer Jones's wheat and Farmer Smith's. Consequently, if the amount of this wheat available exceeds the demand for it, the price drops until all the wheat is sold. Conversely, if the demand exceeds the supply, prices rise until people stop bidding for the wheat. Supply-and-demand forces exert a major impact on commodity prices.

In many respects, the wheat farmers in this example occupy a precarious position unless they can do something to differentiate their products. This differentiation usually occurs when each primary source, or a middleman, attempts to apply his or her own version of the economic values. For instance, manipulating the form in which the product comes to market can earn a seller a stronger competitive position. Consequently, once a basic commodity gets into the channel of distribution, the pressure is on to do something to make the product unique in the buyer's eyes.

If all products were sold strictly on a supply-and-demand basis, sellers would be forced to accept the price that supply-and-demand conditions set. Thus, sellers would worry constantly about producing an excessive supply. Wheat is wheat, period. Consequently, the wheat farmer must accept the established market price.

As products move along in the channel, they acquire various different values. In fact, by the time products reach middlemen, once-similar products may have pronounced differences. This variety means that a seller begins to exercise a bit of control over the price; he or she need not always have to accept the price determined by supply and demand.[1]

But sellers cannot forget supply-and-demand conditions entirely. If a seller is overstocked, for example, he or she may have to lower the price to generate a demand—a situation often associated with perishable goods. Sellers try to avoid this problem, but they remain aware of the old axiom, "Sell it or smell it." And most of them would rather sell.

Buyers can expect to see varying prices for apparently similar products, even products that are in the same quality class. This situation is not so surprising once you realize that each seller can do something to differentiate the product.

Sellers usually strive to emphasize the product's overall value. Value is directly related to the quality of a product, as well as to the supplier services. Hence, a buyer supposedly would be willing to pay more for a product if the price included additional supplier services that the buyer felt provided increased value.

We use the term "value" intentionally, but to be even more accurate, we should use the term "perceived value," since value means different things to different people. Perceived value is equal to the "perceived quality" of a product or service plus the "perceived supplier services" divided by the "perceived edible-portion (EP) cost" (see Figure 4.2 for a diagram of this equation).

The perceived EP cost is the final cost to you of providing, for example, a finished steak dinner. Usually, it is not equal to the as-purchased (AP) price, since some products must normally occasion some waste: fat may have to be trimmed from the steak, resulting in an EP cost per pound that is higher than the AP price per pound; or, depending on the style in which you purchase steak—for example, precut and preportioned versus a whole beef carcass—you incur different

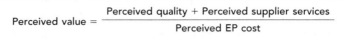

$$\text{Perceived value} = \frac{\text{Perceived quality} + \text{Perceived supplier services}}{\text{Perceived EP cost}}$$

FIGURE 4.2   Value as related to quality, supplier services, and EP cost.

labor costs, as well as different energy costs utilized in the preparation of a steak dinner.

Traditionally, the EP cost of food included only the food-ingredient cost, and the cost of nonfood supplies included only the cost of the usable product. Although the EP cost is difficult to assess, we think that it is more appropriate to expand the tradition and think of the EP cost in a different way. For instance, the labor cost associated with some food items may be higher than that for other similar items. Also, the amount and cost of energy utilized in preparation can differ among similar food products. Further, the labor and energy required to clean can vary according to the type of cleaning solution used.

Throughout this book, we refer to the EP cost, not necessarily as the edible-portion cost of food or beverage, but in the context of an as-served cost of food or beverage or an as-used cost per gallon of liquid cleaner. Our intent is not to provide mathematical formulas to compute these costs. But we want you to adopt a more panoramic view of the AP price—we wish to use the term "EP cost" to mean that the final cost of anything you buy includes several aspects, the least of which might be the initial AP price.

The relationship shown in Figure 4.2 is not a mathematical formula. We present it as an equation to emphasize the point that value is directly related to quality and supplier services, but inversely related to the EP cost. For example, if quality and the supplier services remain the same while the EP cost drops, the value of the product increases. Conversely, if quality decreases and the supplier services and EP cost remain constant, the value of the product decreases.

The possibilities for sellers' manipulation of the value equation and the ubiquitous supply-and-demand conditions create a market situation that economists refer to as "monopolistic competition." Monopolistic competition refers to the idea that each seller enjoys some sort of monopoly to the extent that he or she can manipulate products and services and make them seem to be unique. But the specter of supply and demand remains, and, ultimately, so does the need to be sensitive to price competition: suppliers cannot raise their prices that much higher than their competitors. Thus, most competitors have some sort of monopoly, but just enough to give them some control over prices and some flexibility in attracting customers.

Monopolistic competition is the most common type of marketing environment found throughout the hospitality industry. From the primary source to the retail level, all members of the distribution systems strive to highlight value over price. Suppliers do this in an attempt to convince retailers that no substitute suppliers are capable of satisfying their needs. Restaurant managers similarly manipulate product quality, customer services, and menu prices in order to create repeat patronage. And hotel operators are quick to emphasize their unique sets of room quality, customer services, and room rates.

Buyers must realize that they might need to pay a bit more for a certain unique set of quality, supplier services, and EP cost. But this can easily be the most cost-effective alternative. There is no reason that buyers cannot enjoy considerable financial success by throwing in their lot with only those suppliers who provide the best perceived value. In the long run, a slightly higher AP price can very well generate the most profitable results.

POLITICAL FORCE

Large suppliers and hospitality enterprises exercise considerable political influence in state legislatures and even in the U.S. Congress. These firms frequently lobby for legislation that favors their business and against legislation that is unfavorable to their business. Generally, the primary sources in the channel of distribution have the most political influence. There are fewer sources than middlemen and hospitality operations; thus, the sources can make a well-organized, concentrated effort to assure that their interests are served.

The majority of members in the channels of distribution usually restrict their lobbying efforts to joining the local hospitality association and/or chamber of commerce. Since politics play a large part in how hospitality operators conduct their businesses, it should not be surprising to find many people trying to effect an easier business climate. One unfortunate aspect of this political reality is that as one channel member is accommodated, others may be hurt.

Political activity need not be restricted to local, state, and federal legislative bodies. Many political realities, or "unwritten laws," can affect a channel member's behavior. For instance, it may be politically unwise for a hospitality operator to provide some of his or her own specific values, thereby reducing some middleman's income, particularly if that operator may need the friendship of the middleman later. Alternately, it may be unwise for a hospitality operator to delay paying bills.

There is nothing inherently wrong with trying to influence legislation; this behavior is natural and often beneficial. Also, operators must always remember that politics are not restricted to government. Channel members must coexist, and the political force, as invisible as it may at times be, is there to influence product availability, prices, and channel member behavior.

ETHICAL FORCE

What is the "ethical force"? Better yet, what is "ethical"? Is it ethical for a large meat packer to restrict supply for a few days, hoping that the price for meat will rise? Is it ethical for buyers to browbeat suppliers, especially suppliers who may be in a slump and are, therefore, vulnerable? Is it ethical for a chef to return spoiled products if the items spoiled because the chef purchased too much and could not use them quickly enough? Is it ethical for a salesperson to keep quiet about a product's limitations if the buyer does not ask about them? No doubt, most of us would agree that these practices would be unethical behavior, but we must recognize that not everyone would view such practices as dishonest.

For instance, a study posed the following scenario: A beverage supplier offers a buyer a free case of wine for the buyer's personal use. What should the buyer do? Accept the wine? Reject it? Offer to buy it at a reduced price? Or take it and add it to the bar inventory instead of taking it home?

The results of the study indicated that approximately one-third of the respondents would accept the wine; just over one-half would say thanks, but decline the gift; about 1 percent would offer to purchase it at half price; and approximately 8 percent would accept the wine, but add it to the bar inventory.[2]

Another study also indicated that there is no clear-cut definition of ethical behavior. Respondents were asked to indicate their perceptions of ethical issues in business practices. Interestingly enough, on average, they felt that accepting gifts from suppliers was not considered very unethical.[3]

Some have suggested that questionable ethics are necessary speed bumps in the channel of distribution. The pressure on salespersons and buyers to consummate attractive deals practically compels members to behave unethically at times. The fact is that through the years, a system of rebates and kickbacks has grown up among some traditional operators, and these may be thought of as an unethical force bearing on the channels. In large business firms, control systems quickly detect the inflation of cost, and the wise and ethical manager avoids these practices. An honest manager can advance more surely playing by the rules than can the dishonest person who must constantly devote energy to covering his or her tracks—and who continually risks destroying his or her career.[4]

Several professional purchasing associations, among them the Institute for Supply Management (www.ism.ws)—formerly the National Association of Purchasing Managers (NAPM)—and the Foodservice Purchasing Managers Executive Study Group (FPM [www.restaurant.org/purchasing]) of the National Restaurant Association (NRA), have developed codes of ethics to guide their members.[5] All buyers should be familiar with these codes. The buyers' supervisors should also examine these codes, since purchasing policies to guide a buyer's performance could inadvertently force the buyer toward unethical behavior.

Legislators continue to devote considerable attention to selling and buying practices, particularly the various rebate systems and other forms of economic favoritism. Channel members' adherence to sound ethics can ease this growing pressure, but, regardless of the future role of ethics in the hospitality channel of distribution, ethical and unethical forces continue to influence product availability and prices in the present.

LEGAL FORCE

Many buyers have discovered that a lawyer is a buyer's best friend. Channel members must accept a multitude of rules and regulations if they want to engage in buying and selling. We have already seen how the political force works to influence legislation. The following paragraphs discuss the major pieces of legislation and their relevance to the hospitality channel of distribution.

The Sherman Act (1890)

The Sherman Act was the United States' first piece of antitrust legislation. Basically, it forbids any action that tends to eliminate or severely reduce competition. Interestingly, the language of this law is so general that just about anything relating to unfair competition could be covered under the Sherman Act.

Meat Safety Legislation

In 1906, Upton Sinclair shocked the world with his book *The Jungle* (sunsite.berkeley.edu/Literature/Sinclair/TheJungle/). In it, he depicted the unspeakable sanitation conditions then prevalent in the meat packing industry. His description of these horrendous conditions led immediately to a severe decline in meat consumption in the United States. The book also forced the federal government to pass the Pure Food Act (1906) and the Meat Inspection Act (1907). These acts gave the U.S. Department of Agriculture (USDA [www.usda.gov]), established by Congress in 1862, inspection powers throughout the channels of distribution. Although the USDA technically has the authority to inspect any channel member (except seafood production), it usually confines its activities to the inspection of red meat, poultry, and egg production.

The meat-inspection legislation requires continuous antemortem and postmortem inspection of all meat intended for interstate and international commerce. State agriculture departments normally inspect meat plants that service customers located only within the particular states.

One of the major weaknesses in the original meat inspection laws was the lack of application to poultry products. Although voluntary poultry inspection was begun in 1926, the required inspection of all poultry sold in interstate commerce did not take effect until the passage of the Poultry Products Inspection Act (1957) more than 30 years later.

No further federal legislation affected red meat until 1967, when Ralph Nader and his "Nader's Raiders" focused attention on continuing abuses in the meat industry (http://www.nader.org/). Nader's efforts led to the passage of the Wholesome Meat Act (1967).

Current USDA food-safety authority rests on a series of legislation based primarily on the Wholesome Meat Act (1967), the Poultry Products Inspection Act (1957), and the Wholesome Poultry Products Act (1968). The USDA enforces chemical residue standards and the standards dealing with wholesomeness, general sanitation, packaging, and labeling.

Today's meat inspection system still relies on inspectors' observations of meat products. However, inspection also calls for Pathogen Reduction and Hazard Analysis and Critical Control Points (HACCP) system assessment. This system (similar to one promulgated by local health districts for restaurant operators) requires food processors to identify places within their production cycle where the items can become contaminated (i.e., "critical points") and institute procedures to ensure food safety. It is thought that stronger regulations could reduce the number of food-borne illness outbreaks caused by meat and poultry products.[6] The USDA also requires that safe-handling instructions be placed on all packages of raw meat and poultry (see Figure 4.3).

There are approximately 7000 federal meat and poultry plants and 2900 state plants. Approximately 8000 federal inspectors are employed to supervise the processing of approximately 6 million birds and 125 million beef, pork, and lamb animals per year.

Federal inspection is under the direction of a supervising veterinarian from the Food Safety Inspection Service (FSIS [http://www.fsis.usda.gov]) division of

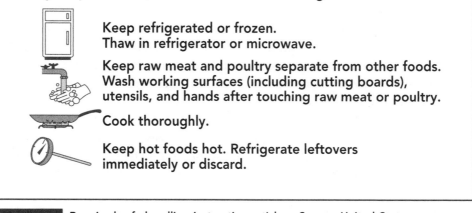

Safe Handling Instructions

This product was prepared from inspected and passed meat and/ or poultry. Some food products may contain bacteria that could cause illness if the product is mishandled or cooked improperly. For your protection, follow these safe handling instructions.

Keep refrigerated or frozen.
Thaw in refrigerator or microwave.

Keep raw meat and poultry separate from other foods.
Wash working surfaces (including cutting boards),
utensils, and hands after touching raw meat or poultry.

Cook thoroughly.

Keep hot foods hot. Refrigerate leftovers
immediately or discard.

FIGURE 4.3 Required safe-handling instructions sticker. *Source:* United States Department of Agriculture Website.

the USDA. Approximately three-quarters of the FSIS's budget is allocated to meat and poultry inspections and operations. The FSIS inspector also oversees all voluntary federal inspection for animals not covered under mandatory inspection, such as buffalo, rabbit, reindeer, elk, deer, antelope, and ratites. This inspection is covered by the Agricultural Marketing Act (1946), which defined grading and inspection services. Hospitality companies that request this inspection pay an hourly fee.

The Federal Food, Drug, and Cosmetic Act (1906)

Although the USDA primarily administers meat inspection, the Federal Food, Drug, and Cosmetic Act (FFDCA) provides the majority of food and drug regulation in the United States. Congress created the Food and Drug Administration (FDA) to administer this law.

The FDA is responsible for random inspections of approximately 50,000 food-processing plants in the United States. It employs about 350 inspectors. And, like the USDA, it has adopted the HACCP system (http://www.cfsan.fda.gov/~lrd/haccp.html) to increase quality assurance.

The FDA has the power to inspect products, records, and premises of food and drug establishments to ensure compliance with the law. Among other powers, the FDA is granted the authority to establish maximum amounts permitted for various classes of contaminants whose presence in food cannot be avoided.

The FDA's power has been increased several times over the years. The major changes occurred in 1938, 1958, 1960, 1962, and 1967, perhaps the most significant one being the Cosmetics-Devices Act (1938). This law gave the FDA injunctive power and the authority to set food standards. Essentially, the FDA has the power to remove from the marketplace any product that does not meet agency standards. Indeed, no other governmental agency can force a company to recall its products as quickly as the FDA can.

Recently the FFDCA was amended by the new Food Quality Protection Act (FQPA) in 1996. This new act provides a single safety standard for pesticide residuals in foods and changes the way the Environmental Protection Agency (EPA [www.epa.gov]) regulates pesticides use in the United States.

Seafood Safety Legislation

Seafood is not subject to the rigorous, mandatory continuous inspection required for meat and poultry products. People have lobbied for a mandatory seafood-inspection system,[7] but as of this writing, there is only a voluntary program.

However, in 1997, the FDA established HACCP requirements for all processors engaged in interstate commerce and/or the importing of seafood. In essence, these operations now have to perform at least a hazard analysis based on HACCP guidelines.

On the voluntary side, a major continuous inspection program is housed in the U.S. Department of Commerce. For a fee, a fish processor can obtain continuous inspection of its processing plant from the National Oceanic and Atmospheric Administration (NOAA [http://seafood.nmfs.noaa.gov/]). In return, the processor can label its packages as "Packed Under Federal Inspection" (PUFI). For an additional fee, the Department of Commerce will provide a quality grading service.

Seafood is subject to the provisions of the FFDCA. This law permits the FDA to periodically inspect fish production to ensure that the foods are wholesome, sanitary, labeled correctly, and stored properly. Since the United States has approximately 5000 fish processing plants, a mandatory continuous inspection program is not feasible. However, as stated previously, the FDA now requires seafood processors to use the HACCP system when establishing and operating their production plants.

The FDA has the authority to examine seafood in interstate commerce and, if the product is defective, to seize it and prohibit its sale. In addition, the FDA is allowed to inspect imported seafood products before they are permitted to enter the United States.

There also is a cooperative program, involving federal and state agencies, that supervises the beds of water that are used to grow and harvest shellfish. This venture, referred to as the Interstate Shellfish Sanitation Commission, certifies areas that are suitable for the production of clams, oysters, and mussels, and designates that they are in compliance with the Department of Commerce's voluntary inspection program.

Some seafood products are subject to legislation that, while not necessarily focused on seafood safety, nevertheless contributes to a safe, wholesome environment. For instance, the 1992 Marine Mammal Protection Act (a federal law) stipulates that only tuna harvested without endangering dolphins can be sold, distributed, or bought in the United States.

Federal Trade Commission (1914), Amended by the Wheeler-Lea Act (1938)

The Federal Trade Commission (FTC) deals with advertising, deceptive promotions, monopolies, and unprofessional conduct in the marketplace. It was established primarily to clarify the Sherman Act and to enhance its power.

The Clayton Act (1914)

The Clayton Act was yet another attempt by Congress to increase the federal government's control over antitrust violations. The act essentially enumerates and amplifies the antitrust duties of the FTC.

Two illegal activities covered in this act are of particular importance to channel members: (1) "Tying agreements," whereby sellers once forced retailers to purchase certain items (e.g., pickles) in order to gain the privilege of purchasing others (e.g., mustard), and (2) "exclusive dealing," whereby a salesperson forced a retailer to buy only his or her product (e.g., beer) and no other brands of that product. Exclusive dealing should not be confused with "exclusive selling," which is a perfectly legal type of franchise arrangement. For example, in most cases, a beer company can legally sell its beer to only a few select retailers, which then become the retailers that customers must contact if they want that particular brand of beer.

More information on the Sherman and Clayton Acts can be found at the U.S. Department of Justice Website (www.usdoj.gov) Specifically, the Antitrust Division Manual for the Statutory Provisions and Guidelines of the Antitrust Division can be found at http://www.usdoj.gov/atr/foia/divisionmanual/table_of_contents .htm. Chapter 2 of the manual details the Clayton and Sherman Acts.

Perishable Agricultural Commodities Act (1930)

The intent of this legislation is to control interstate commerce, specifically by prohibiting unfair and fraudulent practices in the sale of fresh and frozen produce. Wholesalers are required to be licensed by the government. If an individual hospitality operation does a bit of wholesale business on the side and the products sold in this manner cross state lines, the operation also may need such a license.

Agricultural Adjustment Act (1933) and Agricultural Marketing Agreement Act (1937)

This legislation permits primary sources and intermediaries to work together in certain ways to solve their marketing problems and to ensure a steady flow of perishable products. The acts exempt these sellers from some antitrust laws. For example, in certain cases, sellers of these products may join together to form seller co-ops, which market the products of each individual primary source.

The Robinson-Patman Act (1936)

This act, known as the "small-business protection act," was designed to enhance further the power of the federal government to control antitrust violations. The primary thrust of the act was the limitation placed on companies that used various types of price discounts when marketing their goods and services.

Among other things, this act addressed three specific loopholes: (1) Up until 1936, sellers could give "promotional discounts" to buyers of their choice. After 1936, this became a form of illegal price discrimination when the discounts were not offered to all qualified buyers. (2) It is legal for sellers to offer a buyer a discount if the buyer purchases in large amounts. But it has been illegal since 1936 to set this amount so high that only one or two buyers can hope to reach it. In other words, the Robinson-Patman Act incorporated a "quantity limits provision" so that the quantity a buyer must purchase to qualify for a discount must be reasonable. (3) A supplier cannot practice "predatory pricing." That is to say, he or she cannot price goods or services so low that it would drive all other competitors out of the marketplace, thereby affording this lone supplier a monopoly and the opportunity to raise prices significantly in the future.

The Clayton Act and the Robinson-Patman Act do not prohibit all types of price discrimination. Generally, two buyers can pay different prices for the same product if, for example, one buyer provides some value. For instance, purchasing large quantities of products is a way for buyers to provide their own financing as well as storage. As a reward for bulk purchasing, a supplier can legally charge a lower price. In general, sellers can manipulate the price if the goods are of unlike quality or quantity. Sellers also can reduce their prices at a moment's notice to meet a competitor's recently reduced price.

The Hart Act (1966–1969)

The Hart Act altered the way products are packaged, particularly with regard to a package's pictorial aspects. The act, which the FDA enforces, sought to eliminate misleading descriptions and illustrations. It also sought to force companies to adopt standard packaging sizes, which it failed to accomplish. The Hart Act has managed to frighten several channel members, especially primary sources, who quickly adopted many of the late Senator Phillip Hart's informal suggestions voluntarily.

Package Label Regulations

The federal government requires the labels of packaged, processed foods to contain the following information:[8]

1. The common or legal name of the product.

2. The name and address of the food processor, or the distributor, of the items.

3. The net contents in the package, listed according to count, weight, or other appropriate measure.

4. A listing of ingredients, in descending order, from greatest proportion to least proportion. (This requirement may be unnecessary if a "standard of identity" has been established for the product. A standard of identity essentially establishes what a food product is—for example, what a food product must be to

be labeled "strawberry preserves." The federal government has developed standards of identity for approximately 235 products.)[9]

5. A notation of any artificial flavoring or chemical preservative added to the product.

6. Serving size (in typical measures, such as "cups") and number of servings per container. (The federal government has developed standard serving sizes for approximately 150 food categories.)

7. Number of calories per serving.

8. Number of calories derived from fat.

9. Amounts of fat, saturated fat, cholesterol, sodium, sugars, dietary fiber, protein, total carbohydrates, and complex carbohydrates.

10. Amounts of important vitamins and minerals.

11. If the product is a beverage, the amount of juice (fruit or vegetable) it contains.

12. A notation that the product falls below the standard of fill, if relevant. (A "standard of fill" indicates to the processor how full a container must be to avoid deception. This standard prevents the selling of air or water in place of food; prescribed amounts of air and water, though, are permissible.)

13. Also, if relevant, a statement that the product falls below the standard of quality. (A "standard of quality" is the minimum standard a product must meet in order to earn the federal government's lowest possible quality grade. For instance, if canned green beans are excessively broken, the label could read "Below Standard of Quality: Excessively Broken.")

14. All label information must be noted in English unless an imported product with a foreign-language label will not deceive consumers, or if such a product will be distributed in an area where the foreign language is the predominant language.

15. If the food processor makes any nutritional or dietary claims, the package label must carry government-approved terminology. Several terms can be used as long as the processor meets these strict definitions (see Figure 4.4).

16. A standardized list of nutrition facts, as articulated by the Nutrition Labeling and Education Act (1990), must be included on the package label (see Figure 4.5). (Technically, the package labels of processed foods sold only to food services that will process them further and resell them to guests, do not have to include nutrition facts. Today, however, it is unusual to see a package label that does not include this standardized information.)

NUTRITION/HEALTH CLAIM STANDARD DEFINITIONS	
Calorie free	Fewer than 5 calories
Cholesterol free	Fewer than 2 milligrams cholesterol and 2 grams (or less) saturated fat
Fat free	Less than $1/2$ gram fat
Heart healthy	Contains 13 grams of oat bran or 20 grams of oatmeal and is low fat and low sodium
Light (lite)	One-third fewer calories (or 50 percent less fat)
Low calorie	40 calories (or less)
Low cholesterol	20 milligrams (or less) cholesterol and 2 grams (or less) saturated fat
Low fat	3 grams (or less) fat
Low sodium	140 milligrams (or less) sodium
Sodium free	Fewer than 5 milligrams sodium

FIGURE 4.4 Standard definitions of some nutrition/health claims.

17. If the product is raw or partially cooked meat or poultry, it must contain safe-handling instructions on the package label, that is, instructions that indicate how the product should be handled in order to avoid contamination.

In addition to federal-government labeling requirements, many states and local municipalities issue their own label regulations. For instance, in California, a food processor must put a health warning on any food that contains an ingredient(s) suspected of causing cancer or birth defects. A more detailed discussion of food labeling can be found at www.cfsan.fda.gov/label.html.

Franchise Law

A franchisor can legally require franchisees to adhere to standards of quality set forth by the franchisor. For example, franchisors normally prepare strict product specifications that franchisees must use when purchasing all food, beverage, and nonfood supplies. These specifications ensure quality and cost control as well as a consistent appearance.

Usually a franchisor will not force a franchisee to purchase from the franchisor's commissary and/or central distribution center, nor would a franchisee necessarily be required to buy from a supplier designated by the franchisor. However, it would appear that, under some circumstances, a franchisor can impose these

Nutrition Facts

Serving Size 1 cup (228g)
Serving Per Container 2

Amount Per Serving

Calories 250   Calories from Fat 110

% Daily Value*

Total Fat 12g	**18%**
Saturated Fat 3g	**15%**
Trans Fat 1.5g	
Cholesterol 30mg	**10%**
Sodium 470mg	**20%**
Total Carbohydrate 31g	**10%**
Dietary Fiber 0g	**0%**
Sugars 5g	
Protein 5g	

Vitamin A	**4%**
Vitamin C	**2%**
Calcium	**20%**
Iron	**4%**

*Percent Daily Values are based on a 2,000 calorie diet. Your Daily Values may be higher or lower depending on your calorie needs:

	Calories:	2,000	2,500
Total Fat	Less than	65g	80g
Sat Fat	Less than	20g	25g
Cholesterol	Less than	300mg	300mg
Sodium	Less than	2,400mg	2,400mg
Total Carbohydrate		300g	375g
Dietary Fiber		25g	30g

FIGURE 4.5 An example of nutrition facts on a package label. *Source:* United States Department of Agriculture Website.

types of restrictions on franchisees.[10] At one time, the courts found these restrictions to be illegal, citing them as violations of antitrust legislation. More recently, though, court rulings have eased these limitations on franchisors as long as they do not derive an economic benefit from requiring franchisees to carry certain specified products.

The Internal Revenue Service and the
Bureau of Alcohol, Tobacco, and Firearms

Two federal-government agencies, the Internal Revenue Service (IRS) and the Bureau of Alcohol, Tobacco, and Firearms (BATF [www.atf.treas.gov]), are responsible for the orderly and legal sale, distribution, and purchase of alcoholic beverages. These agencies ensure that: (1) no adulterated product enters the marketplace; (2) products are produced, sold, distributed, and purchased by duly licensed entities only; and (3) all appropriate taxes and fees are collected.

State and Local Legislation

All the laws discussed so far are federal. Some states and municipalities have adopted somewhat stricter versions of them, as well as additional legislation not found in the federal statutes. For example, although the federal government does not mandate fish plant inspection, some states do. In addition, many channel members must contend with several state and county liquor codes.

Contract Law

A contract is "a voluntary and lawful agreement, by competent parties, for a good consideration, to do or not do a specified thing."[11] A completed purchase order, once accepted by a supplier, becomes a legally enforceable contract. If buyers renege on their promises, they may be sued by their suppliers and forced to perform according to the terms established in their contracts.

In some instances, a buyer purchases only a small amount of merchandise at one time and may not prepare a formal purchase order document. He or she may simply call in an order to a local supplier instead of mailing in or faxing a written order. In some cases, a verbal commitment of this type can carry the force of a written contract. Article 2-201 of the Uniform Commercial Code (UCC) states that a purchase order of $500 or more is not enforceable in a court of law unless the agreement is reduced to writing. Consequently, a small verbal order of, say, $100, could be considered legally binding for both parties.

After an order is made with the supplier, a buyer might request a written acknowledgement from the supplier. Technically, no contract exists if a supplier does not acknowledge his or her intent to enter into a legally binding agreement.

Presumably, once the goods are delivered, the buyer will deem them acceptable and will pay for the merchandise. However, legal problems might arise if the goods delivered do not meet the agreed-upon standards of quality, quantity, and price. A buyer is able to return these goods if he or she: (1) inspects a representative sample of the goods; (2) indicates why the goods are not acceptable; and (3) informs the supplier that the goods are being rejected. If a buyer fails to inspect and reject the goods and to indicate why this action is being taken, he or she will have accepted the merchandise and will be responsible for paying for it.[12]

A great deal of trust must exist between buyers and suppliers. In some situations, we cannot take time to create written documentation; we must rely on our suppliers to treat us honestly and with good faith. As long as all parties have each other's best interests at heart, all of them can coexist and achieve their long-term goals.

This brief discussion highlights the major issues that a purchasing agent needs to consider when preparing purchase orders. But a buyer must consider other laws—federal, state, and local laws—as well. In fact, an operator should immediately seek legal advice whenever a question arises. For instance, there may be unique deposit and refund laws in your area that must be considered before you enter into a long-term purchase agreement.

Agency Law

Salespersons need to know the precise authority operators delegate to their buyers. In general, buyers have the authority, as their company's agents, to legally bind their companies to purchase order contracts. Hospitality companies usually limit a buyer's authority by setting a dollar limit on the purchases he or she can contract for. If such a limitation exists, however, salespersons and their companies must be notified; otherwise, they can rightfully assume that the buyer has unlimited authority.

Title to Goods

It is important for buyers to know the precise moment when the title to any product passes to their firm because, at the point of title transfer, the buyer's firm assumes responsibility for the item. Title can pass at any one of many points in the market channel. Usually, when purchasing from intermediaries, the hospitality operation takes title when a receiving agent receives, inspects, and signs for the delivered merchandise. Under a direct-buying arrangement (i.e., purchasing directly from the primary source), the hospitality operation takes title when the merchandise leaves the primary source's premises; typically, the primary source places the merchandise on a common carrier "free on board" (FOB), which states that, once the property is on board, the buyer now owns it and takes responsibility for its safe transit.

If the buyer takes title before actually receiving the item, even though he or she may not have actually paid for the product, it, as well as the risk, belongs to his or her company. (Parenthetically, when taking a risk like this earlier than necessary, the buyer may earn a slightly lower AP price.)

Consignment Sales

Although consignment sales are not common in the hospitality industry, and are not allowed for alcoholic beverages, they do appear now and then, especially in seasonal resort areas where buyers must stock up well before the doors are opened to cash-paying guests. Off-premises caterers also tend to rely on consignment sales from time to time, especially for big parties that are allowed to pay most of their catering bills after the functions are over.

A typical consignment sale stipulates that the buyer of a product need not pay until his or her company sells the product. This is a good way for a retailer to work with a supplier's money, but a desire to buy "on consignment" tends to imply that the buyer is in a precarious financial position.

Warranties and Guarantees

Warranties and guarantees may be either "expressed" or "implied." The express warranty or guarantee is written out in, ideally, straightforward language. The implied versions are, as their name suggests, either inferred by the buyer or implied by the seller. Courts of law have been known to let salespersons voice a degree of prideful exaggeration and to include a certain amount of subjectivity, or permissible puffery, in a sales pitch. Consequently, a buyer may face problems if he or she seeks retribution when the product is not, after all, "the best in the land."

Patents

Retailers must be careful to avoid illegally adopting someone else's patented procedures. For example, at one time, only a select few were authorized to use pressure fryers. Nor can copyrights be violated. For instance, you cannot substitute Pepsi for Coke.

Rebates

Rebates, which are gifts of cash or product, are legal as long as suppliers offer all buyers the same rebate possibility. An exception exists in the liquor trade, in which all rebates are illegal on the wholesale level. Oddly enough, a buyer could be unknowingly implicated in a legal action if he or she takes a rebate, assuming that all other buyers have had the same opportunity, when in fact, he or she is the only buyer receiving the rebate.

Rebates are also against the law when a buyer and seller conspire to inflate the price of a product and the buyer takes a personal rebate after the purchase. (See Chapter 16 for a more complete discussion of "kickbacks," which is the term normally used to refer to illegal rebates.)

TECHNOLOGICAL FORCE

Many technological advances in the hospitality channel of distribution have taken place. The following sections discuss some current developments.

Genetically Engineered Foods

Food processing has advanced to the point where several foods can be altered genetically (i.e., bioengineered) in order to improve their shelf life and to increase their flavor and availability in the marketplace. For example, tomatoes that have been genetically engineered can remain on the vine much longer than those produced the traditional way.[13] While there is some question regarding the safety of these items, it would appear that, before too long, buyers will have several options from which to choose.

Product Preservation

Today, foods reach us in many forms. One of the main reasons for this is the sophisticated level of preservation technology we have reached. Although some individuals are wary of some preservation processes, no one can deny that we would not enjoy many of the foods we take for granted if these products deteriorated noticeably through the channel of distribution.[14]

Closely related to the genetic engineering of foods are techniques that food processors can use to increase productivity. For instance, government-approved irradiation techniques can reduce product spoilage.[15] Also, giving government-approved hormones to dairy cows can increase their output of milk significantly.[16] Once again, though, some people are very leery of these practices and feel they result in foods that are unsafe for human consumption. More information on food irradiation can be found at The Food Irradiation Information Website (www. food-irradiation.com). A discussion of hormones in dairy milk can be found at www.dairymax.com/rBGH.htm.

Value-Added Foods

Product processing, from primary source to retailer level, has reached higher and higher levels of sophistication. A very large number of convenience foods are on the market today. It is the rare hospitality operation that does not purchase some of these products. Hospitality operators usually buy these items in order to save money in the long run. While it is generally true that a value-added food is much more expensive than its raw counterpart, the potential savings in labor preparation time, energy usage, and storing and handling chores may reduce the EP cost to the point at which overall profit margins will be attractive.

In some cases, the AP price of a convenience food may actually be less than the AP price of the raw ingredients needed to fabricate the item. This is especially true with "first-generation" convenience foods. For instance, frozen-orange-juice concentrate is a first-generation convenience food and, like many of the older convenience foods, is usually less expensive than its homemade equivalent. Since it usually takes about three oranges to produce one cup of orange juice, an eight-ounce serving of fresh-squeezed juice can easily cost twice as much as some processed products to prepare and serve.

Today, almost every food item purchased has some degree of form value added to it. "Convenience," then, is all a matter of degree. The hospitality buyer can look forward to having an ever-increasing supply of convenience foods from which to choose.

Transportation

In many respects, faster transportation constitutes a form of product preservation. But it is much more. Today, buyers can expect faster, larger, and more predictable deliveries, which often reduce the number of purchase orders buyers must make. Also, the increased dependability of transportation allows the buyer companies, in turn, to fulfill more readily the promises they make to their customers.

Computerization

The computer is firmly entrenched in the hospitality industry. The selection and procurement function enjoys many of the labor- and time-saving aspects of this form of technology.

As we discussed in Chapter 2, suppliers now have the ability to use the computer to plot the most cost-effective delivery truck routes. Salespersons can carry laptop computers with them when making their sales calls in order to expedite the ordering process. Hospitality operators can use the computer to perform a whole host of purchasing-related duties, such as inventory valuation and control, menu planning, recipe costing, forecasting, and online selection and procurement.

Packaging

According to the USDA, packaging accounts for, on average, about 8 percent of the purchase price of food products. The USDA also estimates that in about one-fourth of all food and beverages sold, packaging costs exceed the cost of the edible ingredients. In general, the more processed or complicated a food product is, the higher the packaging costs.

Packaging is extremely important to the hospitality operator because it directly affects the quality, shelf life, and convenience of the food or beverage products. Unfortunately, the higher-quality packaging that our convenience-oriented society demands has caused a consumer backlash in the United States. Our quest for more and more processed "instant" foods has led food fabricators to create packaging materials that may pose risks of long-term harm to our environment.

Today, some packaging not only can make a food product more convenient, but it can also contribute to better taste. For example, many products are packed in controlled atmosphere packaging (CAP), which involves placing an item in waxboard, cardboard, aluminum, and/or plastic; removing all existing gases by creating a vacuum; and then introducing a specially formulated mixture of gases that will extend the shelf life of the particular product in the package.[17]

Some common forms of CAP—also referred to as modified atmosphere packaging (MAP)—are the aseptic packs that are used to package juices, wines, and unrefrigerated milk; shelf-stable, unrefrigerated convenience meals; and processed produce and other grocery products (see Figure 4.6). These items are convenient to use. They do not require expensive refrigerated storage. They tend to taste better than canned food because the aseptic sterilization process requires less heating time than the canning process. Another plus is that these types of containers usu-

FIGURE 4.6 Aseptic packaging. Courtesy of Sysco Corporation.

ally can be stacked more readily and take up less storage space than regular cans or bottles. Some packaging can also increase the safety of the foods we purchase. For instance, some products have time- and temperature-sensitive food labels attached, which will change color if the products have been stored too long and/or have been subjected to unsafe storage temperatures.

As discussed in Chapter 2, another welcome packaging advance is the application of the universal product code (UPC) to the hospitality industry. The familiar bar codes that are present on most grocery store product offerings are being introduced into the hospitality industry, thanks to the efforts of the International Foodservice Manufacturers Association (IFMA [http://www.ifmaworld.com/]) and other like-minded business organizations. Eventually, the use of this technology will lead to more efficient order processing, improved receiving operations, more accurate inventory valuation and control, and increased opportunities to do business electronically, thereby saving a bit of labor cost.[18]

OTHER FORCES

It may be more appropriate to label other forces "intangible forces." For example, such factors as a supplier's advertising and promotion effectiveness, pricing policy, credit terms, and the conviviality of salespersons fall within this category and certainly affect the channel of distribution. Buyers must continually guard against reacting disproportionately to these intangible forces because both primary sources and middlemen use them to differentiate the products and services they sell. The buyer must be a "rational buyer."

Buyers and their superiors must accept all forces as part of the game they have elected to play. In the final analysis, though, the dynamic market forces that most directly affect the availability of products and their cost must be recognized and used to shape the overall purchasing strategy.

KEY WORDS AND CONCEPTS

Agency law

Agricultural Adjustment Act

Agricultural Marketing Agreement Act

Antitrust

Aseptic pack

As-purchased price (AP price)

As-served cost

As-used cost

Basic commodity

Bureau of Alcohol, Tobacco, and Firearms (BATF)

Business ethics

Clayton Act

Computerization

Consignment sale

Contract law

Controlled atmosphere packaging (CAP)

Convenience foods

Cosmetics-Devices Act

Economic force

Edible-portion cost (EP cost)

Environmental Protection Agency (EPA)

Ethical force

Exclusive dealing

Exclusive selling

Federal Food, Drug, and Cosmetic Act (FFDCA)

Federal Trade Commission (FTC)

First-generation convenience foods

Food and Drug Administration (FDA)

Food Quality Protection Act (FQPA)

Food Safety Inspection Service (FSIS)

Foodservice Purchasing Managers (FPM) Study Group of the NRA (National Restaurant Association)

Franchise law

Free on board (FOB)

Genetically altered foods

Hart Act

Hazard Analysis Critical Control Point system (HACCP system)

Intangible forces

Internal Revenue Service (IRS)

International Foodservice Manufacturers Association (IFMA)

Interstate Shellfish Sanitation Commission

Irradiation

Kickback

Legal force

Marine Mammal Protection Act

Meat Inspection Act

Monopolistic competition

National Association of Purchasing Managers (NAPM)

National Oceanic and Atmospheric Administration (NOAA)

Nutrition Labeling and Education Act

Ordering procedures

Packaging

Packed Under Federal Inspection (PUFI)

Patent

Perceived value equation

Perishable Agricultural Commodities Act

Political force

Poultry Products Inspection Act

Predatory pricing

Product preservation

Product processing

Promotional discount

Pure Food Act

Quantity limits provision

Rebate

Robinson-Patman Act

Safe-handling instructions

Seller co-ops

Sherman Act

Standard of fill

Standard of identity

Standard of quality

Supply and demand

Technological force

Time- and temperature-sensitive food labels

Title to goods

Transportation

Tying agreement

U.S. Department of Agriculture (USDA)

U.S. Department of Commerce

Uniform Commercial Code (UCC)

Universal Product Code (UPC)

Value-added foods

Warranties and guarantees

Wheeler-Lea Act

Wholesome Meat Act

Wholesome Poultry Products Act

REFERENCES

1. F. William Barnett, "Making Game Theory Work in Practice," *The Wall Street Journal*, February 13, 1995, p. A14. See also: Wei-yu Kevin Chiang, Dilip Chhajed, and James D Hess, "Direct Marketing, Indirect Profits: A Strategic Analysis of Dual-Channel Supply-Chain Design," *Management Science*, January 2003, 49(1), pp. 1–20.

2. Kim Johnson and Susan Pottorff, "Ethics and Hospitality: Perceptions of Hotel and Restaurant Management Students," *1992 Annual CHRIE Conference Proceedings* (Poster Session), Orlando, FL.

3. Craig C. Lundberg, "The Views of Future Hospitality Leaders of Business Ethics," *Hospitality & Tourism Educator*, Spring 1994, p. 11.

4. See, for example, Thomas L. Trace, John F. Lynch, Joseph W. Fisher, and Richard C. Hummrich, "Ethics and Vendor Relationships," in *Ethics*

in Hospitality Management: A Book of Readings, Stephen S. J. Hall, Ed. (New Delhi: Atlantic Books, 1992), p. 155. See also: Graham Wood, "Ethics at the Sales-Purchasing Interface: A Case of Double Standards?" *Journal of Marketing Practice: Applied Marketing Science*, 1995, (1)3, pp. 21–38.

5. See, for example, Lendal H. Kotschevar and Richard Donnelly, *Quantity Food Purchasing*, 5th ed. (New York: Macmillan, 1998). See also: Patt Patterson, "Certification Adds Professionalism to Purchasing," *Nation's Restaurant News*, March 23, 1992, p. 36.

6. Marilyn Chase, "Food Poisoning Is No Picnic as Bugs Widen Their Reach," *The Wall Street Journal*, May 22, 1995, p. B1.

7. Robin Lee Allen, "New Senate Bill Backs Seafood Inspection Plan," *Nation's Restaurant*

News, April 27, 1992, p. 3. See also: Cathy R. Wessels and Joan G. Anderson, "Consumer Willingness to Pay for Seafood Safety Assurances," *The Journal of Consumer Affairs,* Summer 1995, 29(1), pp. 85–87; Leila Abboud, "Bad Fish Slip Through FDA's Safety Net—Most Seafood Companies Ignore Standards, U.S. Says; Oy! Throw Out the Lox," *Wall Street Journal,* October 9, 2002, p. D1.

8. Rose Gutfeld, "Food-Label 'Babel' to Fall as Uniform System Is Cleared," *The Wall Street Journal,* December 3, 1992, p. B1.

9. Bruce Ingersoll, "Label Rules to Foster Healthful Foods," *The Wall Street Journal,* December 26, 1991, p. 9. See also: "Appendix 8: Foods with Standards of Identity" in *First Choice: A Purchasing Manual for School Food Service,* 2nd ed., retrieved 2002 (Available http://www.nfsmi.org/Information/firstchoice/intro.pdf).

10. "A Big Franchiser of Hotels Wins Dismissal of Antitrust Charges," *The Wall Street Journal,* January 12, 1995, p. B2. See also: Jeffrey A. Tannenbaum, "Franchisees Balk at High Prices for Supplies from Franchisers," *The Wall Street Journal,* July 5, 1995, p. B1.

11. James O. Eiler, "Hotel Contracts and Words," *Hotel and Casino Law Letter,* September 1990, p. 87.

12. John R. Goodwin and Jolie R. Gaston, "Creating Sales Contracts in the Hospitality Industry," *Hospitality & Tourism Educator,* Spring 1994, p. 23.

13. Laurie McGinley, "U.S. Clears Calgene Tomato, the First Genetically Engineered Food

to Be Sold," *The Wall Street Journal,* May 19, 1994, p. B8. See also: Elizabeth Weise, "Four-fifths of U.S. Soybean Crop Is Now Bioengineered," *USA Today,* April 1, 2003, p. D09.

14. Richard Gibson, "'Shelf-Stable' Foods Seek to Freshen Sales," *The Wall Street Journal,* November 2, 1990, p. B1.

15. Bruce Ingersoll, "FDA Approves the Use of Irradiation for the Control of Bacteria on Poultry," *The Wall Street Journal,* May 2, 1990, p. B4. See also: Michael A. Fletcher, "Ban on Irradiated Ground Beef Lifted in School Lunch Program," *The Washington Post,* May 30, 2003, p. A11.

16. Richard Koenig, "Wisconsin Bans Hormone to Raise Cows' Milk Output," *The Wall Street Journal,* April 30, 1990, p. B4.

17. "In Your Opinion, What Are the Three Most Important Advancements Made in Food Products and Packaging in the Past 10 Years?" *FoodService Director,* May 15, 1990, p. 16. See also: Doris Stanley, "Controlled Atmosphere Packaging Keeps Cut Honeydew Melon Fresh Longer," August 21, 1998 (Available http://www.ars.usda.gov/is/pr/1998/980821.htm); Amand Hesser, "Salad in Sealed Bags Isn't So Simple, It Seems," *New York Times,* January 14, 2003, p. A1.

18. "Implementing Technology," *Nation's Restaurant News,* October 28, 2002, pp. T20–T22. See also: Alan J. Liddle, "New Arena Embraces 'Nothing but Net' Outsourced Technology," *Nation's Restaurant News,* September 23, 2002, p. 34.

QUESTIONS AND PROBLEMS

1. Define "monopolistic competition." How does this concept differ from a strict monopoly? From strict price competition?

2. Give an example of how the political force affects the hospitality channel of distribution.

3. Is it ethical for a buyer to cancel an order with one supplier because he or she just found out that he or she can purchase the item at a lower price from someone else? Why or why not?

4. Define the following:

(a)	Sherman Act	(j)	Rebate
(b)	USDA	(k)	Value-added foods
(c)	FDA	(l)	Federal Meat Inspection Act
(d)	FTC	(m)	Perishable Agricultural Commodities Act
(e)	Tying agreement		
(f)	Exclusive dealing	(n)	Poultry Products Inspection Act
(g)	Quantity limits provision of the Robinson-Patman Act		
		(o)	IRS
(h)	Agency law	(p)	BATF
(i)	Consignment sale		

5. Do rebates foster unethical behavior among channel members? Why or why not?

6. Explain how advertising and promotion might influence buyers and sellers.

7. How do supply-and-demand conditions affect prices? Is it ethical to hold products off the market in an attempt to increase their prices? Why or why not?

8. Assume you own a coffee shop that is open 24 hours a day. You have purchased a two-month supply of chicken for a planned fried chicken promotion. Now you have changed your mind and would like to return the chicken. Your supplier refuses to take it back. What would you do?

9. What does the Robinson-Patman Act forbid?

10. Give an example of legal price discrimination and one of illegal price discrimination.

11. What is the major difference between the AP price and the EP cost?

12. Briefly describe the perceived value equation. How might a broker utilize this equation when selling foods?

13. How might a restaurant operator utilize the perceived value equation to increase patronage?

14. What is one difference between a basic commodity and a product that has additional form value added to it?

15. Why do you think the federal government exempts growers from some antitrust laws?

16. What are some advantages and disadvantages of using genetically engineered foods in a restaurant operation?

17. What is the primary duty of the FSIS division of the USDA?

18. Which federal law grants injunctive power to the FDA?

19. If the label on a seafood package contained the notation "PUFI," what would this indicate to the buyer?

20. What is the difference between "exclusive dealing" and "exclusive selling"?

21. Which federal law is known as the "small-business protection act"?

22. What is "predatory pricing"? Why do you think the federal government outlaws it?

23. When would a verbal contract carry the same legal force as a written one?

EXPERIENTIAL EXERCISES

1. Go to three fast food restaurants that do not serve Coca-Cola products. Specifically ask for a "Coke." Determine if the server merely serves you the non-Coke product (such as Pepsi) without mentioning that it is not Coke. If this happens, do you think that the operation has a responsibility to tell you it is not Coke? Why or why not? Provide a one-page report detailing your experience and answers to the above questions.

2. Obtain a copy of the National Restaurant Association (NRA) booklet *Accuracy in Menus* (1977) or a copy of Paul J. McVety, Bradley J. Ware, and Claudette Lévesque, *Fundamentals of Menu Planning*, 2nd ed. (New York: Wiley, 2001). Prepare a one-page report discussing misrepresentation of a brand name.

3. Select one of the acts or laws that are discussed in this chapter. Go online and gather some information on this topic. A good place to start is www.google.com. Write a one-page report discussing the current debates that surround your selected topic.

4. Go online and research genetically altered foods. Write a one-page report discussing the current debate on this topic. Be sure to include both the benefits and negatives of using these controversial products in your hospitality operation.

AN OVERVIEW OF THE PURCHASING FUNCTION

Ode to a Purchasing Agent

The Purchasing Agent stood at the Golden Gate,
His head was bending low.
He merely asked the man of fate,
Which way he ought to go.
"What have you done," St. Peter said,
"to seek admittance here?"
"I was a Purchasing Agent down on earth,
for many and many a year."
St. Peter opened wide the gate,
and gently pressed the bell.
"Come in," he said, "and choose your harp.
You've had your share of hell!!"

AUTHOR UNKNOWN

The Purpose of this Chapter

After reading this chapter, you should be able to:

- Describe the purchasing activities in a hospitality operation.

- Determine the purchasing requirements of a hospitality operation using value analysis and make-or-buy analysis.

- Outline the objectives of the purchasing function and the potential problems that buyers encounter when pursuing those objectives.

INTRODUCTION

As we mentioned in Chapter 1, each hospitality organization must come to grips with the purchasing function. Moreover, each operation, large or small, performs many purchasing activities common to all. Finally, all operations, regardless of size, strive for similar purchasing objectives. These are the unifying facts that this chapter addresses.

The hospitality industry is made up of a surprisingly large number of small operations. For instance, the majority of foodservice operations are single-unit, independent businesses whose annual sales volumes are less than $500,000.[1] These small establishments do not have the resources to perform each operating activity in "textbook fashion." The small operator normally has to conduct some business procedures informally, and purchasing may be one of them. The large company may employ purchasing specialists, but the normal pattern is for an owner-manager to squeeze the purchasing activities into his or her schedule.

As we have said, every operation performs pretty much the same activities. The difference is in the degree of attention the activities receive and the thoroughness with which they are accomplished. Large companies tend toward completeness; smaller firms must trim somewhere. This chapter discusses these purchasing activities and purchasing objectives. Not every organization adheres to our outline, but all hospitality managers or owners must at least consider a definite procedure.

PURCHASING ACTIVITIES

Regardless of the size of a hospitality operation, someone must perform a certain number of purchasing activities (see Figure 5.1). The owner-manager does the best that he or she can under the circumstances. In some cases, though, we tend to abdicate our responsibilities by letting a supplier and/or a salesperson perform some activities for us. For instance, we should determine our own requirements and not allow a salesperson to do this for us. We are not implying that something unfortunate will occur if we enlist the help of a friendly salesperson, but, realistically, we must understand that the salesperson will be prone to enhancing his or her self-interest.

Buyers usually perform a number of activities common to all hospitality operations. One survey of hotel purchasing agents uncovered the following key purchasing responsibilities:

(1) Determine when to order; (2) control inventory levels; (3) establish quality standards; (4) determine specifications; (5) obtain competitive bids; (6) investigate ven-

PREPURCHASE ACTIVITIES

1. Plan menus
2. Determine specifications of
   product qualities needed
3. Determine appropriate inventory levels
4. Determine appropriate order sizes
5. Prepare ordering documents

FORMAL PURCHASING

6. Contact vendors
7. Establish formal
   competitive bid process
8. Solicit competitive bids
9. Evaluate bids
10. Award contract to
    vendor
11. Receive shipment
12. Issue products to
    production and service
    depts.
13. Monitor future
    contract performance
14. Evaluate and follow up

INFORMAL PURCHASING

6. Contact vendors
7. Obtain price quotes
8. Select vendor
9. Place order
10. Receive shipment
11. Issue products to
    production and
    service depts.

 **FIGURE 5.1** As this chart indicates, several activities must be accomplished to fulfill the purchasing function's responsibilities. Of course, the owner-manager can dictate the desired degree of formality. Adapted from *Food Purchasing Pointers for School Foodservice.*

dors; (7) arrange financial terms; (8) oversee delivery; (9) negotiate refunds; (10) handle adjustments; (11) arrange for storage.[2]

A study of large foodservice firms indicated that the purchasing activities center on:

(1) Recipe development; (2) menu development; (3) specification writing; (4) approval of buying source; (5) designation of approved brands; (6) supplier evaluation; (7) negotiation with suppliers; (8) change of suppliers; (9) change of brands; (10) substitution of approved items; (11) approve new products; (12) invoice approval; (13) invoice payment; (14) order placement with supplier.[3]

To do an efficient buying job, hospitality organizations must usually perform, minimally, the activities discussed in the following sections.

Selection and Procurement Plan

Typically, the person charged with purchasing responsibilities needs to determine relevant policies and procedures to guide the purchasing function. The plan should contain a description of how the organization intends to select and procure the products and services needed to conduct normal business activity. The plan also should explain the methods used, why they were selected, and its major goals and objectives. Ideally, the plan also should include discussion of supplier availability, purchasing trends that will have to be considered, and a procedure to follow to allow the plan to be revised when necessary.

Determine Requirements

In most cases, the buyer helps to determine the varieties and amounts of products, services, equipment, and furnishings that the hospitality enterprise requires. It is unusual, though, for a buyer to make these decisions in a vacuum. Normally, they are made collectively: the buyers consult with other management officials and with those individuals who will eventually use the purchased items to decide what the operation needs.

Supplier Selection

Selecting dependable suppliers who will provide consistent values is a very difficult task. Generally speaking, large hospitality firms wield considerable purchasing power and therefore can receive the attention and value commensurate with this power. Unfortunately, smaller firms sometimes find it difficult to enlist this type of consistency; while no supplier would intentionally ignore a customer, a buyer who is not high on the supplier's priority list will eventually be disappointed.

Sourcing

For most products and services, a number of suppliers are capable of meeting a buyer's needs. For some items, though, especially unique products that must be purchased in large quantities, it may be necessary for a buyer's company to help establish a supplier.[4]

When a buyer establishes a supplier, the process is usually referred to as a type of "sourcing." (Another type of sourcing occurs when a buyer must search high and low for the one supplier capable of handling his or her needs.) It is typically a win-win situation, in that the buyer establishes a reliable source and the supplier enjoys a predictable amount of business.[5] It is also a good way for buyers to help establish and support minority-owned suppliers.[6]

Recently "e-sourcing" has become very popular. This type of sourcing allows buyers to identify, qualify, and select suppliers over the Internet. Examples of the capabilities of e-sourcing can be found at 216.183.121.142/ebusiness/e-Sourcing abridged.pdf. This document, titled "Making E-Sourcing Strategic" and prepared by the Aberdeen Group (www.aberdeen.com), defines e-sourcing and its capabilities.

Maintain a Convenient and Sufficient Inventory

An operation must practice optimal inventory management, which is nothing more or less than ensuring that an appropriate inventory of all items is always on hand. If we have too small an inventory, we could run out of some items, which often produces guest dissatisfaction. Conversely, if we have too large an inventory, we tie up extra dollars in these items and require extra storage space.

An operation should strive to maintain an optimal overall level of inventory items. But this is more easily said than done. As much as possible, though, a buyer must try to maintain this optimal level by determining the correct order size for each item and ordering this correct amount at the correct time.

Conduct Negotiations

Someone has to negotiate specific as-purchased (AP) prices, delivery schedules, and other supplier services. The general feeling in the industry is that "negotiating" should not be a euphemism for browbeating suppliers; firm but fair bargaining builds mutual respect. We should point out that your negotiating power is determined largely by the amount of money you expect to spend. Keep in mind, though, that all things, at least theoretically, are negotiable. In many cases, suppliers will provide something extra simply because a buyer asks about it. Although negotiating may require a certain degree of time and effort, the benefits can be considerable.

Research Activities

Buyers often find it necessary to conduct research projects. Purchasing is a very dynamic activity, and, while the general principles and procedures remain the same, their applications may have to be altered to meet perceived trends. Similarly, product availability, prices, supplier services, and customer tastes may change quickly. The wise buyer will undertake research projects in order to improve future operations.

Value Analysis One of the more common research activities, and one that is typically done very frequently, is value analysis. This involves examining a product in order to identify unnecessary costs that can be eliminated without sacrificing overall quality or performance. For example, a buyer who habitually purchases whole milk for cooking purposes may want to research the possibility of using less expensive, low-fat milk instead. If the recipes can be prepared with the less expensive milk without a discernible loss of quality, the buyer will recommend using the more economical low-fat product.

Value analysis usually centers on the perceived value equation noted in Chapter 4. Although the typical value analysis procedure may not be quite this formal, the ultimate purpose of this research activity is to increase value by manipulating quality, supplier services, and edible-portion (EP) cost.

When a buyer performs value analysis on a product or service, he or she should make no changes without consulting the person who uses that product or service. There may be good reasons, for example, why the EP cost is a little higher than it could be—reasons known only to the user. Value analysis usually works best when it becomes a cooperative venture.

Forecasting Forecasting can involve many things, but, usually, the buyer is most interested in predicting the kinds of products and services that will be available in the future and what their prices will be. Buyers often center their forecasting efforts on picking the brains of friendly suppliers and salespersons. Informal chats with them can yield accurate and useful information quickly and easily.

Today, supply availability and future pricing can be tracked with one or more online services. For instance, the National Restaurant Association (NRA) provides *Restaurant Trendmapper* (http://www.restaurant.org/trendmapper). This subscription-based online information service provides current analysis of the U.S. restaurant industry, including current commodities pricing.

What-If Analysis Many buyers use computer spreadsheet software to develop mathematical models that can test various "what-if" proposals. For instance, a simple model buyers can use predicts the overall effect that an increase in the purchase price of one food item will have on the overall food cost. Suppose that the price of prime rib will increase 10 percent and that prime rib represents 50 percent of a restaurant's overall food cost. We want to know what will happen to the overall food cost as a result of this increase. The model equation to use in this case is:

Increase in overall food cost = Percentage price increase for the
ingredient × The ingredient's percentage
of overall food cost

= 10% × 50%

= 0.10 × 0.50

= 0.05 or 5%

Other, more complicated formulas can be developed to show, for instance, the effect of a purchase price increase on overall profits.

Any model is an attempt to predict the future. Some models may be based on shaky estimates, but this has not curtailed their use. Most, if not all, operations rely on models and some of these models become highly sophisticated mathematical devices.

Make-or-Buy Analysis At times, management may consider making a product in-house instead of buying it already prepared, even though several types of value-added products on the market can serve an operator's needs.

Make-or-buy analysis is one of the most critical types of research projects in which a buyer can become involved. There is a lot to lose when the wrong decision is made. Usually, each situation has several advantages and disadvantages.

For instance, value-added products usually offer the following advantages: (1) consistent quality; (2) consistent portion control; (3) an opportunity to serve diversified menu items, regardless of the employee skill level, and, thereby, to attract patrons who enjoy diversity; (4) operating efficiencies, such as less energy needed to reconstitute, rather than prepare from scratch, a menu item; (5) less food-handler supervision, which gives the supervisor more time for merchandising, promoting, and otherwise increasing sales volume; (6) reduced employee skill requirements; (7) reduction in leftovers; (8) reduction of raw-materials inventory, which implies smaller storage costs; (9) reduction in ordering costs since you are not ordering and receiving several raw ingredients; (10) an increase in edible yields since usually there is no waste with convenience items; and (11) with convenience-foods usage, a possible reduction of the size of the storage and the kitchen facility, which leads to more room for dining patrons.

The major disadvantage of convenience foods is, of course, their high price.[7] Since most or all of the economic form value is included, the buyer expects to pay more for a value-added food than for the individual ingredients needed to produce the item in-house. However, there is no average rule of thumb to indicate whether the difference between these two prices favors the buyer or the food processor. Suppose, for example, that we cannot quite decide which alternative is better: cutting our own steaks from a side of beef or buying precut, portion-controlled steaks. The AP price of the uncut sides is cheaper. But considering the waste involved, additional labor costs, and investment in equipment, the precut steaks might represent the better EP cost.

There is no simple way to tell whether you should "make" or "buy." You need to consider so many qualitative and quantitative factors that the decision necessarily involves a great deal of research and analysis.

Plant Visits　Purchasing agents and buyers usually take the time to visit suppliers' facilities. Most industry members recommend this practice, particularly when there is some question about a supplier's ability to fulfill a need. In addition, a supplier who runs a sloppy store, experiences labor management difficulties, or keeps erratic hours may be undependable and, therefore, undesirable.[8]

Maintain Supplier Diplomacy

A buyer works continually with suppliers and salespersons; meanwhile, several other suppliers may wish for the buyer's business. Keeping every potential supplier content is impossible; a buyer should not even try it. Nevertheless, diplomatic, cordial relations help a buyer get along with suppliers and earn the best value from each.

Some operations concentrate heavily on maintaining amicable relations with all reputable suppliers, and many of these companies insist on instituting a trade relations function within the organization.[9] The objective of trade relations is to spread the purchase dollar among as many suppliers as possible. Although trade relations like this may diminish a buyer's alternatives, the goodwill generated throughout the channel of distribution might sometimes prove valuable in the long run—and in short-run emergencies. (Several operations purchase from only one or two purveyors for other reasons. In Chapter 12, we discuss the potential advantages of "one-stop" shopping.)

Educate Suppliers

Buyers must attempt to keep all potential suppliers informed about anything that can help improve their performance. Suppliers who stay abreast of your changing needs can provide the service to match those needs. Moreover, a buyer can continually test a supplier's flexibility and capability.

Another dimension of this issue is the advisability of buyers maintaining close contact with suppliers and salespersons to "pick their brains." This is a time-consuming activity, but many people in our industry think that it is absolutely necessary if a buyer hopes to maintain his or her knowledge of the rapidly changing hospitality market.

Purchase, Receive, Store, and Issue Products

Someone must be responsible for a product until it is ready to be used. No chef, for example, will take responsibility for expensive meat cuts before they actually come within his or her domain. In some cases, a buyer assumes the duties of selecting the supplier, purchasing and receiving the products, and, often, storing and eventually issuing them to the various departments.

Some firms do not like to link these activities together, especially the buying and receiving activities. These companies tend to relieve a buyer of the receiving activity and place this function under the direct supervision of the accounting department. This approach establishes a measure of control. The physical separation of these two activities substantially reduces the possibility of theft.

Disposal of Excess and Unsalable Items

At times, because of menu changes, overbuying, and obsolescence, a hospitality organization finds itself overstocked with certain products. Sometimes, too, when it purchases a new piece of equipment, it must dispose of the old piece. Buyers are usually expected to shoulder these responsibilities and trade the items, sell them, or give them away. Since buyers involve themselves directly in the marketplace, it is logical to expect them to fulfill these duties.

Recycling

In addition to disposing of excess and unsalable items, buyers may be responsible for ensuring that recyclable materials are gathered efficiently and delivered to an approved recycling center. If a buyer can sell these items, he or she may also have the additional responsibility of accounting for the receipts.

Develop Record-Keeping Controls

The activities of purchasing, receiving, storing, and issuing normally require some sort of control. Large firms and, to a much lesser extent, small ones strive to maintain a system of overlapping receipts connecting these activities. For example, as a product moves from one activity to the next, a variety of computerized and/or noncomputerized forms (bills, receipts, inventory records, issue slips, etc.) may trace its movement. The objective of using these forms is to enable management to locate and monitor the product as it moves through the operation. (Chapters 13, 14, and 15 provide thorough discussions of these internal controls.)

A buyer may help design these forms. Alternately, the accounting department takes charge of this duty as part of its overall responsibility for controlling all of the company assets. It is customary, though, for a buyer to contribute, at least, to the development of these forms.

Organize and Administer the Purchasing Function

Where applicable, the person in charge of purchasing must plan, organize, staff, direct, and control this function, especially in large companies that maintain a separate purchasing department. In addition, purchasing must be coordinated with other company activities, including accounting, marketing, production, and service. The purchasing agent, then, must not only see to it that products and services are efficiently and effectively purchased, received, stored, and, where appropriate, issued, he or she must also have the managerial competence to organize and administer these activities expeditiously.

Self-Improvement

All buyers should continually strive to improve their buying performance. Association meetings, seminars, plant visits, trade show visits, and continuing education courses are among some of the more traditional self-improvement methods available. Full-time buyers should seriously consider obtaining the Certified Purchasing Manager (CPM) or at least the Accredited Purchasing Practitioner (APP) designation from the Institute of Supply Management (ISM). Information on these programs can be found at www.ism.ws/Certification. Another excellent choice is to obtain the Certified Foodservice Purchasing Manager (CFPM) certification offered by the Foodservice Purchasing Managers (FPM) Study Group of the NRA, the National Restaurant Association Educational Foundation (NRAEF [www.nraef.org]), and the National Association of Purchasing Managers (NAPM). The Certified Food-service Professional (CFSP) program certification, offered through the North American Association of Food Equipment Manufacturers (NAFEM [http://www.nafem.org/cfsp) is available to qualified purchasing professionals specializing in the equipment side of the business.[10]

Many hospitality operations reimburse their employees for this kind of self-improvement by paying for tuition charges, the cost of books, seminar fees, and travel expenses. In addition, some operators provide in-house training. In the long run, employees who increase their competence usually return management's investment many times by improving their productivity and increasing their readiness to assume more responsible positions within the firm.

Help Competitors

Helping the competition does not always seem to be a logical part of a purchasing agent's duties. An operation is unlikely to go out of its way to aid competitors; nevertheless, competing buyers are in a position to help each other in mutually beneficial ways.

The type of help we refer to consists, for one thing, of lending products to competitors when a crucial need arises. If we run out of a product we desperately need, we try to borrow it from a neighbor. Moreover, in the role of a lender, we have little to gain by refusing such a service: it is unlikely that a competitor's customers will flock to our door simply because the competitor temporarily cannot serve them a particular item.

When we do lend, we set up a reciprocal arrangement by which we feel justified in borrowing. Of course, management needs to make the ultimate decision about these types of loan arrangements. Lending and borrowing are reasonable activities that often come under a buyer's purview.

A buyer might also help his or her less knowledgeable colleague gain the advantage of the more seasoned buyer's experience. Such cordial, professional relations will tend to make everyone's life a bit easier and will significantly increase the industry's ability to serve its customers more effectively and efficiently.

Other Activities

As hospitality companies continue to downsize their managerial ranks, those managers remaining often need to shoulder nontraditional duties. In today's business environment, managers should be prepared to adapt to any situation. For instance, a purchasing manager working at company headquarters may have to take on responsibility for the mail room operation. Similarly, a buyer working at a large hotel may have to oversee a retail gift shop.

PURCHASING OBJECTIVES

Industry experts suggest several goals for the purchasing function. Continuing research into this issue shows that five major objectives must be achieved.

Maintain an Adequate Supply

Few hospitality operators enjoy running out of products. Stockouts are intolerable. Since customer service is really the only thing sold, running out of a key item frustrates an operator's customer service goals. Thus, an adequate stock level, one that prevents running out of items between deliveries, is crucial to good management.

Minimize Investment

This objective seems to conflict with the first. How can buyers maintain an uninterrupted supply while, at the same time, they minimize the number of dollars they tie up in inventory? This question suggests that buyers must find some kind of trade-off between the investment level and the risk of running out. Most operators expect a buyer to compromise by optimizing the investment level and, at the same time, ensuring a continual flow of products.

Maintain Quality

Maintaining quality is not quite the same as establishing the firm's desired level of quality. Some buyers have comparatively little to say about the quality of products they must purchase. They do, however, have a major responsibility to make sure that, once set, the quality standards vary only within acceptable limits. For some products, such as liquor and soap, brand names assure uniform quality. Unfortunately, the quality of fresh foods can change drastically from day to day and from one supplier to the next. This situation can make it particularly difficult to maintain quality standards. In addition, occasional overbuying or a sudden breakdown in storage facilities, particularly refrigeration facilities, can wreak havoc on quality standards. Regardless of the associated difficulties, however, operators insist that their buyers maintain quality control.

Obtain the Lowest Possible EP Cost

As we mentioned earlier, the AP price is only the beginning. Unfortunately, some buyers are entranced by a low AP price and tend to overlook the fact that the EP cost is the relevant price consideration. Many operators think in terms of steak price per pound or liquid detergent price per gallon. What should be paramount in their thinking is the steak cost per servable pound or the liquid detergent cost per square foot of dirty tile. In other words, the EP cost rules, and management understandably expects its buyers to recognize this fact on the way to achieving the lowest possible EP cost and, ultimately, the best possible value.

Maintain the Company's Competitive Position

As far as we have been able to determine, management's main concern here is to get the same, or a better, deal from a supplier that any other comparable hospitality enterprise gets. Unfortunately, this goal is difficult to achieve. Although EP cost and quality may be more or less uniform, suppliers often apply their supplier services unevenly among buyers. You may recall that these supplier services add to the overall value of a product or service, provided that the quality and EP cost remain constant. If we receive fewer supplier services, theoretically, we receive less value for our money. This value loss places us at a competitive disadvantage.

PROBLEMS OF THE BUYER

Buyers encounter several problems while working to attain their objectives. Some of the major problems are:

1. Backdoor selling, whereby a salesperson bypasses the appointed buyer and goes to some other employee, such as the dining room hostess, to make a sales pitch. The hostess then puts pressure on the buyer to consummate a sale.

2. Excessive time may be spent with salespersons. Most operators set aside certain periods during the week to receive sales presentations. On the one hand, these may be wastes of time, but occasionally you need to spend time with others in order to pick up a good bit of advice or information.

3. A variety of ethical traps await the buyer.

4. Sometimes the buyer has full responsibility for purchasing, yet he or she may lack the commensurate authority needed to act accordingly.

5. The buyer might have full responsibility, but he or she does not have enough time to do the job right. This is particularly true for part-time buyers.

6. Sometimes the buyer finds it difficult to work with other department heads and to coordinate their needs.

7. Sometimes department heads, or other users of products and services, make unreasonable demands on the person in charge of buying.

8. Late deliveries and subsequent problems with receiving and storage can ruin the most efficient purchase.

9. Other company personnel do not always consider purchasing a profit-making activity. Actually, a penny saved in purchasing goes directly to the bottom line of the income statement, whereas the typical hospitality operation must sell about 50 cents worth of product or service to realize a 1-cent net profit, since considerable expense must be incurred in the generation of this 50-cent sale.

10. Suppliers do not always have what the buyer orders, sending a substitute that may or may not be acceptable.

11. Some suppliers may not be interested in the buyer's business if he or she is a "small stop" (i.e., does a small amount of business). No salespersons will intentionally avoid the buyer, but, realistically, they must service the large customers first. This means that the buyer may not be on the top of their list of priorities.

12. Receiving and storage inadequacies make it difficult to protect the merchandise after it is purchased. Regardless of the energy expended to procure the best possible value, the effort could all be for nothing if these inadequacies result in excessive spoilage, waste, and/or theft.

13. When suppliers do not have something that a buyer has ordered, they may note on the delivery slip that the item is "back ordered." This means that the buyer will usually receive the item when the next regularly scheduled delivery occurs and be charged for it at that time. The major problem here is that the buyer does not have the item ready for his or her customers.

14. Returns and allowances occur because some delivered merchandise will be unsuitable for one reason or another. The hospitality operator must then ensure that he or she receives fair credit for the rejected items and that this credit is ultimately reflected on the suppliers' bills. This takes time and effort, two attributes that most individuals have in short supply. Furthermore, as with

back orders, there are the stockout problems that must be solved to avoid customer dissatisfaction.

EVALUATION OF THE PURCHASING FUNCTION

The purchasing function involves a great variety of activities and objectives. As noted earlier, all buyers, full-time or part-time, perform most of these activities, one way or another. Buyers also attain, or fail to attain, what we have outlined as the major purchasing objectives.

How much should we be willing to spend to discharge the purchasing activities conscientiously enough in order to achieve these major objectives? This is an especially difficult question because, on one hand, buyers' salaries and receiving costs are highly visible to management, but, on the other hand, the benefits associated with these costs are not so visible. A look at the income statement reveals immediately most of the costs of maintaining a top-flight purchasing function; unhappily, the benefits do not leap out quite so dramatically.

In our opinion, the benefits outweigh the costs for all but perhaps the smallest hospitality operations. The purpose of this book, however, is to present what we perceive to be the relevant aspects of selection and procurement. We leave it to you to decide, gradually, the value of the purchasing function and the relative justification for its cost.

TECHNOLOGY ENHANCEMENTS TO THE PURCHASING PROCESS

With the use of technological purchasing solutions, buyers and suppliers are able to make purchases without spending time dealing with fax machines or telephone calls. Instead, they can complete the purchasing process, including the request for quote (RFQ), purchase order, and final sale, from the convenience of their desktops within seconds. For example, if a hotel manager orders tomatoes for his or her kitchen, he or she can simply access one of the e-procurement solutions, order the tomatoes, and pay for them in a matter of just a few minutes. This saves an enormous amount of time, allowing the manager more time to conduct day-to-day functions without having to worry about calling a supplier, faxing in the order, and waiting for confirmation. Buyers can spend less time on ordering supplies and more time conducting daily business. In addition, as stated in Chapter 2, several e-commerce companies have created software applications that enable buyers to link directly to a supplier's inventory, enabling the buyer to determine if the supplier has the desired product in stock. Timesaving practices like these will continue to develop as purchasing managers are required to do more for their properties.

KEY WORDS AND CONCEPTS

Accredited Purchasing Practitioner (APP)

As-purchased price (AP price)

Backdoor selling

Back orders

Certified Foodservice Professional (CFSP) program

Certified Foodservice Purchasing Manager (CFPM)

Certified Purchasing Manager (CPM)

Company's competitive position

Convenience foods

Disposal of stock

Edible-portion cost (EP cost)

Foodservice Purchasing Managers (FPM)

Forecasting

Institute of Supply Management (ISM)

Make-or-buy analysis

Minimal inventory investment

National Restaurant Association (NRA)

National Restaurant Association Educational Foundation (NRAEF)

Negotiations

North American Association of Food Equipment Manufacturers (NAFEM)

One-stop shopping

Optimal inventory level

Plant visits

Problems of the buyer

Product substitutions

Purchasing activities

Purchasing objectives

Quality standards

Record-keeping control documents

Recycling

Restaurant Association Network

Returns and allowances

Selection and procurement plan

Small stop

Sourcing

Stockout

Supplier diplomacy

Supplier selection

Trade relations

Trade show visits

Value analysis

Value-added foods

What-if analysis

REFERENCES

1. 2003 National Restaurant Association (NRA) estimates.

2. Gregory T. Bohan, "Purchasing for Hotels: A Changing Scene, Survey Reveals," *Lodging,* April 1986, p. 17. See also: John Lawn, "Common Mistakes that Purchasing Managers Make," *Food Management,* February 2003, 38(2), p. 6; John Lawn, "Seven More Mistakes Purchasing Managers Make," *Food Management,* March 2003, 38(3), p. 8.

3. R. Dan Reid and Carl D. Riegel, *Purchasing Practices of Large Foodservice Firms* (Tempe, AZ: Center for Advanced Purchasing Studies [CAPS], 1989), p. 19.

4. Patt Patterson, "Good Buyers Track Orders from Field to Kitchen," *Nation's Restaurant News,* October 5, 1992, p. 42.

5. "McDonald's Recruits Duo to Make Its McCroutons," *USA Today,* January 27, 1989, p. 7B.

6. Udayan Gupta, "Getting Together," *The Wall Street Journal,* February 19, 1993, p. R12. See also: Udayan Gupta, "Where the Money Is," *The Wall Street Journal,* May 22, 1995, p. R6; Amy Zu-

ber, "Minority Franchisees Prosper with Help from McD Support Groups," *Nation's Restaurant News*, February 14, 2000, 34(7), pp. 26–30.

7. Howard Elitzak, "Desire for Convenience Drives Marketing Costs," *FoodReview*, September–December 1999, 22(3), pp. 23–25. See also: Sarah Hart Winchester, "Cutting Costs Without Cutting Quality," *Restaurants USA*, March 1995, p. 12.

8. Tom Wood, "Total Quality Management,"

Restaurants USA, February 1993, p. 19. See also: Mary Clare Brady, "National Restaurant Association Executive Study Groups," *Restaurants USA*, January 1993, p. 15.

9. "Casinos Back Variation on Set-Aside Program," *The Wall Street Journal*, March 30, 1993, p. B1.

10. Patt Patterson, "Certification Adds Professionalism to Purchasing," *Nation's Restaurant News*, March 23, 1992, p. 36.

QUESTIONS AND PROBLEMS

1. Assume that two suppliers sell the same quality of meat for the same price. What type of supplier services would you seek from them? Why? Which supplier service would you value enough so that if one supplier provided it and the other did not, you would purchase your meat from the former? Why?

2. Assume that steak represents 30 percent of your overall food cost. If the purchase price of steak increases 10 percent, by what percentage will the overall food cost increase?

3. Name some potential benefits of trade relations. Name potential difficulties. Would you engage in trade relations? Why or why not?

4. Do you think it is a good idea to allow competitors to "borrow a cup of sugar" once in a while? Why?

5. Explain what is meant by the purchasing function's goal of "maintaining the company's competitive position."

6. Assume that you have decided to serve roast beef on your menu. The AP price of roast beef is $3.98 per pound. The edible yield per pound is approximately 9 ounces. You plan to serve a $4\frac{1}{2}$-ounce portion size.
    (a) Approximately how much raw roast beef must you purchase in order to serve 125 portions?
    (b) KWG Enterprises, a statewide food-merchant wholesaler, offers a precooked, presliced roast beef product for $6.00 per pound. The edible yield is 100 percent.
        (1) Under what conditions would you purchase this convenience item?
        (2) Under what conditions would it be advisable to purchase the raw roast beef product instead of this convenience item?
        (3) Approximately how much of this convenience roast beef must you purchase in order to serve 125 portions?

7. Name the five major objectives of the purchasing function.

8. Name three types of research activities that a buyer might perform.

9. Is it a good idea to allow a salesperson to assist us in carrying out the necessary purchasing activities? Why or why not? If possible, ask a broker and a merchant-wholesaler to comment on your answer. Also, if possible, ask a hotel or restaurant buyer to comment on your answer and the answers of the broker and the merchant-wholesaler.

10. Define or explain:

(a) Value analysis   (e) CFPM
(b) Sourcing   (f) Stockouts
(c) CPM   (g) Backdoor selling
(d) Plant visits   (h) Back orders

11. What problems will a foodservice operation incur if it experiences several back orders?

12. What is a major disadvantage associated with having excess inventory on hand?

13. When should the buyer visit a supplier's facilities?

14. List three advantages and three disadvantages of using convenience foods.

15. A purveyor has offered to sell you fudge cakes for $6.00 each. You try to determine whether you can make the cakes more cheaply. Assuming that you will need to pay an additional employee $9.25 per hour, plus about $1.50-per-hour fringe benefits, and further assuming that this employee can make 24 cakes per hour, what alternative should you select? Should you "make" or should you "buy"? Why?

The recipe for one cake is:

12 ounces shortening   1 pound, 12 ounces cake flour
2 pounds sugar $1/4$ ounce salt
$1/2$ ounce vanilla   1 ounce baking soda
6 eggs $1^1/2$ pints buttermilk
5 ounces cocoa

The AP prices for these ingredients are:

SHORTENING: $0.32 per pound   CAKE FLOUR: $11.09 per 50 pounds
SUGAR: $18.22 per 50 pounds   SALT: $0.11 per pound
VANILLA: $6.85 per pint   BAKING SODA: $0.24 per pound
EGGS: $1.29 per dozen   BUTTERMILK: $2.45 per gallon
COCOA: $2.12 per pound

EXPERIENTIAL EXERCISES

1. Provide the purchasing activity list below to a purchasing manager. Ask the manager if he or she performs all of these tasks. Ask if the manager would add or remove any of these tasks from the list. Provide a report detailing your conversation.

a. Determine when to order.
b. Control inventory levels.
c. Establish quality standards.

d. Determine specifications.

e. Obtain competitive bids.

f. Investigate vendors.

g. Arrange financial terms.

h. Oversee delivery.

i. Negotiate refunds.

j. Handle adjustments.

k. Arrange for storage.

2. **Determine the requirements for an individual to receive the following certifications:**

Certified Purchasing Manager (CPM)

Accredited Purchasing Practitioner (APP)

Certified Foodservice Purchasing Manager (CFPM)

Certified Foodservice Professional (CFSP)

6

THE ORGANIZATION AND ADMINISTRATION OF PURCHASING

The Purpose of this Chapter

After reading this chapter, you should be able to:

■ Describe the methods used to plan and organize the purchasing activities of a hospitality operator.

■ Recognize the issues involved in administering the purchasing activities of a hospitality operator.

INTRODUCTION

Buyers, both full-time and part-time, must plan, organize, and administer their purchasing activities. This principle is crucial in large operations, especially chain organizations, in which more than one person may be involved in purchasing. But small operations cannot afford to be casual about purchasing; even a part-time buyer needs a definite plan of action.

PLANNING

In the initial stages of developing a selection and procurement plan that will be consistent with the hospitality operation's overall thrust, buyers must understand the goals and objectives of the purchasing function. For instance, the five purchasing objectives we discussed in Chapter 5—maintain adequate supply, minimize investment, maintain quality, obtain lowest possible edible-portion (EP) cost, and maintain competitive position—can serve as the initial goals to be achieved in the long run. But buyers devise several ways of working toward these goals. Thus, evaluating possible methods of achieving the goals and eventually selecting one become the major accomplishment in the planning stage.

Consider this example. A small operator may decide that the main objective of the purchasing function is to maintain adequate supplies at all times and that all other objectives are secondary to this one. The overall buying plan, then, must be tailored to ensure the attainment of this objective: the operator may decide to select only those suppliers with the most favorable delivery schedules and, if necessary, to pay a little extra for this supplier service.

Decisions made at the initial planning stage set the tone for future activities. Planning for purchasing is not carried out in a vacuum. It is part of the overall plan of the hospitality organization and cannot exist apart from the overall goals and objectives of the operation. Furthermore, a buyer rarely determines the buying plan without receiving input from other company personnel.

ORGANIZING

Having formulated a general plan, a buyer must organize the human and material resources needed to follow it. At this second stage, however, the buyer's voice may still be only one of many. In some cases, he or she has little to say; superiors may decide how to do the operation's purchasing.

The buying activities of a hospitality firm can be organized several ways. But, generally, we find only two major organizational patterns: one for the independent operator and one for the multiunit chain operations. Most other organizational patterns are variations of these two.

Organizing for the Independent Operation

The many very small hospitality operations are often referred to as "mom-and-pop" places. Most do not have a payroll; that is, they are operated completely by the owners with, perhaps, some assistance from family members. Usually, the selection and procurement responsibilities fall directly on the owner-manager's shoulders. If these organizations have hourly employees, they normally are involved in these activities only sparingly (see Figure 6.1). For instance, an hourly employee may have receiving and storing responsibility whenever the owner-manager is absent.

FIGURE 6.1 A typical purchasing organizational pattern for a very small independent operation.

Medium-sized operations rarely employ full-time buyers (see Figure 6.2). Instead, these firms tend to designate one or more "user-buyers." Ordinarily, the head bartender, the chef, the dining room supervisor, and other supervisors all do some buying as part of their responsibilities. The owner-manager acts as a coordinator among these user-buyers to control their activity and, especially, to supervise the receipt of their orders. The owner-manager also oversees receiving and storing, as well as bill payments.

In some independent properties, including the large hotels and country clubs, an owner-manager may not coordinate the orders of each department head. Instead, a steward or assistant manager may be employed specifically to do this work. The owner-manager then controls and supervises this person's activities.

Another variation of this pattern occurs when a separate steward or food buyer works in the kitchen specifically to coordinate the chef's needs. A kitchen steward may also supervise the warewashing and cleaning employees. Large independents and, in some cases, large chain operations, may follow this pattern.

Organizational variations abound for independent operations; they are limited only by the imagination. But, as noted, a characteristic they share is the need for the owner-manager to be directly involved in purchasing. He or she cannot avoid this activity. And, in many cases, he or she is actually the owner-manager-

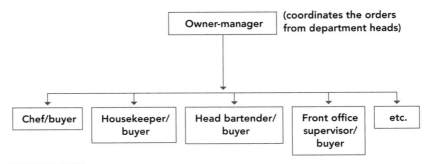

FIGURE 6.2 A typical purchasing organizational pattern for a medium-sized independent hospitality operation.

chef, who not only buys for the kitchen, but may also buy for, or at least coordinate the purchasing for, all the other departments.

Some small- and medium-sized hospitality operations join a communal-buying network. As this term suggests, these independents join together and agree to pool their purchases. The idea is to place one larger order, thereby qualifying for a lower as-purchased (AP) price than the pool members would be entitled to individually. This scheme works not only with food and operating supplies, but also with insurance, advertising, and other service purchasing. The concept works particularly well where independents agree to use the same brand of peas, bread, ice cream, detergent, accounting service, and so on.

The organizational pattern for communal buying, or "co-op purchasing" or "shared buying," as some call it, is relatively simple (see Figure 6.3). Owners and managers from among the group of independents share the task of coordinating all the orders. Alternately, the independents may hire someone to perform this coordination, to place large orders, and to arrange proper delivery schedules. As discussed in Chapter 1, co-ops are now working with aggregate purchasing companies or group purchasing organizations (GPOs) that specialize in streamlining co-op purchases by using the Internet as a vehicle for communication.

The concept of communal or cooperative (co-op) buying has its pros and cons.[1] We discuss the major advantages and disadvantages of co-op purchasing in Chapter 12. In the meantime, an excellent resource to learn more about co-op purchasing can be found at www.ncba.coop, a site sponsored by the National Cooperative Business Association (NCBA).

The large independent is similar to the small one, the major difference being the physical presence of one or more persons assigned full-time to the purchasing, receiving, storing, and issuing of products and services. The most typical setup is to have a purchasing director, with specialists in food buying, beverage buying, and equipment and supplies buying working in the purchasing department. In addition, a receiving clerk might be working for the accounting department and a storeroom manager for the purchasing director (see Figure 6.4).

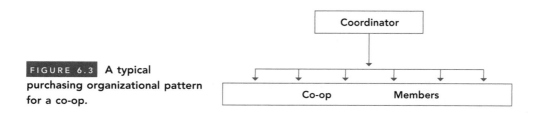

FIGURE 6.3 A typical purchasing organizational pattern for a co-op.

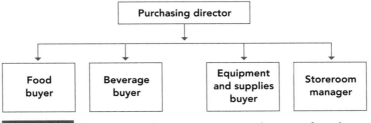

FIGURE 6.4 A typical purchasing organizational pattern for a large independent hospitality operation.

Organizing for Chain Operations

A major difference between independents and chains is the additional level of management found in the chain operation. The purchasing function in a hotel or restaurant that belongs to a chain operation often resembles the purchasing the independents do. What is different is the presence of a vice president of purchasing, or a corporate purchasing director, and a staff of buyers at headquarters overseeing the selection and procurement activities and, if applicable, monitoring the company-owned commissary and/or central distribution activities (see Figure 6.5).

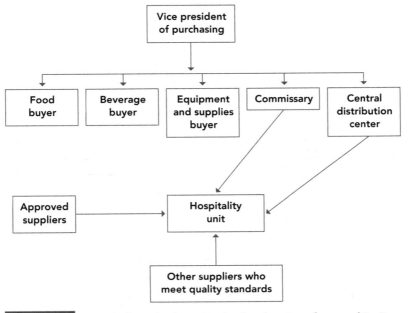

FIGURE 6.5 A typical purchasing organizational pattern for a multiunit hospitality operation.

At the local unit level, in some cases, the unit manager performs all buying activities. In other cases, he or she may serve as coordinator for the users and buyers. Chain operations with large units may have a purchasing system in each unit that is similar to the system of a large independent.

The unit manager in Figure 6.5 can be a franchisee or the manager of a company-owned store. If the former, he or she usually: (1) buys from suppliers approved by the corporate vice president of purchasing; (2) buys from other suppliers as long as they meet the company's quality standards; (3) buys from the franchisor's company-owned commissary and/or central distribution center; or (4) uses a combination of the three approaches. As mentioned earlier, a franchisee typically buys from the commissary and/or central distribution center whenever possible, if only for convenience.

Managers of company-owned stores have the same options as franchisees, but they usually have less flexibility. Once the company's top management determines the buying procedure, there is little chance for variation.

The vice president of purchasing serves as a central coordinator for purchases made by all of the units. His or her major responsibilities usually include: (1) setting purchasing guidelines for unit managers; and (2) negotiating national, long-term contracts for items used by all of the units. The vice president normally negotiates large-quantity buys with set prices—six-month supplies or longer. (Unit managers, by contrast, order and receive just what they need when they need it and then pay the AP price that the vice president negotiated.) The corporate vice president also: (3) sets purchase specifications (to which we devote Chapter 8) for items that must be purchased at the unit level; (4) performs research activities; (5) serves as a resource person for all unit managers and unit buying personnel; and (6) if applicable, supervises the central distribution function and the commissary.

Some advantages and disadvantages accompany this kind of centralized purchasing. The major advantages are the reduction in the AP prices achieved by quantity buys, the presence of a strong negotiator, and cost and quality control. The main disadvantage seems to be the system's potential for alienating local suppliers, especially when the chain deals with one major supplier and bypasses all the locals.[2] But the corporate vice president of purchasing cannot purchase everything, nor can he or she negotiate contracts for all items. At least some buying must remain decentralized and in the hands of the local unit. This slight but inevitable degree of decentralization can soothe ruffled local suppliers, as well as provide the unit personnel with some purchasing experience.

Another major difference between independents and chains is the propensity of the chains to develop a central distribution and commissary network. This network really represents an effort by the chains to provide many of their own economic values and supplier services—that is, to bypass the middlemen. The chains feel it makes sense, dollars and "sense," to centralize their buying, to have products delivered to one location, to process these products (for example, to cut portion-controlled steaks), and to deliver these processed items to each unit.

As we noted in Chapter 3, the commissary and central distribution network is not always a cost-effective system. There certainly are several quality control benefits, as well as the potential benefit of an uninterrupted supply. However, in light of the arguments for and against central distribution and commissary operation, managers who face this difficult decision must undertake a good deal of careful analysis.

STAFFING

Neither small- nor medium-sized operations generally hire full-time purchasing employees. Large operations, especially chains, may hire several buyers, each an expert in one or two product areas. Such operations are also more apt to employ full-time secretarial and clerical personnel in the purchasing department. Also, they may employ receiving clerks and storeroom managers. Again, the small operation would typically settle for a chef-buyer-storeroom manager and a well-trained, generously paid kitchen worker who doubles as a receiving clerk.

The job specification for these employees follows the typical pattern. It is divided into the three broad areas of technical, conceptual, and human skills. For some positions relating to the buying activity, technical skill and extensive experience are very important. For other positions, a desire to learn may be the only requirement. The complicating factor is that purchasing personnel often have responsibilities other than purchasing, receiving, storing, and issuing; thus, these other responsibilities may take precedence when a manager undertakes to develop overall job specifications.

TRAINING

Entry-level purchasing personnel usually require training that consists of an orientation to the job and the company, formal instruction, and on-the-job training (OJT) or experience. In addition, management training seminars and courses sometimes supplement in-house training. The National Restaurant Association (NRA), The National Restaurant Association Educational Foundation (NRAEF), the Institure of Supply Management (ISM), the North American Association of Food

Equipment Manufacturers (NAFEM), and the Foodservice Purchasing Managers (FPM) Study Group of the NRA normally sponsor several seminars and courses every year.

BUDGETING

In operations that employ a full-time buyer, it may be necessary to fund the buying function, which means that annual operating expenses, such as buyers' salaries and clerical costs, must be budgeted. The operations that employ user-buyers rarely construct a separate purchasing budget. (As you will learn in Chapter 7, though, part of a buyer's overall performance can be measured by comparing actual operating expenses with budgeted operating expenses.)

DIRECTING

In addition to fulfilling their other responsibilities, full-time and part-time buyers must supervise the purchasing personnel assigned to them. Supervisory style is, of course, a personal matter; no two successful supervisors ever seem to follow identical supervisory styles. Generally speaking, though, top management, or an owner-manager, dictates some sort of supervisory policy.[3]

CONTROLLING

Buyers usually take responsibility for control over the products they buy until a user takes them from the storeroom and places them in the production flow. It is not always clear at exactly what point this responsibility shifts to the user. Nevertheless, everyone in a hospitality operation should be concerned with controlling waste, spoilage, and theft.

Small operations use a "direct control system" in which the owner-manager keeps a close eye on everything. Larger operations use an "indirect control system," often one in which a system of overlapping computerized and/or noncomputerized forms enables someone, usually the controller, to keep tabs on all the products. The manager can determine, from glancing at the controller's summary of issues and receipts, where these products are in the hospitality operation and how much of each is at its respective location. (Chapters 13, 14, and 15 contain thorough discussions of these controls.)

Controlling the purchasing process of a large organization is always a daunting task, but it is vital to the success of your operation. Today, purchasing technology enables companies with multiregional properties to track, monitor, and control the purchasing activities of its employees.

Large corporations often enjoy deep discounts when they procure products from preferred or contracted vendors. However, ensuring that purchasers at different properties are using these vendors rather than purchasing from non-contracted companies is crucial to cutting costs and increasing a property's profitability. Modern technology permits companies to create systems that track purchases company-wide.

For example, a purchasing agent in Houston seeks to order 1000 pounds of crab from a local vendor. Meanwhile, your company has entered a contract for a certain quantity of crab at a set discount from a national vendor that provides your company with seafood and other products. A corporate manager would then be notified if a purchase order is submitted to a company that has not been approved. Additionally, purchasing managers could be notified if the dollar amount is overly excessive, thereby controlling maverick spending while maximizing company profits.

Consider another example. When the MGM Grand (the largest hotel in the world) first installed its e-procurement system in the late 1990s, executives estimated that each of its purchasing managers averaged a time savings of $1\frac{1}{2}$ to 2 hours per day. Studies found that managers' ability to export vendor pricing from requests for quotes (RFQs) to the e-procurement system, along with other inventory management software systems, greatly reduced redundancy of effort. These studies also found that the MGM Grand was reducing AP prices by 22 percent due to new, more competitive vendors being discovered. In addition, the MGM Grand realized significant reductions in expense involved in long distance faxing when submitting RFQs and orders through the Internet.

Control is further complicated in the hospitality industry by waste and spoilage factors. Furthermore, security becomes more difficult because many of the products we buy are useful, convenient, and attractive to just about everyone. The buyer must do whatever is possible to minimize losses—normally by adhering to the control system approved by company policy.

KEY WORDS AND CONCEPTS

Approved suppliers	Controlling	Cost control
Budgeting	Co-op coordinator	Direct control system
Central distribution center	Co-op purchasing	Directing
Commissary	Corporate vice president of purchasing	Foodservice Purchasing Managers (FPM)
Communal buying		

Indirect control system	National Cooperative Business Association (NCBA)	Quality control
Institute of Supply Management (ISM)		Shared buying
Job specification	National Restaurant Association (NRA)	Small independent organization
Large independent organization	North American Association of Food Equipment Manufacturers (NAFEM)	Staffing
Medium independent organization		Steward
	Organizing	Supervisory style
Multiunit chain organization	Planning	Training
National contracts	Purchasing objectives	User-buyer

REFERENCES

1. Jay Williams and Tom Schrack, "Buying Groups—What Good Do They Do?" *Foodservice Equipment & Supplies,* May 2003, 56(5), pp. 66–68. See also: Timothy L. O'Brien, "Franchises Spearhead Renewed Popularity of Co-Ops," *The Wall Street Journal,* November 29, 1993, p. B2; "Co-Ops: Pool-Buying Grows for the Smaller Independent," *FoodService Director,* May 15, 1990, p. 42. For a history of the co-op, see Craig Cox, *Storefront Revolution: Food Co-Ops and the Counterculture (Perspectives on the Sixties)* (New Brunswick, NJ: Rutgers University Press, 1994).

2. For an in-depth discussion of the advantages and disadvantages of centralized purchasing, see M. C. Warfel and Marion L. Cremer, *Purchasing for Food Service Managers,* 4th ed. (Berkeley, CA: McCutchan, 2001), pp. 44–46. See also: Susan Av-

ery, "MasterCard Creates Global Sourcing Unit to Manage Office Spending," *Purchasing,* November 4, 1999; P. Fraser Johnson and Michael R. Leenders, "The Supply Organizational Structure Dilemma," *Journal of Supply Chain Management,* Summer 2001, 37(3), pp. 4–11.

3. Three volumes that supervisors should consult are: Jack E. Miller, John R. Walker, and Karen Eich Drummond, *Supervision in the Hospitality Industry,* 4th ed. (New York: John Wiley & Sons, 2002); Roger Fulton, *Common Sense Supervision: A Handbook for Success as a Supervisor* (New York: Ten Speed Press, 1988); and Martin M. Broadwell and Carol Broadwell Dietrich, *The New Supervisor: How to Thrive in Your First Year As a Manager,* 5th ed. (New York: Perseus Publishing, 1998).

QUESTIONS AND PROBLEMS

1. Describe the typical organizational patterns for the independent operation and for the multiunit chain operation.

2. Explain how a co-op purchasing organization works.

3. Assume that you are the owner of a small restaurant and you have the opportunity to join a purchasing co-op. Should you do it? Why or why not?

4. What are the major responsibilities of a vice president of purchasing?

5. Why do you think central distribution can be so unprofitable? Are there any benefits, other than monetary, associated with central distribution? If so, what are they? If possible, ask an official of a multiunit chain operation to comment on your answer.

6. Develop a job specification for an assistant food buyer.

7. What is the main difference between a direct and an indirect control system?

8. List three critical issues that should be addressed in a company's selection and procurement plan.

9. A franchisee may purchase from a company commissary. If so, he or she will incur several advantages and disadvantages.
    (a)   List some advantages.
    (b)   List some disadvantages.

10. What do you feel are the major advantage and the major disadvantage of the purchasing co-op? Why?

11. Develop a job specification for a full-time buyer.

12. Briefly describe a national contract. What is the primary advantage of such a contract?

13. When would it be advantageous for a franchisee to purchase from a local supplier instead of from the company-owned commissary?

EXPERIENTIAL EXERCISES

1. What do you think are the major advantages and disadvantages of centralizing the purchasing responsibilities in a hospitality operation?

    a.   What do you think the major advantage is?
    b.   What do you think the major disadvantage is?
    c.   Ask an independent owner-operator of a full-service restaurant to comment on your answer.
    d.   Ask the manager of a company-owned, fast-food operation that is part of a chain to comment on your answer.
    e.   Prepare a report that includes your answer and the owner-operator's and manager's comments.

2. Interview the owner of a small hospitality operation that uses a direct control system. Ask the owner what advantages he or she has with this system that he or she would not have with an indirect control system. Ask the owner what disadvantages he or she does have. Prepare a report providing the owner's comments regarding control systems.

THE BUYER'S RELATIONS WITH OTHER COMPANY PERSONNEL

The Purpose of this Chapter

After reading this chapter, you should be able to:

- Describe the buyer's relationship with others in the hospitality organization.

- Explain various methods used to evaluate a buyer's performance.

INTRODUCTION

In many cases, the buyer and the owner-manager are one and the same person. Only large operations maintain part-time or full-time buyers. In large hotels, for example, it is common to find a full-time purchasing agent as well as several department heads who purchase specialized merchandise for their needs. Similarly, large, multiunit chain restaurants usually employ a corporate purchasing agent with a buyer or a buyer-manager at each individual unit.

The full-time buyer is a member of management. He or she exercises line authority over those purchasing functions for which he or she is personally responsible and, sometimes, supervises other staff members, usually department heads, who accomplish some or all of their own purchasing. In other cases, all buying is part-time in the sense that various department heads and other members of management include among their duties the purchasing function for their areas.

In this chapter, we explore the buyer's relationship with both his or her supervisor and with other supervisory, managerial, and staff members and hourly employees.

THE BUYER'S RELATIONS WITH THE SUPERVISOR

Regardless of the organizational pattern, a buyer or buyer-manager usually answers to a supervisor somewhere in the organization. In Chapter 6, we discussed the various ways of organizing and administering the purchasing function. These methods are a major concern for managers. Of equal concern are the issues that must be addressed before the buyer or buyer-manager can completely organize and administer the buying activity.

The Job Specification

A job specification lists the qualities sought in a job candidate—in our case, a list of qualities to look for when evaluating the employment potential of an applicant for a buyer's position. A supervisor looks for at least four qualities before hiring a buyer (see Figures 7.1 and 7.2).

Technical Skill Buyers must be extremely familiar with the items they will purchase. At the very least, they should have the aptitude to learn the intricate aspects of all these products and services. In addition, a person cannot really aspire to a buyer's job unless he or she is familiar with the ways in which and the conditions under which chefs, bartenders, housekeepers, and so on, will use the purchased items.

Interpersonal (or Human) Skill The buyer must get along with other department heads and employees. After all, his or her performance affects colleagues' performance since they must work with the items purchased. A buyer also must be firm but fair with all types of sales representatives.

Conceptual Skill A buyer should be able to conceptualize the entire hospitality operation and not see things exclusively from the point of view of purchasing. In other words, he or she must make decisions that benefit the entire operation, not just his or her reputation. Sometimes it is difficult to see how, for example, a low as-purchased (AP) price can turn into an exorbitant edible-portion (EP) cost. But it is just this type of general perspective and systems mentality—the ability to view the

TECHNICAL SKILLS

Creating a recipe

Costing a recipe

Preparing a recipe

Preparing a work schedule

Developing a job description

INTERPERSONAL SKILLS

Conducting a performance appraisal

Interviewing a sales representative

Training an employee

Handling a customer complaint

Working with delivery agents

CONCEPTUAL SKILLS

Forecasting food trends

Marketing a restaurant

Organizing a banquet

Budgeting payroll expenses

Researching a new food item

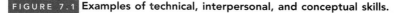

FIGURE 7.1 Examples of technical, interpersonal, and conceptual skills.

whole operation and the multitude of relationships it contains—that supervisors tend to look for in a buyer.

Other Qualities The three skills we just mentioned are fairly routine. Some other characteristics supervisors look for are not so easily discussed, but they are important. These include: (1) the quality and types of an applicant's experience; (2) honesty and integrity; (3) the desire to advance and grow with the operation; (4) the ability to administer a purchasing department, if applicable; and (5) the desire to work conscientiously for the operation.[1] In addition, a supervisor usually develops a set of questions he or she expects an applicant to answer satisfactorily. Also, a supervisor is almost certain to request some personal references.

Labor Pool

The buyer's job can be a full-time position, or it can be part of another job. If a supervisor needs a full-time buyer, he or she may look among the current employ-

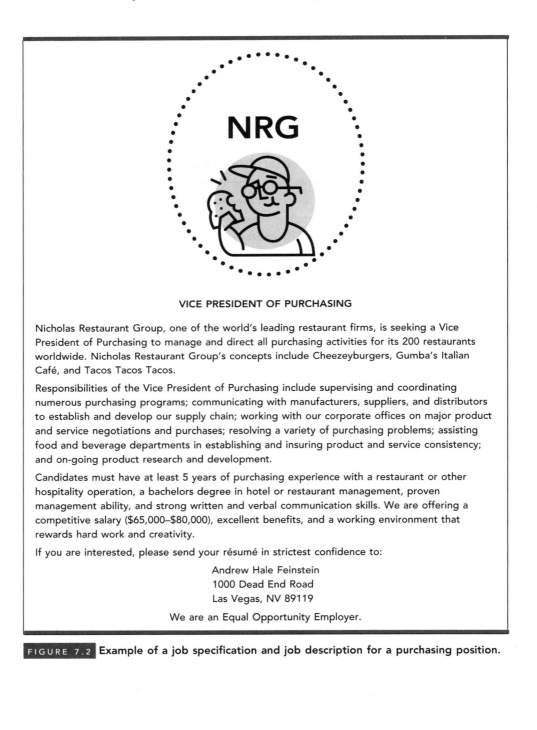

VICE PRESIDENT OF PURCHASING

Nicholas Restaurant Group, one of the world's leading restaurant firms, is seeking a Vice President of Purchasing to manage and direct all purchasing activities for its 200 restaurants worldwide. Nicholas Restaurant Group's concepts include Cheezeyburgers, Gumba's Italian Café, and Tacos Tacos Tacos.

Responsibilities of the Vice President of Purchasing include supervising and coordinating numerous purchasing programs; communicating with manufacturers, suppliers, and distributors to establish and develop our supply chain; working with our corporate offices on major product and service negotiations and purchases; resolving a variety of purchasing problems; assisting food and beverage departments in establishing and insuring product and service consistency; and on-going product research and development.

Candidates must have at least 5 years of purchasing experience with a restaurant or other hospitality operation, a bachelors degree in hotel or restaurant management, proven management ability, and strong written and verbal communication skills. We are offering a competitive salary ($65,000–$80,000), excellent benefits, and a working environment that rewards hard work and creativity.

If you are interested, please send your résumé in strictest confidence to:

Andrew Hale Feinstein
1000 Dead End Road
Las Vegas, NV 89119

We are an Equal Opportunity Employer.

FIGURE 7.2 Example of a job specification and job description for a purchasing position.

ees for someone with an aptitude for purchasing. Alternately, a professional buyer may be sought by advertising in the newspaper and trade journal classified-ads sections or on the Internet, by asking informally among trade association members, or by inquiring among friends and other professional colleagues. The supervisor must adhere to company policy and to federal, state, and local legislation throughout this recruiting process.

Part-time buyers spend relatively little time in purchasing. For example, chefs, kitchen stewards, and housekeepers often are required to do some purchasing. The labor pool for these jobs can be found in the same way employers look for full-time buyers. The main question, and major problem, when you recruit a part-time buyer is the degree of emphasis attached to individual aspects of the job. For instance, when you recruit a chef, how much emphasis should you place on the job candidate's purchasing skill, labor-control skill, cooking expertise, and so on?

Budgeting

As we pointed out in Chapter 6, the large operations that employ full-time buyers may decide to fund their purchasing. This funding usually means that they decide to include annual-salary expenses and other appropriate operating expenses (such as office supplies) as a part of the hospitality operation's overall budget. The operations that employ user-buyers tend to avoid this separate purchasing budget. Nevertheless, since a budget is always a measure of performance, a buyer's overall contribution can be measured by comparing actual operating expenses with budgeted operating expenses.

Job Description

A job description constitutes a list of duties an employee must perform. It is usually prepared before, or in conjunction with, the job specification. In some cases, the supervisor develops the description personally. In others, the purchasing manager may participate in this effort. Even in this situation, however, the supervisor should set the tone of the job by stating its objectives and the broad guidelines a buyer must follow. The buyer, then, is left to iron out the specific details necessary to organize and administer the purchasing function (see Figure 7.3).[2]

Objectives of the Purchasing Function We discussed the general objectives in Chapter 5, noting that buyers attain them by: (1) purchasing the appropriate quality, (2) purchasing at the right price, (3) purchasing in the right amount, (4) purchasing at the right time, and (5) purchasing from the right supplier, who provides

Establish selection and procurement policies

Forecast trends

Develop purchase specifications

Maintain supplier files, price lists, etc.

Negotiate contracts

Monitor deliveries

Select suppliers

Coordinate other departments' purchasing needs

Identify and research new products

Investigate suppliers' facilities

Establish inventory stock levels

Monitor storeroom inventories

Select and train purchasing staff

Monitor operating budget

Establish and monitor inventory and cost controls

FIGURE 7.3 **An example of job description duties for a purchasing manager.**

the needed supplier services. Additional objectives may be more specific. For example, someone in the operation may decide to set rigid quality standards for fresh produce and looser quality standards for the remaining food products. A specific goal, then, would be the maintenance of these various quality standards.

Selection and Procurement Policies These policies are usually broad, flexible rules a supervisor expects a buyer to follow when selecting and procuring products and services. In general, policies guide a buyer in terms of how to act and what to do in several types of situations. As the following discussion shows, precise policies are in the buyer's best interest. Some of these situations are presented next.

Accepting Gifts from a Supplier (This also applies to accepting gifts, pooling them, and distributing them later to all company employees.) Strict rules against this practice are the norm. Drawing the line can, however, be difficult. For example, accepting bottles of liquor may be taboo, but what should a buyer do about a supplier who treats him or her to a free lunch now and then? Similarly, what should a buyer do about a supplier who always has complimentary tickets to major sports events? If the buyer picks up his or her share of the lunch tabs and tickets, everything is probably all right. But whatever the policy, a buyer must realize that accepting gifts, especially those that cannot be returned (such as complimentary meals and tickets) could create a psychological obligation to purchase goods or services from these generous suppliers.[3]

Favoring Suppliers How many potential suppliers should a buyer contact? Should a buyer stick with one or two, or should he or she consider any reputable, capable purveyor? In some cases, other department heads may try to steer a buyer toward a certain supplier, usually a friend. This practice puts the buyer in a difficult position. But a strict policy can protect a buyer from undue pressure from, for example, the bartender who wants all the bar supplies to be purchased from his cousin's supply house. In most instances, the supervisor insists that an approved supplier list be developed, which then serves to restrict all personnel who have purchasing responsibilities.

Limiting Quantity The typical buyer is restricted in the amount he or she can purchase at any one time. If a buyer wants to buy a larger-than-normal amount, generally, he or she must obtain permission. This common policy is strictly enforced to help an operation avoid massive overstocks that tie up large sums of money and extra storage space.

Limiting Prices A supervisor may suggest some flexible price limits for certain products, especially those products that represent the bulk of the purchasing dollar. And, for instance, if an item's price rises above that limit, it may be time to reevaluate the item's place in the operation.

Making Personal Purchases Personal purchases, also referred to as "steward sales," occur whenever the hospitality company allows its employees to take advantage of the company's purchasing power to purchase goods for their personal, private use. Buyers, for example, might be tempted to buy hams, steaks, or roasts for a personal dinner party they are planning. And other employees might like to take advantage of the wholesale price. Usually, however, a supervisor discourages this.

In some companies, employees may be permitted to take advantage of this price on such special occasions as holidays. Also, if employees must buy their own uniforms, they may be able to make these purchases through the buyer or purchasing agent. But abusing this practice can lead to confusion and dishonesty.

Establishing Reciprocity Basically, reciprocity means "you buy from me, I'll buy from you." It is also interpreted to mean "I'll buy from you if you do something special for me." This is a troublesome policy. Other department heads and employees may badger a buyer into entering into some sort of reciprocal arrangement. Not only may the arrangement be illegal, but the best a buyer can do, obviously, is to break even. In fact, the buyer usually winds up purchasing more items from a supplier than the supplier could ever reciprocate; for example, suppliers can refer much less food business to you than you can buy from them. If there is a reciprocal arrangement, the superior normally establishes it, with the buyer then expected to purchase accordingly.

Accepting Free Samples Some buyers collect all sorts of free samples; others accept them only when they have a sincere interest in buying the product; still others purchase the samples they want to avoid obligating themselves to a particular supplier. Perhaps the best policy is to accept a free sample only when there is a serious interest in the product.

Free equipment testing falls under the same guidelines: typically, you test it only if you have more than a casual interest.

The major difficulty with free samples and free equipment testing is the distinct possibility that suppliers will send their most expensive items and then pressure the user to pressure the buyer to purchase them. Consulting with a user of the equipment (the chef, for example) instead of the buyer is an example of "backdoor selling." This selling strategy can be effective, but it also can undermine efficiency and friendship. In any case, hospitality companies should adhere to a strict policy on free samples and test equipment.

Accepting Discounts A buyer can obtain at least four separate types of discounts from a supplier:

1. **Quantity Discount.** This is granted by the supplier if a buyer agrees to purchase a large amount of one specific type of merchandise.

2. **Volume Discount.** This is similar to the quantity discount. The buyer must agree to purchase a large volume of goods; however, he or she can buy more than one type of merchandise. This discount is sometimes referred to as a "blanket order discount," in that the purchase order contains a long list of several items, none of which is ordered in huge amounts. But, when all of these small amounts are totaled, a supplier might reward the resulting large dollar volume with a discount.

3. **Cash Discount.** This is an award for prompt payment, for paying in advance of the delivery, or for using a cash-on-delivery (COD) bill-paying procedure.

4. **Promotional Discount.** A supplier might grant this type of discount if a buyer's company agrees to accept the discount and use it to promote the product in the operation. For example, this promotion might involve letting restaurant customers sample the product at a reduced menu price.

Quantity discounts and volume discounts are relatively common in the hospitality industry, but they often require purchasing amounts that cannot be stored easily. Buyers may or may not be permitted to bargain for cash discounts since the accounting department or the financial officer usually sets up some sort of bill-paying schedule. (We discuss this issue in Chapter 11.)

Some hospitality companies aggressively seek out suppliers who offer generous promotional discount opportunities.[4] For example, some quick-service restaurants will allow a supplier to advertise brand name merchandise in the property if the supplier agrees to give them, free of charge, beverage-dispensing equipment, menu sign boards, and/or countertop display shelving. Some table-service operations like promotional discounts because they can use them to reward servers who sell their quota of a particular item to guests. Also, caterers enjoy having suppliers construct attractive displays of their products in the caterers' sales offices that can be used to entice potential banquet customers into purchasing expensive parties.

Promotional discounts, though, represent a loaded decision. Although a buyer may want to save the money, the company may not want the obligation to promote the product or even to be identified too closely with it.

Following the Written Ethics Code Most hospitality companies have established written ethical guidelines for their buyers. In many cases, these guidelines are adapted from those suggested by one or more professional purchasing associations. The typical code, though, is usually very explicit and pertains to all potential ethical dilemmas. It is normally a major part of a buyer's job description.

Controlling Products When a product is purchased, the buyer is not relieved of the responsibility for that item. He or she may be responsible for its storage and use. In fact, in small operations, the buyer-user or part-time buyer generally takes responsibility for an item until it is used in production. Larger companies often split that responsibility. For example, the food buyer may be responsible for purchasing, storing, and then issuing the food to a user. In hotels, the receiving clerk is often part of the accounting department. He or she checks incoming merchandise and serves as a control on the buyer's purchases. Once users receive an item, they take responsibility for it.

The more times you split responsibility of this kind, the greater control you have, since more people check on each other's performance. This division is practically impossible in small operations. But in smaller places, the operator is usually on the premises to maintain strict supervision. A manager with a sharp eye suffers no loss of control whatsoever.

Supporting Local Suppliers Some owner-managers like to support local suppliers and ensure that a certain amount of business stays in the community. Although this policy of trade relations can limit a buyer's alternatives, in the long run, some local purchasing may be a beneficial strategy.

Adhering to Quality Standards Usually, the owner-manager will set the quality standards, and the person who has ordering responsibilities will abide by them and see to it that, as much as possible, he or she purchases and receives such quality. It is unusual for buyers to have the final say regarding the quality standards to be used in the hospitality operation, but quite often, the person who has the major responsibility for ordering has some leeway and flexibility.

Following Shopping Procedures The buyer's supervisor usually will want to note the exact type of buying procedures, especially the procedures to be used when selecting the appropriate supplier. The shopping procedures that most buyers must use require them to consider the offerings of more than one approved supplier in order to make an intelligent decision regarding the available values and which approved supplier seems to be the best for the buyer's hospitality operation. In some instances, the buyer's supervisor will decide that, for one reason or another, some items should be purchased from one specific supplier, whereas other items should be purchased only from the supplier offering the best value. The supplier offering the best value is determined by shopping around.

Compensation

Full-time and part-time buyers usually receive a straight salary, but in some situations they also receive a bonus. Corporate purchasing agents can expect to receive a good salary and to occupy a top management position within the company. Buyers, too, receive good salaries. Part-time buyers, though, tend to earn salaries based on several duties, not just their buying. For example, a chef may receive a high salary primarily because of his or her staff supervision and culinary expertise.

Where purchasing has been concerned, the major aspect of the compensation issue has always been the bonus. A bonus can be tricky to assign because buyers may be tempted to work toward the bonus alone while sacrificing other important aspects of the job. For example, if a buyer receives a bonus based on the AP prices paid for food, he or she may be motivated to purchase foods with the lowest AP price, even if they are also the ones with the highest EP cost.

Training

A buyer should receive some type of training before being allowed to purchase products. If the buyer is a new employee, he or she must be introduced to the philosophy and goals of the company, to all of its operational aspects, and to the purchasing policies. These introductions actually represent an orientation rather than training.

Full-time buyers and buyer trainees undergo additional training, as needed, in the procedural elements of buying. On-the-job training (OJT) is probably most often used in the purchasing function.

Performance Evaluation

Buyers undergo two types of performance evaluations: (1) how well they operate the purchasing department, if there is one; and (2) how well they have carried out the procurement function.

"Operational performance" refers to how well the buyer has adhered to the budget allocated to the purchasing department; that is, how efficient the buyer has been in discharging the purchasing duties. This evaluation consists of comparing actual secretarial salaries, postage expenses, telephone costs, and so on, with their budgeted counterparts. Small operations tend to skip this type of evaluation even though it can help a manager to isolate the operational costs of the buying function. Unfortunately, it is usually too difficult and costly to separate, for example, telephone calls to suppliers from the rest of the telephone calls. It is not impossible, but in small places it may not be economical.

"Procurement performance" refers to how effectively a buyer has procured products and services. Procuring items is the heart of the buyer's job; thus, procurement performance is extremely important. Unfortunately, we can find little agreement about what to look at when evaluating procurement performance. We discuss several of these performance quality indicators next.

The Materials Budget Some large companies forecast their sales and, concomitantly, the cost of goods sold. For example, the cost of food might be forecast at 35 percent of the food-sales dollar. The food buyer might be expected to spend no more than, say, 30 percent of the sales dollar for food, and the remaining 5 percent to be used to pay for the difference between the AP price and the EP cost—things like trimming loss and other unavoidable waste.

A company could construct a materials budget for such items as advertising costs, detergent costs, and lobster costs. In fact, this procedure is relatively common, even in small operations. But it is uncommon to find a materials budget for all products and services. It would be convenient, however, to have these budgets; they make it easy to compare actual costs, thereby facilitating a fair procurement performance evaluation.

These budgets appear more commonly in hospitality organizations that serve a "captive audience": employee feeding, college feeding, hospital and prison food services, and so on. Indeed, whenever a foodservice catering corporation bids on a foodservice contract of this type, it usually must include the projected expenses as a part of its bid. Consequently, the buyer receives what amounts to a materials budget to work with for the duration of the contract. If, for example, the costs of some foods increase, he or she may be forced to try cheaper substitutes.

Inventory Turnover This refers to the annual cost of goods sold divided by the average dollar value of inventory kept in stock during the course of that year. (The average inventory value is equal to the inventory value at the beginning of the year, plus the inventory value at the end of the year, divided by two.) For example, if a restaurant's annual cost of goods sold equals $250,000, the beginning inventory is $12,000, and the ending inventory is $8,000, the inventory turnover calculation for that particular restaurant is:

$$\text{Average inventory} = \frac{\$12{,}000 + \$8{,}000}{2}$$

$$= \$10{,}000$$

$$\text{Inventory turnover} = \frac{\$250{,}000}{\$10{,}000}$$

$$= 25$$

The normal food turnover is between 20 and 25 times a year on the average. This means that it takes about two weeks for all foods to move from the receiving dock to a customer's stomach; for liquor, the turnover is between 7 and 10 times a year. But since there is no generally accepted rule-of-thumb inventory turnover figure in the hospitality industry, an operation must decide what represents a good turnover figure for its business. So, if 20 turns out to be ideal, 18 or 22 is unsatisfactory. Eighteen would be unsatisfactory because it indicates slow-moving stock. Twenty-two indicates a turnover so rapid that the operation risks the possibility of running out of stock. Most operations can fix an optimal number of turnovers that ensure an appropriate stock level, one that helps the business operate efficiently. (In Chapter 9, we provide further discussion of the optimal stock level.)

Percentage of Sales Volume   Various rules of thumb exist regarding the appropriate amount of inventory that should be on hand at any one particular point in time to accommodate the hospitality operation's expected level of business. For instance, a full-service restaurant should have an inventory of food, beverage, and nonfood supplies that is equal in dollar value to no more than 1 percent of its annual sales volume. An annual sales volume of $1 million, therefore, needs about $10,000 worth of inventory at all times to support it.

A related rule of thumb suggests that the food inventory should be no more than about one-third of the average monthly food costs. The food inventory should not exceed this level unless other financial incentives to purchase unusually large quantities exist. As with all rules of thumb, though, generalizations can be dangerous. However, they provide a quick method that can be used to evaluate the buyer's procurement performance.

Stockouts   A stockout occurs when you cannot serve a customer a particular item because you do not have it on hand. The number of stockouts an operation encounters indicates the amount of inventory held. Several stockouts suggest an unreasonably low stock level. Few or no stockouts indicate a high stock level. Again, an operation wants to reach an optimal stock level, which means it probably must accept some stockouts. How many to accept is, of course, a matter for managerial policy.

Number of Late Deliveries   A buyer may or may not be able to control a supplier's delivery schedule. But he or she certainly can complain when deliveries are late. If too many late deliveries occur, a supervisor may rightfully ask, "Why do you continue to buy from this purveyor?"

Number of Items That Must Be Returned to Suppliers   A buyer cannot always control defective deliveries, but he or she can complain about them. Also, a supervisor can pose the question: "Why continue to buy from a supplier who delivers defective goods?" Returned and late deliveries are to be avoided in the hospitality industry. If a buyer runs out of steak, he or she can hardly tell a customer to come back for it tomorrow.

Number of Back Orders This issue is similar to the previous two. Usually, a buyer does not like back orders and normally will not tolerate many of them.

Checking AP Prices Some companies periodically check the AP prices of other suppliers against the AP prices they are paying their current suppliers. These prices may not always be equal because of differences in overall value between suppliers. But if wide disparities appear, the buyer is either negligent or dishonest. (Dishonesty in these situations usually takes the form of a buyer's overpaying with the operation's funds and then receiving a personal rebate directly from the supplier. This practice, a type of kickback, is discussed more thoroughly in Chapter 16.)

It is, of course, time-consuming and tedious for supervisors to make these comparisons. It is not at all easy to compare values and EP costs. Also, if supervisors do not deal in the marketplace every day, it will be hard for them to keep track of current market prices. Nevertheless, supervisors exercise caution in this area because the practice of paying a little more and receiving a kickback is both tempting and easy to cover up.

Other Performance Indicators There are many other performance indicators, but they are merely variations of the ones we have discussed. For instance, some large companies go to a lot of trouble to calculate such standard ratios as average inventory as a percentage of sales, average inventory as a percentage of total assets, and average inventory as a percentage of annual purchases. These standards, all variations on the materials budget, are subsequently compared with actual percentages.

When evaluating purchasing performance, wise supervisors will establish clearly defined and easily measured goals. In view of the variety of performance evaluations used throughout the industry, the safest conclusion is that supervisors should continually evaluate a buyer's procurement performance by monitoring: (1) the number of stockouts, (2) the inventory stock levels, (3) the percentage of returns, (4) losses due to overbuying, (5) losses due to the user's refusal of an item, and (6) inventory turnover.

Another major problem in performance evaluation is how to evaluate the part-time buyer. The measurements we have already discussed do apply, but the thorny question of how much emphasis to place on this part-time activity remains. For instance, a buyer-chef may be primarily involved in food production. Hence, his or her purchasing performance may be less important to the operation. If buying is a part-time activity, the chef may be unable to devote sufficient attention to it. Is this the chef's fault? Should he or she be reprimanded if the stock turnover is too low? Clearly, another dimension enters the picture whenever the part-time buyer's performance is measured.

Other Relationships Between Buyers and Supervisors

Buyers and their supervisors rightfully have certain expectations of each other. So far in this chapter, we have considered the straightforward aspects of the supervisor's role as it relates to the part-time or full-time buyer. But other more intangible expectations exist between these two employees.

Supervisors expect more than mere job competence. They also expect the buyer: (1) to give pertinent advice when necessary, (2) to be loyal to the company, (3) to put the company's interests ahead of any personal interest, (4) to maintain effective and efficient working relationships with all purveyors and company personnel, (5) to bear in mind constantly that he or she represents the company in the marketplace, (6) to avoid the possibility of legal entanglements, and (7) to avoid the possibility of favoritism and discrimination when dealing with purveyors.

Buyers also have expectations. They expect their supervisor: (1) to give them the necessary authority to perform their jobs adequately, (2) to give them adequate facilities and an adequate budget, (3) to give them a voice in such major decisions as menu planning, and (4) to have an appreciation for the profit potential of the buying activity.

THE BUYER'S RELATIONS WITH COLLEAGUES

All colleagues should strive to help each other. At the very least, a full-time buyer who purchases items for the kitchen, bar, housekeeping department, and so on, can ensure a continuous flow of supplies for all departments of the hotel or restaurant. We have stressed the fact that few operations employ a full-time buyer. Most depend on such buyer-users as the buyer-head bartender, the buyer-housekeeper, and the buyer-chef. But the buying aspect of their jobs can create an additional bond between these colleagues.

For instance, these user-buyers may want to combine some activities. They may agree that the buyer-chef will purchase writing supplies for everyone or that the buyer-housekeeper will purchase soaps and other cleaning supplies for all departments. Sometimes the owner-general manager makes these decisions. Alternately, together, all the part-time buyers can iron out the details. However this process is handled, a greater need for cooperation and coordination among colleagues enters the picture.

Buyers must also work closely with colleagues who have no buying authority. For example, the buyer-chef may work with the accountant to develop various formats to be used for ordering, receiving, storing, and the like. The buyer-chef may work with the sales manager or the owner-manager whenever new menus are contemplated since he or she can advise on food prices, the availability of various items, and the operation's capability of producing the new menu items given its kitchen facilities and employee skills.

Potential Conflicts with Colleagues

Major conflicts can occur between buyers and production supervisors who use the products and services. For example, a full-time buyer may spend a lot of time tracking down good buys, only to see excessive waste and spoilage in food preparation. Although the control of purchased items eventually passes from the buyer to the user, the chef may blame the buyer for purchasing inferior merchandise if food costs are too high because of waste. Conversely, the buyer may blame the waste on the chef's lack of control over the kitchen employees. Either way, the owner-manager has a problem deciding whom or what to believe.

This kind of conflict has encouraged some operations to create several buyer-user positions, thereby keeping control and responsibility together. For example, some restaurants employ a buyer-chef, buyer-head bartender, buyer-wine steward, and buyer-maître d'. The drawback is the buyer-user who has no one checking up on his or her buying activities, no one to uncover buying mistakes. An alert owner-manager, though, can usually minimize this difficulty.

Other, more minor conflicts can occur, but these usually involve the politics that arise whenever colleagues vie for favor with the boss. The major potential problem remains the control issue, which can lead to even larger problems and should never be taken lightly.

THE BUYER'S RELATIONS WITH HOURLY EMPLOYEES

The buyer's main responsibility to hourly employees is to provide the resources they need to carry out their duties properly. Buyers must ensure a continuity of supply. If employees do not have the raw materials, they cannot produce. In addition, idle production workers lead to customer dissatisfaction somewhere down the line. When employees should be producing but cannot because materials are late or unavailable, at some later point, when output is expected, guests will find that their guest rooms are not ready or their food is missing.

The buyer's secondary responsibility to hourly employees involves steward sales. If the hospitality operation permits hourly employees to make personal purchases, the buyer generally incurs the responsibility for supervising and monitoring these purchases.

Potential Conflicts with Hourly Employees

The major potential conflict with hourly employees can occur when a buyer tries to exert control and authority over employees someone else supervises. Generally, this conflict parallels a major conflict that occurs between a full-time buyer and his or her colleagues. Full-time buyers may unknowingly assume more authority than they are entitled to. For instance, if a buyer also manages the storeroom, he or she might alienate the chef's employees by forcing them to follow myriad rules and regulations to obtain the food and supplies they need in their work. These rules can indirectly affect the employees' work patterns; hence, they tend to give the buyer some control over these employees. In the long run, these conflicts must be ironed out between the buyer and his or her colleagues.

KEY WORDS AND CONCEPTS

Approved supplier list	Edible-portion cost (EP cost)	Inventory value as a percentage of sales volume
As-purchased price (AP price)	Ending inventory	
Back orders	Equipment testing	Job description
Backdoor selling	Ethics code	Job specification
Beginning inventory	Evaluating the part-time buyer	Kickback
Bill-paying procedures		Labor pool
Blanket order discount	Favoring suppliers	Late deliveries
Budgeting	Food inventory value as a percentage of food costs	Materials budget
Cash discount		On-the-job training (OJT)
Cash on delivery (COD)	Free samples	Operational performance
Compensation	Gifts from suppliers	Other expectations that exist between buyer and supervisor
Conceptual skill	Interpersonal skill	
Controlling products	Inventory turnover	

Performance evaluation	Reciprocity	Shopping procedures
Personal purchases	Relations and conflicts between buyer and colleagues	Steward sales
Price limits		Stockouts
Procurement performance	Relations and conflicts between buyer and hourly employees	Supporting local suppliers
Promotional discount		Systems mentality
Purchasing objectives	Relations and conflicts between buyer and supervisor	Technical skill
Quality standards		Trade relations
Quantity discount	Returns	Training
Quantity limits	Selection and procurement policies	Volume discount
Rebate		

REFERENCES

1. Patt Patterson, "What Qualities Make a Top-Notch Restaurant Food Buyer?" *Nation's Restaurant News*, January 19, 1987, p. 51.

2. For a detailed job description, see M. C. Warfel, Marion L. Cremer, and Richard J. Hug, *Purchasing for Food Service Managers*, 4th ed. (Berkeley, CA: McCutchan, 2001)

3. Buylines, "Ethical Dangers Multiply," *Purchasing*, October 17, 1996. See also: Pamela Sebastian, "Vendors' Gifts Pose Problems for Purchasers," *The Wall Street Journal*, June 26, 1989, p. B1; Patt Patterson, "'Tis the Season of Gift Giving, a Time to Show Appreciation," *Nation's Restaurant News*, November 23, 1992, p. 128; William Atkinson, "New Buying Tools Present Different Ethical Challenges," *Purchasing*, March 6, 2003 (Available http://www.manufacturing.net).

4. Patt Patterson, "Distributor: Communication Key to Relationships," *Nation's Restaurant News*, February 25, 1991, p. 46.

QUESTIONS AND PROBLEMS

1. Define or briefly explain the following terms:
   - (a) Job specification
   - (b) Job description
   - (c) Purchasing policies
   - (d) Quantity limits
   - (e) Price limits
   - (f) Reciprocal buying
   - (g) Performance evaluation
   - (h) Materials budget
   - (i) Inventory turnover
   - (j) Stockout
   - (k) Approved supplier list

2. Given the following data, compute the inventory turnover.
   Beginning inventory: $15,000
   Cost of goods sold: $325,000
   Ending inventory: $12,000

3. Briefly describe the buyer's major working relationship with the accountant and with the sales manager.

4. What are some specific conflicts that can occur between the full-time buyer and the chef, and between the full-time buyer and the housekeeper?

5. Explain why a hospitality organization might create several buyer-user positions.

6. What is the buyer's typical responsibility regarding the personal purchases employees make?

7. Should full-time buyers have control over a production supervisor's employees and their use of raw materials? Why or why not?

8. Name three advantages of taking the time to shop around for the best value.

9. Name three disadvantages of taking the time to shop around for the best value.

10. What are some disadvantages of accepting promotional discounts from suppliers?

11. What would be the approximate food, beverage, and nonfood-supplies inventory value of a full-service restaurant with an annual sales volume of $600,000?

12. If you had your preference, which method would you use to evaluate a buyer's procurement performance? Which method would you ignore? If possible, ask a hotel manager to comment on your answer.

13. What are the major objectives of the purchasing function?

14. What are some advantages that a hospitality company gains when it insists that all of the company buyers use an approved supplier list?

EXPERIENTIAL EXERCISES

1. Search online, in trade magazines, and in local newspapers for two examples of job specifications and job descriptions for a food buyer or purchasing director (examples are provided in Figure 7.2).
   a. Prepare an advertisement for a food buyer to be used on an online job-posting site.
   b. Prepare an ad for a purchasing manager to be used in a local newspaper.
   c. Provide your two ads to a hotel manager and ask for comments.
   d. Prepare a report that includes your two ads and the manager's comments.

2. Assume that you are a hotel manager.
   a. Devise formal policies for the following:
      Accepting supplier gifts
      Establishing quantity limits
      Accepting free samples
   b. Provide your formal policies to a restaurant manager and ask for comments.
   c. Prepare a report that includes your policies and the manager's comments, and the reasoning that led to your policy statements.

3. Develop a two-week buyer's training program for a bartender who soon will be promoted to liquor buyer-bartender.

4. Assume you are a hotel manager. Develop a list of performance evaluation criteria you would use to evaluate the buyer-housekeeper's procurement activity. Briefly discuss the reasoning that led to your list.

5. Assume that you are a restaurant manager. The food buyer and chef are blaming each other for the low quality of steak dinners. The chef claims that the buyer is purchasing inferior meat. The buyer contends that the chef's employees are abusing the product. How would you solve this conflict?
   a. Prepare a one-page report explaining how you would solve this conflict.
   b. Contact a local restaurant manager and ask him or her to review your answer.
   c. Submit your report and the manager's comments.

6. Assume that you have been instructed to purchase your fresh produce from one specific supplier, who happens to be a close friend of your employer. This supplier has back ordered you on several occasions. What would you do to improve this situation?
   a. Prepare a one-page report explaining how you would improve this situation.
   b. Contact a local restaurant manager and ask him or her to review your answer.
   c. Submit your report and the manager's comments.

THE PURCHASE SPECIFICATION: AN OVERALL VIEW

The Purpose of this Chapter

After reading this chapter, you should be able to:

- List the information included on the purchase specification.

- Identify factors that influence the information included on the purchase specification.

- Explain the potential problems related to purchase specifications.

- Describe how quality is measured, including the use of government grades and packers' brands.

INTRODUCTION

A "product specification," sometimes referred to as "product identification," is a description of all the characteristics in a product required to fill a certain production and/or service need. It typically includes product information that can be verified upon delivery and that can be communicated easily from buyers to suppliers.

Unlike the product specification, which includes only information about the product, the "purchase specification" implies a much broader concept. The purchase specification includes all product information, but, in addition, it includes information regarding the pertinent supplier services buyers require from suppliers who sell them products.

Large hospitality companies normally prepare purchase specifications. They usually seek long-term relationships with several primary sources and intermediaries and, before entering into these relationships, want to iron out every detail concerning product characteristics and desired supplier services. Smaller hospitality firms, on the other hand, tend to shop around for products on a day-to-day basis. These companies concentrate their efforts on preparing and using product specifications. If, for example, a particular supplier's supplier services are found lacking, these buyers will seek an alternative supplier who provides at least some of the desired supplier services.

Preparing detailed purchase specifications is not an easy task. It can be time-consuming, and a shortage of time is a major obstacle to getting this work done. If you plan to invest the time, money, and effort needed to develop adequate purchase specifications, you must be prepared to study the product's characteristics. Among the best sources here are the references the U.S. Department of Agriculture (USDA [www.usda.gov]) distributes. Many libraries carry these materials, or you can procure them from USDA offices or state agriculture offices. (These materials are particularly attractive because you can reproduce them without violating a copyright.) Further, many of these materials are now available online at the USDA's Website.

Other references are available as well. The U.S. government publishes purchasing guidelines for use by school food services that participate in the subsidized school lunch program (www.fns.usda.gov/cnd/Lunch). The various product industries, like the apple growers, also publish literature depicting characteristics of their products (www.bestapples.com). Industry associations, such as the Produce Marketing Association (PMA [www.pma.com]), similarly publish and distribute a significant amount of information that you can use to prepare specifications for fresh produce. And you can always find a supplier waiting to help you, especially if you buy from that supplier.

One decision you must usually make for yourself when preparing specifications is to choose the quality and supplier services you want. You cannot always expect to find a neat formula to guide you. This book offers several considerations that you should examine. But eventually you must make your own decisions concerning these other variables. You must also keep in mind that a purchase specification should contain more than just a brief description of a product.

WHY HAVE SPECS?

"Specs," or specifications, have several basic purposes and advantages, the primary ones being that: (1) they serve as quality control standards and as cost control standards (in these respects, specifications are important aspects of a hospitality operation's overall control system); (2) they help to avoid misunderstandings between suppliers, buyers, users, and other company officials; (3) in a buyer's absence, they allow someone else to fill in temporarily; (4) they serve as useful training devices for assistant buyers and manager trainees; and (5) they are essential when a company wants to set down all relevant aspects of something it wants to purchase, to submit a list of these aspects to two or more suppliers, and to ask these suppliers to indicate (bid) the price they will charge for the specific product or service.

In short, a specification is a sounding board for your ideas through which you detail every relevant consideration. By contrast, a purchase order is much less involved. After you know what you want and from whom you want it, completing the purchase order is a formality. But it is a legal formality: a contract between you and a supplier that he or she will deliver goods at a specific time, for a specific price, to a specific place. The specification lays out the parameters of what you must have. The purchase order is a written or sometimes verbal—for example, over the telephone—contract that arranges an actual transaction.

WHO DECIDES WHAT TO INCLUDE ON THE SPECS?

Four potential decision-making entities are involved here: (1) the owner-manager or another top management official, (2) the buyer, (3) the user, or (4) some combination of these three. It is unlikely that the buyer would write the specs alone, without the advice of the supervisor and of the users of the items to be purchased. All companies seem to approach this issue differently, but the buyers and users do most of the legwork, all the while staying within overall company guidelines. That is, a top company official normally sets the tone for the specs, and the buyers or users complete the details. The biggest problem with this participatory approach is agreeing on what is a main guideline and what is a minute detail.

WHAT INFORMATION DOES A SPEC INCLUDE?

A spec can be very short; it might include only a product's brand name—nothing else. Alternately, it might include several pages of detailed information, which is often the case with equipment specifications.

Be aware that specifications are sometimes categorized as either "formal" or "informal." A formal specification is apt to be extremely lengthy, perhaps several pages of information. Government agencies typically prepare formal specifications. The average hospitality enterprise owner-manager may prepare informal specifications, perhaps just a bit of information regarding product yield, quality, and packaging. You should not assume that the person preparing an informal specification is not cognizant of all of the other information normally found on a formal one. It is just that the typical operator does not spend so much time writing.

The buyer is apt to include at least some of the following pieces of information on a spec:

1.   **The Performance Requirement, or the Intended Use, of the Product or Service.** This is usually considered the most important piece of information. You must have a clear idea of what is supposed to happen.

2.   **The Exact Name of the Product or Service.** You must note the exact name, as well as the exact type of product you want. For example, you cannot simply note that you want olives; you must note that you want black olives, green olives, or anchovy-stuffed olives, or whatever. In some instances, you must be extremely careful to indicate the correct name and/or type of merchandise desired, or you are apt to be disappointed at delivery time.

3.   **The Packer's Brand Name, If Appropriate.** Packers' brands are an indication of quality. Some items, such as fresh produce, do not normally carry instantly recognizable brand name identification. Many other items do, however, and a buyer may be interested primarily in only one or two brands and not any others. If you do indicate a brand name on the spec, you may want to add the words "or equivalent" next to it. This ensures that more than one supplier can compete for your business. By noting merely the brand name, you may reduce the opportunity to shop around, since usually only one supplier in your area will carry that product.

In lieu of the words "or equivalent," some buyers prefer to add the words "equal to or better" to their brand name preferences noted on the specs. This phrase is used in conjunction with a brand name to indicate that the product quality characteristics desired must be similar or "superior" to the brand identified. The drawbacks with these words are that there may be several superior brands and that it may be very difficult for buyers to make a sound purchase decision if they are unfamiliar with some of them.

At times, it is very important to insist on a certain brand name and avoid all other comparable brands. For instance, if a recipe has been developed that calls for a certain brand of margarine, the buyer should not purchase another brand unless it is compatible with that recipe. In this case, the finished product may be unacceptable if a different brand is used.

4. **U.S. Quality Grade, If Appropriate.** The federal government has developed U.S. grades to allow the buyer the option of using an independent opinion of product quality when preparing specifications. A good place to view U.S. quality grades online is at www.ams.usda.gov/howtobuy. This site provides information on how to select numerous food products.

   Unfortunately, since grading generally is a voluntary procedure, many items in the channel of distribution may not be graded. However, you can, at least, indicate a desired grade, along with the notation "or equivalent." This will enable suppliers who do not have graded merchandise to bid for your business. Also, these suppliers then have a quality standard to guide them. Some states also have grading systems. For example, Wisconsin has a grading procedure to use for some dairy items (www.wisdairy.com).

5. **Size Information.** In most instances, buyers must indicate the size desired for a particular item. For some products, such as portion-cut steaks, buyers can indicate an exact weight. For other items, though, such as large, wholesale cuts of beef or whole chicken, usually buyers can only indicate the desired weight range. In some instances, the size of an item, such as lemons or lobster tails, is indicated by its "count," that is, the number of items per case, per pound, or per 10 pounds.

6. **Acceptable Trim, or Acceptable Waste.** For some products, including many fresh foods, you may need to indicate the maximum amount of waste you will tolerate. Another way to say this is to note the minimum edible yield of a product you will accept. For instance, fresh lettuce may have varying degrees of waste, depending on how the food distributor processes it. Some lettuce is a cleaned and chopped, ready-to-serve product, whereas a typical head of lettuce has an edible yield of much less than 100 percent. Of course, you expect to pay much more for the product that has little or no waste.

7. **Package Size.** In most situations, you will need to indicate the size of the container you desire. For instance, the can size must be noted when purchasing canned vegetables.

8. **Type of Package.** In some cases, the type of packaging materials used is highly standardized. For example, dairy products packaging must meet minimum standards of quality. This is not the case for other items. Frozen products, for instance, should come in packaging sufficient to withstand the extreme cold without breaking. Some suppliers scrimp on this, and, while the quality of the product may meet your specification, the poor packaging will result in a rapid deterioration of this once-acceptable item.

Packaging can add considerable cost to the items you purchase. In some cases, the value of the packaging may exceed the value of the item. The cost of packaging of single-serve packets of salt, for instance, can easily be higher than the cost of this food ingredient.

When specifying the desired type of packaging, some buyers may require suppliers to use recyclable packaging materials. Alternatively, buyers may request reusable packaging, such as the plastic tubs some suppliers use to deliver fresh fish.

9. **Preservation and/or Processing Method.** For some products, you will be able to identify two or more preservation methods. For instance, you could order refrigerated meats or frozen meats, canned green beans or frozen green beans, and refrigerated beer or nonrefrigerated beer.

    You also could specify unique types of preservation methods, such as smoked fish instead of salted fish, irradiated poultry instead of nonirradiated poultry, oil-cured olives instead of brine-cured olives, and genetically altered tomatoes instead of natural tomatoes.

    The type of preservation and/or processing method selected often influences the taste and other culinary characteristics of the finished food product. Consequently, it is important for you to be familiar with recipe requirements before altering this part of the spec.

10. **Point of Origin.** You may want to indicate the exact part of the world that a specific item must come from. This is a rather important consideration for fresh fish. For instance, you may need to specify that your lobster must come from Maine and not from Australia.

    Buyers may want to note the point of origin on some specs for several reasons. One is that the flavor, texture, and so forth of an item can differ dramatically among growing regions. Another reason is that the menu may state that an item comes from a particular producing region in the world; if so, it would be a violation of truth-in-menu regulations to serve an alternative product. Freshness can be another important consideration because buyers may specify nearby points of origin in order to ensure product quality. And, finally, buyers may indicate where a product cannot come from, instead of where it must come from, in order to adhere to various company policies and/or legal restrictions. For instance, for political reasons, some companies may refuse to purchase products that come from certain parts of the world.

11. **Packaging Procedure.** Some products are wrapped individually and conveniently layered in the case. Others are "slab-packed," that is, tossed into the

container. The more care taken in the packaging procedure, the higher the as-purchased (AP) price is apt to be. However, carefully packaged products will have a longer shelf life. In addition, they will tend to maintain their appearance and culinary-quality characteristics much longer than those products that are packaged indiscriminately.

Another packaging consideration concerns the number of individual containers that normally come packaged in a case lot. For instance, it is traditional for No. 10 cans of foods to come packed six to a case. However, some buyers cannot afford to purchase six cans, or they cannot use six cans. Will the supplier sell fewer than six cans; that is, will he or she "bust" the case? Buyers who request busted cases run the risk of having few suppliers willing to compete for their business.

12. **Degree of Ripeness.** This is important for fresh produce. The same concept applies to beef items; for example, you may desire a specific amount of "age" on the item. Wines have a similar system that reflects, among other pieces of information, the year of production.

13. **Form.** This is an important consideration for many processed items. For example, do you want your cheese in a brick, or would you rather have it sliced? Do you want your roast beef raw, or do you want it precooked?

14. **Color.** Some items are available in more than one color. For example, buyers can order fresh red, green, or yellow peppers.

15. **Trade Association Standards.** Some trade associations establish minimum performance standards for items. This information can be commonly found in their trade publications (see Figure 8.1). For instance, the National Sanitation Foundation (NSF) International certification (www.nsf.org) seal on a piece of food-production equipment testifies to the equipment's sanitary acceptability.

16. **Approved Substitutes.** Some buyers make it a habit to include on some specs a list of acceptable substitutes that the suppliers can deliver if they are out of the normal item. This can save a great deal of time and effort over the long haul since suppliers would not have to call buyers every time a product shortage occurs. Buyers also may like this convenience. Unfortunately, before determining approved substitutes, buyers must ensure that they are compatible with production and service needs. So, while this notation on each spec saves time and trouble eventually, it can be more difficult in the short run to spend the time needed to test all potential substitute items.

UPDATE

October 2003, Volume 13, Issue 10

The Wheat Foods Council is an industry-wide partnership dedicated to increasing grain foods consumption through nutrition education and promotion programs.

Political cartoon #1 released

WFC's political cartoon series began with two scientists discussing what will be the newest "scapegoat" for selling more fad diet books.

In September, the first of four WFC cartoons was distributed to newspapers nationwide. Cartoons will be released quarterly and will depict clever messages to get consumers thinking about the truth and benefits of grain foods.

10841 S. Crossroads Dr., Suite 105
Parker, Colo. 80138

Phone: 303/840-8787

Fax: 303/840-6877

E:Mail:
wfc@wheatfoods.org

URL:
www.wheatfoods.org
www.homebaking.org

Judi Adams
President

Lori Sachau
Communications
Specialist

Vikki Berry
Office Manager

Sharon Davis
Charlene Patton
HBA/WFC Consultants

Council members are encouraged to reprint articles from this publication.

Grain foods to be featured in "Easy Home Cooking"

WFC recipes, photographs, and grain food information will be featured in the February/March issue of "Best Recipes - Easy Home Cooking" magazine. Since the magazine is sold at grocery checkout stands across the country, it provides an excellent opportunity for the Council to reach it's target audience. Magazines will go on sale February 10, 2004 and will include grains and breads in a special multi-page spread in the magazine's "Heart Healthy" section.

Approved by the WFC Executive Board, the project was made possible because of unanticipated funds that became available after the 2003-04 budget process. The project was included as an add-on for the 2003-04 WFC Communication Plan.

The chapter insert will be approximately eight pages and will feature the headline "A Lovin' Spoonful of Grains." The insert will also include text promoting the healthful benefits of eating grain foods and a description of the WFC. Recipes utilizing pasta, cereal, crackers, tortillas, flour, and bread products were submitted to the publisher. Additionally, the Home Baking Association's "Bake for Family Fun Month" (designated for February) logo will be included to encourage families to bake at home.

FIGURE 8.1 Trade associations provide information useful to buyers. Courtesy of the Wheat Foods Council.

17. **Expiration Date.** Many buyers will not accept products if they are concerned about possible quality deterioration. To avoid this problem, they may indicate on some specs that suppliers must prove that the products delivered are not too old. For instance, some product labels list "sell-by" dates; these are sometimes referred to as "pull dates," "best-if-used-by dates," or "freshness dates." For such items, buyers may want to add to their specs some reference to these dates.

18. **Chemical Standards.** Buyers might decide to specify a particular level of acceptable chemical use for some of the items they purchase. For instance, it is possible to purchase organic produce that is grown in chemical-free soil. Meat and poultry products raised without added chemicals in the animals' diets are also available in the marketplace.

19. **The Test or Inspection Procedure.** This is the procedure you intend to use when checking the items delivered to you or the services performed for you. Generally, this is the logical outcome of specifying the intended use. After you note the intended use, you should be prepared to indicate the tests or inspection procedures you will use to see whether your purchases will perform adequately.

20. **Cost and Quantity Limitations.** Buyers might indicate how much of the item or service is to be purchased at any one time. In addition, they might require an item to be removed from production and a substitute item to be sought when the cost limits are approached.

21. **General Instructions.** In addition to specific details, buyers might include such general details as: (a) delivery procedures, if possible; (b) credit terms; (c) the allowable number of returns and stockouts; (d) whether the product purchased must be available to all units in the hospitality company, regardless of a unit's location; and (e) other supplier services desired, like sales help in devising new uses for a product.

22. **Specific Instructions to Bidders, If Applicable.** Suppliers who bid for your business may want to know: (a) your bidding procedures, (b) your criteria for supplier selection, and (c) the qualifications and capabilities you expect from them.

WHAT INFLUENCES THE TYPES OF INFORMATION INCLUDED ON THE SPEC?

Several factors must be assessed before determining what information to include on a specification. Eight of these are:

1. **Company Goals and Policies.** These are probably most important. Overall managerial guidelines must be consulted before buyers write specs.

2. **The Time and Money Available.** Industry members continually argue the costs and benefits of written specifications. Obviously, we consider the time and money preparing specifications well spent.

3. **The Production Systems the Hospitality Operation Uses.** If, for example, a restaurant broils its hamburgers instead of grilling them, the fat content in its ground beef should be a bit higher than usual to compensate for the additional loss of juices that can occur if meat is broiled to the well-done state.

4. **Storage Facilities.** If, for example, freezer space is limited, a buyer may have to purchase larger amounts of fresh vegetables; a specification might carry this reminder.

5. **Employee Skill Levels.** Generally, the lower the skill level, the more buyers must rely on portion-controlled foods, one-step cleaners, and other convenience items. The trade-off is between a higher AP price and a lower wage scale. The balance in these issues is not always clear-cut; this is a good example of the trade-off concept that usually arises in value analysis (which we discussed in Chapter 5).

6. **Menu Requirements.** For example, live lobster on the menu forces a buyer to include the words "live lobster" on the specification.

7. **Sales Prices or Budgetary Limitations.** If, for example, a restaurant is located in a very competitive market, its menu prices may be fixed by its competition. This fact may force a buyer to include cost limits for some or all food specifications.

8. **Service Style.** A cafeteria, for example, needs some food items that have a relatively long hot-holding life since the food may remain on a steam table for a while. This type of information might be included on the specs, especially the specs for preprepared food entrées.

WHO WRITES THE SPECS?

Generally, four options are available to the hospitality operation, including:

1. Company personnel can write the specs. This option assumes that the necessary talent to write them exists in the company somewhere.

2. Many specs can be found in industry publications, CDs, online services, and in government documents. Although they may not fit your needs exactly, they are at least a good starting point (see Figures 8.2 and 8.3).

American Bakers Association	http://www.americanbakers.org/
American Beverage Institute	http://www.abionline.org/
American Egg Board	http://www.aeb.org/
American Institute of Baking	http://www.aibonline.org/
American Meat Institute	http://www.meatami.com/
American Poultry Association	http://www.ampltya.com/
American Seafood Distributors Association	http://www.freetradeinseafood.org/
Beer Institute	http://www.beerinstitute.org/
Canned Food Alliance	http://www.mealtime.org/
Florida Fruit and Vegetable Association	http://www.ffva.com/
Food and Drug Administration	http://www.fda.gov/
Foodservice Equipment Distributors Association	http://www.feda.com/
International Beverage Dispensing Equipment Association	http://www.ibdea.org/
International Dairy Food Association	http://www.idfa.org/
International Foodservice Manufacturers Association	http://www.ifmaworld.com/
National Cattlemen's Beef Association	http://www.beef.org/
National Fisheries Institute	http://www.nfi.org/
National Food Processors Association	http://www.nfpa-food.org/
National Frozen and Refrigerated Foods Association	http://www.hffa.org/
National Pasta Association	http://www.ilovepasta.org/
National Poultry and Food Distributors Association	http://www.npfda.org/
National Soft Drink Association	http://www.nsda.org/
National Turkey Federation	http://www.eatturkey.com/
North American Association of Food Equipment Manufacturers	http://www.nafem.org/
North American Meat Processors Association	http://www.namp.com/
NSF International	http://www.nsf.org/
Produce Marketing Association	http://www.pma.com/
Quality Bakers of America Cooperative	http://www.qba.com/
Retail Bakers of America	http://www.rbanet.com/
United Egg Producers	http://www.unitedegg.org/
United Fresh Fruit and Vegetable Association	http://www.uffva.org/

FIGURE 8.2 **Some government and private agencies that provide product information useful to buyers.**

U.S. Department of Agriculture	http://www.usda.gov
Agricultural Marketing Service	http://www.ams.usda.gov/
Dairy Market Branch	http://www.ams.usda.gov/dairy/index.htm
Fruit and Vegetable Branch	http://www.ams.usda.gov/fv/
Livestock and Grain Branch	http://www.ams.usda.gov/lsg/
Poultry Market News Branch	http://www.ams.usda.gov/poultry/
U.S. Department of Commerce	http://www.commerce.gov/
National Marine Fisheries Service	http://www.nmfs.noaa.gov/
Wine and Spirits Wholesalers of America	http://www.wswa.org/
World Association of the Alcohol Beverage Industries	http://www.waabi.org/

FIGURE 8.2 **(Continued)**

3. You can hire an expert to help you write your specs. This is a reasonable alternative, as you can control the amount of money you care to spend for this service.

   The USDA operates an "Acceptance Service" (www.ams.usda.gov/gac/) that permits hospitality operators to hire USDA inspectors to help prepare specs. The inspectors check the products you buy at the supplier's plant to make sure they comply with your specs (see Figure 8.4). They then stamp each item or sealed package to certify product compliance. This is often done for meat products. The acceptance service is provided for a fee, which the supplier usually pays. Although this expense may be included in your AP price, the service could save you money by assuring you that you receive exactly what you want.

4. The buyer and supplier can work together to prepare the specifications. The problem with this arrangement is that the buyer usually neglects to send the specs out to other suppliers for their bids. Also, the cooperating supplier may help slant the specs so that only he or she can provide the exact item wanted. Nevertheless, this is the option most independents find realistic, given their limited time resources and prospective order sizes.

The question of who writes the specs is important to hospitality operators because few part-time buyers have enough time to learn this task thoroughly. If operators want to prepare their own specs, they often consult outside expertise.

A. M. Pearson and Tedford A. Gillett, *Processed Meats,* 3rd ed. (New York: Aspen Publishers, 1998).

Arabella Boxer, *The Herb Book: A Complete Guide to Culinary Herbs* (Berkeley, CA: Thunder Bay Press, 1996).

ComSource Canned Goods Specifications Manual (Atlanta: ComSource Independent Foodservice Companies, Inc., 1994) [out of print].

ComSource Frozen Food Specifications Manual (Atlanta: ComSource Independent Foodservice Companies, Inc., 1994) [out of print].

Elizabeth Schneider, *Vegetables from Amaranth to Zucchini: The Essential Reference* (New York: William Morrow, 2001).

Ian Dore, *Shrimp: Supply, Products, and Marketing in the Aquaculture Age* (Toms River, NJ: Urner Barry Pub. Co., 1993).

Ian Dore, *The Smoked and Cured Seafood Guide* (Toms River, NJ: Urner Barry Pub. Co., 1994).

Ian Dore, *The New Fresh Seafood Buyer's Guide,* 2nd ed. (New York: Van Nostrand Reinhold, 1991) [out of print].

James A. Peterson, *Fish & Shellfish: The Definitive Cook's Companion* (New York: William Morrow, 1996).

John R. Romans, *The Meat We Eat,* 14th ed. (Upper Saddle River, NJ: Prentice Hall, 2000).

Kenneth T. Farrell, *Spices, Condiments, and Seasonings,* 2nd ed. (New York: Aspen Publishers, 1999).

Lewis Reed, *SPECS: The Comprehensive Foodservice Purchasing and Specification Manual,* 2nd ed. (New York: John Wiley & Sons, 1993).

North American Meat Processors Association, *The Meat and Poultry Buyers Guide on CD-ROM* (McLean, VA: North American Meat Processors Association, 2002).

North American Meat Processors Association, *The Meat Buyers Guide* (McLean, VA: North American Meat Processors Association, 1997).

North American Meat Processors Association, *The Poultry Buyers Guide* (McLean, VA: North American Meat Processors Association, 1999).

Seafood Business, *Seafood Handbook* (Portland, ME: Diversified Business Communications, 1999).

The Produce Marketing Association Fresh Produce Manual (Newark, DE: Produce Marketing Association, 2002).

FIGURE 8.3 **Some comprehensive reference materials buyers can use to prepare product specifications.**

The reasonable compromise seems to be to hire someone on a consulting basis to help write the specs or, if this is too expensive, to work with the specs found in various trade and governmental sources. The usual approach, to huddle with a supplier, may actually be least advantageous, but it does allow operators to spend more time in other business activities.

FIGURE 8.4 An inspector employed by the USDA Acceptance Service will inspect the buyer's order on the supplier's premises. If the order meets the buyer's specifications, the government inspector will apply a stamp, such as the one shown here, to the package. *Source:* United States Department of Agriculture.

POTENTIAL PROBLEMS WITH SPECS

As in most business activities, you should consider several costs in addition to benefits in specification writing. There are, for example, a number of clearly identifiable costs, and there are some cleverly hidden problems. Some potential problems with specs include:

1. Delivery requirements, quality tolerance limits, cost limits, or quantity limits may appear in the specs. If these are unreasonable requirements, they usually add to the AP price, but it may be questionable whether they add to the overall value.

2. Some inadvertent discrimination may be written into the specs. For example, the spec may read, "Suppliers must be within 15 miles to ensure dependable deliveries." Dealing with a supplier 16 miles away could cause legal trouble because of this.

    Worse, if a spec effectively cuts out all but one supplier, you will have wasted your time, money, and effort if your intention was to use the spec to obtain bids from several sources. You do, of course, still have the benefit of having specified very precisely what you want. This gives you a receiving standard and a basis for returning unacceptable product.

3. The specifications may request a quality difficult for suppliers to obtain. This situation adds to cost, but not always to value. In some situations, the quality you want cannot be tested or inspected adequately without destroying the item. In these cases, however, a sampling approach may ensure the requisite quality. Before you embark on such an expensive process, careful consideration is called for.

4. Some specs rely heavily on government grades. Unfortunately, some may not be specific enough for a foodservice operator's needs. For example, USDA Choice beef covers a lot of possibilities: There are high-, medium-, and low-choice grades. Also, grades do not usually take into account packaging styles, delivery schedules, and so forth. Thus, U.S. grades alone are not adequate for most operations.

5. Food specifications are not static; they usually need periodic revision. For instance, a spec for oranges might include the term "Florida oranges," a perfectly reasonable requirement at certain times of the year. But during some seasons, Arizona oranges might be preferable. It costs time, money, and effort to revise specifications. Moreover, if you cannot determine exactly when to revise, not only might you receive what you do not want, but your customer might also become dissatisfied if you are forced to serve the food because you have no acceptable substitute.

6. The best specs in the world will be of no use to you if the other personnel in the hospitality operation are not trained to understand them and to use them appropriately. For example, a buyer may be adept in the use of specs, but if the receiving agent does not have similar expertise, he or she may accept the delivery of merchandise that is not in accord with the properly prepared specifications.

7. The potential problems and costs multiply quickly if the spec is used in bid buying. Some of these additional problems include the following:

Getting Hit with the "Lowball"

The term "lowball" refers to a bid that is low for some artificial or possibly deliberately dishonest reason. For instance, bidders may meet a buyer's spec head on; that is, they may hit the minimum requirements and might even reduce their normal profit levels in order to win the bid. Once they are in, they may try to trade up the users.

Lowballing is a fairly standard way of doing business for suppliers trying to woo buyers away from their regular suppliers. These suppliers are willing to sacrifice a bit of revenue in the short run for the opportunity to establish a long-term and potentially more profitable arrangement. Suppliers know that once they get their foot in the door, buyers may get comfortable and stick with them through force of habit.

To avoid falling for lowball prices, buyers need to shop around frequently, which means they need to keep their specs current. This tends to keep suppliers competitive and more responsive.

Inequality Among Bidders

If your specs are too loose, that is, if too many suppliers can meet the specs, you run the risk of finding several suppliers of differing reliability bidding for your business. Choosing one of the less reliable suppliers can result in serious operational problems.

This problem is particularly prevalent in the fresh produce trade simply because the available qualities of fresh produce change continually and some buyers do not know exactly when to revise their specs. Several suppliers may bid for your lettuce contract, and several qualities may meet your specifications. Suppose one supplier has a good product, and he bids 60 cents per pound. Suppose, too, that another supplier has lettuce that she could gain good profits on even if she sold it for 55 cents per pound. What she probably will do, though, is enter a bid for 59 cents per pound because she has discovered that the other supplier will bid 60 cents. You gladly accept the 59-cent bid, and—who knows?—the quality may be satisfactory. To avoid this problem, do not use the costly bidding procedure unless you are willing to expend a great deal of effort to keep your specifications current.

A related problem occurs whenever an inexperienced buyer accidentally rigs the procedures by asking a supplier who has a high AP price and high quality to bid for the business. In the preceding example, the 59-cent-per-pound bidder is very happy to include the 60-cent-per-pound bidder in the process. The wise buyer strives to include in the bidder pool only responsible, competent, and competitive suppliers who are able to follow through if they win the buyer's business.

Sometimes, good suppliers may unintentionally differ significantly from others bidding for your business because of unanticipated changing business conditions. For instance, some suppliers who bid for your business may do so only when their regular business is slow. Consequently, you may be forced to continually change suppliers, which could cost you time, trouble, and money in the long run. In addition, although you may indeed receive an AP price break, when their regular business picks up, these suppliers may decide to stop bidding for yours.

Specifications that Are Too Tight

Tight specifications tend to eliminate variables and allow a buyer to concentrate on AP prices. Unfortunately, if only one supplier meets the buyer's specifications, that buyer will end up spending a lot of time, money, and effort to engage in specification writing and bidding, and still find there are only two choices available: take it or leave it.

Large hospitality companies sometimes run into a similar problem when they demand items that only one or two suppliers are able to deliver. For instance, a typical large hospitality firm wants to purchase products that are available nationally; this ensures that all units in the company use the same products, and this, in turn, ensures an acceptable level of quality control and cost control. The number of suppliers who can accommodate national distribution, though, is limited.

Advertising Your Own Mistakes

Bids may be entered on a three-month contract basis. If your specifications are in error, you can look forward to being reminded of your mistake whenever a delivery comes in.

Redundant Favoritism

The buyer who writes several specs, sends them out for bid, and then rejects all of the bids except the one from the supplier he or she usually buys from anyway is a genuine annoyance. This practice is followed by some operations that must use bid buying. The buyer solicits a bid for, for example, corn chips. Three companies bid. But the buyer decides to buy from supplier A because this supplier's product is always preferred. If this is the case, why seek bids?

Too Many Ordering and Delivery Schedules

Another potential problem with bid buying is the possibility that you will have to adjust to several suppliers' ordering and delivering schedules. A large hospitality organization can handle this extra burden. But if a small firm is accustomed to receiving produce at 10:00 A.M., it can be a difficult readjustment for that operator to receive produce at 2:00 P.M. one week and at 9:00 A.M. the next. (We have seen this need to readjust operating procedures cause a great deal of trouble, especially when a delivery must sit on the loading dock for a while because no one is free to store it. When the receiving routine is broken, ordinary problems multiply.)

And Always Remember . . .

The object of bid buying is to obtain the lowest possible AP price. But if the lowest possible AP price does not, somehow, translate into an acceptable edible-portion (EP) cost, you have gained little or nothing.

The costs and benefits of specification writing are never clear, and the subject becomes more confusing when you complicate it with a bid-buying strategy. We believe writing specs is generally necessary because they help you to clarify your ideas on exactly what you want in an item. We are not so confident about the bid procedures, though. For some items, such as equipment, bids may be economically beneficial to the hospitality operator. But on the whole, the buyer who uses this buying plan had better know as much or more about the items as the supplier. Only large operations consistently approach this requirement.

THE OPTIMAL QUALITY TO INCLUDE ON THE SPEC

You frequently hear references to "quality" products. To most people, a "quality" product represents something very valuable. However, when businesspersons talk about quality, they are referring to some "standard" of excellence. This standard could be high quality, medium quality, or low quality. In other words, suppliers offer products and services that vary in quality. In most cases, they can sell you a "high quality," "highest quality," "substandard quality," or almost any other quality you prefer.

It is important to keep in mind that quality is a standard: something to be decided on by company officials and then maintained throughout the operation.

We do not intend to second-guess the types of quality standards that hospitality operators develop or decide upon. Rather, our objective is to examine the typical process by which the optimal quality is determined.

WHO DETERMINES QUALITY?

Someone, or some group, must decide on a quality standard for every product or service the hospitality operation uses. If somebody decides to use a low choice grade of beef, this decision should reflect the type of customers the operation caters to, the restaurant type, and its location, among other factors.

Most analysts agree that a hospitality operator can hardly decide on quality standards without measuring the types of quality standards his or her customers expect. As the AP prices are translated into menu prices and room rates, customers are affected. The quality of the product purchased affects customers' perceptions of the operation, too. On the other hand, for the most part, supplier services are apparent principally to management. It is clear that value has many facets.

Most hospitality operations conduct some sort of market research to determine the types of value their customers, or potential customers, seek. The owner-manager's greatest responsibility is to interpret the results of the market research and translate them into quality standards. In other words, he or she must examine: (1) the overall value retail customers expect; (2) "supplier" services, that is, the property's surroundings, service style, decor, and so on; and (3) the typical menu or room price ranges attributable to his or her type of operation. Then the owner-manager must formulate a definition of quality standards. So, in the final analysis, the consumer really has the major say in determining the quality standards an operation establishes for most of its items.

Company officials may have a bit more latitude in determining the quality standards for those operating supplies and services retail customers do not directly encounter—items such as washing machine chemicals and pest control service. In these instances, it is interesting to note the number of people who may become involved in these determinations. A large group of company personnel may help work out these quality standards. The owner-manager, the department heads, and the buyer often influence the decision. Hourly employees may also be consulted since they constantly work with many of the products and services and are, hence, most familiar with them.

Quality standards for supplies, services, and equipment normally come from the top of the company. Buyers exercise a great deal of influence in these areas, though, because they get involved in such technical questions as "Is the quality standard available?", "What will it cost?", and "Can it be tested easily?" The ultimate decision, though, usually rests with the owner-manager or, in the case of chain organizations, an executive officer.

MEASURES OF QUALITY

A buyer is expected to be familiar with the available measures of quality, as well as their corresponding AP prices and ultimate values. Several objective measures of quality exist. Here are some of them.

Federal-Government Grades

Under authority of the Agricultural Marketing Act of 1946 and related statutes, the Agricultural Marketing Service (AMS [www.ams.usda.gov]) of the USDA has issued quality grade standards for more than 300 food products. These grade standards for food, along with standards for other agricultural products, have been developed to identify the degrees of quality in the various products, thereby helping establish their usability or value.

Federal-government grades are measurements that normally cannot be used as the sole indication of quality. This is true because federal-government grading is not required by federal law, except for foods a government agency purchases for an approved feeding program, or for commodities that are stored under the agricultural price support and loan programs; as a result, a buyer must use other measures of quality for ungraded items. Where possible, though, U.S. grades are the primary measures of quality that buyers use most frequently, at least at some point in the overall purchasing procedure.

The federal government, by legal statute, inspects most members of the channel of food distribution. Generally, the federal government's role is to check the sanitation of production facilities and the wholesomeness of the food products throughout the distribution channel. In some instances, states have set up additional inspector-powered agencies that either complement the federal agencies or supplant them.

Ordinarily, to be graded, an item must be produced under continuous federal-government inspection. Meat and poultry items and items that require egg breaking during their production process are always made under continuous inspection, but other types of items may not be.

The federal government will provide grading services for food processors, usually those at the beginning of the channel of distribution, who elect to purchase this service. Some of these producers buy this service, and some do not. Some opt for U.S. government grading because their customers include these grade stipulations in their specifications. Alternately, in some cases, the state requires federal grading. For example, several states require fresh eggs to carry a federal quality grade shield.

The grading procedure usually takes a scorecard approach with the products, beginning with a maximum of 100 points distributed among two or more grading factors. To receive the highest grade designation, a product must usually score 85 to 90 points or more. As the product loses points, it falls into a lower grade category. In addition, graders work under "limiting rules," which stipulate that if a product scores very low on one particular factor, it cannot be granted a high grade designation regardless of its total score. The grader usually takes a sample of product and bases his or her decision on that sample.

Grading can be a hurried process that can tax the resourcefulness of even the hardest grader. Although some food producers accuse graders of being capricious, unreasonable, and insensitive to production problems, the grading system actually functions fairly well.

Some buyers in the hospitality industry have been conditioned to purchase many food products primarily on the basis of U.S. government grades. The effect of government grading has ultimately been to create demand among retail consumers for specific quality levels; for example, consumers are conditioned to buy USDA Choice beef or USDA Select beef in the supermarket.

A major problem with grading is the emphasis graders place on appearance. Although appearance is an overriding criterion used in U.S. government grading, this sole criterion is dangerous for the foodservice industry because our customers are not making a purchase based solely on visual inspection but, rather, are purchasing and almost immediately evaluating the product based on taste and other culinary factors.

A number of other problems are associated with U.S. government grades. These additional difficulties include: (1) the wide tolerance between grades—so much so that buyers quickly learn that when they indicate U.S. No. 1, they must also note whether they want a high 1 or a low 1 (this tolerance gap is especially wide for meat items); (2) grader discretion—graders operate under one or more "partial limiting rules," which allow them to invoke a limiting rule or not; (3) the deceiving appearance of products—for example, some products can be dyed (like oranges), some can be waxed (like cucumbers), and some can be ripened artificially and inadequately (like tomatoes); (4) the possible irrelevance of grades to EP cost—for instance, a vine-ripened tomato may have a high grade and a good taste, but it may be difficult and wasteful to slice; (5) the fact that graders could slight such considerations as packaging and delivery schedules, which are important in preserving the grade—for example, a lemon may look good in the field, but if it is not packaged and transported correctly, it could be dry and shriveled when it arrives; (6) a raw food item is not a factory-manufactured product, and, therefore, its quality, as well as its U.S. quality grade, can fluctuate and may not be consistent throughout the year; (7) the lack of uniformity among terms used to indicate the varying grade levels—for instance, some items are labeled with a letter, some with a number, and some with other terminology; and (8) the lack of a specific regional designation. There is, for instance, a big difference between Florida and California oranges, particularly during certain times of the year.

AP Prices

To some degree, quality and AP prices go hand in hand. The relationship, however, is not usually direct. One notch up in AP price does not always imply that the item's quality has gone up one notch too. AP prices, though, are considered good indicators of quality by many hospitality managers, especially novices.

Packers' Brands

Some food producers resort to their own brand names and try to convince buyers to purchase on the basis of these names.

The terms "brand names" and "packers' brand names," although often used interchangeably, do differ to some extent. For example, the word "Sysco" is a brand name, but the terms "Sysco Supreme," "Sysco Imperial," "Sysco Classic," and "Sysco Reliance" are the company's packer's brand names. In this case, the Sysco supplier offers several levels of quality, with Sysco Supreme representing its highest quality and Sysco Reliance its lowest (see Figure 8.5).

Both brand names and packers' brand names are indications of quality standards; however, packers' brand names are very specific quality indicators, whereas most brand names are much more general. A packer's brand system is essentially that food processor's personal grading system; that is, the food processor uses his or her personal "grade" in lieu of a federal quality grade. The companies that use such grades usually offer at least three quality levels: good, better, and best. Food processors typically identify their different quality levels by using a particular nomenclature (such as that Sysco uses) or by using different colored package labels (see Figure 8.6).

Even though they are not widely known in many parts of the country, packers' brands exist for many products. In some cases, the food processor uses the brand name in conjunction with U.S. grade terminology. For example, a fresh-produce packer might stencil on a box the designation "No. 1." This would indi-

---

THE TOP TEN BROADLINE DISTRIBUTORS

Food Services of America	www.fsafood.com
Golbon	www.golbon.com
Gordon Food Service	www.gfs.com
J&B Wholesale	www.jbwhsle.com
Performance Food Group	www.pfgc.com
Reinhart FoodService	www.reinhartfoodservice.com
Seneca Foods	www.senecafoods.com
Sysco	www.sysco.com
U.S. Foodservice	www.usfoodservice.com
Zanios Foods	www.zaniosfoods.com

FIGURE 8.5 Some organizations and companies with packers' brands.

FIGURE 8.6 **An example of packer's brand packaging. Courtesy of Sysco Corporation.**

cate that the item was not produced under continuous government inspection, and that, in the opinion of the packer, who is not a government grader, the product meets all U.S. requirements for U.S. No. 1 graded products.

Packers' brands, too, present problems when they are designed to overlap U.S. grades. So, for example, a beef product that might be marked a high USDA Select instead of a low USDA Choice might be switched to the packer's brand. This will permit it to carry a quality designation that food buyers might generally associate with USDA Choice. In addition, packers' branded merchandise, unless it is a meat or poultry item or includes egg breaking in its production, may not be under continuous government inspection. However, even if a food processor does not purchase the U.S. government grading service, he or she must still undergo an inspection procedure. But inspection is concerned only with safety and wholesomeness; it makes no quality statement. Only U.S. grading makes quality judgments.

Brand names may possibly be a little more reliable than government grades because the brand extends over several other considerations, not just the food product's appearance. For example, the brand can also indicate a certain size of fruit and a certain packaging procedure. In addition, for products that do not come under the grading system, brand names may be the logical alternative.

Some food buyers also think that packers' brands are a bit more consistent from day to day and month to month, though not everyone feels this is true. Some argue that the U.S. government graders are not always so consistent. A brand's supposed consistency should effect a more consistent and predictable EP cost. It is critical to recall that the EP cost is more important; the AP price represents only your starting point.

Keep in mind that in this text, we use the term "packer's brand" a bit more frequently than the term "brand name" merely because it seems as if our industry uses such terminology more often.

Samples

It may be necessary to rely on samples, and one or more relevant tests of these samples, when assessing the quality of new items in the marketplace. Samples and testing are commonly used to measure the quality of capital equipment.

Endorsements

Several associations endorse items that we purchase. For instance, NSF International attests to the sanitary excellence of kitchen equipment. The Foodservice Consultants Society International (FCSI [www.fsci.org]) is an association of foodservice consultants whose members must achieve rigorous standards. We find, however, fewer associations endorsing foods and operating supplies.

Trade Associations

Various organizations, such as the National Cattlemen's Beef Association (NCBA [www.beef.org]), and other trade groups, help set quality standards that the buyer can use.

Your Own Specifications

A buyer may use some combination of all of the measures we have been discussing and work them into an extended measure of quality. This lengthy exercise usually finds its way into the specification. In many cases, particularly when a hospitality operation needs a special cut of meat, a unique type of paper napkin, or special cleaning agents, this extended measure is the only appropriate one.

As we imply throughout this discussion, few buyers consider only one of these quality measures. But, in our opinion, too many operators become overreliant on only one measure when it would be more appropriate to consider two or more.

IS THE QUALITY AVAILABLE?

Another aspect of quality a buyer must know is whether the quality desired is available at all. This is quite a practical question. It is useless to determine quality standards if the quality you want is unavailable. Oddly enough, some types of quality are too often unavailable to the hospitality operation. A chef who wants low-quality apples to make homemade applesauce may find that suppliers do not carry such low quality. (Food canners usually purchase them all.)

In addition, a buyer must pay particular attention to the possibility that the quality desired is available from only one supplier. This may or may not be advantageous. In some cases, an owner-manager may take this opportunity to build a long-standing relationship with one supplier. But some company officials are not especially eager to lose flexibility in their supplier selection.

It is easier than you think to restrict yourself unknowingly to one supplier. If this does not happen because of the quality standards you set, it may happen because of the AP price you are willing to accept.

THE BUYER'S MAJOR ROLE

We have noted that the buyer usually provides his or her supervisors with the information they need to determine quality standards. Buyers normally do not set these standards by themselves, but they do generally participate in these decisions. The buyer's major role here is to maintain the quality standards that someone else has determined. Generally, the standards have some flexibility. But whatever the standards are, and whatever the degree of flexibility, a buyer must ensure that all of the items purchased measure up to company expectations.

THE OPTIMAL SUPPLIER SERVICES TO INCLUDE ON THE SPEC

As we noted in Chapter 3, buyers normally have a major voice in determining supplier services, though they generally have less to say regarding economic values that the company should bargain for.

If you want specific supplier services, chances are you will severely restrict the number of purveyors who can provide what you want. Consequently, if you like the bid-buying activity, you must be prepared to put up with a variety of supplier capabilities. In our experience, it is the supplier services that we become so attached to since, for many items, not that much difference in quality usually exists.

KEY WORDS AND CONCEPTS

Advantages and purposes of specs

Agricultural Marketing Service (AMS)

Approved substitutes

Best-if-used-by dates

Bid from a supplier

Busted case

Buyer's major role in setting quality standards

Chemical standards

Color of a product

Cost and quantity limitations

Count

Difference between "brand name" and "packer's brand name"

Endorsements

Equal to or better

Expiration dates

Foodservice Consultants Society International (FCSI)

Formal versus informal spec

Form of a product

Freshness dates

General and specific instructions to bidders

Industry and government publications

Information included on a spec

Intended use

Limiting rule

Lowball bid

Measures of quality

National Cattlemen's Beef Association (NCBA)

National Sanitation Foundation (NSF) International

Optimal quality to include on a spec

Optimal supplier services to include on a spec

Package size and type

Packaging procedure

Packer's brand

Packer's "grade"

Partial limiting rule

Performance requirement of a product

Point of origin

Potential problems with specs

Preservation and/or processing method

Problems associated with the use of U.S. grades as a measure of quality

Produce Marketing Association (PMA)

Product identification

Product specification

Product substitutions

Pull dates

Purchase specification

Returns

Ripeness

Samples

Sell-by dates

Size of a product

Slab-packed

Standards of quality

Stockouts

Test procedures for delivered products

Trade association standards

Trim

Truth-in-menu regulations

USDA Acceptance Service

U.S. Department of Agriculture (USDA)

U.S. government quality grade

Waste

Weight range

What influences the information included on a spec?

Who determines quality?

Who should the spec writer be?

Yield

QUESTIONS AND PROBLEMS

1. What is a purchase specification? How does it differ from a product specification?

2. What are some of the reasons hospitality operations develop purchase specifications?

3. What information is included on a typical purchase specification?

4. Assume you are the owner of a small table-service restaurant.
   (a) How much time, money, and effort would you spend to develop specifications? Why?
   (b) Assume that you do not want to write specifications; you want to rely strictly on packers' brands and government grades to guide your purchasing. What are the advantages and disadvantages of this strategy?

5. Explain how the following factors influence the types of information included on the specification:
   (a) Company policies
   (b) Storage facilities
   (c) Menu requirements
   (d) Budgetary limitations
   (e) Employee skills

6. What are the costs and benefits of hiring an outside consultant to help you write specifications?

7. What are the costs and benefits of writing specifications and using them in a bid-buying strategy?

8. Which items do you think a buyer should receive bids on? Why?

9. Explain how company personnel normally determine quality standards for the food products they use.

10. How does a buyer usually get involved in determining quality standards? What is his or her major role once these quality standards are set?

11. Describe five measures of quality. Name some advantages and disadvantages of each.

12. Why do you think endorsements are used so much in measuring the quality of consulting services?

13. Are AP prices good measures of quality? Why or why not?

14. Some industry practitioners feel that hospitality operators can set quality standards for some non-food supplies without considering their customers' views. Do you think this is true? Why or why not?

15. A product specification for fresh meat could include the following information:
    (a)
    (b)
    (c)
    (d)
    (e)
    (f)

16. Why are expiration dates important to include on fresh-food specs?

17. A food-processing plant normally must undergo continuous federal-government inspection for wholesomeness if:
    (a)
    (b)
    (c)

18. List some problems that the buyer will encounter if he or she is overreliant on U.S. grades.

19. What is the primary difference between a brand name and a packer's brand name?

20. Should a small hospitality operation prepare detailed purchase specifications, or should it prepare product specifications? Why?

21. What is the most important piece of information that can be included on a spec?

22. When should a buyer use packers' brands as an indication of desired quality in lieu of U.S. quality grades?

23. When should a buyer include on the specification "point of origin"?

EXPERIENTIAL EXERCISES

1. What are some potential advantages of limiting yourself to one supplier, the only one who can meet your quality standards?
    a. Write a one-page answer
    b. Provide your answer to a hotel manager and ask for comments.
    c. Prepare a report that includes your answer and the manager's comments.

2. Why would package quality be important to a foodservice buyer? Would you be willing to pay a bit more to ensure high-quality packaging? Why or why not?
    a. Write a one-page answer
    b. Provide your answer to a foodservice manager and ask for comments.
    c. Prepare a report that includes your answer and the manager's comments.

3. Develop a purchase specification.
    a. Write a purchase specification using information provided from one of the agencies in Figure 8.2.
    b. Provide your answer to an executive chef and ask for comments.
    c. Prepare a report that includes your specification and the chef's comments.

4. Identify an agency that provides product information on a Website and that is not included in Figure 8.2. Write a one-page paper explaining how the Website can be used to help purchasing managers to write specifications.

THE OPTIMAL AMOUNT

The Purpose of this Chapter

After reading this chapter, you should be able to:

■ Calculate the correct order quantities and order times using the par stock, Levinson, and theoretical methods.

■ Explain the benefits and problems of using only the theoretical method.

INTRODUCTION

The correct order size and its counterpart, the correct order time, are probably the most important keys to inventory management. Without a reasonable idea of the optimal order size and time, you cannot maintain an ideal inventory level of food, beverages, and nonfood supplies.

OPTIMAL INVENTORY LEVEL

Years ago, few hospitality operators concerned themselves with inventory management concepts. When the industry was smaller and less complex and competitive, and inventory costs were minor, the occasional overbuy or stockout was a forgivable offense. Today, such a casual attitude is rare. Ordering is no longer haphazard. The emphasis now is on holding the optimal inventory; that is, management seeks to determine the amount of inventory that will adequately serve the operation without having to suffer the costs of excess inventory.

A principal objective of inventory management is to maintain only the necessary amount of food, beverages, and nonfood supplies to serve guests without running out of anything, but not to have so much inventory that occasional spoilage and other storage costs result. We also need to develop a cost-effective ordering procedure; for example, a buyer does not want to spend an excessive amount of time, money, and effort to order merchandise because this will increase the hospitality operation's cost of doing business.

These objectives are more easily recited than achieved. Quite commonly, an individual manager may not know the exact value of inventory that should be on hand.

Over the years, hospitality operators have tried to devise ways of computing as accurately as possible the ideal amount of inventory that should be maintained to conduct business effectively and efficiently. Nonetheless, a major portion of the inventory management efforts that are carried out in our industry still rely heavily on rules of thumb. For instance, as mentioned in Chapter 7, many practitioners rely on a percentage of sales to guide their inventory management decisions. Recall that this percentage-of-sales concept suggests, for instance, that a full-service restaurant operation requires an inventory of food, beverage, and nonfood supplies to be equal to about 1 percent of annual sales volume.

A buyer can use other rules of thumb to determine the amount of inventory needed to service guests adequately. As mentioned in Chapter 7, the typical food-service operation could devise an inventory management strategy to ensure that the food inventory that is kept on hand at all times does not exceed about one-third of a normal month's total food costs. Also, in a fast-food restaurant, the general feeling is that the food inventory should turn over about three times per week, or about 156 times per year. Consequently, the buyer's inventory management strategy should include an ordering procedure that maintains this approximate inventory turnover target.

Most industry practitioners view inventory as an investment. Like any other investment, this one must offer a return. Unfortunately, an inventory investment does not lend itself to a precise calculation of return, as does, say, a certificate of deposit, whereby an investor can depend on an exact percentage of return each year.

CORRECT ORDER SIZE AND ORDER TIME: A COMMON APPROACH

Most part-time and full-time buyers use a relatively simple approach to calculate the best order size and order time. This approach is sometimes referred to as the "par stock approach." The buyer usually accepts the supplier's delivery schedule—for example, twice a week. The buyer then determines a par stock, that is, a level of inventory items that he or she feels must be on hand to maintain a continuing supply of each item from one delivery date to the next.

The buyer accepts the supplier's delivery schedule because he or she probably cannot change it without incurring an exorbitant delivery charge. If, however, the buyer's company represents a very large order size, the supplier might make concessions. In addition, the buyer normally accepts the ordering schedule the supplier dictates; he or she places the order at a certain time prior to the actual delivery. For example, a call no later than Monday morning may be required to ensure a delivery on Tuesday morning.

Assume, for example, that the buyer feels that he or she needs six cases of tomato paste on hand to last between orders. On Monday morning, just before placing the order, the buyer counts the number of cases of tomato paste on hand. Suppose that $1^{1}/_{2}$ cases are left. If it is expected that half a case will be used that day, one case will be left on Tuesday morning. The par stock is six. The buyer then subtracts what he or she feels will be on hand Tuesday morning from the par stock $(6 - 1)$ and orders five cases.

Another way to calculate the order size is for the buyer to subtract what is on hand—in this situation, $1^{1}/_{2}$ cases—from the par stock of six cases and enter an order for $4^{1}/_{2}$ cases. Either way, the emphasis is on setting an acceptable par stock level and then ordering enough product to bring the stock up to that level. (This concept is a bedrock of our industry. For example, most bars set up a certain par stock level that must be on hand before opening for the afternoon or evening. The bartender on duty is responsible for counting what is on hand, subtracting this from what should be on hand, and then replenishing the overall inventory of beverages, foodstuffs, and nonfood supplies accordingly.)

Par stocks sometimes change. In a restaurant that does a lot of banquet business, the par stock for tomato paste might fluctuate monthly or even weekly. This fluctuation can complicate matters, but buyers usually can solve the problem just by adding to the par stock the extra amount of tomato paste needed specifically for any emergency or extra business volume, such as a banquet next week. So, for instance, buyers might order enough to reach their par stock level, plus additional product to be their "safety" stock or to use for the banquet.

The buyer, then, normally uses the following procedures when employing the par stock approach:

1. Accept the suppliers' stipulated ordering procedures and delivery schedules.

2. Decide when it would be desirable to order enough product to bring the stock level of any particular item up to par. This decision is normally influenced by the amount of storage facilities the buyer has, how expensive the inventory item is, and the shelf life of the products the buyer orders. For example, if a preferred supplier delivers meat twice a week, and if the meats are expensive, perishable items, a buyer would most likely set a par stock to last about three or four days. For some inexpensive, nonperishable operating supplies, such as paper towels, the buyer might want to order once every three months. Consequently, he or she sets the par stock large enough to last for three months under normal operating conditions.

3. Set par stocks for all food, beverages, and nonfood items—enough to last between regularly scheduled deliveries.

4. When ordering, subtract what is on hand from the par stock. Then include any additional amount necessary to cover extra banquets, increased room service, seasonal patronage, a safety stock perhaps, and so forth.

5. Shop around, if necessary, and enter this order size at the time the supplier designates or at some agreed-upon time.

6. Periodically reevaluate the stock levels, and adjust them as needed. For instance, if you change suppliers and the new purveyor's delivery schedule is different, you must adjust accordingly.

No magic formula is associated with the par stock concept. It is a trial-and-error process. If six cases are too many, the number can be adjusted downward. If it is too low, it can be increased. The trial-and-error procedure requires small amounts of management attention on a continuing basis; in time, however, these can add up to a significant amount. Nevertheless, the work involved is quite simple and lends itself to volume swings in overall sales, as well as in sales of individual products. The par stock concept works quite effectively in the hospitality industry.

The concept works so well for several reasons. Most important, there is only a slight difference in annual storage and ordering costs between a theoretical order size and a more practical order size. (The appendix to this chapter provides an extended discussion of a theoretical calculation of optimal order size and order time.) Another reason is the relative predictability of deliveries. The third reason is that most hospitality operations undergo major modifications in their customer offerings only occasionally. For the most part, menus, sleeping accommodations, and bar offerings remain unchanged, thereby giving a buyer sufficient time to determine acceptable par stock levels for each inventory item. Finally, if a considerable sum has already been invested in a hospitality operation, an inventory level that is a few hundred dollars more than a theoretical optimal amount will tend to generate little concern.

The major drawback to the par stock method is its emphasis on setting only the par stock level, to the possible detriment of the broader view of inventory management. Generally, the optimal amount of inventory on hand is related to annual storage costs, ordering costs, and stockout costs. If acceptable par stocks are achieved, these costs will probably be minimized. But these concepts may not be examined directly, and, as a result, a buyer may be unaware of the complete picture.

This innocence, or ignorance, can cause problems. For instance, buyers often have an opportunity to purchase large amounts of a product at reasonable savings. The problem arises when buyers have little conception of the increase in storage costs that will accompany this huge order. (As with the par stock approach, though, some rule-of-thumb methods can be used to evaluate the economics of large orders, as discussed in Chapter 10.)

Regardless of its potential drawbacks, the par stock approach is common and works fairly well. It does not, however, represent the only approach to determining correct order size and order time.

CORRECT ORDER SIZE AND ORDER TIME: ANOTHER APPROACH

Another approach used in the hospitality industry is just a bit more complicated than the par stock approach. However, it would appear that its use (or a similar one) will become more common as the industry becomes fully computerized and computers can keep track of the data and perform the necessary calculations quickly.

We call this approach the Levinson approach, since Charles Levinson was one of the very first persons to address these ideas formally in his book, *Food and Beverage Operation: Cost Control and Systems Management*, 2nd ed. (Englewood Cliffs, NJ: Prentice-Hall, 1989). Much of the material in this section of our text is adapted from

Levinson's volume. This book is now out of print. However, you might be able to find a used copy at Amazon (www.amazon.com) or eBay (www.ebay.com).

Buyers using the Levinson approach will employ the following procedures:

1. Accept the suppliers' stipulated ordering procedures and delivery schedules.

2. Determine the best time to place orders with the suppliers. For instance, fresh dairy products may be ordered daily, fresh meats and produce may be ordered perhaps every third day, and other less perishable items may be ordered less frequently. Consequently, the buyers' work follows a reasonably predictable routine, in that they have enough work to keep busy each week, even though they are not ordering exactly the same items each day or each week.

3. Before ordering, forecast the amount of merchandise that will be needed during the period of time between regularly scheduled deliveries. The forecasting procedure includes the following steps:

    a. Forecast the expected total number of customers, based usually on past history.

    b. Forecast the expected number of customers who will order each specific menu offering, also based on past history. One way to do this is to compute a "popularity index" for each menu item. To determine a menu item's popularity index, divide the number sold of that particular menu item by the total number of all menu items sold; this will give you a percentage, which is the menu item's popularity index.

    For example, if you project that you will serve 2500 customers next week and you know that, based on past history, 25 percent of all customers eat T-bone steaks, then you can estimate that 0.25×2500, or 625 customers, will eat a T-bone steak.

    c. Determine the number of raw pounds of each ingredient needed to satisfy your projected sales. To do this, first you must figure out the portion factor (PF) and the portion divider (PD) for each ingredient that you need to satisfy your sales forecast. The PF is computed as follows:

    PF = 16 oz. ÷ Amount of ingredient needed for one serving (in ounces)

    The PD is computed as follows:

    PD = PF × ingredient's edible- (i.e., servable) yield percentage

The edible-yield percentage is computed in one of two ways: (1) you accept the supplier's estimate of edible yield, or (2) you conduct your own yield tests for each and every ingredient; that is, you use the ingredients for a while and compute an average of unavoidable waste. This will give you a good idea of the edible-yield percentage you can expect to derive from each ingredient.

   d. Compute the order sizes for all items. An order size is equal to the number of customers you feel will consume an ingredient divided by the PD for that ingredient—this will give you the order size in raw pounds. (Essentially, the PD is the expected number of servings per pound.)

4. Adjust this order size, if necessary, to account for stock on hand, extra banquets, increased room service, seasonal patronage, perhaps a safety stock, and so forth.

5. Shop around, if necessary, and enter the order size at the time the supplier designates or at some agreed-upon time.

6. Periodically revise the order time if necessary, as well as the PD of each ingredient if, for instance, you decide to change suppliers and the new supplier's ingredients have a different yield percentage than those you are currently purchasing. (In Chapter 10, we discuss the procedures used to determine whether another supplier's ingredient provides more value to you, even though it might appear that it has more waste. We also revisit the concept of the EP cost.)

Example I

Given the following data, compute the number of raw pounds needed of each ingredient for a banquet for 500 people.

INGREDIENT	SERVING SIZE	EDIBLE YIELD (%)
Steak	12 oz.	80
Beans	4 oz.	90
Potatoes	4 oz.	75

Solution: *Compute each ingredient's PF:*

$$PF_{(steak)} = \frac{16}{12} = 1.33$$

$$PF_{(beans)} = \frac{16}{4} = 4.00$$

$$PF_{(potatoes)} = \frac{16}{4} = 4.00$$

Compute each ingredient's PD:

$$PD_{(steak)} = 1.33 \times 0.80 = 1.06$$

$$PD_{(beans)} = 4.00 \times 0.90 = 3.60$$

$$PD_{(potatoes)} = 4.00 \times 0.75 = 3.00$$

Compute the order size, in raw pounds, for each ingredient:

$$\text{Order size}_{(steak)} = \frac{500}{1.06} = 472 \text{ lb.}$$

$$\text{Order size}_{(beans)} = \frac{500}{3.60} = 139 \text{ lb.}$$

$$\text{Order size}_{(potatoes)} = \frac{500}{3.00} = 167 \text{ lb.}$$

Example II

Given the following data, compute the number of cases needed to serve 1575 customers.

INGREDIENT: **Iceberg lettuce**

SERVING SIZE: **4 ounces**

EDIBLE YIELD: **75 percent**

MINIMUM WEIGHT PER CASE: **36 pounds**

Solution:

$$PF = \frac{16}{4} = 4.00$$

$$PD = 4.00 \times 0.75 = 3.00$$

$$\text{Number of raw pounds needed} = \frac{1575}{3.00} = 525 \text{ lb.}$$

$$\text{Number of cases needed} = \frac{525 \text{ lb.}}{36 \text{ lb. per case}} = 14.58 \text{ (approximately 15 cases)}$$

Example III

Given the following data, compute the number of gallons needed to serve 2000 customers.

INGREDIENT: **Prepared mustard**

SERVING SIZE: **$^1/_2$ ounce**

EDIBLE YIELD: **95 percent**

Solution:

$$PF = \frac{16}{0.5} = 32.00$$

$$PD = 32.00 \times 0.95 = 30.40$$

Number of raw pounds needed $= \dfrac{2000}{30.40} = 65.79$ lb.

Number of raw ounces needed $= 65.79 \times 16$ oz. per lb. $= 1052.64$

Number of gallons needed $= \dfrac{1052.64 \text{ oz.}}{128 \text{ oz. per gal.}} = 8.22$ (approximately 9 gal.)

CORRECT ORDER SIZE AND ORDER TIME: VARIATIONS OF THE LEVINSON APPROACH

The procedures in the preceding Examples I, II, and III are appropriate for items purchased in pound units. However, the Levinson approach can be adapted for use with any purchase unit. The general formula for the PF needs to be altered to accommodate the specific purchase unit. The unit of purchase is divided by the portion size as depicted in that unit of purchase. For instance, if you purchase liter containers of liquor, the numerator for your PF calculation would be 1000 milliliters, and the denominator would be the portion size of liquor, in milliliters. The computation of the PD remains the same.

Example I

Given the following data, compute the number of liters (l) needed to serve 250 customers.

INGREDIENT: **Gin**

SERVING SIZE: **55 milliliters**

SERVABLE YIELD: **95 percent**

Solution:

$$PF = \frac{1000}{55} = 18.18$$

$$PD = 18.18 \times 0.95 = 17.27$$

Number of liters needed $= \dfrac{250}{17.27} = 14.48$ (approximately 15 l)

Example II

Given the following data, compute the number of cases needed to serve 500 customers.

INGREDIENT: **Lobster tail**

SERVING SIZE: **2 tails**

SERVABLE YIELD: **100 percent**

NUMBER OF TAILS PER CASE: **50**

Solution:

$$PF = \frac{50}{2} = 25$$

$$PD = 25 \times 1.00 = 25$$

Number of cases needed $= \dfrac{500}{25} = 20$ cases

Example III

Given the following data, compute the number of kilograms (kg) needed to serve 125 customers.

INGREDIENT: **Fresh spinach**

SERVING SIZE: **90 grams**

EDIBLE YIELD: **60 percent**

Solution:

$$PF = \frac{1000}{90} = 11.11$$

$$PD = 11.11 \times 0.60 = 6.67$$

Number of kilograms needed $= \dfrac{125}{6.67} = 18.74$ (approximately 19 kg)

CORRECT ORDER SIZE AND ORDER TIME: COMBINATION APPROACH

It is reasonable to expect the typical buyer to use a combination of the procedures just discussed to determine the proper order sizes and order times. For instance, a buyer could use the par stock approach to maintain sufficient stock for the normal, predictable business needs of the hospitality operation. However, when a buyer needs stock for special events, such as banquets and other similar functions, he or she could adopt the Levinson approach, or some variation thereof, when determining the correct order amount and order time.

APPENDIX

Correct Order Size: A Theoretical Approach

In centralized, multiunit purchasing operations, economies of scale make very large purchases realistic. When inventory value reaches the multimillion-dollar level, more formalized modes of analysis are useful in determining order size. This section suggests tools available for use in such cases.

The correct order size is influenced by two costs: the "storage cost," which is sometimes referred to as the "carrying cost," and the "ordering cost." The storage cost is the sum of several little costs associated with holding inventory. The cost of maintaining storage facilities, inventory insurance, and risk of spoilage or obsolescence are three aspects of the storage cost. However, the most important part of the storage cost—the largest aspect of the storage cost—is the need to tie up money in inventory, that is, the "capital cost." Economists refer to this as an "opportunity cost," which is a nice way of saying that if your money is tied up in canned goods on a shelf, you lose the opportunity to invest this money elsewhere, such as in a bank, in shares of stock, or in gold.

Attempts have been made to calculate the storage cost precisely. Unfortunately, no hard figures exist. Annual estimates run from 10 to 25 percent of the value of inventory. This means that for every dollar you tie up on the shelf, you can expect a storage cost of somewhere between 10 and 25 cents per year.

The ordering cost includes primarily the cost of paperwork, telephone, computer, fax, employee wages and salaries, receiving, and invoice processing.

Differences of opinion exist concerning the dollar value of the ordering cost. One company estimates that it costs approximately $20 for each order it makes, another estimates the cost at $30 per order, and others set the cost as low as $3 to as high as somewhere between $100 and $130.[1] No matter. What is important is that you recognize that placing orders is not a cost-free exercise and that the potential savings of reducing the number of orders can and should be determined.

A large order size would ensure a large inventory amount and, hence, a huge annual storage cost. But because you would not order a large amount as often as a small amount, the annual ordering cost would decrease. On the other hand, a small order size would result in a smaller inventory and a correspondingly smaller annual storage cost; however, unfortunately, your annual ordering cost would increase (see Figure 9.1).

The important point is that there is an *optimal* order size, one that leads to the lowest possible total cost per year (annual storage and ordering costs). Note that a small order size (any one to the left of the crosshatched area in Figure 9.1) carries a relatively high total cost per year, as does any order size to the right of the crosshatched area. The optimal range of order sizes is represented by the crosshatched area. Theoretically, there is one optimal order size in that crosshatched area at the point where the storage cost curve intersects the ordering cost curve.

When determining the optimal order size, management must take into account the influence of these two costs. Basically, the intersection of the storage cost curve and the ordering cost curve represents the best balance between the cost of carrying inventory and the benefits derived from having the inventory available for sale to the customer. When calculating this intersection, management has two options. First, a manager could attempt to graph the operation's cost curves and then try to "eyeball" the optimal order size. Second, he or she might use a formula to determine the optimal order sizes.

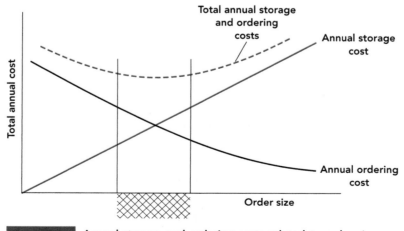

FIGURE 9.1   Annual storage and ordering costs related to order size.

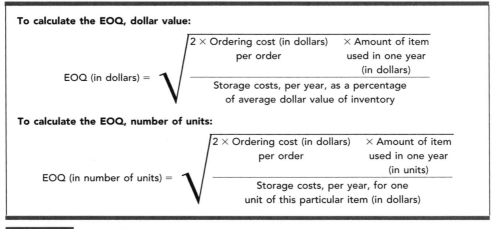

To calculate the EOQ, dollar value:

$$\text{EOQ (in dollars)} = \sqrt{\frac{2 \times \text{Ordering cost (in dollars) per order} \times \text{Amount of item used in one year (in dollars)}}{\text{Storage costs, per year, as a percentage of average dollar value of inventory}}}$$

To calculate the EOQ, number of units:

$$\text{EOQ (in number of units)} = \sqrt{\frac{2 \times \text{Ordering cost (in dollars) per order} \times \text{Amount of item used in one year (in units)}}{\text{Storage costs, per year, for one unit of this particular item (in dollars)}}}$$

FIGURE 9.2 Ways of calculating the EOQ.

The most common option is summarized in the economic order quantity (EOQ) formula, which several industries have adopted. Relatively few hospitality operations use this formula directly. But they do find it useful as a reference insofar as the formula tends to identify the relevant costs and puts them in their proper perspective. Hence, a look at this formula will immediately drive home the concept of optimal order sizes.

You can calculate the EOQ two basic ways, as noted in Figure 9.2. Assume that an operation currently uses 600 cases of tomato paste per year, the ordering cost per order is $3, the annual storage cost is 15 percent of the value of the tomato paste, and the cost of the tomato paste is $8 per case. The question is: How many cases should the buyer purchase at one time? In other words, what is the EOQ?

Applying the formulas noted in Figure 9.2, you determine that the EOQ is about 55 cases, or approximately $440. The calculations follow:

$$\text{EOQ (in dollars)} \approx \sqrt{\frac{2 \times \$3.00 \times \$4800.00^*}{.15}}$$

$$\approx \$440.00^\dagger$$

$$\text{EOQ (in units)} \approx \sqrt{\frac{2 \times \$3.00 \times 600 \text{ units}}{\$1.20^\ddagger}}$$

$$\approx 55 \text{ units (or cases)}$$

*$4800.00 = 600 \times \$8.00$

†$440.00/$8.00 per case = 55 cases

‡$1.20 = \$8.00 \times 15\% = \$8.00 \times .15$

The total cost per year (annual storage and ordering costs) associated with this EOQ of 55 cases is calculated by using the formula depicted in Figure 9.3.

$$\text{Total cost per year} = \frac{\$3.00 \times 600 \text{ cases}}{55 \text{ cases}} + \frac{\$1.20 \times 55 \text{ cases}}{2}$$

$$= \$32.73 + 33.00$$

$$= \$65.73$$

If you order fewer than 55 cases, say, 50 cases, the total cost per year is:

$$\text{Total cost per year} = \frac{\$3.00 \times 600 \text{ cases}}{50 \text{ cases}} + \frac{\$1.20 \times 50 \text{ cases}}{2}$$

$$= \$36.00 + \$30.00$$

$$= \$66.00$$

If you order more than 55 cases, perhaps 60 cases, the total cost per year is:

$$\text{Total cost per year} = \frac{\$3.00 \times 600 \text{ cases}}{60 \text{ cases}} + \frac{\$1.20 \times 60 \text{ cases}}{2}$$

$$= \$30.00 + \$36.00$$

$$= \$66.00$$

You have calculated the order size, 55 cases, that yields the least total cost per year. An order size of 50 cases results in a lower annual storage cost, but your annual ordering cost increases since you have to order more often during the year. Conversely, a larger order size yields a smaller annual ordering cost, but the increase in annual storage cost negates this slight savings.

As a practical matter, it may be inconvenient or impossible to order 55 cases at a time. In addition, some people are disturbed because so many aspects of the

$$\text{Total cost per year} = \frac{\begin{array}{cc} & \text{Number of} \\ \text{Ordering cost} \times & \text{units used} \\ \text{per order} & \text{in one year} \end{array}}{\begin{array}{cc} \text{Order size} & \text{(in units)} \end{array}} + \frac{\begin{array}{cc} \text{Storage cost,} & \\ \text{per year, of} \times & \text{Order size} \\ \text{one unit} & \text{(in units)} \end{array}}{2}$$

FIGURE 9.3 The calculation of the annual total cost associated with a particular order size. (This formula is used in calculating the EOQ formula.)

formulas are merely estimates, not hard-and-fast figures. The question is, then, of what value is this figure of 55 cases? Is it worthwhile to calculate the EOQ if it cannot be used?

Although it may be impractical to order 55 cases at a time, knowing what the optimal order size is can help you make decisions about other more practical order sizes. For instance, if you can order only in blocks of 50 cases, you will have an idea of the annual ordering and storage costs associated with this order size and be able to plan your expenses accordingly.

We do not wish to leave the impression that this theoretical approach is simple or easy to use. It presents several potential problems, which we point out later. These difficulties notwithstanding, however, the concept of EOQ can be used in many productive ways to ensure an optimal overall level of inventory, which is the result of the optimal order size and the topic we turn to next, the optimal order time.

Correct Order Time: A Theoretical Approach

Continuing with the tomato paste example, you should determine when to order your 55 cases, assuming 55 is a practical order size. If you could depend on instant delivery of inventory items, you might be able to wait until you are completely out of tomato paste before you order the next batch of 55 cases. Unfortunately, a lag invariably exists between the time you place an order and when it arrives. In some cases, this time lag is predictable; in other cases, it is not. As a result, you must reduce your supply of tomato paste to some level greater than zero if you want to ensure a continuing, uninterrupted supply.

This level is sometimes referred to as the "safety stock." It is also called the "reorder point" (ROP). You cannot wait until you are out of stock before ordering another batch; you must maintain a safety stock. But what this safety stock should be is open to hunches, theories, and educated guesses.

The trick to calculating the ROP is first to gain some idea of the usage pattern of the particular product in question. In the tomato paste example, you might experience the usage pattern outlined in Figure 9.4.

Normally, this type of pattern is not so predictable as Figure 9.4 implies. But if you keep track of your usage patterns for six months or so, you can determine how many cases you use, on average, every day. For discussion purposes, assume that you have determined that 40 percent of the time, you use one case of tomato paste or less per day; that 90 percent of the time, you use two cases or less; that 96 percent of the time, you use three cases or less; and that 100 percent of the time, you use four cases or less (see Figure 9.5).

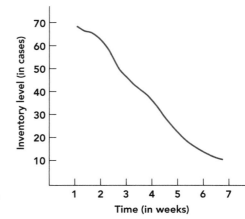

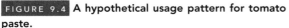
FIGURE 9.4 A hypothetical usage pattern for tomato paste.

Another way of looking at Figure 9.5 is to consider the possibility of using, on any given day, between one and two cases of tomato paste. Note that, in the past, you have used between one and two cases of tomato paste per day 50 percent of the time; hence, there is a 50 percent probability of selling more than one case but less than two cases per day. Similarly, you have sold less than one case per day 40 percent of the time, between two and three cases of tomato paste per day 6 percent of the time, and between three and four cases of tomato paste per day 4 percent of the time.

A conservative safety stock in this situation would be four cases for every day that lapses between the time you place your order of 55 cases and the time you receive this order. The interval of days is sometimes referred to as the "lead time." If you can safely assume that your lead time is three days and you do not want to

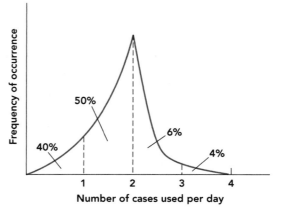

FIGURE 9.5 The percentage of times one, two, three, or four cases are used per day.

take a chance of running out of tomato paste, you would then place your order of 55 cases when your supply of tomato paste reaches 12 cases (see Figure 9.6).

If you use all 12 cases during the three-day lead time, you will be out of stock when your order of 55 cases arrives. If you use only 10 cases, you will have two cases in inventory when the 55 cases are delivered. Your total inventory amount at this point would then be 57 cases.

After your order is delivered, you want to be as close as possible to a total inventory amount of 55 cases. Ideally, you will be at 55 cases exactly, that is, the moment you run out of inventory, the delivery van will be pulling up at the unloading area with the 55-case order.

Hospitality operations that strive for this ideal arrangement practice what is generally referred to in the industry as "just-in-time (JIT) inventory management." While these firms are trying to keep the total ordering and storage costs as low as possible, they are especially interested in minimizing the storage cost. For instance, if, using the figures in the preceding example, they have two cases of inventory in stock when the delivery van arrives, they will then have a current inventory level of 57 cases when the van pulls up. If they have 57 cases, they will incur an additional storage cost—which they are very eager to avoid. However, this additional storage cost must be weighed against the possibility of running out of tomato paste and incurring various "stockout costs."

Stockout costs are expenses associated with being unable to serve a product because you do not have it. These costs are particularly irksome in the hospitality business: you cannot tell customers to come back for a steak tomorrow because you do not have any for them today. If you cannot provide a product, a customer

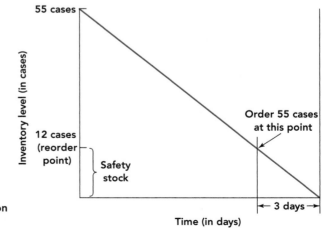

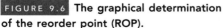 **The graphical determination of the reorder point (ROP).**

usually selects another, the result being no apparent loss in profit. But a customer might be irritated when you cannot supply the product wanted. In essence, you have diminished the customer's favorable opinion of your operation. The cost of goodwill is difficult to determine, and some operators harbor a greater disdain for stockouts than do others. For example, in the tomato paste example, a more liberal manager might decide that he or she needs only two cases per day for the three-day period, thereby taking a slight chance on not needing more than two cases of tomato paste per day. A liberal manager would be willing to risk a stockout since, according to Figure 9.5, there is a 10 percent chance that more than two cases of tomato paste per day will be needed during the lead-time period.

Another problem associated with this safety stock concept is the exactness of the lead time. In most cases, deliveries are reasonably predictable. But the supplier may not have 55 cases of tomato paste. He or she may have only 30 or 40 cases, or perhaps none at all.

The theoretical approach to the optimal order time rests on the assumptions you make about usage patterns, lead times, safety stocks, and supplier capabilities and dependability. By keeping historical records, you can determine the ROP with which you feel most comfortable. If the numbers are correct, the ROP will be optimal. If they are not, at least you will be closer to the optimal ROP than you ever could be by relying on mere hunches.

Although the formality of the approach we have been discussing would not be appropriate for a single operation of modest size, clearly, the logic of the approach has general application. This is a good way to think about ROPs, even if formulas and detailed records do not come into the picture for each hospitality operator.

CORRECT ORDER SIZE AND ORDER TIME: OTHER PROBLEMS WITH THEORETICAL APPROACHES

The basic overriding problem, which we alluded to earlier, is the need for certain assumptions and estimates. Any way you look at it, we deal with some highly variable phenomena here. Some additional variables that tend to detract from the usefulness of these approaches are listed below:

1. Usage rates vary from day to day and do not normally follow a steady pattern, unless the operation caters to a fairly predictable group of repeat customers. Although usage patterns can be approximated, they probably can never be calculated exactly.

2.   Storage and ordering costs can vary; in addition, several opinions exist as to the precise makeup of these costs.

3.   Stockout costs are extremely difficult to assess. Management philosophy is the best guide in this case; consequently, the concept of correct order time can change according to management's tolerance of risk of stockouts.

4.   Lead times are somewhat predictable, but you may qualify for only once-a-week delivery, which hurts any attempt to implement the EOQ and ROP concepts. In fact, the inability to control delivery times, either because of tradition or by law (e.g., some states have strict ordering and delivering schedules for alcoholic beverages), has done more to discourage the use of these concepts in the hospitality industry than any of the other difficulties. With the theoretical approach, the order size stays the same, but the order time varies. The opposite is true with the par stock and Levinson approaches. As a result, since the typical buyer has no control over order times and delivery schedules, he or she cannot implement the theoretical approach.

5.   What items should you consider for EOQ and ROP? All of them? This decision is not very easy when you realize that the average hospitality operation stocks a minimum of 600 to 800 items. Some people suggest considering only those few items that together represent about 80 percent of the value of the total inventory. Others feel that it is possible to construct a few item categories and develop EOQs and ROPs for them. In any case, monitoring all items is impossible without the help of sophisticated computer technology. But as these types of computer applications become increasingly feasible and economical, it is possible that you will be able to overcome this difficulty.

6.   Keep in mind that your supplier normally buys from someone else. Your EOQ may not be consistent with your supplier's EOQ. As a result, you could encounter the problem of receiving an incomplete order. Alternately, you might have to settle for certain substitutions, a situation that may or may not be compatible with your EOQ calculations.

7.   At times, a supplier may be forced to discontinue an item—an item that you find especially profitable in your hospitality establishment. This problem is often associated with wines, particularly those of a certain vintage. Because only so much of a certain type of wine is produced in a certain year, the stock must run out sometime. Before reaching this point, you may decide to order as much as you can in order to maintain your supply as long as possible. Needless to say, this buying decision flies in the face of the EOQ and ROP concepts.

8.   The EOQ assumes that you have adequate storage facilities. You may calculate an EOQ of 55 cases and then discover that you have space for only 30 cases.

9.   Moreover, the EOQ assumes that the products you order will be used before they spoil or become obsolete. Fewer problems concerning obsolescence exist in the hospitality industry than in other industries. But spoilage can be an enormous problem. Although you can expect 55 cases of tomato paste to maintain their quality for two or three months, you cannot assume this storage life for all products.

CORRECT ORDER SIZE AND ORDER TIME: SOME BENEFITS OF THE THEORETICAL APPROACH

Theories can have shortcomings, of course, but they can also have numerous benefits. The EOQ and ROP concepts are cases in point. Some potential benefits associated with these approaches are listed below:

1.   A theoretical approach substitutes fact for fiction. Even if some of your estimates are off, at least you have been forced to consider these variables. This discipline in itself can easily lead to a more favorable profit performance.

2.   A range of order sizes seems to exist in which the total cost per year (annual ordering and storage costs) does not vary dramatically. In the tomato paste example, the total cost per year for 50 cases was $66.00; for 55 cases, $65.73; and for 60 cases, $66.00. Notice that you could go down to 50 or up to 60 cases and incur an additional cost of only $0.27 per year. As a result, you gain insight by using the theory, and you will not have to be overly concerned if your estimates are a little off. And, as mentioned earlier in this chapter, this range is the major reason that the par stock approach to ordering is acceptable for many operations.

3.   As computer services decline in cost, it becomes more feasible to monitor EOQs and ROPs. This, in turn, enables you to extract maximum benefit from these theoretical approaches while at the same time minimizing the time and paperwork involved with analyzing usage patterns, lead times, safety stock, and so on.

4.   While the use of the EOQ and ROP concepts may not be feasible for a single-unit hospitality operation, the multiunit chain organizations, especially

those with company-owned commissaries and/or central distribution centers, would be able to adopt these theories and use them to significantly improve their purchasing performance.

Theoretical approaches may or may not be completely useful in a specific hospitality operation. We believe, however, that all operations can derive more benefit than cost by considering these concepts. A thoughtful consideration of these concepts forces an operator to evaluate all the pertinent variables that influence an overall inventory level. By evaluating these variables, that operator comes as close as possible to an optimal overall inventory level, which is the ultimate objective of the EOQ and ROP concepts.

KEY WORDS AND CONCEPTS

Capital cost

Carrying cost

Correct order size

Correct order time

Delivery schedules

Economic order quantity (EOQ) formula

Edible-portion cost (EP cost)

Edible-(servable) yield percentage

Food-inventory amount as a percentage of monthly food costs

Forecasting

Inventory amount as a percentage of annual sales volume

Inventory turnover

Just-in-time inventory management (JIT inventory management)

Lead time

Levinson approach to ordering

Opportunity costs

Optimal inventory level

Ordering costs

Ordering procedures

Par stock

Par stock approach to ordering

Popularity index

Portion divider (PD)

Portion factor (PF)

Product's usage pattern

Reorder point (ROP)

Safety stock

Stockout costs

Storage costs

Variations of the Levinson approach to ordering

REFERENCES

1. See, for example, Fred R. Bleakley, "When Corporate Purchasing Goes Plastic," *The Wall Street Journal*, June 14, 1995, p. B1; Willem Haneveld and Ruud Teunter, "Effects of Discounting and Demand Rate Variability on the EOQ," *International Journal of Production Economics*, January 29, 1998, 54(2), pp. 173–193; Victor Aguirre-gabiria, "The Dynamics of Markups and Inventories in Retailing Firms," *Review of Economic Studies*, April 1999, 66(227), p. 275; Miles Feitzmann and Adam Ostazewski, "Hedging the Purchase of Direct Inputs in an Inflationary Environment," *Management Accounting Research*, March 1999, 10(1), pp. 61–84.

QUESTIONS AND PROBLEMS

1. Briefly explain how the par stock approach to ordering works. Why does it work so well? What are some of the method's drawbacks?

2. Fill in the blanks: Ordering the correct _____ at the correct _____ leads to _____.

3. Why would a general manager want to determine an optimal inventory amount?

4. Briefly describe EOQ and ROP. What benefits are there for managements that adopt these procedures? What drawbacks are there?

5. What are the elements of the ordering cost? Of the storage cost? How can either, or both, of these costs be reduced without harming the overall hospitality operation's profit performance?

6. You are currently using 750 cases of green beans per year. The cost of one purchase order is $75. Annual storage costs are approximately 25 percent of inventory value. The beans' wholesale price is $24 per case. Each case contains six No. 10 cans. How many cases should you purchase at one time?

7. Given the following data, determine the cost of one purchase order:
    EOQ: 500 pounds (1-month supply)
    Storage cost: 24 percent per year
    Price of the product: $6 per pound

8. The typical owner-operator will accept suppliers' delivery and ordering procedures. What is the primary reason he or she would not try to change them?

9. What is the most important part of the storage cost?

10. What is a safety stock? Why might an operator wish to maintain a safety stock?

11. Briefly describe the concept of an "opportunity cost."

12. Identify one reason the EOQ concept is not particularly useful to the typical hospitality operation.

13. What is the objective of using the JIT inventory management procedure?

14. Given the following data, compute the number of raw pounds needed to serve 250 customers:
    INGREDIENT: Pork chops
    SERVING SIZE: 14 ounces
    EDIBLE YIELD: 75 percent

15. Given the following data, compute the number of liters needed to serve 500 customers:
    INGREDIENT: Scotch
    SERVING SIZE: 60 milliliters
    SERVABLE YIELD: 95 percent

16. Given the following data, compute the number of kilograms needed to serve 750 customers:
    INGREDIENT: Belgian endive
    SERVING SIZE: 75 grams
    EDIBLE YIELD: 65 percent

17. Given the following data, compute the number of cases needed to serve 1000 customers:
    INGREDIENT: Hash brown potatoes
    SERVING SIZE: 4 ounces
    EDIBLE YIELD: 100 percent
    WEIGHT PER CASE: 50 pounds

18. Given the following data, compute the number of cases needed to serve 1250 customers:
    INGREDIENT: Dinner rolls
    SERVING SIZE: 4 ounces (two rolls)
    SERVABLE YIELD: 100 percent
    NUMBER OF ROLLS PER CASE: 250 (500 ounces)

19. Given the following data, compute the number of gallons needed to serve 1500 customers:
    INGREDIENT: Ice cream
    SERVING SIZE: 4 ounces
    EDIBLE YIELD: 90 percent
    WEIGHT PER GALLON: $4^{1}/_{2}$ pounds

EXPERIENTIAL EXERCISES

1. **What are some advantages and disadvantages of utilizing rules of thumb to direct your inventory management procedures?**
    a. Write down the advantages and disadvantages of utilizing rules of thumb to direct your inventory management procedures.
    b. Interview at least two restaurant managers and ask them what rules of thumb they use to direct their inventory management procedures (i.e., amount of inventory to have on hand). Prepare a list of all rules of thumb that you identify.
    c. Ask each manager to comment on what they think are the advantages and disadvantages of utilizing rules of thumb.
    d. Submit a list of rules of thumb used to direct inventory management procedures. Include a report detailing the advantages and disadvantages of utilizing these rules of thumb.

2. **Can the Economic Order Quantity (EOQ) model assist foodservice managers?**
    a. Go online (start with www.google.com) and research the EOQ model in detail. Prepare a two-page report that you will use to persuade a manager of a large or multiunit foodservice operation to incorporate the EOQ model into his or her inventory forecasting procedures.
    b. Submit the report to a foodservice manager of a large or multiunit foodservice operation.
    c. Ask the manager for comments regarding the EOQ model.
    d. Submit a report that includes your two-page persuasion and the manager's comments.

Purchasing from the Chef's Perspective

Jean Hertzman, CCE, *Chef Instructor, UNLV Department of Food and Beverage Management*

Do all these PF and PD calculations seem a little confusing to you? Don't feel alone. They would be a mystery to the average chef. Although executive chefs spend more and more of their time performing cost control and human resources functions, most chefs would rather cook and develop new menu items than spend a lot of time crunching numbers. Therefore, they want to use as simple a formula as possible to determine the quantity of food to purchase.

Chefs rely on the formula of AP (As purchased) = EP (Edible-portion) / Edible-yield percentage to determine the amount of product to order. They basically cut out one step from the Levinson approach. But before we use the formula, let's make sure that you know exactly what that "Edible-yield percentage" means.

Let's use the example of broccoli. If you buy whole broccoli, but cut it into florets for service, you trim off a lot of stems and leaves in the process. The amount cut off would be the trim loss, and the amount left would be the edible portion. If you started with one pound of broccoli and had 12 ounces of broccoli florets after cutting, your yield percentage would be 12 ounces divided by 16 ounces per pound, or 75 percent. If you were determining the yield percentage of other products, for example a roasted meat, you might also have to take into account trimming off the fat, shrinkage during cooking, having unusable portions after cutting, and other factors.

As the text says, the most accurate method to determine the yield percentage is to conduct your own yield test. In that way, you know exactly what you have left using your particular foodservice operation's specific procedures. However, calculating yield percentages for all the different foods you use can be time and labor intensive. Therefore, the book says you can use supplier estimates of edible-yield percentages. However, suppliers may overstate the percentage so that their product looks like a better buy or understate the percentage so that you buy more of their product. If you don't have time to determine your own percentages, there is a third alternative. There are two excellent books that give yield percentages for just about every product you can think of: *The Book of Yields* (Hoboken: Wiley, 2004) by Francis Lynch and *Chef's Book of Formulas, Yields, and Sizes* by Arno Schmidt (Hoboken: Wiley, 2003). These chefs have spent years calculating portion sizes and percentages just to make your life a little easier.

Here's how to use the yield percentage in the AP formula: Suppose a banquet chef wants to serve 4 ounces of broccoli florets as a side vegetable to 600 people. Therefore, she needs 4 ounces × 600, or 2400 ounces (150 pounds) EP of florets. But she knows that the yield percentage on broccoli is only 75 percent. Therefore, she really needs 2400 ounces divided by 0.75, or 3200 ounces as purchased (AP). Translate that to pounds, and she would order 200 pounds of broccoli. If she only ordered 150 pounds, she would have to skimp on the portion sizes or lots of guests would not be getting their vegetable that evening.

Just to make sure you understand, let's do another example. A chef serves a great hot turkey sandwich using turkey roasted fresh daily. A 10-pound turkey breast yields 9 pounds of turkey meat after cooking, removing the skin, and slicing it. Each sandwich uses 6 ounces of turkey, and the restaurant sells them to 200 hungry guests daily. How many turkey breasts does the chef need to buy for each day?

1. 9 pounds EP/10 pounds AP = 0.90 or 90 percent edible yield percentage.

2. 6 ounces × 200 sandwiches = 1200 ounces EP.

3. 1200 ounces ÷ 0.90 = 1333 ounces or 83 pounds AP.

4. If the turkey breasts weigh 10 pounds each, then the chef has to decide whether to order eight and run out of product, or whether to order nine and have some left for sandwiches or turkey soup the next day. Most would play it safe and order nine turkey breasts.

Chefs use this method because the most important thing for them to know is how much food to purchase, regardless of whether they are calling the order in to a supplier themselves or handing in a requisition to a central purchasing agent. It also allows the chef the ability to accurately calculate the cost of preparing a recipe and the individual cost per portion. Once you have the correct AP amount for each ingredient, you can multiply that amount by that ingredient's purchase price to determine the total ingredient cost. Add up the cost of all the ingredients in the recipe and divide it by the number of portions the recipe makes, and voilà, you have the cost per portion. There are a few additional twists to recipe costing, but this procedure will get you started in the right direction.

THE OPTIMAL PRICE

Buying a cheap article
to save money is like stopping
the clock to save time.
JACOB M. BRAUDE'S *COMPLETE SPEAKER'S AND TOASTMASTER'S LIBRARY*

Some people know the price of everything,
but the value of nothing.
ANONYMOUS

The Purpose of this Chapter

After reading this chapter, you should be able to:

- Explain how purchase prices influence buyers.
- Describe how suppliers determine their purchase prices.
- Identify methods buyers employ to reduce purchase prices.
- Calculate cost information, including edible portion cost, servable portion cost, and standard cost.
- Evaluate the advantage of an opportunity buy.

INTRODUCTION

The optimal price is the price that, when combined with the optimal quality and supplier services, produces the optimal value. The optimal price represents the lowest possible edible-portion (EP) cost consistent with the optimal value of a product, service, furnishing, or piece of equipment. Remember, the best EP cost may or may not be the lowest as-purchased (AP) price. When a buyer struggles to assess the optimal AP price, therefore, he or she must be able to translate a quoted AP price into the hospitality organization's relevant EP cost. The buyer could quickly make this conversion by using the following formula:

EP cost = AP price ÷ Edible- (or servable-, or usable-) yield percentage

For example, if a roast beef has an AP price of $2.45 per pound and an edible-yield percentage of 75 percent, the EP cost per pound is $3.27 ($2.45/0.75 = $3.27).

After computing the EP cost, the buyer must then relate it to product quality and supplier services and conclude with the optimal value (see Figure 10.1). The buyer cannot evaluate AP price without concomitantly evaluating EP cost, product quality, and supplier services. The buyer must examine all of these components simultaneously and must seek the optimal value. We now show how the optimal price or, more appropriately, the optimal EP cost, relates to this overall value.

HOW AP PRICES INFLUENCE BUYERS

The AP price can influence buyers in many ways. At one extreme are the buyers who shop entirely on the basis of AP price. This practice succeeds only when the buyers know exactly what they want in terms of quality and supplier ser-

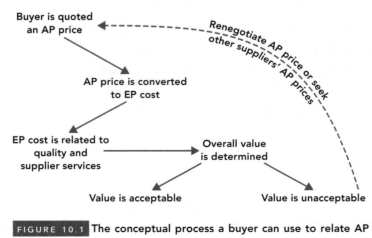

 FIGURE 10.1 The conceptual process a buyer can use to relate AP price to value.

vices and can get two or more relatively similar suppliers to quote AP prices that permit adequate comparisons. At the other extreme are buyers concerned almost exclusively with quality and supplier services. These buyers do not hesitate to pay a premium AP price. The majority of buyers fall somewhere between these extremes—or, more realistically, some buyers may be close to one extreme for some products and close to the other extreme for other products.

The supplier, in turn, must obtain some measure of a buyer's reaction to AP prices. In Chapter 12, we elaborate on "buyer profiles," which are sometimes referred to as "buyer fact sheets." These are diaries in which suppliers and salespersons record information on buyers' purchasing habits, as well as, invariably, reactions to AP prices.

Eventually, suppliers and salespersons can accurately gauge the influence AP prices have on various buyers. However, suppliers and salespersons use certain predictable reactions to AP prices to their advantage when selling the products and services to buyers for the first time. Some of the ways that buyers' and sellers' attitudes affect the purchasing process are discussed in the following paragraphs.

1. For the most part, novice buyers, and particularly novice managers, overrate AP prices. The AP price is, after all, a number, something that can be compared and measured. Inexperienced shoppers are more apt to grasp a number until they gain sufficient practice in relating AP prices to EP costs, quality, and supplier services. Top management is usually aware of the tendency to focus on numbers, which probably explains why buyers are expected to have previous experience in other areas of the hospitality firm. This previous experience generally helps buyers relate AP prices to overall value.

2. Price usually follows quality; a higher quality is normally accompanied by a higher price. To some extent, most buyers accept this reasoning. Unfortunately, at a certain point, the AP price keeps rising, but the quality fails to keep pace. Exactly when this difference between rising price and declining value occurs is not always clear, and inexperienced buyers and managers are liable to guess wrong. Even experienced purchasing personnel can be confused, especially if the products or services in question have just been introduced into the marketplace. Thus, suppliers and salespersons pushing a new item expect the AP price to receive more attention because no matter how much experience buyers have, they will have had little familiarity with new items.

    Price also may not necessarily correlate with quality if, for example, it is due primarily to the exemplary supplier services a particular supplier offers.

Nor will there be a significant relationship between price and quality if a supplier encounters considerable difficulty attaining an item and, therefore, must extract a higher price to compensate for this problem.

3.   Generally, suppliers work under the assumption that what they sell to a hospitality firm is heavily influenced by a "derived demand." A buyer's demand for any particular item is derived from the ultimate customer's demand on the buyer's hospitality operation. As a result, an analysis by suppliers of their customers' customers can be enlightening. For example, price-conscious hospitality customers are a signal to the supplier that the buyer might be price conscious. Suppliers, then, would expect a budget-motel buyer to be price conscious and would tailor their sales presentations and offerings accordingly.

4.   Sometimes, price is secondary. Suppliers sense this whenever an analysis of the buyer's customers shows that the ultimate consumers are not price conscious. Salespersons react by emphasizing other factors. Prices may also be relatively unimportant to buyers when the suppliers are the exclusive distributors for one or more items. Furthermore, if suppliers feel that a buyer is in dire need of something, they may expect a corresponding decrease in concern about the AP price.

5.   A buyer who seeks an itemized bill is almost certainly price conscious. By "itemized," we mean a bill that notes separate charges for the item, for delivery, and for various other supplier services. In most cases, suppliers total all these charges and note only one AP price per item. But suppliers regard a buyer who asks for an itemized statement as being one step away from an attempt to provide many of his or her own economic values and supplier services.

6.   If the products a buyer purchases represent a huge expense to the hospitality operation, chances are the buyer will be price conscious. Similarly, the AP prices of certain items are usually scrutinized more closely than others. Meat, for example, may receive disproportionate attention from a buyer.

7.   Some buyers operate on a tight materials budget. If so, they are liable to become more price conscious than usual as the budget period approaches the end of its cycle. Also, some hospitality firms operate on a tight overall budget, and hard times cause them to examine AP prices more thoroughly. During difficult periods, in fact, some operators begin to assess the profit potential of providing their own economic values, such as purchasing raw food ingredients instead of a preprepared menu entrée, thereby providing their own form value in lieu of paying suppliers for it. Suppliers recognize this thought pattern, and many of them tailor their sales efforts to meet it.

HOW AP PRICES ARE DETERMINED

In Chapter 4, we considered economic forces and their probable effects on the channels of distribution. We suggested two main effects: availability of products and services, and their relevant AP prices. Availability and AP prices usually go hand in hand as one factor, particularly for perishable food products and basic commodities. But additional price-setting procedures exist. Basically, suppliers use at least four general methods for determining AP prices. These approaches are discussed in the following sections.

AP Prices as a Function of the Supplier's Cost

Suppliers add all their operating and nonoperating costs and attempt to allocate a certain portion of these costs to each product and service they sell. Then they add predetermined profit markups to these figures. The result is AP prices based on the suppliers' costs of doing business.

This approach is quite common, if only as a starting point in AP price determination. Hospitality operators, too, typically start setting their retail prices this way. For example, menu prices usually begin with the cost of food. To this cost, management may add labor and other variable costs. A markup to cover profit and overhead is the final touch to reach an initial retail price for the menu item.

In practice, of course, each item is not always approached as a separate case. Instead, the average cost of doing business is known in relationship to sales volume, and a standard profit markup percentage may be derived.

Some products in the channel of distribution include conventional profit markups, which are sometimes referred to as "rules." A rule is a numerical factor that suppliers use to set their AP prices. For example, in the fresh-tomato market, one might find a "rule of three," which tells the supplier to take his or her cost of tomatoes, multiply this amount by three, and use the resulting figure for the AP price.

A cost-based AP price is a useful starting point. The supplier begins by applying a certain profit markup to the cost of his or her products. Then the supplier looks at his or her customers to see if they can pay, or will pay, this AP price. If they cannot, or will not, the supplier may lower the AP price, add more supplier services to justify the price, or, most typically, refuse to carry the item. The restaurant operator works much the same way: he or she will be reluctant to offer a low-profit menu item unless, of course, it is traditional and customers expect it.

It is important to keep in mind that while profit margins vary depending on the type of product, the average supplier in our industry earns an overall after-tax profit of only about 1 to 3 percent.[1] In many cases, a supplier earns only a few pennies per unit sold.[2]

AP Prices as a Function of Supply and Demand

Supply and demand have a great effect on perishable food prices and on commodity prices. Generally, the supply-and-demand force has its biggest impact at the beginning of the channel of distribution. Bread prices, for example, do not vary as much as flour prices. Similarly, flour prices do not vary as much as wheat prices.

To a certain extent, suppliers lower some AP prices to sell a slow-moving item. Hospitality operators do this when they offer certain menu specials or special rates during the off-season.

Most of us would not prefer to participate in a market that sets prices strictly on the basis of supply and demand. Consider, after all, the yearly financial uncertainties farmers and cattle ranchers face. But supply and demand will be extremely influential as long as buyers perceive no differences among competing suppliers' offerings. Wheat is wheat, and choice steak is choice steak.

Most sellers want to reduce the supply-and-demand effect; they consider it much too risky to carry several items other suppliers can duplicate exactly. The most common way to minimize the effect is to differentiate the products somehow. How can suppliers do this? Recall that quality is just one part of value. EP costs and supplier services are important too. Suppliers know this, and, as a result, most of them try to maintain profitable AP prices by manipulating supplier services. In other words, they make one or more attempts to differentiate the overall value, not just the AP price. This differentiation comes into play whenever suppliers use the following method of determining AP prices.

AP Prices as a Function of Competitive Pressure

Suppliers operate in a reasonably competitive market, but they have different ways to turn various sorts of competitive pressures to their advantage. By differentiating a product's overall value, or by convincing buyers that a product's overall value is unique, suppliers can minimize competition.

In Chapter 4, we suggested that hospitality-related organizations operate in a market characterized by monopolistic competition. That is, price competition is a big factor simply because many of the products such organizations sell are so similar. But each firm has some type of monopoly. A steak served in a truck stop diner might be as good as or better than the same type of steak served in a gourmet restaurant. Yet the menu prices will be different because the supplier services—in this case, certainly, service style and physical surroundings—are different, so different in fact that the overall value of each product might be quite acceptable to consumers. For the most part, many people are willing to pay more for the same item served in a gourmet restaurant than in a diner because the different supplier services justify the higher price.

Suppliers seem more willing to operate under this third method of setting AP prices. It gives them an edge since they can claim that there is no substitute for the value they provide. Moreover, it allows them numerous combinations of quality, supplier services, and AP prices sure to confuse even the most tight-fisted, objective buyer. The crucial factor, then, would seem to be supplier services. Delivery schedules, sales courtesy, general reliability—all these factors, and more, work their way into a product's overall value.

Buyer Pricing

Without a doubt, suppliers prefer this type of price determination. Unfortunately, the buyer who practices this procedure is almost certain to overpay.

Buyer pricing comes about in one of two ways. It will occur if a buyer does not have a detailed purchase or product specification; in this situation, the supplier "assists" the buyer in developing the spec, which, of course, will tend to place the buyer in a precarious financial position. Buyer pricing also will rear its ugly head if a buyer consistently engages in "panic buying," that is, if he or she continually runs out of products and relies on suppliers to make emergency deliveries. These emergencies will most assuredly result in significantly higher AP prices. There may also be penalties charged for unscheduled deliveries.

Price determination seems to be one of the last managerial "arts." It is not entirely amenable to mathematical formulas; hunches and experience come into play. Suppliers, however, normally want to maintain some perceived differences among one another's items. As long as they can do this, you will continue to see varying AP prices for the same type of product, unless these prices are controlled, either directly or indirectly, by state or product association bylaws or by legislation. Theoretically, though, the resultant values should be acceptable to all concerned because of variations in supplier services.

WAYS TO REDUCE AP PRICE SO THAT OVERALL VALUE IS INCREASED

A quick way to increase a product's value is to pay less for that product yet keep the same quality and supplier services. This is not only a quick method, but it also leads to dramatic results: the buyer's superiors can easily see and appreciate a lower AP price, whereas a bit more quality and supplier services do not make so deep an impression, at least not immediately. Buyers in large organizations are quick to note that their superiors notice a lowered AP price. Chances are they will be asked to explain how they obtained the lower AP price, which gives them an opportunity to publicize their excellent performance. Consequently, buyers continually seek a lower AP price to increase an item's overall value.

Nevertheless, buyers should be cautious when seeking a lower AP price. The most important consideration is how well the purchased item fulfills its intended use. If a buyer pays a slightly higher AP price, all that will be lost is money. But if an item performs poorly, a buyer will waste money and time. In addition, he or she may create some long-run employee or customer relations problems.

When seeking a lower AP price, the buyer should emphasize increasing or maintaining overall value. At no time should a buyer accept a lower AP price if the overall value of a product or service is reduced disproportionately, unless this is done with management's approval. The buyer should also fix a value on the time it takes to find or negotiate a lower AP price.

A buyer can use several methods in an attempt to decrease an AP price. A thorough value analysis of all products and services purchased will reveal the most feasible ones. Theoretically, a buyer can use some or all of the methods discussed in the following sections of this chapter.

Make-or-Buy Analysis

Buyers should periodically perform make-or-buy analyses, at least for more expensive purchases. For example, a hospitality operation might find that it can save a great deal of money by cutting its own steaks instead of purchasing them precut. When performing these analyses, though, buyers must be absolutely certain to consider all relevant cost data because it is very easy to overestimate these types of cost savings.

Provide Your Own Supplier Services and/or Economic Values

Several possible cost-cutting opportunities exist. As is true with make-or-buy analysis, buyers benefit from considering the many alternatives available. For example, buyers can save money by purchasing products from a no-frills wholesale club, where customers are expected to pay with cash, credit card, or debit card, and provide their own delivery.

Buyers may also be able to select and pay for only those supplier services or economic values they desire. For example, some suppliers may offer high-priority, regular, and low-priority delivery options, with payment according to the speed of delivery. Some suppliers may offer price concessions for online orders, which are more cost-effective than orders placed during personal sales visits or over the phone. Still other suppliers may allow buyers to earn what is sometimes referred to as a "forklift discount" if they unload their own deliveries instead of requiring the drivers to do the unloading.[3]

While these and other similar options may prove tempting, unfortunately, many hospitality operations have not fared well when pursuing such cost reduction strategies. Earlier, we discussed the potential costs and benefits of buyers providing many of their own supplier services and economic values. The conclusion seems to be that many firms attempting to do this have achieved mixed results and, in many cases, do not save nearly as much as they anticipated or have actually lost money.

Shop Around More Frequently

Buyers who shop around frequently usually practice a technique that is sometimes referred to as "line-item purchasing." This purchasing strategy is used to obtain competitive bids for several products from two or more suppliers. Buyers then select each individual product from the supplier who has given the lowest bid for it. For example, each supplier may bid on a total list of ten products. However, the only products an individual supplier will be able to sell will be the ones he or she has priced lower than those the competing bidders have priced.

Suppliers do not like buyers to "cherry pick" their bids in this manner. They prefer buyers who use a purchasing technique that is sometimes referred to as "bottom-line, firm-price purchasing." Using this buying procedure, buyers agree to purchase a group of products from the supplier who bids the lowest total price for the group. In this case, the successful bidder comes away with the complete order, while the unsuccessful ones leave empty-handed.

Although it takes considerable time, money, and effort to shop around, the potential rewards may make this strategy very profitable. If buyers have the time to develop specs and seek bids and do not mind dealing with several potential suppliers, generally they will obtain lower AP prices. As always, though, it is not quite clear whether the lower AP prices translate into increased values.

Lower the Quality Standard

Although it is possible to lower the quality one notch while lowering the AP price two notches, it is unlikely that this tactic will be successful. We have suggested elsewhere that buyers seldom have the authority to reduce the quality standard unilaterally. Management input is normally required. Also, a few suppliers are unwilling to stock a product line of more than two or three qualities, thereby minimizing the opportunity to purchase lower quality items. Therefore, even if you decide to accept a lower quality, you may be unable to purchase it, though it is possible some suppliers might carry those qualities you desire.

Lowering the quality standard for all items purchased is unusual, but it is not uncommon to do this for a few items. Whenever you do this, though, you risk confusing or alienating your steady customers. A hospitality operation's image and reputation are very fragile and could easily be tarnished irreparably if quality standards are altered.

Blanket Orders

A blanket order is a form of volume discount. It usually includes quite a few miscellaneous items, no one of which is particularly expensive. However, the sum of the large number of low-cost items included in the blanket order makes it worth the supplier's time and effort, and some AP price concessions may be granted.

The basic question with blanket orders seems to be whether you should try to order on an optimal-size basis or to order these items only a few times a year. In most cases, such as for personalized matchbooks, it would probably benefit you to place a large order once in a while because any optimal order size you might calculate would almost certainly be impractical. In fact, most buyers opt for a reasonably large par stock for these miscellaneous items and order up to par only once every three or four months.

When you place a blanket order for miscellaneous items, their AP prices may or may not decrease. Even without a reduction in AP prices, you can expect some savings if you use blanket orders because you significantly reduce your annual ordering costs while experiencing only a slight increase in annual storage costs.

Improved Negotiations

It is possible to lower the AP price by adopting a strict negotiating posture. For many products, AP prices are pretty well set and are not normally subject to negotiation. But supplier services and economic values can be manipulated, which might result in a higher overall value. Also, it is sometimes possible to negotiate more favorable credit terms or payment schedules. Although this does not lower the AP price, it does increase overall value since you can delay paying your bills and can use that money elsewhere, if only for a little while.

AP prices are generally a little more flexible for long-term contracts and certain types of services. The AP price of a product purchased on a six-month contract basis is usually lower than the AP price for the same item purchased on a day-to-day basis. Also, strict AP prices do not always accompany such services as contract cleaning and consulting.

Substitutions

Whenever AP prices become too onerous, or appear to be heading that way, management can take at least one of four actions: (1) pay the price and pass it on to the consumer, (2) lower the quality and/or reduce the supplier services and economic values provided to the hospitality operation's customers, (3) drop the item, or (4) stop offering the item but carry a substitute.

The fourth alternative is often used in the restaurant business and to some extent in the lodging industry. This strategy does not necessarily lower the AP price of any item, but it can lower the total cost of operating the business. Buyers and suppliers should be encouraged to offer substitute possibilities to management since they are the first to notice price trends, availability trends, and increased costs of preparation or service. They also are the first to evaluate new items on the market. Furthermore, in some situations, these substitute items save money.

The big disadvantage with substitutes is that not all firms can use them. For instance, a family restaurant can manipulate menu offerings quite easily, but a steak house finds this substitution road a little rougher. Nevertheless, substituting products is a useful alternative that hospitality organizations often employ effectively.

Cash Discounts

A supplier may be willing to accept a lower AP price, provided he or she receives cash in advance, at the time of delivery, or shortly thereafter. This is particularly true if the supplier is cash-starved. This practice is referred to as a "cash discount."

The cash discount is a viable alternative only when the buyer has the authority to promise a quick payment and only when enough cash is available. In large firms, the accounting department or financial officer decides the payment schedule (in small operations, it is the owner-manager's decision) unless, of course, suppliers have strict payment demands or buyers have the authority to negotiate payment schedules that do not require a quick cash outlay. The accounting department usually does this as a part of its own cash management program, and because it may be more efficient to pay bills on a periodic basis. In addition, companies rarely have large amounts of cash available on a moment's notice. Nevertheless, paying cash up front can be extremely economical. The immediate cash payment, sometimes coupled with the proviso that you are buying an item "as is," can be such an attractive money-saving opportunity that sometimes it might even pay to borrow the funds to complete such a transaction.

A concept related to the cash discount is the "cash rebate," which is sometimes also referred to as a "coupon refund." Essentially, the supplier will charge you the full AP price, but later on, after you send him or her some proof of purchase, you will receive a bit of money back—a cash rebate. It does not appear to us that this activity saves as much money as it might seem to initially. Generally, you have to pay postage, absorb the costs of reproducing bills or other proof-of-purchase records, and endure the long wait for your money. Most large hospitality organizations do not like this procedure because of the extra work involved; they prefer bargaining for lower AP prices up front. Nevertheless, these types of rebates are quite common for many items, and, if economical, they should be pursued as much as possible.

Hedging

The idea behind hedging is to maintain a specific AP price, not to reduce it. For example, assume that you wish to maintain the AP price of chicken for the next month. To do this, you would determine how much product you need for one month and enter into an agreement, usually a "futures contract," to purchase this amount one month from now at a specific price. During the month, you would purchase product as needed on the open market at the current AP price. If the AP price is higher than it was at the beginning of the month, you would be paying more for the product. However, your agreement, or futures contract, theoretically would be worth more. That is, the value of your agreement, which can be sold on the futures market, would increase. This increase would offset the higher, open-market AP price for the commodities. Consequently, you offset your high purchase price by selling your futures contract at a profit that you would then use to subsidize your "loss" on the open market. Where hedging is successful, the tendency is to maintain a stable AP price for the month.

But buyers should consider several problems associated with hedging: (1) a lot of cash may be necessary to buy futures contracts because the minimum amount of product involved in each agreement is relatively large; (2) hedging can be done for only a few items, though these items may account for the bulk of your purchasing dollar; (3) transactions costs are involved—you must pay people to trade the contracts for you, as you cannot do this yourself unless you own a seat on a commodity exchange; (4) few small hospitality operations can muster the time necessary to engage in this activity; (5) the transactions costs might easily overpower the benefits you could derive from this type of protection against AP price fluctuations; and (6) it is possible, though unlikely, that no one would want to purchase your contract when you need to sell it to break even.

At one time, the hospitality industry appeared to be well on its way toward making the hedging procedure a common component of the overall procurement strategy. However, the industry has had second thoughts about this procedure. While some large hospitality organizations maintain at least a modicum of hedging as part of their overall purchasing arsenal, few companies currently seem to follow this pattern. Examples of this practice, such as fuel hedging, are common in the airline industry.[4]

Economical Packaging

Every now and then, interest reemerges in changing some of the packaging methods manufacturers use. Some of the containers in use force an operator to waste storage space. For example, cylindrical cans and slope-necked bottles require more shelf space than cube-shaped boxes. In addition, a lot of packaging contains such cosmetic touches as pictures and suggested recipes, which tend to increase the overall cost.

Since you buy products for production and not, like supermarkets, for immediate resale, you gain no benefit from attractive but inefficient packaging. Theoretically, more standardized packaging should reduce the AP price. Furthermore, efficient packaging reduces your storage capacity needs, thereby providing another saving. Nevertheless, manufacturers do not like to abandon this type of advertising and promotional appeal.

The buyer should consider purchasing products that are packed in adequate, not luxurious, packaging materials, if at all possible. In addition, large volume packs are normally cheaper per unit of weight than their smaller counterparts. For instance, a 1-gallon container of sliced peaches probably costs less than four 1-quart containers.

Another advantage to large containers is that they tend to lessen the possibility of petty pilferage.

Odd-Hours Deliveries

If suppliers deliver at night or very early in the morning, they should be able to handle more delivery stops because of the decrease in road traffic and other distractions. To some extent, these types of deliveries are done in large, downtown urban areas that have particularly troublesome traffic jams during the day. It is not clear just what type of AP price reduction you could expect with these deliveries. Theoretically, you should gain some monetary benefit by increasing delivery efficiency.

Night deliveries might produce other cost savings, notably reductions in receiving costs. However, these savings would be possible only if all receiving was done at night, since night deliveries by just one supplier probably would increase costs; this is because the receiving and storage areas would need to be open for an extended period of time. These savings can materialize, though, if you trust the driver with a key to your premises.

A concept related to night deliveries is the possibility of receiving some monetary considerations from a supplier if you agree to receive deliveries during the "sacred hours." The sacred hours are those surrounding the lunch period, typically from 11:30 A.M. to 1:30 P.M. In some cases, the foodservice buyer who agrees to receive deliveries during this time period may earn some price concessions.

Co-op Purchasing

Recall that a purchasing co-op is a group of buyers, each representing a different hospitality operation, who pool their individual small orders. The resulting single large order more than likely qualifies the group for a lower AP price.

Several advantages and disadvantages are associated with co-op purchasing, and some of these are addressed in Chapter 12. It does seem clear that AP prices decrease whenever you purchase a large amount of a product or service. However, what is not clear is the effect on EP costs.

Cost-Plus Purchasing

Under the cost-plus purchasing procedure, the AP price is equal to the supplier's cost of the product, which is sometimes referred to as the "landed cost," plus an agreed-upon profit markup. The markup can be a set dollar amount or a percentage of the supplier's cost. Either way, if the supplier's cost decreases, the buyer will enjoy a price reduction. However, if the supplier's cost increases, so will the AP price.

Buyers must be willing to incur a bit of risk if they participate in this type of buying process. A sudden price increase is the most obvious risk. However, buyers must also be careful to monitor suppliers so that they do not subcontract products to their friends several times, thereby creating an artificial "daisy-chain" type of distribution channel, whereby the suppliers' costs are illegally inflated. In addition, if the profit markup is a percentage, suppliers have no incentive to control their costs. (Note that government buyers usually are not allowed to enter into a cost-plus purchase agreement if the profit markup is a percentage of cost; however, they can usually agree to a set dollar amount.) Wise buyers normally have, and exercise, the right to audit the supplier's records to determine whether the correct AP price has, in fact, been charged.

Large hospitality operations generally prefer a long-term arrangement in which both the availability of a product and its AP price are predictable. While suppliers usually do not mind agreeing to provide a certain amount of product to a hospitality company, they do not like to enter into a long-term, fixed-price contract. So, the use of a cost-plus arrangement seems to be the logical compromise. Negotiations center on the agreed-upon profit markup, not on the actual AP price itself. It appears that a hospitality corporation must follow this strategy if it wants to develop long-term contractual arrangements with its suppliers.

Promotional Discount

A promotional discount is a rebate from the supplier that the buyer's company must use to promote the retail sale of the product. For example, a cheesecake manufacturer might grant a 2-percent rebate if you agree to promote his or her product in your foodservice operation.

Today, the traditional promotional discount is not so common. More often, suppliers provide free promotional materials now and then (see Figure 10.2). Many suppliers also like to do joint promotions with hospitality operations.[5] For example, a liquor distributor may split the cost of a special event with a local nightclub operator. In this case, although the nightclub operator does not receive a lower AP price, he or she does enjoy an increased promotional budget.

If the option to gain a promotional discount arises, management should not jump too quickly. The extra money is, of course, tempting, but you need to do some serious thinking about how such a promotion will affect your operation's reputation. This decision can have several ramifications, and some of them may prove troublesome in the long run.

Exchange Bartering

Exchange bartering is simply the practice of trading your products or services for something you need. This is a relatively common practice in the hospitality industry (see Figure 10.3).[6] For instance, it is not unusual for a hotel company to ex-

FIGURE 10.2 (a) A promotional discount. Courtesy of Allens Canning Co. 2003.

FIGURE 10.2 (*b*) **A promotional discount. There is no direct reduction in the AP price, but the buyer can receive free promotional materials. Courtesy of Dole Food Company, Inc.**

change room nights, restaurant meals, and beverages for radio and billboard advertising. Industry experts think that as long as bartering represents no more than approximately 10 to 15 percent of a hospitality operation's total sales revenue, it can be a very profitable arrangement.

Bartering does, however, have its costs. For instance, you may have to join a barter group. More than 500 such barter groups exist in the United States. A few charge a fee to join (around $400) but most typically charge a 10 to 12 percent commission for each transaction.[7]

You may be able to avoid these costs if you engage in what is sometimes referred to as "direct bartering," whereby you personally make a deal with another business to swap goods and/or services.[8]

Bartering presents other potential difficulties. For example, you may have image problems to contend with. At times, you may have to deal with price gouging and poor selection availability. Furthermore, the Internal Revenue Service (IRS)

FIGURE 10.3 An announcement by an organization that matches individual businesses that want to trade. Courtesy of ITEX.

may be more apt to audit your income and expense records if you engage in a significant amount of bartering because the agency suspects bartering might become the prelude to unreported income. In 1982, the IRS recognized bartering as a legitimate purchase strategy so long as "trade" dollars are reported correctly for tax purposes.

The savings associated with bartering can be significant. For example, when you pay a bill of $100 with $100 worth of menu items, you have been able to discharge the obligation for much less out-of-pocket cost to you. Furthermore, if you restrict your trading partners' ability to exchange their meal credits—say, allowing them to eat during only the slow periods—you may gain even more financial benefit.

Introductory Offers

New products continually come on the market. Some suppliers move these items by selling them for an inexpensive AP price, at least for the first one or two orders. Alternately, you might buy one and get one free. The obvious problem, of course, is that these offers are temporary. You can hardly make a career of moving from one introductory offer to the other. This strategy is inconvenient, and suppliers do not like it. However, you could take advantage of an offer and stock up on the merchandise in anticipation that you can use it later, for example, for special parties.

Reevaluate EP Costs

You should get into the habit of revising the portion divider (PD) and portion factor (PF), if necessary, of currently used ingredients and ingredients that you expect to use at some later time. You should do this for all of the ingredients that you are procuring from current suppliers and for all of the ingredients that you might consider buying from other suppliers from whom you are not currently purchasing. Furthermore, you should occasionally consider purchasing an ingredient in some other form, such as a form that provides less edible yield, because it just might turn out that the ingredient purchased in that form offers the lowest EP cost.

You can never ignore an ingredient's overall value, of which the EP cost is only one factor. But, assuming that the quality and the supplier services are the same across the board, and also assuming that your other expenses will not increase if you purchase different types of ingredients, you owe it to yourself to examine the potential of purchasing another product that can be cheaper for you in the long run.[9]

You need to have a storehouse of data to perform this type of analysis. Each ingredient that you currently purchase, as well as each ingredient that you could conceivably purchase, must be listed, along with its PF and PD. As such, as we discussed in Chapter 9, food services that have sophisticated computer technology would more likely do this type of analysis.

If you have these data, you can proceed to evaluate the EP costs of each ingredient. Simply divide the AP price per pound for any ingredient by its PD, and, instantly, you have the EP cost for one serving of that ingredient.

Example 1

Given the following data, determine the EP cost for one serving of each ingredient.

INGREDIENT	EDIBLE YIELD (%)	SERVING SIZE	AP PRICE PER POUND
(a) Raw corned beef brisket	50	4 oz.	$1.38
(b) Raw corned beef round	75	4 oz.	$1.45
(c) Cooked corned beef brisket	90	4 oz.	$2.98
(d) Cooked corned beef round	95	4 oz.	$2.45

Solution: *Compute each ingredient's PF:*

(a) $PF = \dfrac{16}{4} = 4$ (c) $PF = \dfrac{16}{4} = 4$

(b) $PF = \dfrac{16}{4} = 4$ (d) $PF = \dfrac{16}{4} = 4$

Compute each ingredient's PD:

(a) $PD = 4 \times 0.50 = 2.00$ (c) $PD = 4 \times 0.90 = 3.60$

(b) $PD = 4 \times 0.75 = 3.00$ (d) $PD = 4 \times 0.95 = 3.80$

Compute each ingredient's EP cost:

(a) $EP \ cost = \dfrac{\$1.38}{2.00} = \$0.69$ (c) $EP \ cost = \dfrac{\$2.98}{3.60} = \$0.83$

(b) EP cost = $\dfrac{\$1.45}{3.00}$ = $0.48   (d) EP cost = $\dfrac{\$2.45}{3.80}$ = $0.64

Example II

Given the following data, determine the EP cost for one serving of each ingredient.

INGREDIENT	EDIBLE YIELD (%)	SERVING SIZE	AP PRICE PER KILOGRAM
(a) Fresh raw spinach	60	90 g	$1.75
(b) Frozen leaf spinach	100	90 g	$2.95
(c) Frozen chopped spinach	100	90 g	$3.25

Solution: *Compute each ingredient's PF:*

(a) PF = $\dfrac{1000}{90}$ = 11.11

(b) PF = $\dfrac{1000}{90}$ = 11.11

(c) PF = $\dfrac{1000}{90}$ = 11.11

Compute each ingredient's PD:

(a) PD = 11.11 × 0.60 = 6.67

(b) PD = 11.11 × 1.00 = 11.11

(c) PD = 11.11 × 1.00 = 11.11

Compute each ingredient's EP cost:

(a) EP cost = $\dfrac{\$1.75}{6.67}$ = $0.26

(b) EP cost = $\dfrac{\$2.95}{11.11}$ = $0.27

(c) EP cost = $\dfrac{\$3.25}{11.11}$ = $0.29

Example III

Given the following data, compute the servable portion cost for one serving of each ingredient.

INGREDIENT	SERVABLE YIELD (%)	SERVING SIZE	AP PRICE PER LITER
(a) Scotch (750 ml bottle)	95	50 ml	$8.25
(b) Scotch (1 liter bottle)	95	50 ml	$7.95
(c) Scotch (1.75 liter bottle)	100	50 ml	$7.25

Solution: *Compute each ingredient's PF:*

(a) $PF = \dfrac{1000}{50} = 20$

(b) $PF = \dfrac{1000}{50} = 20$

(c) $PF = \dfrac{1000}{50} = 20$

Compute each ingredient's PD:

(a) $PD = 20 \times 0.95 = 19$

(b) $PD = 20 \times 0.95 = 19$

(c) $PD = 20 \times 1.00 = 20$

Compute each ingredient's servable portion cost:

(a) Servable portion cost $= \dfrac{\$8.25}{19} = \$0.43$

(b) Servable portion cost $= \dfrac{\$7.95}{19} = \$0.42$

(c) Servable portion cost $= \dfrac{\$7.25}{20} = \$0.36$

As mentioned earlier, unless you have access to specific computer technology, it is very difficult to maintain current EP costs per serving for all food and beverage ingredients. However, you could develop some useful cost data in a relatively short amount of time if you knew each ingredient's: (1) AP price per unit, and (2) its edible- (or servable-, or usable-) yield percentage. For instance, if you know that raw corned beef brisket carries an AP price of $1.38 per pound and that its edible-yield percentage is 50 percent, you can determine very quickly the EP cost per pound for this item by using the formula noted at the beginning of this chapter and repeated here:

$$\text{EP cost} = \frac{\text{AP price}}{\text{Edible- (or servable-, or usable-) yield percentage}}$$

$$\text{EP cost per pound of raw corned beef brisket} = \frac{\$1.38}{0.50} = \$2.76$$

This type of cost information is very useful to buyers because it provides a solid base upon which they can make sound purchasing decisions. But buyers are not the only ones who will find this information useful; so will other managers and supervisors, who rely on product cost data to perform their jobs. Production managers, for instance, also use these data when performing their menu-planning duties. Specifically, product cost data are needed whenever a supervisor or manager has to "precost" the menu and calculate suggested menu prices.

Precosting a menu involves costing out each menu offering. This is done by first calculating the EP cost of each ingredient included in a menu offering and then obtaining a total EP cost per serving. The result of this work is the calculation of each menu item's "standard cost," that is, the expected (or theoretical) cost of the menu item.

To see how a standard cost is calculated, consider the following example:

Example

Menu Item: Steak Dinner

INGREDIENT	SERVING SIZE	EDIBLE YIELD (%)	AP PRICE PER POUND
Steak	12 oz.	80	$4.75
Beans	4 oz.	90	$0.65
Potatoes	4 oz.	75	$0.90

Solution: *Compute each ingredient's PF:*

$$PF_{(steak)} = \frac{16}{12} = 1.33$$

$$PF_{(beans)} = \frac{16}{4} = 4.00$$

$$PF_{(potatoes)} = \frac{16}{4} = 4.00$$

Compute each ingredient's PD:

$$PD_{(steak)} = 1.33 \times 0.80 = 1.06$$

$$PD_{(beans)} = 4.00 \times 0.90 = 3.60$$

$$PD_{(potatoes)} = 4.00 \times 0.75 = 3.00$$

Compute each ingredient's EP cost:

$$EP\ cost_{(steak)} = \$4.75 \div 1.06 = \$4.48$$

$$EP\ cost_{(beans)} = \$0.65 \div 3.60 = \$0.18$$

$$EP\ cost_{(potatoes)} = \$0.90 \div 3.00 = \$0.30$$

Compute the standard cost:

$$\begin{array}{r} \$4.48 \\ 0.18 \\ +0.30 \\ \hline \$4.96 \end{array}$$

Once a standard cost is computed, a manager can calculate a suggested menu price by dividing the standard cost by the target (i.e., desired) product cost percentage. For example, if the manager wanted the food cost of the steak dinner menu item to be 30 percent of its menu price, the suggested menu price would be $16.53 ($4.96/0.30 = $16.53).

Note that if $4.96 = 0.30 × menu price, then

$$Menu\ price = \frac{\$4.96}{0.30} = \$16.53$$

The $16.53 figure is only a suggested menu price. The wise hospitality operator will usually begin with this price, but he or she typically will adjust it somewhat so that it is consistent with local market conditions. Furthermore, the manager would not normally adopt a menu price of $16.53; more than likely, he or she would use a price of $16.50 or $16.95, figures that are more recognizable to the typical customer.

The standard cost can also be used in a hospitality operation's overall cost control system. For instance, if you find that at the end of the month you sold 500 steak dinners, the total standard food cost for the ingredients needed to prepare and serve these meals would be $2480.00 (500 × $4.96 = $2480.00). This total standard cost can then be compared with the total actual cost, which may be calculated in the following way:

Inventory value (in dollars) at beginning of month
+ Purchases for the month (in dollars)
_____
= Inventory available for the month (in dollars)
− Inventory value (in dollars) at end of month
_____
= Actual cost (in dollars)

The actual cost should be close to the total standard cost. If a significant "variance" exists between them, the hospitality operator will need to diagnose the situation, uncover the problem(s), and take corrective action.

OPPORTUNITY BUYS

One general category of purchases that can reduce AP prices dramatically deserves a separate discussion. Some single event may occur that causes a supplier to offer a bargain. A number of examples of the kind of opportunity we refer to appear in the discussion that follows.

Suppliers offer opportunity buys for several reasons: (1) Sometimes they give a normal quantity discount for large purchases of one item. When you buy larger and larger amounts at one time of a particular item, the per-unit AP price decreases. For example, when you buy 50 cases at one time, the AP price per case might be $8.00. But if you increase your order size to 100 cases, the AP price per case might be $7.95. (The figures 50 and 100 cases are sometimes referred to as "break points.") (2) Many suppliers offer volume discounts for large purchases that include several items. (In our experience, quantity discounts and volume discounts are the most common types of opportunity buys.) (3) Suppliers may have a "blowout sale," "buy-out sale," or "closeout sale." These "sales" generally refer to merchandise that may be unsalable for one reason or another, or merchandise that must be sold at a loss. In most instances, the buyer of these "sales" is in a position to take advantage of someone else's misfortune. (4) Some suppliers have move lists, or "muzz-go" lists, which include items that are on the verge of spoiling or, for one reason or another, are of poorer quality. These items, though, are wholesome and some hospitality operations can use them. (5) Suppliers might have received an excellent buy and want to pass some of the savings on to their good customers. (6) Suppliers may be cash-starved and willing to offer cash discounts on large purchases. (7) New suppliers may be trying to break into the market and will sell items at a loss in order to introduce their company. (8) Established suppliers may be introducing a new product line and, while so doing, may reduce their AP price. (This is referred to as an "introductory offer" when the amount you can purchase is relatively small.)

To take advantage of an opportunity buy, a buyer usually must agree to purchase in very large amounts. The buyer may have to purchase the item when he or she already has a complete stock. In addition, the buyer usually has to produce the cash in advance or on delivery.

Buyers must, of course, evaluate both the quantitative and the qualitative factors when exploring the attractiveness of an opportunity buy. On the quantitative side, buyers first must consider the numbers: they must determine the potential savings. If the savings are insufficient, buyers do not need to evaluate any qualitative factors.

For example, assume that you normally purchase 600 cases of canned peaches once a month. The AP price is $5.00 per case, for a total of $3000.00. You have an opportunity to purchase a two-month supply, or 1200 cases, for $4.95 per case, for a total of $5940.00. Your ordering cost for each order is $25.00. Storage costs are 24 percent per year, or 2 percent per month. What should you do?

Figure 10.4 depicts a quantitative analysis of this opportunity buy. In the usual situation, you would spend $6050.00. In the proposed situation, you would spend only $6023.80. You would save $0.05 per case and $25 with one less order. By deciding to take the option of buying 1200 cases, you make two savings, but you also incur an additional cost. You must buy next month's supply right now and store these 600 cases for an extra month, incurring a 2-percent storage charge on $2940.00, which comes to $58.80. You would not have to do this if you continued your monthly ordering schedule—that is, your normal storage costs would prevail. The upshot of this quantitative analysis, assuming that your ordering and storage cost estimates are reasonably correct, is a savings of $26.20. So, based on the numbers, which reveal a very small savings, management could either take this opportunity or leave it.

There is a simpler way to evaluate the quantitative aspects of this opportunity. In the first place, many buyers do not consider the ordering cost, mostly because of confusion about the makeup and magnitude of this cost. Basically, these buyers look at the opportunity buy as an investment. In the peach example, you

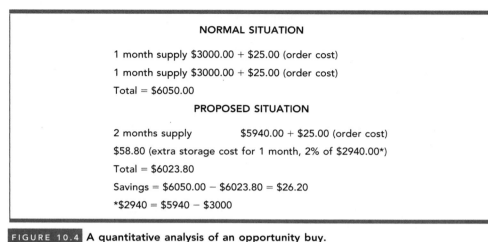

NORMAL SITUATION

1 month supply $3000.00 + $25.00 (order cost)

1 month supply $3000.00 + $25.00 (order cost)

Total = $6050.00

PROPOSED SITUATION

2 months supply $5940.00 + $25.00 (order cost)

$58.80 (extra storage cost for 1 month, 2% of $2940.00*)

Total = $6023.80

Savings = $6050.00 − $6023.80 = $26.20

*$2940 = $5940 − $3000

FIGURE 10.4 **A quantitative analysis of an opportunity buy.**

must buy an additional 600 cases for $2940 and store these cases for one month. In short, you have been asked to invest $2940 in inventory for one month. If you do, you save $60. The return on this investment, then, is 2.04 percent ($60/$2940) per month, or 24.48 percent per year. This percentage is normally compared with some cutoff percentage rate, usually a rate that represents the storage cost.

Regardless of which quantitative method the buyer uses, the emphasis should not be on a formula but on the estimates used in the calculations. Management must spend its time determining the relevant storage cost. (Recall that varying opinions exist surrounding the makeup of this cost.) Management must also determine what percentage rate of return it requires to take advantage of an opportunity buy. (In our experience, a buyer may be willing to purchase an additional one-month's supply of a product if the supplier discounts the AP price by at least 2 to 3 percent.)

Normally, management takes a conservative approach when setting this percentage rate and sets a relatively high rate. That way, if the savings of an opportunity buy exceed this high rate, the buy is, indeed, an excellent opportunity. But if management sets an unreasonably high rate, it may needlessly reject opportunity buys that, in reality, it should accept.

We think that the percentage rate should differ according to the storage requirements of the product. Dry storage products would have a low annual rate, perhaps 12 percent, whereas refrigerated and frozen products would require a higher rate, perhaps 18 percent or more, to offset the higher costs of refrigerated storage.

These quantitative analyses can be more complex than our discussion so far has indicated. For instance, you may have to consider the probabilities of large AP price increases or decreases during the next month, as well as the possibility that you may suddenly start using less of the product. If management sets a reasonable cutoff percentage rate, however, you usually will not need to examine these additional possibilities. As noted, the conservative approach seems popular and is, in itself, normally sufficient to cover most of these extra potential costs.

Once a buyer is satisfied with the numbers, he or she can evaluate several qualitative aspects of the opportunity buy before making a purchasing decision, including:

1. Is the quality the same? Does it compare favorably with the normal purchase?

2. What is the probability of a large decrease in the item's AP price after the opportunity buy?

3. Are cash reserves available? How will the purchase affect the overall cash position of the company?

4. Are storage facilities available? Will this buy pose an excessive burden on these storage facilities?

5. What is the storage life of the product?

6. Will insurance premiums, security risks, and the like increase dramatically, or will the current annual storage cost (in the peach example, 2 percent per month) remain pretty much the same?

7. Will personal property taxes increase now that the overall inventory level is higher?

8. Will the usage rate of the item remain the same over the next few weeks or months? Is it possible that management will discontinue the item? Technically, you do not save money when you buy the product; you save money only when you use it.

9. Does the opportunity buy require a change of suppliers? If so, your current supplier may become disgruntled. Also, what happens if the new supplier cannot maintain the overall value?

10. Are the supplier services the same? If not, how do they differ? Are these differences being considered when the numbers are being evaluated?

11. Is the opportunity a legitimate one? Are you buying legitimate merchandise from licensed suppliers? You should never purchase anything if you doubt the legal status of the item.

12. Furthermore, a buyer should not engage in any illegal activity when trying to save money. For example, you may save sales taxes on a piece of equip-

ment if you buy it in another state and arrange to have it delivered to you. Alternately, you may accomplish the same objective by purchasing equipment through an out-of-state Internet supplier. However, even though you do not pay sales taxes to the supplier's state, you are required to pay them in your state (usually in the form of "use taxes").

13. Another problem is purchasing from unlicensed independent food distributors. You never know where they get their merchandise or whether they are under government inspection. Local producers often are not required to undergo federal inspection. Most states have laws preventing the purchase of home-canned and other home-prepared products. But local egg farmers and fishermen, who sell only in their local area market, usually require no inspection. Furthermore, they are not likely to obtain the necessary business license. Hence, you incur a risk by purchasing these products.

14. Sometimes a hospitality operation that is going out of business attempts to sell its inventories and equipment. Perhaps the operation is selling items that actually belong to its creditors.

15. Another example is the salvage opportunity. For instance, a refrigerated railroad car overturns. Someone tries to sell the frozen-food merchandise for 20 cents on the dollar. Should you take such a deal? No, since buying food salvage or food from unlicensed purveyors is a violation of local health codes. The violation is referred to as "purchasing food from an unapproved source." It is permissible, however, to purchase nonfood and nonbeverage salvage items. For example, you could purchase a freight-damaged table if the damage will not interfere with the hospitality operation's production and service or tarnish the company's image. A buyer must realize, though, that he or she could be purchasing an item that suffers more than cosmetic bruises. Indeed, a freight-damaged item might be unusable and might not be a bargain at any price. Since products of this type generally are sold with no guarantee, the buyer must be willing to gamble that such a purchase will enhance the company's profits.

16. You may be able to save a great deal of money if you purchase used merchandise. Unfortunately, these items normally are sold or auctioned off in an "as-is, where-is" condition (i.e., there is no guarantee, and you would need to provide your own transportation). The high probability of a much shorter useful life for these types of items makes their purchase a risky endeavor. However, you may come out ahead if you are the lucky one who can spot a good opportunity. This is especially true if you can purchase a little-used demonstration model or a new one displayed only at a trade show exhibit.

Opportunity buys are clearly challenging. The quantitative aspects are relatively simple when the ordering and storage costs used are reasonably accurate. But the qualitative aspects are much more difficult to assess. This probably explains why most managements usually take a cautious approach when evaluating opportunity buys.

KEY WORDS AND CONCEPTS

"As-is, where-is" condition

Actual cost

AP price and its influence on buyers

As-purchased price (AP price)

Barter group

Beginning inventory

Blanket orders

Blowout sale

Bottom-line, firm-price purchasing

Break point

Buyer fact sheets

Buyer pricing

Buyer profiles

Buyout sale

Cash discount

Cash rebate

Cherry picking

Closeout sale

Commodity

Commodity exchange

Competitive pressure

Conventional profit markup

Co-op purchasing

Cost-plus purchasing

Coupon refund

Credit terms

Daisy chain

Demonstration model

Derived demand

Direct bartering

Economic values

Economical packaging

Edible yield

Edible-portion cost (EP cost)

Ending inventory

Exchange bartering

Fixed-price contract

Forklift discount

Freight-damaged item

Futures contract

Hedging

How the AP price is determined

Introductory offer

Inventory available for the month

Itemized bill

Landed cost

Line-item purchasing

Long-term contract

Make-or-buy analysis

Menu price calculation

Monopolistic competition

Muzz-go list

Negotiations

Odd-hours delivery

Opportunity buy

Ordering cost

Panic buying

Portion divider (PD)

Portion factor (PF)

Precosting the menu

Product cost percentage

Product substitution

Profit markup

Promotional discount

Qualitative aspects of opportunity buys

Quality standard

Quantity discount

Sacred hours

Sales taxes

Salvage opportunity

Servable portion cost

Servable yield

Shopping around

Standard cost

Storage cost

Supplier services

Supplier's costs

Supply and demand

Target product cost percentage

Usable yield

Use taxes

Used merchandise

Variance

Volume discount

Wholesale club

REFERENCES

1. Patt Patterson, "Finding 'Bargains'—and Knowing How to Police Them," *Nation's Restaurant News*, April 5, 1993, p. 37.

2. Michael L. Facciola, "Supply & Dementia," *Food Arts*, May 1992, p. 112.

3. Marj Charlier, "Existing Distributors Are Being Squeezed by Brewers, Retailers," *The Wall Street Journal*, November 22, 1993, p. A6.

4. Warren Getler and Scott Kilman, "Cheddar Lovers May Take a Slice of These Futures," *The Wall Street Journal*, January 14, 1993, p. C1. See also: Scott Kilman, "Broilers May Return to Roost at Merc," *The Wall Street Journal*, November 19, 1990, p. C1; Leslie Scism, "Derivatives May Deliver Postal Savings," *The Wall Street Journal*, November 11, 1993, p. C1; "Business Brief—AirTran Holdings Inc.: Subsidiary Enters Program to Hedge on Fuel Costs," *The Wall Street Journal*, January 5, 2001, Eastern edition, p. 1. More examples of hedging can be found by searching "hedging" at www.google.com.

5. Patt Patterson, "Suppliers Offer Free Promo Help for the Asking," *Nation's Restaurant News*, March 2, 1992, p. 39. See also: Paul Moomaw, "Two Heads (and Two Pocketbooks) Are Better Than One," *Restaurants USA*, January 1991, p. 12; Katie Fairbank, "TV Advertisers Seek to Cash in on Movie Characters' Cachet," *Dallas Morning News*, June 11, 2003, p. 1A.

6. James W. Damitio and Raymond S. Schmidgall, "Bartering Practices in the Lodging Industry," *Hospitality Research Journal*, 1994, 17(3), p. 101. See also: Mark Robichaux and Michael Selz, "Small Firms, Short on Cash, Turn to Barter," *The Wall Street Journal*, November 26, 1990, p. B1; Peter D. Meltzer, "Bartered Bucks," *Food Arts*, July/August 1993, p. 41; Michael Selz, "Health-Care Bartering Seen as a Money-Saver," *The Wall Street Journal*, December 23, 1993, p. B1; Sarah Hart Winchester, "Cutting Costs Without Cutting Quality," *Restaurants USA*, March 1995, p. 13; M. Franner, "Creative Financing," *Foodservice and Hospitality*, July 1995, pp. 15–16; Leon Stafford, "Tourism Officials Barter to Stretch Tight Advertising Budgets," *Atlanta Journal-Constitution*, May 15, 2003, p. D1.

7. Ira Apfel, "Trading Places," *Restaurants USA*, May 2001 (Available: http://www.restaurant.org/rusa). See also: Bob Ortega, "Swap the Sweat of Your Brow for a Suite Right on the Beach," *The Wall Street Journal*, June 16, 1995, p. B1; J. Damitio, M. Malk, and R. Schmidgall, "Smarter Barter," *Lodging*, July/August 1993, pp. 45–48.

8. Robert Liparulo, "Food as Currency," *Restaurants USA*, September 1993, p. 20. See also: James W. Damitio and Raymond S. Schmidgall, "Bartering Activities of the Fortune 500 and Hospitality Lodging Firms," *International Journal of Hospitality Management*, March 1995, pp. 3–9.

9. Jacquelyn Lynn, "Profiting from Smart Purchasing," *Restaurants USA*, April 1996 (Available http://www.restaurant.org/rusa). See also: Patt Patterson, "Review Purchasing List with Your DSR to Cut Costs," *Nation's Restaurant News*, October 11, 1993, p. 18.

QUESTIONS AND PROBLEMS

1. Assume that your economic order quantity (EOQ) is 500 cans. If you purchase 500 cans, you pay $343.50. If you buy 1000 cans, you pay $650.00; 500 cans represents a three-month supply,

and 1000 cans represents a six-month supply. Storage charges are 12 percent of inventory value per year. The cost of preparing one purchase order is $25.00.

  (a)   Should you purchase 500 or 1000 cans? Why?

  (b)   Even if it is cheaper to purchase 1000 cans, why might you reject such a huge order?

2. Consider the following problem data:

  EOQ = 500 pounds (one-month supply)
  Normal price = $1.00 per pound
  Storage cost = 24% per year, or 2% per month

  The product is ordered monthly. The cost of one purchase order = $20.00. You have an opportunity to purchase 1000 pounds of this product this month at $0.95 per pound. How much will you save if you purchase 1000 pounds?

3. Assume that you normally purchase 60 cases of Canadian whiskey once every three months. The cost of the whiskey is $3600. The distributor wants to sell you a six-month supply, 120 cases, for $6768. What do you suggest?

4. Explain how a buyer relates AP price to EP cost.

5. What are the four methods that suppliers use to determine their AP prices? As a buyer, which method would you prefer? Why? Which method would the supplier prefer? Why?

6. Review the various ways of reducing AP prices. Which method do you think is best? Why? Which is worst? Why?

7. What is the major objective of hedging?

8. Assume that you normally purchase 100 cases of Scotch per month at an AP price of $32.50 per case. You could purchase a two-month supply at an AP price of $30.00 per case. Your ordering cost is $25.00 per order, and your storage cost is 24 percent per year. How much would you save if you purchased a two-month supply?

9. Briefly describe the concept of "derived demand."

10. What are some major disadvantages of lowering your quality standard to reduce your costs?

11. What is the primary difference between a quantity discount and a volume discount?

12. List some advantages and disadvantages of exchange bartering.

13. Given the following data, determine the EP cost of each ingredient.

INGREDIENT	EDIBLE YIELD (%)	SERVING SIZE	AP PRICE PER POUND
Lettuce A	70	3 oz.	$0.22
Lettuce B	80	3 oz.	$0.29
Lettuce C	90	3 oz.	$0.32

14. What are some advantages and disadvantages of purchasing used merchandise?

15. Define or briefly explain the following terms:
    (a) Blanket order
    (b) Cash discount
    (c) Introductory offer
    (d) Quantity discount
    (e) Break point
    (f) Move list
    (g) Promotional discount
    (h) Coupon refund
    (i) Sacred hours
    (j) Salvage buying
    (k) Buyer profile
    (l) Buyer pricing
    (m) PD
    (n) PF
    (o) Make-or-buy analysis
    (p) Direct bartering

16. Under what conditions would salvage buying be illegal?

17. Given the following data, compute the EP cost for a 6-ounce portion:
    ITEM: Prime rib
    AP PRICE: $2.85 per pound
    EDIBLE YIELD: 12 ounces per pound
    (One pound = 16 ounces)

18. What are the advantages and disadvantages of purchasing merchandise from a no-frills whole-sale club?

19. Under what conditions would management consider a product substitution strategy in order to reduce costs?

20. What are the major problems associated with the hedging strategy?

21. Given the following data, compute the standard cost for one seafood dinner:

INGREDIENT	SERVING SIZE	EDIBLE YIELD (%)	AP PRICE PER POUND
Fish	12 oz.	75	$8.98
Rice	4 oz.	100	$0.22
Beans	4 oz.	90	$0.65

22. What is the name of the difference between the standard cost and the actual cost?

23. How can the actual cost be computed?

24. Given the data in Question 21, compute the suggested menu price for a seafood dinner, assuming that the target food cost percentage is 40 percent.

25. What could cause the actual cost to be greater than the standard cost? What could cause the standard cost to be greater than the actual cost?

EXPERIENTIAL EXERCISE

1.   How can you reduce the overall AP price and increase overall value?

  a.   Interview a restautant or hotel manager involved in purchasing for his or her operation. Ask the manager to comment on specific methods he or she employs to reduce the overall AP prices of products.

  b.   Compare the manager's methods with the following ones described in this chapter:
  Make-or-buy analysis
  Provide your own supplier services and/or economic values
  Shop around
  Lower the quality standard
  Blanket orders
  Improved negotiations
  Substitutions
  Cash discounts
  Hedging
  Economical packaging
  Odd-hours deliveries
  Co-op purchasing
  Cost-plus purchasing
  Promotional discounts
  Exchange bartering
  Introductory offers
  Reevaluate EP costs
  Opportunity buys

  c.   Identify any reduction methods that the operation is not employing and ask if they have been considered. If a particular method has been considered but not implemented, ask for an explanation. If it has not been considered, ask if the operation might benefit from this type of reduction method. Provide a report to include:

    i.   *The identification of AP price reduction methods used by your selected hospitality operation.*

    ii.   *A discussion of why particular reduction methods are not currently being used.*

    iii.   *A discussion of the possible benefits of implementing new reduction methods.*

11

THE OPTIMAL PAYMENT POLICY

The Purpose of this Chapter

After reading this chapter, you should be able to:

■ Identify the major objective of a payment policy.

■ Explain the costs of paying sooner than necessary and of paying too late.

■ Compare the bill-paying procedures that can be employed by hospitality operators.

INTRODUCTION

Buyers usually have little influence on their company's payment procedures unless they are, themselves, the owners who pay the bills. Usually, the controller or some other financial officer is responsible for these decisions. But buyers cannot be divorced entirely from this issue for at least four reasons: (1) Payment terms, cash discounts, opportunity buys, and so on, represent supplier services, and buyers must consider them in value analyses. (2) At times, these supplier services are negotiable, implying that buyers need at least some limited authority to bargain effectively. (3) Opportunity buys normally require quick payment. (4) Buyers must continue to work with suppliers who are sometimes "stalled" at bill-paying time. Such stalling tends to place buyers in a relatively poor negotiating position in future dealings; hence, buyers need to be able to influence any such "stalling" decision (see Figure 11.1).

PLEASE PAY FROM THIS INVOICE

22058

Sheldon's Meats

100 MAIN ST.   LAS VEGAS, NEVADA 89123
555-1212
Federal Inspected Meat Plant Est. 1000

IMPORTANT
MAIL REMITTANCE TO:
P.O. BOX 1000
LAS VEGAS, NV 89123

SOLD TO _____
ADDRESS _____

☐ C.O.D.   ☐ CASH   ☐ CHARGE   P.O. NO. _____   DATE ___/___/___

QUAN	DESCRIPTION	WEIGHT	PRICE	AMOUNT
	PATTIES			
	PATTIES			

All claims must be made immediately upon receipt of goods. If any discrepancy, please call (702) 555-1212; otherwise late claims will not be allowed.

TOTAL →

Received by _____

Boxes _____   Pkgs _____   Pcs. _____

All accounts are due the 10th of the month following date of purchase and after such date are past due accounts subject to an interest charge of $1\frac{3}{4}$% per month, which is **AN ANNUAL PERCENTAGE RATE OF 21%.** In the event legal proceedings are instituted to collect any sums due, the purchaser agrees to pay reasonable attorney's fees and costs.

I hereby certify that the above described product, which is offered for shipment in commerce, has been U.S. inspected and passed by the U.S. Department of Agriculture, is so marked, and at this date is not adulterated or misbranded.

FIGURE 11.1 Some suppliers are reluctant to allow the hospitality operator to work with their money. Notice that this supplier exacts an interest penalty if the buyer's company fails to pay in the allotted period of time.

THE OBJECTIVE OF PAYMENT POLICY

The tenets of cash management are: (1) keep your money as long as possible; (2) pay your bills at the correct time, neither too early nor too late; and (3) collect monies due as fast as you can.

While it is usually a good idea for a hospitality organization to hang onto its money as long as possible, sometimes it clings to its money too long, such as when financial incentives exist for paying earlier than it normally does. In Chapter 10, we considered the cash discount and the opportunity buy. In some cases, it could be costly to keep your money for 30 days when, by paying on the first day, you could receive a discount of 2 percent of your bill.

The specific aim, therefore, is to determine the optimal payment policy. Such a policy dictates that you should pay your bills at that moment when you will receive the most benefit. To accomplish this, the buyer or accountant must balance the costs of paying money too early with the potential ill will created among suppliers who must wait too long for payment.

COST OF PAYING SOONER THAN NECESSARY

Theoretically, it is easy to calculate this cost. For example, if you pay $40,000.00 today instead of one week from today, and the bank in which you keep your money pays 5.5 percent simple interest per year on deposits, you would lose approximately $42.31:

$40,000.00 × 0.055 = $2200.00 Interest income per year

$2200.00 ÷ 52 Weeks per year = $42.31 Interest income per week

You also could invest your money in some type of marketable security for one week and, perhaps, earn a bit more interest income than the typical rates paid on bank deposits. From this interest income, you must subtract whatever it costs to engage in this type of investment-disinvestment routine. Whatever profit you have left over is an opportunity cost incurred by paying the bill today instead of one week from today.

Investing money in this fashion, though, is not typical of the vast majority of hospitality firms, especially since few of them have cash balances large enough to justify the time and effort needed to keep cash invested productively. For the most part, if you avoid paying your bills for one week, you immediately find another use for these funds in the business. For instance, you might decide to replace an oven and hope that this week's sales receipts will be sufficient to pay the current bills seven days from now. Alternatively, you might want to use the money to pre-pay an insurance policy. In other words, some sort of priority within the organization always awaits an application of cold, hard cash. Shuffling the priority list—borrowing from Peter to pay Paul—is often necessary in the hospitality industry.

Another potential cost of paying sooner than necessary is that such action can leave you cash-starved and vulnerable to excessive financial risks. For example, if you needlessly drain your bank account too soon, you might be unable to take advantage of a once-in-a-lifetime opportunity buy. Conversely, you might find yourself in a precarious position if you suddenly need to pay cash to a serviceperson to make an emergency call to fix, for example, a refrigerator.

COST OF PAYING TOO LATE

Some hospitality operators attempt to preserve capital by stretching their accounts payable. Unfortunately, if a buyer abuses the suppliers' normal credit period, he or she will incur several potential costs. For instance, a buyer's company could: (1) gain a reputation as a slow payer, (2) jeopardize future credit potential, (3) damage credit ratings, (4) be put on a cash-on-delivery (COD) basis by all suppliers, (5) incur interest charges and/or penalty charges, (6) lose cash discounts or other favorable as-purchased (AP) price reductions, (7) incur legal difficulties, (8) find that many suppliers will not do business with a poor credit risk, and/or (9) be able to purchase only from those suppliers who provide shoddy merchandise and poor supplier services.

WHAT IS THE BEST POLICY?

The best policy is probably the one that allows you to keep your money as long as possible, unless you have an incentive, such as a cash discount, to pay early. Always keep in mind that the longer you can delay paying your bills, the more you operate with someone else's money.

Unfortunately, the average hospitality operation finds it impossible to negotiate specific payment terms. Most suppliers expect you to pay COD unless you have established credit, in which case you will normally be put on a monthly credit term period.

The typical hospitality operation also tends to incur interest charges on any balances that are not paid off at the end of the 30-day period. For instance, it is not unusual for you to be able to pay a minimum monthly payment and let the remaining balance "ride" until the end of the next month. This "ride," though, is usually accompanied by a monthly percentage charge of about $1^{1}/_{2}$ to $1^{3}/_{4}$ percent. In this situation, a buyer's company has some latitude in planning its payment schedule since suppliers allow more time. However, at these high interest rates, it probably benefits the buyer to pay his or her bills at the end of every month to avoid such charges.

Usually, large hospitality organizations are able to negotiate a more favorable set of credit terms than smaller organizations. Since large firms represent huge amounts of business, suppliers generally are willing to treat them more leniently and with more respect. In our experience, the typical large hospitality company generally seeks a 45-day credit term period; that is, it expects to pay its bills every 45 days.

Small hospitality operators should try to set up a periodic payment schedule, perhaps setting aside one day a week to pay bills. Although this may not allow them to keep their money as long as they would like, it will at least systemize their payments. This systemized procedure is often more efficient in the long run than the juggling of bills and payment periods throughout the year. The only exception should be when suppliers offer some type of discount in exchange for quick payment. In this situation, small firms should perform the appropriate opportunity buy analysis.

THE MECHANICS OF BILL PAYING

Hospitality operators can employ four bill-paying procedures. These are discussed in the sections that follow.

Paid-Outs

A method that is fairly popular with small hospitality operators is the paid-out. That is, assuming that everything is acceptable when the delivery is received, the receiver reaches into the cash register and pulls out the appropriate amount of cash to pay the delivery driver. Instead of pulling out cash, the receiver could pull out a prepared check and give it to the delivery driver. Either way, the emphasis is on paying COD.

This procedure does not allow you to work with the supplier's money, but it is very convenient. You eliminate having to plan for and execute periodic payments, to spend money on postage or electronic funds transfers, and to pay for the printing cost of a check and other bank charges.

Some suppliers will not allow their delivery drivers to accept paid-outs because of security reasons. It also is possible that paying COD is illegal for some purchases; for example, in some parts of the United States, it is illegal to pay COD for liquor purchases. However, most suppliers will agree to the paid-out procedure as long as the amount of money involved is not too large.

Invoices on Account

When a delivery is made, an invoice usually accompanies it. That is, you ordinarily receive a written description of the delivery, noting such things as items delivered, prices paid, and so forth (see Figure 11.1).

During this process, the receiver normally is asked to sign the delivery driver's copy of the invoice, attesting to the fact that everything is acceptable. If a problem with the delivery exists—say, some merchandise is damaged and must be sent back—the delivery driver may give the receiving agent a credit slip, or the hospitality operation may need to seek the appropriate credit directly from the supplier's main office. Once the driver and receiver are satisfied, the driver leaves and the receiver arranges for storage of the shipment. No money changes hands at this point.

At the end of the credit period (e.g., at the end of the month, or at the end of a 45-day period), the hospitality operation receives a statement listing all the invoice amounts delivered during the period; the previous balance, if any, that was left unpaid from the previous period; credits applied to the account, if any; and, if applicable, interest charges on last period's unpaid balance. The organization then needs to reconcile this statement with its copies of invoices and credit slips accumulated during the period and to report any discrepancies to the supplier.

The operation's copies of the invoices and credit slips may also be reconciled with its copies of purchase orders, or some similar order records, to ensure that it did, in fact, order all of the merchandise received. After the reconciliation, the hospitality operation then sends the supplier a check for the agreed-upon minimum payment or, perhaps, pays the entire balance.

Credit Card Payments

Some hospitality operations, especially small ones, prefer using a credit card to charge purchases and pay for them at the end of the credit period.[1] This is very similar to the invoices-on-account system described in the preceding section, but with this procedure, the credit card company handles the billing instead of the suppliers.

When you use a credit card, suppliers must pay a fee to the credit card company. The fee is usually a percentage of the amount of money charged. The percentage amount ordinarily depends on which type of credit card you use. For instance, a bank card, such as Visa or MasterCard, is normally less expensive than a travel-and-entertainment card, such as American Express.

While these fees increase the suppliers' costs of doing business, many suppliers may save money in the long run if they receive their payments quickly. For example, if buyers pay with a Visa credit card, suppliers should receive payment in about 2 or 3 days instead of waiting 30 to 45 days for their money. This gives suppliers the option of investing this money and earning a bit of interest income. Furthermore, since the credit card companies handle a good deal of the paperwork, suppliers will experience some administrative savings as well.

Bill-Paying Service

At times, a hospitality operation might prefer depositing money into an escrow account and authorizing a bill-paying service to use this money to pay its accounts payable. For instance, if you hire a contractor to build an addition on your hotel, it is common practice for a bill-paying service to inspect the contractor's progress and pay off the project in stages—say, one-third of the price when the contractor begins work, one-third when the framing is up, and the final one-third when the addition is completed satisfactorily.

A bill-paying service will charge a fee, but in exchange it will provide an extra margin of security. In addition to handling the paperwork and other assorted details, the service ensures that purchases meet buyers' specifications.

ANOTHER WORD ABOUT DISCOUNTS

Large hospitality operations tend to have more opportunity for discounts, especially promotional, volume, and quantity discounts—and, to a certain extent, cash discounts as well. Many chain operations can earn considerable income just by keeping track of the cash discount period, which is usually 10 days, and paying at the last possible moment before the end of this period. But discounts raise some problems:

1. Hospitality operations may become too intent on the discounts and may lose track of the real cost of purchases. Fortunately, keeping the books according to the *Uniform System of Accounts for Hotels and Restaurants* can separate the real cost from any discount.

2. Cash discounts may interfere with the firm's normal accounts payable schedule. Unless the operation has several cash discounts, which is no longer likely, it may be too much trouble to pay bills on different days.

3. The operation might stay with a "discounting" supplier longer than it should. For instance, if the supplier delivers slightly inferior foods from time to time, the firm may begin to overlook this problem in order to retain the discount.

4. Even if it is profitable for the hospitality operation to take advantage of a discount, it may be necessary to undergo a costly borrowing procedure to get the cash. The firms must add the interest cost of such borrowing to the cost of the purchase for decision-making purposes.

5. If the hospitality operation is lucky enough to receive a cash discount, it needs to know whether the payment due date will be extended if it has to return the delivered merchandise and wait for two or three days for an acceptable replacement. Does the cash discount period start when the replacement arrives, or does it start when the first, unacceptable delivery was made? This has caused many a strained relationship between buyers and sellers.

KEY WORDS AND CONCEPTS

Bank charges	Credit rating	Payment terms
Bill-paying service	Credit risk	Reconciling the supplier's end-of-period statement
Cash discount	Credit slip	Some problems with the acceptance of discounts
Cash management	Escrow account	
Cash on delivery (COD)	Interest charge on unpaid balance	Stalling a supplier
Cost of paying too early		Stretching the accounts payable
Cost of paying too late	Invoices on account	Supplier services
Credit card payments	Opportunity buy	The objective of a payment policy
Credit period	Paid-out	

REFERENCE

1. Steven Lipin, "Office Supplies Are Battlefield for Credit Cards," *The Wall Street Journal*, July 22, 1993, p. B1.

QUESTIONS AND PROBLEMS

1. What is the main purpose of cash management?
2. How is cash management similar to inventory management? How do they differ?
3. If you pay a $10,000 bill today instead of two weeks from today when it is due, approximately how much money will you lose if you have to take the $10,000 out of a bank account that pays 2.75 percent simple interest per year?
4. What are the costs and benefits of "stalling" a supplier?
5. What should a manager do if he or she forecasts a temporary shortage of cash and will not be able to pay the bills on time next month?
6. What are some of the potential problems managers who accept discounts might experience?
7. Are there any advantages to paying your bills as early as possible? If so, what are they?
8. What are the major disadvantages of paying your bills too late?
9. What are some advantages and disadvantages of using paid-outs?
10. Define or briefly explain the following terms:
    (a) COD
    (b) Credit terms
    (c) Optimal payment policy
    (d) Interest charge on the unpaid balance
    (e) Invoices on account
    (f) Credit rating
11. When should a hospitality operator request a credit slip from the supplier?
12. What are some advantages and disadvantages of using a bill-paying service?

EXPERIENTIAL EXERCISES

1. **Interview an owner-operator of a small restaurant.**
    a. Ask this owner-operator to discuss how he or she does business with suppliers regarding credit.
    b. Have the owner-operator describe how he or she initially received credit from the first supplier.
    c. Prepare a one-page report detailing your interview.

2. **Interview a purchasing director or buyer of a hotel.**
    a. Ask this person to discuss how the hotel does business with its suppliers regarding credit.
    b. Have the director or buyer describe how he or she negotiates credit terms with a new supplier.
    c. Prepare a one-page report detailing your interview.

THE OPTIMAL SUPPLIER

The Purpose of this Chapter

After reading this chapter, you should be able to:

- Determine a buying plan by selecting a single supplier or bid buying.
- Explain additional criteria used when choosing suppliers.
- Describe the relationship between suppliers and buyers.
- Describe the relationship between salespersons and buyers.

INTRODUCTION

Buyers have a good deal more to do with selecting suppliers than fixing quality standards and economic values. The major exception to this rule occurs when another company official insists that a buyer purchase from a certain supplier. This insistence usually means that some sort of reciprocal buying arrangement has been reached or that the owner-manager has prepared an approved-supplier list without consulting the buyer.

THE INITIAL SURVEY

The first step in determining the optimal supplier is to compile a list of all of the possible suppliers, or at least a reasonable number of potential suppliers. Local suppliers' names can be gathered from the local telephone directories, local trade directories, local trade magazines, other similar publications, and other hospitality operators.

National suppliers' names can be obtained from similar sources. They also can be gathered from national buying guides and directories such as:

The *Thomas Food and Beverage Market Place* (see Figure 12.1) (www.tfir.com)

Restaurants & Institutions Marketplace (www.rimarketplace.com)

The National Restaurant Association's Online Buyer's Guide

    (www.restaurant.org/business/buyersguide)

Foodtrader (www.foodtrader.com)

FIGURE 12.1 The *Thomas Food and Beverage Market Place.* **Courtesy of Grey House Publishing, www.greyhouse.com.**

Nation's Restaurant News Marketplace (www.nrn.com)

Foodservice Product Link (www.fsdmag.com)

Suppliers can also be found and evaluated at live trade shows and conventions, including:

American Culinary Federation National Convention (www.acfchefs.org)

National Restaurant Association Show (www.restaurant.org)

The Foodservice Symposium (www.thefoodservicesymposium.com)

Fresh Summit (www.pma.com)

Multi-Unit Food Service Operators (MUFSO) Conference (www.mufso.com)

North American Association of Food Equipment Manufacturers (NAFEM) Show
   (www.nafem.org)

Hospitality Information Technology Conference (HITEC) (www.hitec.org)

International Foodservice Technology Expo (FS/TEC) (www.fstec.com)

The International Hotel/Motel & Restaurant Show (www.ihmrs.com)

Multi-Unit Restaurant Technology Conference (www.htmagazine.com)

Large corporations take the time to compile lengthy lists of suppliers. The procedure most small operators follow is to seek out a more limited number of suppliers that carry most of the required items. In some cases operators may contact only one supplier for a particular product line. This is true especially for such items as liquor and dairy products because the middlemen dealing in these product lines usually have few competitors.

Whatever initial survey is undertaken, it can present three major problems. First, it may be difficult to determine which suppliers to include on the initial list. Many potential suppliers carry several product lines; consequently, the list can become larger than you would wish.

A second problem stems from the first. In the buyers' haste to shorten the potential supplier list, they may stop adding suppliers when they reach a certain number. The longer the list, the more time is required for interviewing, checking references, touring plants, and completing the other analytical work involved in culling the list. But indiscriminate culling can eliminate a good potential supplier. Furthermore, it tends to limit the pool of potential suppliers in the future when buyers stick with the original list. It can be costly to a hospitality firm to lock out a good supplier in this way.

The third problem is less common. It occurs when buyers need to purchase a unique item. In such situations, the search for a supplier can be extremely time-consuming.

TRIMMING THE INITIAL LIST

Buyers begin to narrow their initial list into an approved-supplier list by looking closely at each supplier's product quality, as-purchased (AP) price, and supplier services. (We assume that, at this stage, a buyer knows what types of products are wanted.) These factors help to separate acceptable suppliers from the initial list.

It is relatively easy to ascertain the quality standards and AP prices of suppliers. The major obstacle occurs when buyers examine supplier services. What is the best way to evaluate these supplier services? Basically, this process becomes a matter of taste. But the important considerations come under the rubric of "performance." When evaluating performance, buyers should be interested in prompt deliveries, the number of rejected deliveries, how adjustments on rejected deliveries are handled, how well suppliers take care of one or two trial orders, the capacity of their plants, and their technological know-how.

It might be easier to narrow a supplier list by trial and error. But a supplier's poor performance can leave buyers without a product, as well as with disgruntled customers demanding that particular product. It might be best, then, to accept the list-narrowing procedure as an essential aspect of purchasing.

THE RELATIONSHIP OF PURCHASING POLICY TO SUPPLIER SELECTION

The actual selection of the optimal supplier is the next logical step. Buyers cannot do this, however, without considering the type of procurement policies best for them. For instance, buyers might want to work with one particular supplier and negotiate long-term contracts for some items. If this is the case, they must keep these requirements in mind when going over the approved supplier list. Some suppliers may wish to be accommodating; others may not.

Large corporations have a bit more latitude in formulating their preferred buying policies and then convincing suppliers to cooperate. Small operators have less discretion; that is, they may have to accept the buying procedures their suppliers prefer. But at least a few procurement policies are available to any size operator. And, just as important, most suppliers are willing to adjust to more than one policy.

BUYING PLANS

Generally speaking, the hospitality industry has two basic buying plans: (1) the buyer selects a supplier first, and they work together to meet the buyer's needs;

or (2) the buyer prepares lengthy specifications for the items needed and then uses bid-buying procedures.

The first plan, which involves selecting one or more suppliers to work with, is not common. Usually, a buyer chooses this plan only when: (1) a reciprocal buying policy is in effect; (2) only one supplier provides the type of item needed; (3) the buyer or owner-manager, for some reason, trusts the supplier's ability, integrity, or judgment; or (4) the buyer, for some reason, wants to establish a long-term relationship with a supplier. This plan is, however, used somewhat more often in small operations in which management, already spread thin with other operational problems, decides to limit the number of suppliers, even in some cases to a single supplier, for as many products as possible. This practice is called "one-stop shopping," and we discuss it below.

Bid buying is more common, particularly for items that several suppliers sell.[1] It works fairly well as long as buyers realize that all suppliers are not created equal. Also, buyers must keep in mind that obtaining the lowest bid may not ensure the lowest edible-portion (EP) cost.

Deciding which plan to use is a matter of judgment for buyers. For some items, the first plan may be appropriate. For example, since the quality of fresh produce tends to vary significantly, buyers may opt to select only one or a few suppliers whom they can trust. However, those same buyers might purchase canned goods strictly on a bid-buying basis.

Buyers who use bid buying generally take two approaches: (1) the "fixed bid," and (2) the "daily bid." Typically, buyers use the fixed bid for large quantities of products purchased over a reasonably long period of time. This is usually a very formal process.

The fixed-bid buying plan usually begins with a buyer sending a "Request for Bid" or "Request for Quote" to prospective suppliers, asking them to submit bid prices on specific products or services. The request includes detailed specifications and outlines the process bidders need to follow, as well as the process the buyer will use to award the contract.

Buyers send bid requests only to eligible, responsible bidders. An ineligible bidder is a company that, because of financial instability, unsatisfactory reputation, poor history of performance, or other similar reasons, cannot meet the qualifications needed in order to be placed on the approved-supplier list.

Responsible bidders usually need to send in sealed bids when participating in the fixed-bid process. A sealed bid is almost always required on major purchases to ensure fair competition among bidders. After the buyer opens the sealed bids, he or she awards the business to the responsible bidder with the lowest bid. The buyer awards the contract to this bidder because the unit price is lower, or the value per dollar bid is higher than what the other bidders quoted. Furthermore, the bid winner's reputation, past performance, and business and financial capabilities are judged best for satisfying the needs of the contract.

The daily bid is often used for fresh items, such as fresh produce. (The daily-bid method is sometimes referred to as "daily-quotation buying," "call sheet buying," "open-market buying," or "market quote buying.") Buyers also use this type of bid when purchasing a small amount—just enough to last for a few days or a week. The daily bid usually follows a simple, informal procedure: (1) the suppliers that form a list of those with whom the buyer wants to do business—the approved-supplier list—are given copies of the buyer's specifications; (2) when it is time to order some items, the buyer contacts these suppliers and asks for their bids; (3) the buyer records the bids or analyzes them electronically; and (4) the buyer usually decides on the supplier selection by choosing the supplier with the lowest AP price quote.

Some sort of value analysis could be used here to determine the optimal plan to use, given the types of items being purchased. The optimal procedure, though, is not an easy formula to develop because several good reasons exist for buyers to choose either plan. Convenience, degree of buyer skill, product availability, and so on, come into play when buyers determine the optimal plan. In the final analysis, the plan used will result from examining several factors.

Regardless of the plan or combination of plans a buyer chooses, he or she must ascertain the suppliers' willingness to participate in the plan. Most suppliers will jump at the chance to be a part of the first plan. Buyers, though, normally start with some type of bid-buying procedure, if only to determine which supplier they want to use all the time. Alternately, at the very least, buyers use bid buying in order to select the suppliers they plan to use for the next three, four, or six months.

Not all suppliers like to become involved with bid buying, especially when they feel that the other bidding suppliers are not in their league. These nonparticipating suppliers frequently balk at bid buying because their AP prices look high, due to the amount of supplier services they include. Generally, high AP prices do not win bids. Furthermore, the competing bidders may inflate their AP prices to fall just under those legitimately high AP prices. High-priced, reputable suppliers do not like to be involved in this type of practice.

Many suppliers try to circumvent a buyer's desire to bid buy by offering various discounts, other opportunity buys, introductory offers, and so forth. In addition, suppliers may try to become exclusive distributors for some items: if a buyer wants to purchase them, he or she will have no choice in supplier selection.

OTHER SUPPLIER SELECTION CRITERIA

After determining a supplier's response to the two basic buying plans, a buyer must assess the supplier's willingness to participate in additional aspects that are related to these two basic plans. Furthermore, buyers must evaluate several other related variables when developing a list of acceptable suppliers. Some of the more common aspects and variables are discussed next.

Cost-Plus Purchasing

A buyer might want to be charged whatever the suppliers paid, plus an agreed-upon profit markup. Recall from Chapter 10 the possibility of arranging this type of purchasing procedure. In this situation, the buyer may be able to negotiate with suppliers for the agreed-upon profit markup percentage or set dollar amount to be added to the suppliers' cost of obtaining the products. Large hospitality firms are usually able to negotiate, whereas smaller operators may have to settle for the suppliers' normal profit markup.

Suppliers are not always fond of cost-plus buying because it usually requires considerable work to alter AP prices. It also is necessary for the suppliers to share cost data with buyers, a practice upon which competitive businesspersons tend to frown. Large hospitality firms, though, tend to prefer cost-plus purchasing because experience suggests that it can reduce AP prices, lessen the buyer's administrative effort, raise the level of supplier services, and improve product quality. In short, cost-plus purchasing can increase value.

One-Stop Shopping

One-stop shopping, which is sometimes referred to as "sole-source procurement," "prime-vendor procurement," or "single-source procurement," appeals to many buyers because of its simplicity. A one-stop shopper tries to purchase as many items as possible from one supplier. The main advantage of this procedure is the reduction of the ordering cost. There is considerably less effort involved with fewer orders: less paperwork, less receiving activity, fewer deliveries, and less opportunity for error. Another advantage is the possibility of qualifying for a volume discount when you purchase a large dollar amount of merchandise; the one-stop buyer usually enters relatively large purchase orders and, hence, is more apt to qualify for a volume discount.[2]

Unfortunately, one-stop shopping carries its share of disadvantages. One obvious disadvantage is the reduction in supplier selection flexibility. Another potential disadvantage is the possibility that the total dollars spent for purchases over the long run may be higher than if the buyer shopped around a bit.

The reason for this second disadvantage is simple. Many suppliers carry reasonably large product lines, perhaps as many as 4000 products, under one roof. Some of these products are strong sellers, which are good-quality items that are competitively priced. Other products are not so good, nor are they as inexpensive as comparable items a competing supplier carries. As a result, although the one-stop supplier makes a minimum profit on some items, he or she typically makes up for it somewhere else, much the same as the foodservice menu that carries several items, all with varying profit potentials. The idea of shopping around is to get the minimum-profit items from each supplier, and to do this without spending more money, time, and effort than might be saved in AP prices.

No supplier can really provide complete one-stop service, just as no one supplier can carry every item an operation needs. But some suppliers can and do carry much of what an operation needs. The fact that most suppliers cannot provide a broad range of products severely limits the one-stop shopper's pool of potential suppliers. If, for example, a buyer wants to use bid buying for most products, and solicits bids from suppliers with the stipulation that the bidders must be prepared to provide all of the items the buyer includes on the bid, it is likely that only one supplier will be able to meet this requirement.

One-stop shopping may be more valuable for small operators. Although some AP prices may run a bit higher, chances are that the eventual costs of items used in production will be optimal. The AP price at the back door may be higher, but if the planned EP cost holds up with the additional time the buyer can now spend in supervision and guest service, the eventual costs of products sold may be quite acceptable.

Stockless Purchasing

When a buyer purchases a large amount of product—for example, a three-month supply—and takes delivery of the entire shipment, the procedure is usually referred to as "forward buying."[3]

When the buyer purchases a large amount of product, but arranges for the supplier to store it and deliver a little at a time, as needed, the procedure is called "stockless purchasing." For instance, a buyer might foresee an impending shortage of a 2000 vintage Bordeaux wine and, in order to offer this wine to his or her customers as long as possible, he or she might buy all the distributor has. Since the storage area might be limited, the buyer asks that the wine distributor store the wine and deliver a bit at a time.

A buyer may also use stockless purchasing when he or she suspects that the AP prices for some items are about to increase drastically.

Buyers often use this procedure when purchasing such products as ashtrays, dinnerware, and flower vases, especially when the hospitality operation wants a particular logo on these items. A large purchase of personalized items usually results in a lower AP price per unit. But the buyer may not be able to take advantage of this tradition if he or she has no place to store the items, unless, that is, the supplier will provide that storage as a supplier service.

Cash and Carry

The cash-and-carry procedure, which is sometimes referred to as "will-call purchasing," appears to be a marginal practice in the hospitality industry because most buyers rely heavily on supplier services (especially delivery services) and are unwilling, or unable, to sacrifice them even though it may result in price concessions.[4] Some buyers, however, like this idea if it means a considerably lower AP price in exchange for providing their own delivery.

Some hospitality buyers are very dependent on the cash-and-carry option. For instance, off-premises caterers cannot always plan their purchases as carefully as local restaurateurs who enjoy more predictable business cycles. Small independent operators may not qualify for delivery or volume discounts.[5] Cash and carry, then, is very important to these buyers.

Some suppliers resist cash and carry mainly because they have already invested heavily in the delivery function. Some do not want to deal with small buyers because of the inherent inefficiencies. Some suppliers, though, have set up one or more cash-and-carry locations, which are sometimes referred to as "wholesale clubs" or "warehouse wholesale clubs," to service small accounts. In fact, a few suppliers have aggressively pursued this type of business, seeking small accounts as well as the large corporate and institutional buyers.[6]

Standing Orders

A standing order is an order placed with a supplier who regularly delivers just enough to bring the buyer's stock level up to par. A driver with a fully stocked truck shows up, takes inventory of what the buyer has, drops off enough merchandise to bring the buyer up to par, writes up an invoice, and leaves it with the bookkeeper. (The delivery drivers in this type of situation are usually referred to as "route salespersons.")

Buyers like to use standing orders for items that have a standard usage pattern, such as milk and bread. Also, buyers sometimes like the convenience that standing orders provide. Buyers appreciate this method of purchasing even though some purchasing professionals suggest avoiding it because the procedure contradicts the basic principles of security and cost control.

With some products, such as ice cream, standing orders are traditional. But when such orders are not traditional, buyers will probably be unable to obtain this concession from suppliers, since most of them want some sort of minimum order before they schedule a delivery. They prefer a more precise order to justify sending a delivery truck.

Use of Technology

Ordering that takes place when the buyer's computer communicates with the supplier's computer has been used for almost two decades. Some suppliers still offer complimentary software and hardware to their large customers that can be used to electronically transmit orders to the suppliers' distribution centers. This technology usually includes additional software packages that buyers can use to manage inventories, price menus, and calculate food costs.[7]

However, as discussed in Chapters 1 and 2, this system of selection and procurement is rapidly changing. Many suppliers are now moving toward the use of e-marketplaces to sell their products rather than relying upon expensive configurations that require buyers to install proprietary software on their computers. One of the main causes of this change is that buyers are migrating away from online one-stop shopping and using e-marketplaces as a method to "shop around." A side benefit of e-marketplaces is that they do not require user-installed software. Rather, e-enablers that develop these e-marketplaces act as Application Service Providers (ASPs) and permit users to download any needed software directly into their Web browser.

Not all suppliers participate in e-marketplaces, and some do not offer any type of computer-based communication solution. However, most suppliers who wish to continue to be competitive are considering some form of e-procurement.

Other forms of computerization are on the increase. For example, many suppliers have armed their salespersons with laptop computers equipped with cellular communication capabilities with which to communicate a buyer's order directly to the supply house computer. This hastens the order procedure by shortening the lead time, verifying product availability, eliminating inaccuracies, and providing an additional supplier service to the buyer.

Co-op Purchasing

Recall that co-op purchasing is the banding together of several small operators in order to consolidate their buying power. A lower AP price is the major advantage. Few suppliers argue with the co-op concept. Many participate in this procedure as long as no glaring inefficiencies or inconveniences result—that is, as long as the supplier makes one delivery to one location and receives one bill payment, he or she is willing to cooperate.

The major disadvantage of co-op purchasing is the cost of developing and operating the co-op. Someone must coordinate all of the members' needs and take on the challenge of supplier selection, negotiations, and so forth. A buyer also should realize that co-op purchasing may limit an individual member's influence in supplier selection. Each member surrenders a bit of flexibility as he or she goes along with the rest.

Co-op purchasing has recently enjoyed renewed popularity, primarily because it is seen as an effective way to reduce product costs.[8] In the past, when the co-op members had to do all the work, fewer buyers were interested in this type of buying plan. But, lately, several "buying services"—which are sometimes referred to as "buying clubs," "contract houses," or "aggregate purchasing companies"—have emerged to streamline the process and make it more efficient.[9]

Recall from Chapter 1 that many of these buying services have migrated to the Web. It is no longer necessary to join a local co-op and be confined to procuring food from a limited list—one from which a neighboring competitor might be selecting as well. Instead, these international online services enable the buyer to select and procure products from a variety of suppliers, products that, many times, are delivered directly from the supplier. In essence, these buying services merely contractually negotiate prices for their members.

A buying service is a private company that buyers can join. For a fee, buyers can take advantage of the service's purchasing power, as well as other subtle benefits, such as the service's willingness to share many profitable ideas with its members. In effect, the buying service is an easy way for small, independent operators to "hire" a highly skilled, professional purchasing executive.[10]

Each buyer or owner-manager has to make his or her own decision concerning the potential costs and benefits of co-op buying. The practice is, however, worth careful investigation. In some instances, it can be a very profitable option.

Local Merchant-Wholesaler or National Source?

A small operator normally deals with local suppliers. But larger operators sometimes bypass these middlemen and go directly to the primary source; this is especially common with equipment purchases. Large hospitality operations normally require national distribution, so that all of the units in the chain organization can use the same type of products. As a result, they usually seek out the large suppliers who can provide this alternative.

Operations must address the question of providing their own economic values, especially transportation and risk, before they make a decision. And, as we have already pointed out, several advantages and disadvantages must be weighed here.

On a dollars-and-cents basis, small operations find it economical to purchase from local suppliers. Chains and other larger operations might, however, save money buying directly from the primary source. But they must consider the possible enmity engendered among the local suppliers. Disgruntled locals are, perhaps, the biggest, though not an immediately apparent, disadvantage associated with centralized buying and direct purchases. A buyer can expect little sympathy from bypassed local suppliers if he or she needs an emergency order or service on a piece of equipment.

A compromise is possible. For instance, a vice president of purchasing might go directly to the source and negotiate a long-term contract, for, perhaps, six months. Then he or she might "hire" local suppliers to take delivery from the sources and distribute the items to the local unit operations. Parceling out these end-user services is usually an acceptable and profitable compromise for all parties involved in the transaction.

Delivery Schedule

All hospitality operations have preferences regarding the time(s) of day and the day(s) of the week when they accept delivery from their suppliers. For instance, if buyers had their druthers, most of them would demand morning delivery.

Realistically, hospitality operations often must make do with what is available to them. However, this does not mean that they cannot swing their purchase dollars toward the supplier(s) who most closely matches their desired delivery schedule. This is a valued supplier service, and, although buyers often must expect to pay a little more for a preferred delivery routine, the overall effect may prove profitable for both the hospitality operation and the supplier.

Ordering Procedure Required by Supplier

As with the delivery schedule, buyers will be partial to those suppliers who most closely meet their needs. Suppliers who offer very convenient ordering procedures will most likely have a valuable competitive edge in the marketplace.

Credit Terms

Buyers are interested in the credit terms that are available from the various suppliers with whom they might consider conducting business. It is important to note such factors as the availability of cash discounts, quantity discounts, volume discounts, cash rebates, and promotional discounts; when payments are due (i.e., the credit period); the billing procedures; the amount of interest charges buyers may have to pay on the outstanding balance; and the overall installment payment procedure available, if any.

A preferred buying plan often will be bent to accommodate superior credit terms. That is, many hospitality operators are quite enamored with credit terms and will do what is necessary, within reason, to deal with suppliers who offer generous credit terms. This criterion conceivably could be the major consideration in supplier selection.

Minimum Order Requirement

Before a supplier will agree to provide buyers with "free delivery," they must, normally, order a certain minimum amount of merchandise. This is true even when they want to pick up the merchandise on a will-call basis, although the minimum order requirement usually is much lower in this situation.

Most buyers have little trouble in meeting minimum order requirements, so it is unlikely that such a criterion would be a concern. But a small operator might be very concerned with these stipulations; in this case, this aspect becomes an important supplier selection standard.

Variety of Merchandise

This concept is related to the one-stop shopping opportunity discussed earlier. In general, a supplier may or may not have the one-stop shopping capability, but he or she can, at least, offer a reasonable range of options. The supplier may offer a variety of quality grades, brand names, and/or packers' brand names for the merchandise he or she carries.

If a supplier specializes, for example, in fresh produce, he or she could offer tremendous variation even within such a relatively narrow product line. A supplier who can offer buyers a variety of qualities of fresh produce may conceivably be more valuable than a one-stop supplier who carries only one quality level of fresh produce along with several other product lines.

Lead Time

The shorter the lead time, the more convenient it is for a buyer, since he or she can wait until the last possible moment before entering an order for delivery at a predetermined time. All other things being equal, buyers would probably want to deal with a purveyor who offers them the ability to call tonight for an order to be delivered tomorrow morning, rather than a supplier who requires two or three days' notice.

Free Samples

Suppliers will often give buyers one or two free samples for their evaluation, particularly if the buyers represent a potentially large amount of business. However, some suppliers may not want to do this. Also, some buyers may not feel comfortable accepting free samples because it could compromise them.

Returns Policy

This is a very sensitive issue, and buyers should evaluate it well before it ever becomes necessary to return merchandise and/or refuse to pay for goods or services. Needless to say, the more liberal the returns policy, the more buyers expect to pay in the long run.

A related issue is the return of prepayment for merchandise that buyers ordered but for some reason must refuse its delivery. For instance, it often is necessary for buyers to put up a significant deposit for equipment purchases. If they then decide that they do not want or need the item, what happens to their deposit? It would be prudent for buyers to iron out any potential problems early.

Reciprocal Buying

One day, buyers may want to initiate a reciprocal buying arrangement, that is, an arrangement whereby "you buy from me, and I'll buy from you." If so, they should inquire as early as possible about the suppliers' willingness to do this.

A related concept is the notion of doing business only with those who do business with you, or who send other business your way. In our experience, if you allow yourself to get entangled in a web such as this, replete with so many interlocking obligations, one little slip can cause the whole house of cards to tumble.

Willingness to Barter

As trading becomes more popular, buyers might decide to adopt it as part of their overall buying plan. If so, they must test the suppliers' desires to accommodate this request.

Cooperation in Bid Procedures

Most suppliers realize that a buyer will want to shop around, at least occasionally. In addition, most of them will respond to a buyer's request for bids and other related information. However, some suppliers are not particularly eager to spend this time or are so secretive about their price quotations that it becomes a burden for a buyer to deal with them. These suppliers probably will not make a buyer's approved-supplier list if he or she is a bid buyer.

Size of Firm

If a buyer has a large amount of business, he or she must be assured that suppliers are large enough to accommodate the buyer. On the other hand, large suppliers may be more impersonal. Perhaps the buyer would prefer dealing with small firms, allowing him or her to talk to the owners regularly. If nothing else, dealing directly with owners generally makes a buyer feel that his or her concerns will be met consistently.

A related issue is the amount of time suppliers have been in business. Some buyers will consider suppliers only after they have established acceptable performance track records that indicate they can handle buyers' needs and will most likely be around for a while.

Number of Back Orders

It seems to us that a supplier who has a history of excessive back orders will not be part of a buyer's approved-supplier list. A buyer can probably forgive a back order once in a while. But if this is a recurring problem, he or she cannot do business with such a purveyor. The buyer will want to do business with suppliers who have very high "fill rates." A fill rate is a ratio calculated by dividing the number of items delivered by the number ordered. Ideally, it would always equal 100 percent.

Substitution Capability

On occasions when back orders cannot be avoided, it is nice if the supplier can provide a comparable substitute. Generally, though, only suppliers who offer a one-stop shopping opportunity are capable of doing this.

A related possibility is the supplier who runs out of an item but who would be concerned enough about buyers personally to secure the products necessary to complete their order from another supplier or from one of his or her competitors. This type of purveyor is rare, but one or two of them may be in your area.

Buyout Policy

We can recall years ago when suppliers who wanted a buyer's business would agree to purchase his or her existing stock of competitors' merchandise. For instance, if a soap salesperson was soliciting a buyer's business, he or she might agree to buy out the existing stock so that the buyer could begin immediately to use the new merchandise. This is an uncommon policy today, but it may exist somewhere. If it does exist in your area, it represents one more criterion on which to judge a potential supplier.

A related issue is the willingness of a supplier to buy back outdated or obsolete merchandise. For example, when buyers purchase replacement equipment, a major supplier selection factor would be the trade-in allowance that competing suppliers offer. All other things being equal, the supplier who has the most favorable policy is apt to have an edge over his or her competitors.

Suppliers' Facilities

Buyers should be particularly concerned with a potential supplier's storage and handling facilities, the delivery facilities, and the facilities' sanitation. For instance, if the supplier uses old, dirty, and uncooled vans to deliver fresh produce, you may want to avoid that purveyor regardless of the AP price and other supplier services provided. Inadequate facilities harm product quality, and this is intolerable. As the industry moves more and more toward e-procurement, it will become increasingly more difficult to evaluate this supplier selection criterion.

Outside (Independent) Delivery Service

Shopping on the Internet may yield several suppliers who do not provide delivery service personally, but who outsource it to an independent service, such as UPS or FedEx. Buyers should be leery about e-suppliers who use no-name delivery services that have no verifiable track record. Delivery inconsistencies will wipe out any good deals that buyers obtain by shopping around. Furthermore, independent drivers, even from major delivery services, are unable to rectify mistakes on the spot.

Long-Term Contracts

Some suppliers are unwilling or unable to enter into long-term contracts for AP price and/or for availability of the product during the contract period. If buyers prefer some type of long-term commitment, they may have to settle for a relatively short approved-supplier list.

Case Price

When buyers purchase a case of merchandise, such as a six-can case of tomatoes, they will pay a certain price for it, say, $12.00. If buyers wish to purchase one can of tomatoes and can purchase it for $2.00, they are receiving what is normally referred to as the "case price" for that can.

Few, if any, suppliers will give a buyer a case price when he or she purchases less than a case. If he or she is lucky, suppliers will "bust" a case for a buyer, but they will usually charge a premium to do this. Typically, either the buyer purchases the whole case or does business elsewhere.

When a buyer purchases some items in small batches, it is important to deal with suppliers who understand his or her needs. In some situations, a buyer cannot afford to purchase a whole case of, for example, soup bases if he or she expects the contents to sit around for a period of time losing flavor and otherwise deteriorating. This buyer will need to look for those suppliers who can and will accommodate him or her. In many cases, he or she may have to settle for warehouse-club suppliers.

Bonded Suppliers

A buyer is concerned about the capability of suppliers to cover the cost of any damage they might inflict on his or her property. Usually, before the appropriate government authority will issue a business license to a supplier, that supplier must display adequate insurance coverage; that is, they must be bonded. However, what is adequate for the licensing bureau may not be adequate for the buyer.

A related issue is the fact that buyers may inadvertently be dealing with an unlicensed supplier. This situation should be avoided because, if, say, a customer gets ill from products this supplier provided, the buyer's organization could become entangled in all sorts of litigation.

Consulting Service Provided

To a great extent, salespersons, and suppliers in general, are the primary sources of product, and related, information for the typical hospitality operator. Buyers are interested in data concerning product specifications, preparation and handling procedures, nutrition, merchandising techniques, and other similar types of advice.[11]

Small hospitality operators are especially loyal to suppliers and salespersons who willingly share their expertise. For example, a small caterer who is bidding for an unusually large banquet contract will appreciate the salesperson who takes the time to help prepare the proposal.

Formal consulting, though, is not something that every purveyor is able or willing to provide. For instance, when purchasing equipment, buyers may find that some dealers stock it, sell it, and deliver it—period. Other dealers provide some additional advice, such as providing blueprints or seeking the appropriate building permits. Buyers pay more for this type of service, but they may be willing to do so. When this is the case, buyers must seek suppliers who can provide for their needs.

Deposits Required

For some products, buyers may need to put up a deposit. For example, if they purchase soda pop syrup in reusable containers, they may need to put up a cash deposit for them. Usually, deposit requirements are not burdensome, but if they are, buyers probably will want to eliminate such a demanding supplier from their approved supplier list.

Willingness to Sell Storage

Some suppliers will sell storage, which can be a tremendous service if, for example, a buyer needs space to house a large amount of merchandise that he or she purchased through a favorable opportunity buy. A supplier's storage space is usually better than one rented from a generic warehouse or storage locker location because it is apt to be appropriately cooled and/or heated for items the typical hospitality buyer purchases.

A supplier who will sell storage probably is a rare find, but if buyers are fortunate enough to have one in their area, they must be certain to inquire not only about the fees for this service, but also about any other sort of requirements. For instance, to qualify to purchase storage, buyers may need to purchase $1000 worth of merchandise per week. This may or may not be attractive to them, however, and they should be alert to these kinds of restrictions, which could place them in an unprofitable position.

Suppliers Who Own Hospitality Operations

Some hospitality operations own commissaries and/or central distribution centers that sell merchandise to other hospitality companies. For instance, many quick-service restaurants purchase Pepsi-Cola products. In the past (prior to the sale of its foodservice division to Tricon Global Restaurants, Inc., and subsequent renaming of the company to YUM! Brands [www.yum.com]), PepsiCo competed directly with restaurants through company-owned and franchised Pizza Huts, Taco Bells, and KFC outlets. In a similar situation, General Mills, whose foodservice brands include Gold Medal Baking Mixes, Betty Crocker Potato Buds, Cheerios, and Yoplait, also owned restaurants such as Red Lobster and Olive Garden. However, General Mills spun off its restaurant division to Darden Restaurants, Inc., in 1995. The main issue, of course, is: Could such a purchasing strategy be beneficial for the buyer?

At first glance, it would seem foolish to buy from a competitor. Buyers would think that the competitor would learn too much about their business. Furthermore, would the competitor favor his or her hospitality units at the buyers' expense?[12]

On the other hand, some people feel that buying from another hospitality operator has its advantages. For example, the competitor understands the business much better than a conventional supplier and is much more conscious of the required supplier services.

Socially Responsible Suppliers

Some buyers prefer to work with suppliers who promote socially responsible agendas. For instance, some buyers will not purchase from suppliers that sell products manufactured by employees in foreign countries who do not receive a basic level of wages and/or benefits.[13] Alternately, some buyers will not purchase from suppliers carrying products whose processing damages the earth's rain forests. Also, some buyers prefer to purchase from suppliers who employ minorities and deal with minority-owned subcontractors.[14]

Buyers can use subscription services to search for socially responsible firms. For example, for an annual fee, buyers can subscribe to referral services, such as Thomas Publishing Company (www.thomaspublishing.com), that list suppliers that are owned by minorities and/or women. Suppliers are typically listed by product category, and, with little more effort than picking up a Touch-Tone™ phone or visiting the referral service's Website, buyers can quickly secure the information they need.[15]

References

Usually, a large part of a buyer's supplier selection work is devoted to obtaining personal references. This is normally an informal process, whereby the buyer talks with friends in the industry who may be able to provide meaningful input about certain suppliers. The buyer might also consider contacting credit-rating firms to uncover a potential supplier's financial strength. Generally, though, if a friend whose opinion the buyer trusts has had a good experience with a particular supplier, the buyer would want to do business with that firm.

It would appear that the buyer is most anxious about a potential supplier's integrity and overall dependability. These are the characteristics the buyer tries to uncover when conversing with friends. These factors can mean many things to many persons, but if a friend is impressed with a supplier's dependability and integrity, the buyer will probably want that supplier on his or her approved-supplier list.

MOST IMPORTANT SUPPLIER SELECTION CRITERIA

No one can dictate the criteria that buyers should consider when selecting their suppliers. This is something that only buyers can judge for themselves. It is interesting, though, to note those criteria that are most important to members of the hospitality industry.

Generally, most buyers are interested primarily in product quality. Suppliers must be able to consistently provide the quality needed, or else buyers cannot deal with them.

Supplier service is, usually, a close second to product quality. Dependability is critical. Suppliers must ensure that buyers receive what they need when they need it.

The AP price seems to trail quality and supplier services in most buyer surveys. While this does not necessarily imply that buyers are unconcerned with product costs, it does emphasize the point that AP prices do not unduly influence purchase decisions in the hospitality industry.

Typical hospitality buyers seem to follow the supplier selection process that Walt Disney World food services adopted. When selecting its suppliers, Disney is concerned with product quality, supplier service, whether the purveyor is large enough to handle the account, and AP price.[16]

Regardless of the number and type of supplier selection criteria the hospitality operation employs, the common thread running through them is one of consistency, dependability, loyalty, and trust.[17] If suppliers can render consistent value, chances are they will be on the approved-supplier list of several hospitality operations. Furthermore, suppliers who consistently provide acceptable value will continue to grow and prosper.

MAKE A CHOICE

As buyers gradually complete their basic buying plan, they simultaneously reduce the potential supplier pool. Eventually, common sense and company policy guide them toward the optimal suppliers. Buyers do not want too many restrictions placed on their basic buying plan. On the other hand, they do not necessarily want to ignore all of the suppliers' needs. Buyers must strike a balance, within reason, so that both they and the seller feel confident that profit will result from the relationship. The best relationship is one in which both the buyer and the seller are satisfied.

SUPPLIER–BUYER RELATIONS

The buyer's principal contact with suppliers is through salespersons. In the initial stages of supplier selection, the buyer may meet an officer of a supply house. But after this meeting, a supply house officer almost never usurps the salesperson's role. The top management of a supply house is never out of the picture, although it may be out of sight. Those officials work hard to improve business; some of their major activities include those discussed next.

Supply House Officers Set the Tone of Their Business

Usually, supply house officers set this tone by establishing the quality standards of the items they carry, by determining the types of economic values and supplier services they provide, and by planning their advertising and promotion campaigns. While considering these aspects of the business, moreover, suppliers seek a balance between what they want to do and what their customers, the hospitality operations' buyers, need.

Supply House Officers Set the Overall Sales Strategies

Two basic sales strategies exist: (1) the "push strategy," in which suppliers urge their salespersons to do whatever is necessary to entice the buyer to purchase the product—the normal push is AP price discounts of one type or another, and (2) the "pull strategy," in which suppliers influence those who use the items the buyer purchases. For example, suppliers may advertise heavily on television, exhorting ultimate customers to demand the suppliers' product in their favorite restaurant. If they do, the restaurant buyer has little choice but to purchase the product. In other words, the ultimate customer "pulls" the product through the channel. Alternately, if backdoor selling can be implemented successfully, a user in the company "pulls" the product through by influencing the buyer's purchasing decisions (see Figure 12.2).

You have undoubtedly seen many types of pull strategies. If, for example, a restaurant customer orders a Coke®, which is a brand name, what choice does the buyer have? This also applies to catsup or hot sauce on the tables. Restaurant patrons typically prefer Heinz® and Tabasco® brands.

Of course, various shades and combinations of these two basic strategies exist, but, generally speaking, suppliers lean toward one, or, at least, they lean toward one for some items and toward the other for their remaining items.

The pull strategy can be risky and extremely costly for suppliers to implement and maintain. But if it works, the rewards are fruitful indeed.

The pull strategy also is a major weapon suppliers use to steal business from one another.

Another satisfied customer.

Let's be frank. She ordered that dish for one reason: the Sugar Snap Peas just made it sound so good. Then she experienced their crisp-tender texture and fresh, sweet flavor. And pretty soon, she was smiling. And so were you. Because premium Classic IQF Sugar Snap Peas from Simplot makes staying in step with the trends... well, a snap! And that's what we call satisfaction guaranteed.

Simplot
We're on your side.®

FOR FREE RECIPES AND MORE SNAP-PEA IDEAS: **1-800-572-7783** *OR WWW.SIMPLOTFOODS.COM*

FOR FURTHER INFORMATION CIRCLE 56 ON READER SERVICE CARD.

FIGURE 12.2 The pull strategy. Courtesy of J. R. Simplot and Company.

Supply House Officers Sponsor a Great Deal of Product and Market Research

Suppliers also spend considerable time and effort evaluating the bids they make for buyers' business. Furthermore, they continually prepare and revise files that contain information about current and potential customers. These information files are sometimes referred to as "buyer fact sheets" or "buyer profiles." They constitute a selling tool and contain as much or as little information as thought necessary to facilitate the sales effort.

The following pieces of information are usually found in these files:

1. Does the buyer have a favorable impression of the supplier's reputation? Generally speaking, a favorable impression makes it easier for a salesperson to get his or her foot in the door on the first sales visit.

2. What are the major characteristics of the ultimate customers of the buyer's company? If, for example, the ultimate consumers are price conscious, the buyer will probably adopt a similar posture.

3. Is the buyer concerned with AP prices?

4. Is the buyer concerned with fast and dependable deliveries?

5. Will the buyer take a chance on new products? Does he or she have the authority to suggest new products to the respective hospitality departments?

6. Does the buyer have a great deal of confidence in his or her purchasing skill, or will second-guessing prevail?

7. Does the buyer have other duties? For example, is he or she a buyer and a user? Will these other duties minimize the time he or she spends with salespersons?

8. Does the buyer insist on rigid quality control, or will he or she accept certain exceptions or substitutions from time to time?

9. What is the possibility of setting up a reciprocal buying arrangement?

10. What is the payment history of the buyer's company?

11. How does the buyer treat suppliers and salespersons?

12. Do any little things irritate the buyer? For example, does he or she get annoyed if a salesperson is a few minutes late for an appointment?

Suppliers Train Their Sales Staffs

Suppliers expend tremendous efforts in sales training, for both new salespersons and, continually, for salespersons currently on staff. Quite often, the training materials are based on market research, new products, and buyer profiles.

Suppliers Keep Their Salespersons' Promises

Suppliers must, for example, make sure that orders are handled properly and delivered on time.

SALESPERSON–BUYER RELATIONS

Salespersons, who are sometimes referred to as "distributor sales representatives" (DSRs), are buyers' main contact with supplier firms. Buyers must usually meet several DSRs every week. Many of them are familiar faces; others are new. Establishing firm and fair business relations with DSRs, and particularly setting the ground rules regarding sales visits, is essential to efficient procurement.

Buyers need to be aware of the sales tactics salespersons use. Generally, on the first sales call, salespersons might: (1) make some attempt, however slight, at backdoor selling (i.e., they might try to interest users in the supplier's wares), (2) attempt to use free samples and literature in an effort to interest and possibly to obligate a buyer, (3) try to establish a justification for their presence, (4) try to talk buyers away from the current supplier, or (5) try to be invited to return, thereby starting a nominal business relationship.

Sales professionals are usually adept at practicing what is usually referred to as "relationship marketing."[18] Salespersons after a buyer's business will bend over backward to start some type, any type, of business relationship. They will usually take any order, no matter how small, so that future sales visits are justified. Even if the buyer purchases only one item once, the salesperson still feels, as "one of your suppliers," free to drop in periodically. It may seem ludicrous that salespersons would hang around once a buyer makes it clear that he or she probably will not buy from them again. Also, you would think that supply house officers would prohibit salespersons from taking small orders. But buyers may not always respond the same way. The next buyer, or manager, may be more receptive. Today, it may be a small order; tomorrow, who knows? Hence, salespersons continue their efforts.

Small operators enamored of one-stop shopping like to avoid excessive contacts with salespersons and to minimize their ordering procedures. These preferences turn them into house accounts. House accounts are regular, steady customers for whom suppliers are not always motivated to provide generous supplier services. However, they may continue to provide exceptional supplier services in order to keep these customers happy.

This is a touchy issue. Dealing with many salespersons is time-consuming. But never seeing them at all is poor local public relations, shuts off good sources of information, and prevents them from helping buyers check inventories, production techniques, and any equipment they may have loaned for use with their products. Good trade relations might dictate that buyers spread their orders out a bit more. But this, too, can be costly. Each operation must, therefore, balance the potential ill will with this loss of time and make its decision in the light of such factors as order size and management availability, as well as public relations.

A full-time buyer for a large operation, though, is expected to spend a good deal of time with salespersons. The company pays the buyer to minimize the AP prices. In these large organizations, other people are responsible for the steps the product follows from purchase to use. Someone watches for pilferage, shrinkage, and spoilage in storage. Another individual is responsible for using cooking or other production techniques that prevent waste and shrinkage. Someone else is responsible for minimizing overportioning of finished product. How these responsibilities are distributed is not relevant to the present point. Our point is that, in a large operation, the achievement of a good EP cost results not only from a good AP price, but also from the proper working of a complex, skilled organization.

Several volumes have been written on sales tactics, strategies, and procedures. Buyers would be wise to read some of these materials, paying particular attention to such topics as: (1) personal characteristics of good salespersons, (2) types of salespersons, (3) what to avoid when dealing with salespersons, (4) what to do when dealing with salespersons, (5) types of sales tactics, and (6) techniques for evaluating salespersons.

We do not want to suggest that an adversarial relationship necessarily exists between buyers and salespersons. But buyers must expect salespersons to go to whatever ethical lengths they can to make sales. Salespersons come to sell, not to entertain. They want to meet your expectations, but for a price.

Good salespersons will never sell a buyer something he or she does not need. But keep in mind that the main objective is to convert the buyer into a regular customer, not by pressuring the buyer, but by providing satisfaction. Within reason, then, salespersons do what is necessary to turn a buyer into a house account.

An alert buyer should be able to compete in the game of sales strategy and tactics. Objectivity helps a buyer, as does an understanding supervisor. In most cases, the buyer and salesperson work together for each other's benefit. Remember, though, business being business, a buyer should never become too friendly with a sales representative.

EVALUATING SUPPLIERS AND SALESPERSONS

Suppliers and salespersons sometimes become such integral parts of a business that a buyer starts treating them as he or she would an employee. For this reason, a buyer should periodically evaluate the suppliers' and salespersons' performance and consider disciplining or rewarding them as necessary. The ultimate discipline is to switch to another source of supply. The ultimate reward is to become a house account. (This may be no reward for salespersons, though. Some supply houses pay no sales commissions on house account sales; the theory is that little effort has gone into making the sales. These salespersons may, however, receive a bonus when they obtain a house account for their firm.) Obviously, there is a considerable range between these extremes and several discipline-reward combinations.

Most analysts agree that an operator should rate suppliers and their salespersons as part of the discipline-reward cycle. However, few analysts agree on the criteria to use in these evaluations. For instance, some buyers are appreciative of the salespersons who take the time to listen to what the buyers have to say. Other buyers seek only those salespersons who can answer the buyers' questions completely and correctly. Still other buyers are more enamored with effective and impressive sales presentations.

In any case, once again the common thread running throughout is consistency: consistent quality, consistent supplier services, and so forth. If suppliers and salespersons consistently fulfill their part of the bargain, whether it was made yesterday or last year, buyers should have no complaint. Our suggestion, then, is for buyers to enumerate those factors on which they and the suppliers and salespersons agree and, from time to time, to use a consistency yardstick to measure performance. While buyers look for consistency, though, they must remember that a high AP price often accompanies high levels of consistency, especially consistent supplier services.

If buyers expect suppliers and salespersons to be consistent, they themselves must be consistent. That is, they should never change their evaluation criteria unilaterally. Professional buyers generally try to be consistent, but users who also buy, in contrast to professional buyers, tend to be more subjective about the items they purchase, as well as more abusive toward suppliers and salespersons. User-buyers, therefore, should be especially leery of finding these traits in themselves.

In the final analysis, evaluation is probably a combination of art and science. Having evaluated consistency, buyers could examine other subjective factors. But buyers should resist being too hasty in this process. It is true that, unless buyers have a long-term contract, they can drop their supplier quite abruptly. But this may do more harm than good. If a supplier is deficient, buyers should give him or her a chance to improve, just as they would give a poor-performing employee a chance to improve. Buyers should never "fire" the supplier or salesperson without allowing a second chance. If buyers acquire a reputation for rash decisions, other suppliers or salespersons may become gun-shy, especially those who consider themselves fair and reputable performers. Buyers do not want to be left with only the poorest supply choices.

A step short of cutting a supplier off completely, a step that is often used, is to cut him or her off for a week or so, just to make certain that this supplier realizes that he or she can lose the buyer's business. This discipline supposedly helps keep suppliers in line. Buyers want to be certain, though, that the supplier really did something to deserve this treatment and that the problem is not in their operation rather than the supplier's.

GETTING COMFORTABLE

Supplier selection is not something to be done once and then forgotten. But small operators often seem to think it is, even when competing suppliers and salespersons bombard them with sales pitches.

Salespersons will fight to prevent a buyer from settling in with one or two suppliers unless they are among those he or she has selected. They do not want the buyer to enter into the "comfort stage" of the supplier selection procedure. Their sales efforts will, in fact, become increasingly insistent. On the other hand, a buyer's current suppliers and salespersons will see to it that he or she is satisfied in order to discourage the advances of other suppliers and salespersons. Of course, the buyer's current sources may get comfortable themselves and need to be brought up short now and then.

Many buyers and user-buyers become comfortable with a salesperson, but at least they remain aware of the need to examine alternate suppliers and to make a switch if necessary. However, flitting continually from one supplier to another involves a certain amount of emotional strain, broken loyalties, and disrupted business patterns. The switching becomes particularly difficult when a buyer's favorite salesperson goes to work for another supplier and the buyer wants to continue doing business with him or her. In effect, the buyer allows this salesperson to carry the buyer's business to his or her new employer.

Generally, a supplier who takes good care of buyers' needs deserves some type of reward. Suppliers and salespersons are, indeed, just like partners, or employees. Good employees are rewarded with continuous employment, and a salary raise or a bonus. Suppliers and salespersons should be treated with equal consideration. We are not sure whether it is always a good idea to become a house account, but we do believe that, at the very least, good current suppliers and salespersons deserve first crack at a buyer's business, now and in the future. A restaurant manager once expressed this sentiment precisely when he remarked:

> We don't believe in getting locked into one supplier, because it would make us too vulnerable. But, on the other hand, we don't switch suppliers just to gain a few cents. We try to find suppliers who appreciate our dedication to quality and then stay with them. That doesn't mean we don't check the market every Monday and maintain a continuing check on prices. But we believe in commitment—on both sides.[19]

KEY WORDS AND CONCEPTS

Approved supplier	Consulting service	House account
Approved-supplier list	Contract house	Ineligible bidder
As-purchased price (AP)	Co-op purchasing	Lead time
Back order	Cost-plus purchasing	Long-term contract
Barter	Credit period	Market quote buying
Bid-buying procedures	Credit terms	Market research
Bonded supplier	Daily bid	Minimum order requirement
Bust a case	Daily quotation buying	National distribution
Buyer fact sheets	Delivery schedule	One-stop shopping
Buyer profiles	Deposits	Open-market buying
Buying clubs	Distributor sales representative (DSR)	Ordering cost
Buying plans		Ordering procedures
Buying services	End-user services	Par stock
Buyout policy	Evaluating suppliers and salespersons	Potential supplier
Call sheet buying		Prime-vendor procurement
Case price	Fill rate	Product substitution
Cash and carry	Firing a supplier	Profit markup
Cash discount	Fixed bid	Promotional discount
Cash rebate	Forward buying	Pull sales strategy
Consistency	Free samples	Push sales strategy

Quantity discount	Size of a supplier firm	Suppliers who own hospitality operations
Reciprocal buying	Socially responsible supplier	
Relationship marketing	Sole-source procurement	Trade show
Request for bid	Standing order	Trade-in allowance
Responsible bidder	Stockless purchasing	Value analysis
Returns policy	Supplier facilities	Volume discount
Route salesperson	Supplier references	
Salesperson-buyer relations	Supplier selection criteria	Warehouse wholesale club
Sealed bid	Supplier services	Wholesale club
Single-source procurement	Supplier-buyer relations	Will-call purchasing

REFERENCES

1. Michael Guiffrida, "Saying What You Mean on Bids," *FoodService Director*, May 15, 1990, p. 78. See also: Patt Patterson, "Bid Buying Saves Time and Cuts Food Costs for Red's Seafood," *Nation's Restaurant News*, October 28, 1991, p. 58; Foster Frable, Jr., "Strange Business: How Kitchen Equipment Is Sold," *Nation's Restaurant News*, September 1994, pp. 183–185.

2. Patt Patterson, "Effective Purchasing in Recessionary Times," *Nation's Restaurant News*, February 4, 1991, p. 48. See also: Annie Stephenson, "Shopping Habits," *Hospitality*, April/May 1995, p. 20; Mack Tilling, "One-Stop Shopping," *Restaurant Hospitality*, June 1999, pp. 84–86; Lisa Bannon, "CTF Hotel's Suit Queries Purpose Behind Avendra," *Wall Street Journal*, May 23, 2002, p. D.8.

3. Patt Patterson, "Now May Be the Time for Distributors to Buy Ahead," *Nation's Restaurant News*, February 17, 1992, p. 24. See also: Rajiv Lal, John D. Little, and J. Miguel Villas Boas, "A Theory of Forward Buying, Merchandising, and Trade Deals," *Marketing Science*, 1996, 15(1), p. 21; Terence A. Brown and David M. Bukovinsky, "ECR and Grocery Retailing: An Exploratory Financial Statement Analysis," *Journal of Business Logistics*, 2001, 22(2), pp. 77–90; Craig A. Hill, "Information Technology and Supply Chain Management: A Study of the Food Industry," *Hospital Material Management Quarterly*, August 2000, 22(1), pp. 53–58.

4. Patt Patterson, "Warehouse Clubs: A Foodservice Supply Source?" *Nation's Restaurant News*, December 14, 1992, p. 49. See also: C. Lazaro, "The Survival of the Fittest," *Caterer and Hotel Keeper*, April 1995, pp. 13–19; Colm O'Gorman, "The Sustainability of Growth in Small- and Medium-Sized Enterprises," *International Journal of Entrepreneurial Behaviour & Research*, 2001, 7(2), p. 60.

5. Patt Patterson, "Back to Warehouse Clubs: Are They Good Supply Sources?" *Nation's Restaurant News*, February 8, 1993, p. 18.

6. Anonymous, "Sam's Club: Back to Business—History: Twenty Years Young and Building for the Future," *DSN Retailing Today*, April 2003, 42(7A), pp. 16–20. See also: Anonymous, "Focus on the Core Customer," *Chain Store Age*, May 2003, 79(5), pp. 52–56; Anonymous, "1982 to 1992: Clubs and Category Killers Arrive on the Scene," *DSN Retailing Today*, August 2002, 41(15), pp. 21–25.

7. Julie Ritzer Ross, "Challenges Abound, But Lack of Standards Slows e-Business Progress," *Na-*

tion's Restaurant News, May 21, 2001, 35(21), p. 28. For examples, see http://www.sysco.com/esysco/esysco.html and https://www.usfood.com/. For historical information, see also Bill Eacho, "Quality Service Through Strategic Foodservice Partnerships: A New Trend," Hosteur, Spring 1993, p. 28. See also: R. Burns, "Food and Beverage: Linking the Electronic Supply Chain," Lodging, November 2000, pp. 8–10.

8. Margaret Sheridan, "Class Clout," Restaurants & Institutions, April 1, 2003, 113(8), pp. 84–90. See also: Peter D. Meltzer, "Bartered Bucks," Food Arts, July/August 1992, p. 42; Timothy L. O'Brien, "Franchises Spearhead Renewed Popularity of Co-ops," The Wall Street Journal, November 29, 1993, p. B2.

9. Patt Patterson, "Purchasing Power: Getting a Little Help from HSG," Nation's Restaurant News, March 16, 1992, p. 46. See also: Patt Patterson, "A New Breed of Co-ops: Team Purchasing Can Work," Nation's Restaurant News, August 30, 1993, p. 20; G. Tyler, "On-line Purchasing," Hotel and Restaurant, November/December 2001, pp. 43–46.

10. Anonymous, "ecFood buys Master Dairies," Dairy Foods; November 2001, 102(11), p. 10. See also: Anonymous, "E-Boz Developments: Niche Players, Requests for Competitive Price Quotes Becoming More Common," Nation's Restaurant News, January 24, 2000, p 51; Anonymous, "Beverage Media Group Launches Online Buying Service," Empire State Foodservice News, January 2002 (Available http://www.theheadtable.com).

11. Peter Matthews, "What Constitutes Excellence in In-Store Supplier Service?" Retail World, November 25–December 6, 2002, 55(23), pp. 38, 45. See also: Phil Roberts, "Looking for a Supplier 'Partner,' Not a Salesman," Nation's Restaurant News, September 9, 1991, p. 30; Phil Roberts, "WholeSELLERS: Putting Wind in Our Sales," Nation's Restaurant News, September 21, 1992, p.

122; Patt Patterson, "Commercial Electric Contest Can Spark Bright Ideas," Nation's Restaurant News, January 11, 1993, p. 18.

12. Ted Richman, "Suppliers' Demands Are Too High a Price to Pay," Nation's Restaurant News, December 19, 1994, p. 21. See also: Martha Brannigan, "Coke Is Victim of Hardball on Soft Drinks," The Wall Street Journal, March 15, 1991, p. B1.

13. G. Pascal Zachary, "Starbucks Asks Foreign Suppliers to Improve Working Conditions," The Wall Street Journal, October 23, 1995, p. B4.

14. James Morgan, "How Well Are Supplier Diversity Programs Doing?" Purchasing, August 15, 2002, 131(13), pp. 29–35. See also: Carolyn Walkup, "MultiCultural Confab Weighs Supplier Diversity as Rising Bottom-Line Issue," Nation's Restaurant News, May 10, 1999, 33(19), p. 46; Dale K. DuPont, "Minority Markets Offer Diverse Opportunities," Hotel and Motel Management, April 5, 1999, 214(6), pp. 30–31.

15. Leon E. Wynter, "Supplying a Minority or Female Supplier," The Wall Street Journal, September 21, 1993, p. B1.

16. Stephen M. Fjellman, Vinyl Leaves: Walt Disney World and America (San Francisco: Westview Press, 1992), p. 390.

17. John R. Farquharson, "And These Doctors Make House Calls!" Nation's Restaurant News, September 21, 1992, p. 116. See also: Michael L. Facciola, "Supply & Dementia," Food Arts, May 1992, p. 113; Rob Johnson, "A Deal of Time and Effort," Supply Management, April 10, 2003, 8(8), pp. 30–31; Vijay R. Kannan and Keah Choon Tan, "Supplier Selection and Assessment: Their Impact on Business Performance," Journal of Supply Chain Management, Fall 2002, 38(4), pp. 11–21; Michael Tracey and Chong Leng Tan, "Empirical Analysis of Supplier Selection and Involvement, Customer Satisfaction, and Firm Performance," Supply Chain Management, 2001, 6(3/4), pp. 174–188.

18. John Bowen, "Don't Imitate, Differentiate," *Nevada Hospitality*, July/August 1996, p. 20. See also: Susanne Frey, Roland Schegg, and Jamie Murphy, "E-Mail Customer Service in the Swiss Hotel Industry," *Tourism and Hospitality Research*, March 2003, 4(3), pp. 197–212; Isabelle Szmigin and Humphrey Bourne, "Consumer Equity in Relationship Marketing," *Journal of Consumer Marketing*, 1998, 15(6), pp. 544–557.

19. Patt Patterson, "Shere Sets High Standards for Coach and Six," *Nation's Restaurant News*, January 13, 1986, p. 4.

QUESTIONS AND PROBLEMS

1. What major problems are associated with the initial-survey stage of supplier selection? What would you suggest to alleviate these difficulties?

2. The buyer usually has a minor role in selecting equipment suppliers. What do you think is the usual role? Why would an owner-manager take the initiative in selecting equipment suppliers?

3. Identify the two basic buying plans. Suggest items that would be purchased under each plan.

4. Why do you think bid buying is so popular in our industry? What are the costs and benefits of this plan, as opposed to those of the other basic buying plan?

5. What are the advantages and disadvantages of one-stop shopping? Suggest the types of hospitality operations you feel would most likely benefit from one-stop shopping.

6. A buyer often takes a daily bid before placing a meat order. What does this procedure involve?

7. What are the major advantages and disadvantages of co-op purchasing?

8. What are some of the advantages of using a computer online service to search for potential suppliers? Do CDs offer the same advantages?

9. What is the difference between a formal bid procedure and an informal bid procedure?

10. What are the major advantages and disadvantages of will-call purchasing?

11. What are some advantages and disadvantages of purchasing only from socially responsible suppliers?

12. What is the difference between the push sales strategy and the pull sales strategy? Which strategy do you think a supplier prefers?

13. When is it appropriate for a buyer to use a fixed-bid buying procedure?

14. Why might a supplier be reluctant to participate in a cost-plus purchasing procedure?

15. How could a buyer save money by using the stockless purchasing procedure?

16. What are some advantages and disadvantages of the standing-order purchasing procedure?

17. Why is it important to purchase merchandise from licensed and bonded suppliers only?

18. Develop a checklist that you would use to evaluate your suppliers. Assign degrees of importance to each item on the list. If possible, ask a hotel manager and/or a food buyer to comment on your list.

19. Define or briefly explain the following:

(a)	Call sheet buying	(j)	Lead time
(b)	Approved supplier list	(k)	Returns policy
(c)	Forward buying	(l)	Buyout policy
(d)	Cash rebate	(m)	Case price
(e)	Credit period	(n)	Buyer fact sheet
(f)	Buying club	(o)	House account
(g)	Direct purchase	(p)	National distribution
(h)	Credit terms	(q)	Trade-in allowance
(i)	Minimum order requirement	(r)	Ineligible bidder

EXPERIENTIAL EXERCISES

1. Assume that you are very happy with your current supplier, who has been supplying most of your needs for over a year. A new supplier comes along with what appears to be a better deal: a promise of lower AP prices, along with the same quality and supplier services.

    a. Write a one page report on what you would do.
    b. Ask a hotel or restaurant manager to comment on your answer.
    c. Prepare a report that includes your answer and the manager's comments.

2. Create a list of national hospitality suppliers that you might use if you owned a hospitality operation. Prepare a report that explains what type of hospitality operation you would own and how/why you identified specific national suppliers. (Hint: start by searching for suppliers using the Websites discussed at the beginning of this chapter.)

3. Create a list of hospitality suppliers in your local area that you might use if you owned a hospitality operation. Prepare a report that explains what type of hospitality operation you would own and how/why you identified specific local suppliers.

CHAPTER 13

TYPICAL ORDERING PROCEDURES

The Purpose of this Chapter

After reading this chapter, you should be able to:

- Explain the use of a purchase requisition.
- Describe the elements of a purchase order and its use.
- Recognize methods to streamline the ordering process.

INTRODUCTION

When actually engaged in buying products and services, a buyer is most concerned with obtaining the right amount and the right quality at the right time with the right supplier services for the right edible-portion (EP) cost. In addition, he or she does not, technically, complete the buying procedure until all products and services are properly received, stored, and issued to employees. In short, the buying responsibilities end only when the buyer turns these products and services over to those who will use them.

It is, of course, true that when the department head is a user-buyer, he or she may simply call in the order to an approved supplier. Similarly, many hospitality operations do not use a formal issues system. It is important to note that even when a hospitality operation has an "open storeroom," someone still keeps a close eye on what employees have removed from the storeroom. In very large operations, and in many smaller clubs and hotels, however, the practice of requiring written issues, approved by the department head, to draw food or supplies from a storeroom is more common. The discussion that follows describes the system found in places using a formal issues system.

PURCHASE REQUISITIONS

At times, before the buyer places any orders or the unit manager coordinates any, the department heads of the hospitality operation—for example, the chef, the executive housekeeper, the maître d'—prepare "purchase requisitions." These forms list items or services that the particular department heads need (see Figure 13.1 for a typical purchase requisition, and Figure 13.2 for a requisition sheet). Generally speaking, these requisitions grant the buyer the authority to go out into the marketplace and procure the items the department heads have listed.

Typically, a purchase requisition is used in the hospitality industry whenever a manager or supervisor needs an item that the buyer does not order regularly. For instance, if a chef wants to try a convenience item, such as a frozen beef stew, and if this type of item is not regularly ordered, the chef must petition the buyer, and possibly other management people, for permission to use this item in production.

If the hospitality operation's buyer orders an item regularly, a purchase requisition is unnecessary. If the item is kept in a separate storage facility, the employee needs to complete a stock requisition and give it to the storeroom manager

PURCHASE REQUISITION		
DATE _____		PAGE _____ OF _____
DEPARTMENT(S) _____		
COMPLETED BY _____		
ITEM	QUANTITY NEEDED	OTHER INFORMATION?

FIGURE 13.1 A purchase requisition.

Group:				Date: _____		REQUISITION SHEET			
Job Code: _____				Date Needed: _____					
Circle One:	DAIRY	DRY GOODS		PRODUCE	MEATS/SEAFOODS				

| | | Estimated | | | | | | Actual | |
Quan.	Unit	Unit Cost	Total Cost	Item Description		Quan.	Unit	Unit Cost	Total Cost

Received by: _____   Date: _____

Issued by: _____   Date: _____

FIGURE 13.2 **A requisition sheet.**

in exchange for the item. (See Chapter 15 for a discussion of stock requisitions and issuing procedures.) If no separate storage facility exists, such as in a typical small restaurant unit, no formal stock requisition system may be in place. However, an employee usually must obtain permission from a supervisor before he or she is allowed to take products, especially expensive products, from the shelves for use in production and service.

Potential problems are associated with the purchase requisition system. For example, it tends to dilute the selection and procurement function, in that too many people may be involved in deciding the types and qualities of products and services that the hospitality operation should purchase and use. Another problem is that the procedure tends to invite backdoor selling. Still another disadvantage is the time and effort required to implement and operate a purchase requisition system.

Certain benefits are associated with the purchase requisition system. First, it can be a useful training device for those department heads who aspire to become full-time buyers. Second, it can relieve a buyer of responsibility for ordering mistakes; he or she can simply point out that so-and-so improperly completed the purchase requisition. Third, this system can relieve the buyer of a good deal of paperwork. Fourth, it is a way of controlling the use of the products and services in the various departments.

This control can be easily accomplished by requiring additional information from the department head via the "other information" section (see Figure 13.1). For example, the buyer may want to know how much product the department has on hand, how much was sold yesterday, how much waste was incurred during the past week, which supplier to contact, and so on. Requiring all this information does little to endear a buyer to the department heads, but this control mechanism is, nevertheless, one of the strongest aspects of the purchase requisition systems.

ORDERING PROCEDURES

Before placing an order, the buyer must determine the appropriate order size. The most common way to do this is to use the par stock approach, for which the buyer or user-buyer must note what is on hand in the main storeroom areas and in the department areas (stock that departments hold is normally referred to as the "in-process inventory"), subtract what is on hand from the par stock, and add products needed for banquets or other special functions. The buyer must then prepare the appropriate purchase orders (POs) and send them to the suppliers or call them in, keeping one or more copies for his or her records. The buyer may interact with department heads and buyers, but the full-time buyer usually relieves the department head of the major responsibilities associated with ordering.

In operations that have sophisticated computerized record-keeping and control systems, there is a greater tendency to use the Levinson approach to ordering (or some variation of it), as discussed in Chapter 9.

These procedures are commonly used in both small and large operations. The major differences between small and large properties are the degree of formality and the presence or absence of a full-time buyer. In small properties, the user-buyer is more common.

Large operations usually have at least one full-time buyer who is deeply involved in the purchasing function. In chain restaurants, for example, recall that, usually, a vice president of purchasing works in a home office and sets policies and procedures, while the unit manager handles only the paperwork for his or her particular store. Thus, the unit manager prepares the POs based on the format and procedure that the corporate headquarters office has designed. The unit manager then places the orders with designated suppliers, commissaries, or central distribution centers and sees to it that the products and services are properly received, stored, and issued to the respective departments.

The paperwork used in placing orders varies from one establishment to the next. But among hospitality operations that use various types of forms, the information in them is reasonably standard throughout the industry.

Once the various order sizes are determined, a buyer can place the order in one of several ways. The old-fashioned method is to physically give a hard copy of the order to the supplier's salesperson or distributor sales representative (DSR). Alternatively, the buyer can telephone in the order and leave it with a person who answers the telephone, or leave it on voice mail. The buyer can also send the order via an e-mail attachment to the supplier, or, as is becoming more common, can send the order directly to the supplier electronically.[1]

Another method is the use of a fax machine to convey ordering information. This is an inexpensive alternative to the computerized ordering process and, like the computer, enables the buyer to call in an order at any time. Unlike the computerized process, though, a buyer cannot verify his or her order with the fax procedure. When a buyer uses a computer or talks to a person, most often he or she can obtain verification on the spot; that is, the buyer knows immediately whether the products he or she desires are available.

Unless an approved supplier has a specific requirement, management usually decides which ordering procedure to use. Small hospitality operations commonly follow one-stop shopping procedures and seek to minimize the ordering effort. Some large organizations, though, particularly the multiunit chain operations, normally contract to purchase large supplies of merchandise from several primary sources and/or intermediaries. Unit managers, therefore, may need to spend a bit more time when placing their orders if they must deal with several distributors.

THE PURCHASE ORDER

A purchase order (PO) can take many forms. At one extreme, an operation may not use one at all. At the other extreme, one may find a mind-boggling jumble of paper. Whatever shape it takes, a purchase order represents a request that a supplier deliver what the buyer wants, ideally at the time he or she wants it (see Figure 13.3 for a typical purchase order).

A purchase order usually resembles a purchase requisition. The date of the order enables buyers to keep track of product usage patterns, and to know when to pay the bills. Some buyers may note the transportation requirement and packaging instructions. It is usual to indicate the desired receiving date, but, as a prac-

Date _____   Name of operation _____   Order No. _____

Account No. _____   Page _____ of _____

TO: _____ (supplier) _____

Please send the following items

via _____ (transportation requirements?) _____

By _____ (date) _____

SIZE OF UNIT	QUANTITY	ITEM	UNIT PRICE	EXTENDED PRICE
			PAGE TOTAL	
			GRAND TOTAL	

TERMS OF PAYMENT _____

for use by receiving clerk:

Rec. by _____   Condition of goods _____

Date rec. _____   Other remarks _____

 **FIGURE 13.3** **A purchase order.**

tical matter, buyers probably have only two choices: either take the supplier's pre-determined delivery schedule—or leave it. The quantity desired, the item type, the unit size (the size of the can, the weight per unit, etc.), the unit price, and the extended price (the number of units times the unit price)—all these entries are clear instructions to the supplier about what buyers want, as well as their understanding of the pertinent as-purchased (AP) price, either the current AP price or the AP price contracted for.

Recording prices also makes it easier for buyers to keep track of the value of stock on hand and serves to remind them that several thousands of dollars pass through their hands every year. The information the receiving clerk uses to compare the order with the delivery may or may not be included on the purchase order. But if buyers send a carbon copy of the order to the receiving clerk to be used when checking the delivery, it may be appropriate to include this information for the receiver. On the other hand, the receiving clerk may have a separate form he or she uses for this purpose.

Different operators have different opinions about the number of copies of the purchase order to prepare. It is possible to prepare and use up to eight copies. One copy goes to the supplier (1). The supplier might also receive a second copy, which he or she would use as the bill that accompanies the delivery of the various items or services (2). The supplier might receive yet a third copy, which he or she would initial and send back to the buyer, indicating that he or she acknowledges the order and is entering into a binding contract (3). The buyer normally keeps a copy for his or her files to monitor usage patterns for future reference, as well as to keep track of which suppliers receive orders (4). The receiving clerk might get a copy so that he or she knows which deliveries to expect; he or she also might use this copy to check against the deliveries (5). The requisitioner, usually a department head, might like a copy for the department's files (6). The accountant or bookkeeper might want a copy to keep track of bills coming due and to compare that copy with the copy of the bill that accompanies the particular delivery (7). Finally, if there is a separate head office, its accounting office may want a copy for its use and records (8).

Much more commonly, only three copies are made: one for the supplier, one for the receiving clerk, and one for the buyer's records (see Figure 13.4). A little less frequently, a fourth copy, which the supplier uses as the bill and sends back with the delivery, is prepared. The acknowledgement, requisitioner, accountant, and main-office copies do not appear so frequently.

The buyer's decision about how many copies to use is, however, important. An essentially inescapable aspect of the buying procedure is the need to begin controlling the purchased products and services. In addition, the buyer must exercise control from the moment he or she purchases an item, until the time that item is used in a productive capacity and the hospitality operation's customer pays for it. The objective is to control the cost and quality of all merchandise as it travels throughout the hospitality operation from one operating activity to another.

Another method for controlling the cost and quality of all merchandise is to use a limited purchase order (LPO). This form restricts the overall amount that a buyer can purchase on a particular purchase order form (see Figure 13.5 for an example).

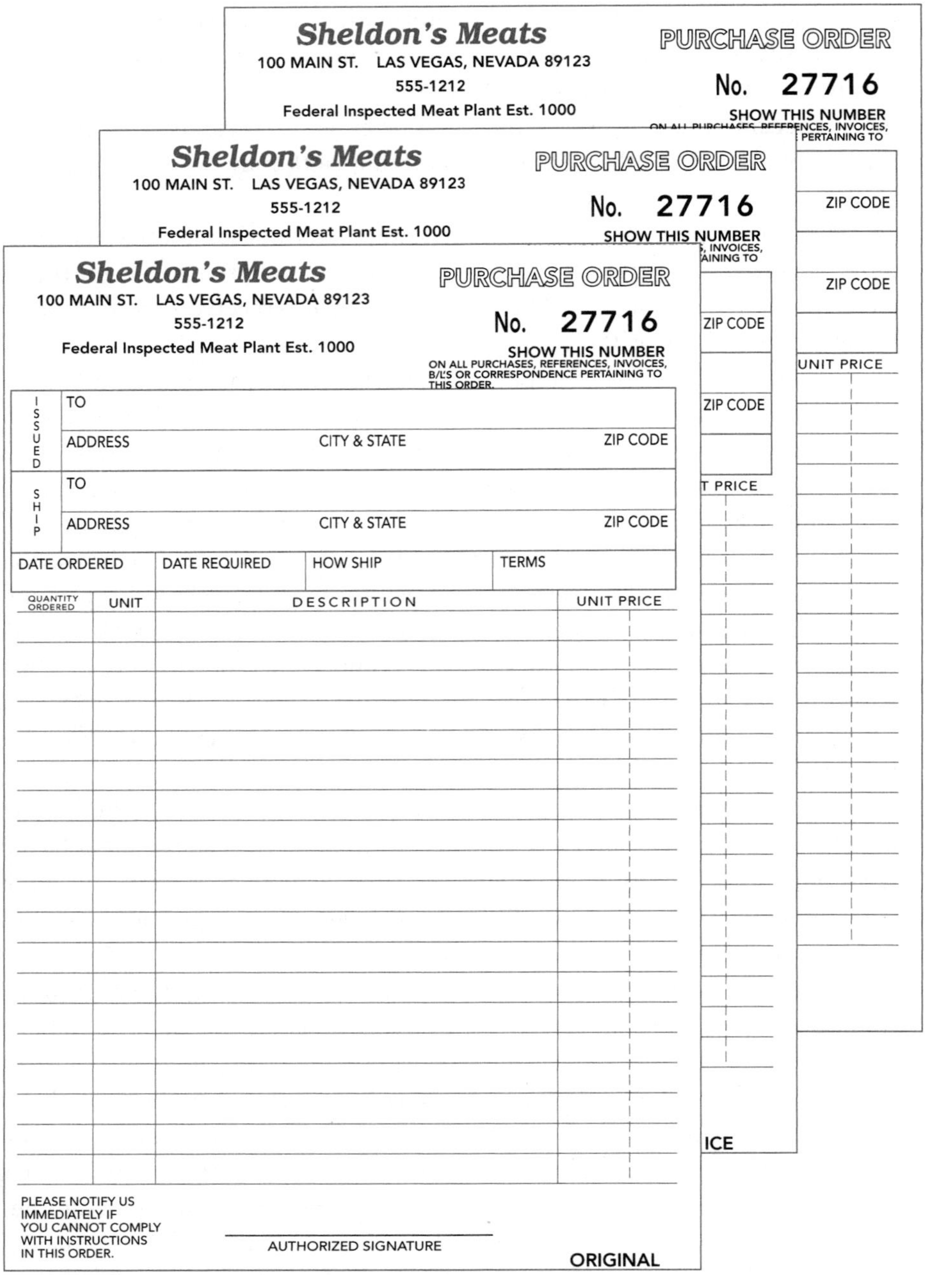

Sheldon's Meats
100 MAIN ST.   LAS VEGAS, NEVADA 89123
555-1212
Federal Inspected Meat Plant Est. 1000

PURCHASE ORDER

No. **27716**

SHOW THIS NUMBER
ON ALL PURCHASES, REFERENCES, INVOICES,
B/L'S OR CORRESPONDENCE PERTAINING TO
THIS ORDER.

I S S U E D	TO		
	ADDRESS	CITY & STATE	ZIP CODE
S H I P	TO		
	ADDRESS	CITY & STATE	ZIP CODE

DATE ORDERED	DATE REQUIRED	HOW SHIP	TERMS

QUANTITY ORDERED	UNIT	DESCRIPTION	UNIT PRICE

PLEASE NOTIFY US
IMMEDIATELY IF
YOU CANNOT COMPLY
WITH INSTRUCTIONS
IN THIS ORDER.

AUTHORIZED SIGNATURE

ORIGINAL

FIGURE 13.4 A three-part purchase order.

LIMITED PURCHASE ORDER
NOT VALID OVER $500.00
University of Nevada, Las Vegas
Federal Tax ID# 88-6000024
Business Center South • Las Vegas, NV 89154-1033
702-895-3521 • FAX 702-895-3859

ORDER #: 2LPOB

Page 1 of _____ **26554**
Agreement or Bid #_____

CONFIRMING ORDER?
☐ No   ☐ Yes
TO _____   ON_____

PLEASE PRESS HARD

Date: _____

To: _____

Address: _____

City, State, Zip _____

Federal Tax ID No: _____

Telephone: (____) ____-_____ Fax: (____) ____-_____

SHIPPING INFORMATION
UNLV/Receiving Department
Business Services Building
4505 Maryland Parkway
Las Vegas, NV 89154-1033
(No deliveries after 4:00 PM)

LINE #	QUANTITY	UNIT	COMPLETE DESCRIPTION	A/R	UNIT PRICE	TOTAL
001						
					TOTAL	

Required Delivery Date: _____
Contact Name: _____
Phone Number: (702) _____ FAX No: (702) _____

DEPARTMENT INFORMATION
Requesting Dept. Name: _____
Bldg: _____ Room: _____ Mail Code: _____
Have items been received ☐ Yes ☐ No

INVOICE TO:
Business Center South
Disbursements
P.O. Box 71590
Las Vegas, NV 89170-1590

ACCOUNTING INFORMATION

LN	FUND	AREA	ORGN	SORG	OBJT	SOBJ	JOB #	TOTAL
01								
02								

COMMODITY CODE: _____
COMMODITY APPROVAL: _____
SIGNATURE AUTHORITY: _____

PR/1033-12/12-94 DISTRIBUTION: *White and Yellow Vendor, Pink - Purchasing, Gold - Department*

NOTICE TO VENDOR
1. NO PARTIAL SHIPMENTS ACCEPTED
2. DO NOT CHARGE SALES OR EXCISE TAX.
3. ORIGINAL INVOICE AND ONE COPY REQUIRED FOR PAYMENT.
4. PURCHASE ORDER # MUST APPEAR ON *LABEL, INVOICE AND PACKING SLIP.*

FIGURE 13.5 A limited purchase order. Courtesy of the University of Nevada, Las Vegas.

Purchased products normally follow a chain of operating activities (see Figure 13.6). The control chain begins with buying; that is, it begins when the products and services legally become the buyer's. To control these items, a great deal of record keeping may be essential. Keep in mind that management may want to

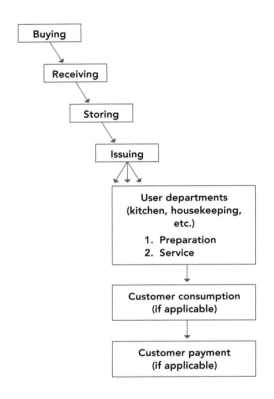

FIGURE 13.6 **Typical operating activities in a hospitality operation.**

know: where the item is within the chain, how much of the item is at any one point within the chain, and whether the product is being used according to plan. The more management wants to know, the greater the potential record-keeping burden; hence, the greater the need for purchase order copies, as well as for the various other types of paperwork used. The sole reason for all this paper, or all these computerized records, is to control products and services. The greater the degree of control the buyer wants, the more complex a system he or she needs. Consequently, at the very least, a purchase order record should exist so that deliveries can be compared to it. This is probably the minimum control a buyer should have.

It is not our purpose to present a full discussion of control concepts; many excellent discussions of this subject already exist.[2] The best buying strategy in the world will be worthless, however, if by the time the product is supposed to have reached the user department, some of it is spoiled, misplaced, stolen, or otherwise wasted. Large firms can afford the paperwork burden or the computerized record-keeping procedures available in the hospitality industry. Fortunately, smaller operators can minimize the paperwork and/or computerization because, generally speaking, they can substitute eyes and ears for these more formal controls.

CHANGE ORDER

At times, a buyer may need to alter an original purchase order. Faced with this situation, a buyer normally contacts the supplier and effects changes with little difficulty. But the original purchase order, once acknowledged by the supplier, is a legal contract, and the supplier could, therefore, sue the buyer's company if any unwarranted attempt is made to alter the contract. To be on the safe side, a buyer should be sure to get it right the first time and not burden a busy supplier with change order requests.

EXPEDITING

Expediting is a buyer's effort to monitor suppliers from day to day to ensure that products and services arrive at the right time and in acceptable condition. Expediting is not a common practice among most buyers unless there is a chance that a large order, required at a precise time, might arrive late. For instance, a banquet for 1000 people on a particular night might depend on a delivery of 1000 steaks that afternoon. In this situation, an extra telephone call to the supplier is recommended.

Expediting is most often used, at least in the hospitality industry, when purchasing furniture, fixtures, and equipment (FFE). These items have a habit of showing up late, especially, for example, long after the planned grand opening of a new restaurant. In addition, purchased services may not always be performed at the exact time desired. In these situations, the buyer, and probably even the senior management, will nag the suppliers.

STREAMLINING THE ORDERING PROCEDURE

Ordering is a time-consuming affair, and the paperwork and/or computerization can be costly. This process can, however, be streamlined. Unfortunately, some of the methods involved force an operation to surrender a bit of control. We do not advocate dropping all paperwork and record keeping. We suppose that small hospitality operations could omit most paperwork. But this drastic step would almost certainly encourage theft, waste, and overall employee carelessness. However, the point is well taken: if buyers can be in the hospitality operation at all times, they can use their eyes as a direct control system, instead of paperwork, an indirect control system.

Of course, larger organizations require some sort of an indirect control system. But even in these cases, some potential cost-cutting approaches exist.

Blanket Order

One method of streamlining ordering procedures that we have already discussed deserves review here. Several items hospitality organizations use have a low dollar value, and the time and effort involved in ordering them can sometimes be costly, especially if they are ordered frequently. Recall that a blanket order is one that includes a large amount of miscellaneous items—enough products to preclude, for example, weekly ordering. In other words, if a large par stock of miscellaneous items is set, the resultant order size usually saves ordering costs, but it is not so valuable as to increase drastically the cost of storing them.

Purchase Order Draft System

A purchase order with an attached check to cover the cost of the ordered items is referred to as a "purchase order draft" and amounts to a prepaid order. Alternately, a supplier can charge a buyer's credit card or debit card number that is noted on the purchase order. This can, in some cases, save the buyer some money. For example, the supplier might be so glad to get the cash ahead of time that he or she grants a discount. Also, this system eliminates the need for a great deal of clerical work. This type of system, however, requires firm trust between the supplier and the buyer, especially in the sensitive area of returned merchandise and other adjustments that must be made. These always seem to be more difficult after the buyer paid the bill.

Supplier's Forms

Some suppliers provide preprinted paper or Web-based order forms. These may not be exactly what buyers would like, but the forms may be less expensive than their own. If a hospitality operation uses several expensive multipart forms, buyers can save a considerable amount of money by using a supplier's order blanks. Of course, the cost of all "free" items and services is recaptured somehow. However, the supplier should be able to get these forms in huge quantities, thereby saving a little money, which, perhaps, is passed on to buyers.

Standing Order

Recall that a standing order generally is a procedure whereby you set par stocks and the supplier's route salesperson, who might come to your place twice a week, leaves just enough product to bring you up to par. This procedure minimizes ordering costs and eliminates the need to prepare purchase orders.

Computerization

The cost of computerization has declined to the point where all hospitality operators can afford it. In fact, because most of these new e-procurement applications do not rely upon proprietary software, all that is needed is an inexpensive computer, a browser, and an Internet connection.

E-procurement applications represent tremendous streamlining opportunities for both the supplier and the buyer. The costs associated with paper use can be drastically reduced. Purchase requisitions and purchase orders, and the purchases themselves, can all be done electronically (see Figure 13.7). There is no need for multiple paper copies of these forms; instead, an unlimited number of electronic copies of these documents can be sent anywhere at an insignificant cost. Not only do these applications significantly reduce costs, they also reduce the amount of time needed to complete an order, thus allowing employees and management to focus on other aspects of their jobs. Additional benefits include increased order accuracy and lead-time reduction that can result in minimizing stockouts and investment in inventories (thereby reducing opportunity costs).

E-commerce enablers empower purchasing managers to source across a base of hundreds of thousands of businesses of all sizes for products ranging from linens to fresh seafood. Additionally, e-procurement technology can be set up to restrict lower-level employees from being able to source products and services unless directed by a supervisor, effectively allocating employees' time and efforts to tasks that fit their job descriptions. Applications can also be configured to permit key employees to select and procure products themselves based on prescribed criteria. For example, a purchasing manager might allow the director of housekeeping to procure linen so long as it is from one of three approved vendors and a single order does not exceed $1000. In this example, a purchase requisition can be completely eliminated, thereby streamlining the ordering process even further.

Managing purchasing employees is an ever-expanding task for purchasing managers. While these managers should be focused on securing goods and services, they may spend a good part of their day supervising employees. Technological ad-

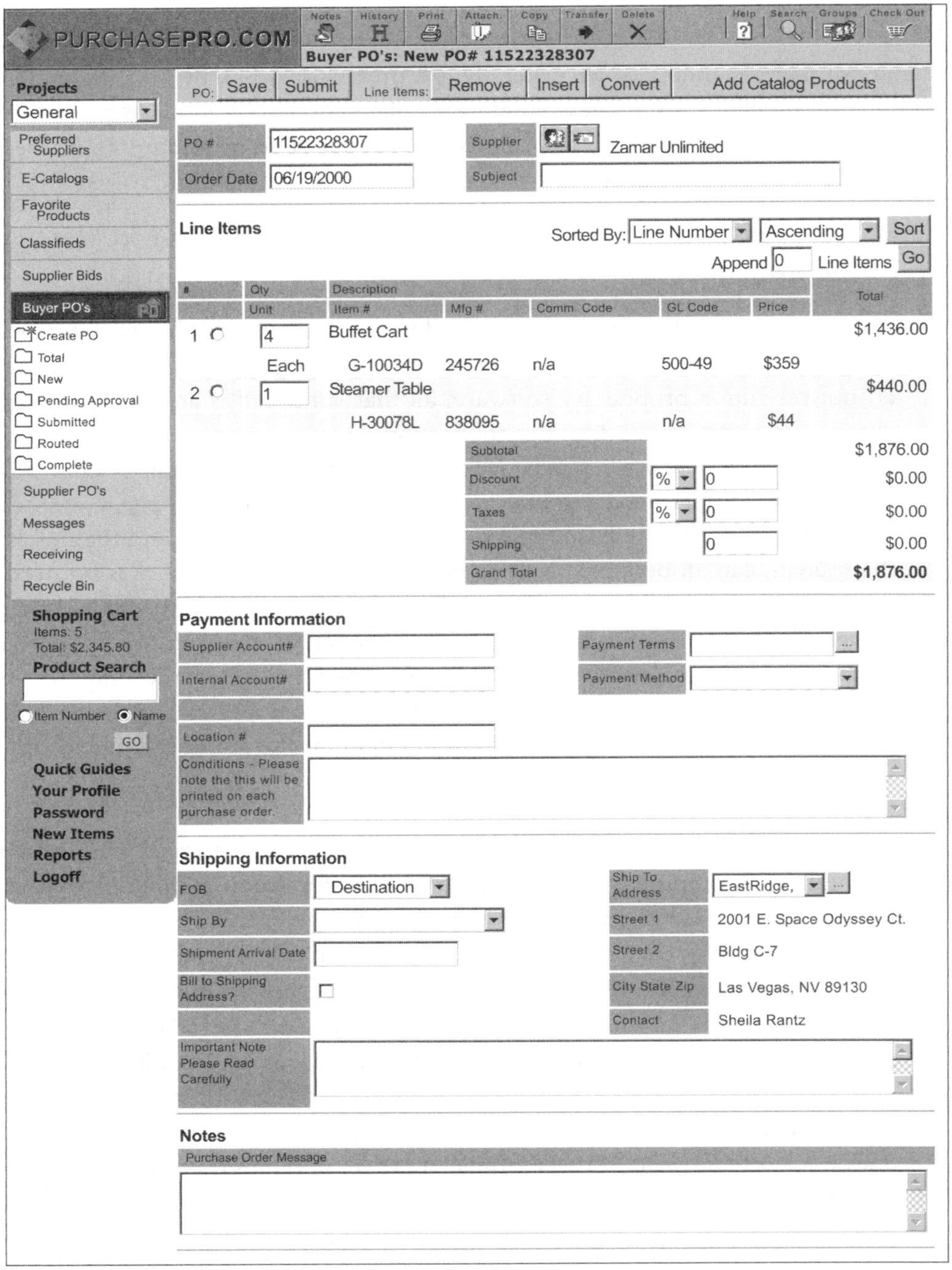

FIGURE 13.7 An example of an online purchase order. Courtesy of PurchasePro.com, Inc. PurchasePro and PurchasePro.com are registered servicemarks of PurchasePro.com, Inc.

| step1: standard | step2: shipping details | step3: billing details | step4: optional details |

STEP 1 OF 4: PURCHASE ORDER Standard Details

Accounting Options:	Billing and Shipping by Purchase Order
TO:	Supplier Name change supplier
From:	ADMINISTRATION transfer this PO
CC:	select internal user
SUBJECT:	
REQUIRED BY DATE:	11 / 20 / 2000

PO NUMBER: 123456789123

PO STATUS: NEW

PARTIAL ORDERS ACCEPTED: ⊙ yes ○ no

ATTACHMENTS: 📎

PO ITEM LIST **Printer-Friendly Format**   ▶ collapse all   ▽ expand all

ADD ITEMS FROM: Catalog, Shopping Cart, Favorite Products, or Manually Insert [- ▾] Items

LINE	DETAIL	ITEM #	NAME/DESCRIPTION	QTY	UNIT	PRICE	TOTAL	ADD	SELECT
1	▶	0458H	wash cloth	4	box	$38.00	$152.00	📎	☐
2	▶	0556H	hand towel	2	box	$59.99	$108.00	📎	☐
3	▶	0787H	towel rack	3	box	$5.99	$26.99	📎	☐

UPDATE   🗑 ALL   🗑 SELECTED

ADD ITEMS FROM: Catalog, Shopping Cart, Favorite Products, or Manually Insert [- ▾] Items

SUBTOTAL:		$286.97
DISCOUNTS:	5 [% ▾]	$14.35
TAXES:	0 [% ▾]	$0.00
SHIPPING:	0 [$ ▾]	$0.00
TOTAL:		$272.62

SUPPLIER RESPONSE

No Response From Supplier

CONTINUE TO STEP2	Click here to proceed to step 2.
SAVE	
CANCEL	Click here to exit and return to the previous screen.

FIGURE 13.7 (Continued.)

vances, such as the ones described above, allow management to be conducted more effectively, enabling managers to keep tabs on many aspects of employees' work duties from their computers. Technology will never have the power to replace a caring and sincere manager, but it *can* increase management's effectiveness.

Alternative Ways to Cut Costs

Other potential cost-cutting procedures exist, but all of these are some variation of the five just noted. Essentially, management must decide which course to follow. For many hospitality organizations, control and a certain amount of costly paperwork go hand in hand. The most economical compromise between control and record keeping seems to be an e-procurement application that can be used and viewed by whoever receives the deliveries, the buyer or user-buyer, the person who pays the bills, and the supplier. This is sufficient control at the initial stage of the cost-control chain of operating activities. The receiver knows what to expect. The buyer and bill payer can compare the PO with the bill, or invoice, that accompanies the delivery. The supplier also has a copy for his or her records.

It now remains for us to explore how control is maintained throughout the receiving, storing, and issuing functions.

KEY WORDS AND CONCEPTS

Backdoor selling

Blanket order

Chain of operating activities

Change order

Computerized ordering and record-keeping procedures

Distributor sales representative (DSR)

Expediting

Formal issues system

In-process inventory

Issuing

Levinson approach to ordering

Methods of placing the order

Methods of streamlining the ordering procedure

Open storeroom

Ordering procedures

Par stock approach to ordering

Purchase order (PO)

Purchase order draft system

Purchase requisition

Receiving

Source

Standing order

Stock requisition

Storage

Supplier's forms

Variations of the Levinson approach to ordering

REFERENCES

1. Andrew Hale Feinstein and Greg Dunn, "Target Sector: Hospitality Industry Strives to Welcome B2B Initiatives," *Purchasing Today,* May 2001, pp. 24–28. See also: Anonymous, "Distributors Put More Value into e-Commerce," *Purchasing: Electronics News—Web Exclusive,* June 6,

2001 (Available http://www.purchasing.com); Alan J. Liddle, "NRA Tech Poll Bolsters Think-Tank's 2010 Forecast," *Nation's Restaurant News,* November 25, 2002, pp. 4, 42; Dickinson Waters, "NRN Survey Reports E-Business Is on the Upswing," *Nation's Restaurant News,* December 11, 2000, p. 80. See also: Alan J. Liddle, "E-Business Could Learn a Thing or Two from Plastic Pioneer," *Nation's Restaurant News,* December 11,

2000, p. 29; Margaret Sheridan, "Keyboard Shoppers," *Restaurants and Institutions,* September 1, 2000 (Available http://www.rimag.com/017/Busb.htm).

2. See, for example, Paul R. Dittmer and the NRA Educational Foundation, *Principles of Food, Beverage, and Labor Cost Controls Package,* 7th ed. (New York: John Wiley & Sons, 2002). Other texts on cost control can be found at http://www.amazon.com.

QUESTIONS AND PROBLEMS

1. What is the difference between a purchase requisition and a purchase order?

2. What information should you note on a purchase order? Why?

3. What is the purpose of expediting?

4. Describe the chain of operating activities for the typical hospitality operation.

5. What are some advantages and disadvantages of using a purchase requisitioning system?

6. What is the difference between a purchase requisition and a stock requisition?

7. How could an e-procurement application save a buyer money and time?

8. Assume that a restaurant with an annual sales volume of $7.5 million can computerize its ordering procedures via an initial investment in computers and other machinery of $14,500. What should you know about the current ordering procedures so that you can decide whether this initial cash outlay is economically feasible?

9. Briefly describe the purchase order draft system. Do you feel that this is an advantage or a disadvantage to the hospitality operator? Why? If possible, ask a food buyer to comment on your answer.

10. When would you be likely to prepare a change order document?

11. Specifically, how does a hospitality operator save money by using the standing order method of purchasing?

12. How might a buyer save money by using the blanket order procedure?

13. What are the advantages and disadvantages of the open storeroom form of issuing?

14. How might an e-commerce enabler assist in streamlining the ordering process?

EXPERIENTIAL EXERCISES

1. Call one or more suppliers in your area. Find out whether they provide their customers with order forms and, if so, how much, if anything, they charge for this supplier service.

2. Contact a buyer for a hospitality establishment and ask for an interview to discuss buying procedures. Prepare a report that provides the interviewee's answers to the following questions:

    a. How are order sizes determined?
    b. Please explain the purchase order form in use.
    c. List the information the purchase order calls for, and explain why that information is needed.
    d. How many copies of a purchase order are prepared? Why?
    e. What, do you suppose, is the cost of the ordering procedure?
    f. How might that cost be reduced?

3. Contact a buyer for a hospitality establishment and ask for copies of the following forms, so you can bring the documents into class and discuss them:

    a. Purchase requisition
    b. Purchase order
    c. Limited purchase order (LPO)

    Note: It might be difficult to acquire these documents as the Purchase Order and the LPO can be used as legal tender if they are not voided. A suggestion would be to ask the manager of the hospitality establishment to void out the order form by writing "Void" across all copies. Another idea would be to create your own forms based on examples in this chapter.

14

TYPICAL RECEIVING PROCEDURES

The Purpose of this Chapter

After reading this chapter, you should be able to:

■ Explain the objectives of receiving.

■ Explain the essentials of effective receiving.

■ Describe invoice receiving and other receiving methods.

■ Outline additional receiving duties.

■ List good receiving practices and methods to reduce receiving costs.

INTRODUCTION

Someone once said, "Receiving is the proof of purchasing." It's at receiving that you determine what it is you actually got—not what you ordered but what you received. And there could be a lot of difference between the order you placed and the delivery you received. That's why receiving is so important to the proper control of purchasing.[1]

Receiving is the act of inspecting and either accepting or rejecting deliveries. It is an activity with many facets. In any particular hospitality operation, receiving can range anywhere from a buyer letting delivery truck drivers place an order in his or her storage facilities, to having various receiving clerks waiting at the delivery entrance to check every single item to see that it meets the specifications set forth in the purchase order (PO).

Although many varieties of practice exist, the variety of correct procedures, though subject to debate, is considerably less. For instance, many operations permit the bread route salesperson to come into the kitchen and storage areas, remove bread left over from the previous delivery, restock the operation, and leave the bill with someone. Purists could argue that this is poor practice on two counts: (1) the delivery agent could cheat on both returns and delivery; and (2) the delivery agent could steal other items while he or she was there.

Operators following this practice, however, would probably argue that the cost of a unit of product—a loaf of bread, for instance—is so small that the cost of a receiving clerk or management time to physically check returns and delivery is unwarranted. Moreover, the delivery agent in this case saves time. As for the theft issue, the delivery agent is no more likely to steal than employees because he or she is subject to the same controls they are. No hard-and-fast rules exist for a case like this. Each operator or company must weigh the advantages and disadvantages in order to arrive at a policy.

On the other hand, consider a situation in which a supplier provides a very large portion of an operation's goods and offers, as a supplier service, to check the storeroom for all of the items this supplier provides and to determine what needs to be replenished. This might be done "to save the operator some time." Most people would argue, here, that both the receiving and the purchasing functions have been turned over to a supplier, and allowing a supplier to do this is inappropriate.

THE OBJECTIVES OF RECEIVING

These objectives resemble the objectives of the purchasing function itself. Recall the main objectives: obtaining the correct amount and correct quality at the correct time with the correct supplier services for the correct edible-portion (EP) cost. The main objective of receiving is to check that the delivered order meets these criteria.

Another important objective of receiving is controlling these received products and services. Once the receiver accepts the items, whatever they are, they become the property of the hospitality organization. Thus a cycle of control begins at this point.[2] For the most part, an owner-manager requires a certain amount of documentation during this receiving function in order to ascertain what was delivered and where the delivered items were sent within the organization. Keep in mind that this control activity can be simple or elaborate, depending on management's policy. At the risk of being redundant, though, we repeat that the best buying plan in the world is useless if someone or something goes awry during the cycle of control and causes a reduction in quality or an increase in costs.

In some large firms, additional control is exerted in the receiving function by placing receiving personnel under the direction of the accounting department. Thus, management minimizes the possibility of any fraudulent relationship between the buyer and the receiver. Small firms cannot afford this luxury.

On the other hand, some small firms often use their very smallness—their lack of personnel—as an excuse to avoid receiving control. Although the small operator may not be able to afford the elaborate receiving department of a large hotel, he or she certainly can adapt the techniques it uses to some degree. For instance, many small- to medium-sized operations can designate a specific employee, perhaps a line cook, to act as receiver and the only person authorized to sign for received products. This person might warrant a modest salary increase for the added responsibility assumed. To make the task easier, he or she should be responsible for verifying counts and weights; quality evaluations can be left to some members of management.

ESSENTIALS FOR GOOD RECEIVING

To ensure that the receiving function is performed properly, several factors must be in place:

1. **Competent Personnel.** Such personnel should be placed in charge of all receiving activity. By "competent," we mean persons, full-time or part-time, who are reasonably intelligent, honest, interested in the job, and somewhat knowledgeable about the items to be received. Once this person is designated, it is necessary to train him or her to recognize acceptable and inferior products and services. However, where the line cook-receiver combination is used, management may need to make quality checks and to supervise the receiving activity more closely.

    It is very important to provide the receiving agent with appropriate training. This can be a time-consuming, costly procedure, but it is absolutely essential. The receiver must be able to recognize the various quality levels of merchandise that will be delivered to the hospitality operation. He or she also must be able to handle the necessary paperwork and/or computerized record keeping adequately. Furthermore, the receiver must know what to do when something out of the ordinary arises. While the training costs may be considerable, they will be recovered many times over if the receiver is able to prevent merely one or two receiving mistakes per month.

2. **Proper Receiving Equipment.** This is a must. Since many deliveries must be weighed, accurate scales are, perhaps, the most important pieces of equip-

ment in the receiving area. Temperature probes let receivers check the temperatures of refrigerated and frozen products. Rule measures are useful in checking trim of, for example, fat on portion-cut steaks. Calculators are needed to verify costs. Cutting instruments, such as a produce knife, are handy when product sampling is part of the receiving process. Conveyor belts, hand trucks, and motorized forklift trucks can help transport the received items to the storage areas or, in some cases, directly to a production area. And, where applicable, receiving agents must have the technology to read existing bar codes on product packaging in order to process shipments correctly. In short, receivers should have enough of the proper equipment to do the most efficient, thorough job possible.

In a smaller operation, a reliable scale is a bare minimum. It is surprising how many small operations "save money" by purchasing an inexpensive scale that is often inaccurate. Then, because "it doesn't work anyway," they do not use it. This is the falsest of economies since, even if the operators trust their suppliers, unintentional errors can still occur.

3. **Proper Receiving Facilities.** If an operation wants a receiver to perform adequately, he or she must have the facilities that will make that possible. By "facilities," we are referring to the entire receiving area. By "proper," we mean, for example, that the area should be well lit, big enough to work in comfortably, reasonably secure, and convenient for both delivery people and receivers.

In some old buildings, or in a hospitality operation built into another kind of building—for example, an office building—management may not see exactly what we have described, but the closer management can move to this ideal, the better the receiver can do his or her job.

4. **Appropiate Receiving Hours.** Deliveries should be scheduled carefully. If possible, deliveries should be staggered so that a receiver is not rushed. Also, all delivery times should be relatively predictable so that a competent receiver will be on hand and receiving will not be left to whoever happens to be handy. Remember, we mentioned that one of the biggest benefits of one-stop shopping is to minimize any difficulties and expense arising from too many deliveries. Perhaps now you can appreciate why many managers are swayed by this potential benefit. It not only reduces the number of hours a receiver must work, but it also allows for a more secure backdoor routine and, because of fewer transactions, minimal theft opportunities.

5. **Available Copies of All Specifications.** The receiver will need these as references. This can help whenever ambiguity arises, as it sometimes will. When

a supplier is out of a particular brand of soap, for example, he or she might deliver what is believed to be a comparable substitute. When this occurs, it becomes necessary for the deliverer and receiver to have a reference handy, unless the buyer insists on handling any substitutions personally, in which case the receiver will ask him or her to inspect the substitute. In many cases, though, drivers are not eager to wait for this decision; it is expensive for them to leave their trucks idle. As a result, decisions must often be made quickly, and a copy of the specifications can, therefore, be quite helpful.

6.   **Available Copies of Purchase Orders.** Most hospitality operators feel that a receiver should know what is due to be delivered so that he or she can be prepared. These purchase order copies are necessary to ensure this preparedness.

INVOICE RECEIVING

The most popular receiving technique is sometimes referred to as "invoice receiving." In this scheme of things, an invoice, or bill, accompanies the delivery (see Figure 14.1). An invoice is an itemized statement of quantity, price, and other information that usually resembles the purchase order depicted in Chapter 13. An invoice may, in fact, be nothing more than a photocopy of the original purchase order. The receiver uses the invoice to check against the quantity, quality, and prices of the items delivered. He or she may also compare the invoice with a copy of the original purchase order as a further check. The order is either accepted or rejected. If accepted, it is stored or delivered to a production department. If rejected, appropriate credit must be obtained. Sometimes, an invoice does not accompany the delivery. In these situations, the receiver normally fills out some type of form right there on the spot and treats this completed form as the invoice. The following sections discuss the typical invoice receiving sequence in more detail.

Delivery Arrives

When arriving at a large operation, the delivery person must usually announce that he or she is there, sometimes by ringing a doorbell and asking the receiver for access. These procedures are, of course, less formal in a small operation, but they represent good security precautions.

The receiver opens the receiving area and, using the invoice and, perhaps, a copy of the original purchase order, checks immediately for the proper quantities.

PLEASE PAY
FROM THIS
INVOICE

Sheldon's Meats

100 MAIN ST.   LAS VEGAS, NEVADA 89123
555-1212
Federal Inspected Meat Plant Est. 1000

22058

IMPORTANT
MAIL REMITTANCE TO:
P.O. BOX 1000
LAS VEGAS, NV 89123

SOLD TO
ADDRESS

☐ C.O.D.   ☐ CASH   ☐ CHARGE   P.O. NO.   DATE   /   /

QUAN	DESCRIPTION	WEIGHT	PRICE	AMOUNT
	PATTIES			
	PATTIES			

All claims must be made immediately upon receipt of goods. If any discrepancy, please call (702) 555-1212; otherwise late claims will not be allowed.

TOTAL ⟶

Received by

Boxes   Pkgs   Pcs.

All accounts are due the 10th of the month following date of purchase and after such date are past due accounts subject to an interest charge of 1¾% per month, which is **AN ANNUAL PERCENTAGE RATE OF 21%.** In the event legal proceedings are instituted to collect any sums due, the purchaser agrees to pay reasonable attorney's fees and costs.

I hereby certify that the above described product, which is offered for shipment in commerce, has been U.S. inspected and passed by the U.S. Department of Agriculture, is so marked, and at this date is not adulterated or misbranded.

FIGURE 14.1 **A typical invoice.**

The receiver's first step, then, is to check each item's weight, count, and/or volume as quickly and efficiently as possible and compare them to the invoice and the original purchase order, or some other purchase record. The comparisons should match.

Next, where applicable, the receiver checks for the proper quality. Unfortunately, except for a check of the packers' brand names, this is the most difficult kind of check to make and, in some cases, is almost impossible to complete. For example, it is difficult to determine the overall quality of lobster tails. A receiver might be able to tell whether they have been refrozen. But he or she can never be sure if any particular tail is bad until it has been cooked; a bad lobster tail crumbles after it is cooked.

Some establishments expect the receiver to check for quantities only and to call someone else to inspect for quality. In these situations, the receiver calls the chef, housekeeper, maître d', or whatever department head is appropriate to come check the quality of the items that will eventually be used in his or her department. The big drawback of this procedure is the potential time lag in waiting for the department head to arrive. Another problem is the possibility of the items, especially frozen ones, deteriorating while waiting for a quality check.

Large operations, particularly commissaries, usually engage quality control, or quality assurance, inspectors who check deliveries, as well as the products prepared in the commissary. These inspectors do not normally work for the purchasing agent. In fact, they act as a check on the purchasing agent by keeping tabs on the quality that the purchasing agent procures.

If a quality discrepancy is present, the buyer should be notified as soon as possible since it is his or her duty to deal with suppliers and salespersons. Moreover, the buyer may want occasionally to be on hand in the receiving area in order to gain a firsthand impression of the types of items that are actually delivered as compared to what was ordered.

After the quality inspection—unless the entire order has been rejected—the receiver in some operations checks all prices and price extensions. [A price extension for a particular item on the invoice is the as-purchased (AP) price per unit of that product times the number of units purchased.] The receiver might also check all sales tax and other use taxes that are noted on the invoice to ensure accuracy. For instance, in most states, a hospitality operator must pay sales tax for merchandise that he or she will not resell, such as cleaning chemicals, but not for products earmarked for resale to consumers, such as meats and produce.

Unfortunately, checking all of these figures can take too long, usually because a receiver must compare the prices on the invoice with those that the supplier quoted prior to ordering the merchandise. It is necessary for the receiver to compare the invoice with the purchase order, or some other written purchase record, both to check the prices and to note whether the merchandise delivered actually was ordered in the first place. To save time, many operations have the accountant or bookkeeper check invoices later, before paying the bill.

It is probably a good idea to handle any AP price discrepancies as soon as possible. Waiting too long can produce confusion and distrust among business partners. Also, a supplier may be honest with the buyer and would want to know immediately if, for instance, a driver has altered the prices on the invoice. The opposite can also be true; that is, the supplier, for example, may have quoted a much lower AP price over the telephone than the one now written on the invoice. If so, the receiver should notify the deliveryperson so that he or she will be a witness to this discrepancy.

Rejection of Delivery

In some cases, a receiver may merely note a discrepancy regarding prices and/or taxes noted on the invoice. Alternately, he or she may have to reject all or part of an order. When this occurs, the receiver might prepare a Request for Credit memorandum, which is a written statement attesting to the fact that the particular item or items did not meet quality, quantity, or price standards (see Figures 14.2 and 14.3 for typical Request for Credit memoranda). The deliveryperson's signature shows that a representative of the supplier has agreed that the hospitality operation's account must be credited. The objective of this memo is to ensure that your account is credited and that all costs are accurate.

A receiver also may need to prepare a Request for Credit memo if he or she should receive credit for product substitutions, such as when a less expensive item than the one ordered is delivered. Also, the invoice might contain arithmetic errors that require adjustment. A back order may have been charged to the hospitality operator, in which case the receiver might want to ensure that the firm does not pay for the items, thereby tying up its money unnecessarily, until it receives them.

When the accounting office pays the invoices, it will reduce the invoice total by the amount indicated on the credit memorandum itself, which comes from the supplier after the receiver sends him or her a copy of the Request for Credit memo. Alternately, the supplier will give credit to the operator on the next delivery. Some operations eliminate credit memos when the supplier either agrees to give his or her deliverypeople authority to "reprice" the invoice on the spot or allows the de-

```
┌─────────────────────────────────────────────┐
│        ┌──────────────────────┐             │
│        │  NAME OF HOSPITALITY  │             │
│        │      OPERATION        │             │
│        └──────────────────────┘             │
│                                              │
│          Request for Credit Memorandum       │
│                                              │
│   Date _____                        │
│                                              │
│   To Supplier:  Please credit our account    │
│   because:                                   │
│                                              │
│          1. _____   │
│          2. _____   │
│          3. _____   │
│                                              │
├──────────────────────────────────────────────┤
│                                              │
│   Return ordered by _____  │
│                                              │
│   Invoice no. _____           │
│                                              │
│   Date received _____             │
│                         _____ │
│                         Deliverer's signature│
│                                              │
└──────────────────────────────────────────────┘
```

FIGURE 14.2 A Request for Credit memorandum.

liverypeople to prepare a credit memorandum, or "credit slip," right then and there and give it to the receiver. However, if a common carrier (i.e., an independent trucking firm) delivers the shipment, the receiver must complete a Request for Credit memo because the driver will have no authority to alter the delivery.

When credit paperwork is prepared, the original copy is usually sent to the supplier. In addition, the receiver or buyer might call the supplier; this serves as a check on the deliverypersons, who, for example, may have stolen the original item and substituted an inferior product. Another copy usually goes to whoever pays the bills. Some receivers might want to keep a copy as a reminder to be especially

Sheldon's Meats

100 MAIN ST.   LAS VEGAS, NEVADA 89123
555-1212
Federal Inspected Meat Plant Est. 1000

2336
CREDIT REQUEST

DATE

P.O. NUMBER

INVOICE NUMBER	DATE	WEIGHT	ITEM	PRICE	CREDIT AMOUNT	REASON NUMBER

AUTHORIZATION

CODE KEY ➡

1 - REFUSED   5 - NOT ON TRUCK
2 - WRONG PRODUCT   6 - PRICE ERROR
3 - SPOILED   7 - INVOICE ERROR
4 - SHORT WEIGHT   8 - OTHER

FIGURE 14.3 A Request for Credit memorandum used by customers of Sheldon's Meats.

careful of any future deliveries from this particular supplier. In addition, the buyer may want a copy in order to keep up to date on the supplier's performance.

Whenever rejection is contemplated, the owner-manager must not act too hastily. It may not be a good idea to reject a product that deviates only slightly from the hospitality operation's standard, for at least two reasons: (1) suppliers may not like to do business with a customer who focuses on small details, particularly one who sends back a reasonable substitute that the supplier sent because the ordered item was unavailable; and (2) in many cases, a rejection leaves a receiver short. It might be good business occasionally to accept some slight deviation since the potential ill will generated among suppliers and customers by hasty rejections may be detrimental.

Returning Merchandise

The receiver may have something from a previous delivery that the deliveryperson must return to his or her company's warehouse. For example, say the buyer has arranged to send back an unintentional overbuy of canned pears from the preceding week. Usually, in this situation, the supplier has given the deliveryperson a "Pick-Up" memorandum, authorizing him or her to take back the merchandise (see Figure 14.4).

Whenever a belated return must be arranged, the deliveryperson leaves a copy of the Pick-Up memo with the receiver. This copy serves as a receipt for the returned goods. The supplier will issue a credit memo later on, once he or she inspects the returned merchandise and is satisfied that the return is justified.

Acceptance of Delivery

When an order has been accepted, the receiver normally initials some paperwork attesting to the fact that everything is correct. The deliveryperson usually produces a delivery sheet or a copy of the invoice for the receiver to sign.

Unless the items are definitely substandard, the receiver accepts most deliveries. Even if only part of a shipment is acceptable, the customary practice is to keep what is good and return the rest along with a Request for Credit memo. For the most part, an owner-manager is reluctant to send back everything because the resultant shortages can, as we said, lead to dissatisfied customers.

Upon acceptance of the deliveries, the receiver usually places the items in the proper storage location or, in some cases, delivers them to a production department.

To ensure that all pertinent checks have been made, the receiver normally applies an ink stamp with a predetermined format to the invoice (see Figure 14.5 for a typical invoice stamp format stamped on incoming invoices).

This format notes all checks that must be performed and provides a space for those responsible to affix their initials. The receiver normally initials the first three entries; the accountant or bookkeeper, number 4; the buyer, number 5; and the owner-manager, number 6.

Sheldon's Meats

100 MAIN ST.   LAS VEGAS, NEVADA 89123

555-1212

Federal Inspected Meat Plant Est. 1000

CUSTOMER NAME

_____   **PICK-UP MEMO**

_____

_____

DATE	DRIVER	CUST NO		PICK UP MEMO NO	
QTY	GRADE	PROD CODE	DESCRIPTION	WEIGHT	PRICE

THIS IS NOT AN INVOICE OR CREDIT MEMO. IT IS A RECEIPT FOR MERCHANDISE RETURNED TO OUR PLANT FOR INSPECTION. YOU WILL BE ADVISED OF OUR FINDINGS AND DECISION AT THE COMPLETION OF THE INSPECTION.

DISPOSITION	DATE

FIGURE 14.4 A typical Pick-Up memorandum.

1. Date received _____

2. Received by _____

3. Prices checked by _____

4. Extensions checked by _____

5. Buyer's approval _____

6. Payment approval _____

FIGURE 14.5 **Typical invoice stamp information.**

After processing the invoice, the receiver may record the delivery on a "receiving sheet," or "receiving log." This sheet is nothing more than a running account of deliveries (see Figure 14.6 for a typical receiving sheet).

To a certain extent, the receiving sheet is a redundant exercise: it contains a good deal of information already on the invoice or affixed to the invoice via one or more invoice stamps. Large hospitality operations traditionally use the sheet, but the whole process may be avoided without any significant loss of control by merely photocopying invoices or scanning them into the computer for the buyer's and receiver's files.

One reason many operators like the receiving sheet is that it forces the receiver to record information, however redundant. Thus, mistakes previously overlooked sometimes come to light. Also, a copy of the receiving sheet usually stays in the receiver's files, which makes it handy for the receiver if he or she needs to evaluate a certain supplier's past performance. Furthermore, the sheet is useful to cost accountants who prepare daily food, beverage, and nonfood cost reports. Since the receiving sheet notes the deliveries on one page, it is convenient. In addition, the "Other Information" column can contain several comments that are not easily recorded on the incoming invoices. Such elements as the deliveryperson's attitude and the cleanliness of the delivery truck may be important to the buyer in future negotiations with that particular supplier.

Another reason for some managements' continuing desire for the receiving sheet is that it can be treated as the receiver's daily report of activities. This type of report is particularly attractive to the accountant in a large hotel who is responsible for the receiver's actions.

Overall, however, it is far more economical to record all such information on the incoming invoices or on invoice copies, or to attach a small Post-It note to these invoices if space is insufficient, and then make a copy of this completed invoice for the receiver's files.

DATE	TIME DELIVERED	QUANTITY	INVOICE NO.	PURVEYOR	DESCRIPTION OF ITEM(S)	UNIT PRICE	EXTENSION	*DIRECT			†STORES			OTHER INFORMATION?
								FOOD	BEVERAGE	NONFOOD	FOOD	BEVERAGE	NONFOOD	

* The receiver notes in this column the amount of food, beverage, and nonfood items that go directly to the production department, bypassing the main storage area. In other words, these items go directly into the in-process inventory.

† The receiver notes in this column the amount of food, beverage, and nonfood items that go into main storage.

FIGURE 14.6 A receiving sheet.

After making the necessary entries to the records, the receiver normally sends the incoming invoices, any credit slips, and a copy of the receiving sheet if one is used, to the accountant or bookkeeper. If a bill of lading, which is a piece of paper that represents title to the goods, comes with the delivered items, he or she sends this along also.

If the storage areas are supervised and controlled by someone other than the receiver, this person may want a copy of the receiving sheet to compare what is on the sheet with what has been put in storage. This is yet another type of control serving as a check on the receiver, although the buyer's and the accountant's copies can serve as more than sufficient control.

At this point, the receiver normally has stored the items or delivered them to production departments, completed the necessary paperwork, and sent the appropriate paperwork to the right office(s), along with any bills of lading that may have arrived at the receiving dock that day. He or she also keeps a copy of the receiving sheet.

Additional Receiving Duties

As a general rule, the receiving procedure is now complete. But the receiver may have other, less routine duties to perform. He or she may have to do one or more of the following:

Date the Delivered Items If it is too costly to do this, the usual compromise is to date only the perishable items. This dating is usually done with colored tags or with an ink stamp. This can facilitate proper "stock rotation," a process by which older products are used first.

Price All of the Delivered Items Like dating delivered items, this pricing may also be too costly, but it can have such benefits as costing of inventories for accounting purposes and providing an easy cost reference. Some operators like to price the items for the psychological effect it supposedly provides. Items that an operator has priced are no longer just merchandise to employees, but articles of value to be treated accordingly.

Many properties use the "Dot System" to date and price inventories. These are color-coded, stick-on dots (usually a different color for each day) that have sufficient space to pencil in dates, times, and prices. Incidentally, this procedure is also used to identify and code preprepared products that the kitchen staff has made. For instance, grated cheese to be used later on can be coded so that all cooks use any older grated cheese first (see Figure 14.7).

Create Bar Codes In some large hospitality operations, the receiving agent may need to create bar codes and apply them to incoming products that do not have them on their package labels. This is usually done to enhance the inventory management and control process, in that it makes it very easy to track inventories and their AP prices throughout the operation. While investing in the technology needed to adopt this procedure can be very expensive, in the long run it could prove very cost-effective.

Apply "Meat Tags" A meat tag contains information similar to that on an invoice stamp. The major difference between the two is that the typical meat tag contains two duplicate parts (see Figure 14.8). During the receiving procedure, one part of the tag is put on an item, and the other part goes to the accountant or bookkeeper for control purposes. When an item moves from the storage area to production, the part on the item is removed and sent to the accountant or bookkeeper, who matches it with the other part and removes it from the inventory file.

Specifically, meat tags are used as a check on the overall use of an item. For instance, comparisons are made between meat tags and stock requisitions (requests from a production department for items that are held in storage). Also, meat tags are sometimes compared with the service department's record of guest services. For example, with steak items, the meat tags can be compared with the sales of steaks to customers, thereby producing a check on the waitstaff. If everything goes right, all these comparisons will reveal that what was used from storage actually went to the paying customer, with no loss of product along the way. The units recorded on the meat tags should correspond exactly to the amounts used in production and the amounts sold to customers.

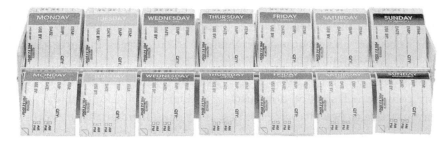

FIGURE 14.7 **An example of a Dot System. Courtesy of DayDots.**

```
                                                      No. 100

                    Date rec'd _____

                    Item _____

                    Grade _____

                    Wt. _____

                    Purveyor _____

                    Date issued _____

                    Date used _____
- - - - - - - - - - - - - - - - - - - - - - - - - - - - - - - - - -
                                                      No. 100

                    Date rec'd _____

                    Item _____

                    Grade _____

                    Wt. _____

                    Purveyor _____

                    Date issued _____

                    Date used _____
```

FIGURE 14.8 A meat tag.

The meat tag control is, however, cumbersome, unless it can be computerized and/or bar coded. And, like the receiving sheet, it tends to be redundant as well. If meat tags are used, they tend to be used only for high-cost products. Nevertheless, both meat tags and receiving sheets are used in operations that desire close control over their stock.

Housekeeping Management usually requires the receiver to maintain a clean, efficient workplace. Also, he or she usually ensures that all equipment and facilities are kept in good working order (see Figure 14.9).

Update AP Prices Hospitality operations that use a computerized management information system normally maintain updated AP prices for all merchandise they

FIGURE 14.9 An example of a modern storage area. Courtesy of Summit Foods.

buy. They also might maintain updated portion factors, portion dividers, and EP costs for all of the ingredients they currently serve, as well as all of the ingredients they might serve in the future. Furthermore, computerized hospitality operations also tend to maintain costed recipes in a recipe file for those menu items that are currently being offered to customers, as well as those that may be offered at a future date.

A computerized system includes the necessary formulas and databases to make the necessary calculations quickly. Since AP prices tend to vary from day to day in our industry, someone must continually "load the computer" with the new, current AP prices. In some operations, this task falls on the receiving agent. He or she, after performing the other required receiving duties, must follow the procedures needed to enter the new AP prices and to remove the old, outdated AP prices. Someone in the accounting department might just as easily do this task, but a receiving agent may be deemed the best person to do this work, especially if the task involves scanning the bar codes of all of the incoming products.

Backhaul Recyclables Some operations save their recyclables, such as corrugated cardboard, glass bottles, and metal cans, and hold them until a common carrier hired by a primary source to deliver a product shipment uses the emptied truck to "backhaul" the recyclables on the return trip. In this case, the receiving agent usually needs to help the driver load the truck and see to it that the driver has all of the necessary paperwork and authorizations.

OTHER RECEIVING METHODS

Occasionally, other receiving procedures are used. For the most part, though, they are variations of invoice receiving. Some of these alternate approaches are described in the following sections.

Standing-Order Receiving

This receiving procedure may not differ at all from invoice receiving. But receivers sometimes tend to "relax" a bit when checking items received on a standing-order basis. Also, delivery tickets rather than priced invoices may accompany the delivery, since the operation may make a regular, periodic payment to the supplier in exchange for the same amounts delivered at regular intervals.

It is really best to use invoice receiving to receive standing orders. Otherwise, deliverypeople, receivers, and bill payers can grow careless. In addition, deliveries may begin to "shrink" in both quantity and quality if strict receiving principles are not maintained.

Blind Receiving

The only difference between blind receiving and invoice receiving is that the invoice accompanying the delivery contains only the names of the items delivered, and no information about quantity and price. A duplicate invoice, which contains all of the necessary information, is usually sent to the accountant or bookkeeper one day before delivery.

Another form of blind receiving involves the need for the receiver to complete a "Goods Received Without Invoice" slip whenever a shipment comes in that does not have an invoice or delivery slip. For instance, a mailed delivery or shipment delivered by a messenger service may not have accompanying paperwork. When this happens, the receiver must check with management and, if the shipment is legitimate, inspect the products and complete the in-house invoice slip.

The whole idea behind blind receiving is to increase the margin of control. The receiver is forced to weigh and count everything and then record this information. Such a procedure effectively prohibits the receiver from stealing part of the delivery and altering the invoice. Also, the procedure precludes any fraudulent relationship between the receiver and the deliveryperson.

A good deal of disagreement exists regarding the benefits of blind receiving. The general feeling in the industry is that the receiving agent should have some idea of what to expect; otherwise he or she might receive the wrong product, too much product, too little product, and so forth. Such unintentional errors can destroy an operation's production planning.

Blind receiving is a time-consuming, costly method of receiving and processing deliveries. Operations can employ technology to speed up the process, but it normally is too expensive to be used for only a short period each day or in a small operation. Furthermore, drivers do not like to wait for a receiver to record every last detail of information.

Although we can appreciate the control benefits of blind receiving, we consider it an archaic method, similar to receiving sheets and meat tags. We know of few establishments that still use it. It is too expensive; besides, a receiver under suspicion can be checked with the accountant's copy of the original purchase order. The invoice should look just like the original purchase order; if they look different, management should ask for a good explanation—or look for a new receiver.

Odd-Hours Receiving

The major difference with this receiving method is that the regular receiver is not on hand to accept the delivery. In most cases, an assistant manager is then entrusted with this duty. Although the invoice method may be applied during odd hours, an inadequate receiving job may result. The stand-in receiver usually has other pressing duties and, as a result, tends to rush the receiving process. Usually, the owner-manager recognizes this potential danger and tries to arrange for deliveries when the regular receiver is on duty. But some deliveries must be made at odd hours. As a result, it may be a good idea for the owner-manager to print the regular receiving procedure on a poster and hang it in the receiving area to aid the stand-in receiver.

Drop-Shipment Receiving

When a buyer purchases products from a primary source, that source usually hires a common carrier to "drop ship" the merchandise to the hospitality operation. Remember, the common carrier is typically an independent trucker hired to provide only the transportation function.

When a common carrier delivers a shipment, the receiving procedure used is very similar to the standard invoice receiving process. The major difference is that the driver is not involved with any disputes that may arise between the buyer and the primary source, unless he or she is directly responsible for the problem. For instance, if the driver damages the goods along the way, the buyer must deal with the driver or the driver's employer. But, as is more often the case, if the products do not meet the buyer's specifications, the receiver usually must take the shipment from the driver and hold it until the problems are rectified. Ordinarily, the driver is not in a position to take back returned merchandise.

When disagreements arise between the buyer and the supplier in this situation, it is difficult to resolve them. For example, the buyer may have to arrange for another common carrier to return the shipment. Alternately, he or she may have to wait for the supplier's representative to arrive and check the items personally before a settlement can be reached. In addition, if the shipment is insured by an independent insurance company, its representative may need to inspect the claim and monitor the negotiations. When hospitality operators buy directly from primary sources, especially unfamiliar ones on the Web, seemingly little problems can add a great deal of stress to the transaction before they are cured.

Mailed Deliveries

When orders are delivered by mail, or by similar means, such as United Parcel Service (UPS) or FedEx, the invoices that come with them are normally referred to as "packing slips." These slips are treated like any other invoice except when the order does not match the packing slip's description. In this instance, a Request for Credit memo or some similar record must be completed, but usually management, not the receiver, does this. The receiver notes any discrepancy and then turns the shipment over to his or her supervisor.

Cash-on-Delivery (COD) Deliveries

Under this system, the receiver has the added duty of paying the delivery agent or, more commonly, sending the delivery agent to the office for the payment check. It is also possible that the receiver accompanies the delivery agent to the office so that he or she can attest to the adequacy of the delivered items.

GOOD RECEIVING PRACTICES

Receivers should follow a number of sound procedures. Most of them fall mainly under the security category:

1. Receivers should beware of excess ice, watered-down products, wrapping paper, and packaging that can add dead weight to the delivered items. Receivers must subtract the amount of this dead weight, which is sometimes referred to as the "tare weight," from the gross weight in order to compute the net weight of the merchandise.

2. Receivers should always check the quality under the top layer. Make sure that all succeeding layers are equal to the facing layer.

3. Receivers should always examine packages for leakage or other forms of water damage. This could indicate that the package contents are unusable. If the packages, especially cans, are swollen, the contents are probably spoiled and receivers should reject the shipment.

4. If a package label carries an expiration date, receivers should ensure that it is within acceptable limits. Receivers should also make sure that the dating codes are correct.

5. Receivers should not weigh everything together. For example, they should separate hamburger from steak and weigh each product by itself. If they weigh these items together, they might begin to buy hamburger at a steak price.

6. Receivers should be wary of deliverypersons eager to help them carry the delivered items to their storage areas. Trust is not the issue. The big problems with letting people on the premises are the distraction they cause among employees and the possibility that liability insurance premiums will increase.

7. Receivers should watch for incomplete shipments, as well as for the deliveryperson who asks them to sign for a complete order after telling them that the rest of the order will arrive later. Later may never come.

8. Receivers should spot-check portioned products for portion weights. For example, if receivers buy portioned sausage patties by the pound and sell them by the piece, a 2-ounce sausage patty that is consistently $1/4$ ounce overweight will inflate the food cost. But operators will not reflect this in their sales since their menu price will still reflect a 2-ounce portion. It is equally troubling if the sausage patties are underweight and are purchased by the piece; a short weight of as little as $1/8$ ounce can cost quite a bit of money in the long run.

9. Receivers should be careful of closed shipping containers with preprinted dates, weights, counts, or quality standards. Someone may have repacked these cartons with inferior merchandise. It might be wise to weigh flour sacks, rice sacks, potato sacks, and the like, once in a while. Receivers might even open a box of paper napkins occasionally to count them.

10. Receivers should also be careful that they do not receive merchandise that has been refrozen. In addition, they should be on the lookout for supposedly fresh merchandise that is actually "slacked out" (i.e., has been frozen, thawed, and made to appear as if it is fresh).

11. At times, receivers may confuse brand names and/or packers' brand names. This is easy to do when receivers are in a hurry.

12. When receiving some fresh merchandise, such as meats, fish, and poultry, receivers normally give suppliers a "shrink" allowance. For instance, dehydration might turn 25 pounds of fresh lobster today into 24 pounds of lobster tomorrow. The product specification normally indicates the minimum weight per case that receivers will accept, but in some circumstances, they may not be able to judge the delivery as closely as they would like. When they weigh the shipment, it might be within the accepted tolerance; however, it is not easy for receivers to determine acceptability quickly when they are busy weighing several packages of various sizes. Delivery drivers know this, and, as such, some may be tempted to test a receiver's skills to see how much shrink he or she is willing to accept.

13. In general, receivers are concerned about any product that they receive that does not live up to their specifications. It is absolutely essential to prepare adequate specifications because this is the only way receivers can ensure that they have the appropriate standard upon which to judge incoming merchandise.

We do not intend to criticize suppliers or delivery agents. A good rule in business is to maintain a cautious optimism when receiving, but remember that it is possible to get "stung" in at least four ways: (1) the unintentional error, (2) the dishonest supplier with an honest delivery agent, (3) the honest supplier with a dishonest delivery agent, and (4) a dishonest supplier with a dishonest delivery agent. Keep in mind that once receivers sign for a delivery, the items are theirs. So receivers must verify that they receive the right quantity, quality, and AP price.

REDUCING RECEIVING COSTS

Receivers can reduce receiving costs a few ways without losing a proportionate amount of control. Some common cost-saving methods are described in the following paragraphs.

1. **Field Inspectors.** Large firms sometimes use field inspectors, which saves some time for receivers in that they do not have to check for quality and quantity. This is because the inspector often seals the packages to be delivered. The overall cost, though, may not decrease; field inspectors, like receivers, must be paid.

2. **Night and Early-Morning Deliveries.** These odd-hour deliveries are often the rule in the downtown sections of many large cities in order to avoid daytime traffic congestion. With fewer distractions, delivery agents can make more deliveries, and part of the lower transportation cost per delivery may be passed on to hospitality operations. A variation of this procedure is the "night drop," in which a delivery agent uses a key to get in, places the items inside the door, locks up, and leaves. Opinion varies among operators regarding the degree of trust required for this practice.

3. **One-Stop Shopping.** This is, perhaps, the most common method of reducing receiving costs. Although some people are not enthusiastic about this buying method, everyone agrees that it can reduce receiving costs.

In trying to reduce receiving costs, receivers must be careful that they do not simply shift the costs around. For instance, low receiving costs accompany one-stop shopping, but the savings from reducing the number of potential suppliers may be wiped out by higher AP prices from a single supplier.

Certain inescapable costs must be incurred if receivers expect to meet the objectives of the purchasing and receiving functions. It is absolutely essential not to negate the effective job the buyer may have done. In the end, the receiving function affords few cost-cutting possibilities unless receivers are willing to give up a certain amount of control.

KEY WORDS AND CONCEPTS

Accepting a delivery

As-purchased price (AP price)

Backhaul

Bar codes

Bill of lading

Blind receiving

Cash on delivery (COD)

Checking the quantity, quality, AP price, sales tax, and other use tax

Common carrier

Computerized record keeping

Credit memo

Credit slip

Cycle of control

Date and price items that are delivered

Delivery ticket

Dot system

Drop shipment

Early-morning deliveries

Edible-portion cost (EP cost)

Equal to facing layer

Essentials for good receiving

Expiration date

Field inspectors

Good receiving practices that should be followed

Goods Received Without Invoice slip

Gross weight

Handling an invoice discrepancy

Incomplete shipments

Invoice

Invoice receiving

Invoice stamp

Loading the computer with current AP prices

Mailed deliveries

Meat tags

Net weight

Night deliveries

Night drop

Odd-hours receiving

One-stop shopping

Packing slip

Pick-Up memo

Price extensions

Purchase order (PO)

Quality assurance

Quality control

Receiving objectives

Receiving sheet

Rejecting a delivery

Request for Credit memo

Returning merchandise

Route salesperson

Sales tax

Shrink allowance

Slacked out

Specifications

Standing-order receiving

Stock requisition

Stock rotation

Tare weight

Use tax

Water damage

Ways to reduce receiving costs

REFERENCES

1. Patt Patterson, "Checks and Balances Prevent Disputes Over Orders," *Nation's Restaurant News*, November 22, 1993, p. 82.

2. Robert B. Lane, "Food and Beverage Management," in *VNR's Encyclopedia of Hospitality and Tourism*, Mahmood Khan, Ed. (New York: Van Nostrand Reinhold, 1993), p. 39.

QUESTIONS AND PROBLEMS

1. You hear that your competitors are using a control device called "blind receiving." What is blind receiving? Under what conditions would you use this procedure?

2. Explain how one-stop shopping can reduce your overall receiving costs.

3. At 10 A.M. on September 27, the A & H Foods Company delivered the following items:

UNIT	QUANTITY	ITEM DESCRIPTION	UNIT PRICE	EXTENSION
Pound	80	T-bone steaks	$ 6.85	$548.00
Pound	18	Sliced bacon	2.80	50.40
Pound	20	Flank steak	4.25	85.00
Case	2	Floor wax, gallon cans	28.00	56.00
Case	2	Boston lettuce	16.50	33.00
Case	1	Canned green beans, No. 10 cans	17.50	17.50
Total				$789.90

Upon inspection, you determine that the sliced bacon is inferior and that you must return it to the supplier.

(a) Using Figure 14.2 as a guide, prepare a Request for Credit memo for the bacon.

(b) Using Figure 14.5 as a guide, complete the information on the invoice stamp that the receiver usually completes.

(c) Using Figure 14.6 as a guide, transfer the acceptable items to the receiving sheet. *Note:* The flank steak goes directly into the in-process inventory.

4. What type of information would you like to have in the "Other Information" column on the receiving sheet? Why?

5. Many operators feel that the receiving sheet is useful in calculating daily food, beverage, and nonfood costs. How do you think the receiving sheet is helpful in this matter?

6. What should a receiver do when a question arises regarding the quality of merchandise received?

7. What should a receiver do if a delivery is made without an accompanying invoice?

8. A receiver will prepare a Request for Credit memo when:

(a)

(b)

(c)

9. List some objectives of the receiving function.

10. List the primary essentials that are needed for proper receiving.

11. What is the primary difference between invoice receiving and blind receiving?

12. Briefly describe the computation of price extensions.

13. Describe one purpose of using an invoice stamp.

14. What is the primary reason for using meat tags?

15. Briefly describe the concept of stock rotation.

16. What is a bill of lading?

17. What does it mean when we say that a food item has been "slacked out"?

18. Why should you separate meat items before weighing them?

19. What is the primary purpose of the Pick-Up memo?

20. Assume you must pay sales tax for all nonfood items you purchase. If the sales tax rate is 6 percent, recalculate the invoice total for Question 3.

21. What is the significance of the expiration date placed on the package label of some food products?

22. Assume you are checking in a shipment of canned goods. You notice some dried water spots on the bottom of one of the cases. You open the case and notice nothing leaking from the cans. Should you accept the shipment? Why or why not?

23. What are the advantages and disadvantages of the standing-order receiving procedure?

EXPERIENTIAL EXERCISES

1. Visit a local supplier and arrange to ride with a deliveryperson as he or she makes the rounds. Compare and contrast the receiving procedures you see in each hospitality operation. In addition, take the time to examine how the supplier processes his or her copy of the invoice.

2. Arrange to spend one day in the receiving area of a hotel or restaurant. Evaluate the receiving procedures the receiver uses. In addition, try to follow the paperwork, from invoice processing, receiving-sheet completion, and so on, up to the end of the receiver's paperwork duties. If management allows, pick out one invoice and stay with it as it travels from the receiving area to the accounting department. While in the accounting department, see whether you can determine how and when this particular invoice will be paid.

CHAPTER 15

TYPICAL STORAGE MANAGEMENT PROCEDURES

The Purpose of this Chapter

After reading this chapter, you should be able to:

- **Explain the objectives of storage.**

- **Identify space, temperature, humidity, and other requirements of proper storage.**

- **Describe the process of managing storage facilities, including inventory.**

- **List important storage-management practices for small hospitality operators.**

INTRODUCTION

Storage is an activity typically performed in conjunction with receiving. As soon as receivers inspect incoming merchandise, they ensure that it is put in the proper storage facility. In some instances, receivers may send some items directly to a production department. For example, steaks scheduled for tonight's banquet should go directly to the kitchen. (Items sent directly to the production departments are usually referred to as "direct purchases" or "directs" when an internal issues system is used.)

Often, the same person who receives also stores. Large operations may divide this responsibility by assigning, for example, the receiving function to a receiving supervisor and the storage function to a storeroom manager. But typically, the receiver and storeroom manager are the same person. In small operations, the user-buyer or the chef might receive and store products and even manage the storage facilities. Good control, however, implies some separation of responsibilities.

THE OBJECTIVES OF STORAGE

The basic goal of storage management is to prevent loss of merchandise due to: (1) theft, (2) pilferage, and (3) spoilage.

Theft is premeditated burglary. It occurs when someone drives a truck up to the back door of an operation and steals all of the expensive foods, beverages, and equipment. Generally, storage facilities are not designed to prevent this. Management would need a citadel to eliminate theft. Storage security is normally designed to discourage employee theft by keeping honest employees honest. In some parts of the United States, and the rest of the world, theft is common. Thus, hospitality operators must see to it that storage facilities are designed so as to make theft more difficult, generally by some combination of clear visibility of general access storage and very tight security on locked, limited-access storage located elsewhere. Locking storage areas when not in use and minimizing the number of persons who have access to the keys appear to be good practices.

Pilferage is a serious problem in the hospitality industry and centers on the employee who sneaks off with a bottle of mustard or a couple of ashtrays. Eating on the job is another form of pilferage, unless the owner-manager allows it. Shoplifting also falls in this category.

Pilferage is sometimes referred to as "inventory shrinkage" or "skimming." The estimated dollar losses resulting from pilferage vary considerably, but industry experts feel that approximately 2 to 4 percent of every sales dollar is lost to employee and customer dishonesty. Several potential ways to control pilferage exist, some of which we discuss in the next chapter. Unfortunately, in some cases, the cure may be more expensive than the disease.

Spoilage can be controlled a little more easily than either theft or pilferage. Generally, spoilage can be minimized by adhering to rigid sanitation practices, rotating the stock so that old items are used first, and providing the proper environmental conditions for each item in storage.

Rigid sanitation is, in fact, a must in all storage facilities. This involves two quite different kinds of steps. First, products that might induce spoilage in others through migration of odors or chemicals must be separated properly. For example, fresh fish is not stored with butter, and cleaning agents are segregated from food products. A second and more obvious sanitation activity involves keeping the storage facility clean, for instance, by mopping it daily.

Any sanitation slipup not only hastens spoilage, but also increases the risk of customer or employee sickness. Some states and local municipalities have legislation that requires hospitality management personnel to successfully pass some sort of a sanitation test or to satisfactorily complete an approved sanitation course. There is also discussion suggesting that eventually all of the hospitality employees will have to pass some type of sanitation certification exam.

The proper environmental conditions for storage seem easy enough to achieve. But the expense of providing for all the various temperature and humidity requirements for an entire spectrum of food products can be burdensome for small restaurants. Nonfood storage is not so large a problem, but a good deal of valuable space may be required.

Freezers; separate produce, dairy, and meat refrigerators; and separate dry storage areas for groceries, beverages, and cleaning supplies can all add up to a large investment. This can be so large, in fact, that small operations often try to make do with outdated facilities, which can get them into trouble with the local health department.

The benefits of proper environmental conditions are definite but sometimes not readily apparent. The prevention of food-borne illness does not carry a price tag. Moreover, improper storage can cause a significant loss of nutritional value and taste. The value here is difficult to quantify. Lost nutrition does not necessarily concern restaurant customers, but school foodservice operations might consider this loss unacceptable. Fortunately, even though a hospitality operation may maintain an old, erratic refrigerator, proper stock rotation and a reasonably quick stock turnover can minimize quality loss.

It would probably be enlightening for operators to monitor the losses attributable directly to improper environmental conditions. For example, how much cheese has to be discarded because it absorbed onion flavors? How much flour attracts excessive moisture? Most operations experience some losses because of complete spoilage or because products, while technically not spoiled, have passed their peak of culinary quality and are not suitable for guest service. But when these losses are compared with the cost associated with providing the proper environment, they may seem insignificant.

They are not insignificant, however, when operators go beyond mere dollars and cents. Operators must be very concerned, for example, with the loss of their operation's reputation should a customer get sick after eating in their establishment. How do they compare this reputation loss with the cost of proper environmental conditions?

There is an old saying in the hospitality industry: "The most important asset a hospitality company has is its reputation." This asset should be protected first. Clearly, a few thousand dollars pales in comparison with a loss of goodwill. But how many operators are able to make this connection? We see the few thousand dollars easily. But we do not necessarily see the loss of goodwill as the primary concern.

WHAT IS NEEDED TO ACHIEVE STORAGE OBJECTIVES?

The major factors needed to achieve the storage objectives are discussed in the following sections.

Adequate Space

Of all requirements, this is probably the hardest for hospitality operators to comply with. Usually, they must accept what they have to work with unless they are willing to remodel or add more floor space to the building.

If hospitality operators are constructing the building from the ground up, designers can plan for optimal space, for today and for the future. But when building costs must be cut somewhere, the storage area is vulnerable. This is unfortunate because it not only hampers current storage demands, but also limits the types of products operators can store in the future. Also, this more or less permanently limits what they can offer customers.

Generally, the space needed for all storage is between 5 square feet per dining room seat and 15 square feet per hotel room, depending on the amount of sales, types of items sold, the quantity of nonfood items held in storage, and the local health district space requirements. A well-managed facility usually allocates about 10 to 12 percent of the total property for the storage function.[1] Typically, owner-managers try to minimize the storage space so that they can add more dining room seats or rooms. Real estate is expensive, and no one can blame owner-managers if they prefer tables and chairs that generate sales to storage shelves whose direct relation to sales is not so clear. But the smaller the storage space is today, usually the more limited are an operator's offerings tomorrow.

Adequate Temperature and Humidity

A hospitality operation that houses one or more foodservice facilities will need to follow its local health district temperature requirements and space requirements.

In general, the health district mandates that all potentially hazardous food—such as meats, seafood, and poultry—must be stored at 40°F, or below, or at 140°F, or above. However, the Food Safety and Inspection Service of the United States Department of Agriculture (USDA) has suggested more stringent hot-storage temperatures for cooked hamburger meat and poultry (see Figure 15.1). Nonhazardous food and nonfood items usually have no temperature requirements. Furthermore, they usually have no mandated humidity requirements.

A local health district typically mandates certain space requirements, so that good housekeeping practices can be performed. For instance, merchandise usually must be stored about 4 inches from the walls, ceiling, and floor. Food items usually must be stored on shelving that is not solid, so that proper air circulation can

FIGURE 15.1 Temperature rules suggested for cooking foods at home. *Source:* USDA's Food and Safety Inspection Service (FSIS).

be maintained. Food cannot be stored under any exposed or unprotected sewer lines or water lines, or in rooms with toilet or garbage facilities. Furthermore, such material as soaps, chemicals, and pest control supplies must be stored in a separate storage area so that they can neither contaminate food and beverage products, nor be picked up by accident by someone obtaining food supplies.

While health district requirements are important, they represent *minimum* standards of sanitation and wholesomeness. Wise hospitality operators will go beyond these requirements in order to ensure that the shelf life of all stored merchandise is maximized. You can accomplish this objective by following the temperature guidelines presented by the National Restaurant Association Educational Foundation (NRAEF).[2] Its recommendations are:

- Meat and poultry: 32°F to 41°F

- Fresh fish: 32°F to 36°F

- Live shellfish: 30°F to 41°F

- Eggs: 40°F to 45°F

- Dairy products: 35°F to 41°F

- Most fruits and vegetables: ranging from 32°F to 50°F

- Freezer storage: 0°F to 10°F

To maintain these suggested temperature requirements, hospitality operators must invest in a considerable amount of expensive storage facilities. For instance, in large hotels, it is common to find several walk-in refrigerators and freezers, each one serving a particular environmental need. Typical hospitality operators cannot afford this investment. Consequently, they must ensure rapid inventory turnover, so that product quality does not deteriorate to the extent that customer dissatisfaction would result.

Adequate Equipment

A proper storage area requires at least three major types of equipment: shelving/racks, trucks, and covered containers. Shelving, wall racks, and floor racks (i.e., "dunnage racks" or "pallets") are essential because you cannot store anything directly on the floor. Motorized and/or nonmotorized trucks are needed to transport products in and out of storage. Furthermore, covered containers, including see-through plastic buckets and pans, are needed to hold products, such as cored lettuce, that you may want to remove from shipping crates before placing into storage.

Proximity of Storage Area to Receiving and Production Areas

To the extent possible, you should install the storage facilities close to the receiving dock and to the production departments. In addition, it is desirable to place the receiving, storage, and production areas on the same floor level. This saves time and ensures that products are not out of their storage environments for excessive periods.

Access to Proper Maintenance Is Essential

Depending on the size of the operation, thousands, tens of thousands, even hundreds of thousands of dollars worth of inventory can be on hand at any one time. One freezer breakdown can ruin a considerable amount of frozen food. A leaking water pipe can damage huge amounts of food in the dry storage areas.

A maintenance contract is, therefore, useful, even though it carries no guarantee that the service person can get there precisely when needed. Some operations hire their own maintenance personnel to ensure that service is available at a moment's notice. Unfortunately, small operations cannot afford this luxury. Their best bet is to purchase good equipment in the first place.

Proper Security Is a Must

Chapter 16 contains a discussion of relevant security considerations, not only for storage, but also for other aspects of the selection and procurement function.

Competent Personnel Are Needed to Supervise and Manage the Storage Function

Typically, one person receives, stores, and issues items to production departments. It is even more common for one person to buy, receive, store, and eventually use the items in production. A working chef, for example, may perform all these tasks.

Large firms usually impose some separation of responsibility; small firms often have to rely on whoever is available at the time to receive and store incoming merchandise. When a production department needs an item, quite often someone just goes into an unsecured storage area to get it.

Experts often assert that the savings from good receiving, storage, and issuing can be quantified; some experts put the potential savings at 2 percent of a hospitality operation's sales, although others would opt for the lower figure of 2 percent of its purchases. Since no actual cost studies are available to back up either figure, it is hard to assert a hard-and-fast rule beyond saying that good procedures in this area of logistics are important, involving potential savings of, perhaps, as much as 2 percent of sales.

Any savings a hospitality operation achieves in this area will correspond closely with the competence of the person(s) performing these functions. Having a rule that states that nothing leaves the storeroom without permission is one thing; implementing and enforcing this rule is something else again. Hence, the ability of people working in these areas is critical. The best-designed receiving and storage facilities and receiving, storing, and issuing procedures are useless if the right person is not on the job.

Finally, we have to realize that ideal circumstances do not always occur. Sales volume may not be large enough to permit the operation to "follow the book" and have people available for all functions. Conversely, volume may be large enough to afford proper support staff, but the labor market may be too tight and the kind of people you want for this function may be unavailable. Developing ways to secure goods under these less than ideal conditions is challenging.

Sufficient Time to Perform the Necessary Duties Is Almost Always Missing

Adequate time is just as important as employee talent. Receiving, storing, and issuing involve more than just weighing food and putting it into storage. Hospitality operations have many other tasks, such as monitoring the necessary control procedures, maintaining sanitation, rotating the stock, keeping track of usage patterns, and so on.

Small operations cannot always afford the time to do all of these tasks. But even large companies tend to load down the receiver-storeroom clerk with such extraneous duties as sorting mail.

It is unfortunate when hotels, restaurants, institutions, and clubs go to the expense of hiring good people and designing excellent receiving, storing, and issuing procedures, but then stop short at providing enough time to discharge these functions adequately.

Storeroom Regulations Are an Absolute Must, for Both Control and Predictability

Regulations dictate who is allowed to enter storage areas and who is allowed to obtain items from storage. Also specified is the required procedure to use to obtain these items. In some cases, the senior management determines these guidelines. But large firms that set broad guidelines often expect the storeroom manager to work out the day-to-day details necessary for a smooth-running operation.

MANAGING THE STORAGE FACILITIES

Small operations usually hope that the storage facilities will manage themselves. An idle food server, for example, might be sent into the storeroom now and then to clean up. Similarly, the chef may have a few moments to rotate the stock. Often, though, the storage areas of small operations are not managed systematically.

The one exception seems to be the liquor storeroom. An owner-manager keeps this area locked at the very least. In addition, he or she may personally receive these items. And since the liquor control commission requires bars to maintain records of their liquor purchases, considerably more bookkeeping and record keeping is done here than elsewhere. Liquor storage tends, then, to be well organized almost everywhere, but the same cannot be said for soap, paper towels, and light bulbs. The food storage area falls between these two extremes, but the degree of attention here varies dramatically from one operation to another. For instance, in some places, food servers enter the storeroom at will to retrieve salt, pepper, catsup, and so on. In others, only a predetermined number of hours during the day are set aside for issuing supplies of any sort.

Larger operations that can afford the luxury of a receiver-storeroom manager assign him or her several activities. The major ones are discussed in the following sections.

1. Inventories must be classified and organized in a systematic fashion (see Figure 15.2). This procedure simplifies general control and also helps with the preparation of reports that deal with inventories and their costs.

    Some storeroom managers label the shelf location with the name of the item that occupies that spot; they take this step in dry, refrigerated, and frozen storage. Furthermore, a diagram of a storage facility, complete with a guide noting where each particular item is located, is often displayed on the door-

FIGURE 15.2 **An example of classifying by date food items in inventory using DayDot stickers. Courtesy of DayDots.**

way of the facility. Other operators, however, take a considerably more flexible approach to control the use of storage space.

It is important for operators to organize and classify their inventories in a manner that satisfies the local legal requirements. For instance, normally the local health district stipulates that toxic materials must be housed in a separate storage facility and that this location must be locked unless it is necessary to enter it. It is conceivable that in your locale, alcoholic beverages must be kept in a separate area because underage employees must not be exposed to this merchandise.

2. Usage rates must be determined for all inventories. Storeroom managers must keep track of the usage patterns so that they can revise and help improve ordering procedures and par stock levels. In addition, this information can help determine the optimal reorder point.

3. Storeroom managers must occasionally make an emergency order or travel to the supplier's location to pick up extra items, particularly if a stockout threatens. The storeroom manager may also need to pick up an order right away rather than wait for the scheduled delivery. This is sometimes necessary when a supplier must alter his or her normal delivery schedule.

4. Storeroom managers also keep track of accumulating surpluses. The chef may fail to inform the buyer that certain items have been removed from the menu. This communication breakdown happens now and then. It is more liable to occur in the largest operations—those that have two or more dining facilities and two or more food production areas.

5. Storeroom managers may be responsible for disposing of items that the hospitality operation no longer uses. Buyers may want to do this personally, but often storeroom managers may arrange to return merchandise to the supplier, trade it, or otherwise get rid of it.

6. Storeroom managers may need to effect transfers of merchandise to other company outlets. For instance, if another unit in the restaurant chain needs frozen french fries, the manager may need to send it some of its own. Storeroom managers might also do this if they are overstocked and another unit is understocked. Whatever the case, when doing this, storeroom managers usually must complete a Transfer Slip (which is similar to an invoice) so that the stock is controlled and accounted for properly.

7. Storeroom managers may keep track of all inventories and their corresponding dollar value. This important and time-consuming duty is discussed in detail below.

Some companies want to keep a perpetual inventory system; that is, they want to know what is on hand in the storeroom at all times. These firms might even keep track of all in-process inventories in addition to the storeroom inventories. As a rule, however, this kind of control requires a considerable amount of computer technology.

Because such a system costs a good deal of time and money, it is sometimes used, usually without a computer, for only a few items. In such cases, it is generally used for the most expensive items. And, to a great extent, it is used for most liquor.

Because storeroom managers must keep records of liquor purchases, it is only a bit more trouble to keep a perpetual inventory by keeping a "bin card" next to each type of liquor in storage (see Figure 15.3).

A bin card is a record of all liquor, or other items, delivered, all liquor sent to the production areas—bars, kitchen, and service areas—and, in some cases, all liquor sent back to storage from the production areas.

At one time, several large hotels and clubs kept no inventories in the production areas when these areas were closed. That is, at the beginning of a shift, a

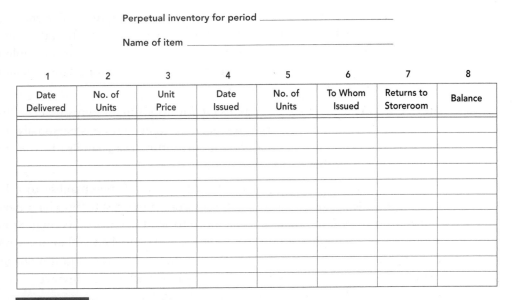

Perpetual inventory for period _____

Name of item _____

1	2	3	4	5	6	7	8
Date Delivered	No. of Units	Unit Price	Date Issued	No. of Units	To Whom Issued	Returns to Storeroom	Balance

FIGURE 15.3 A bin card.

bartender, for example, would pick up and sign for a complete par stock of all the items needed during the shift. Any necessary replenishment was usually handled by an assistant manager. At the end of the shift, the bartender would send everything back to storage. Storeroom managers then would determine what had been used during the shift, and this amount should correspond to the bar sales amount. This type of procedure is no longer in widespread use in our industry, but it is still followed for banquet bars.

Such a procedure is time-consuming and requires someone in the storeroom to set up the par stocks for each user. But this approach does eliminate the need for stock requisitions—a concept we address in our discussion of issuing later in this chapter. Some operations do insist that at least the more expensive items be treated this way. For instance, a chef may follow this procedure with meat and fish. Also, a bartender may have to follow it for some liquors. In other words, storeroom managers closely monitor the costly items and require users to pick up and return them; it is unacceptable to keep any of them in the in-process inventory except during working hours.

The perpetual inventory has some advantages, such as providing for a tight degree of control. Moreover, many operators believe that if they continually monitor inventory levels, they will remain close to the optimal levels because they will have accurate par stocks.

Today, the cost of maintaining a perpetual inventory "by hand" for more than a few items is almost prohibitive. Not only does the labor cost of accomplishing it loom large, but experience teaches that hand-posted records often contain a good deal of human error, often to the point of making their value questionable. Consequently, the greatest use of perpetual inventory for a total inventory is found in hospitality operations in which all departments are integrated into a computerized management information system (MIS).

Operators who once swore by the perpetual inventory system now tend to take a complete physical inventory once weekly, every ten days, semimonthly, or monthly. In this way, they keep track of their overall performance.

A physical inventory, in contrast to a perpetual inventory, is an actual counting and valuing of all of the items in storage and, in some cases, of all of the items in the in-process inventory. Three good reasons exist for taking a physical inventory: (1) It is useful for operators to have this information before calculating order sizes and preparing purchase orders. (2) It is necessary for accountants who must calculate product costs. For example, they might want to compute the actual food cost for the month (see Figure 15.4). (3) Assuming some type of perpetual inven-

---

The cost equations are:

$$BI + P - EI = C$$

$$C \div S = C\%$$

where BI = beginning inventory

P = purchases for the month

EI = ending inventory

S = sales

C = food cost

C% = food cost percentage

Note that in the example below, some operations may make other adjustments, such as granting a credit for employee meals, in order to determine the actual food cost for food sold to guests.

BI (which is last month's EI)	$12,000
P	+20,000
EI	−14,000
Credit for employee meals	−2,000
C	$16,000

If S = $49,000, C% = $16,000/$49,000 = 32.6%

FIGURE 15.4 The calculation of this month's actual food cost.

tory is used, the physical-inventory count can be compared with the "theoretical-inventory" count shown on bin card records. In this case, if the actual inventory does not equal the theoretical inventory, an inventory control problem may exist.

Taking a physical inventory can be very time-consuming, especially when every item, including the inventory of goods in production, is counted. It is not, however, as time-consuming as maintaining a perpetual inventory.

Regardless of the amount of time needed to perform a physical inventory, the hospitality operation usually must do it at least once a month. The monthly profit-and-loss statement for the operation must be prepared. This cannot be done unless the operator knows his or her cost of goods sold, and the operator cannot compute this expense unless he or she takes a physical inventory.

Several ways exist to take the inventory. One method requires two persons, one calling and the other writing. Usually, when this or any other procedure is used, the storage facilities are laid out in a predetermined pattern, such as alphabetically. The inventory sheets are preprinted with the items' names and spaces where the writer can record the numerical entries. In a computerized installation, the sheets can be printed by the computer via manual entry or entered directly on a portable computer. Those operators without computers must prepare these sheets in some other way.

Another inventory-taking method that has become popular in the hospitality industry is to use a handheld bar code scanner to record stock levels. In a hospitality operation that has a fully integrated, computerized MIS, such a procedure is a natural addition to the overall inventory management process.

Operators who do not have access to the latest computer technology can adopt shortcuts that speed the inventory-taking process with only minor sacrifices of accuracy. These shortcuts include: (1) Operators count everything in the storage areas and then add on a certain predetermined percentage to represent the amount of items in the in-process inventory. (2) They count only full-case equivalents. That is, operators do not add in half a can of baking powder; they just count full cases, boxes, or cans. (3) Operators combine inventory taking with the ordering procedure. If the storage manager's count is sufficiently accurate, correct purchase orders can be prepared. This does, however, have a drawback: it offers the storeroom manager the opportunity to manipulate the count, a risk that must be judged acceptable if this procedure is to be followed. (4) Operators use a tape recorder to recite units and dollar values, and later on, someone transcribes the information. (5) Operators may use a handheld computer device to encode their inventories, and later on, this electronically gathered information can be processed and printed.

Some operators do not want their storeroom manager taking inventory, at least not all the time. They would rather have someone else do it periodically to serve as a check on the storeroom manager. For instance, the storeroom manager may keep some type of perpetual inventory, and a representative of, for example, the accounting department may take a physical inventory once or twice a month both to check on the storeroom manager's accuracy and to calculate various product costs so that financial statements and reports can be prepared.

Sometimes, small operators do something similar. For example, they might ask the head bartender to take a physical inventory of the food-storage areas while the chef or head housekeeper inventories the liquor. Each of these user-buyer-storeroom managers may keep some type of perpetual-inventory system while deferring the actual physical counting to another department head. Alternately, the owner-manager might do the actual physical counting once or twice a month, while the department heads keep some sort of a perpetual inventory for some or all items. Finally, some member of management who is not attached to any one department may assist the department representative with this inventory.

In some cases, especially for liquor, an owner-manager may periodically hire an outside service that specializes in the hospitality industry to take a physical inventory. This is sometimes done to get an absolutely unbiased inventory report. It is also traditionally done as part of the audit of the entire operation by someone who wants to buy the business.

Exercising Tight Control Over the Stock

Tight control exists when only a few persons are authorized to withdraw items from the storeroom. It also exists when effective and efficient security precautions prevail. These control and security aspects are, perhaps, the most important parts of the storeroom manager's job. Unfortunately, many operations neglect them. It is also true that many operations do not have storeroom managers. In some of these operations, this represents a wildly uncontrolled situation. But this is not always the case.

Some operations with no specific storeroom person manage to have excellent product costs with open storerooms. These firms, however, limit storeroom entry to persons who are under close, continuous supervision. Commonly, these firms also maintain minimal stocks so that pilferage is more noticeable to supervisors. In some cases, only small "working storerooms" are open to employees, and large storerooms that are used to stock the working storerooms are accessible only to a limited number of management personnel.

Ideally, when a storeroom manager is present, he or she issues items only to authorized persons and only when they present an official stock requisition. A stock requisition is a formal request made by a user for the items needed to carry out necessary tasks (see Figures 15.5, 15.6, and 15.7). The primary purposes of stock requisition are to control who gets the items and to record how much of an item is issued and when it is issued.

	1	2	3	4	5
	Item	Amount Requested (in units)	Unit Cost	Extended Value	Other Information

No. 873

Date ____   Page ____ of ____

Department ____

Requested by ____

col. 2 × col. 3

such as: how much of the item is in process? what's the forecasted usage of the item?

Signature of requisitioner ____

Requisition filled by ____

FIGURE 15.5 A stock requisition.

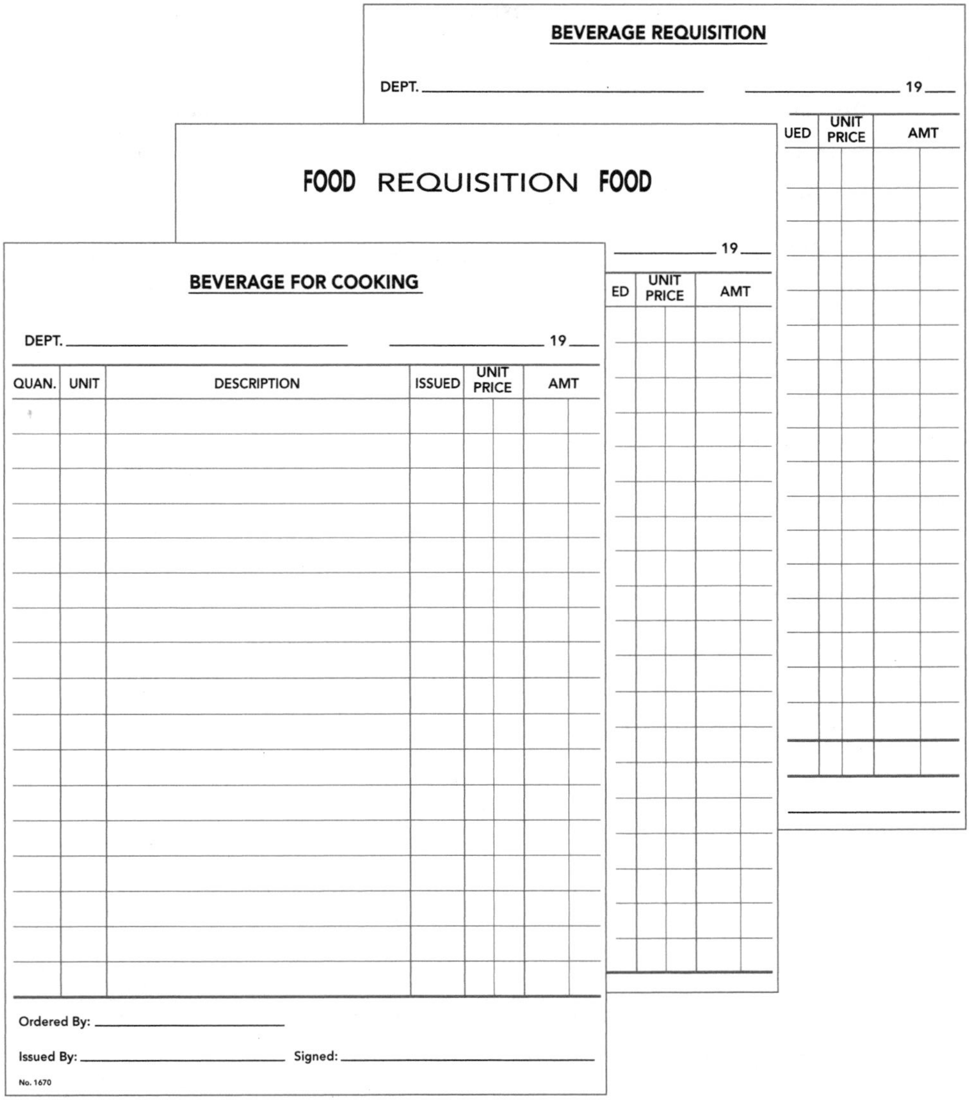

BEVERAGE REQUISITION

DEPT. _____   _____ 19 ____

	UED	UNIT PRICE	AMT

FOOD REQUISITION FOOD

_____ 19 ____

	ED	UNIT PRICE	AMT

BEVERAGE FOR COOKING

DEPT. _____   _____ 19 ____

QUAN.	UNIT	DESCRIPTION	ISSUED	UNIT PRICE	AMT	

Ordered By: _____

Issued By: _____   Signed: _____

No. 1670

FIGURE 15.6 Large hospitality operations tend to have a variety of stock requisitions. In this example, food is separate from beverage, and beverage used for cooking warrants its own stock requisition slip.

The control is not over the storage stock alone, but also extends, to some degree, to the in-process inventories. For example, if the requisitioner (the user) has to note how much of an item is currently held in the in-process inventory, he or she would hesitate to requisition too much, thereby preventing in-

WAREHOUSE REQUISITION

Department: _____ Date: _____

Cast Member: _____ Extension: _____

Remarks: _____

Item Number	Item Description	Quantity

Approval: _____
WHS0600 (10/93)   White - Originator   Yellow - Warehouse

FIGURE 15.7 An all-purpose stock requisition.

process items from slipping to the back of the shelf, eventually to spoil (see Figure 15.5).

The accountant or bookkeeper might use the requisitions to calculate product costs. For example, he or she might merely add up all the food requisitions and direct purchases for the week and use this computation as the week's food cost. This procedure can be reasonably accurate if operators set strict par stocks on all items in the in-process inventory. (Keep in mind, however, that this approach may be impractical, especially for liquor. After all, how do you issue half a bottle of liquor?)

Some operators hold the accountant responsible for issues, not only for the purpose of calculating product costs, but also for serving as an additional check on the receiver or storeroom manager. This approach is impractical for small firms, even though it is theoretically sound to have a separate person responsible for each operating activity.

The issuing activity is, as you can imagine, time-consuming, especially if requisitioners can drop in any time. Some operations allow the storeroom to issue only at certain times during the day. In some operations, the users must prepare their requisitions in the morning, send them electronically to the storeroom manager's computer terminal or put them in the storeroom manager's mailbox, and then wait for the storeroom manager to deliver the items on a predetermined schedule. If users run out of items during their shift, some member of management may enter the locked storage facilities; complete a stock requisition, time permitting; and take the necessary items to the users. If time is precious, the manager may complete the necessary forms a little later.

In the rare situation in which each user picks up a complete par stock from the storeroom manager at the beginning of the shift and then returns what is left at the end of the shift, the time spent filling out and processing forms might be reduced considerably.

Additional control is achieved when the storeroom manager issues exact amounts of ingredients needed for either one day or one shift. For instance, a storeroom employee may weigh out the ingredients according to the recipes to be prepared during the shift. (When this is common practice, the storeroom usually houses an area referred to as the "ingredient room" to do this type of work.)

A VALUE ANALYSIS OF STORAGE MANAGEMENT PROCEDURES

Proper storage management has never been a hallmark of the hospitality industry. This has resulted in unnecessary merchandise loss. Nevertheless, we can sympathize with managers faced with potentially large storage management costs.

It costs a great deal of money, time, and effort to adequately manage inventories. In most large operations, receiving, inspecting, storing, tracking, and properly issuing merchandise constitute a full-time job. The benefits supposedly consist of the traditional 2-percent saving mentioned earlier. But when you compare an easily noticed cost with a relatively hazy benefit, it is no wonder that most operators have forgone systematic storage management techniques. The issue becomes more cloudy when we add the customer dissatisfaction that can arise because of stale or spoiled products resulting from improper storage management.

Large operations have more to gain by employing a full-time receiver-store-room manager. They can usually afford more personnel, and that 2-percent saving translates into many dollars for them. Small operators, in contrast, face a bigger dilemma. No one can really blame them for refusing to spend several hundred dollars per month managing the storage function. Clearly, these operators need control as much as anyone, but what they truly need is some sort of truncated method of storage management that is reasonably effective yet fairly economical.

Our suggestions for these small operators follow: (1) Use one-stop shopping to significantly reduce the number of deliveries. (2) Have the owner-manager, or assistant, receive and inspect all incoming merchandise; send expensive items to the main storage facilities and less expensive items to the production areas—that is, to the in-process inventory. (3) Have the owner-manager, or assistant, issue par stocks of the expensive items to the users—the cooks, housekeepers, bartenders, and servers—at the beginning of their shifts. (4) Lock the main storage facilities. (5) If additional expensive items are needed during the shift, have the owner-manager, or assistant, retrieve them. (6) At the end of the shift, have the owner-manager, or assistant, open the main storage facilities to accept the expensive items that were not used during the shift. (7) Have the owner-manager, or assistant, record the number of expensive items used during the shift and pass this information along to the bookkeeper, who will compare what was used during the shift with what was sold. This comparison procedure is sometimes referred to as a "critical-item inventory analysis" or "product analysis." It is also sometimes referred to as "auditing the inventory sales," that is, calculating the amount of sales that should have been recorded and collected for based on the amount of inventory that is missing. If the comparison reveals a significant difference between what is missing and what was sold, the owner-manager, or assistant, must diagnose the cause(s) of this problem and correct it (them) as soon as possible.

Operators will have to devote some time to these procedures, but much less than more complete inventory control methods. This system can be very useful, assuming that management supports and enforces it. Moreover, we see no reason why it would not work for every operator. It should grant small operators an additional element of control, because it is certainly a constructive alternative to leaving storage facilities open and unattended most of the time.

Of course, this system has a couple of disadvantages: (1) it must be done regularly, that is, you cannot miss a day, and (2) it requires adequate physical space, refrigerators, and freezers to hold in-process inventories; otherwise, the owner-manager must run back and forth to the locked storage facilities too frequently. This can create stress, so that, in time, he or she may leave the main storeroom open.

We have not directly addressed the cost-benefit analysis of storage management procedures. But any such analysis ultimately rests upon the analyst's interpretation of relevant costs and benefits, as does every other economic analysis. The 2-percent argument is too vague; it fails to incorporate such noncash benefits as smooth operations and a no-nonsense image that investors and employees appreciate. In the end, management must decide the appropriateness of accepted storage management principles. It is not an easy decision, but few important managerial decisions are.

KEY WORDS AND CONCEPTS

A typical issuing procedure

Auditing the inventory sales

Bin card

Computerized management information system

Controlling only the most expensive merchandise

Critical-item inventory analysis

Direct purchase

Disposing of merchandise no longer required

Factors needed to achieve the storage objectives

Food cost equals beginning inventory plus purchases minus ending inventory minus other credit

Food Safety Inspection Service (FSIS)

Health district storage requirements

Ingredient room

In-process inventory

Inventory classification

Inventory control and security

Inventory shrinkage

Inventory usage rates

Management information system (MIS)

Managing the storage facilities

National Restaurant Association (NRA)

National Restaurant Association Educational Foundation (NRAEF)

One-stop shopping

Open storeroom

Par stocks

Perpetual inventory

Physical inventory

Pilferage

Product analysis

Purposes of taking a physical inventory

Skimming

Speeding up the inventory-taking process

Spoilage

Stock requisition

Storage objectives

Storage space

Storage temperature and humidity

Storeroom layout

Storeroom manager

Theft

Theoretical inventory value

Transfer slip

Working storeroom

REFERENCES

1. M. C. Warfel, Marion L. Cremer, and Richard J. Hug, *Purchasing for Food Service Managers*, 4th ed. (Berkeley, CA: McCutchan Publishing, 2001).

2. *ServSafe® Coursebook*, 3rd ed. (Hoboken, NJ: John Wiley & Sons, 2004).

QUESTIONS AND PROBLEMS

1. List the objectives of storage management. What is normally needed to achieve these objectives?

2. What are the typical storeroom manager's activities? Which one do you feel is most important? Why?

3. Briefly describe how a perpetual-inventory system works.

4. In most operations, it is too expensive to maintain a perpetual inventory for all items. However, it may be beneficial for some items. Which items would you like to keep on a perpetual-inventory basis? Why?

5. What is one of the main purposes of taking a month-end physical inventory?

6. What are some ways of shortening the inventory-taking procedure? Which seems best? Which seems worst? Why?

7. Assume that you own a small table-service restaurant. Annual sales are approximately $1.2 million. Should you hire a receiver-storeroom manager? What are the potential costs and benefits? If you think that this person might be too expensive, could you assign additional tasks to the person's job description to justify the expense? If yes, what would some of them be? Why? If possible, ask an independent restaurateur to comment on your answer.

8. Assume that a storeroom manager notices that a shipment received by the receiving agent had an accompanying invoice with the notation "Direct Purchase" stamped on it. What should the storeroom manager do with this shipment?

9. What is the main difference between theft and pilferage?

10. Given the following data, compute the food cost percentage:

    TOTAL SALES: $500,000

    FOOD SALES: 75 percent of total sales

    BEVERAGE SALES: 25 percent of total sales

    BEGINNING FOOD INVENTORY: $25,000

    ENDING FOOD INVENTORY: $30,000

    TOTAL FOOD PURCHASES: $200,000

    EMPLOYEE MEAL COST: $6000

11. Briefly describe the temperature guidelines suggested by the National Restaurant Association Educational Foundation.

12. What are the advantages and disadvantages of computerized inventory management procedures?

13. If the beginning food inventory is $12,500, the food purchases are $40,000, and the food cost is $47,500, what is the ending food inventory (dollar amount)?

14. Define or briefly explain the following terms:

(a)	Skimming	(i)	Working storeroom
(b)	Bin card	(j)	Health district storage requirements
(c)	Theoretical inventory value	(k)	In-process inventory
(d)	Full-case inventory-taking procedure	(l)	Credit for employee meals
(e)	Stock requisition	(m)	Open storeroom
(f)	Ingredient room	(n)	Par stocks
(g)	Inventory sales	(o)	Authorized access to storage areas
(h)	Shoplifting	(p)	Critical-item inventory analysis

EXPERIENTIAL EXERCISES

1. Contact a hotel manager and ask permission to observe a physical-inventory procedure. Follow up the inventory procedure to determine its purposes and to see the uses for this information. Ask the manager to discuss the inventory-taking process.

2. Ask the manager of a local hospitality operation if you can evaluate his or her storage areas.

   a. Prepare a draft report that evaluates the operation's storage areas based on the following criteria:

   Adequate space
   Adequate temperature and humidity
   Adequate equipment
   Proximity of storage area to receiving and production areas
   Proper maintenance
   Proper security
   Competent personnel
   Sufficient time given to storeroom employees to perform the necessary duties
   Proper storeroom regulations

   b. Provide your draft report to the manager and ask for comments.

   c. Include the comments with your final report.

16

SECURITY IN THE PURCHASING FUNCTION

The Purpose of this Chapter

After reading this chapter, you should be able to:

- Describe the security problems associated with the purchasing function.

- Identify methods used to prevent security problems related to purchasing.

INTRODUCTION

Several years ago, many hospitality operators considered theft and pilferage manageable costs of doing business and routinely added a slight markup to menu and room prices to compensate for these losses. In fact, credit card companies supposedly continue these practices today. But because of increased competitive pressure and shrinking profit margins, the hospitality industry has become more concerned about these problems.

This concern with security should come as no surprise. After all, Ernst & Young (www.ey.com), a large business consulting company, estimates that employees steal almost $23 billion a year from their employers.[1] More startling facts of employee theft include:

- One in every 27 employees is apprehended for theft from their employer each year.

- Dishonest employees steal almost eight times the amount stolen by shoplifters.[2]

- One-third of employees steal from their companies at least once a year.[3]

- Approximately 70 percent of all merchandise losses are the result of inside stealing.[4]

- The foodservice industry loses approximately $20 billion a year to theft and cash mishandling.

- Approximately 5 to 8 percent of foodservice gross sales are lost to internal theft.

- Seventy-five percent of inventory missing in restaurants is from theft.

- The majority of foodservice employees caught stealing have worked for an operation for an average of five to seven years.[5]

The heightened interest in security that is found in the foodservice industry can be attributed to at least four factors: (1) hospitality operators find it increasingly difficult to pass on security losses to the consumer in the form of higher menu and room prices; (2) in general, the public has become more security conscious; (3) the cost of insurance coverage has skyrocketed; and (4) a good deal of unfavorable publicity has focused on the hospitality purchasing function.

Much of this unfavorable publicity centers on the willingness of purchasing agents to accept gifts and other economic favors. For example, a five-unit Dunkin' Donuts operator was sentenced in 2003 to eight months in jail, two years probation and had to pay a $2000 fine for his acceptance of more than $284,000 in kickbacks from one of his suppliers.[6] A president of Rax Restaurants resigned after an internal investigation indicated "improprieties in supplier relations," such as the awarding of some supply contracts without competitive bidding.[7] A president of Whataburger, Inc., resigned amid allegations of supplier kickbacks.[8] A buyer for JC. Penney Co. admittedly "supplemented his salary with as much as $1.5 million in bribes and kickbacks."[9] Some dairy companies admitted that they schemed "to fix milk prices at an artificially high level by colluding on bids to supply milk for school lunch programs."[10] Similarly, "more than 30 Louisiana chefs, restaurateurs, and fishermen were arrested on charges of buying and selling banned fish."[11] And in case you think today's employees are the only ones who steal, two well-known celebrities of the nineteenth century, César Ritz (said to be the greatest hotelman ever) and Auguste Escoffier (said to be the "king of chefs, and the chef to kings"), "were sacked for stealing from the hotel larder and taking kickbacks from food purveyors, to the tune of roughly $20,000."[12]

Theft and pilferage are probably no more common today than they were in the past, but they certainly have been more widely publicized. This notoriety has forced hospitality operators to reexamine their attitudes toward security. Management is no longer willing to dismiss theft, fraud, pilferage, and shoplifting as minor problems.

Security has, of course, always been important in the hospitality business. But it can be difficult to provide adequate security, particularly in the service areas and those areas that customers frequent, because physical facilities are not always designed with security in mind. Security can be more of a consideration during the designing of storage areas, but it often must take a back seat in dining rooms, lounges, front offices, and other public areas.

In many respects, however, buyers can enforce a good measure of security in their realm of responsibility. The activities and duties of buyers, receivers, and storeroom managers, among others, are hidden from public view. If desired, then, management can set policies that go so far as to resemble an armed-camp atmosphere in the receiving and storage areas of the hospitality operation.

SECURITY PROBLEMS

Several potential security problems arise in connection with purchasing, receiving, storing, and issuing, and an owner-manager must be on guard against them. The major ones are discussed next.

Kickbacks

A buyer, or user-buyer, could easily collude with a supplier, salesperson, or delivery agent. The operation could, thus, pay for a superior product but receive inferior merchandise, while the buyer and accomplices pocket the difference between the as-purchased (AP) prices. This difference is referred to as a "kickback."

Sometimes two or more conspirators "pad an invoice," that is, add on a phony charge. This is a form of kickback that requires the cooperative efforts of at least two thieves.

A form of kickback also occurs when a conspirator sends an invoice that has already been paid to the bookkeeper, who pays it again. The thieves then pocket the payment.[13]

Another form of kickback happens when supposedly defective incoming merchandise is "returned" (returned to the thieves, that is, who hope that the bookkeeper will forget or ignore this transaction).

Much the same kind of kickback occurs when "short orders" are delivered or when half an order is delivered in the morning, with the other half promised in the afternoon—the afternoon that never comes. Again, the thieves depend on the bookkeeper or management to overlook the shortage.

Perhaps the most common type of kickback happens when the buyer agrees to pay a slightly higher AP price and, unknown to the owner-manager, receives an under-the-table payment from the supplier. The payment sometimes comes in the form of merchandise, such as a new watch or PDA computer. This collusion is extremely difficult to detect, especially when, overall, the product costs appear to be in line.

Keep in mind one important point about kickbacks: although the hospitality operator usually loses, the honest supplier always loses if his or her salespersons or delivery agents conspire with receivers, buyers, or bookkeepers. It is difficult, however, for continuing theft to go undetected if the supplier is honest because he or she usually is constantly alert to these practices. Thus, the supplier's management and the buyer's management have the same interests at heart.

Invoice Scams

A problem related to kickbacks occurs when someone diverts a bill payment to a fictitious company or a fictitious account. The conspirators then pocket the payment. Similarly, someone might present a fictitious invoice to the bookkeeper, which the bookkeeper pays—and mails directly to the thief's post office box.

At first glance, it would seem difficult for a buyer to set up an invoice scam. However, even the largest hospitality companies are not immune to this type of fraud. For instance, a buyer for the Marriott Corporation pleaded guilty to stealing more than $1.4 million from the company over a 14-year period by altering invoice copies and having them paid into a dummy bank account that he controlled. He admitted doing it at first because he needed the money. But as time went on, he continued the scam because "it just seemed so easy after it got started."[14]

Supplier and Receiver Error

Incoming invoices must be checked for arithmetic errors. It is surprising how many unintentional mistakes occur, but intentional mistakes are also possible. These could be a form of kickback. Either way, the loss is the same.

Several other more or less unintentional mistakes can occur. Most of them are relatively minor. But, in the long run, little losses add up. Some of the typical errors are: (1) losing credit for container deposits or returned merchandise; (2) receiving a substitute item of a slightly lower quality than that ordered and failing to issue a Request for Credit memo, or otherwise ensuring that the cost difference is corrected; (3) receiving the wrong items unintentionally (such as receiving bulk butter instead of butter pats); and (4) weighing items with an inaccurate scale.

Inventory Theft

To prevent inventory theft, operators should restrict access to all storage areas and receiving facilities. Only authorized persons should be allowed to enter these areas. Furthermore, these areas should be locked when not in use.

The most common type of "inventory shrinkage" is pilferage by employees. Restricted access can reduce pilferage opportunities. Adequate supervision in the production and service areas of the hospitality operation also can reduce or eliminate pilferage and shoplifting opportunities.

Inventory Padding

Recall from Chapter 15 our discussion of the physical-inventory-taking process, and that one of the reasons for doing this was to compute various product costs. The formula used to compute, for example, the actual food cost for the month is:

Beginning inventory
+ Purchases
= Food available for sale
− Ending inventory
− Other credit (e.g., food used for employee meals)
= Cost of food sold

If the beginning inventory is $12,000, the purchases are $20,000, the ending inventory is $14,000, and the other credit is $2,000, the actual food cost is $16,000 ($12,000 + $20,000 − $14,000 − $2,000 = $16,000).

Suppose a food supervisor wants to reduce this food-cost figure in order to earn a greater performance bonus. An easy way, albeit an illegal way, is to increase the ending inventory amount, that is, to "pad" the inventory so that top management believes that the supervisor produced a highly favorable food cost for the month. (Notice that, in this example, if the ending inventory were artificially inflated to $15,000, the cost of food sold would drop to $15,000 from $16,000.) Unless management supervises the inventories carefully, a person could easily steal the merchandise and alter the inventory records, and no one would ever uncover the fraud unless an independent audit was conducted.[15]

Inventory Substitutions

In hospitality operations with an open-storeroom policy, it is relatively easy for an employee to remove high-quality merchandise and substitute inferior goods. The employee can consume the stolen merchandise or can sell it on the black market. This potential security problem is similar to inventory padding in that an independent audit may be needed to uncover it.

Telephone and E-Mail Sales Scams

All companies are susceptible to telephone solicitors who use illegal tactics and high-pressure selling techniques to defraud buyers. These salespersons, sometimes referred to as "WATS-line hustlers" (Wide Area Telecommunications Service), rarely deal with the authorized purchasing agent. They usually attempt backdoor selling and offer free gifts and other inducements to clinch a sale.

A common type of telephone fraud involves offers of sweet deals on replacement toner used for copying machines and laser printers.[16] These telephone solicitors, sometimes referred to as "toner-phoners," typically portray themselves as representing major supply houses offering once-in-a-lifetime low prices, although the unsuspecting buyer usually receives watered-down merchandise and high service charges.

A related problem occurs whenever an unauthorized and unordered shipment arrives at a buyer's doorstep. If he or she mistakenly pays for this shipment, it is unlikely that the buyer will ever get the money back.

E-mail is quickly becoming the ideal medium for perpetrating these same types of sales scams on unsuspecting hospitality operators. The rapid growth of e-mail scams can be attributed to the fact that sending large quantities of unsolicited e-mail is relatively inexpensive. It is also much more difficult for authorities to trace these e-mail solicitors, as many of them operate overseas and use sophisticated programming techniques to mask their true identities.

Inability to Segregate Operating Activities

Ideally, a hospitality operation separates the buying, receiving, storing, and bill-paying procedures. Usually, a separate person pays the bills, but this is not the case with the other operating activities.

The most common potential problem is the buyer, or user-buyer, who receives the products he or she orders. There is nothing inherently wrong with this practice, but it can enable buyers to order one item and receive another, which may be inferior. Even worse, buyers can substitute inferior merchandise for the ordered products, converting the better products for their own use.

Nevertheless, buyers who receive are common in the hospitality industry, usually because: (1) they are the only ones who can recognize the various product quality standards (this is especially true of buyers who command an expertise in an area in which the rest of the staff has little knowledge, such as wine stewards); (2) the buyer must do other things to justify his or her job (buying may not be enough work); and (3) management just cannot afford to hire a separate receiver.

Suspicious Behavior

A variety of employee behaviors call for management scrutiny. The owner-manager should be wary of employees who: (1) seem unduly friendly with suppliers, salespersons, or delivery agents; (2) hang around storage areas pointlessly; (3) needlessly handle keys or locks; (4) make too many trips to the garbage area, bathroom, locker room, or parking lot (perhaps to move stolen merchandise); (5) requisition abnormally large amounts of supplies; (6) make frequent trips to the storage areas for no apparent good reason; (7) have relatives working for his or her suppliers; (8) stray from their assigned workstations too frequently; (9) are seen passing packages to guests; (10) are seen stuffing boxes or packages under a couch in a public area, which a conspirator may pick up later; (11) permit delivery agents to loiter in unauthorized areas; and (12) have visitors on the work site. The list could go on. Since many employees cannot be restricted to one work area, theft and pilferage opportunities are always a part of the workplace.

PREVENTING SECURITY PROBLEMS

In general, an owner-manager can take three main steps to prevent security breaches: (1) select honest suppliers, (2) employ honest employees, and (3) design the physical facilities so that tight, effective security conditions can be maintained.

It is difficult to assess the honesty of potential suppliers. Even if they are willing to talk about dishonesty, the most that they usually say is, "We don't do anything like that." The more dishonest the suppliers, the salespersons, or the delivery agents, the less likely they will be to admit it. It is useful, though, to ask other hospitality operators for their advice. Whatever report an owner-manager receives on a supplier, he or she must remember that bad practices may have been corrected. As with so much else, management's own informed judgment must be the guide.

Assuring employee honesty is no simple matter. Hospitality operators have trouble with pilferage for two reasons. First, many of the products they use can easily be converted into cash. Second, few hospitality operators do anything more than simply firing a dishonest employee. Having petty thieves arrested is still uncommon, and, as a result, a thief has little to lose if caught.

Lately, however, more employers are beginning to prosecute dishonest employees and dishonest customers. If this becomes the rule, this type of swift, stern action should help minimize the number of dishonest people who are employed by hospitality enterprises.

An effective personnel recruiting and selection procedure is a hospitality operator's main weapon in the fight against employee theft and pilferage. One aspect of personnel selection that represents a highly controversial issue is the use of background investigations, particularly the investigation involving the use of "integrity"—that is, "honesty"—tests or other similar reference-checking techniques. These tests are thought to be the most effective weapons in the war against theft and pilferage.[17]

Integrity testing has become more popular in the past few years primarily because employers cannot use polygraph machines or other similar devices to determine employee honesty during the recruiting and hiring stages. Any type of honesty testing, though, will be controversial because these types of tests are not completely accurate. Furthermore, many people feel that these tests, as well as preemployment drug tests, are invasions of privacy.

Being certain that a new employee is honest is no simple or sure matter. Reference checks can tell what a previous employer knows—or what that employer wants to reveal—about past behavior. But stresses and strains could convert an honest employee to a dishonest one. Probably the best rule here is a cautious optimism about people, combined with a set of controls that make dishonesty difficult to engage in and relatively easy to check.

Designing the physical facilities to ensure proper security is relatively easy in back-of-the-house storage facilities if the operation is being built from the ground up, if the operation is undergoing extensive remodeling, and if the owner-manager can spare the necessary funds. Unfortunately, many existing operations have flaws that prevent tight security. These flaws are often impossible to correct or, if correctable, require large expenditures.

In most cases, then, hospitality operators fall short in attempting to arm themselves with the previously cited three basic weapons in the fight against crime. These operators must learn to work, instead, with the resources available to them. Nevertheless, all operators can take several specific steps to prevent theft and pilferage:

1. The owner-manager should document cash paid-outs carefully. Be certain that the deliveryperson receiving them initials the copy of the invoice properly. A canceled check always is the preferred receipt, but the convenience of paid-outs is important to many small operators. Nevertheless, operators must be certain that their accounts are credited properly.

2. The owner-manager should never pay an invoice that shows a post office box number as the supplier's address without checking further. For that matter, do not pay a bill unless the supplier's name and address are familiar. But it is the box number that is more suspicious. If employees are trying to cheat by sending fraudulent invoices to the bookkeeper, a box number can be the tip-off.

3. Those who buy should never pay the bills. A buyer who pays may be tempted to pay himself or herself once in a while.[18] Most companies require the manager to verify all invoices for payment and then forward them to the accounting office or to company headquarters. Someone at headquarters then pays. Small firms can copy this practice to some degree by separating the buying and paying functions.

4. The owner-manager should cancel paperwork on all completed transactions. At the very least, operators should mark an invoice paid as soon as they pay it so that this same invoice will not be paid again. Sometimes, a type of perforating machine is used to punch a series of holes in the invoice, indicating that payment has been made.

   In addition to canceling all documentation, make sure it has been completed. For example, if part of a delivery must be returned, see to it that a Request for Credit memo is prepared or that credit for the return has been otherwise received.

   As an added precaution, bill payers should compare the invoice with the original purchase order or other ordering record to ensure that they do not pay for nonexistent merchandise. If no purchase order copies exist, take steps to remedy this situation; it is just too easy to pay a fraudulent or padded invoice, particularly if the amount involved is relatively small.

Furthermore, be especially careful to compare the AP prices, delivery charges, and other costs noted on the invoice with those that were quoted earlier. The number of times the quotations are less than the prices noted on the invoices is surprising. In most instances, this probably represents an innocent mistake (e.g., perhaps the computer at the supplier's warehouse was not programmed correctly). However, if operators are not diligent in their comparisons, an unscrupulous supplier can earn a bit of extra income by indicating one price and charging another.

5. The owner-manager should arrange, now and then, for an independent audit of the hospitality organization's operating procedures. If done on a random, unannounced basis, an audit can be an excellent deterrent to theft and pilferage. The independent auditor should: (1) analyze invoices and payment checks to determine their accuracy, completeness, and consistency; (2) check the receiving routine and equipment; (3) inspect the storage facilities, taking a physical inventory and noting how consistent it is with the inventory figures recorded on accounting records; the physical inventory should also be consistent with the sales volume and purchase expenditures; (4) check receiving sheets and stock requisitions for consistency with invoices, purchase orders, and payment checks; and (5) check consumption against reported units of sales—for example, compare the stock requisitions of steaks with guest checks in the dining room and the in-process inventory in the kitchen.

Surprise audits are used successfully in such other enterprises as banks, in which the audit team enters the premises, shuts down some teller windows, and begins the audit procedure. Operators cannot always shut down a hospitality facility, but a surprise audit can be performed during slow periods.

The surprise audit is undoubtedly a powerful control in terms of theft and pilferage. It can easily have the same effect on employees as a surprise integrity test. In addition, it is not unduly expensive. Most operations can easily afford such audits.

6. Hospitality employers do not use undercover agents as a rule in the back of the house. But spotters, or "shoppers," are quite often used in the front of the house.[19] For instance, many bars pay a shopping service to periodically send around someone who, posing as a customer, observes all pertinent activities. This person then prepares a report for management, commenting on such

factors as product quality, service, and an employee appearing to pocket cash illegally. A shopping service is relatively inexpensive and, like the surprise audit, represents a powerful crime deterrent.

7. Related to the surprise audit is the use of integrity or personality tests and drug tests. These tests are relatively inexpensive. However, they may not be 100 percent accurate. In the hands of a competent evaluator, though, they may be a fair evaluation of employee honesty.

   Some hospitality operations do not like to use any sort of honesty or drug-testing program. They do not wish to use something that may not always be accurate. Nor do they want to invade a person's privacy, which could hinder the development of a favorable employer/employee relationship.

8. If operators do not relish pre-employment testing (sometimes referred to as pre-employment screening or background checks) and are not satisfied with a surprise audit now and then, they can resort to a fidelity bonding company. A "bonding company" insures a hospitality operator against employee theft of cash. Not all employees are bonded, but cashiers usually are. Since the bonding company performs a thorough background check of all employees it insures, however, operators can conceivably bond everyone for the sole purpose of investigating each applicant (though this might prove a fairly expensive way of getting thorough background checks). In lieu of bonding, an operator could employ a less expensive background-checking firm, which is sometimes referred to as a "résumé-checking" service, as an alternative.[20] Many major payroll service companies—such as Automated Data Processing (ADP [www.adp.com])—also offer pre-employment screening services to their customers. These services typically include multiple types of employee testing and background checks.

   Bonding is expensive. In addition, it tells you only about the past, not the future. Also, if a thief has never been caught, he or she will obviously receive a clean bill of health from the bonding company. Moreover, you must first determine the legality of this activity. Some states and municipalities restrict background investigations of this type.

9. The owner-manager might consider investing in a trash compactor. A lot of stolen items are removed from the operation in trash cans, to be retrieved later by an off-duty employee or an accomplice. A compactor minimizes this opportunity.

10. Whenever possible, employees should be allowed to enter or leave the premises through only one door. This door should not be used to receive deliver-

ies, unless there is some sure way of guarding and controlling access to it. If necessary, it is better to insist that employees use the front door, the same door customers use. As irritating as this requirement might sound, it helps to minimize theft and pilferage.

11. Employees should not be allowed to park their cars close to the building or near a doorway or large window that can be opened. This prevents employees from sneaking out quickly with merchandise, stashing it in the car, and returning to the workplace.

   A related difficulty involves an outside area replete with such hiding places as tall shrubs, storage or garbage bins, and other nooks and crannies. Whenever possible, eliminate these potential repositories or limit employee access to them.

12. If possible, employee locker rooms and rest rooms should be within a reasonable distance so that the operator can check them once in a while. But they should not be too close. An employee can use either complete isolation or quick access to hide stolen items.

   If the owner-manager cannot place these facilities in an optimal place in the building, the best alternative is to equip the employee lockers with heavy see-through screens instead of solid doors (see Figure 16.1). This eliminates an attractive hiding place for stolen items. Also, these facilities should not be too close to an exit or large window that can be opened.

13. The owner-manager should not allow delivery agents to enter the premises or loiter in unauthorized areas unless their presence is necessary, such as for standing orders. Some of these agents merely want to be helpful by putting items in storage. But some may have sticky fingers. Furthermore, they tend to distract employees.

   A lot of socializing goes on in the receiving and storing areas. The owner-manager must make the decision concerning this and any related activities.

14. The owner-manager should not rush receivers. They should take their time and inspect all deliveries adequately, keeping in mind some of the common receiving problems we discussed in Chapter 14.

15. As much as possible, the operator should not let anyone who has no business being there remain in the back of the house. Friends of employees should be kept out of these areas. Salespersons and delivery agents cannot always be barred, but they can be restricted to certain places in the back of the house.

   The owner-manager should restrict these people because, not only do they distract employees, they also might try to establish some sort of pilfer-

FIGURE 16.1 Mesh lockers. Courtesy of Penco Products, Inc.

ing arrangement with an unscrupulous employee. Moreover, the seeds of backdoor selling could find fertile ground.

16. The owner-manager should invest in some cost-effective physical barriers. These include: (1) time locks that can be opened only at certain times by certain persons; Marlock computerized locking systems (or an equivalent) are excellent choices as they will print out reports that indicate who accessed the system (and whether such persons were authorized to do so), as well as access times; (2) heavy-duty locks that are rotated occasionally, with the keys or key cards entrusted only to those who absolutely must have them; Medeco

locks (or an equivalent) are good choices as they are very secure;[21] (3) adequate lighting in the storage areas so that thieves cannot hide; (4) reasonably priced closed-circuit television (CCTV) or digital video recorder (DVR), which can be an excellent deterrent to theft, and some of which can be accessed remotely online;[22] (5) uniformed guards, who may inspect employees, their packages, and their time cards when they leave work; (6) see-through screens on all storage facility doors—heavy screens can keep thieves out, while allowing a supervisor to spot-check the storage areas quickly; and (7) perimeter and interior alarm systems; a sound control system is especially useful for areas in the property that are not continuously open.

17. The owner-manager should try to eliminate collusion opportunities by separating the buying, receiving, storing, and issuing activities. He or she might even go as far as to separate the bookkeeping and bill-paying functions. This is good control, but it may be impractical for all but the largest firms.

    Some separation is, however, possible. For example, an owner-manager might ask an assistant manager to help the receiver-storeroom manager or the chef-buyer-receiver to inspect incoming merchandise. In addition, a surprise audit can go a long way toward achieving the type of control a complete separation of these operating activities usually affords.

18. An owner-manager should compare what he or she is paying current suppliers with AP prices available from other suppliers for the same type of merchandise. It would, of course, be more reliable to compare edible-portion (EP) costs whenever possible, since a premium AP price can be, as we have said, entirely justifiable under certain circumstances. But an owner-manager must make the effort to compare AP prices periodically because it is just too easy for buyers, or user-buyers, to pay a bit more for a little kickback. This practice is extremely hard to discover, but it is essential not to overlook this all too tempting opportunity within the reach of most buyers.

19. If possible, an owner-manager should try not to hire employees who have relatives working for suppliers. Better to eliminate this and other similar conflicts of interest from the start.

20. The owner-manager should make sure that whoever pays the bills checks them over carefully. Sometimes a phony invoice gets slipped in. This is especially true with bills for regularly scheduled periodic services, such as waste removal. Another potential problem is receiving a solicitation that looks just like an invoice from a company. If the owner-manager is not careful, some-

one might honor the solicitation, thinking that it is just another bill that must be paid.

If possible, the owner-manager should develop an approved-payee list, which is a list of names of individuals or companies eligible to receive payments from his or her firm. If a bill pops up and the supplier's name is not on the approved-payee list, the bill should not be paid unless management personally approves.

21.   As much as possible (and without compromising quality), an owner-manager should take everything out of its shipping container before storing it. This practice minimizes the problem of "inventory shrinkage" occurring before he or she even opens the case.

In addition, when an owner-manager takes a physical inventory, he or she should actually lift a few containers in order to make sure there is something in the container. It is possible for someone to take a full one and leave an empty one or to substitute an inferior product.

22.   The owner-manager should be leery of putting up cash deposits. A supplier or, more commonly, someone who does remodeling work or other types of service, will request a deposit for one reason or another. The owner-manager must be careful that this person does not take the deposit and skip town. This does not happen too often in the hospitality industry, but it does occur now and then with people who, for example, do some remodeling work and need some cash up front to buy their materials. Also, an owner-manager could get stung if he or she sends away for something advertised in a trade paper: the sales advertisement may be disguising some sort of sham operation. Unless the owner-manager knows his or her suppliers and other vendors, he or she probably should avoid paying anything until receiving the purchase.

23.   A hospitality operation might find it worthwhile to become a house account for one or more suppliers whose integrity it trusts completely. Although being a house account usually increases the AP prices a firm must pay, at least for some items, the operation is assured that its friends will not conspire with others to defraud the establishment.

24.   Management must develop a procedure to prevent the possibility of unrecorded merchandise getting into the storage facilities or into the in-process inventory. For instance, nothing should be received unless an invoice accompanies it or unless the receiver records it somehow. If this is not done, there will be more stock in inventory than that recorded. Employees could somehow pilfer this excess inventory and no one would be able to detect the

problem. An old bartender's trick is to deliver his or her own personal bottles to the establishment, sell drinks made with the contents of these bottles, and pocket the cash.

25. When ordering merchandise, the owner-manager should make certain that he or she is not rushed into purchasing inadequate products. For instance, it is possible that a telephone salesperson can call unexpectedly, offering what at first might appear to be sterling goods. Some telephone solicitors may resort to deceptive practices.

    An owner-manager also might misinterpret, for example, an advertisement and end up ordering something through the mail that he or she does not want. He or she might mistakenly order an off-brand artificial sweetener packaged in blue-colored, individual packets, assuming the product is the nationally recognized Equal® brand merchandise.

26. The owner-manager should develop an approved-supplier list and instruct all persons who have ordering responsibilities to use the suppliers on the list. Of course, there are exceptions to any rule, but management must be informed if, for example, someone in the operation wishes to purchase something from an unfamiliar supplier. The owner-manager would want to investigate this supplier, utilizing the procedures discussed in Chapter 12, and then make a final decision regarding the admissibility of this supplier to the approved-supplier list.

    Using an approved-supplier list appears to be one of the most effective controls for such problems as kickbacks and other forms of skullduggery. The vast majority of large hospitality operations follow this practice.

27. The hospitality operator should avoid purchasing merchandise in small, single-service packages. These items are very easy to pilfer, although their convenience in terms of customer service may override the requisite need for greater security.

28. One of the most effective deterrents to theft and pilferage is to restrict access to all high-cost products. While it is not always feasible to lock up everything, management must maintain close control over those items that represent the bulk of the purchase dollar.

29. The owner-manager should maintain close tabs on all expensive items throughout the production and service cycles. For instance, each day a manager should conduct a critical-item inventory analysis; that is, he or she should balance the use of key, expensive ingredients with the stock requisitions and

guest checks. The actual usage of these items and their expected (i.e., "standard") usage should be the same.

30. If affordable, management should adopt computer technology available to calculate the theoretical-inventory value, which is sometimes referred to as the inventory "book" value, so that it can be compared with the value determined by a physical-inventory count. Unlike hand-posted records, a computer facilitates a quick, convenient compilation of bin card balances that, when compared with the physical-inventory count, will immediately highlight inventory control problems.

31. Management must ensure that access to all records is restricted to only those individuals who are authorized to make entries in those records or to those persons who must analyze them.

32. An owner-manager must also be concerned with additional security precautions in other parts of the operation. We have discussed the principal ones associated with the back of the house, that is, those that are pertinent to the purchasing function. Several security considerations are, of course, relevant to the front of the house. An owner-manager should take the time to peruse some of the excellent materials dealing with these concerns.[23]

Control and security have become popular terms in the hospitality industry. They are increasingly becoming the subjects of books, seminars, newspaper features, and magazine articles. But some of these often omit a crucial factor: employee supervision.

The best systems fail without proper supervision. Physical barriers, audits, separation of responsibilities, and so on are the machines, but supervision is the grease. Without it, security cannot operate. The owner-manager should use his or her two eyes instead of depending too much on indirect control and security systems.

An owner-manager may well slip into one of two camps: (1) security will become a mania, and he or she will use everything possible to protect the property; or (2) security will occupy a low position on the priority list: visiting with guests, for instance, may be more important to some managers than overseeing production.

Control, security, and supervision go hand in hand. Successful operators find the time to supervise properly. Unfortunately, these operators seem to be in short supply; otherwise, the losses due to employee theft and pilferage would not increase as they seem to do every year.

The glamour of the hospitality industry sometimes tempts people to forget the mundane aspects of employee supervision and motivation. Many buyers are no different. They would much rather write specifications, test new food products, and bargain with salespersons than supervise employees. Effective supervision may not guarantee success, but inadequate supervisory attention practically guarantees failure.

WHO CHECKS THE CHECKER?

Who watches over the manager, especially if the operation has an absentee owner? Also, who watches the chef while he or she is watching someone else? We have to draw the line somewhere and eventually trust someone. It is virtually impossible to have a complete set of checks and balances. An adequate management information system (MIS), however, should help monitor the operating results in a way that will indicate where, if at all, problems may exist in the purchasing-receiving-storage cycle.

KEY WORDS AND CONCEPTS

Accept gifts

Actual product cost calculation

Actual usage

Alarm system

Approved-payee list

Approved-supplier list

Backdoor selling

Background-checking firm

Background investigations

Bonding company

Bribery

Cancel transactions appropriately

Cash deposits

Closed-circuit television (CCTV)

Compare bid as-purchased (AP) prices with those listed on invoice

Critical-item inventory analysis

Digital video recorder (DVR)

Document paid-outs

Fictitious invoices

Honest, unintentional mistakes

House account

Independent surprise audits

Indirect control system

Integrity test

Inventory book value

Inventory padding

Inventory shrinkage

Inventory substitutions

Inventory theft

Invoice padding

Invoice scams

Kickbacks

Marlock system

Medeco locks

Physical barriers

Physical inventory

Pre-employment screening

Pre-employment testing

Reference checks

Restricted access

Résumé-checking service

Returned merchandise

Security problems

Segregate operating activities

Select honest suppliers and employees

Separate buyer from bill payer

Shoppers

Short orders

Standard usage	Telephone sales scams	Undercover agents
Stock requisition	Theoretical inventory value	WATS-line hustlers (Wide
Supplier and receiver error		Area Telecommunications
Suspicious behavior	Toner-phoners	Service)

REFERENCES

1. Anonymous, "Ernst & Young Estimates Retailers Lose $46 Billion Annually to Inventory Shrinkage: Employee Theft Is Biggest Problem," May 13, 2003 (Available http://www.ey.com/global/Content.nsf/US/Media_-_Release_-_05-13-03DC).

2. Bill Zalud, "Outsiders, Insiders and Theft," *Security,* July/August 2002, 39(6), p. 62. See also: Anonymous, "Consumer Watch," *Discount Store News,* July 26, 1999, 38(14), p. 18.

3. Gregory Goussak, "Employee Theft and Fraud in the Food Service Industry," *The Bottomline,* October/November 1993, p. 20. See also: R. Ghiselli and J. A. Ismail, "Employee Theft and Efficacy of Certain Control Procedures in Commercial Food Service Operations," *Journal of Hospitality and Tourism Research,* 1998, 22(2), pp. 174–187.

4. Donald E. Lundberg and John R. Walker, *The Restaurant: From Concept to Operation,* 3rd ed. (New York: John Wiley & Sons, 2000), p. 101.

5. Beth Lorenzini, "Internal Security," in *Winning Foodservice Ideas,* Michael Bartlett, Ed. (New York: John Wiley & Sons, 1994), p. 242.

6. Anonymous, "Dunkin' Franchisee Sentenced over Kickback Plot," *Nation's Restaurant News,* Daily Specials, QSR Briefs—April 18, 2003 (Available http://www.nrn.com/story.cfm?ID=7183203108). See also: Richard Martin, "Franchisee Sentenced amid Dunkin' Lawsuit Barrage," *Nation's Restaurant News,* April 28, 2003, p. 4, 111.

7. Carolyn Walkup, "Former Rax Prexy to Pay $400K," *Nation's Restaurant News,* January 6, 1992, p. 1.

8. Ron Ruggless, "Whataburger Prexy Jim Peterson Resigns," *Nation's Restaurant News,* January 17, 1994, p. 1. See also: Rick Van Warner, "Kickbacks Can Trip Up a Company: Set Honesty as the Only Policy," *Nation's Restaurant News,* January 24, 1994, p. 19.

9. Andrea Gerlin, "How a Penney Buyer Made up to $1.5 Million on Vendors' Kickbacks," *The Wall Street Journal,* February 7, 1995, p. A1.

10. Anonymous, "Milk Price-Fixing Case Yields Guilty Plea, Prosecutors Say," *The Wall Street Journal,* August 27, 1991, p. B5. See also: Stephen Chapman, "Fixing Milk Prices: Crime, Blessing or Both?" *Las Vegas Review Journal,* September 13, 1991, p. 11B; Anonymous, "Mrs. Baird's Bakeries Found Guilty of Fixing Bread Prices in Texas," *The Wall Street Journal,* February 15, 1996, p. B5.

11. Anonymous, "Louisiana Chefs Arrested in Illegal-Fish Sting," *Nation's Restaurant News,* May 1, 1995, p. 2.

12. Paul Levy, "Skimming at the Savoy: Britain's Foodiegate," *The Wall Street Journal,* May 30, 1985, p. 28. See also: Anonymous, "Taking Aim at Crime: Crime Concerns: Polling the Restaurateurs," *Nation's Restaurant News,* May 22, 2000, p. 120.

13. Cinda Becker, "Partners in Crime?," *Modern Healthcare,* June 9, 2003, 33(23), pp. 8–9. See also: Howard Schultz, "Washing Away the Sin of Overpayment," *The Wall Street Journal,* August 9,

1993, p. A12; Pat DiDomenico, "Don't Get Scammed," *Restaurants USA*, June/July 1992, p. 18.

14. Michael York, "Ex-Marriott Official Pleads Guilty in Theft," *The Washington Post*, August 29, 1992, p. C7. See also: Anonymous, "Rite Aid Sues Man over Invoice Scam," *Las Vegas Review—Journal*, June 16, 2000, p. 6B.

15. Lee Berton, "Inventory Chicanery Tempts More Firms, Fools More Auditors," *The Wall Street Journal*, December 14, 1992, p. A1. See also: Office of Internal Audit, Northwestern University, "Fraud Awareness," retrieved July 11, 2003 (Available http://www.nsula.edu/internalaudit/fraudaware.htm).

16. Jess Bravin, "Court Rules Feds Can Use State Law to Collect Restitution in Phone Scams," *The Wall Street Journal*, July 29, 1998, p. CA6. See also: Timothy L. O'Brien, "Copier-Toner Phone Scams Are Targeting Small Firms," *The Wall Street Journal*, July 16, 1993, p. B2; Anonymous, "Beware of the Scam," *Nevada State Purchasing Newsletter*, June 1995.

17. Terry Franklin, "Honesty Tests Are Best Weapon vs. Theft," *Nation's Restaurant News*, May 1, 1995, p. 26. See also: Gilbert Fuchsberg, "Integrity-Test Firms Fear Report Card by Congress," *The Wall Street Journal*, September 20, 1990, p. B1; M. Williams, "Baring the Soul," *Caterer and Hotelkeeper*, October 1994, p. 64; John W. Jones, Arnold W. David, and William G. Harris, "Integrity Testing: The Debate Continues," *Security Management*, January 1991, 35(1), p. 71; Joan Axelrod-Contrada, "Personality Assessments' Value Draws Some Debate," *Boston Globe*, October 20, 2002, p. 10; Anonymous, "Winning' Culture, Lower Theft," *Chain Store Age*, August 1999, 75(8), p. 38.

18. Anonymous, "For a U. of California Campus, a Purchasing Agent Seemed the Ideal Employee—Until He Got Caught," *The Chronicle of Higher Education*, April 10, 1991, p. A26.

19. Dina Berta, "It's No Mystery: Secret Shoppers Can Improve Service," *Nation's Restaurant News*, November 6, 2000, 35(45), pp. 14, 118. See also: John Stefanelli, "Using Mystery Shoppers to Maintain Hospitality Company Service Standards," *Hospitality & Tourism Educator*, Winter 1994, p. 17; D. Silver, "Hidden Agenda," *Restaurants & Institutions*, June 15, 2000, pp. 63–64; Bob Krummert, "Show Them the Money," *Restaurant Hospitality*, May 2003, 87(5), p. 14; Ed Watkins, "The Road to Five Diamonds," *Lodging Hospitality*, March 1, 2003, 59(3), p.12.

20. Carroll Lachnit, "Protecting People and Profits with Background Checks," *Workforce*, February 2002, 81(2), pp. 50–54. See also: Kirstin Downey Grimsley, "Security Concerns Enrich Background-Checking Companies," *The Washington Post*, November 24, 2001, p. E.1; Eugene Carlson, "Business of Background Checking Comes to the Fore," *The Wall Street Journal*, August 31, 1993, p. B2; Phillip M. Perry, "StopThief," *Restaurants USA*, November 1995, p. 13; Jenny Hedden, "Sorting Out the Bad Eggs," *Restaurants USA*, February 1996, p. 13; J. Farr, "To Catch A Thief," *Restaurant Hospitality*, October 1998, pp. 72–73.

21. Jim W. Moffa, "50 Ways to Increase Restaurant Security, Safety," *Nation's Restaurant News*, January 17, 1994, p. 18.

22. Ameet Sachdev, "Tighter Security on Restaurant Menus: Video Recorders, Alarms Installed," *Chicago Tribune*, May 23, 2002, p. 3.1 See also: Kerry Lydon and Bill Zalud, "Fast-Food Mass Murder Triggers CEO Involvement," *Security*, June 1997, 34(6), pp. 59–60.

23. See, for example, Bill Copeland, *Absolutely Complete Retail Loss Prevention Guide* (Phoenix, AZ: Absolutely Zero Loss Inc., 2000); Robert J. Fischer and Richard Janoski, *Loss Prevention and Security*

Procedures: Practical Applications for Contemporary Problems (Woburn, MA: Butterworth-Heinmann, 2000); Russell Bintliff, *Crimeproofing Your Business: 301 Low-Cost, No-Cost Ways to Protect Your Office, Store, or Business* (New York: McGraw-Hill, 1994); Rudolph Kimiecik, *Loss Prevention Guide for Retail Businesses* (New York: John Wiley & Sons, 1995); Robert L. O'Block, *Security and Crime Prevention*, 2nd ed. (Boston: Butterworth-Heinemann, 1991). See also *Security Management*, American Society for Industrial Security (ASIS), http://www.asisonline.org/.

QUESTIONS AND PROBLEMS

1. What security problems do you risk when you allow the buyer to receive deliveries? When you allow the buyer to pay for the items he or she orders?

2. Is employee supervision the best deterrent to theft and pilferage? Why or why not? If possible, ask a hotel manager or restaurant manager to comment on your answer.

3. What are some of the relatively inexpensive physical barriers that an owner-manager can use to deter theft and pilferage?

4. Assume that you do not want to use an integrity test. How would you check a job applicant's honesty?

5. Why is an owner-manager generally reluctant to put up a cash deposit?

6. Why is paying with a check preferable to using a cash paid-out?

7. List three examples of kickbacks.

8. Why does a buyer often double as the receiving agent? Identify at least two reasons.

9. What is the primary purpose of using an approved-payee list as part of the overall bill-paying procedure?

10. The approved-supplier list represents a major security precaution that is popular among large hospitality companies. Explain some of the reasons for its popularity.

11. Why would a hospitality operator use a shopping service?

12. Why would a hospitality operator require employees to be bonded?

13. What is inventory padding? What can you do to avoid it?

14. What are the major advantages and disadvantages of becoming a house account?

15. What is the primary reason for not hiring an employee who has a relative working for one of your suppliers?

16. Why would you be reluctant to purchase an item from a telephone salesperson?

17. What is the most common type of kickback arrangement?

18. What can a hospitality operator do to protect his or her company from being defrauded by an invoice scam?

19. What can you do to prevent shoplifting?

20. When should a hospitality operator use undercover agents in his or her operation?

21. What are inventory substitutions? What can you do to prevent them?

EXPERIENTIAL EXERCISES

1. Assuming that it is legal, should a hospitality operator use an integrity test during employee selection? Why or why not? What are the potential advantages and disadvantages of the test?

    a. Speak to an operator who likes to use integrity testing and one who does not.
    b. Write a one-page report comparing and contrasting their thoughts.

2. Are there any benefits associated with independent, random audits? Do you think they are worth the time and expense?

    a. Ask a local accounting firm what it would charge for an independent, random audit of a small restaurant.
    b. Ask a representative of this company to comment on the costs and benefits of surprise audits.
    c. Write a one-page report detailing your findings.

3. Assume that your buyer is purchasing all meat items from one purveyor. You notice, however, that other meat purveyors offer the same type of meat products, and that their AP prices are consistently 2 to 3 percent lower than what you are paying. You decide to talk to the buyer about this situation. What questions would you ask? Why? If possible, ask a hotel or restaurant manager to comment on your answer. Prepare a report that includes the questions you would ask and the manager's comments.

17

FRESH PRODUCE

The Purpose of this Chapter

After reading this chapter, you should be able to:

■ Explain the selection factors for fresh produce, including government grades.

■ Explain the process of purchasing, receiving, storing, and issuing fresh produce.

INTRODUCTION

Purchasing fresh produce calls for a great deal of skill and knowledge. Next to fresh-meat procurement, fresh-produce buying is, perhaps, the most difficult purchasing task the hospitality buyer faces.[1] In fact, it can be so difficult that some operators hire professional produce buyers to select and procure these products for them.[2] Fresh-produce buyers must have the wherewithal to purchase products that fluctuate in quality, quantity, and price on a daily basis. The real mark of an amateur in this area is to insist on top quality when none is available anywhere, or to accept poor quality when he or she should know good quality is available.

Fresh-produce buyers, especially those who work for supply houses, are extremely well paid. This fact alone indicates the difficulty and huge responsibility associated with the job. Even assistant fresh-produce buyers for a supply house require about two years of on-the-job training (OJT) before being allowed to make major purchasing decisions.

When a buyer purchases fresh, natural food products, several quality variations within the same product line can appear daily. Soil and climatic conditions can affect the quality of the product he or she receives. Different geographical areas favor different plant varieties and can have a significant impact on the quality of the crop. Seasonal changes, natural or manmade disasters, or changes in demand have effects on the availability of quality product as well. As a result of variations in quality and quantity, the buyer should expect as-purchased (AP) prices to fluctuate throughout the year for produce, both within a given grade and among grades. For this reason, a single year-round price is unrealistic.

To stay abreast of these changes, the savvy buyer subscribes to trade publications that include information on both price and quality. The *Daily Fruit and Vegetable Report*, available online (http://www.ams.usda.gov:80/fv/mncs/fvdaily.htm) or by written request from the U.S. Department of Agriculture (USDA), Washington, DC, is one such publication. The Agricultural Marketing Service (AMS) also provides market news for fruit and vegetables online at http://www.ams.usda.gov/fv/mncs/fvwires.htm. Other subscription services, such as *The Packer: The Business Newspaper of the Produce Industry* (http://www.thepacker.com), and *The Produce News: National News Weekly of the Produce Industry since 1897* (http://www.producenews.com) are additional sources of current fresh-produce data.

In addition to the natural variations outlined above, another difficulty in buying fresh produce is choosing from the tremendous number of varieties and sources. Several hundred varieties of fresh-produce items are regularly available at any given time from various primary sources and intermediaries. Some supply sources stock more than 500 varieties of fresh produce.[3] Without research, it is difficult to decide which variety to use for a particular purpose.

Another major problem that the buyer may face is a lack of acceptable sources of fresh produce. Different varieties of produce grown in different regions come to market throughout the growing season. At times, it may be impossible to find suppliers that can obtain the quality the buyer wants, the quantity he or she needs, or both. On the other hand, it may be fortuitous if the buyer is located near an orchard or farm where the produce is harvested: he or she may be able to obtain fruits and vegetables at the peak of freshness.

SELECTION FACTORS

The owner-manager usually specifies the quality levels of fresh produce desired. The buyer normally carries out these specifications, as much as possible. Management personnel, often in concert with other individuals in the hospitality operation, usually consider one or more of the following fresh-produce selection factors when determining the quality standards as well as the preferred supplier(s).

Intended Use

As with any product or service a buyer plans to purchase, it is very important to identify exactly its performance requirement or intended use. This could save money in the long run because the buyer will not purchase, say, a superb-quality product to be used for a menu item if a lower-quality, lower-priced product will suffice. For instance, apples that must be on display on a buffet line should be very attractive, and the buyer would probably pay a premium price for this appearance. But if apples were to be used in a fruit cup, where their appearance would be camouflaged to some degree, perhaps lesser-quality apples would be adequate.

Exact Name

With the development of so many new types and varieties of fruit and vegetables and the advent of genetically modified foods,[4] the fresh-produce market is filled with a lot of terminology. Keeping track of the types, varieties, and styles of fresh produce can be a challenge. However, understanding this terminology is an absolute necessity for foodservice operations that prepare many menu items from raw ingredients because each item serves a specific culinary purpose. Therefore, a buyer must stay carefully and closely in tune with the needs of the hospitality operation and must find a supplier who is likewise aware.

It is not sufficient for a buyer to specify only the type of fresh produce required; he or she must also specify its variety. If a particular foodservice operation requires lettuce, then the variety must be known (e.g., romaine, iceberg, or red or green leaf). The same is true for potatoes (e.g., Burbank russet or Norgold russet potatoes), apples (e.g., Jonathan, Winesap, Golden Delicious, or McIntosh), and so forth.

U.S. Government Inspection and Grades (or Equivalent)

Grade standards were developed out of the necessity for common terminology of quality and condition in the produce industry (see http://www.ams.usda.gov/fv/ for more discussion on this topic). The first U.S. grade standard for fresh produce was established for potatoes in 1917. "U.S. No. 1" was the term given to the highest grade. It covered the majority of the crop and meant that the product was of good quality. "U.S. No. 2" represented the remainder of the crop that was worth packing for sale under normal marketing conditions.

To enforce these standards, the U.S. Inspection Service for fresh produce was established that same year. In 1930, the Perishable Agricultural Commodities Act (PACA) was signed; it prohibited unfair and fraudulent practices in the interstate commerce of fruits and vegetables. By 1946, the Agricultural Marketing Act was signed into law and provided for the integrated administration of marketing programs. This act also gave the Agricultural Marketing Service (AMS) basic authority for major functions, including federal standards, grading and inspection services, market news services, market expansion, and consumer education. Currently, the USDA, through its AMS, Fruit and Vegetables Division, has grading standards for approximately 150 types of fruits, vegetables, and nuts.

Although government grades are used as a quality guideline, the buyer should be aware that each vegetable or fruit might have a different grading schedule. For example, the grades for grapefruit are U.S. Fancy, U.S. No. 1, U.S. No. 2, U.S. Combination, and U.S. No. 3; the grades for carrots are U.S. Extra No. 1, U.S. No. 1, U.S. No. 1 Jumbo, and U.S. No. 2; and the grades for apples are U.S. Extra Fancy, U.S. Fancy, U.S. No. 1, and U.S. Utility (see Figure 17.1).

FIGURE 17.1 A federal grade stamp used for fresh produce. *Source:* United States Department of Agriculture.

Since most specifications for fresh produce include some reference to federal grades, buyers need to know where to find this information. In addition to the USDA, they can locate grading data in *The PMA Fresh Produce Manual* (see Figure 17.2). This reference manual is available for purchase at http://www.pma.com.

The U.S. government grader considers several factors when grading fresh produce, but appearance is the most important factor. The critical appearance factors include size, size uniformity, maturity, shape, color, texture, and freedom from disease, decay, cuts, and bruises. Other factors sometimes come into play. For example, if produce is to be shipped long distances, say from California to Chicago, a more stringent examination may be applied to ensure that it represents the grade stated at the delivery point (as opposed to the shipping point). The wise buyer is aware of the potential product change during transit and will insist that the fresh produce meet the specified grade at the time of delivery, not at the time the products were shipped from the supplier's warehouse.

Several grading terms exist in the marketplace for fresh-produce items. The most commonly used terminology for fresh fruit, vegetables, and nuts are as follows:

- Fancy—the top quality produced; represents about 1 percent of all produce

- No. 1—the bulk of the items produced; the grade that most retailers purchase

- Commercial—slightly less quality than U.S. No. 1

- No. 2—much less quality than U.S. No. 1; very superior to U.S. No. 3

- Combination—usually a mixture of U.S. No. 1 and U.S. No. 2 products

- No. 3—low-quality products just barely acceptable for packing under normal packing conditions

- Field run—ungraded products

The grades most commonly used in food service are the top grades since the low grades yield less, require additional labor for trimming, and often have a shorter shelf life. Thus, they are not generally a good buy, even at a low price.

The grade most often ordered is the high end of U.S. No. 1, or the equivalent. Clubs, hotels, and restaurants normally order the high end of U.S. No. 1 or the U.S. Fancy grade; the low end of U.S. No. 1 usually is reserved for supermarkets and grocery stores. The few items that fall into the lower-grade categories may not make it to market in any fresh form. Typically, they find their way to some of

Cherries, Sweet

Availability

Some major production areas include:

	January	February	March	April	May	June	July	August	September	October	November	December
California					•	•	•					
Oregon						•	•	•				
Washington						•	•	•				
Chile												•

Variety/Type Descriptions

Bing – Large firm cherry with mahogany skin and flesh; sweet rich flavor.

Chelan – Firm, round, heart-shaped fruit.

Lambert – Dark red, heart-shaped cherry with sweet rich flavor.

Lapins – Mahogany red cherry that exhibits excellent firmness and flavor.

Rainier – Firmly-textured cherry; golden skin with pink-red blush and clear-colored flesh. Sweet delicate flavor.

Sweetheart – Bright red, heart-shaped cherry with mild, sweet flavor and outstanding firmness.

Ordering Specifications

Common packaging:
11- to 20-lb. cartons or lugs
32-lb. crates

Grades:
U.S. No. 1
U.S. Commercial

NOTE: Differences between grades are based primarily on external appearance. Individual growing areas may also set their own grades.

Sizes:
9, 9.5, 10, 10.5, 11, 11.5, and 12 row

Equivalents

80 cherries = 2 cups pitted and sliced
1 pound cherries = 1½ cups juice

Receiving and Inspecting

Look for cherries that are plump with firm, smooth, and brightly colored skins. Avoid cherries with blemishes, rotted or mushy skins. Avoid those that appear either hard and light-colored, or soft, shriveled, and dull. Good quality cherries should have green stems intact.

Storing and Handling

Temperature/humidity recommendations for short-term storage of 7 days or less:
32-36 degrees F/0-2 degrees C
90-98% relative humidity

Retail display tips:
Water sprinkle: No
Top ice: No

Ethylene production/sensitivities:
Produces ethylene: Yes–very low
Sensitive to ethylene exposure: No

Storing tips:
Maintain high humidity while storing cherries. Keep separated from foods with strong odors.

Handling tips:
Cherries bruise easily; handle with care.

Nutrition*

Serving Size 1 cup Cherries (140g)

Amount Per Serving	% Daily Value
Calories 90	
Calories from Fat 5	
Total Fat 0g	0%
Saturated Fat (Not Available)	
Cholesterol 0mg	0%
Sodium 0mg	0%
Total Carbohydrate 23g	8%
Dietary Fiber 3g	12%
Sugars 20g	
Protein 2g	
Vitamin A	2%
Vitamin C	15%
Calcium	2%
Iron	2%

*These values are based on the proposal published by FDA in the Federal Register of March 20, 2002. While PMA believes that use of these data should not result in FDA regulatory action, such a result can never be assured. Consultation with Company counsel is suggested before the data is used in conjunction with the marketing of specific products.

PMA

Produce Marketing Association

Troubleshooting

Pitted skin:
Pitting is the result of damage caused by rough handling. To prevent pitting, keep handling to a minimum and do not dump cherries from shipping containers.

Shriveling; dry, dark stem:
These are indications of moisture loss due to low humidity. For best quality, maintain humidity level of 90-98% during storage.

Loss of flavor; dull color:
These are indications of age. For best quality, inspect cherries carefully upon arrival and use soon after receiving.

Hard, light-colored cherries with dry, acidic flavor:
These are indications of immature fruit; do not use.

FIGURE 17.2 An example of the type of product information noted in *The Produce Marketing Association Fresh Produce Manual.* Courtesy of the Produce Marketing Association. © November 2002.

the food-processing plants that produce juices, jams, and generic-brand canned fruit and vegetables.

Generally, purveyors are knowledgeable about the grading system. If a buyer expresses interest in U.S. No. 1, they will know what he or she wants. However, grades are sometimes unavailable for some fresh produce because: (1) the buyer may be purchasing an item for which there is no grading standard; (2) the suppliers refuse to have an item graded; or (3) more commonly, the produce may come from a foreign country that may not carry a grade, though it must be inspected before it is allowed to enter the United States.

Since considerable problems exist regarding variation in quality due to several seasonal factors, the use of government grades in buying fresh produce typically is not the sole selection criterion. The grade is just one factor, and buyers usually do not base their purchase strictly on it. However, if they bid buy and U.S. grades are a major criterion in their specifications, they must be sure to use the appropriate grade terms.

Packers' Brands (or Equivalent)

Because branded fresh produce is not as commonplace as branded canned and frozen goods, some buyers commonly use both U.S. government grades and packers' brands when developing their fresh-produce buying procedures. Perhaps the most familiar brands are the Sunkist® brand used for citrus fruits and the Blue Goose® brand used for several high-quality fruits and vegetables.

With fresh produce, a packer's brand may also indicate that a particular packing process has been used or that a particular cleaning and cooling process has been followed in the field (see Figure 17.3). U.S. grades may or may not indicate these attributes, depending on the area of the country the products come from.

Consistency, which should be a hallmark of packers' brands, is particularly important with fresh produce. It can result in a much more predictable edible-portion (EP) cost, which is always difficult to calculate for fresh produce in the best of situations. Consistency helps to minimize the variation both between and within case packs. For example, many products, such as whole lettuce, are sold by the case. Some types of lettuce are firm and weighty; others have a lot of space between the leaves. Citrus fruit varies in juice content from one crop to the next; fruits carrying a packer's brand may be more consistent. Asparagus may be old and woody or young and pleasantly crisp, but a packer's brand usually is consistently sound.

Even though a packer may not purchase the U.S. government grading service, government inspections, which consist of random visits by an official

FIGURE 17.3 A packer's brand is a useful selection factor when the buyer wants to purchase precut fresh produce. Courtesy of Fresh Western Marketing Inc.

inspector, are mandatory. In addition, if a packer wants to use a brand name, most states require that this name be registered with the state's department of agriculture.

Packers' brands exist for many varieties of fresh produce. Packers' fresh-produce brands that do not include some reference to federal grades make up only a small portion of the fresh-produce business, and they are not widely known in most parts of the country. In most situations, packers use the brand name in conjunction with the U.S. grade designation (e.g., U.S. No. 1). Beware of a stencil on the box with the designation "No. 1." This sign indicates that the product is not under continual government inspection, nor has it been graded; but, in the opinion of that packer, the product meets all U.S. requirements for U.S. No. 1 graded products.

A major problem found with packers' brands for produce is that packers sometimes put out two categories of the same brand. For example, some packers have been accused of putting the same brand name on demonstrably different qualities of the same product—and trying to imply that the qualities are the same since they both carry the same name. For instance, on a high No. 1 and on a low No. 1, the high No. 1 produce typically goes to hospitality operations, while the low No. 1 produce goes primarily to supermarkets. The possibility of a switch should disturb and alert hospitality buyers.

Product Size

Product size is a very critical selection factor for at least two reasons. First, it would be embarrassing to serve guests items of varying sizes. Second, if the products were sold by the piece rather than by weight, buyers would find it impossible to achieve effective cost control if varying sizes are served.

Many buyers, especially novices, are unaware of the many fresh-produce sizes available. Indicating this selection factor is sometimes overlooked when buyers purchase fruits and vegetables. Buyers should not merely order a box of lemons; they should indicate the size of the lemon wanted by specifying the count per box—the lower the count, the larger the lemon. A great many types and varieties of fresh fruits are sold this way.

Still another common way to indicate produce size is to indicate the desired number of pieces per layer of the "lug," or box. This is particularly true when you buy a lug of tomatoes. For example, a "4 by 5" preference indicates a specific tomato size: the lug has layers of tomatoes with 4 on one side and 5 on the other, or 20 tomatoes per layer.

Some products carry a unique nomenclature. For instance, a packer may classify onions into four product sizes: pre-pack, large medium, jumbo, and colossal.

Furthermore, buyers may find that some produce sold in their area is sized according to the approximate number of pieces per pound. For example, a "3 to 1" item size indicates that there are approximately three items per pound. Moreover, agribusiness has advanced to the point where several sizes exist within narrow product lines; for instance, Idaho potatoes come in 12 sizes, ranging from 4 to 18 ounces each.

Size of Container

Foodservice buyers prefer to purchase the size of container that is consistent with the needs of the operation. Generally, most fresh-produce items are packed in at least two, sometimes more, container sizes, and buyers usually find one of these sizes more suitable for their operation's needs. For instance, if buyers do not require a particular type of produce in large quantities, it would be appropriate for them to purchase it in small containers so that waste and spoilage are minimized.

As with many other types of foods and beverages, the fresh-produce product line has uniform container sizes. For instance, avocados typically come in a "flat," which is one layer of product, or a "lug," which consists of two layers of product. Some suppliers may be willing to "break" a case. However, chances are that you will need to pay for this added supplier service.

Type of Packaging Material

Several standardized types of packaging materials are available in the fresh-produce product line. However, these materials vary quite a bit in terms of quality and price. The AP price variation for some fresh produce is related solely to the quality of packaging; less expensive merchandise may be scantily packed, and more expensive products may be wrapped in high-quality packaging. Certain assurances come with the type of packaging material used. For instance, high-quality fiberboard costs more than thin brown-paper wrappings. With the former, the merchandise will be protected, whereas with the latter, you will probably lose some of it to damage during shipping and handling.

Packaging Procedure

Packing generally takes two forms: layered merchandise and slab-packed merchandise. With the layered style, the product is arranged nicely, usually between sheets of paper or cardboard. With the slab-packed style, the product is randomly placed into a container with no additional packaging. If it is important to preserve the edible yield of an item, buyers should probably purchase better packaging arrangements, or the savings associated with slab packing will be illusory.

For some products, buyers can request each item to be individually wrapped and layered in the case. They may also be able to purchase products that are layered in a "cell pack," which is a cardboard or plastic sheet with depressions in it; the items can sit in the depressions and not touch each other. Some apples are packed this way. These procedures are expensive, but if this process is necessary to preserve the appearance of the apples, probably no better way exists for buyers to accomplish their goal than to insist that cell packs are used.

Minimum Weight Per Case

Since so much fresh produce is purchased by the case, or by the container, the case weight can vary considerably. This has implications on the bid price because the weight will vary from case to case. Therefore, buyers should indicate the minimum acceptable weight during the bidding process and write it in the specifications. Also, fresh produce tends to "shrink," or dehydrate, while in transit. Thus, specifying a minimum weight enables buyers to receive the appropriate amount while simultaneously giving suppliers some shrink allowance. In some cases, buyers might also indicate a "decay allowance" on a fresh-produce product specification. For example, when buyers purchase ripe plums, slab packed, a few unusable ones are bound to be in the lot. Buyers and suppliers should agree on the number of bad pieces that will be acceptable.

Another dimension of this selection factor is the possibility that buyers might wish to indicate a weight range per case of produce they order. This gives suppliers a bit more flexibility and ensures that, once in a while, buyers might receive more weight, and, therefore, more usable servings of product than they would if they indicated only a minimum weight required on the specification.

Product Yield

Some of the fresh produce buyers purchase will be subject to a certain amount of "trim," or unavoidable waste. For example, when purchasing whole, fresh turnips, buyers should note on the product specification the minimum edible yield expected or, alternatively, the maximum amount of acceptable trim loss.

Point of Origin

If buyers shop around, they must be careful that they understand the differences in quality, texture, appearance, and taste that will accompany products from different areas of the world. If buyers do business with only one or two purveyors, generally these suppliers will try to provide fresh produce whose characteristics are somewhat consistent. But this may not be the case if buyers wish to deal with multiple purveyors.

Another dimension of this selection factor is the problem associated with noting on the menu the point of origin for certain menu offerings. For instance, if a hospitality operation indicates that it serves Idaho potatoes, the operator must be certain that its potatoes actually come from Idaho or it will be in violation of truth-in-menu legislation.

Color

Generally, when buyers specify the type or variety of merchandise desired, that in itself will indicate color. However, with the growing number of varieties of fruits and vegetables available, buyers may need to specify the color preferred. For example, peppers come in many colors, including green, red, purple, yellow, and orange.

Product Form

Buyers can purchase fresh produce in many forms. From the whole "fresh-off-the-vine" items, to the ready-to-serve products, to anything in between, buyers must determine which product best meets the requirements of their operations. When they purchase an item in anything other than its original form, varying degrees of value have been added: different degrees of economic "form" have given value to the item. These value-added products are more expensive, but in the long run may be more economical than whole products that require considerable labor and handling before service.[5] Today, many operators prefer purchasing value-added, "precut" fresh produce that has been subjected to additional cleaning, chopping, and so forth. For example, buyers can purchase peeled and sliced onions, potatoes, and similar items.

Degree of Ripeness

Buyers can purchase some fresh produce at varying stages of ripeness. Usually, buyers will purchase mature, fully ripened produce. However, immature, green produce can also be found. For some items, such as bananas and tomatoes, several stages of ripening can be ordered; these options may be quite suitable for an operation that wants to ripen some of its own fresh produce so that it is at its peak of quality when served.

Ripening Process Used

Buyers should be aware of the types of ripening processes. Some produce is naturally ripened on the plant. These items are a bit more expensive because of the difficulty of handling and the loss producers experience; they often end up with some rotting merchandise in their fields. The taste of the item, though, may be so desirable that buyers are willing to pay for it.

Some produce is ripened in a "ripening room." In this situation, the produce is picked when it is green and then is placed in a room, train car, or truck. Ethylene gas is then introduced into the "room." When some types of produce ripen naturally, they emit ethylene gas, so the introduction of this gas into the "room" speeds up the ripening process. Unfortunately, if the process is hastened too much, the fresh-produce item will not mature properly. Bananas, for example, will turn bright yellow, but the fruit under the skin will not have kept pace (i.e., it will not be very flavorful because it has not ripened fully even though the skin color suggests that it has).

Preservation Method

Fresh produce is not considered a potentially hazardous food; consequently, the federal government does not require any type of preservation. Nonetheless, storage conditions throughout the fresh-produce channel of distribution affect culinary quality and availability of produce. These conditions may also create unsanitary conditions that can cause a food-borne illness outbreak. However, this problem is typically due to contaminants present in the soil or water. The food itself is not usually the issue.

Some fresh produce items are refrigerated, while others can be left unrefrigerated. Buyers must note on their specification their refrigeration requirement, if any. Refrigeration is unnecessary for some items, such as bananas, potatoes, and most onions. However, they still should be kept in a cool environment so that they do not overripen or rot.

Refrigeration is expensive, so operations expect to pay more for refrigerated fresh produce. But unrefrigerated or uncooled product can rapidly deteriorate. As a result, the EP cost for such produce will usually be much greater than the EP cost associated with refrigerated produce.

If buyers are purchasing precut, convenience fresh produce, refrigeration is mandatory. The supplier must preserve the appropriate "pulp" temperature, otherwise, the produce will quickly deteriorate. For instance, chopped salad greens should be delivered at a pulp temperature of approximately 34°F to 36°F in order to preserve their culinary quality.

Waxing is another method used to preserve some produce. The wax prevents moisture loss and also contributes to the appearance of the produce. Mother Nature uses this process for such foods as peppers and cucumbers. Producers are also allowed to apply wax to some items, especially when they remove the natural wax when cleaning the product. Some items are traditionally waxed, and operators will receive them in this state unless they specify otherwise. Fresh-produce items most likely to be waxed by producers are apples, avocados, bell peppers, cantaloupes, cucumbers, eggplant, grapefruit, lemons, limes, melons, oranges, parsnips, passion fruit, peaches, pineapples, pumpkins, rutabagas, squash, sweet potatoes, tomatoes, and turnips.

Some fresh produce is preserved in controlled-atmosphere storage. The produce is put into a room, and the room then is sealed. Oxygen is removed, and a variety of other gases are introduced. The lack of oxygen reduces the rate of respiration, hence retarding spoilage. The produce held in atmosphere-controlled chambers will remain as is for a considerable period of time. Unfortunately, when this produce is removed from this environment, it deteriorates very rapidly. Generally, suppliers do not sell this type of merchandise to hospitality operators; rather, they sell it to the retail trade. But when buyers shop around, they should note on their specification that they prefer merchandise that has not been stored in a controlled environment.

Some of the fresh produce that comes to market has been chemically treated in order to preserve its shelf life and palatability. If buyers do not want this type of merchandise, they can opt to purchase fresh produce that has been "organically" grown—that is, grown without the use of synthetic chemicals and fertilizers.[6]

Organic food products have become so popular with consumers that in October of 2001, the USDA set up stringent guidelines and standards for products to be called "organic."[7] You can review these guidelines at www.ams.usda.gov/nop.

Buyers can also purchase fresh produce that has been grown in nutrient-rich water instead of chemically treated soil. This "hydroponic" fresh produce is especially popular with fine-dining establishments because they can grow it in the food-service operation and serve it almost immediately after harvest. If, however, buyers purchase organic or hydroponic produce, they can expect to pay a premium AP price.

Trusting the Supplier

Specifying U.S. grades, packers' brands, and one particular supplier can make you a "house account" of the highest order, which may or may not be in accord with company policy. However, buyers building a trusting relationship with their suppliers may be the key to the success of their operations. This is because suppliers are linked to several crucial factors associated with operating an establishment. These may include: delivery schedules, seasonal changes, weather factors, the suppliers' buying capabilities, the transportation and storage facilities, and the speed with which the suppliers rotate products.

With fresh produce, and to a lesser extent with processed items, suppliers must assure buyers that they will get the quality they need and want, and that this will be as good on the table as it was in the field. If buyers do not work closely with a fresh produce supplier, they take some risks. For instance, just because you specify Sunkist and U.S. No. 1, there is no guarantee that you will receive them. The box might note U.S. No. 1, but it can easily have been repacked with lower-quality product.

Additionally, fresh-produce buying does not lend itself easily to bid buying. Buyers have many points to consider, and, in some parts of the United States, there are few suppliers to bid for their business. Consequently, this is an area in which they may wish to rely on the suppliers' highly developed expertise.

PURCHASING FRESH PRODUCE

The first step in purchasing fresh produce is to obtain *The PMA Fresh Produce Manual*. This unique publication contains very detailed specifications for many fresh-produce items. It also includes information on receiving, storing, and handling techniques.

The next step is to decide on the exact type of produce and quality wanted. Buyers may not be the ones to make this decision, unless they are user-buyers or owner-user-buyers. Once the decision on the type and quality of produce to be ordered has been made, the buyer should prepare specifications for each item. These specifications should be as complete as necessary and should include all pertinent information, especially if the buyer intends to engage in bid buying. (See the guidelines noted in Chapter 8. For examples of fresh-produce product specifications and a product specification outline, see Figures 17.4 and 17.5, respectively.)

After buyers prepare the specifications, the next step is to consider the suppliers likely to satisfy their needs. Here, again, they can become a house account, use bid buying, or settle on some procedure in between. (Note that bid buying is not as prevalent in the fresh-produce trade as it is for processed foods and nonfoods.)

Over the years, several fresh-produce buying groups and trade associations have evolved. This, in turn, has made such products more readily available in the local markets. Buyers may also find several suppliers handling a few fresh-produce items as a sideline to their regular business of canned goods, frozen foods, and various nonfood items. Generally, though, it is difficult to find more than one or two consistently capable full-line, fresh-produce suppliers. Because of this, buyers may find it difficult to engage in bid buying.

An added attraction in the fresh-produce area is the independent farmers. These small businesspersons may occasionally want to sell buyers "farm-fresh pro-

Red Delicious apples Used for fruit plate item U.S. Fancy Washington State 72 count 30- to 42-pound crate Moisture-proof fiberboard Layered arrangement, cell carton Whole apples Fresh, refrigerated Fully ripened	Cauliflower, white Used for side dish for all entrées U.S. No. 1 (high) 12 count 18- to 25-pound carton Moisture-proof fiberboard Loose pack (slab pack) Pretrimmed heads Fresh, refrigerated Fully ripened
Sweet Spanish, yellow globe onion Used for onion rings U.S. No. 1 (high) Jumbo size 50-pound plastic mesh bag Whole onions Fresh, unrefrigerated Fully ripened	Iceberg lettuce Used for tossed salad U.S. No. 1 (high) 10-pound poly bag Loose pack (slab pack) Chopped lettuce Fresh, refrigerated Fully ripened

FIGURE 17.4 An example of fresh-produce product specifications.

Intended use:

Exact name:

U.S. grade (or equivalent):

Packer's brand name (or equivalent):

Product size:

Size of container:

Type of packaging material:

Packaging procedure:

Minimum weight per case:

Product yield:

Point of origin:

Color:

Product form:

Degree of ripeness:

Ripening process used:

Preservation method:

FIGURE 17.5 **An example of a product specification outline for fresh produce.**

duce." Some may sell on the roadside. Others may allow customers to come in and "pick their own." Still others may gather together one or two days a week in what is referred to as a "farmers' market." Over the years, farmers' markets have become more visible, numerous, and popular.

In some instances, the small, local farmer will be a wise choice. For example, as part of a college project, some students were required to compare an independent farmer's AP prices and supplier services a restaurant purchased to the same products and supplier services offered by other fresh-produce suppliers. The results of the study indicated that the restaurant's management was paying the farmer about 7 percent more per month. But it was the opinion of the class that the quality of the farmer's fresh produce was far superior. In addition, the farmer delivered daily. Unfortunately, he could not supply all the needs of this restaurant. But, for what he did supply, the class judged it to be the best overall value.

Reliable, independent farmers are, however, hard to find. Some of these "farmers" purchase their products from supermarket suppliers and then give the impression that the produce is home-grown. Another problem that might concern buyers is that neither the state or federal government is likely to inspect the farmer's facilities and products.

Adventurous operators might consider developing their own fresh produce gardens. Lately, several restaurant chefs have taken this unique step.[8] Gardens located on the premises ensure freshness. They can also be excellent marketing and promotional tools used to attract guests.

RECEIVING FRESH PRODUCE

Taking delivery of the correct amount of the specified quality is a major challenge. Some receivers may merely look at the box of lettuce, read "24 heads," and take it for granted that 24 heads of lettuce are in the carton. A skillful receiver resists the temptation to examine only the printing on the containers and cartons and to look at only the top layer of merchandise.

Before accepting a produce shipment, the receiver should conduct a visual inspection of the top layer, and check the weight of the entire carton. This inspection provides a quick and accurate idea of the quantity and quality of the shipment. The receiver should also conduct a random sampling of a proportion of containers. Here, a receiver carefully unpacks a box of produce to check the count, size, and quality throughout the carton. A good place for this inspection is in refrigerated quarters, such as a walk-in refrigerator, so that the produce does not become too warm, thus decreasing its shelf life.

Although receiving fresh produce can be a daunting task, we are not suggesting that receivers break open every carton to see whether it really contains full count. This undertaking can cause extensive damage to fragile fruit and vegetables, particularly if they are packaged in special protective films designed to extend their shelf life (see Figures 17.6 and 17.7 for signs of acceptable and unacceptable quality in some fresh-produce items). However, buyers can make the task less stressful by establishing a partner-like relationship with vendors. If buyers have concerns about trusting their suppliers and receivers completely, it will be in their best interest to continually review their receiving practices very carefully. At the very least, they should verify that the produce is acceptable by checking to see that the quality is equal throughout and to make certain that no repacking has occurred.

After checking quality and quantity, receivers should check the prices and complete the appropriate accounting documents.

FIGURE 17.6 Signs of acceptable and unacceptable quality in some fresh fruit items. Reprinted with permission from *Applied Foodservice Sanitation Certification Coursebook*, 4th ed. Copyright 1992 by the National Restaurant Association Educational Foundation. All rights reserved.

	SIGNS OF GOOD QUALITY	SIGNS OF BAD QUALITY, SPOILAGE
Apples	Firmness; crispness; bright color	Softness; bruises. Irregularly shaped brown or tan areas do not usually affect quality.
Apricots	Bright, uniform color; plumpness	Dull color; shriveled appearance
Bananas	Firmness; brightness of color	Grayish or dull appearance (indicates exposure to cold and inability to ripen properly)
Blueberries	Dark blue color with silvery bloom	Moist berries
Cantaloupes (Muskmelons)	Stem should be gone; netting or veining should be coarse; skin should be yellow-gray or pale yellow	Bright yellow color; mold; large bruises
Cherries	Very dark color; plumpness	Dry stems; soft flesh; gray mold
Cranberries	Plumpness; firmness. Ripe cranberries should bounce.	Leaky berries
Grapefruit	Should be heavy for its size	Soft areas; dull color
Grapes	Should be firmly attached to stems. Bright color and plumpness are good signs.	Drying stems; leaking berries
Honeydew melon	Soft skin; faint aroma; yellowish white to creamy rind color	White or greenish color; bruises or water-soaked areas; cuts or punctures in rind
Lemons	Firmness; heaviness. Should have rich yellow color	Dull color; shriveled skin
Limes	Glossy skin; heavy weight	Dry skin; molds
Oranges	Firmness; heaviness; bright color	Dry skin; spongy texture; blue mold
Peaches	Slightly soft flesh	A pale tan spot (indicates beginning of decay); very hard or very soft flesh
Pears	Firmness	Dull skin; shriveling; spots on the sides
Pineapples	"Spike" at top should separate easily from flesh	Mold; large bruises; unpleasant odor; brown leaves
Plums	Fairly firm to slightly soft flesh	Leaking; brownish discoloration
Raspberries, Boysenberries	Stem caps should be absent; flesh should be plump and tender	Mushiness; wet spots on containers (sign of possible decay of berries)
Strawberries	Stem cap should be attached; berries should have rich red color	Gray mold; large uncolored areas
Tangerines	Bright orange or deep yellow color; loose skin	Punctured skin; mold
Watermelon	Smooth surface; creamy underside; bright red flesh	Stringy or mealy flesh (spoilage difficult to see on outside)

	SIGNS OF GOOD QUALITY	SIGNS OF POOR QUALITY, SPOILAGE
Artichokes	Plumpness; green scales; clinging leaves	Brown scales; grayish-black discoloration; mold
Asparagus	Closed tips; round spears	Spread-out tips; spears with ridges; spears that are not round
Beans (snap)	Firm, crisp pods	Extensive discoloration; tough pods
Beets	Firmness; roundness; deep red color	Gray mold; wilting; flabbiness
Brussels sprouts	Bright color; tight-fitting leaves	Loose, yellow-green outer leaves; ragged leaves (may indicate worm damage)
Cabbage	Firmness; heaviness for size	Wilted or decayed outer leaves. (Leaves should not separate easily from base.)
Carrots	Smoothness; firmness	Soft spots
Cauliflower	Clean, white curd; bright green leaves	Speckled curd; severe wilting; loose flower clusters
Celery	Firmness; crispness; smooth stems	Flabby leaves; brown-black interior discoloration
Cucumber	Green color; firmness	Yellowish color; softness
Eggplant	Uniform, dark purple color	Softness; irregular dark brown spots
Greens	Tender leaves free of blemishes	Yellow-green leaves; evidence of insect decay
Lettuce	Crisp leaves; bright color	Tip burn on edges of leaves. (Slight discoloration of outer leaves is not harmful.)
Mushrooms	White, creamy, or tan color on tops of caps	Dark color on underside of cap; withering veil
Onions	Hardness; firmness; small necks; papery outer scales	Wet or soft necks
Onions (green)	Crisp, green tops; white portion two to three inches in length	Yellowing; wilting
Peppers (green)	Glossy appearance; dark green color	Thin walls; cuts, punctures
Potatoes	Firmness; relative smoothness	Green rot or mold; large cuts; sprouts

FIGURE 17.7 Signs of acceptable and unacceptable quality in some fresh vegetable items. Reprinted with permission from *Applied Foodservice Sanitation Certification Coursebook*, 4th ed. Copyright 1992 by the National Restaurant Association Educational Foundation. All rights reserved.

	SIGNS OF GOOD QUALITY	SIGNS OF POOR QUALITY, SPOILAGE
Radishes	Plumpness; roundness; red color	Yellowing of tops (sign of aging); softness
Squash (summer)	Glossy skin	Dull appearance; tough surface
Squash (winter)	Hard rind	Mold; softness
Sweet potatoes	Bright skins	Wetness; shriveling; sunken and discolored areas on sides of potato. (Sweet potatoes are extremely susceptible to decay.)
Tomatoes	Smoothness; redness. (Tomatoes that are pink or slightly green will ripen in a warm place.)	Bruises; deep cracks around the stem scar
Watercress	Crispness; bright green color	Yellowing, wilting, decaying of leaves

FIGURE 17.7 **(Continued.)**

STORING FRESH PRODUCE

To prevent rapid quality degradation and loss of some nutritional value, it is imperative that hospitality operations properly store fresh fruits and vegetables. If buyers can arrange for frequent deliveries from their fresh-produce supplier and move the produce rapidly through production, they can be a little more flexible with their storage duties. But because many suppliers are not equipped to provide daily delivery, operators should plan for a suitable storage facility.

Fresh produce must be stored immediately at the proper temperature and humidity (see Figure 17.8 for requirements for some vegetables). Large foodservice operations usually have a separate cool area or refrigerator for these items. But any cool temperature is better than none. Hospitality operations must avoid all delays: most fresh produce deteriorates considerably when it is left at room temperature. In fact, most fully ripened produce becomes inedible quite quickly if it is held in the wrong storage environment. For example, fresh corn loses about 50 percent of its sugar in the first 24 hours after it is picked; proper refrigeration, however, can slow this deterioration.

To extend the shelf life of fresh produce, buyers must research the best possible storage environment for each fruit and vegetable. This includes knowing how the produce is packaged since some packages are designed to extend shelf life. Some fruits and vegetables, packed in a box, carton, or in cello wrap, are best stored by

USDA RECOMMENDED STORAGE REQUIREMENTS FOR VEGETABLES			
COMMODITY	STORAGE TEMPERATURE	RELATIVE HUMIDITY	MAXIMUM TOTAL STORAGE PERIOD*
Asparagus	32–36°F	95%	2–3 weeks
Broccoli	32–35	90–95	10–14 days
Carrots (topped)	32–35	90–95	4–5 months
Cauliflower	32–35	90–95	2–4 weeks
Celery	32–35	90–95	2–3 months
Lettuce	32–34	95	2–3 weeks
Onions, green (scallions)	32–35	90–95	—

*This maximum storage includes commercial storage of produce before it is delivered to your loading dock. If you intend holding fruits and vegetables in your walk-in for any length of time, consult your produce house or distributor to determine how long you can safely store produce that has already been in storage.

FIGURE 17.8 Recommended storage requirements for some fresh vegetables. Courtesy of *Restaurants & Institutions* magazine, a Cahners publication.

merely placing them in the refrigerator. On the other hand, some produce arrives in crates that are not designed to extend shelf life. Celery, for example, usually arrives in a crate and rapidly loses moisture and becomes limp if not repacked. Cello bags or plastic, reusable, see-through tubs are excellent for repacking. Contrary to popular opinion, produce should not be washed before it is stored. Moisture enhances the growth of soft-rot microorganisms and invariably decreases the shelf life of the fruit or vegetable. Washing may also remove protective wax coating designed to extend the shelf life of vegetables such as green peppers and cucumbers. Products should be washed, if necessary, when they enter the production cycle.

Operators also should expect to extend fresh-produce shelf life if they practice proper fresh-produce handling techniques. The techniques are quite simple. The general rule is to handle the merchandise only when it is absolutely necessary. Employees should not pick it up, move it around, bend it, or bounce it because this will cause unnecessary bruising that will manifest itself in excessive spoilage and waste.

ISSUING FRESH PRODUCE

Fresh-produce purchases often bypass the central-storage facility and go directly to the food production department. If employees first move the fresh produce

	RAW WEIGHT	APPROXIMATE EDIBLE YIELD	APPROXIMATE WASTE
Apples	1 lb.	13 oz.	19%
Apricots	1 lb.	12 oz.	25%
Asparagus	1 lb.	9 oz.	44%
Avocado	1 lb.	12 oz.	25%
Bananas	1 lb.	13 oz.	19%
Beans, green	1 lb.	14 oz.	13%
Broccoli, whole head	1 lb.	10 oz.	38%
Brussels sprouts	1 lb.	16 oz.	0%
Cabbage	1 lb.	13 oz.	19%
Cantaloupe	1 lb.	11 oz.	31%
Carrots, no tops	1 lb.	12 oz.	25%
Cauliflower, trimmed	1 lb.	16 oz.	0%
Celery, whole stalk	1 lb.	12 oz.	25%
Cranberries	1 lb.	16 oz.	0%
Cucumbers	1 lb.	14 oz.	13%
Eggplant, whole	1 lb.	13 oz.	19%
Grapefruit	1 lb.	11 oz.	31%
Lemons	1 lb.	11 oz.	31%
Limes	1 lb.	11 oz.	31%
Lettuce, untrimmed	1 lb.	12 oz.	25%
Melon, honeydew	1 lb.	11 oz.	31%
Mushrooms	1 lb.	16 oz.	0%
Onions	1 lb.	14 oz.	13%
Oranges	1 lb.	11 oz.	31%
Pears	1 lb.	13 oz.	19%
Peppers, green	1 lb.	13 oz.	19%
Potatoes, sweet	1 lb.	11 oz.	31%
Potatoes, white	1 lb.	12 oz.	25%
Squash, summer	1 lb.	14 oz.	13%
Strawberries	1 lb.	14 oz.	13%
Tangerines	1 lb.	11 oz.	31%
Tomatoes	1 lb.	14 oz.	13%
Turnips	1 lb.	12 oz.	25%

FIGURE 17.9 **The preparation waste of some fresh-produce items.**

STORAGE TIMES FOR FRUITS AND VEGETABLES

APPLES, Fresh	Store in fruit or vegetable box three weeks to a month. Inspect daily to remove rotten fruit so that the balance will not be contaminated. Watch for blue mold or black rot.	**CUCUMBERS**	These are not sturdy and should be used within a week.
APRICOTS	Easily stored for one to two weeks.	**EGGPLANT**	Should not remain in storage more than a week.
ASPARAGUS	Can be kept for two weeks but must be crated with the heels packed in moss.	**GARLIC**	Can be kept for about two months at temperatures from 55 to 65 degrees. In a vegetable cooler at temperatures 32 to 36 degrees, garlic will last four months.
AVOCADO	May be kept in refrigerator one week after ripening.	**GRAPEFRUIT**	Will last six weeks at 32 to 36 degrees.
BANANAS	May be kept at 50 to 60 degrees and used within two to three days after ripening. Do not store in the cooler at any time.	**GRAPES**	White seedless or red Tokay grapes will keep for four weeks. Red Emperor, obtainable in late fall, will keep for two months.
BERRIES	All fresh berries can be kept for a week to 10 days. However, it is recommended that these be used as quickly as possible for best flavor.	**KALE**	In temperatures from 32 to 36 degrees, kale will remain in good condition for three weeks.
BROCCOLI	Can be stored for 8 to 10 days.	**LEMONS**	May be kept from one to two months at 50 to 60 degrees.
CABBAGE	EARLY VARIETY will keep about two weeks. LATE VARIETY is much sturdier—will last two months.	**LETTUCE, Iceberg**	If in good condition and inspected regularly, iceberg lettuce may be kept for four weeks. The leaves should not be removed until the lettuce is to be used, unless they have begun to rot. However, to obtain a maximum quality, lettuce should be used as soon as possible after arrival.
CANTALOUPE	Inspect daily for ripeness. When ripe, may be held in the cooler for one week.		
CARROTS	If in good condition, they may be kept in the storeroom for a few days. Under refrigeration, they will last three months.	**LIMES**	Will not last in storage over two weeks.
CAULIFLOWER	May be kept for two weeks if the leaves are not cut away. After the leaves are removed, it deteriorates rapidly.	**MELONS**	May be stored a maximum of three weeks. However, it is recommended that they be used as soon as the proper degree of softness is achieved.
CELERY	Should not be kept longer than a few days. If it is wilted, placing in water will freshen it.	**MUSHROOMS**	Fresh, should not be kept more than one or two days.
CORN	Corn is one of the most sensitive of vegetables and should be used within 24 hours after arrival.	**ONIONS, Green**	If kept under refrigeration, they will last a week or 10 days.
CRANBERRIES	May be stored in a vegetable box for as long as two months.	**ONIONS, Yellow**	If stored in a cool, dry place, un-refrigerated, they will last three months.

FIGURE 17.10 Storage times for some fresh-produce items. Reprinted from *Lodging* magazine.

ORANGES	Should be used within a week if possible. If necessary, they may be held in a reasonably good condition for a month or six weeks.	POTATOES, Sweet	These do not have the staying power of white potatoes. They require a cool place, 50 to 60 degrees, and should not be kept for more than a week. They will last for three or four weeks if the air is extremely dry.
PARSNIPS	Can be stored two to three months at 32 to 36 degrees.		
PARSLEY	A week is about the time limit for parsley. Keep it well iced.	PUMPKIN	Can last for a month at temperatures from 50 to 60 degrees. However, it is better to buy the canned variety.
PEACHES	Most varieties will last about a week; the yellow cling variety about two weeks. Peaches must be inspected and sorted each day.		
PEARS	Summer or Bartlett variety—before ripening, they may be kept three weeks at 65 to 75 degrees. After ripening, they must be refrigerated and used within a few days. They require gentle handling to prevent bruising and must be sorted every 5 days. Bosc or Comice variety—may be kept six weeks before ripening if sorted weekly. After ripening, must be used within a few days. Winter Anjou or Winter Nelis variety—will keep eight to ten weeks before ripening.	RADISHES	Should not be kept longer than a week, and it is wiser to use them within a few days. The leaves should be removed as soon as possible.
		RHUBARB	May be kept for a week, but since it loses flavor after a short time, it should be used as soon as possible.
		ROMAINE	Will generally last about 10 days.
		SPINACH	Must be properly iced to last any time at all. Even then, one week is its time limit.
		SQUASH, Summer	Will last only two weeks
		SQUASH, Winter	Can be held at 50 to 60 degrees for three months
PEPPERS	May be held for about three weeks.	STRAWBERRIES	Must not be kept longer than 2 days and require a temperature from 32 to 36 degrees.
PINEAPPLES	May be kept as long as two weeks on a ripening table at temperatures from 65 to 75 degrees. Once ripe, they should be used within 2 or 3 days.		
		TOMATOES	Should not be kept over a week after ripening. They require daily sorting for ripeness.
PLUMS	Green Gage or red—will keep for two weeks but after ripening must be used within a few days.	TURNIPS	White—they will keep about 10 days or two weeks without refrigeration. Under light refrigeration, they will last three months.
POTATOES, White	May last four months in cool, dry, well-ventilated place that is refrigerated. New potatoes, however, should not be kept for more than five or six weeks.		
		WATERMELON	May be held a week or 10 days, but no longer.

FIGURE 17.10 (Continued.)

to a central-storage facility and issue it later to the food production department, they may want to issue these items as ready-to-go. That is, they may consider issuing cleaned, chopped onions instead of whole onions; sliced tomatoes instead of whole tomatoes; or topped, peeled, and cut carrots instead of whole carrots (see

Figure 17.9 for preparation waste of some fresh fruit and vegetables). By doing this, they may be able to effect a labor cost savings or extract better value from higher-paid cooks and chefs.

Employees should follow proper stock rotation when issuing produce (see Figures 17.8 and 17.10 for storage times for some fresh-produce items). Since these items spoil quickly, make sure that the requisitioner takes no more than necessary. It may be wise to ask him or her to note the in-process inventory before asking for more stock.

IN-PROCESS INVENTORIES

Buyers will discover that control of purchasing, receiving, storing, and issuing fresh produce is easier than control of produce production and service. For instance, a great deal of supervision is required to ensure that salad greens do not sit out at room temperature too long.

Generally, once the fresh produce is issued to a user, buyers are relieved of their responsibility. But since this book is directed toward managers who need a more panoramic view of the hospitality industry, we offer commentary on how the production and service staffs use these purchased items.

We have known several restaurants that undertook considerable expense to purchase fresh produce efficiently, only to see the savings disappear because an inexperienced manager did not, or could not, supervise its use. Many operations protect the AP price, or backdoor cost, very well, but the EP cost, or front door cost, does not often enjoy equal consideration. Figure 17.9 shows that considerable unavoidable loss is associated with fresh produce; the chances for excessive loss increase if proper supervision is absent.

KEY WORDS AND CONCEPTS

Agricultural Marketing Service (AMS)

Approximate waste percentages

As-purchased price (AP price)

Broken case

Cell pack

Color

Controlled atmosphere storage

Decay allowance

Degree of ripeness

Difference between two levels of U.S. No. 1

Edible-portion cost (EP cost)

Ethylene gas

Exact name

Farmers' market

Field run

Flat

Form value

Genetically altered fresh produce

Grading factors

Hydroponic fresh produce

Independent farmer

In-process inventories

Intended use

Layered packaging

Lug

Minimum weight per case

Organic fresh produce

Perishable Agricultural
Commodities Act (PACA)

Packaging material

Packaging procedure

Packers' brands

Point of origin

Precut fresh produce

Preservation method

Produce Marketing
Association (PMA)

Product form

Product size

Product yield

Pulp temperature

Purchasing, receiving,
storing, and issuing fresh
produce

Ready-to-serve produce

Reference books that can be
used when preparing
specifications

Ripening process used

Ripening room

Shelf life

Shrink allowance

Size of container

Slab-packed

Storage requirements for
fresh produce

Trim

Trusting the supplier

Type of product

United States Department
of Agriculture (USDA)

U.S. grades

Value-added products

Variety of products

REFERENCES

1. Patt Patterson, "A Hard Sell: Buying Produce Is No Day in the Park," *Nation's Restaurant News*, January 25, 1993, p. 23.

2. Thomas M. Burton, "Buying Fine Produce for Finicky Chefs Is No Bowl of Cherries," *The Wall Street Journal*, August 6, 1991, p. A1.

3. Kathleen Deveny, "America's Heartland Acquires Global Tastes," *The Wall Street Journal*, October 11, 1995, p. B1.

4. Brian O'Reilly, "Reaping a Biotech Blunder," *Fortune*, February 19, 2001, p. 156. See also: Scott McMurray, "New Calgene Tomato Might Have Tasted Just as Good Without Genetic Alteration," *The Wall Street Journal*, January 12, 1993, p. B1; Anonymous, "European Ruling Backs Banning of Biotech Crops," *The Wall Street Journal— Eastern Edition*, September 10, 2003, p. A22; Rick Charnes, "Genetically Altered Food: Myths and Realities," *EarthSave International*, Retrieved on September 16, 2003 (Available http://www. earthsave.org/ge.htm).

5. Meg Major, "Produce Perspectives 2000," *Supermarket Business*, October 15, 2000, pp. 89–94.

See also: Food Spectrum, "Retail Prepared Refrigerated Foods: The Market and Technologies Mini Study on Value-added Produce," Retrieved on September 16, 2003 (Available http://www .foodspectrum.com/value_added_produce.htm); Patt Patterson, "Fresh-Cut vs. Raw Produce: Where's the Value?" *Nation's Restaurant News*, September 13, 1993, p. 95; Elizabeth Schneider, "Veggies in Volume: Beating the Buffet and Banquet Blahs," *Food Arts*, November 1991, p. 76.

6. Betsy Block, "What You Need to Know About Organic Food," *Boston Globe*, March 29, 2000, p. E.1. See also: Charles Thienpont, "More Growers Plant Organic Crops—See Prices 50% Below Last Year," *FoodService Director*, April 15, 1990, p. 58; Diane Welland, "Chefs Consider Organic Produce," *Restaurants USA*, September 1991, p. 26; David Belman, "The Time Is Ripe for Organics," *Restaurants USA*, August 1995, p. 18.

7. Betsy Spethmann, "Planting the Seed," *Promo*, August 2002, 15(9), pp. 26–28. See also: Stephanie Salkin, "USDA Unveils Final Organics

Rules," *ID: The Information Source for Managers & DSRS*, February 2001, 37(2), p. 20.

8. Ken Macqueen, "Kitchen Garden," *Maclean's*, July 1, 2003, 116(26/27), p. 77. See also: Amy Zuber, "On the Menu: Foodlife, Chicago," *Nation's Restaurant News*, September 4, 2000, p. 38; Kathy Blake, "New Herb Garden Spices Up Offerings at NYC's Lenox Hill Hospital," *Nation's Restaurant News,* August 10, 1998, 32(32), p. 78; Jennifer Batty, "Restaurants with Farms Start a Blooming Revolution," *Restaurants USA*, August 1992, p. 30.

QUESTIONS AND PROBLEMS

1. Name the U.S. grades for fresh produce.

2. What is the most frequently ordered grade of fresh produce in the hospitality industry?

3. A product specification for fresh lemons could include the following information:
   (a)
   (b)
   (c)
   (d)
   (e)

4. Why does the foodservice operator normally not care for fresh produce that has been in controlled atmosphere storage?

5. Why should buyers note on their specifications for fresh produce the minimum weight per case?

6. Why is the point of origin for fresh produce very important?

7. What is an appropriate intended use for green tomatoes?

8. When would a buyer use a packer's brand in lieu of a U.S. grade when preparing a product specification for fresh tomatoes?

9. When would a buyer purchase fresh produce from a farmers' market?

10. Why might it be difficult to engage in bid buying when purchasing fresh produce? When would a buyer bid buy? Why? If possible, ask a school foodservice director to comment on your answer.

11. Outline the specific procedures a buyer would use to purchase, receive, store, and issue salad greens—lettuce, red cabbage, and carrots—and baking potatoes. Assume that these products will be used in a steak house. If possible, ask a steak house manager to comment on your answer.

12. Prepare product specifications for the products noted in Question 11.

13. Assume that you manage a cafeteria and have run out of salad greens at 7:30 P.M. on a Saturday night. What do you do? If possible, ask a cafeteria manager to comment on your answer.

14. Supplier A offers lettuce at $16.75 per case, and Supplier B offers it at $18.50 per case. The yield for Supplier A is 88 percent; for Supplier B, 94 percent. Supplier A expects a COD payment; Supplier B gives seven days' credit terms. Which supplier should a buyer purchase from? Why?

15. Why is it important to note the exact variety of fresh produce desired, instead of merely noting the type of item needed?

16. What is an appropriate intended use for U.S. No. 2 grade tomatoes?

17. What does the notation "3 to 1" indicate to a buyer?

18. Precut fresh produce usually carries an AP price that is much higher than that of raw fresh produce. Identify some of the reasons for this difference.

19. What are some of the methods fresh-produce suppliers can use to extend the shelf life of fruits and vegetables?

20. When would a buyer specify organically grown fresh produce on a product specification for fresh produce?

21. What is a "decay allowance"?

22. What critical information is missing from the following product specification for onions?
    Onions
    Used to make onion rings
    U.S. No. 1 Grade (or equivalent)
    Packed in 50-pound mesh bags

23. What is the advantage of purchasing genetically altered fresh tomatoes?

24. What is an appropriate intended use for "field run" fresh produce?

25. For which types of products is "pulp temperature" an important selection factor?

18

PROCESSED PRODUCE AND OTHER GROCERY ITEMS

The Purpose of this Chapter

After reading this chapter, you should be able to:

- Identify management considerations surrounding the selection and procurement of processed produce and other grocery items.

- Identify the selection factors for processed produce and other grocery items, including government grades.

- Describe the process of purchasing, receiving, storing, and issuing processed produce and other grocery items.

INTRODUCTION

The purchasing procedures for convenience items, such as processed fruit and vegetables, and for other grocery items, such as spices, pastas, fats, and oils, are more routine than those required for fresh products. In general, the qualities are more predictable, and the as-purchased (AP) prices do not fluctuate so widely as those for fresh products.

To prevent the mistaken idea that this area of purchasing does not present difficulties, we must stress that purchasing processed items requires several management considerations. As is almost always the case, these considerations center on the determination of what a hospitality operation wants, what type of product is best suited for its needs, and which supplier can accommodate these needs.

MANAGEMENT CONSIDERATIONS

It is probably impractical to imagine any storeroom without a few cans of tomatoes on its shelves. Thus, the decision here is not an either/or proposition. It is more a question of which products should be fresh and which should be processed. In addition, some methods used to cook certain fruits and vegetables do not produce food that tastes substantially different from its processed counterpart. For example, a tomato sauce made with canned tomatoes may taste about the same as one made with fresh tomatoes. Finally, you can combine some fresh products with processed ones. For instance, a tomato and green bean casserole can be made with fresh tomatoes and canned or frozen beans, or with fresh beans and canned tomatoes.

Food processors process produce for many reasons in addition to preserving them. Food processors seek to smooth out seasonal fluctuations and to capture items at their peak of flavor while simultaneously adding value to the items. In doing so, food processors transfer some work from the foodservice kitchen to the food-processing plant. Thus, processing fruits and vegetables can be viewed as the procedure of extending the availability of perishable items.

One of the ironies about processed produce is that most items are processed to increase shelf life. When these items are lost due to mishandling in the foodservice operation, one of the main reasons why they were processed in the first place is defeated. Many processed products, once thawed, opened, or heated, have extremely short in-process shelf lives. In addition, reheating or reusing many of these items usually results in inferior finished products. Processed produce shares this problem with most convenience products.

Consequently, a major management decision involving processed produce items is whether to use them at all. (Hospitality operations usually have little choice for other grocery items, although some properties make their own pasta, render their own fat, and blend their own condiments.) Taking into consideration the current interest in "natural, whole foods," operators cannot take this decision lightly. Some make a point of reminding their patrons that all vegetables on their menus are cooked from the fresh state. Whether this approach has marketing value may be a matter of opinion.

Once hospitality operators realize that at least some processed produce and other grocery items will be used in preparing menu items, they face the question of which processing method to choose. For some products, they have little choice. For example, if buyers must purchase plain pasta, they must keep in mind that it is a dried product, though some fresh refrigerated and some precooked frozen pas tas are available. They must also consider additional processing techniques, like pickling and other fermentation methods. Buyers almost exclusively purchase foods processed in these ways for the taste the processing imparts and not necessarily for convenience, AP price considerations, or other reasons. Also, some other preservation methods, such as adding chemical preservatives and refrigerating some soup bases, have become standard. Unless buyers specify otherwise, they will receive the product this way. The buyers' selection of a processing method, then, is affected by: (1) food quality, (2) AP price, and (3) the need for convenience. Although the standards of quality vary within each processing method, by and large, the processing method itself predetermines the taste, AP prices, and convenience.

If buyers opt for canned goods or shelf-stable products packed in aseptic packaging, they will receive the benefits of standardized packaging, longer shelf life, and less expensive storage costs. But the buyers also get a distinctive "canned" taste. For some items, such as tomato sauce, cans or aseptic packages may be the only choices. For others, such as white asparagus spears, buyers may have to settle for a can or a bottle.

When buyers choose frozen processing, they have the benefit of fresher flavor, or at least a taste as close as possible to natural flavor. Moreover, purveyors claim that only products picked at their peak of flavor are frozen. Some processed items usually are sold only in the frozen state. For example, corn on the cob and french fries are normally available only fresh or fresh-frozen.

Unfortunately, frozen-fruit and frozen-vegetable packaging is not quite as standardized as the cans used for produce packed that way. Buyers also take greater risks with frozen items: the chances of thawing and refreezing, of a freezer breakdown, and of freezer burn. The shelf life of many frozen items is not as long as that of canned and bottled items. The AP prices tend to be higher, and a higher storage cost is associated with frozen products.

One of the biggest difficulties with any frozen product is the possibility of thawing a larger amount than is needed. The excess cannot be refrozen without a considerable loss of quality. Usually, the item is then wasted entirely. But frozen products are just too costly to throw out; consequently, a hospitality operator may try to work them into the menu somehow at the risk of alienating customers.

When choosing dried products, buyers are obviously going to save on storage. In addition, if buyers care for the items properly, they will have a long shelf life. Also, since the food is lightweight and does not require refrigeration, its transportation costs remain low, which, in turn, reduces AP prices. On the other hand, the AP prices of many dried items may still be high because of the amount of time and energy used to process them. Unfortunately, buyers cannot purchase very many food items in a dried state. However, some processed items, including instant mashed potatoes, dried onion flakes, and dried spices, are usually sold only in a dried state.

Many dehydrated foods are expensive. For example, dried fruit requires very ripe fruit with a high concentration of natural sugar. These qualities are costly; however, they make such fruit particularly desirable. For example, dried pineapple rings used in making upside-down cakes probably have an AP price that exceeds that of the canned counterpart, but the taste is different—dried pineapple is extremely sweet and strong.

A major difficulty with some dried items is the need to reconstitute them. A mistake here, even a tiny one, can ruin the product. Another difficulty is the style of packaging. For instance, macaroni products come in all sorts of packaging materials and package sizes. Dried fruit is sometimes nicely layered on waxed paper and lined up neatly in a box. But it may also be slab-packed, or tossed in randomly and pushed together so that by the time buyers get it, some of it may be damaged.

In addition to deciding which processing method best suits the needs of the operation, management must make another major decision regarding processed products, which centers on the question of substitution. For example, a recipe for mixed vegetables could include some fresh product, to use leftovers; some frozen product, bought at bargain prices; and some dried product, to take advantage of the excess sweetness. But consider the problem of inertia: since these purchases do not usually represent a large percentage of the purchase dollar, few operators devote much effort to determining the least expensive recipe unless they have access to a computerized management information system (MIS). Although this area may not seem to offer a great deal of money-saving potential, some money can, nevertheless, be saved.

When buyers purchase processed food, they usually obtain what they want. They name it, and somebody will make it if the purchase volume is large enough. For instance, fats and oils can be manufactured almost according to individual specifications, but operators must pay for this service. Nevertheless, when buyers purchase these products, it is good to know that they can get what they need.

Some other management considerations involving processed food that occur intermittently are outlined below.

1.   Some buyers tend to neglect generally accepted purchasing principles when it comes to some processed produce and grocery items. This is probably because only a small amount of the total purchase dollar is involved, as the majority goes toward meat, fish, poultry, alcoholic beverages, and some desserts.

For example, the temptation is strong for buyers to set the par stock for condiments and let it go at that. Manufacturers and suppliers who rely heavily on "pull strategies" for some of these items further foster this tendency. Some products, such as Heinz® ketchup and A-1® steak sauce, that grace a dining room table seem almost traditional. To a lesser extent, other condiments, such as olives, pickles, and relishes, fall into this category.

2. The neglect mentioned earlier might also be nurtured by the cavalier attitude with which some employees approach inventory. For instance, some managers allow service personnel to bypass the normal issuing system when they need steak sauce, hot sauce, or similar condiments. In many small operations, service staff walk into the storeroom and take what they need. If a bottle or two spills or disappears, few supervisors get upset.

3. Numerous "impulse" purchases flood the market. For example, buyers can purchase devices to: drain near-empty catsup bottles, check the pressure in canned goods, and determine whether a product has been thawed and refrozen. These may be used once or twice and then tossed into the back of a drawer.

4. For one reason or another, several new products are introduced each year in grocery product lines. Of course, many food products are not really new, just new variations of existing foodstuffs. For example, buyers can find all sorts of new vegetable combinations and sauce variations. The same is true for rice and pasta concoctions. Taking the time to examine all these "new" ideas can finally force buyers to neglect other more important business.

5. Sometimes buying one processed item entails buying something else. For instance, if buyers purchase semolina flour to make their own pasta, they must also buy the pasta machine. Similarly, if they buy corn flour to make their own tortillas and taco shells, they may need a special basket to hold the shells in the fryer.

6. Processed foods present several "opportunity buys," such as introductory offers, quantity discounts, volume discounts, salvage buys,* and other hospitality operations' going-out-of-business sales. For operators who control a lot of purchase money, long-term contracts may also be available. These opportunities usually require a bit of extra analysis. Buyers must decide whether

---

*Recall that these purchases may be outlawed by local health authorities. At any rate, these are questionable opportunities because buyers cannot be sure that the products have not been exposed to prolonged heat, chemicals, or other contamination.

they are going to buy these items on a day-to-day basis or to succumb to a salesperson who comes in with a flamboyant special offer.

7.   Buyers must decide which container size they should buy. Smaller packages have higher AP prices per unit, but they sometimes provide the best edible-portion (EP) cost. A related concern exists: Should buyers purchase individual, filled catsup bottles, or should they keep the empty bottles and refill them with catsup from a No. 10 can or some other bulk pack? The latter choice may entail some waste and labor, but it may also produce the best EP cost.

8.   A final major consideration relates to Point 6. Should buyers accept an offer that looks appealing but that would involve changing the form of the product they usually purchase? For instance, they may be offered a bargain in canned green beans, but they normally use the frozen form. Buyers should not take this temptation lightly. If profits are running a little low for the business, or if a particular buyer is just naturally conservative with money, it's surprising how big a few pennies can look. (This problem also arises with introductory offers or other types of "push strategies." Suppliers often try to switch a buyer from one item to another by temporarily manipulating the AP price.)

SELECTION FACTORS

Management, either alone or in conjunction with others, decides the quality, type, and style of food wanted for each processed item. During this decision-making process, the owner-manager should evaluate the selection factors in the following sections.

Intended Use

As always, owner-managers want to determine exactly the intended use of the item so that they will be able to prepare the appropriate, relevant specification. For example, canned fruit used in a recipe that has several other ingredients need not be as attractive as that used alone in a pie filling.

Exact Name

Confusing terminology clutters the market, especially the processed-produce market. For instance, buyers cannot simply order pickles; they must order Polish pickles, kosher pickles, sweet pickles, and so on. Similarly, they must specify canned Bartlett pear halves if that is what they desire, or extra virgin olive oil if they want olive oil with the lowest possible acidity.

The list of these designations can grow incredibly long, and more esoteric terms seem to exist in the area of processed produce and other grocery items than in most other areas. Nonetheless, buyers must become familiar with the market terminology.

The federal government has provided some assistance to buyers who are responsible for ordering many processed foods. Recall from Chapter 4 that it has issued several "standards of identity" that essentially establish what a food product is (e.g., what a food product must be in order to be labeled "strawberry preserves"). Some standards set specific processing requirements, such as heating at very high temperatures in hermetically sealed containers. This is necessary to ensure the wholesomeness and safety of the finished product. Other standards are related to composition. For instance, any food that purports to be organic or to contain organically produced food ingredients—that is, the product label or labeling bears the term "organic" or makes any direct or indirect representation that the food is organic—must meet a particular set of standards. For example, canned organic vegetables must contain at least 90 percent organic ingredients, which are ingredients that are grown without added hormones, pesticides, herbicides, or synthetic fertilizers. If a can of soup, for instance, simply states "made with organic vegetables," then the percentage of organically produced ingredients in the soup must be stated on the label as "Contains _____ percent organic ingredients" (with the blank filled in with the actual total percentage of organically produced ingredients in the soup).

These types of standards, however, do not keep different companies from making distinctive recipes. For example, the United States Department of Agriculture (USDA) content requirement for beef stew specifies only the minimum percentage of beef (25 percent) that the stew must contain. The USDA requirement does not prevent a manufacturer from using its own combinations of other ingredients or increasing the amount of beef to make the product unique. As such, all brands of stew probably will taste somewhat different, which makes it risky for buyers to rely only on standards of identity when selecting processed produce and other grocery items, as well as some meat, dairy, fish, and poultry items.

Standards of identity are available for approximately 235 items if you care to use them. The USDA has established standards for meat and poultry products (see: www.ams.usda.gov), and the Food and Drug Administration (FDA) has set them for cocoa products; cereal, flour, and related products; macaroni and noodle products; bakery products; milk and cream products; cheese and cheese products; frozen desserts; sweeteners and table syrups; food flavorings; dressings for food; canned fruits and fruit juices; fruit butters, jellies, preserves, and related products; soda water; canned and frozen fish and shellfish; eggs and egg products; oleomargarine; nut products; canned and frozen vegetables; and tomato products.

For some items, buyers may be able to make do with only a standard of identity. For instance, although all types and brands of frozen orange juice are not the same, most of them are close. This is true of other frozen juices, too. Thus, buyers might be governed primarily by the AP price for these products.

U.S. Government Inspection and Grades (or Equivalent)

The USDA's Agricultural Marketing Service (AMS) Fruit and Vegetables Division and the FDA conduct mandatory inspections of processors' facilities. If any meat is incorporated in a product or if any items require egg breaking, the inspection falls under the jurisdiction of the USDA's Food Safety and Inspection Service (FSIS). Recall that continuous federal inspection or equivalent state inspection exists for any type of meat product that is sold. If no meat is involved, the foodstuffs are, nonetheless, inspected for wholesomeness, though less frequently. Of course, some state and local inspection may also be involved.

Government inspection is mandatory, but U.S. grading service is voluntary and food processors must pay for it. However, they have the option to pay for continuous inspection with or without a grade. Many buyers include federal-government grades in their specifications to ensure that the products are produced and packed under continuous government inspection. Understandably, bid buyers also seek out the relevant grading standards for their specifications.

Buyers can also specify that the products desired must carry the federal-government inspection shield. This shield indicates that the product was "packed under continuous inspection of the U.S. Dept. of Agriculture." The USDA provides this fee-based service to those primary sources who want inspection only and who do not want to purchase the federal-government grading service.

Federal grades have been established for canned, bottled, frozen, and dried produce and grocery items (see Figure 18.1).[1] Specific grading factors exist for different items. For instance, the grading factors for canned and bottled foods include the color, the uniformity of size and shape, the number of defects and blemishes, and the "character," which refers to the texture, tenderness, and aroma. Also, the quality of the packing medium—the water, brine, or syrup—may be important for

FIGURE 18.1 Federal grade and inspection stamps used for processed produce and other grocery items. *Source:* United States Department of Agriculture.

some products. For some items, such as canned, whole tomatoes, during the evaluation process the grader considers the "drained weight," which is the servable weight that remains after the juice is removed.

Grading factors for frozen foods include the uniformity of size and shape, maturity, quality, color, and number of defects and blemishes.

Grading factors for dried foods include uniformity of size and shape, color, number blemishes and defects, moisture content,* and the way the products are packed—are they carefully layered or packed tightly together in a container, thus distorting their natural shape?

As with fresh produce, no single categorization of grading nomenclature exists for processed foods. As a matter of convenience, buyers could rely on the following grading categories for canned, bottled, and frozen items:

1. Grade A. The very best product with excellent color, uniform size, weight, and shape, and few blemishes.

2. Grade B. Slightly less perfect than Grade A.

3. Grade C. May contain some broken and uneven pieces, perhaps some odd-shaped pieces; the flavor usually falls below Grades A and B, and the color is not so attractive.

---

*No federal standard exists for moisture content. The usual dried item has at least 75 percent of its moisture removed, but this is not enough to make the product last for an extended period. The term "sun-dried" implies high moisture residual, about 25 percent, whereas foods dehydrated in other ways usually contain 5 percent moisture.

Again, for convenience, you could rely on the same nomenclature for dried foods:

1.   Grade A. The most attractive and most flavorful product.
2.   Grade B. Not quite so attractive as Grade A.
3.   Grade C. More variations in taste and appearance, and usually broken pieces.

Although this convenient grading system for canned, bottled, frozen, and dried products might be ideal, it is not reality. Not all these types of foods use the grading system A, B, and C. For example, canned mushrooms, frozen apples, and several dried foods carry Grades A, B, and Substandard. Frozen apricots carry the Grades A, B, C, and Substandard. Sometimes you hear the terms "Fancy," "Choice," or "Extrastandard." These are alternate terms for U.S. grades that several people in the channel of distribution use. For example, many buyers use the following U.S. grade designations when purchasing canned fruit and canned vegetables:

CANNED FRUIT	CANNED VEGETABLES
Fancy	Fancy
Choice	Extrastandard
Standard	Standard

Another confusion in this area is that some processed items carry two grade designations, some carry three, and many carry four.

Still another difficulty: some products may display "Grade A," and not "U.S. Grade A" on the label. This is an indication that a federal inspector has not graded the products. Food processors are allowed to use "Grade" on their labels, as long as a nongovernmental graded item does not carry the "U.S." prefix. As a general rule, an item could carry types of grading nomenclature similar to those the federal government uses, even if the appropriate government agency did not grade the product. Since some discrepancy exists between these terms, to avoid any potential confusion, buyers should carefully note whether "U.S. Grade A" or "Grade A" is listed on the package label. (As we noted in Chapter 17, buyers usually can communicate with a purveyor and make their desires known.)

Packers' Brands (or Equivalent)

We noted in Chapter 12 that a bit of "pull strategy" is inherent in certain product lines. As such, buyers can sometimes be "coerced" into purchasing Heinz ketchup, A-1 steak sauce, Del Monte® relish, and so on.

In addition, many processed items come and go. So, if buyers want a particularly esoteric combination of fruit, they might find only one producer who handles it.

Also, since packaging can be unstandardized, buyers may seek out brands that meet their particular packaging requirements. (Recall that a brand normally implies more than just product quality.)

For some items, particularly something like frozen peas in cream sauce, a packer's brand may be the most important indication of quality and flavor. The quality of a fruit or vegetable varies from year to year and from place to place. The top-of-the-line brands make an effort to smooth out these annual fluctuations.

Packers' brands may be desirable, therefore, if only because subtle differences occur between, for example, tomato packers. After all, canned tomatoes can vary tremendously, not only in appearance, but in taste as well. Consequently, some buyers may be wary about trading Heinz for Del Monte simply because they detect a slightly different flavor.

A tremendous variety of brands is available to buyers. For instance, some companies package only the best-quality merchandise and will pack lower-quality products only if these items carry some other brand name. These firms refer to themselves as "premium" brands. Recall from Chapter 8 that some companies prepare several qualities under the same brand-name heading; that is, they carry several "packers' grades" (i.e., packers' brands) in their sales kits. For instance, buyers can sometimes purchase a specific producer's brand of carrots, but they will notice that different-colored labels exist for each quality of carrots that specific producer packs. These different-colored labels represent the packer's "grades" produced by the company.

Buyers can also opt for generic brands. These brands are not as plentiful in the wholesale-distribution channels as they are in retail grocery stores and supermarkets, probably because if buyers desire this type of quality, a packer's brand already exists to satisfy their needs. If they insist on purchasing generic brands, they probably will need to shop at the numerous warehouse wholesale clubs that cater to small businesses.

Generic brands can be very economical. Generally speaking, they typically are offered at very low AP prices for at least three reasons: (1) lower, or nonexistent, selling and advertising costs; (2) lower packaging costs; and (3) in some cases, lower quality. Keep in mind that lower quality does not necessarily imply lower nutritional value. Also, buyers are apt to receive a more uniform quality when ordering single-ingredient, generic-brand food. For instance, canned sliced peaches would tend to have better and more consistent quality than, say, mayonnaise, which includes several ingredients and involves relatively complicated processing.

Product Size

A very important consideration is the question of size, or count. For example, when buyers order pitted green olives in a No. 10 can, they should also indicate the olive size they want. They can do this by stating a specific count, which, in turn, implies a number, or count, of olives in a particular can. The higher the count, the higher the number of olives in the can and the smaller the olives. Sometimes, too, buyers can specify the approximate number of product pieces they would like in a can. They will, however, usually be limited in the count that they can have. Only a few choices are available (see Figure 18.2).

In lieu of specifying the count, buyers could use other marketing terms that essentially serve the same purpose. For instance, while it is true that buyers can indicate olive sizes by stating the count desired, they can also use such terms as "large," "extra large," "jumbo," or another appropriate marketing term to convey the necessary size information to their suppliers.

Buyers also may want to know how many cups they can get from a can or a frozen pack. Although these volume measurements appear on consumer products' package labels, buyers must be careful with volumes listed on commercial labels; they are sometimes misleading. For instance, on an instant mashed potato can label, there could be a reconstituted, or ready-to-serve, volume of 3 gallons stated—a volume that may be attainable only if you whip the potatoes long enough to incorporate a great deal of air.

Size of Container

Buyers must indicate on the specification the exact size of the container that they wish to buy (see Figure 18.3). To do this, they should determine whether the size of each package meets their needs. It costs more per ounce to buy dried oregano in a little bottle than in a much larger container. But if hospitality operations do not use much dried oregano, some product in the big container will go to waste. So the EP cost becomes the buyers' main consideration when they evaluate appropriate container sizes.

Type of Packaging Material

For frozen and dried products, especially frozen, the packaging materials are not nearly so standardized as those for cans and bottles. If buyers purchase large

FIGURE 18.2 Typical product sizes for peach and pear halves. Courtesy of Canned Fruit Promotion Service.

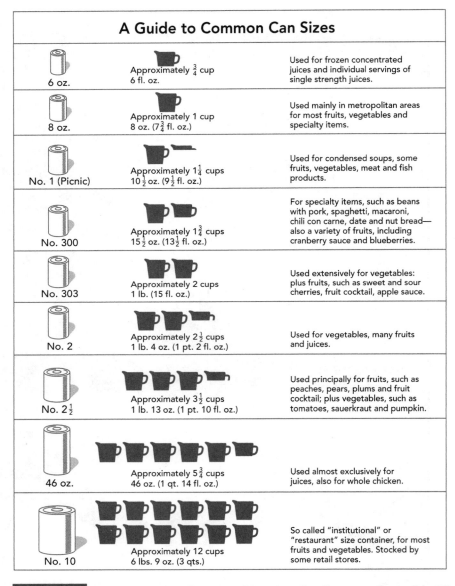

A Guide to Common Can Sizes

6 oz.	Approximately $\frac{3}{4}$ cup 6 fl. oz.	Used for frozen concentrated juices and individual servings of single strength juices.
8 oz.	Approximately 1 cup 8 oz. ($7\frac{3}{4}$ fl. oz.)	Used mainly in metropolitan areas for most fruits, vegetables and specialty items.
No. 1 (Picnic)	Approximately $1\frac{1}{4}$ cups $10\frac{1}{2}$ oz. ($9\frac{1}{2}$ fl. oz.)	Used for condensed soups, some fruits, vegetables, meat and fish products.
No. 300	Approximately $1\frac{3}{4}$ cups $15\frac{1}{2}$ oz. ($13\frac{1}{2}$ fl. oz.)	For specialty items, such as beans with pork, spaghetti, macaroni, chili con carne, date and nut bread— also a variety of fruits, including cranberry sauce and blueberries.
No. 303	Approximately 2 cups 1 lb. (15 fl. oz.)	Used extensively for vegetables: plus fruits, such as sweet and sour cherries, fruit cocktail, apple sauce.
No. 2	Approximately $2\frac{1}{2}$ cups 1 lb. 4 oz. (1 pt. 2 fl. oz.)	Used for vegetables, many fruits and juices.
No. $2\frac{1}{2}$	Approximately $3\frac{1}{2}$ cups 1 lb. 13 oz. (1 pt. 10 fl. oz.)	Used principally for fruits, such as peaches, pears, plums and fruit cocktail; plus vegetables, such as tomatoes, sauerkraut and pumpkin.
46 oz.	Approximately $5\frac{3}{4}$ cups 46 oz. (1 qt. 14 fl. oz.)	Used almost exclusively for juices, also for whole chicken.
No. 10	Approximately 12 cups 6 lbs. 9 oz. (3 qts.)	So called "institutional" or "restaurant" size container, for most fruits and vegetables. Stocked by some retail stores.

FIGURE 18.3 Average can sizes. Courtesy of American Can Company, Greenwich, CT.

amounts of these products, such as an annual supply, they should examine the packaging very carefully. Will it hold up for a few weeks or a few months in the freezer? Also, especially for dried products, can moisture seep into the containers?

Another packaging consideration that emerges occasionally is ease of opening. Also, can the package be reclosed tightly enough to save the rest of the contents for later? Sometimes an item comes in an inconvenient package, which can lead to waste. In this case, the EP cost goes up. A more convenient package generally costs more. But as long as the EP cost is acceptable, it may be worth it.

We should address the need to use environmentally safe packaging whenever possible. When buyers purchase cans or bottles, these items may not be as convenient as, say, plastic pouches or aseptic containers. However, buyers can recycle them. This helps protect the environment and, in some parts of the United States, buyers may even be able to earn a small amount of income from recycling plants that purchase these materials.

Another packaging consideration is the issue of "personalized" packaging (see Figure 18.4). For some processed items, such as sugar packets, buyers can order packaging that contains the hospitality operation's logo or another form of advertisement. Sometimes these options will increase the AP price of the underlying food item; however, the advertising value may more than offset the added expense.

Packaging Procedure

This is an important consideration for some processed produce and other grocery items. As a general rule, packing usually has two styles: slab-packed merchandise and layered merchandise. Most processed produce and other grocery items are necessarily slab-packed—that is, they are poured into the container and the container is then sealed. Some products, though, such as dried fruit, can be slab-packed or neatly layered between sheets of paper or cardboard. Furthermore, some layered merchandise, such as frozen, double-baked, stuffed potatoes, might be individually wrapped.

As usual, the layered and/or individually wrapped products cost more, at least in terms of higher AP prices. However, because better packaging and a more care-

FIGURE 18.4 An example of a personalized package. Courtesy of Lady Luck.

ful packing style minimize product breakage and other forms of product loss, the resulting EP costs may be quite acceptable.

Drained Weight (Servable Weight)

Considering weights instead of volumes is usually a good idea. The weight of the contents of a can can vary. It is good practice for buyers to calculate "drained weight" (servable weight) when purchasing canned items; this is the weight of the product less its juice. To compute this figure, buyers drain a product in a specific sieve for a certain amount of time. Some packers' brands offer a great deal of fruit and little juice. Other brands could have more juice and less fruit. Buyers must be concerned with portions per can and drained weights—and with EP costs, to be sure.

Recall that food processors need to note on consumer package labels the serving size and number of servings in the package. Processors may eventually be required to list the weight of the fruit and, separately, the weight of the juice, water, or syrup. To a certain extent, buyers can estimate the amount of juice by the absence or presence of the words "heavy pack" or "solid pack." If these words do not appear, buyers should expect a lot of liquid—for example, about $5^{1}/_{2}$ ounces of liquid in a typical 16-ounce can of fruit. The term "solid pack" means no juice added; "heavy pack" means some juice added, but not much.

Best of all, however, buyers should measure the drained weight. It is more reliable than estimating weight by looking at a can's label.

When buyers compare the weights of two or more packers' brands of frozen products, they should thaw frozen fruit and cook frozen vegetables from the frozen state before weighing them. Buyers should also do the same with dried products: weigh them only after reconstituting them.

Buyers should be wary of purchasing anything after considering only the volume. Remember from Chapter 4 the standard of fill, which protects buyers from a packer who fills a can only halfway and pretends to give a lot for the money. Remember, too, the possibility that an unscrupulous supplier may pump air into a product or lower the specific gravity of a product (by decreasing the product's density, he or she makes it lighter). Some possible examples here include ready-to-serve potato puffs. (Should buyers purchase them by count or by weight?) Similarly, tomato puree can vary in density; it can weigh about as much as an equal amount of water, which has a specific gravity of 1.00. Alternately, the puree can have a specific gravity of 1.06 or even a little more, and, thus, a greater weight.

Type of Processing

Buyers must indicate the type of processing desired. The type of processing implies certain flavor and texture characteristics, as well as specific product-preservation techniques. Generally, buyers will purchase canned, bottled, frozen, and/or dried merchandise.

Color

In some cases, buyers will need to specify a preferred color. Suppose, for instance, canned red apple rings are available but no green ones are. The same choices are available for bottled maraschino cherries. Generally, when buyers specify the exact name of the item wanted, they indicate the color required. If the exact name of a product does not include this notation, buyers must be sure to point it out elsewhere on the specification if it is relevant.

Product Form

At times, buyers will need to indicate the specialized form of the merchandise they want. Usually this is not necessary if they are purchasing common, ordinary processed produce and grocery items. But if buyers are purchasing, say, a particular vegetable casserole, they may want to note the amounts and types of vegetables desired. Alternately, buyers may find it necessary to point out that they want a minimum number of almonds in the frozen green beans almondine they want to procure for their establishment.

Packing Medium

For some products, several packing mediums are available. For example, for canned fruit, buyers can select fruit packed in water, in syrup, or with no added medium. They also can specify the syrup density desired by noting the minimum "Brix" level. Thick syrup has a higher Brix (i.e., more sugar) than light syrup. The federal government sets minimum Brix levels for some products, yet buyers may want higher levels. For instance, a higher Brix carries a higher AP price, but since fruits packed in heavy syrup do not break easily, the resulting EP cost may be quite satisfactory.

When purchasing vegetable products, buyers may be able to specify the type and amount of sauce desired. For instance, frozen broccoli could be packed with butter sauce, cheese sauce, or some other specialized sauce.

The Use of Additives and Preservatives

The concern some hospitality operators show regarding the issue of preservatives in canned, bottled, frozen, and dried items appears to be less than they exhibit regarding dairy and meat products. Operators could not get the products they need if they had to settle for "fresh" produce all the time. Moreover, they could not store fresh produce efficiently and would probably waste a great deal of it. But some processors are more discreet with their use of additives and preservatives than others.

If the thought of additives and preservatives bothers buyers, they may have difficulty weeding out the offending packers' brands. Furthermore, they will find "organic," "whole," and "natural" foods to be expensive. Why? Buyers have entered a market with few suppliers. Furthermore, shelf life is reduced, resulting in greater handling costs and subsequently greater spoilage loss.

Other Information That May Appear on a Package Label

The federal government requires a great deal of information to be displayed on consumer product labels. However, required label information aside, typical hospitality operators would be much more interested in other kinds of information that may or may not appear on a package label. Many operators would like to see packing dates, freshness dates (or shelf lives), and serving cost data noted on package labels. Many also would like to see the lot number on a package label. (Since the quality of product shifts, it would be nice to be able to reorder, for instance, corn of not only the same packer's brand but also from the same batch as the previously ordered corn.) School foodservice buyers seek out products that carry Child Nutrition (CN) labels, which indicate how the products conform to the nutritional requirements of the USDA. When food processors put these details on their package labels, buyers must expect to pay a bit for this added information value.

One-Stop-Shopping Opportunities

Small operations tend to prefer one-stop shopping for many items, including processed products. To capitalize in this area, some national corporations carry extensive lines of processed produce and other grocery items and compete directly with local and regional distributors. For instance, General Mills (www.generalmills.com/corporate/), Green Giant (www.greengiant.com/), Pillsbury (www.pillsbury.com), and McCormick (www.mccormick.com/index.cfm) produce, market, and distribute wide varieties of processed products. These companies normally offer only one level of product quality, and they usually control all aspects of production and distribution. As a result, their products are often referred to as "controlled brands."

Some national corporations carry extensive lines as well as extensive qualities of processed produce and other grocery items. For instance, U.S. Foodservice (www.usfoodservice.com)—a broadline distributor—distributes many types of products, as well as many different "packer's grades" (i.e., packer's brands) in most product lines.[2] U.S. Foodservice uses the name "Cross Valley Farms®" on their signature brand line of fruits and vegetables.

As the typical hospitality operation grows, it shows less and less of a tendency to use one-stop shopping for processed produce. Too many opportunity buys and long-term contracts at a good savings are available, but they can usually be exploited only if buyers shop around. Large firms usually have the time to do such shopping around. In addition, as its menu gets larger and incorporates more variety, an operation has less opportunity to satisfy its needs with the one-stop-shopping method.

However, one-stop shopping for processed produce, other grocery items, and meat products provides a subtle advantage. Shortages sometimes occur for these items, and being a good customer may ensure a buyer a continual supply. In fact, some suppliers "allocate" certain product lines; that is, they predetermine how much a buyer can purchase. This amount is referred to as the buyer's "allocation."

AP Price

The EP cost is the only relevant concern for a buyer. The EP cost includes not only the cost of the product, but, indirectly, the cost of the labor it takes to prepare and serve it, the cost of the energy needed to work with it, and other overhead expenses. Making these judgments is difficult. But a buyer must look beyond, for example, the drained weight of canned mushrooms.

Since an interminable number of varieties, styles, and packaging methods exist for processed foods, there are correspondingly different AP prices. It is not easy to tell whether it is advantageous to take a Grade C instead of a Grade B for a savings of, perhaps, 5 cents a can. In most cases, the trade-off here would be a matter of opinion. Since lower grades are perfectly acceptable in some recipes, lower qualities can save money without reducing a recipe's acceptability.

For similar items, a buyer usually pays similar AP prices. But some suppliers may give better quantity discounts and volume discounts than others. Typically, these discounts are quite lucrative. Therefore, bid buying can save money, but only if a buyer is willing to accept a large supply, put the cash up front, and make the buy at new pack times, that is, when packers process that year's products.

Unfortunately, there may not be enough bidders for a buyer's business, especially if the local supplier cannot find enough of a product to satisfy his or her requirements. But even if the buyer finds only one supplier, a large buy can be valuable: a substantial savings may result if he or she can store and protect a large supply. However, this has subtle disadvantages: if a buyer is "locked in" for a year, his or her menu is somewhat set. Also, if AP prices for similar items fall, the buyer cannot easily take advantage of them when his or her storage area is full.

Supplier Services

Normally, canned products require only nominal supplier service. Most of these items are not readily perishable, so buyers are not likely to be concerned with how quickly the supplier moves them. But this cannot be said of frozen items. If buyers doubt the capability of a supplier to maintain frozen products at 0°F or below, they should avoid this person. Frozen food costs more because it maintains a better culinary quality, but this quality rapidly deteriorates when storage temperatures are above zero or if they fluctuate; in addition, these problems reduce shelf life drastically.

Occasionally, buyers may want to obtain a stockless purchasing deal, in which they protect an AP price for six months to a year. This tactic rarely saves as much as traditional forward buying, in which buyers take delivery of a large amount. But now and then it can produce a reasonable saving.

Buyers would also like to receive reasonable "break points." They may not want to buy, for example, 100 cases before they get a price break or quantity discount. Fifty cases may be more acceptable. We have noticed that break points are somewhat standard among suppliers.

Sometimes an AP price shoots up dramatically. Buyers like to be warned about this beforehand, if possible. If buyers use bid buying exclusively, they may not receive that warning. If buyers are house accounts, chances are they will.

Together with fluctuating AP prices, which really are not so common with processed products as they are with fresh foods, comes the potential for shortages. A rainstorm can reduce the canned-peaches supply. Only certain buyers may be on the list of those slated to get some of that supply. Again, bid buyers may be left behind. They always take a chance that nobody will answer their solicitations for bids. House accounts may be better serviced.

Buyers should consider another supplier service: If they want a low grade, can they get it? Low-grade products, generally, are not in plentiful supply. Here again, house accounts find themselves in a better position than bid buyers.

Yet another service is the delivery schedule. Realistically, though, most buyers can live with one delivery every week, or even one every two weeks. If, however, buyers have only a limited storage area, they might want other arrangements.

Local Supplier or National Source?

Buyers can easily go to the primary source for a direct purchase and have the carload of canned tomatoes "drop-shipped" (which means that they will be delivered straight to the back door). Buyers can also buy direct and arrange for a local supplier to distribute the merchandise.

We have already expressed our views on buying directly and bypassing the local supplier. Still, buyers must do what they believe is best given their circumstances.

PURCHASING PROCESSED PRODUCE AND OTHER GROCERY ITEMS

A buyer's first step in purchasing processed produce and other grocery items is to obtain copies of reference materials that contain useful information that they can use to prepare specifications. Most suppliers publish several in-house materials, particularly individual brochures that detail their major product lines. They also have very informative Websites. These references usually include considerable product information, as well as detailed descriptions of grading factors used by U.S. government graders.

The buyer's next step is to determine precisely what he or she wants. This may not be an easy task since several management decisions are involved. Some items are traditionally purchased canned or bottled, some frozen, others dried. But the tradition does not hold true for all products.

Once buyers know what they want, they can make the actual purchase simple or difficult. It will be relatively simple if they buy on a day-to-day basis. If they become dissatisfied with a particular packer's brand, they can just switch to another brand. It is, however, a little more adventurous to enter the bid-buying route, especially when buyers seek to lock up a six-month or one-year supply.

If buyers enter into a long-term contract on a bid basis, they will need detailed specifications. They may find it beneficial to prepare these detailed specs even if they do not use bid buying; it is good discipline for buyers to put their ideas on

Pineapple slices Used for salad bar Dole® brand (or equivalent) 66 count No. 10 can Unsweetened clarified pineapple juice	White cake mix Used to prepare cupcakes Pillsbury® Food Service brand 5 pounds Cardboard box
Whole canned onions Used for plate granish U.S. Fancy 350 count No. 10 can Water pack	Confectioners' powdered sugar Used for baking C & H® brand 1-pound cardboard box Packed 24-pound per case

FIGURE 18.5   **An example of processed produce and other grocery items product specifications.**

paper before they actually commit to any type of purchase. (See Figure 18.5 for some example product specifications and Figure 18.6 for a sample product specification outline for processed produce and other grocery items.)

If buyers go the long-term route, which is usually available in this product area even for small operations, they will have a bit of work ahead of them. Before

Intended use:

Exact name:

U.S. grade (or equivalent):

Packer's brand name (or equivalent):

Product size:

Size of container:

Type of packaging material:

Packaging procedure:

Drained weight:

Type of processing:

Color:

Product form:

Packing medium:

FIGURE 18.6   **An example of a product specification outline for processed produce and other grocery items.**

they sign a long-term contract, they should examine the bidders' products very carefully. A mistake in this area can be extremely costly, and unintentional mistakes happen easily. For example, buyers may examine three brands of canned tomatoes. They may perform all sorts of tests—comparing drained weights, looking for tomato skins, noting the clearness of the juice—but they may discover too late that one brand has slightly less acid, which may be unsuitable for some recipes. These tests are called "can-cutting tests." If competing salespersons or suppliers are in attendance, the testing is sometimes referred to as "holding court." Buyers usually complete a checklist for each brand and then compare each brand's scores (see Figures 18.7 and 18.8). If buyers are purchasing for large commissary production, a little oversight like insufficient acid in a recipe can significantly impair the culinary quality of the finished product.

Another problem can occur through purchasing errors. How do buyers return a year's supply of canned tomatoes to a supplier if they make an error? Buyers should consider a related problem: If they buy a year's supply and later notice that the product is not quite as good as what they contracted for, they must protect themselves by retaining a few unopened packages that were available for their cutting test just prior to signing the contract. Buyers then have on hand a standard of quality they can use to prove that they actually contracted for something better.

SAMPLE	1	2	3
Vendor/brand			
Drained weight			
Color			
Size			
Uniformity of size			
Defects			
Clearness of syrup			
Grade			
Flavor			
Case price			
Unit price			
Serving size			
EP cost/serving			

FIGURE 18.7 A checklist for canned sliced peaches.

	CLING PEACHES	BARTLETT PEARS	FRUIT COCKTAIL
Color:			
Grade B:	Reasonably bright, possibly slight discoloration.	Reasonably uniform in color, may show tint of pink, appear translucent.	Fairly clear liquid and distinct color.
Grade C:	Reasonably bright, yellow-orange, possibly greenish-yellow.	May vary noticeably, appearance could be either white or brown.	
Texture/Character:			
Grade B:	Reasonably good texture, no more than 10% of fruit being mushy.	Reasonably tender, may possess moderate graininess.	Texture of fruits may vary, from firm to soft.
Grade C:	Fairly good texture.	Texture may vary noticeably, with soft or frayed edges.	
Defects:			
Grade B:	Reasonably free of pit material, not more than 5% crushed or broken.	Major defects may not exceed 10% of fruit and minor defects by 20%.	Refer to USDA guidelines for acceptable defects for each individual fruit in fruit cocktail.
Grade C:	Fairly free of pit material, less than 20% of fruit may be blemished.	Major defects may not exceed 20% of fruit and minor defects by 30%.	
Uniformity:			
Grade B:	Largest unit may not exceed smallest unit by more than 60%.	Largest unit may not exceed smallest unit by more than 75%.	No more than 20% of fruit may vary substantially in size.
Grade C:	Largest unit may not exceed smallest unit by more than 100%.	Largest unit may not exceed smallest unit by more than 100%.	
Smell:	No offensive odors should be present in fruit or liquid of any grade.		
Taste:	Distinct and fruity.	Similar to mature pears.	Ability to detect flavor of individual fruits.
Sample Size:	#10 can equals 30 halves or 100 slices.	#10 can equals 30 halves or 100 slices.	#10 can
Pack Ratio:	N/A	N/A	Peaches 30%–50% Pears 25%–45% Grapes 6%–20% Pineapple 48 pieces Cherries 24 halves

FIGURE 18.8 Guidelines for examining some canned fruit products. *Source:* United States Department of Agriculture.

Buyers can consider other suggestions for cutting tests: (1) Always check frozen fruit after it has thawed; in particular, check the fruit's texture, which tends to suffer in the freezing process. (2) Be sure to cook frozen vegetables from the frozen state before testing them. (3) Check all canned goods immediately after opening them, especially their odor. Canned products are cooked during the canning process to kill harmful bacteria so that the products will stay wholesome and not deteriorate. Thus, they are ready to eat. (4) Conduct tests of dried and concentrated products, such as soup, on the reconstituted product.

Generally, then, buyers should test products after they have been prepared for customer service. In some instances, buyers may even want to prepare a full recipe with each one of the competing bidder's products and then perform their tests.

Unless buyers are invited to a supplier's headquarters for some type of product introduction or abbreviated cutting test, these tests can take time and effort. But it is normal practice in large organizations to spend a great deal of effort when considering a quantity buy.

Once buyers enter into a long-term contract, salespersons carrying similar products will still undoubtedly approach them. For instance, each competing supplier with its new brand of spaghetti sauce will bring it to a buyer's attention. Alternately, thanks to backdoor selling, a cook may urge the buyer to purchase a new type of soup base.

Actually, buyers will not see too many revolutionary products. But they may see subtle changes, such as different packaging. For instance, they may buy a new packer's brand of soup base if it is similar to the one they currently use simply because it comes in a 30-pound pack instead of the 1-pound packs they usually buy. If buyers purchase the new product, their old supplier may come out with a 22-pound pack, so testing tends to be a continuing process.

A very complicated test arises when buyers want to evaluate, say, canned peas and frozen peas by using each in two versions of the same recipe, and when buyers want to try other combinations of canned, frozen, and dried. For instance, one stew recipe might be made three ways, with frozen onions, canned onions, and fresh onions. Buyers have to decide which meets their criteria the best.

We have not seen very many local small producers in the processed produce area. But suppose somebody in the family has won a state fair blue ribbon for his or her canned pears and now wants to sell them. We do not consider it a good idea to buy these items. Indeed, recall that most states prohibit the use of home-cooked products in foodservice operations because they come from unapproved sources.

Having struggled successfully with all these details, buyers will find the actual buying, at last, relatively easy. The ordering procedures themselves rarely present any burdensome difficulties.

RECEIVING PROCESSED PRODUCE AND OTHER GROCERY ITEMS

Generally accepted procedures for inspecting the quality of delivered processed produce and other grocery items have been established:

1. **Canned and Bottled Products.** Check the containers for any swelling, leaks, rust, dents, or broken seals. These characteristics, especially swelling, indicate contamination problems. Refuse damaged containers, as well as those that are dirty, greasy, or generally unkempt.

2. **Dried Products.** Check the condition of the containers. If the dried foods are visible, look for mold, broken pieces, and odd appearance.

3. **Frozen Products.** Check the condition of the container, looking for any indication of thawing and refreezing; stained packaging indicates this. Check the food temperature. Look for $-10°F$, but $0°F$ is acceptable. If the frozen foods are visible, check for "freezer burn," the excessive, often brownish dryness that occurs if food has not been protected properly in frozen storage.

Occasional problems occur with quantity checks. Most of these processed products come in cases, and when the cases are full, buyers may assume that these cases are full of exactly what they ordered. Repacking is rare, but it can happen. In any event, buyers should open at least some cases when they are receiving these items. This is particularly true when receiving a large quantity.

Carefully check incoming products against the invoice and a copy of the purchase order. Some packers' brands resemble one another. Also, be careful of supplier substitutions, which can occur from time to time, especially for these types of products.

Quality checks are not always easy, mainly because what you can actually see is limited. Rarely will a chef, for example, come to the receiving dock to check the quality of processed products, unless a large quantity is being delivered.

After checking the quality and quantity, check the prices, and complete the appropriate accounting documents.

STORING PROCESSED PRODUCE AND OTHER GROCERY ITEMS

Generally accepted procedures for storing processed products have also been established:

1. **Canned and Bottled Products.** Store these products in a dry area at approximately $50°F$ to $70°F$. Avoid any wide fluctuation in temperature and hu-

midity. Heat can be especially damaging. For instance, it robs spices of their flavor; it hastens the oxidation of frying fats, which means that these fats will not retain flavor or last as long in the french fryer; and it hastens the chemical changes in canned items, which means taste changes. Avoid dampness, too, which causes rust and attracts dust and dirt. In hot climates, consider refrigerating such items as spices and fats. Keep all canned and bottled products tightly covered, opening only what is necessary; otherwise, they will lose some shelf life.

2. **Dried Products.** Be especially careful of dampness as it can hasten the growth of mold, thereby ruining the products. Try to keep these products a little cooler than canned items so that insects are not attracted to them.

3. **Frozen Products.** If at all possible, store these products at −10°F or lower. This temperature will preserve the maximum flavor, especially if the other distribution channel members have maintained this temperature. Be careful not to damage any packages because that will eventually lead to freezer burn. Also, avoid fluctuations in temperature, which reduce shelf life drastically.

Perhaps the most unfortunate aspect of storing processed produce and other grocery items is that so many of them require slightly different storage environments. As a practical matter, we can hardly satisfy each requirement, so we try to reach a happy medium by paying especially close attention to proper stock rotation.

However, it is not always easy to ensure proper rotation because many employees grow complacent in their handling of processed items, thinking they will hold forever. Theoretically, canned, bottled, and dried food will last a long time, but no one would try to keep them very long. Nor will frozen food last forever; freezing merely slows, but does not eliminate, deterioration.

Other storage considerations include: (1) keeping the items off the floor, where they can attract dirt; and (2) when filling flour bins, and other such storage bins, trying not to mix the new flour with old. If possible, use bins that load from the top and unload from the bottom.

ISSUING PROCESSED PRODUCE AND OTHER GROCERY ITEMS

Hospitality operators often find a good deal of neglect for many processed items. Such products as individual containers of catsup, salt, and sugar—usually food that goes to the service personnel stations—are not always controlled closely. The best way to avoid this waste is to ensure that written stock requisitions exist for every item and that no requisitioner asks for more than necessary. Buyers can control a requisitioner by asking him or her to take note of the in-process inventory prior to asking for additional stock.

Buyers need to consider how they would issue half-cans or some similar amount. The fact is, if this problem arises frequently, they might be better off with smaller containers.

Finally, the EP cost is more vulnerable to attack in the area of in-process inventories. Here, as elsewhere, supervision is the key. Without effective and efficient supervision, it is futile to spend time and effort to save money in purchasing.

KEY WORDS AND CONCEPTS

Additives and preservatives

Advantages and disadvantages of the various processing methods

Agricultural Marketing Service (AMS)

Allocation

Aseptic packaging

As-purchased price (AP price)

Break points

Brix

Can-cutting test

Child Nutrition label (CN label)

Color

Common can sizes

Controlled brands

Drained weight

Drop shipment

Edible-portion cost (EP cost)

Environmentally safe packaging

Exact name

Food and Drug Administration (FDA)

Food Safety and Inspection Service (FSIS)

Forward buying

Freezer burn

Freshness dates

Generic brands

Going-out-of-business sales

Grading factors

Heavy pack

Holding court

Impulse purchase

In-process inventories

Institutional can size

Intended use

Layered packaging

Lot number

Management considerations when purchasing processed produce and other grocery items

New pack time

One-stop shopping

Opportunity buys

Organic, whole, natural foods

Packaging material

Packaging procedure

Packed under continuous government inspection

Packers' brands (grades)

Packing dates

Packing medium

Personalized packaging

Premium brands

Product form

Product size

Product-testing factors

Pull strategy

Purchasing, receiving, storing, and issuing processed produce and other grocery items

Push strategy

Quantity discount

Recommended storage procedures

Reference books that can be used when preparing specifications

Salvage buys

Shelf life

Shelf-stable products

Single-ingredient, generic-brand food

Size of container

Slab-packed	Sun-dried versus other drying methods	U.S. grades
Solid pack	Supplier services	U.S. Grade A versus Grade A
Specific gravity	Type of processing	Volume discount
Standard of identity	United States Department of Agriculture (USDA)	Warehouse wholesale club
Stock rotation		

REFERENCES

1. For a detailed dicsussion of processed fruits and vegetables grades, see http://www.ams.usda.gov/fv/ppb.html. Retrieved October 2, 2003.

2. For a list of U.S. Foodservice's signature brands, see http://www.usfoodservice.com/products/signature/signature.html. Retrieved October 2, 2003.

QUESTIONS AND PROBLEMS

1. What are the U.S. grades for canned, bottled, frozen, and dried items?

2. Give an example of optional information a packer could note on a package label.

3. Assume that you own a small coffee shop and that you have no franchise affiliation. Your annual volume (open 24 hours, every day) is $825,000.00. You sell hamburgers, and you are currently using Heinz individual catsup bottles. You can save about 8 percent of your $438.00-a-year catsup expense (i.e., 0.08 × $438.00 = $35.04 per year) if you buy a different brand of bulk-pack catsup and plastic containers and fill these containers from the pack. What course do you recommend? If possible, ask a coffee shop manager or owner-manager to comment on your answer.

4. What is an appropriate intended use for canned peas?

5. Give an example of the pull strategy in the processed produce and other grocery items channel of distribution.

6. What is the primary difference between U.S. Grade B and U.S. Grade C products?

7. What are the grading factors for canned and bottled products?

8. What are the grading factors for frozen products?

9. What are the grading factors for dried products?

10. What critical information is missing from the following product specification for canned peach halves?
    Peach halves
    Packed in light syrup
    CODE brand, red label (or equivalent)
    Packed in No. 10 cans, 6 cans per case

11. Why is organic food more expensive than nonorganic, processed-produce products?

12. Note three examples of grocery products that you have seen in a restaurant operation that carry personalized packaging. What are some of the advantages and disadvantages of personalized packaging?

13. Assume that you normally purchase 1200 cases of canned peaches every three months. (You order once every three months.) The AP price per case is $8.75. Your supplier offers you a one-year supply for $8.60 per case, cash on delivery (COD). (You currently have 30 days in which to pay your invoices from this supplier.) Assume you are the purchasing director for a 400-room hotel that does excellent restaurant and banquet business. What course of action do you suggest? If possible, ask the manager of a comparable property to comment on your answer.

14. What is an appropriate intended use for dried apricots?

15. Assume that you are the purchasing director for a university food service with 15 campus housing buildings, 8 snack bars, a large dining commons, and an unpredictable banquet business. Currently, you operate a central commissary and a central distribution center. Outline the specific procedures you would use for the purchasing, receiving, storing, and issuing of canned peach halves. If possible, ask a university foodservice purchasing director to comment on your answer.

16. Your supplier calls to say that the price of tomato paste is due to rise soon and suggests that you purchase at least 2500 cases immediately. Assuming that you find your supplier completely trustworthy, what specifically should you consider before making your decision about this potential purchase?

17. What are the recommended storage temperatures for canned and bottled products and for frozen products?

18. Assume that you manage a steak house. You have been using individually wrapped half-ounce portions of catsup. One Saturday afternoon, you notice that you have very few of these packets left because the previous night's business was especially brisk. At first glance, you do not believe you can get a delivery from the commissary—the steak house is part of a national chain—until Monday morning. But you are open tonight until 9 P.M. and all day tomorrow, 11 A.M. to 9 P.M. What course of action do you take? If possible, ask a steak house manager to comment on your answer.

19. Assume that you manage a college foodservice facility. You want to purchase your annual requirement of canned tomatoes. You have four brands of tomatoes from which to choose, three reasonably well-known brands and one generic brand. The AP prices vary only slightly among the three name brands, but the generic brand offers a 22 percent savings. Unfortunately, the generic brand contains mostly broken pieces and has a drained weight that is 15 percent less than the name-brand merchandise. In addition, the supplier warns you that the quality of the generic brand is not predictable from year to year. Which type of merchandise would you purchase? Why? If possible, ask a college foodservice manager to comment on your answer.

20. A product specification for frozen corn could include the following information:
    (a)
    (b)
    (c)
    (d)
    (e)

21. The choice of which food-processing method a buyer selects is usually affected by three major criteria. Identify these three criteria.

22. Why would a canned tomato puree with a high specific gravity usually be more expensive than one with a lower specific gravity?

23. What is the difference between the designations "U.S. Grade A" and "Grade A"?

24. What is an appropriate intended use for frozen asparagus spears?

25. Define or explain the following terms:

    (a) AMS   (i) New pack time
    (b) CN label   (j) Can-cutting test
    (c) Standard of identity (k) Holding court
    (d) Stock rotation   (l) Freezer burn
    (e) Break point   (m) Solid pack
    (f) Drained weight   (n) Premium brand
    (g) Heavy pack   (o) Generic brand
    (h) Specific gravity   (p) Packer's grade

DAIRY PRODUCTS

The Purpose of this Chapter

After reading this chapter, you should be able to:

■ Explain the selection factors for dairy products, including government grades.

■ Describe the process of purchasing, receiving, storing, and issuing dairy products.

INTRODUCTION

Purchasing dairy products can be an arduous task. Foodservice buyers are inundated with numerous varieties and forms of these products, including milk, cheeses, and frozen concoctions. Whether the product is fresh, aged, dried, or fermented, the savvy buyer is knowledgeable in the distinguishing factors that characterize each product. The most noted component of dairy products is butterfat. The butterfat content affects quality, including flavor and mouthfeel. Because it is such a key component, the amount of butterfat in a dairy product has a direct correlation with the as-purchased (AP) price.

Buyers may ask what the difference is between one whole-milk brand and another? There should be little, since most dairies use fairly standardized management techniques. But dairies may vary somewhat in their quality control programs and their processing methods, so that, perhaps, a taste comparison between dairies is not a wasted effort. The type of feed, seasonal variation, and the stage of lactation of the dairy herds can also cause slight flavor variations.

Chances are that even though little difference in flavor may exist between one brand of whole milk and another, the same cannot be said of other dairy products. The taste of many of these products, especially cheese, tends to be unique to each producer. Once buyers settle on a particular brand—for example, a specific cheese—especially if the cheese is served alone, they may find it difficult to discontinue it in favor of another brand. If they do, their customers probably will notice any change. Thus, for these items, there is a good possibility that buyers will inevitably become a house account with the supplier of the chosen brand.

As mentioned, butterfat is an important component in dairy products, and it is considered an expensive fat. Since butterfat content is almost directly related to the AP price of a dairy item, many products have been manufactured in which the butterfat has been either reduced or replaced. These types of substitutions can be cost-effective. For that reason, the owner-manager should evaluate the types of substitution possibilities. Will it be butter or margarine; half-and-half or nondairy coffee cream; and natural cheese or cheese food made with vegetable fat? The type of foodservice establishment will help answer these questions on the number and types of allowable substitution possibilities. For example, margarine chips are not a suitable substitute for butter pats in a gourmet dinner house.

Buyers face another series of substitution issues: one dairy item may be substituted for another in food-production recipes. More possibilities exist for dairy products than for other ingredients because any time an item contains fat, at least one substitution is a possibility: for example, yogurt for sour cream, skim milk for whole milk, and pasteurized process cheese for natural cheese. These factors can complicate the decision-making process for buyers. For example, they do not have to use sour cream on the baked potato; they have at least two alternatives: a cultured dressing, which is like a low-fat sour cream, or an imitation nondairy product.

Whatever the decision, if hospitality operations use a suitable dairy substitute product, the possible flavor and nutrition alterations in the final product must be addressed. To a certain extent, it is a matter of opinion whether these flavors are different. Whenever operators combine two or more ingredients in a recipe, the possibility of recipe change always exists. So it is to the firm's benefit to experiment (see Figure 19.1, which notes some dairy product substitutions).

Proper representation of substitute products is critical. Truth-in-menu legislation in some parts of the country prohibits misrepresentation—plus it is unethical. In addition, operators must be careful not to serve one product and imply that

1 cup butter	1 cup margarine
	$7/8$ to 1 cup hydrogenated fat plus $1/2$ teaspoon salt
	$7/8$ cup lard plus $1/2$ teaspoon salt
	$7/8$ cup rendered fat plus $1/2$ teaspoon salt
1 cup coffee cream (20 percent)	3 tablespoons butter plus about $7/8$ cup milk
1 cup heavy cream (40 percent)	$1/3$ cup butter plus about $3/4$ cup milk
1 cup whole milk	1 cup reconstituted nonfat dry milk plus $2 1/2$ teaspoons butter or margarine
	$1/2$ cup evaporated milk plus $1/2$ cup water
	$1/4$ cup sifted dry whole milk powder plus $7/8$ cup water
1 cup milk	3 tablespoons sifted nonfat dry milk powder plus 1 cup water
	6 tablespoons sifted nonfat dry milk crystals plus 1 cup water
1 cup buttermilk or sour milk	1 tablespoon vinegar or lemon juice plus enough sweet milk to make 1 cup (let stand 5 minutes)
	$1 3/4$ teaspoons cream of tartar plus 1 cup sweet milk

FIGURE 19.1 **Some dairy product substitutions.**

it is another; for example, they cannot serve half-and-half and imply that it is cream, a richer product that has more butterfat and is more expensive.

Once operators decide what dairy products they want, they must then determine the exact products and supplier(s) they would like to use. The typical food-service operation can use one supplier for its dairy products—a sort of built-in one-stop buying strategy. Alternately, a buyer can take the time to evaluate the wide variety of suppliers available for each type of dairy product.

Small operators may prefer one-stop shopping for the majority of their dairy products. But a single supplier may not have everything needed. Consequently, the decision sometimes involves a choice between one or two suppliers, who may not always have exactly what the firm wants and who make fewer deliveries, versus several suppliers who carry what the firm needs and who make more frequent deliveries.

This decision is not easy to make. On the one hand, dairy products do not usually represent a great deal of the purchase dollar. Hence, hospitality operators could argue that little potential gain is associated with evaluating every available brand and supplier. Conversely, the substitution possibilities can be lucrative. A single sure way of an operation knowing whether it has examined all the substitution possibilities is to plow through every available brand and supplier. To complicate matters, many new products come and go. In some cases, it is preferable to procure the desired dairy products from one or two suppliers. But bear in mind that in many instances, a more careful search of the possibilities may pay for itself.

SELECTION FACTORS

Management personnel usually determine the varieties and qualities of dairy products they want to include on the menu. They may or may not work in concert with other company personnel in making these decisions. Regardless, they usually consider many of the selection factors outlined below.

Intended Use

As always, buyers want to determine exactly the intended use of the item so that they will be able to prepare the appropriate, relevant specification. For instance, if a cheese is needed primarily for flavor and only secondarily for appearance, the specification should reflect this.

Exact Name

It is very important for buyers to note the exact, specific name of the item they want. The majority of dairy products carry a standard of identity established by the federal government. This standard is based primarily on the minimum amount of butterfat content. For some products, the standards of identity also prescribe minimum or maximum amounts of milk solids allowed (see Figure 19.2 for some dairy products' legally defined minimum fat contents).

If an operation can use these minimum governmental standards, it may find bid buying the easiest procedure. Assuming that everything else is equal, the buyer could write the specifications with just a few words, for example, "vanilla-flavored ice cream." So, assuming that every bidder meets the required standard, a buyer could save money when one supplier bids lower than the rest.

U.S. Government Grades (or Equivalent)

The Agricultural Marketing Service (AMS) of the United States Department of Agriculture's (USDA's) Poultry and Dairy Division has set federal grading standards for poultry, eggs, and dairy products. U.S. grades, however, do not exist for every type of dairy product.[1] But milk, which is the base for all natural dairy products, usu-

ITEM	MINIMUM PERCENTAGE FAT
Cheddar cheese	30.5%
Cottage cheese, creamed	4.0%
Cottage cheese, dry curd	0.5% (Maximum)
Cottage cheese, low fat	0.5% to 2.0%
Cream cheese	33.0%
Ice cream	10.0%
Ice milk	2.0% to 7.0%
Milk, evaporated	7.9%
Milk, low fat	1.0% to 2.0%
Milk, skim	0.1% to 0.5%
Milk, whole	3.25%
Mozzarella cheese	18.0% to 21.6%
Mozzarella cheese, part skim	12.0% to 18.0%
Neufchatel cheese	20.0% to 33.0%
Pasteurized process American cheese	26.8%
Pasteurized process American cheese food	23.0%
Pasteurized process American cheese spread	20.0%
Ricotta cheese	11.0%
Ricotta cheese, part skim	6.0% to 11.0%
Sour cream	18.0%
Whipping cream	30.0%

FIGURE 19.2 **Some dairy products' legally defined minimum fat contents.**

ally is graded. As is true with most foods, the grading of milk and milk products is voluntary; however, many states require milk to be graded by the federal government (see Figure 19.3).

Like most foods high in protein, milk is a good medium for harmful bacteria. Consequently, most states and local municipalities have stringent health codes covering milk production. As such, milk must be produced and bottled under government-prescribed conditions. The U.S. Public Health Service's Milk Ordinance and Code (termed the Pasteurized Milk Ordinance [PMO]) contains provisions covering such activities as the approved care and feeding of dairy cows, the handling of the milk, the pasteurization* requirement, and the holding temperature of the milk.[2]

---

*Heating the milk to kill pathogens (disease-causing but not spoilage bacteria). Milk that is not pasteurized is referred to as "raw milk." Hospitality operators usually are not allowed to serve raw milk to their customers.

FIGURE 19.3 Federal grade and inspection stamps used for dairy products. *Source:* United States Department of Agriculture.

Because of these safety controls, dairies have little influence regarding milk production. They do, however, have the option of homogenization. This is the dividing of the butterfat globules so that they stay suspended in the milk and do not rise to the top. The dairies can also dictate what to do with their milk: sell it to ice cream makers, sell it to dry-milk producers, market it to households, and so on.

Fluid milk grades are based primarily on the finished product's bacterial count. There are two federal-government grading designations for fluid milk:

1. **Grade A.** This is the milk the government considers to be fluid milk, to be sold in retail stores and delivered to consumers (see Figure 19.4).

2. **Manufacturing Grade.** This milk is sometimes called Grade B. More bacteria are allowed in Manufacturing Grade milk than in Grade A; this milk is used for manufacturing milk products, such as butter, cheese, and ice cream.

Some persons discuss a third grade of milk, a certified grade. This refers to milk that has very little bacteria and can be used for infants and sick persons; technically, "certified" is not classified as a grade, but some buyers treat it as such.

Some spoilage bacteria always exist in pasteurized milk, but they are harmless. In addition to the number of bacteria, the grader also considers the milk's odor, taste, and appearance.

Milk can be fortified with vitamins A and D, and some states allow other types of nutrient additives.

As we noted previously, few dairy products are graded; this is primarily because the fluid milk used to produce them is usually graded and produced under continuous government inspection. Furthermore, the federal government has not established grading standards for most dairy products. In addition to fluid milk, U.S. grading standards have been determined for dry milk, Cheddar, Swiss, Colby, and Monterey Jack cheeses, and butter.

An example of a retail carton of milk. Courtesy of Anderson Dairy, Inc.

The federal grades for dry nonfat milk are:

1. Extra

2. Standard

The federal grades for dry whole milk are:

1. Premium

2. Extra

3. Standard

The grading factors for dry milk that the grader evaluates include the product's color, odor, flavor, and bacterial counts, how scorched the milk is, how lumpy it is, how well it will go into solution, and how much moisture it contains.

The federal grades for Cheddar, Swiss, Colby, and Monterey Jack cheeses are:

1.   AA

2.   A

3.   B

4.   C

The grading factors for cheeses that the grader evaluates include the product's color, odor, appearance, flavor, texture, finish, and plasticity (i.e., body).

The federal grades for butter are:

1.   AA

2.   A

3.   B

The grading factors for butter that the grader evaluates include the product's flavor, odor, freshness, texture, and plasticity.

Some states use their own grading systems. For example, Wisconsin imposes grades for cheese. Also, the "U.S. Grade A" designation on a package label indicates that the federal government graded the dairy product, whereas the notation "Grade A" on the package label signifies that the dairy product meets specific criteria that a state, county, and/or local government agency established.

Additional terminology sometimes appears in the dairy products market, but this terminology does not necessarily represent governmental grades. Instead, this terminology tends to comprise terms and designations that, for one reason or another, have become popular. For example, ice cream carries several designations. It can be called "premium," "regular," or "competitive" (premium has 15 to 18 percent butterfat, regular has about 12 percent, and competitive has 10 percent—see Figure 19.5). Alternately, ice cream might be called "French," which means that eggs have been used as a thickening agent.

Another type of terminology especially prevalent on dairy product package labels is dating information. In some states, "pull" dates must be listed on dairy products' package labels. These dates tell supermarket managers, suppliers, and consumers the last day that the products can be sold. If states do not require pull dates to be listed, they usually require some sort of coded dates, or "blind" dates, to be noted on the package labels.

Typically, foodservice buyers opt for Grade A milk and a comparable quality for all the other dairy products. Since several dairy products differ in taste as one

FIGURE 19.5 Premium quality and regular French vanilla ice cream. Courtesy of Anderson Dairy, Inc.

goes from one supplier to the next, it is not difficult to understand why U.S. Grades, and even local government grades, are not the major selection criterion.

Packers' Brands (or Equivalent)

The difference in taste between one supplier and another can be remarkable for cheese, yogurt, ice cream, sherbet, and dry milk. It is, in fact, amazing how different the taste can be between two brands of apparently equal merchandise.

Consequently, brand names tend to become important to buyers. Foodservice managers cannot be easily persuaded to drop their current ice cream for competing products. Of course, the bid buyer, or the buyer who has the time, occasionally checks out different brands of dairy products. New dairy items enter the market periodically, and some of them may be deemed to be good substitutes. Some of these new products may even save hospitality operators a bit of money.

Product Size

A few dairy products require size designations. For instance, butter could be ordered in 1-pound prints, 50-pound slabs, or one or more "chip" sizes. Cheese slices usually come in two or more sizes; for example, you might order a 1-ounce size for the cheeseburger platter and a 2-ounce size for the grilled cheese sandwich plate.

Size of Container

Dairy products are sold in various package sizes. Because of the highly perishable nature of dairy items, experience shows that the size of the container is very important. Buyers should purchase only the necessary amount in order to minimize leftovers and reduce waste.

Naturally, the smaller the package size unit—for example, half-pint milk containers in contrast to half-gallons—the higher the AP price. The edible-portion (EP) cost could, however, be lower. For instance, bartenders use cream in some drinks. A small package could carry a premium AP price, but if the cream drink volume is low, bartenders may waste cream if you use large containers. In this case, the EP cost would jump to an unacceptable level.

Not every supplier carries the package sizes buyers want. For example, a buyer may be satisfied with a particular brand but find that the supplier does not stock that brand in the individual portion packs the buyer desires.

Type of Packaging Material

Generally, dairy products packaging materials are quite standardized throughout the hospitality industry. One of the major reasons for this is that dairy regulations usually specify minimum packaging requirements that protect the culinary quality and wholesomeness of the products.

This standardization does not mean, however, that all dairy products are packaged alike. Buyers usually can select from a wide variety of packaging materials. There are plastic, fiberboard, metal, glass, and aseptic containers. Typically, two or more choices are available for many products.

Custom-packaging options may also be available for some dairy products. For instance, some dairies will include an operation's name and/or logo on individual half-pint containers of milk, individually wrapped butter chips, and single-serve creamers. Of course, the buyer must be prepared to pay a bit more in exchange for this added value.

Packaging Procedure

This can be an important consideration, especially for the single-serve dairy product items many restaurant operators purchase. For instance, buyers can purchase butter chips that are layered in a 5-pound container and separated by pieces of waxed paper. Alternately, buyers can obtain individually wrapped butter chips (which, by the way, the local health district may require in order to protect the wholesomeness and cleanliness of the butter).

As mentioned several times, the layered and/or individually wrapped products will carry premium AP prices. But the end result—that is, the EP costs—may be quite acceptable if buyers purchase premium packaging and packaging procedures that tend to protect the shelf life of the merchandise.

Product Yield

For some dairy products, buyers may need to indicate the maximum waste they will accept (or the minimum yield acceptable). For instance, they might need to indicate whether they would accept rind on the cheese they want to buy. Similarly, buyers should note on the specification that, for example, they will not accept more than two broken cheese slices per hundred.

Product Form

For some dairy items, buyers may need to note the exact form of the product. For example, they might need to note sliced, whole, grated, shredded, or crumbled cheese. Similarly, they might need to note whipped butter, if applicable, instead of just butter.

Preservation Method

Most dairy items are kept under continuous refrigeration. Although refrigeration is not required for some items, such as certain cheeses, if buyers want these types of items kept under refrigerated conditions, they need to note this on the specification.

Some dairy items are frozen. The obvious ones are ice creams and frozen yogurts. However, some suppliers freeze the cheeses and butter they sell. So if buyers do not want frozen dairy items, they may have to specify this for some items that they purchase.

A few dairy items are traditionally canned. Evaporated milk, sweetened condensed milk, and canned whole milk are usually marketed in metal containers. Whole milk also comes in aseptic packages and can be kept at room temperature for months. This "shelf-stable" product is pasteurized using "ultra-high temperatures" (UHT), and its taste is very similar to fresh, refrigerated, whole, fluid milk and coffee creamers. This technique is sometimes referred to as "ultra-pasteurized"

(UP). Although individual UP creamers are used extensively in foodservice operations, the whole-milk product has yet to gain widespread popularity in the United States.

When considering preservation methods, wise buyers also take the time to specify the maximum pull date allowed at time of delivery. If stored correctly, dairy products will remain safe to consume for a few days after the pull date; however, their culinary quality could be compromised to the point where these products should not be served to guests. Furthermore, the local health district may not allow the use of out-dated products.

Butterfat Content

In general, as the butterfat increases, so does the AP price, but more butterfat also makes for a better product. Moreover, producers tend to treat dairy products with a high butterfat content with more respect. For example, a premium ice cream typically contains high-quality flavorings—fresh fruits rather than fruit syrups, for example.

If buyers are satisfied with the amount of butterfat mandated by the federal government's standard of identity, they can ignore this selection factor. However, if they want a product that is more or less "creamy," they must note this requirement on the specification.

Milk Solids Content

The federal government also mandates the maximum amount of nonfat, dried milk solids that some dairy products can have. If these standards are acceptable, this selection factor is irrelevant. However, if buyers desire fewer solids than the maximum allowed, they must indicate their exact requirement on the specification.

Overrun

The amount of air in a frozen dairy product is referred to as "overrun." Most people in the foodservice industry consider overrun to be the amount of air incorporated into any type of dairy product. Some dairy products contain a good deal of air. When a chef whips butterfat, he or she incorporates air. Also, butterfat holds the air for quite a while, and even longer when the product is frozen or contains some added emulsifiers.

The air content is crucial to the flavor of such items as ready whipped cream in an aerosol can and ice cream.

Whipped cream is usually sold by the number of ounces in the can. But it can also be sold by volume, which is a typical measure of quantity for many types of dairy products. If buyers start to compare AP prices on the basis of volume, they must keep in mind that air costs nothing. So they could be buying more volume but less solid product.

The federal government standard of identity for ice cream dictates that 1 gallon must weigh at least $4^1/2$ pounds and contain at least 1.6 pounds of total food solids. Therefore, for this type of product, buyers are protected to some extent. But this is not the case for such items as whipped topping. For these types of products, buyers must be ever mindful of the exact value of the purchase.

Chemical Additives

Because milk is a food for babies, it has been kept natural for many decades. However, a few dairy products contain chemical additives that stabilize, emulsify, and preserve them, and at times, the dairy industry has been unjustly criticized for this. It is easy to assume that all dairy items include several chemical additives. But this is just not the case. The products that typically contain chemicals are nondairy items. All things considered, dairy products in their natural form, processed or relatively unprocessed (pasteurized), have significantly fewer chemical additives than other processed foods.

Untreated Cows

In this age of biotechnology, dairies are able to treat their herds with synthetic and naturally occuring hormones—such as bST (bovine somatotropin) and rBGH or rBST (Recombinant Bovine Growth Hormone)—designed to increase milk production. Some buyers, though, may not want to purchase products made from this type of milk.[3] If so, they need to note on the specification that they will accept only products coming from cows that have not been treated this way.

How the Product Is Processed

Dairy processing methods usually fall under government inspection. But these inspections ensure only wholesomeness, not flavor, convenience, or packaging.

The type of processing can be very important for some dairy products. For example, all Swiss cheeses are a bit different. Although they all meet a minimum standard of identity, substantial differences in aging methods and aging times can exist. The packer's brand usually indicates these processes.

Buyers may want to know whether or not the process is "natural." For example, some cottage cheeses contain an absolute minimum of additives; others may contain extra acid, such as phosphoric acid to set the curd, and artificial flavorings. If buyers want all of the dairy items they purchase to be natural, they will have to search out the appropriate brand.

Nondairy Products

Many operators may use nondairy items for several reasons, including: (1) AP prices may be lower; (2) nondairy products, being less perishable, save on storage costs and reduce waste; and (3) weight watchers and those people who cannot tolerate lactose (milk sugar) may represent a clientele worth accommodating (see Figure 19.6).

Unfortunately, most imitation items contain some chemical additives and usually are not nutritionally equivalent to the products they imitate; consequently, some customers may refuse to use them. The fat substitutes being marketed today do not impress many nutritionists, who doubt very much that these products will make people healthier or slimmer. Furthermore, nondairy products may not work in some recipes that call for dairy ingredients.

FIGURE 19.6 A nondairy item. Courtesy of Sysco Corporation.

AP Price

In a free-market area, some opportunities to reduce the AP price may exist. In a controlled state, you must legally pay at least the minimum AP price.

Most states have a variety of price control and credit control policies; that is, the local governments regulate the price and the type and amount of credit a dairy can extend to its customers. Periodically, someone starts a drive to eliminate the local government and the federal government's power in this area. But the price and credit controls seem to weather these attacks very well.

Dairy products provide few quantity buy opportunities, although there may be money-saving long-term contracts for some items if it is legally possible.

Also, some dairy products, especially cheese, are imported. Import taxes tend to add up, thereby increasing AP prices.

One-Stop Shopping

Most foodservice operators like one-stop dairy shopping because of the standing order they can bargain for and some dairy suppliers provide. If buyers can get a supplier to bring his or her current stock of dairy items just up to par, this supplier service is an added plus. However, the supplier then controls the inventory level. But since dairies often provide frequent deliveries, this reduces the amount of inventory of perishable items hospitality operations must carry.

One-stop shopping tends to entail a higher AP price. To receive the convenience we noted, however, operators may be willing to pay more.

PURCHASING DAIRY PRODUCTS

Since most dairy products are highly perishable, the buyers' first purchasing steps are to determine precisely what they want and then to determine the delivery schedule they think will be appropriate. Buyers prefer daily delivery; however, they should negotiate for and follow any supplier service or purchasing tactic that helps control the quality of these items.

Preparing elaborate specifications for dairy products usually is not necessary unless the buyer is a bid buyer or if he or she expects to enter into a long-term contractual arrangement with the supplier. As always, it might be good discipline for a buyer to reduce his or her ideas to detailed written specifications before committing to purchasing any item. (See Figure 19.7 for some example product specifications and Figure 19.8 for an example product specification outline for dairy products.)

Butter Used for customer service U.S. Grade AA Butter chips 90 count Layered arrangement, easily separated 5-pound box Waxed, moisture-proof, vapor-proof Refrigerated	Nondairy coffee whitener, liquid Used for customer service House brand $3/8$-ounce portion, single serve 400 servings per case Loose pack (slab pack) Moisture-proof carton Unrefrigerated
Bleu cheese Used for tossed salad Frigo® brand Crumbles 5-pound poly bag 4 bags per case Moisture-proof, vapor-proof Frozen	Half-and-half Used for customer service U.S. Grade A $3/8$-ounce portion, single serve 400 servings per case Loose pack (slab pack) Moisture-proof carton Refrigerated

FIGURE 19.7   An example of dairy product specifications.

If a hospitality operation uses the ordinary types of dairy products and is located in a noncontrolled state, bid buying might be profitable. But as a percentage of total purchase dollars, these savings are liable to be small. However, if operators can live with some variations, their savings can add up through the optimal selection of many suppliers and packers' brands.

Intended use:

Exact name:

U.S. grade (or equivalent):

Packer's brand name (or equivalent):

Product size:

Size of container:

Type of packaging material:

Packaging procedure:

Product yield:

Product form:

Preservation method:

FIGURE 19.8   An example of a product specification outline for dairy products.

If buyers can live with variations and/or purchase a large quantity of dairy products, they should take the time to evaluate some of the substitution possibilities. Several products are capable of providing comparable culinary quality in a recipe, and a few minutes of cost calculation might indicate that a particular recipe is much less expensive to produce with one of these instead of with a comparable one. For instance, if buyers use large quantities of fresh milk to prepare breads, a switch to dry milk may yield a comparable-quality finished product at a lower EP cost.

Sometimes independent farmers seek to do business with hospitality operations. It might be best to avoid them no matter how "natural" their products may seem or how good the deals they offer appear to be. The products might not come under the rigid quality control standards the federal and state governments have established.

RECEIVING DAIRY PRODUCTS

When receivers get dairy products, they should take the time to carefully examine them for dirt, broken containers, and faulty wrapping. Milk cartons can get dented, and cheese wrappings sometimes crack or split. Since these products deteriorate quickly, receivers should be reluctant to accept anything that does not look clean and properly packaged.

Receivers also must check to see that they receive everything that was ordered. This check can be difficult for at least two reasons. First, with so many dairy items on one invoice, either the receivers or the suppliers may miss something. Second, some dairy items are delivered on a standing-order basis. This is typical with ice cream and sherbet, and it may allow the delivery agent to work alone stocking an operation's freezers. When leaving, the agent may present an invoice for the receiver to sign. If the receiver is busy, he or she may not thoroughly check what has been delivered. Alternately, an unscrupulous delivery agent may tell a receiver that a container that already was in the dairy box was delivered that day.

A related problem centers on supplier substitutions. For example, a supplier may be out of Roquefort cheese and send bleu cheese instead, not wanting to see the operation serve guests without at least a similar item. But some substitutes in the dairy line do not always match well, especially cheeses.

Although receivers do not often take the time to make planned but random taste tests, they should. This may not be necessary if buyers purchase a proprietary brand; they will then have some assurance of quality.

Since most dairy items are perishable, receivers might consider moving everything into a refrigerated area before they make their inspection. After checking qualities and quantities, receivers should check the invoice arithmetic and complete the appropriate accounting procedures.

STORING DAIRY PRODUCTS

Most dairy products should be stored in a refrigerator or freezer as soon as possible. Dried, canned, and bottled items can go to the storeroom, as can, possibly, some nondairy products.

If chefs are going to serve a certain dairy product—for example, if they plan on presenting a cheese platter on that evening's menu—they should bring the cheese to the correct serving temperature by leaving it out at room temperature before serving. If they are going to serve the cheese later in the week, it should be refrigerated, since room temperatures cause most cheeses to age. This will have a detrimental effect on the cheese by causing it to quickly change in odor, flavor, and appearance.

Most dairy items readily pick up odors. Therefore, maintaining a separate dairy refrigerator is recommended. If that is impossible, hospitality operators should keep dairy products tightly covered, in a segregated area in the common refrigerator, and away from odorous foods.

As much as possible, operators should also keep dairy products, particularly cheeses, in their original packaging. When they store these items, they should try not to nick or cut the packaging. This is easy to do and hastens spoilage and waste.

When storing dairy products, operators should take a bit of extra time to ensure that they rotate the products on the shelves properly. They cannot take a chance that a customer will get sour milk. It is not easy to tell whether the food is rotated properly unless they take the extra time to check the pull dates many dairies put on their products. Dairy products are not like lettuce: if a head of lettuce is bad, you know it, but whole milk in individual half-pints is harder to monitor.

ISSUING DAIRY PRODUCTS

Hospitality operators should issue older dairy products first. Many of these items, especially ice cream, go straight from receiving to a production area. If they are issued from a central storeroom, make sure that the requisitioner receives the correct product. For example, if the requisitioner wants milk for a cake recipe, make sure that he or she gets the appropriate dry milk.

Since most dairy products deteriorate rapidly, hospitality operators should try not to handle them any more than necessary. Also, they should make sure that requisitioners do not take more than they need for any one particular work shift or job. Operators might consider asking the requisitioner to make a note of the in-process inventory before asking for more stock.

IN-PROCESS INVENTORIES

Dairy products fall victim to spoilage, waste, and pilferage whenever they stay in-process for any extended period. They spoil because butter, cheese slices, and coffee cream, for example, are often left at room temperature too long. Also, employees waste dairy products by failing to empty milk containers and cans of whipped cream completely. Pilferage is particularly common. For instance, employees may help themselves to a quick glass of milk once in a while.

As usual, supervision is the key. It helps both to head off waste and pilferage and to prevent, as well, such embarrassing situations as a customer tasting curdled coffee cream or rancid butter.

KEY WORDS AND CONCEPTS

Agricultural Marketing Service (AMS)

As-purchased price (AP price)

Blind dates

Bovine somatotropin (bST)

Butterfat content

Chemical additives

Custom packaging

Disease-causing bacteria

Edible-portion cost (EP cost)

Exact name

Fortified milk

Grading factors

Homogenization

In-process inventories

Intended use

Lactose

Manufacturing grade

Milk solids content

Nondairy products

One-stop shopping

Overrun

Packaging material

Packaging procedure

Packers' brands

Pasteurization

Pasteurized Milk Ordinance (PMO)

Preservation method

Price and credit controls

Processing method

Product form

Product size

Product yield

Pull dates

Purchasing, receiving, storing, and issuing dairy products

Raw milk

Recombinant bovine growth hormone (rBGH or rBST)

Shelf-stable products

Size of container

Spoilage bacteria

Standard of identity

Substitution possibilities

Synthetic hormones

Truth-in-menu legislation

Ultra-high temperature (UHT) pasteurization

Ultra-pasteurized (UP)

U.S. grades

U.S. Grade A versus Grade A

U.S. Public Health Service's Milk Ordinance and Code

Vitamins A and D

REFERENCES

1. For a detailed dicsussion of dairy grades, see http://www.ams.usda.gov/dairy. Retrieved October 2, 2003.

2. See, for example, Anonymous, "Milk Safety References," U. S. Food and Drug Administration Center for Food Safety and Applied Nutrition, Retrieved October 3, 2003 (Available http://www.cfsan.fda.gov/~ear/prime.html).

3. See, for example, Anonymous, "POSILAC® bovine somatotropin," Monsanto Dairy Website, Retrieved October 3, 2003 (Available http://www.monsantodairy.com/). See also: Deana Grobe and Robin Douthitt, "Consumer Risk Perception Profiles Regarding Recombinant Bovine Growth Hormone (rbGH)," *Journal of Consumer Affairs*, Winter 1999, 33(2), pp. 254–276; David Smith and Robert Skalnik, "Biotechnology in the Agricultural Sector: A Challenge to Consumer Welfare," *International Journal of Consumer Studies*, September 2003, 27(4), pp. 277–283.

QUESTIONS AND PROBLEMS

1. What are the U.S. grades for fresh fluid milk?

2. What are the U.S. grades for butter?

3. What is the minimum weight of a gallon of ice cream?

4. What is the minimum butterfat content for ice cream?

5. What is an appropriate intended use for nondairy creamer?

6. What is an appropriate intended use for margarine?

7. What is an appropriate intended use for dry nonfat milk?

8. Assume that you operate the food service in a minimum security prison. You serve approximately 500 inmates and 120 civilian staff members a day, three meals and various snacks. You have a severely tight food budget. Outline the specific procedures you might use to purchase, receive, store, and issue whole, fluid milk for use in cooking and as a beverage. Note: The prisoners are your workers. If possible, ask a prison foodservice official to comment on your answer.

9. What is the primary purpose of pasteurization?

10. What is the primary purpose of homogenization?

11. What are the U.S. grades for dry nonfat milk?

12. What are the grading factors for Cheddar, Swiss, Colby, and Monterey Jack cheese U.S. grades?

13. What critical information is missing from the following product specification for milk?
    Milk, fluid
    U.S. Grade A
    Used for cooking and baking
    Bulk container

14. What is the primary difference between premium ice cream and competitive ice cream?

15. What is an appropriate intended use for low fat milk?

16. Explain why dairy products should not be stored with fresh produce.

17. A product specification for an ice cream bar could include the following information:
    (a)
    (b)
    (c)
    (d)
    (e)

18. One-stop dairy product shopping is especially popular among small operators. Why do you think this is the case? What advantages are there? What disadvantages are there?

19. Why do most government jurisdictions prohibit restaurants from serving raw milk?

20. Define or explain the following terms:
(a) Pull dates	(i)	Custom packaging
(b) Certified milk	(j)	Product form
(c) Fortified milk	(k)	Aseptic container
(d) Lactose	(l)	Nondairy products
(e) Minimum butterfat content	(m)	Product yield
(f) Overrun	(n)	Standard of identity
(g) Controlled AP prices	(o)	U.S. Grade A versus Grade A
(h) UHT pasteurization		

20
EGGS

The Purpose of this Chapter

After reading this chapter, you should be able to:

- Explain the selection factors for eggs, including government grades.
- Describe the process of purchasing, receiving, storing, and issuing eggs.

INTRODUCTION

The most important egg purchasing considerations center on determining what hospitality operations want and which type of product is best suited to their needs. Purchasing fresh shell eggs is a relatively easy task. Buying processed eggs, whether frozen, dried, or imitation eggs, or preprepared egg products, can be more of a challenge.

SELECTION FACTORS

As with all products, management personnel, either alone or in cooperation with others, normally decide in advance the quality of eggs the operation needs. They use the following selection factors to evaluate the standards of egg quality and, to a certain extent, the egg suppliers.

Intended Use

As always, buyers want to determine exactly the intended use of an item, so that they will be able to prepare the appropriate, relevant specification. For instance, an egg product may be needed primarily for flavor and only secondarily for appearance. If so, the specification should reflect this.

Exact Name

Generally, this selection factor causes very little difficulty. Fresh eggs are chicken eggs, so if buyers use the term "eggs," they will receive chicken eggs (see Figure 20.1). The term "fresh shell eggs" refers to eggs that are fewer than 30 days old. Conversely, "storage eggs" are shell eggs older than 30 days.[1]

Storage eggs are rarely utilized in the foodservice industry, as egg production has been stabilized throughout the year and most shell eggs are now distributed within a few days. Shell eggs kept under refrigeration or in a controlled atmosphere for long periods of time are now considered unacceptable. However, if an operator's specification notes "shell eggs" or "eggs" instead of "fresh shell eggs," he or she may be disappointed with the purchase.

FIGURE 20.1 A flat of chicken eggs. Courtesy of the American Egg Board.

The term "egg products" refers to eggs that have been removed from their shells for processing at facilities called "breaker plants." Whole eggs, whites, yolks, and various blends—with or without added ingredients—that are processed and pasteurized, are basic types of egg products (see Figure 20.2). These products are available in liquid, frozen, and dried forms. Because of the different combinations of types and forms, buyers need to carefully consider their selection factors when ordering processed egg products. Buyers must be absolutely certain that they indicate the exact name of the desired item to prevent receiving an unacceptable product.

U.S. Government Inspection and Grades (or Equivalent)

The Egg Products Inspection Act (EPIA) of 1970 requires the United States Department of Agriculture (USDA) to ensure that egg products are safe, wholesome, unadulterated, and accurately labeled, for the protection of the health and welfare of consumers (www.fsis.usda.gov/OPPDE/rdad/Acts/epia_toc.htm). The original impetus for this act was driven by states' concerns regarding the contamination risk present with eggs and egg products. Under the EPIA, breaker plants must sub-

 **Processed egg products.
Courtesy of Michael Foods, Inc.**

mit to continuous government inspection. (Conversely, federal shell egg inspection is a voluntary program and is under the jurisdiction of the Food and Drug Administration [FDA].)

In most states, an egg producer must submit to either a federal-government inspection or a state-operated inspection. These inspectors also examine the condition of the laying hens, their environment, and their feed. The USDA's Food Safety and Inspection Service (FSIS) employs inspectors to examine egg products at official breaker plants. However, federal and state agencies often work together to perform inspections.

Unlike the FSIS, the USDA's grading service is voluntary. Therefore, shell egg processing plants can elect whether or not to purchase the egg quality grading program the USDA's Agricultural Marketing Service (AMS) administers. The USDA grade shield can be placed on the carton when eggs are graded for quality and checked for weight (size) under the supervision of a trained USDA grader.

The shell eggs produced under continuous federal-government inspection as mandated by certain states for monitoring the compliance with quality standards, grades, and weights can bear the USDA grade shield. States that elect not to purchase the USDA grading service but that use their own agencies to monitor egg packers for compliance can allow the cartons to bear such a term as "Grade A" without the USDA shield.

Three federal-government consumer grades for fresh shell eggs have become familiar quality guidelines (see Figure 20.3).

1. **U.S. Grade AA.** These eggs have whites that are thick and firm; yolks that are high, round, and practically free from defects; and clean, unbroken shells. Because these eggs are the top quality produced, only the freshest products earn this grade. The grade is very hard to obtain because once an egg is about a week old, its quality deteriorates to Grade A.

2. **U.S. Grade A.** These eggs have characteristics of Grade AA eggs except that the whites are "reasonably" firm. This is indicative of slightly lower quality. A fresh egg older than about a week usually falls into this grade category. This product's egg white and egg yolk are not quite as firm as those found in Grade AA merchandise. However, both Grade A and Grade AA eggs are generally suitable for all finished menu products where appearance is important.

3. **U.S. Grade B.** These eggs have whites that may be thinner and yolks that may be wider and flatter than eggs of higher grades. The yolks are also susceptible to breaking under even the slightest pressure. The shells must be unbroken but may show slight stains. Therefore, because of these appearance prob-

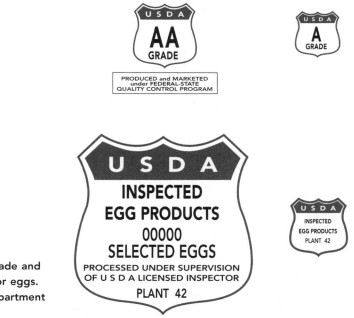

FIGURE 20.3 Federal grade and inspection stamps used for eggs. *Source:* United States Department of Agriculture.

lems, Grade B merchandise is suitable only for finished menu products in which eggs are used as an ingredient or as scrambled eggs (or omelettes).

Within these grade categories, an egg can be rated "high," "medium," or "low." As such, nine possible grades exist.

Fresh eggs are graded mainly on interior and exterior quality factors. Interior quality, such as the firmness of the egg yolk and egg white, is determined primarily by freshness. The exterior quality factors, such as shape, cleanliness, and soundness, are determined by the age of the hen, the feed eaten, and the general management of the flock and of the egg-laying facilities. The fresher an egg, the better it is, assuming that the laying hen is the right age (from 6 months to $1\frac{1}{2}$ years old), is eating a proper diet, and is living in an appropriate environment.

The grader uses a process called "candling" to check the interior quality of fresh eggs. This involves passing the egg over a light source, which reveals the yolk (a dead center implies freshness), the size of the air space (which gets larger as the egg becomes older), impurities, and cracks. The grader may also crack open randomly selected eggs to determine the height and firmness of the egg white. He or she might also evaluate the condition of the shell, especially if the laying hens are relatively old. Older hens produce eggs that have rougher and thinner shells.

The use of U.S. grades for fresh-egg purchasing is widespread, even though a wide tolerance exists between egg grades. A major advantage of graded shell eggs is that they have been produced under continuous government inspection. It is a good idea for buyers to insist on this type of inspection because shell eggs are on the FDA's list of potentially hazardous foods. Fresh shell eggs, even those that appear to be sound, can be contaminated with salmonella bacteria by the hens on rare occasions. Continuous government inspection, as well as buyers insisting on constant refrigeration at 45°F, should help mitigate this problem.

Foodservice buyers usually purchase Grade A eggs. Grade AA eggs are difficult to obtain. In addition, Grade A eggs normally suffice, particularly for fried and scrambled eggs and omelettes.

Packers' Brands (or Equivalent)

Some supermarkets pack their own eggs, so these eggs carry a packer's brand. But foodservice buyers do not show a great deal of brand loyalty for fresh shell eggs. The federal grade is the most common quality indicator.

However, packers' brands can be extremely important when buyers purchase processed and convenience forms of eggs, such as frozen, refrigerated liquid, and dried egg products. Processed egg products, while produced under continuous government inspection, do not have established grading standards. As a result, in almost every instance, brand names are the only reliable indication of quality.

Product Size

Buyers are normally interested in the size and uniformity of the shell eggs they purchase. The U.S. government helps in this area because graded eggs must meet quality and size standards. If a federal inspector grades the eggs, the producers are required to indicate the egg size somewhere on the container. Buyers should choose the size most useful and economical. Shell eggs are available in six sizes (see Figure 20.4).

Peewee eggs, sometimes called "pullet eggs," come from younger hens, usually at the beginning of their laying life. Jumbo eggs come from relatively older hens, usually at the end of their laying life. These extreme sizes are not common in the fresh-egg trade. If buyers want these sizes, normally they must visit a farmer with very young and very old laying hens.

When choosing eggs to be fried, scrambled, poached, or prepared in omelettes, buyers usually prefer the large size. These eggs have a very acceptable

SIZE OR WEIGHT CLASS	MINIMUM NET WEIGHT PER DOZEN (OUNCES)
Jumbo	30
Extra large	27
Large	24
Medium	21
Small	18
Peewee	15

FIGURE 20.4 **U.S. weight classes for shell eggs.** *Source:* **United States Department of Agriculture.**

appearance and show up well on the plate. Also, those who purchase fresh eggs for use in cake, batter, or drink recipes tend to choose large eggs because most quantity recipes, as well as recipes found in most cookbooks, assume a 2-ounce egg.

Buyers who keep close track of the as-purchased (AP) prices for each size might be able to save a few pennies when purchasing fresh shell eggs. For instance, in a recipe calling for eggs by weight, if large eggs cost $1.20 per dozen and medium eggs cost $1.00 per dozen, buyers could determine the best price per ounce in the following manner:

$1.20 per dozen ÷ 24 ounces per dozen = $0.05 per ounce

$1.00 per dozen ÷ 21 ounces per dozen = $0.0476 per ounce

So, medium eggs represent a slightly better buy.

We do not normally see buyers use this procedure; it is probably more helpful to homemakers than to commercial buyers, who are often restricted to the large-size egg. But if buyers want to purchase a large volume of eggs for use in various recipes and the labor is available to process them, such a procedure might save money.

Size of Container

For shell eggs, the normal package size is a 15-dozen or 30-dozen case. At times, buyers might order one or more "flats"; a flat contains $2^1/_2$ dozen fresh eggs. It is unusual to purchase eggs in 1-dozen or $1^1/_2$-dozen containers.

Processed egg products offer a bit more variety in package sizes, so buyers must be prepared to describe the exact packaging characteristics that best suit their needs.

Type of Packaging Material

For fresh shell eggs, the packaging is standardized. Buyers probably will not need to consider this selection factor if they order only fresh eggs. The same may not be true with processed egg products, since a considerable variation in packaging quality can exist. Buyers must be concerned with this selection factor because improperly packaged products can support tremendous bacterial multiplication. This is especially true if hospitality operators must store the processed egg products on their premises for a reasonably long period of time.

Usually, frozen egg products are packaged in moisture-proof, vapor-proof containers. In most instances, a processed product, such as frozen, precooked scrambled eggs, normally is packaged in a heavy plastic pouch; these pouches are sometimes referred to as "Cryovac® bags," or "Cryovac packaging." (Cryovac is a brand name. It is the company that developed the "vacuum shrink-wrap" technology that enables food processors to store products for considerable lengths of time.)

Some frozen items are also packed in metal or plastic containers. For instance, frozen eggs, frozen egg yolks, and frozen egg whites are typically packaged in 30-pound plastic containers, tankers, or poly-lined drums.

Dried egg products—which are becoming less frequently used in the hospitality industry—are, generally, sold in 6-ounce pouches, and 3-pound and 25-pound poly packs, which are airtight, plastic-lined bags. Some of these products are also packaged in metal or plastic containers.

Packaging Procedure

The packaging process is not a concern for most egg products that the typical hospitality buyer purchases. The types of packaging and packaging procedures for fresh shell eggs are very standardized, as they are for most processed products.

In a few instances, buyers may need to specify a desired packaging procedure. For example, if they want to purchase frozen, precooked, plain omelettes, they could purchase them individually wrapped and stacked neatly in the case, or in a layered arrangement, where they are separated by sheets of waxed paper. In some cases, then, it is possible for buyers to specify a combination of inner wrapping and outer wrapping that meets their needs.

Color

The breed of the hen determines the color of an egg. White-feathered chickens, such as the Leghorn, White Rock, and Cornish chickens, lay white eggs. Chickens with red feathers, such as the Rhode Island Red, New Hampshire, and Plymouth Rock chickens, lay brown eggs. Although no differences in flavor and nutrition have been proved, in some parts of the United States, such as New England, consumers request brown eggs. Consumers may perceive some psychological difference in shell color. So, in addition to a potential price difference between brown- and white-shell eggs, buyers must keep this customer preference in mind.

Product Form

In some instances, buyers may wish to purchase one or more convenience egg products. For example, they may want to buy precooked, refrigerated, whole, peeled eggs and use them to garnish their salad bar offerings. Alternately, buyers might wish to purchase cheese-stuffed, frozen, precooked omelettes. As always, the added value of the desired form will increase the AP prices, but the ultimate edible-portion (EP) costs may be quite affordable.

Preservation Method

Buyers should know how fresh and processed egg products are preserved, so that they can make additional judgments concerning the items' quality. The most common preservation methods are discussed in the following paragraphs:

Refrigeration This is the most common preservation method for fresh shell eggs. As fresh eggs get older, they lose quality: moisture dissipates, the white gets thinner, and the yolk becomes weaker. Refrigeration is the best deterrent to this quality loss. The FDA recommends that state and local health districts require fresh shell eggs to be received and stored at 45°F or less in order to minimize food-borne illnesses that can result if the eggs are contaminated with small amounts of salmonella bacteria. However, no federal law requiring egg refrigeration exists. Wise buyers do not jump to the conclusion that the fresh shell eggs they have purchased have been kept under constant refrigeration.

Oil Spraying or Dipping When a hen lays an egg, it puts a protective coating on the outside of the egg. At the plant, federal-government regulations require that

USDA-graded eggs be carefully washed and sanitized using a special detergent, which removes this coating. To counteract this, usually the egg is coated by the supplier with a tasteless, natural mineral oil. This helps to preserve egg freshness. Oil spraying is not quite as effective as refrigeration, though it is a reasonably effective alternative.

Overwrapping To retard moisture loss and the tendency for its yolk and white to thin, an egg can be doubly wrapped in heavy plastic film. If wrapped correctly, this method is superior to oiling eggs.

Controlled-Atmosphere Storage Some producers hold eggs in an oxygen-free environment. The oxygen is removed and replaced by carbon dioxide. As an egg ages, it loses moisture and carbon dioxide. The carbon dioxide in the environment acts as a counterpressure, thereby preventing the loss of carbon dioxide and keeping the egg white firm. This is an expensive method, but producers who wish or need to hold shell eggs for a while use it.

As a general rule, suppliers do not sell controlled-environment eggs to food-service operators. These eggs are intended for supermarket and grocery store distribution. As with fresh produce, once eggs are removed from the controlled atmosphere, their quality deteriorates very rapidly; hospitality operators cannot tolerate this problem.

The Processing Method When buyers purchase processed egg products, they are actually purchasing eggs that have been preserved in a manner other than in the shell. Among the most common forms of processed eggs are frozen whole eggs, frozen egg yolks, and frozen egg whites. Large bakeries normally use these products. Some labor savings are associated with these products since no one in the operation has to process them.

But problems are associated with these egg products, too. First, the freezing process must be conducted using optimal conditions and techniques. Frozen yolks will become rubbery if sugar or glycerine is not added to them before freezing and if they are not frozen correctly. Second, the thawing process for frozen eggs should be done in a controlled refrigerated temperature. (Operators should allow three to five days in the refrigerator for thawing a 30-pound can.) Unsupervised employees may not be patient enough to wait out this relatively long thawing procedure. Also, if frozen eggs are thawed at room temperature, harmful bacteria can multiply rapidly.

Other familiar forms of processed eggs used in food-service operations and large bakeries are dried eggs, dried egg yolks, and dried egg whites. Since reconstitution may be problematic, dried eggs are not normally used for scrambling. They tend to work better in recipes that call for eggs because cooks can measure them easily. The only possible problem associated with dried eggs, other than their reconstitution, is that some of the product may be scorched during the drying process. This is much less of a problem today due to improved processing technology. Spray drying, or spraying the liquid egg mixture into a heated environment, is a superior method. Freeze-drying, or freezing liquid eggs and going from the frozen state directly to the dried state, is also successful.

Buyers can purchase other types of processed egg products. For instance, they can order frozen deviled eggs and frozen, cooked scrambled eggs. These items are expensive because of the convenience they offer, but the potential labor savings might more than offset the high AP price.

Trust the Supplier

The problem with buying eggs is not so much selecting the quality: buyers will rarely go wrong if they stipulate U.S. grades for fresh shell eggs or if they settle on a particularly desirable brand name for a processed egg product. Buyers must be concerned with choosing the right supplier. Since suppliers abound in the egg trade, the choice can be wide. Buyers must make sure that a supplier can make adequate deliveries and moves only fresh product. Also, if buyers expect that fresh eggs be refrigerated, they may need to check that the supplier maintains the specific storage environment.

In addition to supplier services, buyers must consider purchasing options. Bid buying and becoming a house account are two alternatives. Both have their advantages and disadvantages, and buyers must make their choice.

PURCHASING EGGS

As usual, the first step in egg purchasing is for hospitality operators to determine precisely what they want. As noted earlier, fresh shell eggs present few problems: the most widely used quality is U.S. Grade A, and the normal size is large. However, considerably more combinations of qualities and sizes are available. As a result, management, either alone or in conjunction with other key employees, must determine the efficacy and usefulness of these combinations as they relate to a particular operation.

The qualities and styles of processed egg products are not so easily chosen. If buyers purchase these items, their best bet is to consider brand names. No federal quality standards exist for processed egg products (although buyers could specify that the processed product be prepared with fresh eggs of a certain U.S. grade); the convenience and reliability of the packer's brand name eventually become the overriding factors.

Once buyers make their decision, they need to prepare a complete specification that includes all pertinent information, whether or not they use it in bid buying. If nothing else, the discipline of preparing this document will help to ensure that buyers have considered all of the relevant factors and are, indeed, purchasing the egg product that suits their needs (see Figure 20.5 for some sample product specifications and Figure 20.6 for an example of a product specification outline for egg products.)

After determining what they need and when they need it, buyers must evaluate potential suppliers. Buyers will find a reasonable number of potential suppliers in the fresh-egg trade, which is good news for those who like the bid-buying strategy. The biggest problem in supplier selection probably involves determining which supplier provides the freshest eggs. A "U.S. Grade A" designation on the box is no guarantee of the quality of the eggs inside.

Fresh shell eggs
Used for fried, poached, scrambled eggs
U.S. Grade AA
Large
30 dozen per shipping case; 20 cases
Cartons labeled with an expiration date
   not to exceed 28 days from date of
   packaging
Eggs delivered within 7 days of official
   grading
White shell

Scrambled egg mix
Used for scrambled eggs on buffet
Fresh Start® brand
2-pound carton
Moisture-proof, vapor-proof carton
6 cartons per case
Refrigerated liquid

Meringue powder
Used to prepare dessert topping bakery
   products
R & H® brand
6-pound container
Plastic, resealable container
Unrefrigerated

Frozen, whole, shelled eggs
Used to prepare bakery products
McAnally® brand
30-pound container
Metal can

FIGURE 20.5   An example of egg product specifications.

Intended use:

Exact name:

U.S. grade (or equivalent):

Packer's brand name (or equivalent):

Product size:

Size of container:

Type of packaging material:

Packaging procedure:

Color:

Product form:

Preservation method:

FIGURE 20.6 **An example of a product specification outline for egg products.**

The processed-egg trade does not offer as many suppliers or brands. If buyers want dried eggs, the limited number of purveyors stocking them may be a surprise. Furthermore, if buyers want reduced-cholesterol eggs, they may find even fewer suppliers. Similarly, not too many producers carry such specialty items as frozen deviled eggs.

As we found with fresh produce, independent farmers are very active in the fresh-egg trade. But buyers should be wary of them. Keep in mind that their flocks may be too young or too old, and the hens may not be well managed. Also, independent farmers can purchase eggs from someone else and then resell them, implying that the eggs are from their own farms. Moreover, government inspectors may not check these farmers.

One potential advantage of buying from independent farmers is that they may be able to get shell eggs to buyers one or two days after laying. When purchasing from a typical supply house, buyers can expect to receive eggs that are almost a week old. But if the farmer does not provide refrigerated storage, the older egg may be a better buy because an unrefrigerated, 2-day-old egg has less quality than a refrigerated 7-day-old egg.

Another potential advantage might be the willingness of the independent farmer to bargain for an AP price based on an agreed-upon markup of the wholesale egg market price. This might represent a reasonable saving. Ordinarily, most suppliers are not eager to use this type of pricing technique except for their large customers.

Before purchasing any egg product, buyers should take some time to evaluate the substitution possibilities. Several processed items substitute nicely for fresh eggs, and vice versa. If buyers purchase a lot of eggs, it may pay for them to have recipes printed several ways to include various forms of eggs and egg substitutions. For example, cake recipes might be written to incorporate fresh eggs, dried eggs, or frozen eggs. If the AP prices vary favorably, a few minutes of cost calculation might signal that one of these recipes is demonstrably more economical than the others.

RECEIVING EGGS

When receiving fresh shell eggs, receivers should take the time to examine them carefully for cracks, dirt, and lack of uniformity. They should also check the temperature to see if the eggs are at 45°F or lower without being frozen. In addition, receivers should make sure that all of the eggs are there. Weighing the containers might be the easiest quantity check.

It is difficult for receiving personnel to determine the age of fresh eggs. The American Egg Board recommends that receivers randomly break a few eggs and inspect them to determine if they meet the guidelines of their given grade.[2] The delivery agents may think that the receivers have lost their mind if they expect the agents to wait around while they conduct this ritual. But a little skepticism never hurt a buyer.

Processed eggs usually require other sorts of inspection. Assuming that all of the products ordered have been delivered, receivers then need to assess the quality of the items. This is not very easy. Receivers can check frozen egg products to see whether any crystallization has occurred; this is an indication of refreezing. They can also use a temperature probe to test frozen egg products.

Furthermore, receivers are able to check the can pressure of any canned dried egg products; devices on the market make this quick, simple test possible. An abnormally high pressure could indicate that a can's contents are contaminated.

If receivers do not take or make the time to check egg quality, or if they do not have the time, they must trust their supplier and delivery agent. Because processed-egg quality is always difficult to determine, we suppose that a certain degree of trust is inherent here in any case.

After checking the quality and quantity, receivers should check the prices and complete the appropriate accounting procedures.

STORING EGGS

Fresh eggs should be refrigerated as soon as possible at 45°F or below, but do not freeze them. Eggs stored at 45°F or below will retain their quality for weeks. In addition, since these items pick up odors quickly, they should be kept in their original containers. Some large operations maintain a dairy refrigerator to keep fresh eggs away from particularly odorous products, such as onions, fish, cabbage, and apples (see Figure 20.7). Processed eggs also require a specific storage environment, either frozen or dry storage, suggested by the form in which they come.

Egg Safety and Quality

STORAGE
* Refrigerate at 45°F or below (do not freeze)
* Store away from strong odors
* Rotate—first in/first out

HANDLING
* Wash hands
* Use only clean, uncracked eggs
* Use clean, sanitized utensils and equipment

PREPARATION
* Cook eggs thoroughly
* Hold cold egg dishes below 40°F
* Hold hot egg dishes above 140°F
* Never leave egg dishes at room temperature more than 1 hour (including preparation and service)

The incredible edible egg

American Egg Board
1460 Renaissance Drive
Park Ridge, Illinois 60068

FIGURE 20.7 An American Egg Board egg safety and quality flyer. Courtesy of the American Egg Board.

ISSUING EGGS

Hospitality operators should properly rotate stock, so that the oldest items are issued first. This may be accomplished by dating containers as they are received. In some cases, the egg purchases go straight into production. If operators issue eggs from a central storeroom, they must make sure, for example, that the requisitioner who wants eggs for a cake recipe gets the frozen or dried eggs, if applicable.

Because fresh shell eggs deteriorate rapidly once they leave refrigeration, operators must ensure that the requisitioner takes no more than he or she needs for any one particular work shift or job. They might consider asking the requisitioner to take note of the in-process inventory before asking for additional stock.

IN-PROCESS INVENTORIES

The benefit of good purchasing effectiveness can be immediately offset if hospitality operators do not control in-process inventories. For example, if breakfast cooks leave fresh shell eggs out at room temperature all day, the egg quality could drop a grade. The same is true of processed eggs. As always, supervision is the key. Without it, there is little sense in buyers taking care to purchase the proper items for the production staff. The best a supervisor can do is insist that all eggs be kept in the recommended environment at all times and removed from this environment only when necessary.

KEY WORDS AND CONCEPTS

As-purchased (AP price)

Breaker plants

Candling

Color

Controlled-atmosphere storage

Cost per ounce of fresh shell eggs

Cryovac

Edible-portion cost (EP cost)

Egg Products Inspection Act (EPIA)

Exact name

Food Safety and Inspection Service (FSIS)

Fresh-egg flat

Fresh shell eggs

Grading factors

Independent farmer

In-process inventories

Intended use

Large egg, most typical size purchased

Packaging material

Packaging procedure

Packers' brands

Potentially hazardous food

Preservation method

Processed eggs

Processing method

Product form

Product size

Purchasing, receiving, storing, and issuing eggs

Shrink-wrap

Size of container

Storage eggs

United States Department of Agriculture (USDA)

U.S. grades

REFERENCES

1. American Egg Board, *Eggcyclopedia,* 3rd ed. (Park Ridge, IL: American Egg Board, 1994).

2. American Egg Board, *The Incredible Edible Egg: A Natural for Any Foodserive Operation* (Park Ridge, IL: American Egg Board, 2003). See also:

American Egg Board, *Egg Handling and Care Guide,* 2nd ed. (Park Ridge, IL: American Egg Board, 2000); for more information about eggs, visit http://www.aeb.org.

QUESTIONS AND PROBLEMS

1. What are the U.S. grades for fresh shell eggs?

2. List the sizes for fresh shell eggs.

3. What procedure can receivers follow to determine the freshness of shell eggs?

4. What will be the AP price per ounce of a large shell egg at $1.25 per dozen?

5. Assume that you are the manager of an employee food service. Outline the specific procedures you would use for the purchasing, receiving, storing, and issuing of fresh shell eggs that will be used for 3-minute eggs. If possible, ask an employee foodservice manager to comment on your answer.

6. Assume that your buffet brunch has another hour to go and that you have just run out of fresh eggs. You were preparing omelettes and scrambled eggs for use on the buffet line. You have a couple of cans of dried eggs and one can of frozen eggs in storage. Can you use these processed eggs to tide you over? If not, what do you suggest? If possible, ask a foodservice manager to comment on your answer.

7. An independent farmer calls on your country club to solicit its fresh-egg business. The following offer is made: daily delivery, eggs no more than a day old, an AP price 2 cents higher than the AP prices other suppliers charge. What do you suggest? (*Hint:* Eggs that are too fresh should not be used for hard-boiled eggs because the shells may be difficult to peel; otherwise, we know of no problems with very fresh eggs.) If possible, ask a country club manager to comment on your answer.

8. Assume that you are the kitchen supervisor for a resort hotel. Your Sunday brunch normally includes scrambled eggs. Your cooks have been preparing them in a steamer and serving them in a chafing dish; customers then help themselves. The quality of this product is not as good as you would like it to be, but the alternative of scrambling a few eggs at a time to order is not viable. You could purchase frozen scrambled eggs packed in 5-pound Cryovac bags. These eggs need only to be steam-heated for 20 minutes. Their quality, in your opinion, is superb. But the AP price is very high—approximately three times the price of fresh eggs. What do you suggest? If possible, ask a resort hotel's food and beverage director or kitchen supervisor to comment on your answer.

9. What is an appropriate intended use for frozen whole eggs?

10. What is an appropriate intended use for dried egg whites?

11. A product specification for dried eggs could include the following information:
    (a)
    (b)
    (c)
    (d)
    (e)

12. A foodservice buyer normally specifies the large-size fresh egg because:
    (a)
    (b)

13. What are the two typical package sizes for fresh shell eggs?

14. Fresh shell eggs can be preserved in the following ways:
    (a)
    (b)
    (c)

15. What happens to a fresh shell egg as it becomes older?

16. What is the preferred preservation method for fresh shell eggs?

17. When is a fresh shell egg at its highest quality?

18. A "flat" contains _____ dozen fresh shell eggs.

19. What are the primary grading factors for fresh shell egg grades?

20. What is the primary indication of quality of a processed egg product?

21. What is the difference between the designations "U.S. Grade A" and "Grade A"?

22. When would buyers purchase reduced-cholesterol egg products?

23. A product specification for frozen omelettes could include the following information:
    (a)
    (b)
    (c)
    (d)
    (e)

24. What is an appropriate intended use for U.S. Grade B shell eggs?

25. What critical information is missing from the following product specification for a frozen egg mix?
    Frozen egg mix
    Used for low-fat entrées
    EggBeaters® brand

21
POULTRY

The Purpose of this Chapter

After reading this chapter, you should be able to:

- Explain the selection factors for poultry, including government grades.
- Describe the process of purchasing, receiving, storing, and issuing poultry.

INTRODUCTION

"Poultry" is a term applied to all domesticated birds used for food. Poultry is not an especially difficult item to purchase, unless you are in the market for certain types of processed items. Generally, raw poultry is still considered to be a "commodity," which means the typical buyer does not perceive a great deal of difference between one frying chicken and another.

The poultry that food services typically buy are chicken, turkey, and duckling. On occasion, some might also purchase goose, squab, and Cornish hen (see Figure 21.1). For the most part, a specific class of bird is raised the same way all over the country. For example, frying chickens are raised in about eight weeks. They consume a relatively standardized diet—standardized, at least, according to nutritional needs—and are slaughtered, cleaned, and packed with similar produc-

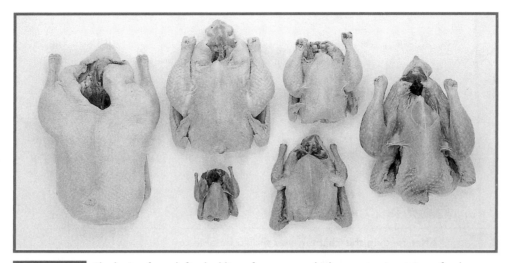

FIGURE 21.1 Clockwise from left: duckling, free-range chicken, poussin, guinea fowl, squab, quail. Copyright © 2003, John Wiley & Sons, Inc. This material is used by permission of John Wiley & Sons, Inc.

tion line techniques. In short, raising any bird these days is a standard, scientific undertaking. Hospitality operators find very few small-scale producers, although a few independent farmers here and there may seek their business.

As with other products, the operators' major problem is deciding exactly what they want. If they want fresh or fresh-frozen poultry, they will have several suppliers from which to choose. Also, unless the buyers include packers' brands of fresh poultry, the as-purchased (AP) price will be about the same among the suppliers, provided, of course, that these suppliers offer the same quality and supplier services.

If buyers want other types of processed poultry, they obviously face the question of the degree of convenience they would like built into the products. They can usually purchase whole, dressed birds (it is not easy to purchase live birds today); cut-up birds; and precooked, prebreaded, presliced, and prerolled poultry. Numerous processed poultry products, as well as some imitation items, are available.

Only a few food processors undertake some types of processing. For instance, buyers can purchase cut-up frying chickens from a variety of sources. But they can purchase canned, cooked whole chickens from only a few suppliers.

In general, buyers will encounter little difficulty when purchasing poultry items. Numerous suppliers exist, and numerous styles of poultry items are available in the market.

SELECTION FACTORS

As with all products, the owner-manager normally decides the quality, type, and style of poultry products desired. Either alone or in cooperation with other employees, the owner-manager usually evaluates the following selection factors when determining the desired standards of quality and, to a certain degree, the supplier for poultry items.

Intended Use

As always, buyers want to determine exactly the intended use of the item so that they will be able to prepare the appropriate, relevant specification. For example, poultry used for soup will differ from that needed for a deep-fried menu item.

Buyers may want to select a poultry item they can use for two or three purposes. This approach is not ordinarily recommended because each item has one best use. However, poultry has a short shelf life, especially if it is fresh. Consequently, fresh poultry should be turned quickly. One way for buyers to do this is to use the poultry they purchase in several different dishes.

If buyers purchase a lot of poultry, they should examine the substitution possibilities because bargains may await them. They might, for instance, substitute turkey rolls for turkey breasts or for whole turkeys. They could also substitute canned poultry for fresh; purchase precooked, chopped chicken pieces if the intended use is for chicken salad; and use precooked sliced turkey breast instead of cooking their own.

Substitutions can disrupt the production and service functions, however. In addition, buyers must, of course, keep track of the distinctive culinary differences between these items. The culinary quality varies for at least two reasons: (1) for different menu items, food processors use poultry of different ages; and (2) the processing method itself could rob or add favorable qualities.

A major issue with any processed product centers on the substitution possibilities and on how much convenience buyers want built into it. Whatever type of processing they want, they have a generous number of suppliers from which to choose, which gives them additional flexibility. Poultry products encourage bid buying.

Exact Name

This is an important consideration because the federal government has established standards of identity for many poultry items. For example, some fresh products are standardized according to the birds' sex and/or age at the time of slaughter (see Figure 21.2).

Age can affect the intended use of the poultry. Poultry to be cooked with dry heat should be young if buyers want a tender product. (As poultry ages, it becomes less tender. However, it also develops more fat, which carries flavor.) If chefs want to simmer a chicken for chicken soup, buyers would probably opt for an old bird. It will have more flavor, and moist heat will ensure tenderness. As a bonus, an old bird tends to have a high conversion weight, that is, a high edible yield. If a bird gets too old, though, much of the weight begins to collect in the abdominal fat. This fat can be collected and used for, perhaps, a roux for cream of chicken soup. But the yield of cooked meat per pound of raw chicken may be less than expected because of the extra fat.

Sex is not particularly important for young birds, but in older birds, the differences in taste, texture, and yield diverge dramatically between the sexes. Females tend to be tastier, juicier, and have higher conversion weights than males. So, if

---

CHICKEN

Young (tender) birds

Broiler/fryer—9 to 12 weeks old; $1^1/_2$ to $3^1/_2$ pounds; either sex

Roaster—3 to 5 months old; $3^1/_2$ to 6 pounds; either sex

Capon—less than 8 months old; 6 to 10 pounds; desexed male bird

Cornish game hen—5 to 7 weeks old; 1 to $1^1/_2$ pounds; immature bird

Old (less tender) birds

Stewing hen—more than 10 months old; 3 to 7 pounds; mature female bird

Stag—more than 10 months old; 3 to 7 pounds; mature male bird

TURKEY

Fryer/roaster—less than 16 weeks old; 4 to 8 pounds; either sex

Young hen—5 to 7 months old; 8 to 14 pounds; female bird

Young tom—5 to 7 months old; over 12 pounds; male bird

Yearling hen—under 15 months old; up to 30 pounds; mature female bird

Yearling tom—under 15 months old; up to 30 pounds; mature male bird

DUCK

Duckling—under 8 weeks old; under 4 pounds; either sex

Duck—over 16 weeks old; 4 to 6 pounds; either sex

FIGURE 21.2 **Definitions of some poultry products.**

buyers purchase mature poultry, they should take note of the birds' sex, especially if they are bid buying.

As with other product lines, buyers occasionally encounter market terminology that defines very specifically what a poultry product is. For instance, "free-range" chickens are allowed to roam free instead of spending their lives in cages. "Kosher" chickens, prepared according to Jewish dietary laws, are also allowed to roam free, are usually a strong breed, tend to be a little older at the time of slaughter in order to promote flavor development, and are free of hormones and other chemical and artificial ingredients. Since these types of poultry products are usually much more expensive than those raised in the traditional way, buyers must not use this terminology carelessly.

If buyers purchase processed poultry products, merely noting the exact name may not be enough because even though standards of identity exist for such products as chicken pot pies, the producers of these items need to meet only some minimum standard. Also, even though buyers may not be averse to a producer's particular formula, they must keep in mind that chicken pot pies can come with several onion varieties and potato varieties. If buyers are dealing with fresh poultry, either whole birds or standardized parts, using the exact name is normally adequate because these fresh items are more consistent among producers. But the same cannot be said for processed products. These items can and will vary significantly among producers, so overreliance on standards of identity for them can be a bit chancy.

U.S. Government Grades (or Equivalent)

Poultry inspection became mandatory with the 1957 Poultry Products Inspection Act. This law applies to all raw poultry sold in interstate commerce, as well as to such processed products as canned and frozen items.

Some states conduct their own poultry inspection programs, and the 1968 Wholesome Poultry Products Act requires state programs to be at least equal to the federal inspection program. Poultry inspected under a state program, however, can be sold only within that state. Any poultry product transported across state lines or exported to another country must be produced under continuous federal inspection. In states that do not conduct inspection programs, all plants are required to be under continuous federal-government inspection (see Figures 21.3 and 21.4).

The Food Safety and Quality Service (FSQS) of the United States Department of Agriculture (USDA) performs federal inspection for wholesomeness and federal grading (see Figure 21.4a and 21.4b). Assuming that the product is wholesome, a poultry producer can elect to purchase the grading service.

FIGURE 21.3 Federal grade and inspection stamps used for poultry products. *Source*: United States Department of Agriculture.

Some states leave poultry producers no choice: they must have their products federally graded after they are inspected. As a practical matter, most poultry product specifications contain a U.S. grade designation. Consequently, producers have little choice in the matter.

Federal inspectors grade poultry according to several grading factors. Inspectors, or graders, consider: (1) conformation (Does the bird have good form?); (2) fleshing (Does the bird have a well-developed covering of flesh?); (3) fat covering (Does any flesh show through the skin—that is, is it a "thin-skinned" bird?); and (4) other factors (Does the bird have any bruises, excessive pin feathers left after cleaning, broken bones, missing parts, or discoloration?).

Several poultry grades exist. The consumer grades are as follows:

1. **Grade A.** This is the top poultry quality produced. It indicates a full-fleshed bird that is well finished and has an attractive appearance.

2. **Grade B.** This bird usually has some dressing defects, such as a torn skin. Also, the bird is, generally, less attractive. For example, it might be slightly lacking in fleshing, and the breast bone may be very visible.

3. **Grade C.** This bird resembles a Grade B bird, but it lacks even more in appearance. Also, parts of its carcass might be missing.

In addition to consumer grades, the federal government offers a "procurement" grading system, which consists of two procurement grades: I and II. These grades are intended for use by noncommercial, "institutional" food services and are based almost entirely on the amount of edible yield the poultry products contain. The appearance of the birds is deemphasized.

Some state and local markets use the following three commercial grades: Extra, Standard, and No Grade. They are similar to procurement grades, although the tolerances between these grades are wider than those of the consumer and procurement grades.

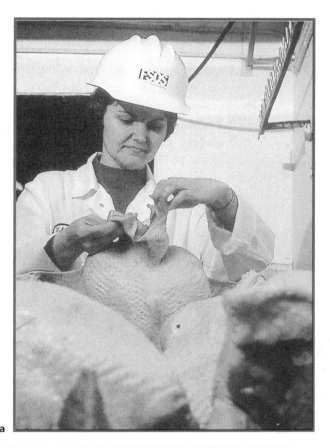

FIGURE 21.4 (*a*) and (*b*) FSQS inspecting the wholesomeness of poultry. *Source:* United States Department of Agriculture.

a

b

A specification for poultry products usually contains some grade reference. This is especially true when buyers purchase fresh or fresh-frozen whole birds or parts. If buyers purchase processed products, such as prebreaded, precooked chicken patties, they are more apt to rely on a packer's brand name to specify the desired quality.

The use of U.S. grades for poultry, especially the consumer grades, is very popular in the foodservice industry. Buyers usually opt for U.S. Grade A products when appearance is very important. For instance, chefs would most often prepare a fried-chicken entrée with the highest-quality raw products. Lower grades of poultry are usually sold to food processors. These grades are often referred to as "manufacturing grades" because they are not usually intended for foodservice operations unless they undergo some sort of processing that alters their appearance and culinary quality. When appearance is not as important to a hospitality operation, such as when poultry is used to prepare chicken salads, turkey casseroles, or pot pies in the operation's kitchen, these lesser grades may be adequate.

More information on grading regulations and standards of poultry is available online. Buyers can find regulations governing the grading of poultry and rabbits (7 CFR Part 70) at www.ams.usda.gov/poultry/regulations. In addition, they can find U.S. classes, standards, and grades for poultry (AMS 70.200 *et seq.*) at www.ams.usda.gov/poultry/standards.

Packers' Brands (or Equivalent)

For fresh and fresh-frozen poultry, brand loyalty rarely comes into play. Buyers seem to rely a little more on specific brands of raw turkey or duck. But this does not seem to be the case with raw chicken, which is usually viewed as a basic commodity.

Some manufacturers attempt to take poultry out of the commodity class and instill brand loyalty in consumers, who have several brands from which to choose. For instance, Perdue®, Tyson®, and Foster Farms® are some of the brand labels buyers can specify for fresh chicken.

Some value, as well as a higher AP price, is associated with proprietary chicken brand names. For example, producers generally slow down the assembly line to use a "soft-scald" procedure, which removes feathers at a lower temperature, thereby significantly increasing the tenderness of the birds. Some producers use a "chill pack" preservation procedure for their finished products. This maintains the chickens' temperature at about 28°F to 29°F (they freeze at about 27°F to 28°F), which extends the products' shelf life without freezing them. Furthermore, these brand name items are usually produced in exceptionally clean environments. Very high levels of sanitation will increase the products' shelf life because it is directly related to the numbers of bacteria found on the skin of the birds.

The brand name campaign seems aimed primarily at homemakers, however. Hospitality operations that list a lot of poultry signature items on their menus strive to ensure that their customers identify such poultry with the operations that prepare it, and not with a particular packer's brand name. Generally, packers' brands are important to hospitality buyers only when they purchase processed poultry products.

Product Size

When purchasing raw poultry products, buyers usually cannot specify an exact product size. Instead, they must indicate the acceptable weight range. For example, they need to indicate a weight range for whole birds and, to some extent, for raw poultry parts, such as chicken thighs and turkey breasts.

As a general rule, the larger the bird, the higher its edible yield. Buyers might find it helpful—and interesting—to know that, for example, a turkey's bone structure stops developing when it reaches about 20 pounds. Turkeys that weigh more than 20 pounds have more fat and a bit more meat on the same-size skeleton as "thinner" birds. If the operations' intended use allows, their buyers should purchase large birds because these may be the most economical choice.

Buyers also must note the product size of any processed products that their operations need. Fortunately, they normally can specify an exact size for these items and do not have to rely on weight ranges. Many sizes are available for such products as precooked, breaded chicken breasts; chicken patties; and turkey pot pies.

Product Yield

For some poultry products, such as frozen, breaded chicken patties, buyers may want to indicate the maximum yield, or the minimum trim, expected. For example, they may want to note on the specification that they will accept no more than two broken pieces in a 48-piece container of chicken patties.

Size of Container

As always, buyers must indicate the package size that they prefer. If necessary, they would need to note the size of any inner packs. For instance, buyers may want a

30-pound case of frozen chicken chow mein, with six 5-pound plastic pouches per case.

Type of Packaging Material

A reasonable variety of packaging quality is available, so buyers would do well to consider this selection factor when preparing their specifications. The variety is considerable for fresh product—for instance, fresh poultry may arrive at your back door wrapped in butcher paper; packed in cardboard or wooden crates; packed in shrink wrap, or packed in large, reusable plastic containers that the suppliers will pick up when they deliver the next shipment. The relatively brief shelf life of fresh items makes it necessary for buyers to reject packaging that would do anything to shorten a product's shelf life drastically.

When buyers purchase several types of processed products, they will experience a greater variety of packaging qualities. Normally, processed items used in the hospitality industry are packed in moisture-proof, vapor-proof materials that are designed to withstand freezer temperatures. Buyers must be certain that the items they purchase in this manner are packaged properly so that they can avoid any unnecessary loss of product.

Packaging Procedure

Like most products, poultry is packaged in many different ways. For instance, most raw, refrigerated items are slab-packed, while their frozen counterparts are usually layered. Whole birds, typically, are individually wrapped if they are frozen, whereas fresh, refrigerated birds may not be; in fact, fresh birds may be slab-packed with crushed ice covering them, which is sometimes referred to as an "ice pack procedure."

Fresh or frozen boneless poultry products are sometimes packaged in "cello packs." Products packed this way usually come in a 5-pound box that has six cello-wrapped portions, each of which contains two to four poultry pieces.

Fresh birds or bird parts can also come in "gas-flushed packs." In this arrangement, the poultry is placed in plastic bags, and the air is "flushed" out of the bag and replaced with carbon dioxide. This packaging procedure, which is a type of controlled-atmosphere packaging, is done primarily to extend the fresh poultry's shelf life.

Some fresh, refrigerated products can be purchased in a "marinade pack." Here, suppliers pack individual poultry parts, for example, chicken wings, in a reusable plastic tub and pour a specific marinade solution over them. The chicken wings then absorb the required flavor as they journey through the channel of distribution, so that by the time they are delivered to the hospitality operation's back door, they can be put directly into production.

Most processed poultry products that the typical hospitality operation purchases are frozen and layered. These items are usually referred to as "individually quick frozen" (IQF). This designation indicates that the products are flash-frozen and layered in the case. In some instances, they may even be individually wrapped.

IQF is sometimes referred to as a "snap pack" or "shatter pack." When you remove a layer of product and drop it onto a counter top, the pieces should snap apart cleanly. If they don't, it's likely the product has been refrozen.

Product Form

One of the amazing aspects of the poultry trade is the seemingly endless number of products available and the forms in which buyers can purchase them. At one extreme are the raw products, while at the other extreme several artificial meat items, such as "ham" and "hot dogs," are produced with poultry.

If buyers purchase whole birds, they will have the option of receiving them whole or they can request that the birds be cut into a specific number of pieces. Buyers also may be able to specify a particular cutting pattern, although the standards of identity the federal government has established address this issue fairly well; hence, it is often unnecessary to dwell on this aspect.

When purchasing whole birds, buyers can opt to have the variety meats included or excluded. These are the organ meats, such as the liver and heart. Because they are not usually included with whole birds intended for use by foodservice establishments, if buyers want them, they normally will need to indicate this desire on the specification. Ordinarily, if foodservice operators need to purchase variety meats, they will buy them separately; for example, chicken livers are normally purchased separately, packed in a 5-pound Cryovac® bag.

Sometimes raw poultry, especially raw-poultry parts, includes a bit of cutting and trimming that adds to the AP price of the items, but enhances their convenience. For example, buyers can order boneless, skinless chicken breasts. This convenience, while initially a costly alternative, could, in the long run, result in the most economic edible-portion (EP) costs.

If buyers need to purchase a good deal of highly processed poultry products, such as precooked turkey rolls or frozen, preprepared chicken chow mein, and are not satisfied with the federal-government minimum standards of identity, they will need to do something to indicate the particular type of formula they want. For example, they may find it necessary to specify in great detail a chicken patty's proportion of white and dark meat, the amount and type of breading, and so forth. Buyers might be able to utilize a packer's brand, one that resembles what they want, but this convenience may not always be available.

Preservation Method

Most poultry purchased for use in the hospitality industry is preserved in one of two ways: refrigerated or frozen. Many refrigerated products are packed at chill pack temperatures. If suppliers do not provide the chill pack alternative, usually they will provide the ice pack method, which tends to accomplish the same effect as the chill pack—namely, the reduction of the storage temperature to just above freezing. Both chill packs and ice packs maintain temperatures of about 28°F to 29°F.

Foodservice operations that strive for a good poultry reputation usually purchase fresh, ice-packed, or chill-packed poultry. For instance, if fried chicken is an operation's signature item, it is very unlikely that the firm will use a frozen item because it can cause several problems. These items can, for example, very easily thaw just a bit during the receiving cycle and become freezer-burned when they refreeze in storage. In addition, frozen poultry products get a red tinge around the bones when they are cooked. Furthermore, these items lose flavor and moisture when they are thawed too long before cooking.

Some fresh poultry (as well as fresh meat, fish, and produce) may be preserved with irradiation. Irradiation removes almost all traces of harmful bacteria in meat and fish, and spoilage bacteria in fresh produce. However, many critics maintain that nutrients are lost during the irradiation process and that not enough information is known about the safety of this procedure. As a result, many food services are not eager to embrace this technology.

Generally, buyers purchase processed poultry products in the frozen state. Some canned products exist, but the typical hospitality operation seldom uses them. For instance, buyers could purchase either frozen or canned chicken noodle soup. The canned item is usually less expensive, but many foodservice operators opt for the frozen variety because the culinary quality is superior.

AP Price

Raw-poultry products offer little spread in AP price from one supplier to another. The distance that a finished poultry item must travel to get to a hospitality operation's back door, does, however, make a difference. For example, Colorado free-range chicken usually costs more than a similar item raised closer to home. But given the same style of poultry, the same quality, and the same supplier services, the AP prices are pretty much identical.

In addition, AP prices for raw products tend to be more predictable because farmers can produce poultry much more easily and quickly than many other foods. For instance, it takes about two years to bring a steer from birth to the dining room table. With a frying chicken, this process takes only a few weeks. Also, fresh-poultry AP prices reflect the standardized, scientific management used in raising poultry. For instance, suppliers use pretty much the same feeding formulas and environments so that the poultry looks the same, tastes the same, and has the same conversion weight. Since AP prices vary little, the EP costs, theoretically, should also be similar between competing suppliers' raw products.

AP prices vary quite a bit for processed items, however, and this requires buyers to estimate EP costs as well as customer acceptance of these processed products. So, if buyers purchase a lot of chicken, they should consider entering into long-term contracts or, at least, using the hedging technique discussed in Chapter 10. Buyers may be able to maintain an AP price that they can live with by hedging in the commodity futures market. In addition, quantity buys offer reasonably good savings.

Trust the Supplier

No matter what type of poultry buyers purchase—fresh or processed—they can find several potential suppliers in the marketplace. Hospitality operations do not need to become house accounts unless they want to.

The AP prices of raw poultry do not vary significantly among suppliers. Consequently, bid buying these items may not be as profitable as it is for processed products, unless, of course, buyers can get some additional service. For instance, if they purchase fresh poultry, they will want to keep it at a temperature of at least about 30°F to 35°F. Also, they might want the supplier or processor to cut up the poultry and put it into a marinade. Alternately, they might want a whole chicken cut into eight, nine, or ten parts, depending on the intended use. Not every supplier can provide these services. But if two or three have these capabilities, buyers might consider bidding out their business once in a while.

In our experience, buyers tend, eventually, to become fresh-poultry house accounts; that is, they tend to purchase from one trusted supplier. This product requires at least a 30°F to 35°F temperature environment, as well as one that is very sanitary. We have known buyers whose only evaluation of a fresh-poultry supplier centered on the odor emanating from his or her poultry storage refrigerator. To these buyers, a clean refrigerator meant a reliable supplier.

Several suppliers sell various processed poultry items. The exact one buyers want, though, may be available from only one purveyor.

If buyers are very particular, they may find that they have to cast their lot with one supplier. If they are satisfied with a variety of choices, bid buying and extra negotiating might generate rewards.

PURCHASING POULTRY

As always, the first step in purchasing is for buyers to decide on the quality and type of product they want. For fresh poultry, and even for some processed poultry, they may find few suppliers who can provide exactly what they want, particularly if they have special requirements. As we have noted, though, usually enough potential suppliers exist to satisfy bid buyers.

Buyers normally use U.S. Grade A quality for poultry, especially when appearance is important. Of course, they can buy several combinations when other grades are available. However, buyers cannot always assume that Grade B is available for every item, since most producers strive to achieve the Grade A.

Once buyers know what they want, it is usually beneficial for them to prepare a complete specification. This should include all pertinent information, whether or not they use it in bid buying, simply because the discipline of preparing this written document helps to ensure that buyers have considered all relevant factors and are, indeed, purchasing the right quality and quantity (see Figure 21.5 for some example product specifications, and Figure 21.6 for an example product specification outline for poultry products).

After preparing the specs, buyers must evaluate potential suppliers. Keep in mind that for raw poultry, the important consideration probably is supplier services, since quality and AP prices usually vary only a little. Buyers need to consider such matters as freshness, delivery capabilities, temperature control, and plant appearance. Buyers usually can find many processed poultry product suppliers, but not too many if they have strict requirements. For example, if buyers want turkey or chicken cold cuts, they will not find many suppliers.

As in the fresh-produce and fresh-egg trades, independent farmers can probably supply poultry. We do not recommend this, however, unless a farmer's products and plant are under continuous inspection.

Broiler/fryer, raw
Used for fried chicken lunch entrée
U.S. Grade A
Quarter chicken parts, cut from
    whole birds weighing between
    $2^{1}/_{2}$ to $3^{1}/_{4}$ lb. dressed weight
No variety meats
Ice packed in reusable plastic tubs
Approximately 30 lb. per tub

Boneless chicken breast, raw
Used for dinner entrée
Tyson® brand
4-oz. portions
48, 4-oz. portions packed per case
Moisture-proof, vapor-proof case
    with plastic "cell-pack" inserts;
    products layered in cell packs
Frozen

Chicken base
Used to prepare soups and sauces
Minor's® brand
16-oz. resealable plastic containers
12 containers packed per case
Refrigerated

Turkey breast, raw
Used for sandwiches
U.S. Grade A
Bone in, skin on
Under 8 lbs.
Wrapped in Cryovac® (or equivalent)
Refrigerated

FIGURE 21.5 An example of poultry product specifications.

Intended use:

Exact name:

U.S. grade (or equivalent):

Packer's brand name (or equivalent):

Product size:

Product yield:

Size of container:

Type of packaging material:

Packaging procedure:

Product form:

Preservation method:

FIGURE 21.6 An example of a product specification outline for poultry products.

RECEIVING POULTRY

First, when accepting poultry, receivers must make the customary quality and quantity checks. Because harmful bacteria can multiply rapidly on poultry, especially at room temperatures, many hospitality operations receive and inspect poultry in refrigerated storage. The delivery agent and the receiver go straight to this area.

The raw-poultry quality check is not difficult. The grade shield is usually displayed prominently on the carton, and with whole poultry, on the wing of each bird. But receivers must be careful that the boxes have not been repacked. They can never be quite sure of what is in the boxes, regardless of the grade noted on the carton. A trustworthy supplier is the best insurance.

The quality check can cause some trouble if receivers are concerned with the age of the poultry. For instance, buyers might purchase hens to get the flavorful meat. But how do receivers know whether the hens are as old as they should be? Receivers can look at their size and amount of abdominal fat. To the trained eye, this check is routine. But some receiving agents lack this skill.

Processed products usually require other types of quality checks. Receivers must perform the normal checks of frozen products—looking for proper temperature, signs of thawing and refreezing, and inadequate packaging—and of canned products—looking for leaks, rust, and swollen cans.

Once receivers are satisfied with the quality, they must check quantity. Normally, buyers purchase poultry by the pound or by the bird. Also, some poultry comes packed in ice, which tends to make weighing difficult. Receivers might have to weigh enough birds to see whether they are within the weight range that the buyers have specified. As such, they may have to dig around in the ice a little or weigh the poultry with the ice on it. It is preferable, however, to temporarily remove the ice before weighing the poultry. Another option is to weigh the packer's brand, prepackaged, chill pack chicken to compare it with the weight stated on the label.

Receiving agents also need to check the types of parts, variety meats, and processed items they get. Sometimes, buyers order legs and receivers get wings, buyers order chicken livers and receivers get gizzards, or buyers order chicken franks and receivers get turkey franks. These are usually honest mistakes, but they can ruin a production schedule.

Receiving agents can streamline the poultry-receiving process by using the USDA's Acceptance Service. This service is popular among large foodservice operators for meat and poultry items. Remember also that buyers can hire an inspector to help them write specifications. Also, under the Acceptance Service, the federal inspector, or the state counterpart, will accept or reject the product according to what the buyers specify.

Finally, after making quality and quantity checks, receivers must check the prices and complete the appropriate accounting procedures.

STORING POULTRY

Hospitality operators should store fresh and frozen poultry immediately and at the proper temperatures and humidity in the environment its form suggests.

Fresh poultry has a short shelf life. Following proper storage practices can extend this shelf life from three to four days to up to a week. For example, if chickens are received in an ice pack, they should be stored as is, but in such a way that any melted ice runs out of the storage package and does not soak into the birds. As the ice melts, operators should add more ice, but usually not more often than every other day. When receivers get poultry items packed without ice, they can increase the shelf life by placing them in a perforated pan, layering in ice, and refrigerating them. This maintains the temperature at approximately 28°F to 29°F.

Some operations may wish to marinate their poultry to lengthen the shelf life; this imparts a distinctive flavor as well. They can also extend poultry's shelf life by precooking it, though this could hamper their standard production schedule. Whatever storage procedures they follow, operators should not handle poultry any more than is absolutely necessary. If improperly handled, it will become contaminated.

Since poultry is expensive, operators might consider keeping a perpetual inventory of it. To do this, they need to enter the appropriate information into their inventory management system.

ISSUING POULTRY

If hospitality operators use a perpetual inventory system, they must deduct the quantity issued. If applicable, they will need to make the following decision: Should they issue the item as is, or should they issue it as ready-to-go (for example, cut-up and breaded, or precut)? Recall that any choice involves several advantages and disadvantages.

Operators should follow proper stock rotation guidelines when issuing these items. Also, since these products, especially fresh ones, deteriorate rapidly and are expensive, operators must make sure that the requisitioner does not take more than is absolutely necessary. If they can, they should force this person to note the in-process inventory before asking for more poultry.

IN-PROCESS INVENTORIES

Depending on the type of poultry product, several degrees of waste are possible. For example, it is easy for a chef to burn a breaded poultry item on the outside while failing to cook it thoroughly on the inside. Similarly, if a chef is carving a whole roast turkey, a lot of usable meat can stick to the bones. Also, leaving a roast turkey under a glow lamp too long can make a once beautiful roast turkey collapse into charred rubble.

If hospitality operators use several types of poultry, they need to keep them straight. For example, a cook might unknowingly use the chopped, cooked chicken slated for chicken salad in the soup.

Probably the biggest consideration with in-process poultry inventory is the sanitation problem. Staphylococcus and salmonella bacteria should not be present on cooked poultry products. However, when poultry items are contaminated after cooking, usually by a human handler or by being placed on a contaminated surface, bacteria grow very quickly at warm temperatures (40°F to 120°F). For example, a finished chicken à la king kept in a warm instead of a hot steam table for four or five hours can become sufficiently contaminated to cause an outbreak of food-borne illness.

KEY WORDS AND CONCEPTS

Age of bird at time of slaughter

As-purchased price (AP price)

Cello pack

Chill pack

Commodity

Contamination problems

Conversion weight

Edible-portion cost (EP cost)

Exact name

Food Safety and Quality Service (FSQS)

Free-range chicken

Gas-flushed pack

Grading factors

Ice pack

Independent farmer

Individually quick frozen (IQF)

In-process inventories

Intended use

Irradiation

Kosher chicken

Manufacturing grade

Marinade pack

Material used in processed products

Number of pieces per bird

Packaging procedure

Packers' brands

Poultry Products Inspection Act

Poultry used for more than one menu item

Preservation method

Procurement grades

Product form

Product size

Product yield

Purchasing, receiving, storing, and issuing poultry products

Sex of bird	Standard of identity	U.S. grades
Shatter pack	State grades	Variety meats
Shelf life	Substitution possibilities	Weight range
	Trust the supplier	Wholesome Poultry
Signature item	Type of packaging material	Products Act
Size of container	United States Department of Agriculture (USDA)	
Snap pack	Acceptance Service	

QUESTIONS AND PROBLEMS

1. What are the U.S. consumer grades for poultry?

2. Why is the age of a bird at the time of slaughter an important selection factor?

3. Why do hen turkeys generally have a higher AP price than tom turkeys?

4. What is an appropriate intended use for a broiler-fryer?

5. The primary grading factor for the poultry grades "Procurement I" and "Procurement II" is:

   _____.

6. What are lower-quality poultry products generally used for?

7. Outline the specific procedures hospitality operators should use for purchasing, receiving, storing, and issuing frozen, prebreaded broiler-fryer parts. Assume that these parts will be used in a school food service or in a hospital food service. If possible, ask a school foodservice director or a hospital dietitian to comment on your answer.

8. Which type of poultry product would buyers purchase if they were planning to prepare chicken and dumplings and wanted to use fresh chicken? Why?

9. When hospitality operators serve turkey and dressing, they could use fresh turkey or a processed turkey product, such as a turkey roll. What are the potential advantages and disadvantages of using the fresh product? What are the potential advantages and disadvantages of using the processed product?

10. What is another name for the term "conversion weight"?

11. What is the primary difference between the poultry grades U.S. Grade A and U.S. Grade B?

12. Why is the weight range of a fresh, whole bird an important selection factor?

13. What critical information is missing from the following product specification for sliced, cooked chicken breast?

    Sliced, cooked chicken breast
    Used for deli sandwiches
    Country Pride® brand (or equivalent)
    Packed in Cryovac bags
    Refrigerated

14. Describe the necessary storage conditions for fresh and processed poultry.

15. Prepare a product specification for the product mentioned in Question 8.

16. Why are free-range and kosher chickens more expensive than chickens raised in the typical way?

17. Why are frozen chicken parts, such as breasts and thighs, unacceptable to many foodservice operators?

18. What method can hospitality operators use to extend the shelf life of fresh poultry?

19. Explain why chicken is referred to as a "commodity item."

20. Assume that you manage a school food service. You serve lunch only—5000 lunches per day, five days a week. A poultry purveyor calls to tell you that he is going out of business. He has about 7500 pounds of frozen, cut-up broiler-fryers. He will sell you this stock for 50 percent of the current AP price. You have to let him know your decision tomorrow. What do you do? If possible, ask a school foodservice manager to comment on your answer.

21. A product specification for turkey franks could include the following information:

    (a)
    (b)
    (c)
    (d)
    (e)

22. What are the major advantages of the chill pack procedure?

23. When would buyers substitute a processed chicken patty for a boneless, skinless chicken breast?

24. Prepare a product specification for the following poultry products:

    (a)   Chicken wing
    (b)   Turkey
    (c)   Chicken egg roll
    (d)   Duckling
    (e)   Chicken patty

25. What is the difference between the ice pack procedure and the marinade pack procedure?

22
FISH

The Purpose of this Chapter

After reading this chapter, you should be able to:

- Explain the selection factors for fish, including government grades.
- Describe the process of purchasing, receiving, storing, and issuing fish.

INTRODUCTION

Buying fresh fish can be one of the most frustrating jobs in all of purchasing. Processed—that is, canned, salted, and frozen—fish is easier to buy. With fresh items, not only will buyers find very few suppliers, but they may also have to take whatever fresh fish is available. If hospitality operations want fresh fish on the menu, they might have to offer whatever their supplier has in stock. At times, however, the supplier may have nothing.

Obtaining a wide variety of fresh fish is very difficult unless operators are willing to deal with all potential suppliers. It also is very difficult for operators to maintain consistent culinary quality unless they have a working relationship with all of the suppliers. It is not unusual for a foodservice operator to purchase only one type of fresh fish from as many seafood suppliers as possible in order to obtain a steady supply and consistent quality.

One nice feature of fish is that operators can usually get by with processed products, unless they want to advertise fresh items. If they insist on fresh fish, it is not particularly difficult to buy something fresh; it is just that, as we said earlier, they have few suppliers from which to choose.

Moreover, fresh fish can cause other challenges. Unless operators are close to a major transportation hub, the "fresh" fish can be in tired condition; its as-purchased (AP) prices can fluctuate, which can force operators to price their menu almost every day; once they get the fish, production employees may not be able to handle it properly unless they are highly skilled in this area; and some choice items, like Dover sole, Maine lobster, and Alaska king crab, cannot always be purchased fresh. So, unless operators can obtain a reasonably steady supply, they might want to reconsider any decision to feature fresh fish on the menu.

Some companies take the guesswork and the difficulty out of the selection and procurement of fresh fish by "growing their own," or by purchasing products that suppliers grow under controlled conditions. For instance, large restaurant companies that own commissaries can practice "aquaculture," or fish farming, which serves to produce fish items of consistent size and culinary quality. Any foodservice operation, though, can purchase farm-raised fish from suppliers who provide this option.

Aquaculture is not a new development; in fact, its roots go back to China, where the Chinese people have farmed fish since before the birth of Christ. However, the procedures have become very popular only in the last few years.

Many buyers are fond of farm-raised fish because it eliminates a lot of the risk from the fish-purchasing process. It also ensures stable quality and a consistent supply.

Each year sees an increase in the amount of farm-raised fish purchased in the United States. According to the National Restaurant Association (NRA), farm-raised catfish is the largest segment of the aquaculture industry. Other popular farm-raised fish are trout, tilapia, salmon, oysters, mussels, clams, scallops, abalone, crawfish, and shrimp. While aquaculture, technically, can be expanded to include other fish species, such as halibut and flounder, the technology needed to do it effectively and efficiently is still being refined.

Fresh-fish buyers must be very knowledgeable about the fish products they purchase. These items are not very standardized, and, unlike other fresh products, such as fresh produce and fresh meats, few market guidelines are available for most items. So operators who are responsible for purchasing fresh-fish products can never know too much about them.

SELECTION FACTORS

Management must determine the varieties and qualities of fish they want on the menu. Remember, they usually make this type of decision in cooperation with other company personnel. Management usually considers several of the following selection factors.

Intended Use

As always, hospitality operators want to precisely determine the intended use of an item so that they will be able to prepare the appropriate, relevant specification. For example, a whitefish that will be broiled needs a more attractive appearance than a whitefish that will be used in breaded fish patties.

Exact Name

Many varieties of fish exist in the world. In the United States, more than 200 varieties are sold. Obviously, then, buyers must be especially careful and indicate the precise name of the item they want (see Figure 22.1) for some of the more popular varieties of fish product used in the foodservice industry).

Unfortunately, even if buyers indicate an exact name, they could receive an unwanted item because the fish industry is fond of renaming fish. For example, on the East Coast of the United States, the name "lemon sole" refers to a particular size of flounder, while on the West Coast and in Europe, it refers to other fish species. A similar problem occurs with the name "snapper." It sometimes seems that almost every fish under the sun is called snapper.

The federal government actually encourages renaming fish because it would like to see the public eat products that are quite good, yet suffer from an image problem because they have unappealing names. Many perfectly delicious and nutritious fish species abound primarily because they are protected by repugnant names. Lately, though, several "trash" fish have become more popular.

Renaming fish is also done as an attempt to increase its marketability and profitability. For example, we recall that years ago a fish product called "slime-heads" or "Australian perch" was on the market. There was little demand for it. However, once Australians renamed it "orange roughy," sales skyrocketed. And, we might add, so did its price.

Renaming fish is a particularly sensitive issue in the hospitality industry. Receivers must be careful to get only those products that buyers actually order. If cus-

SALTWATER SPECIES	FRESHWATER SPECIES
Cod	Catfish
Flounder	Lake perch
Haddock	Lake trout
Halibut	Pike
Mackerel	Rainbow trout
Mahi Mahi (Dolphin)	Smelt
Monkfish	Tilapia
Ocean catfish	Whitefish
Ocean perch	
Orange roughy	SHELLFISH SPECIES
Pollock	Abalone
Salmon	Clam
Sea bass	Crab
Sea trout	Crawfish
Snapper	Lobster
Sole	Mussel
Swordfish	Oyster
Tuna (Ahi, Bluefin, Yellowfin, etc.)	Scallop
Turbot	Shrimp
Whiting	

a

b

FIGURE 22.1 (*a*) Varieties of fish. (*b*) Varieties of fish that are popular in the foodservice industry. Top row from left: tilapia, blue runner. Middle row: jack, mahi mahi. Bottom row: trigger fish, two red mullets. Source: Gisslen, *Professional Cooking*, 4th ed. Copyright © 1999, John Wiley & Sons, Inc. This material used by permission of John Wiley & Sons, Inc.

tomers are adventurous and accept more exotic species, then buyers will order them. If not, buyers must be certain to select only those suppliers who will help them achieve their purchase objectives.

In addition to the exact name of the product, operators must be careful to use, where applicable, the appropriate market terminology in their particular area that further identifies what they want. While some market terms are common, each growing and harvesting area tends to adopt its own peculiar nomenclature to identify some items (see Figure 22.2 for some of the most common marketing terms).

A few fish products meet federal-government standards of identity. For instance, a "lightly breaded" shrimp product must contain at least 65 percent shrimp, whereas a "breaded" shrimp product must contain at least 50 percent shrimp. As

Block—a solid cube of raw fish; usually skinless; normally weighs about 10 to 20 pounds.

Breaded/battered—fish product coated with a seasoned crumb or batter mixture.

Butterfly fillet—two small fillets held together by a small, thin piece of skin.

Chunk—cross section of a large, dressed fish. It contains the cross section of the backbone. It is similar to a bone-in beef pot roast.

Drawn—whole fish that has been eviscerated, i.e., the entrails have been removed.

Dressed—a completely clean fish; can be cooked as is or processed into steaks, fillets, portions, etc.

Fillet—boneless fish, cut away from the backbone.

Fin fish—fish that has fins and a backbone. There are "fat" fin fish and "lean" fin fish. There are saltwater and freshwater species.

Green, headless—usually refers to a raw, unprocessed shrimp.

Peeled and deveined (P&D)—a shrimp without its shell or black vein.

Portion—a piece of fish cut from a block of fish. It is similar to a fillet, but it does not meet the exact definition of the fillet.

Shellfish—fish products that are completely or partially covered by a shell. There are crustaceans, whose shells are soft (e.g., shrimp), and mollusks, which have hard shells (e.g., oysters).

Shucked—fish that has been removed from its shell. Normally used when ordering shell-less mollusks.

Steak—a cross section of a large fish that has been cut from a dressed fish carcass.

Stick—a small piece of fish usually cut from a fish block.

Whole (round)—fish right out of the water; nothing has been done to it.

FIGURE 22.2 (a) Common marketing terms for fish products.

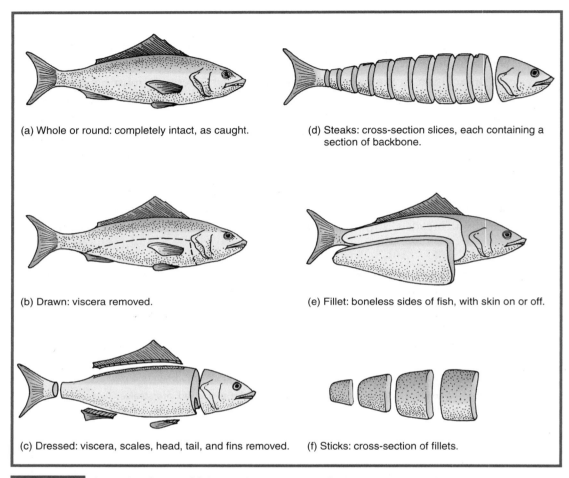

(a) Whole or round: completely intact, as caught.

(d) Steaks: cross-section slices, each containing a section of backbone.

(b) Drawn: viscera removed.

(e) Fillet: boneless sides of fish, with skin on or off.

(c) Dressed: viscera, scales, head, tail, and fins removed.

(f) Sticks: cross-section of fillets.

FIGURE 22.2 (b) **Market forms of fish. Source: Gisslen, *Professional Cooking*, 5th ed. Copyright © 2003, John Wiley & Sons, Inc. This material is used by permission of John Wiley & Sons, Inc.**

with all standards of identity, though, the figures represent minimal requirements. Furthermore, in the fish trade, only a handful of processed products are subject to the standard of identity regulations. Consequently, wise buyers usually do not rely on standards of identity when preparing specifications for fish products.

U.S. Government Grades (or Equivalent)

The U.S. Department of Commerce's (USDC) National Marine Fisheries Service publishes grade standards and offers grading services for fishery products similar to those that the United States Department of Agriculture (USDA) established for other foods. The USDC's grading program also provides for official inspection of the edibility and wholesomeness of fishery products, and many of its grade standards specify the amount of fish component required in a processed product.

The U.S. government grades few fish items. The products for which the federal government has established grading standards are processed products, such as breaded and/or precooked items.

Fish grades are based on several grading factors. Normally, the grader evaluates the fish's appearance, odor, size, uniformity, color, defects, flavor, and texture, as well as its point of origin. The federal grades for fish products are:

1. **Grade A.** This is the best quality produced. The appearance and culinary quality are superior. Grade A products have a uniform appearance and are practically devoid of blemishes or other defects.

2. **Grade B.** This is good quality and, generally, is suitable for many foodservice applications. Grade B items have significantly more blemishes and/or defects than Grade A products.

3. **Grade C.** This grade resembles Grade B, but it is lacking in appearance. It is suitable only for finished menu items, such as soups and casseroles, where appearance is not critical.

When buyers use U.S. grades as one of their selection factors, normally, only the U.S. Grade A designation is specified (see Figure 22.3). Lower grades usually do not carry a federal grade shield; rather, these manufacturing grades are left unmarked and are usually sold to food processors who will process them into several types of convenience fish products.

FIGURE 22.3 Federal grade stamps used for fish.
Source: United States Department of Agriculture.

Packed Under Federal Inspection Seal

Recall from Chapter 4 that fish products are not subject to mandatory, continuous, federal-government inspection. The Food and Drug Administration (FDA) provides periodic inspections for all food-fabricating plants, monitors imported and interstate fish shipments, and requires fish processors to adopt the Hazard Analysis Critical Control Point (HACCP) system to increase food safety. Also, a cooperative agreement exists between federal and state agencies that monitors the farm beds where oysters, clams, and mussels are raised. However, these inspections fall far short of those the USDA uses to monitor meat-packing, poultry-packing, and egg-breaking plants.

Fish are cold-blooded animals; hence, the diseases afflicting them supposedly do not threaten the humans who eat them. However, fish can be exposed to many toxins, bacteria, and parasites that can be harmful to humans. Even though properly prepared and served fish causes no more health problems than meat products and fewer problems than poultry items, many fish buyers seem to be reluctant to purchase fish that has not been produced under continuous government inspection.

One way for buyers to ensure this type of inspection is to demand that all fish products they purchase carry a U.S. grade designation. Fish products that are produced and graded under the USDC inspection program may carry the USDC "Federal Inspection" mark or the U.S. grade shield. Unfortunately, grading designations, as mentioned earlier, are available only for a few fish items.

Another problem is that only fish produced in the United States can carry the federal government's grade or inspection shield; according to the NRA, about two-thirds of the fish consumed in the United States comes from approximately 120 other countries.

An alternative to requiring a U.S. grade designation or federal inspection is to purchase only those fish products that are produced under the continuous inspection of a state or local government agency. However, these agencies normally do not provide an extensive array of inspection services, and the ones they do provide usually are not very comprehensive.

The only sure way to obtain fish items that are produced under continuous government inspection is to demand that any fish product purchased carry the Packed Under Federal Inspection (PUFI) seal (see Figure 22.4). This seal indicates that the product is clean, safe, and wholesome, and that it has been produced in an establishment that meets all of the sanitary guidelines of the USDC's National Marine Fisheries Service. The product is not graded for quality, but it meets the acceptable commercial quality standards the federal inspection agency has set.

FIGURE 22.4 This seal signifies that the fish product is clean, safe, and wholesome and has been produced in an acceptable establishment with appropriate equipment under the supervision of federal inspectors. *Source:* United States Department of Commerce.

Specifying that all of the fish buyers purchase must carry the PUFI seal probably will significantly reduce the potential number of suppliers who can bid for their business. Continuous fish inspection is a voluntary program, and not many fish-processing plants participate. Furthermore, time-consuming inspection is not easily adaptable to many fish suppliers who sell fresh fish products; in many instances, the products are caught in the morning and sent via air express to a foodservice operation, where they will be used on the menu that evening.

Packers' Brands (or Equivalent)

Because most fresh fish does not carry a brand name, this criterion is not a useful selection factor for fresh items. But packers' brands for processed fish items, especially canned fish, abound. In fact, a brand name, as well as the reputation of the item's producer and distributing suppliers, is very important to many buyers. For example, we probably could safely assume that StarKist® and Chicken of the Sea® brands instill a good deal of confidence in the marketplace.

In some instances, a brand name may be the only guide to seafood consistency. In addition, the type of processed product you want may be available from only one company. For example, not too many firms are producing marinated baby sardines.

Few beginning purchasers are familiar with the brand names in the seafood area. As a result, these brands may not be very useful until a buyer has studied the brands and experimented with them for awhile.

Some brand-name, processed fish products carry the U.S. Grade A designation. Items like fish sticks and raw breaded shrimp usually carry this type of grading mark. The brand is indicative of a certain culinary quality, and the grade shield assures wholesomeness.

Product Size

As usual, size information is a very important selection factor. Fish products come in so many sizes that a specification without this type of information is seriously deficient.

Some shellfish items, such as crab legs and lobster tails, are usually sized by count. For these two products, the count is based on 10 pounds. For example, if lobster tails are sized "10/12," a 10-pound lot comprises approximately 10 to 12 pieces.

For many fresh fish products, buyers may be able to specify a weight range only. For example, if buyers are purchasing large salmon fillets, the supplier may be unable to accommodate an exact size.

If buyers are purchasing whole-fish products, they will also need to settle for a weight range. For instance, they cannot specify an exact size for whole lobsters. They must be satisfied with one of the five traditional sizes available: "chickens" (approximately 1 pound), "quarters" (1 to $1\frac{1}{2}$ pounds), "selects" ($1\frac{1}{2}$ to $2\frac{1}{2}$ pounds), "jumbos" ($2\frac{1}{2}$ to 5 pounds), and "monsters" (more than 5 pounds).

For processed products, buyers are normally able to indicate the exact desired weight per item. For instance, when purchasing breaded fish sticks, they usually can choose among several available sizes.

The sizing system is an informal procedure that has developed over the years. No federal-government standards deal with this issue. Furthermore, many producers attach their own type of size designation to their items. When this happens, buyers will need to determine the exact nomenclature so that their specifications are adequate.

Product Yield

Buyers may need to indicate the minimum yield they will accept, or the maximum trim they will allow, for the fish products they receive. For example, buyers could note on their specification that they will accept no more than, perhaps, 2 percent broken fish sticks in every 20-pound case purchased. Alternately, the buyer will accept no more than 2 percent dead oysters for each barrel purchased.

Size of Container

When considering the size of the individual fish products buyers purchase, they must also give some thought to the size of the container they would prefer. Container sizes vary sufficiently to satisfy most buyer preferences. Generally speaking, the size and type of packages available for fish products are very similar to those used to package poultry products.

Type of Packaging Material

Fresh fish often is delivered in reusable plastic tubs or styrofoam containers. The products normally also are packed in crushed ice—that is, fresh product is often "ice packed."

Processed fish items usually are packaged in cans, bottles, or moisture-proof, vapor-proof materials designed to withstand freezer temperatures.

Live-in-shell fish items usually are packaged in moisture-proof materials. These products also may be packed in seaweed, or some other similar material designed to prevent dehydration. Usually, these products are not packed in ice or in fresh water because these packing media reduce their shelf lives.

As mentioned, fish products are generally packaged in the same type and variety of materials used to package poultry products. Buyers, therefore, have several choices.

Packaging Procedure

Once again, we note the similarity between poultry and fish products. As with poultry, fish items are slab-packed, layered, chill-packed, ice-packed, cello-packed, and individually quick frozen (IQF). Some items are also available in a marinade pack; for example, buyers may be able to purchase Cajun-seasoned sole fillets.

Fresh shellfish are, typically, slab-packed. Fresh fin fish normally are ice-packed in order to preserve their culinary quality and extend the shipment's shelf life. Some fresh fin fish are placed in "modified-atmosphere packaging" (MAP), which is a type of controlled-atmosphere packaging that involves chilling freshly harvested fish; placing it in plastic wrap; and pumping a combination of carbon dioxide, oxygen, and nitrogen into the wrap. The shelf life of fresh fish packaged this way can be as long as three weeks.

Fresh-frozen fish products are usually trimmed, cut, IQF, and packaged on board a fish-factory ship. These items are often cello-wrapped and placed in moisture-proof, vapor-proof containers.

Processed frozen-fish items are most often processed, IQF, layered on plastic or waxed sheets or plastic "cell packs," and placed in moisture-proof, vapor-proof containers. As with similarly processed frozen poultry products, this type of packaging procedure is sometimes referred to as a "snap pack" or "shatter pack."

Product Form

Fish is processed into many forms. Foodservice operations that strive for a high-quality seafood reputation normally need to use dressed fresh fish and, if further processing is necessary, to perform these tasks in the operation's kitchen. High-quality processed convenience items, though, are usually available. For example, breaded/battered, portion-control products are very popular, as are portion-control stuffed, marinated, and other preseasoned fish products.

Many unique types of convenience fish products are available. For example, "flaked and re-formed" "shrimp" items, which consist of odd scraps of shrimp material shaped to look like whole shrimp, are available. Also, several imitation fish products, such as imitation shrimp and seafood salad, are made with a fish-based paste called "surimi." Surimi is also used to produce various "meat" products—such as imitation frankfurters and bacon bits. While these items do not necessarily provide the same health benefits as the real products, some of these low-cost substitutes are very attractive to budget-conscious restaurant operators.

If buyers purchase a good deal of processed fish, they may need to rely exclusively on packers' brands as an indication of quality and other desired product characteristics. If buyers do not use brand name identification and are purchasing, say, a frozen-fish patty, they need to note on the specification the types of fish and other food matter that must be used to process these items. Buyers also would need to note the proportion of these materials desired. If they do not note these characteristics and do not wish to specify a particular packer's brand name, they cannot expect to maintain quality control. While federal standards of identity exist for some fish products, hospitality operators cannot rely on them exclusively because they represent only minimum guidelines to which commercial fish processors must adhere.

Usually, the major issues that need to be resolved when contemplating the purchase of processed fish products are: (1) what are the substitution possibilities, and (2) what degree of convenience do you want?

Several substitution possibilities exist. Processed fish products come in many forms. For example, buyers can substitute fillets for steaks, butterfly shrimp for headless shrimp, and imitation crab for real crab. These alternatives are limited because, as buyers go from one item to the next, the culinary quality changes. Managers must not risk alienating their customers.

The degree of convenience desired usually is related to the labor skill, equipment, and utensils available to produce menu items, and the size of the kitchen and storage facilities. Today, the economics of the foodservice industry tend to favor the use of many convenience products, and so long as the culinary quality is acceptable, managers will seriously consider using them.

Whatever the degree of processing buyers desire, they will, typically, have more than one supplier from which to choose. Fresh fish may be scarce, but buyers usually have two or more brands of processed fish from which to choose. This makes it easier for buyers who like to shop around and bid buy. It also makes it convenient for hospitality operators who want to move fish items around on their menus. This gives buyers a greal deal of flexibility.

Preservation Method

Fish is preserved in many ways: frozen, dried, smoked, refrigerated, ice-packed, cello-packed, chill-packed, live, live-in-shell, and canned.

The operation that offers fish signature menu items prefers live, live-in-shell, and/or ice-packed or chill-packed dressed fresh fish. If fresh product is unavailable, the frozen item is normally the preferred alternative, because at least it ensures a steady, year-round supply.

For some products, canned is the preferred choice. For example, snails and sardines are usually purchased in cans or bottles. Indeed, Americans buy more canned fish than any other type, fresh or processed.

Packing Medium

In some instances, buyers need to indicate the specific packing medium desired. For example, canned tuna is packed with water or with several varieties of oil. The same is true for other canned fish products. Since the packing medium significantly affects a product's culinary quality, buyers must be careful to include this selection factor on the specification.

Point of Origin

A lobster is not simply a lobster. If a lobster comes from the Gulf of Mexico, it is not the same type as the lobster that comes from Australia. This is true of any other type of fish, fresh or processed: the area it comes from influences its distinctive character, flavor, and texture. Hence, buyers sometimes carefully specify the origin of the fish they buy, especially if they purchase a great deal of fresh fish.

Many foodservice operators note on their menus the points of origin for some menu offerings. This seems to be a very popular practice for fish products. For instance, it is quite common to see menus that advertise Lake Superior whitefish, Alaskan salmon and crab legs, Australian lobster tails, and Chilean sea bass (see Figure 22.5). This menu nomenclature forces buyers to purchase fish products that originate from these locales. Substitute items cheat the customer. Furthermore, in some parts of the United States, any substitutes would violate truth-in-menu legislation.

Trust the Supplier

When buyers use a great deal of fresh fish, they may have to cast their lot with one primary supplier, assuming that they are satisfied with his or her capability. Together, a buyer and a supplier take what they can get from several sources, usually dictated by season, from the various seafood-producing areas of the world.

For instance, if a buyer purchases fresh, live-in-shell lobsters, the typical scenario may go something like this. The buyers will either go through a local supplier or purchase directly from a supplier on the East Coast, and order what is wanted for the next two or three days. The lobsters will be shipped FedEx air freight. At the airport in the buyer's city or a nearby city, the lobsters will be put into a local FedEx van, and brought right to the buyer's back door. The buyer will pay the East Coast fish supplier the going rate for that day, usually on a cost-plus basis. Alternately, the buyer may pay a local supplier, and he or she will then take care of all the details. Scenarios like this often take place for other types of fresh fish as well. But with other types, buyers may need to accept what is available.

The cost-plus purchasing procedure will influence an operator's menu pricing procedures. When buyers purchase fresh-fish products, they may wish to set a different menu price every day or every week. In the live-lobster example, a typical price-setting strategy is as follows: Pay for the lobsters. Throw out any dead ones, perhaps two out of 24. Divide the total as-purchased (AP) price plus any freight cost by 22. Add a markup to cover labor, overhead, and profit, and use this figure as the live-lobster menu price for today or for however long it takes to sell this batch of lobsters.

It is a good idea for buyers to deal consistently with trusted suppliers when they purchase a great deal of fresh fish. The items are not standardized, the quality is variable, the supply is erratic, and the prices change continuously. Buyers need the supplier's expertise. Also, they must be confident that he or she will charge the correct market price for the items and not try to take advantage of the buyers' inability to track the fresh-seafood market on a daily basis. Furthermore, the suppliers must ensure that the products they distribute are wholesome and safe for hu-

FIGURE 22.5 An example of point of origin. Courtesy of and © Ocean Garden Products, Inc.

man consumption. Fresh fish are very difficult items to move successfully through the distribution channels; several contamination opportunities exist. The competent fresh-fish supplier deserves the buyer's respect.

When buyers purchase processed fish, they do not need to become a house account. Processed-fish buying, like most other processed-food purchasing, lends itself nicely to bid buying. Buyers learn, in time, the qualities associated with particular brand names. They can also learn to specify the type of processing they want and the area from which the fish should come.

Bear in mind, too, that there is a "new pack time" for canned and frozen fish, similar to the new pack time for canned fruits and vegetables. If hospitality operators have the money and the expertise, and large firms often have both, bid buying for a six-month or one-year supply can be rewarding.

PURCHASING FISH

The first step in purchasing fish is to acquire some of the indispensable reference materials available. For instance, fish buyers might want to have a copy of *The New Fresh Seafood Buyer's Guide: A Manual for Distribution, Restaurants, and Retailers* (New York: Kluwer, 1991—although it is now out of print). They should consult some of the leading trade journals, such as *The Seafood Leader*; the March/April annual buyer's guide issue is especially useful. Buyers should also consider subscribing to the *Seafood Price-Current*. This report contains twice-weekly market prices for many fish products from various regions of the United States. The Web also has a large amount of current seafood information. For instance, Seafood.com provides daily price information and news regarding the seafood industry.

The next step is for buyers to contact the FDA Office of Seafood Safety and ask for a list of approved interstate fish suppliers operating in their area. The local health district can provide a list of suppliers who operate only in their local market.

Next, buyers and other management personnel need to decide the exact type of product and quality they want. Once they determine what they want to include on the menu and what quality they want, the buyers should take the time to prepare a specification for each product. However, we do not think that specs are very valuable for fresh fish since buyers usually have to take what is available or go someplace else. They might prepare a statement of quality and give it to their suppliers, who then might call them when something meeting their standard comes in. A statement of quality might include the area the fish is to come from, as well as its size, form, and preservation method. If the fish is grown under controlled conditions, buyers might be able to specify its feed and nurturing techniques.

If buyers purchase processed fish, they should prepare detailed specifications so that they compile ideas as to exactly what they want. The specs must include all pertinent information, especially if buyers will use them in bid buying (see Figure 22.6 for some examples of product specifications and Figure 22.7 for an example product specification outline for fish products).

If buyers purchase processed fish in quantity, it might be worth a little trouble for them to shop around. For instance, purchasing a lot of frozen fish, such as a six-month supply, can save buyers a bit of money, as long as the storage costs are reasonable. Many frozen-fish suppliers will set up a stockless purchase plan for you or will provide the same type of supplier service for a slight carrying charge.

Another interesting aspect of buying processed fish is the reasonable spread in the AP prices between one brand name and another. Naturally, when the AP price is lower, buyers usually suspect a lower quality. Although this conclusion is typically true when buyers purchase other processed products, especially canned fruits and vegetables, it is not always the case with processed fish. For example, buyers will see a big difference in AP price between canned dark-meat tuna and white-meat tuna. Some people care very little about this color differential. Another

Tuna, solid white, albacore Used to prepare tuna salad Chicken of the Sea® brand Water pack 66.5-ounce can 6 cans per case Moisture-proof case	Australian lobster tails Used for dinner entrée U.S. Grade A (or equivalent) 16/20 count 25-pound moisture-proof, vapor- proof container Layered pack Frozen
Seafood Newburg Used for banquet service Overhill® brand 6-ounce individual portion pack 48 portions per case Packaged in moisture-proof, vapor- proof material To be reconstituted in its package Frozen	Clam juice (ocean) Used for beverage service Nugget® brand 46-ounce can 12 cans per case Moisture-proof case

FIGURE 22.6 **Examples of fish product specifications.**

Intended use:

Exact name:

U.S. grade (or equivalent):

PUFI seal:

Packer's brand name (or equivalent):

Product size:

Product yield:

Size of container:

Type of packaging material:

Packaging procedure:

Product form:

Preservation method:

Packing medium:

Point of origin:

FIGURE 22.7 An example of a product specification outline for fish products.

example is the processed fish stick: a little more cod and a little less haddock may yield a fine-tasting product at a more economical AP price. Similarly, different formulas for fish patties, fish stews, and other processed entrées can yield substantially different AP prices while maintaining acceptable quality standards.

Minimum-order requirements may trouble buyers. If they buy fresh fish, but only a little, they might find that a high minimum-order requirement and freight cost hinder their desire to serve a high-quality fish entrée.

Sometimes, buyers may be tempted to purchase fish from a neighbor who has just returned from a fishing trip. No mandatory federal-inspection requirement exists for the neighbor, and the fish may be perfectly good. The state or local health district, however, may have some regulations prohibiting the sale of this fish. We believe that buyers should avoid this practice since they never really know where the fish came from or how it has been handled.

Since fish availability can be somewhat unpredictable, buyers can sometimes find real seafood bargains. For example, a supplier may have some merchandise on a "move list." Perhaps more shrimp has suddenly shown up on the market and its AP price has gone down, or the tuna industry has a larger promotional effort. Before buyers jump at these bargains, though, they need to consider four factors: (1) Can their employees handle the item properly if it is a new item to them? (2) Do they have the proper equipment to prepare and serve the new item? (3) If the item is currently on their menu, should they drop its menu price? (4) Should they use this bargain as a loss leader on their menu? That is, would they be willing, for instance, to serve bargain shrimp in their lounge at a very inexpensive menu price in order to attract customers who supposedly will then order more profitable merchandise from them during a subsequent visit to the restaurant? This type of promotion may establish a trend whereby buyers would be forced to continue it well after the AP price of shrimp soars.

Management and buyers must decide what fish they want. Then they must engage the supplier that can handle their needs. For processed fish, bid buying may be the answer, but this is not always possible when purchasing fresh merchandise.

RECEIVING FISH

When a fish shipment is delivered, the receivers' first step is to check its quality. When they examine fresh fin fish or fresh, shucked shellfish, the product should have a mild, not fishy, scent. Its flesh should be firm, and it should spring back when slight pressure is applied. The product should be slime-free. Gills should be bright pink or red. If the head is attached, the eyes should be clear and bright. To ensure quality and maximum shelf life, the product should be ice-packed or chill-packed.

Sometimes, suppliers will send "slacked-out" fish, that is, thawed fish, instead of the fresh product ordered. Usually, this product looks a little dry, or it has "ice spots," which are dried areas on its flesh.

When examining live fish, receivers should see a product that is very active. They do not want live fish that seem sluggish or tired. Also, the product should be heavy for its size.

Live-in-shell crustaceans, upon examination, should also be very active and feel heavy for their size.

When receivers evaluate live-in-shell mollusks, the shells should be closed, or they should at least close when tapped with fingers. Open shells indicate that the products are dead and are past their peak of culinary quality. Live-in-shell also should feel heavy for their size.

Frozen fish should be frozen solid. They should be packaged in moisture-proof, vapor-proof material. No signs of thawing or refreezing, such as crystallization, dryness, items stuck together, or water damage on the carton, should be visible. Also, if applicable, the amount of "glaze" on the items—a protective coating of ice on the frozen items that the producer adds to prevent dehydration—should not be excessive.

Canned merchandise should show no signs of rust, dents, dirt, or swelling. Canned fish is especially dangerous if it is contaminated, so the receiving agent can never be too careful when evaluating the containers.

One problem receivers have when checking the quality of fresh fish is knowing whether or not they have gotten the right species—the item they ordered. Many fish products look similar to the untrained eye. For example, it is not easy to distinguish bay scallops from shark meat cubes, red snapper from Pacific rockfish, or cod fillets from haddock fillets.

Here is a corollary problem: What represents good quality to one nose may be offensive to another. We have seen receivers try to send back fresh-fish items because these items did not "look right" or "smell right." They had to be convinced that the slipperiness or ocean aroma was natural.

Another problem with receiving fresh fish arises when receiving agents do need to return it. Suppose that the deliveryperson made a mistake. If he or she takes the fish back, chances are that the product will go bad before the supplier can resell it. Also, operators are left without a fresh-fish item they may need that very night. Consequently, they might keep it and use it if the quality is acceptable in spite of its being the wrong variety. Receivers then would complete a Request for Credit memorandum or make some mutually agreeable settlement with the supplier.

An unfortunate problem with some processed fish is that it is hard to tell whether they will be acceptable once they are prepared for customer service. For instance, chefs may not know whether a frozen lobster tail is bad until they cook it and it falls apart. With a fresh lobster tail, experienced chefs can usually judge its quality before cooking it.

After satisfying their nose and eyes, receiving agents should go on to weigh, preferably without the ice, or count the merchandise and then get it into the proper storage environment as quickly as possible. Fresh fish will deteriorate right before their eyes if they fail to keep it refrigerated. Whatever receivers do, they should not let fresh and frozen fish stay on the receiving platform any longer than is absolutely necessary. Some companies put scales and checking equipment in the walk-in refrigerator to receive fish, poultry, and meat. Others roll the scale into the refrigerator temporarily.

If receivers are getting a shipment of shellfish from a supplier on the FDA's Interstate Certified Shellfish Shippers List, a tag in the container will note the number of the bed where the shellfish were grown and harvested. Operators are required to keep this tag on file for 90 days if the products are fresh and two years if they are frozen. If an outbreak of food-borne illness is traced to the shellfish, health officials must be able to determine the lot number of the offending products so that any as-yet-unused parts of that batch can be removed from the channel of distribution.

In some areas, other tags may accompany a fish shipment. For instance, some parts of the United States do not allow the importation of fish from other areas unless they carry identifying tags. These tags are usually issued to indicate that the products are acceptable to the local Fish and Game office and the local health district, and that they have not been purchased from unapproved local sources.

After doing the quality and quantity checks, receivers must verify the prices and complete the appropriate accounting documents.

STORING FISH

Fresh fin fish and fresh, shucked shellfish should be maintained at approximately 32°F and at no less than 65 percent relative humidity. These products are best stored on a bed of crushed ice and covered with waxed paper to prevent dehydration. If hospitality operators cannot use crushed ice, they should wrap the products tightly in plastic wrap, aluminum foil, or some other suitable container and store them in the coldest part of the refrigerator. The maximum shelf life for these items is about two days.

Operators must store live fin fish in tanks specifically designed to hold the particular types of products they are purchasing. Operators can also store live-in-shell fish in the appropriate water tanks, although they could be kept in their original containers and covered with damp cloths. Generally, these shellfish items should not be stored in fresh water or crushed ice. This is especially true for mollusks because the fresh water can kill them.

Hospitality operators should store frozen fish at or below 0°F. Ideally, these fish should be stored at −10°F to −15°F because these temperatures are conducive to maximum shelf life, which is about three months. If the products have the correct amount of glaze on them, they could maintain acceptable culinary quality for up to one year.

Operators should keep canned or bottled fish products in a dry storeroom. The ideal temperature of this storeroom would be 50°F, though 70°F is acceptable. The storeroom's relative humidity should not exceed 60 percent.

ISSUING FISH

Most fresh fish goes directly into production. But if fish enters an issue-controlled storage area, hospitality operators will need to prepare issue documents when it goes to production. Just as when operators issue most items, they have a choice: Should they issue the product as is, or should they issue it as ready to go? For example, oysters can be shucked ahead of time. Similarly, escargot can be preprepared, and someone might portion a fresh snapper, put it in pie pans, and season it, so that all the cook has to do is pop it into the oven.

Operators should try to avoid the temptation of prepreparing the snapper and then storing the portions in a freezer. On the one hand, this practice allows the cook to take the preprepared snapper out of the in-process freezer and put it in the oven. This is convenient; it also reduces leftovers, which usually go straight into the garbage can. On the other hand, some of the flavor is lost when fish are frozen this way. Besides, if operations have fresh fish on their menu, they have to risk some loss; they will also have to price these menu items so as to take into account these probable losses.

Of course, it is absolutely essential for operators to follow proper stock rotation when issuing fish products. Also, since these items deteriorate rapidly and are expensive, operators must make sure that requisitioners do not take more than absolutely necessary. Management should ask them to note the in-process inventory before requisitioning more fish.

IN-PROCESS INVENTORIES

A great deal of risk—spoilage, especially—is associated with fish, particularly fresh fish. This risk increases dramatically when fish is not handled properly at this step. Merely listing fish on the menu probably places hospitality operators in a high "risk category."

Operators must try to reduce losses in the in-process inventories; typically, however, some loss occurs, particularly if several fresh fish items appear on the menu. But two rules are paramount: (1) Employees should not handle the product needlessly because this spreads bacteria and hastens the deterioration of fish quality. (2) Do not preprepare any more fish than chefs can use during the shift. Conservative prepreparing can cause production problems later on if the operation gets an unexpected rush, but it is necessary if the firm wants to avoid excessive leftovers.

KEY WORDS AND CONCEPTS

Aquaculture	Chill pack	Fish and Game office requirements
As-purchased price (AP price)	Crustacean	Fish "frankfurter"
	Exact name	Flaked and re-formed fish products
Cello pack	Fin fish	

Food and Drug Administration Office of Seafood Safety (FDA Office of Seafood Safety)

Glaze

Grading factors

Hazard Analysis Critical Control Point system (HACCP system)

Health district requirements

Ice pack

Ice spots

Individually quick frozen (IQF)

In-process inventories

Intended use

Interstate Certified Shellfish Shippers List

Live

Live-in-shell

Loss leader

Lot number

Manufacturing grade

Marinade pack

Marketing terms for fish products

Modified-atmosphere packaging (MAP)

Mollusk

Move list

National Marine Fisheries Service

New pack time

Packaging procedure

Packed Under Federal Inspection (PUFI) seal

Packers' brands

Packing medium

Point of origin

Popular varieties of fish products

Preservation method

Processed fish

Product form

Product size

Product yield

Purchasing, receiving, storing, and issuing fish products

Renaming fish

Shatter pack

Shelf life

Shellfish

Shucked fish

Size of container

Slacked out

Snap pack

Standard of identity

Statement of quality

Stockless purchase plan

Substitution possibilities

Surimi

Tagged fish

Trash fish

Trust the supplier

Truth-in-menu legislation

Type of packaging material

United States Department of Agriculture (USDA)

United States Department of Commerce (USDC)

U.S. grades

Voluntary inspection

QUESTIONS AND PROBLEMS

1. List the U.S. grades for fish.

2. A product specification for frozen, breaded shrimp could include the following information:
   (a)
   (b)
   (c)
   (d)
   (e)

3. Briefly describe the necessary storage environments for fresh-fish products.

4. The deliveryperson arrives at 5 P.M. with 20 pounds of fresh whitefish. The buyer ordered 20 pounds of fresh snapper. The supplier was out of snapper and sent whitefish. He tried to call earlier about it, but could not get through. What should the buyer do in this situation? If possible, ask a foodservice manager to comment on your answer.

5. Outline the specific procedures hospitality operators should use for purchasing, receiving, storing, and issuing frozen lobster tails. Assume that the tails will be used in a steak house for a steak and lobster tail entrée. If possible, ask a steak house manager to comment on your answer.

6. What is an appropriate intended use for canned, dark-meat tuna?

7. What does the acronym PUFI stand for?

8. What are the differences between fin fish and shellfish?

9. What are the two main types of shellfish?

10. What is the difference between a fish fillet and a fish portion?

11. KWG Enterprises sells a frozen, breaded shrimp, eight to a pound, for $7.69 per pound. Its fresh, raw shrimp, 14 to a pound, sell for $6.24 per pound. A restaurant normally sells about 24 orders of fried shrimp each day. Which product should its buyer purchase? Why? If possible, ask a food-service manager to comment on your answer.

12. Why is the point of origin of a fish product an important selection factor?

13. What does the term "14/16 crab legs" indicate to a foodservice buyer?

14. What is the primary difference between "round" fish and "drawn" fish?

15. A supplier calls to tell a buyer that he has just gotten a good buy on frozen ocean perch. The hospitality operation has never used this item before on its menu, but, with the low AP price the supplier quoted, the buyer is tempted. She has to buy 500 pounds, but this does not seem too troublesome. Assume that you operate a family-style restaurant. What would you do in this situation? Why? If possible, ask a family-style-restaurant manager to comment on your answer.

16. What critical information is missing from the following product specification for shrimp?
    Whole, raw, headless shrimp
    Used for shrimp cocktail
    U.S. Grade A (or equivalent)
    Packed in 5-pound laminated cardboard containers

17. List the grading factors for fish products.

18. Under what conditions would buyers purchase an imitation fish product?

19. What is the purpose of the tagging system that is in effect for shellfish products?

20. When would buyers purchase a flaked and re-formed fish product?

MEAT

The Purpose of this Chapter

After reading this chapter, you should be able to:

- Identify the management considerations surrounding the selection and procurement of meat.

- Explain the selection factors for meat, including government grades.

- Describe the process of purchasing, receiving, storing, and issuing meat.

INTRODUCTION

Meat represents a major portion of the foodservice purchase dollar. Consequently, buyers tend to be especially careful when making meat-purchasing decisions. Although the meat industry and the federal government provide buying guidelines, purchasing meat is a time-consuming experience.

TYPES OF MEAT ITEMS PURCHASED

Many foodservice operations purchase some type of beef, veal, pork, or lamb item in addition to many types of processed meats, such as cold cuts, sausages, ham, and bacon. Operations use preprepared meat entrées, such as beef stew, and other less familiar products to a lesser extent (see Figure 23.1 for some of the more popular types of meat products the foodservice industry uses).

BEEF

Brisket
Bottom sirloin butt
Butt steak
Chicken fried steak
Chuck
Cubed steak
Eye of round
Ground beef
Inside round
Outside round
Porterhouse steak
Rib
Ribeye roll
Ribeye steak
Short loin
Skirt steak
Strip loin steak
T-bone steak
Tenderloin
Tenderloin steak
Top sirloin butt
Top sirloin steak

CURED MEAT AND SAUSAGE

Bacon
Bologna
Bratwurst
Breakfast sausage
Corned beef
Frankfurter
Ham
Italian sausage
Knockwurst
Luncheon meat
Pepperoni
Polish sausage
Salami

LAMB

Breast
Hotel rack
Leg
Loin
Loin chop
Rib chop
Shoulder

PORK

Back rib
Boston butt
Center-cut chop
Cutlet
Fresh ham
Ground pork
Loin
Loin chop
Rib chop
Spare rib
Tenderloin

VARIETY MEAT

Calf liver
Steer liver
Sweetbread

VEAL

Breast
Cubed steak
Cutlet
Hotel rack
Ground veal
Leg
Loin chop
Rib chop
Shank
Tenderloin

FIGURE 23.1 Types of meat products that are popular in the foodservice industry.

MANAGEMENT CONSIDERATIONS

As a rule, deficient supervision is not an issue in the purchasing, receiving, storing, and issuing of meat, nor is it an issue in production. But management finds that deciding on the quality they want and the cuts they prefer is not easy.

They must seek suppliers who can provide what they want on a continuous basis. Managers who are responsible for the ordering, expediting, and receiving of meat products can attest that this is no simple task.

Some of the major managerial meat-purchasing decisions are discussed in the following sections.

Should Management Offer Meat on the Menu?

Or should you minimize the amount of meat items that you offer? The question usually is, how tied do you want to be to meat? (In other words, how much of your image do you want to be associated with it?) Although some operations, such as vegetarian restaurants, exclude meat on the menu, realistically, most operations offer meat entrées. As such, it is difficult to alter an image of the establishment when the concept is tied to meat. This is evident in theme restaurants, such as a steakhouse, where meat represents the "signature item." Consequently, you must stay with your specialty, regardless of availability or increases in the as-purchased (AP) price.

Given the high cost of meats in relation to that of other foods, the restaurateur's goal is to utilize every edible morsel. As such, meat may appear as menu items in discreet ways. What is intended to be served once sometimes blossoms into an unwieldy number of meat-related menu items: the luncheon chef's special created from the preceding night's leftovers, a meat loaf or beef stew prepared from the trimmings from a large piece of meat, and new menu selections based on customer request.

Alternatives

Many alternatives for conventional meat items exist. Fish and poultry are excellent substitutes. Also, hospitality operators can take a chance on exotic types of meat dishes, such as buffalo, bison, and venison. Additionally, they can experiment with different grades of meat. For instance, operators can use a lower meat grade from an older, tougher, but more flavorful animal when a moist cooking method is employed. Otherwise, they can purchase lower grades of meat and tenderize them chemically or mechanically. Meat recipes that contain several ingredients make good candidates for some lower-cost substitutions. Meat loaves, stews, and casseroles can be manipulated by including or excluding certain fats, meat qualities, and fillers. Also, meat alternatives, such as soybean extender, can be incorporated into certain recipes.

Although the list of meat alternatives is seemingly endless, operators always take a chance when they make substitutions. This is especially true when customers are used to one item and taste a substitute product that is unfamiliar, or when the replacements are visible to consumers, such as when a low-quality steak that has been mechanically or chemically tenderized is substituted for a naturally tender steak of higher quality.

The Quality Desired

As always, the quality hospitality operators need reflects the intended use of the product and the image they wish to project. Spending considerable time determining the quality of the product they want does not guarantee that the desired item is readily available.

One reason for this is that differences exist from animal to animal and, since many meat items come fresh, quality variations result. To minimize this phenomenon, most livestock farmers have standardized the care and feeding of their animals. In addition, this variability is generally less of a problem with processed meats. For example, pork that is cured for ham and bacon offers a great deal of predictability.

A second reason buyers cannot always find desired items is that meat of the highest- (or lowest-) quality grade may be in short supply. Because this can also thwart the operators' plans, buyers may need to rethink their strategy.

A third challenge relates to bid buying. Obtaining consistent quality should be a concern when purchasing in this manner. When bids are accepted, they often cover a long period. Changes in quality may become evident over time. The problems associated with finding consistent quality and a continuous supply of meat may drive buyers to stay with one supplier.

Type of Processing

While buyers can still purchase a "side of beef," which is half of an animal carcass, most buy fresh meat items that are butchered to some extent. Although many dining establishments prefer only fresh cuts of meats, numerous foodservice operations rely on frozen meat products in order to operate efficiently. Also, when it comes to some processed-meat items, such as bacon, ham, and bologna, most operations would never consider purchasing fresh meat and processing it in-house. Ultimately, buyers must decide on what type and amount of processing is most economical for the meat's intended use.

A key factor used in making this decision is the AP price; usually, it has a direct correlation with the degree of fabrication. A considerable spread may exist between the AP price per pound for "portion-cut" meat that needs nothing more than some cooking or heating, such as ready-to-cook sirloin steak, and the AP price per pound for "wholesale cut" meat, such as a whole loin, which can be butchered into sirloin steaks. An even greater AP-price-per-pound spread may exist between a portion-cut steak and a side of beef.

Many restaurants find it more economical to let suppliers wield the cutting tools because it is too expensive to devote a great deal of space to a butcher shop. They prefer to concentrate on devoting as much space as possible to a revenue-generating dining room and lounge.

Still, some foodservice operations perform a great deal of fabrication in-house. They may have determined that in-house processing is more economical or that it enables them to have better control of the quality. Some may even use this feature in their marketing efforts. In any case, the hospitality industry generally thinks that in-house meat fabrication presents four major problems:

1. This practice requires additional labor hours and skilled laborers, which may lead to increased operating expenses and recruiting cost.

2. This practice tends to increase the level of pilferage; it is easy to steal items that are being preprepared, usually in a remote area of the kitchen.

3. Avoidable waste also tends to increase whenever hospitality operators engage in major production efforts.

4. Meat production creates a considerable amount of "working" dirt and waste products that must be removed continuously in order to prevent contamination. As such, an operation's sanitation needs increase substantially. The typical restaurant kitchen does not have the equipment, time, and skill needed to perform these duties adequately.

Conversely, some disadvantages exist with portion-cut meats. These drawbacks include:

1. A premium may be charged for uniform weight, shape, and thickness. (This uniformity, however, may be very useful to relatively inexperienced cooks.)

2. Pilferage may increase with portion cuts of meat; they are easy to steal, especially since they usually come in convenient packages.

3. Sometimes, a case of precut steaks contains one or two steaks of demonstrably lower quality. Can the receiver catch this problem or will the cook notice the difference?

When purchasing in large quantities, some buyers may find it advantageous to choose frozen-meat items. With today's processing technology, freezing does not harm the products. Proper freezing, thawing, and cooking methods can make any quality differences in taste or texture almost imperceptible. Quality problems are usually due to improper handling.

Another option buyers can consider is convenience foods. Frozen-meat entrées, including fajitas, baked and sliced meat loaf, and stuffed peppers, may not be popular in some hospitality operations, but college, hospital, and other institutional food services use these products readily. These preprepared, portion-control items are sometimes used for large banquets and employee meals, too.

Reducing the AP Price and the EP Cost

Meat purchasers can find all sorts of ways to reduce the AP price while keeping the edible-portion (EP) cost, profit margins, and dollar profits acceptable. Some opt for substitutions, such as replacing meat with fish, offering casseroles instead of sandwich steaks, and widening the menu to include lower-cost products. This latter tactic, though, reduces both AP prices and menu prices. The food cost as a percentage of menu sales prices may decrease, but the sales revenue may also decline and cut into the number of dollars left to cover labor, overhead, and profits.

Buyers can also substitute meat of lower quality and tenderize it; purchase some "formed-meat" products, which are less expensive cuts of meat that have been "flaked," then re-formed and sliced to resemble a steak; or add soybean extenders, as long as chefs follow the legal requirements. (For example, soybean-extended ground beef cannot be called hamburger.)

Furthermore, hospitality operations can reduce the AP price and the EP cost by shrinking portion sizes. Alternately, instead of including a baked potato with the steak, they can charge extra for it. (This reduces the EP cost of the steak dinner, not the EP cost of the steak itself.) Yet another option is to consider serving coleslaw as a substitute for tossed salad. Remember, these substitution strategies always carry a certain amount of risk.

One way to protect the AP price and EP cost is to enter into a long-term contract with the supplier. This arrangement can help operators retain their standards of quality while considerably reducing the risk of both blurring their image and annoying their customers—a risk that may accompany the other cost-cutting strategies just noted. Buyers may realize a saving if they contract for, perhaps, a six-month supply of beef. Of course, they must have the wherewithal to procure the huge quantities that are necessary to interest a supplier. Consequently, only large chains regularly use this method. Not everyone in the hospitality industry thinks that firms can save money this way. For instance, the daily cash price for meat may drop considerably at any time during the contractual period.

The hedging procedure (see Chapter 10) may be a viable way of maintaining a relatively stable AP price. Large foodservice companies that have the resources and skills needed to practice this procedure may save money in the long run.

As a practical matter, small operators may have to make do on a day-to-day basis. If they try to spend too much time concentrating on the AP price, they may neglect the EP cost. It may be better for small operators to concentrate on the EP cost, especially on ways of reducing it that represent little or no risk. For instance, they should ensure that there is minimal waste in production and service, minimal shrinkage, zero pilferage, and so forth.

Every once in a while, buyers may find a bargain. Unfortunately, most bargains come from new suppliers in the form of temporary introductory offers. In addition, bargains may force buyers to purchase a new convenience entrée at a special AP price or to take fresh-frozen meat in lieu of fresh-refrigerated meat.

Normal quantity buy opportunities do appear. But, aside from items on a move list, fewer meat bargains are available in comparison to those offered in other product areas. Furthermore, buyers do not shift suppliers or meat specifications quickly. Meat is a major purchase, so meat buyers practice discretion more widely.

SELECTION FACTORS

As with all products, management decides on the quality and style of meat desired. Then, either alone or in concert with other personnel, management evaluates several of the following selection factors when determining standards of quality desired and suppliers.

Intended Use

As always, buyers want to determine exactly what the intended use of an item is so that they will be able to prepare the appropriate, relevant specification. For instance, bacon used on the breakfast menu should be cut differently from bacon that will be cooked, crumbled, and used as a salad topping.

Exact Name

As with all other products, it is very important for hospitality operators to note the exact name of the meat items they want so they do not receive products that will not suit their needs. To some extent, identifying the exact product that they prefer is a bit easier in this channel of distribution than it is in some other product lines. Over the years, a great deal of standardization has evolved, which the meat industry, meat users, and the United States Department of Agriculture (USDA) have spurred.

The federal government has set several standards of identity for meat products. For instance, if buyers specify that they want hamburger, they will get a mixture that is 70 percent lean meat and 30 percent fat. Of course, as with all standards of identity, a producer is free to improve upon the government definition. In this example, the producer can use beef from just about any part of the animal. So, if buyers expect to receive a specific type of meat in their hamburger, they must include this information in their specification.

Using standards of identity, therefore, is a bit risky unless buyers include additional appropriate information on the specification. They will be able to reduce this amount of information considerably if they utilize in the specification the Institutional Meat Purchase Specifications (IMPS) numbering system for meat items. These numbers take the place of part of a meat specification. For example, if buyers order a 1112 ribeye steak, they will get a particular style and trim.

The IMPS numbers evolved from a cooperative effort by the National Association of Meat Purveyors (NAMP [now called the North American Meat Processors Association]), the National Live Stock and Meat Board, foodservice purchasing agents, and the USDA's Agricultural Marketing Service (AMS) Livestock Division. These numbers are included in *The Meat Buyers Guide (MBG)*, published by the NAMP. In addition to the numbers, a description and a picture of each item are included. This is very desirable to buyers who can then "order by the numbers" and be assured of receiving the exact cut of meat they want.

The IMPS numbers, sometimes referred to as the IMPS/NAMP numbers or the *MBG* numbers, provide a considerable degree of convenience. Typical buyers would never think of preparing meat product specifications without first consulting this major reference book. IMPS numbers are indexed according to product category. The first digit of the number refers to the type of product; the remaining digits indicate a specific cut and trim (see Figure 23.2 for the IMPS numbers for some meat cuts and Figure 23.3 for the *MBG* Table of Contents).

If, for some reason, buyers do not wish to use the IMPS numbers when preparing specifications, they must at least be able to indicate the exact cut of meat they

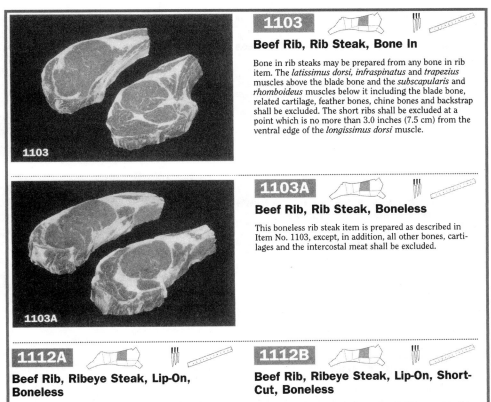

1103
Beef Rib, Rib Steak, Bone In

Bone in rib steaks may be prepared from any bone in rib item. The *latissimus dorsi, infraspinatus* and *trapezius* muscles above the blade bone and the *subscapularis* and *rhomboideus* muscles below it including the blade bone, related cartilage, feather bones, chine bones and backstrap shall be excluded. The short ribs shall be excluded at a point which is no more than 3.0 inches (7.5 cm) from the ventral edge of the *longissimus dorsi* muscle.

1103A
Beef Rib, Rib Steak, Boneless

This boneless rib steak item is prepared as described in Item No. 1103, except, in addition, all other bones, cartilages and the intercostal meat shall be excluded.

1112A
Beef Rib, Ribeye Steak, Lip-On, Boneless

Boneless ribeye steaks, lip-on shall be prepared from a rib item meeting the end requirements of Item No. 112A. The lip shall be cut on the short rib side with a straight cut which is ventral to, but no more than 2.0 inches (5.0 cm) from the *longissimus dorsi,* leaving the lip firmly attached.

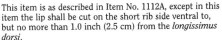

1112B
Beef Rib, Ribeye Steak, Lip-On, Short-Cut, Boneless

This item is as described in Item No. 1112A, except in this item the lip shall be cut on the short rib side ventral to, but no more than 1.0 inch (2.5 cm) from the *longissimus dorsi.*

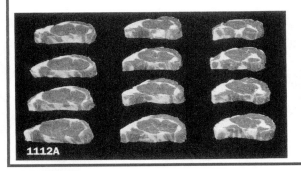

FIGURE 23.2 IMPS numbers for some meat products. Reprinted from *The Meat Buyers Guide,* Author and Publisher: The North American Meat Processors Association. Copyright 1997, Third Printing—May 2003. All rights reserved. Visit www.namp.com for further product information.

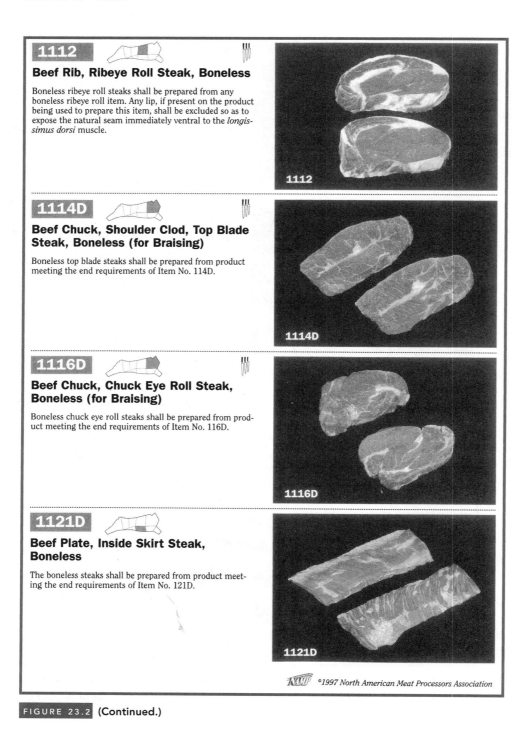

1112

Beef Rib, Ribeye Roll Steak, Boneless

Boneless ribeye roll steaks shall be prepared from any boneless ribeye roll item. Any lip, if present on the product being used to prepare this item, shall be excluded so as to expose the natural seam immediately ventral to the *longissimus dorsi* muscle.

1112

1114D

Beef Chuck, Shoulder Clod, Top Blade Steak, Boneless (for Braising)

Boneless top blade steaks shall be prepared from product meeting the end requirements of Item No. 114D.

1114D

1116D

Beef Chuck, Chuck Eye Roll Steak, Boneless (for Braising)

Boneless chuck eye roll steaks shall be prepared from product meeting the end requirements of Item No. 116D.

1116D

1121D

Beef Plate, Inside Skirt Steak, Boneless

The boneless steaks shall be prepared from product meeting the end requirements of Item No. 121D.

1121D

©1997 North American Meat Processors Association

FIGURE 23.2 (Continued.)

Table of CONTENTS

FIGURE 23.3 *The Meat Buyers Guide* Table of Contents. Reprinted from *The Meat Buyers Guide*, Author and Publisher: The North American Meat Processors Association. Copyright 1997, Third Printing—May 2003. All rights reserved. Visit www.namp.com for further product information.

want or the exact type of processed item they need. Fresh meat comes in four basic cuts: (1) the whole carcass; (2) a side, essentially half a carcass; (3) a wholesale (primal) cut; and (4) a retail cut. Numerous other cutting terms, such as hotel-sliced bacon, Spencer-cut prime rib of beef, and square-cut chuck, are involved, too. Buyers are responsible for becoming familiar with these cuts and related terminology, especially if they decide to forgo the use of IMPS numbers.

In addition to cuts of meat, buyers need to be knowledgeable about other commonly used trade terms. Two major ones are "variety meats" (sometimes referred to as "edible by-products"), which refer to such organs as the liver, tongue, and heart, and "sausages," which are preserved, usually dried or salted, chunked or chopped meat and spices shaped into tubes. Some sausages have skins; some do not. Some are cooked; some are not.

The federal government can modify the existing list of terms via additions or deletions. It can also include definitions of the terms used in its grading practices and grading standards. Buyers should stay abreast of these changes if they purchase a great deal of meat.

If buyers need a great deal of processed meat products, they must be concerned with the exact name, specific form, and culinary quality of these items. Standards of identity exist for many products; for example, a minimum formula exists for preprepared beef stew. Generally, though, these identity formulas are not very useful as a major selection factor for processed-meat products.

U.S. Government Inspection and Grades (or Equivalent)

The inspection of meat for wholesomeness has been mandatory since the passage of the Federal Meat Inspection Act in 1907. This law applies to all raw meat sold in interstate commerce, as well as meat exported to other countries. Processed products, such as sausages, frozen dinners, canned meats, and soups made with meat, must also be inspected. An exception is rabbit meat; it is not required to be federally inspected. However, the rabbit industry has a voluntary program that requires rabbit meat packers to pay for inspection.

Federal inspection falls under the jurisdiction of the UDSA's Food Safety and Inspection Service (FSIS) (www.fsis.usda.gov). The principal inspection system the FSIS uses for most meat-slaughtering and -processing facilities is the Hazard Analysis Critical Control Point (HACCP). The food industry instituted HACCP to ensure food safety and nonfood safety conditions exist in all critical stages of food handling by reducing and eliminating defects that pass through traditional inspection. FSIS inspectors conduct online carcass inspection and verification inspection to make certain that plants are meeting the FSIS's performance standards for food safety or nonfood safety defects (www.fsis.usda.gov/OA/haccp).

States with companies that sell meats solely through intrastate commerce channels have the discretion of conducting their own meat-inspection programs. Under the 1967 Wholesome Meat Act, these state inspection programs are required to be at least equal to the federal inspection programs.

The federal inspection program begins with the approval of plans for a slaughtering or processing plant to ensure that the facilities, equipment, and procedures can adequately provide for safe and sanitary operations. Facilities and equipment in plants must be easy to clean and to keep clean. The floor plan, water supply, waste disposal methods, and lighting must be approved for each plant facility. Each day before operations begin, the inspector checks the plant and continues the inspection throughout the day to ensure that sanitary conditions are maintained. If, at any time, he or she finds that the equipment is not properly cleaned or an unsanitary condition is present, slaughtering or processing operations are stopped until corrective steps have been taken.

The inspection of animals is done both before and after slaughtering. Before slaughter, USDA inspectors examine all livestock for signs of disease, and any animal appearing sick undergoes a special examination. No dead or dying animal is allowed to enter the slaughtering plant. After slaughter, the inspectors examine each carcass and its internal organs for signs of disease or contamination that would make all or part of the carcass unfit as human food (see Figure 23.4). To ensure uniformity in the inspection process, veterinary supervisors regularly monitor the inspectors' procedures and work.

Meat that passes the rigorous USDA inspection is marked with a federal-inspection stamp (see Figure 23.5). This stamp indicates the number of the meat-processing plant where the meat was slaughtered and packed. The stamp does not appear on all meat cuts; usually, it is visible only on wholesale cuts of meat. Some retail cuts, however, may include remnants of an inspection stamp unless it is completely removed during the cutting and trimming process.

The inspection program the USDA provides is the most trusted inspection program available. The program the United States military uses to inspect its meat products before use in troop feeding is comparable to the USDA's procedures. Although several types of inspection programs exist, they are not the same as USDA inspection for wholesomeness. For instance, religious inspections are performed in some meat plants. These inspections certify only that the meat items satisfy the religious codes, not that they have met a certain standard of quality.

FIGURE 23.4 Federal inspector checking a beef carcass. Courtesy of National Cattlemen's Beef Association.

In addition to its meat inspections, the federal government also prepares guidelines on such topics as humane slaughter techniques, animal husbandry, and transportation techniques.

In addition to mandatory inspection, the USDA offers voluntary grading programs. It has long recognized the importance of a uniform system of grading slaughter animals to facilitate the production, marketing, and distribution of livestock and meats. These grading programs also provide an objective evaluation of the culinary quality and edible yield of fresh meat items. The initial U.S. standards for grades of beef were formulated in 1916, with the official standards adopted in 1928. Today, these services are conducted under the regulations of the Agricultural Marketing Act of 1946. The AMS Live Stock & Feed Division publishes the grades (see Figure 23.6).

Quality grading systems exist for beef, lamb, pork, and veal; voluntary yield grading systems are available for beef and lamb. While no formal yield grading sys-

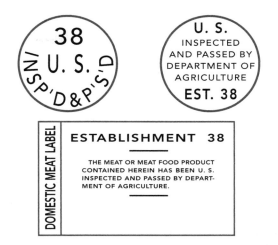

FIGURE 23.5 Federal inspection stamps used for meat products. The number appearing in the stamp identifies the meat plant where the meat was processed and inspected. *Source:* United States Department of Agriculture.

tem exists for pork, these items' quality grades are based primarily on yield; other culinary characteristics play a lesser role. Veal is not graded for yield.

Because grading services are not mandated, they must be purchased. Nonetheless, purchasing such services is popular with many manufacturers, distribution intermediaries, and retailers since it is quite common for buyers to use

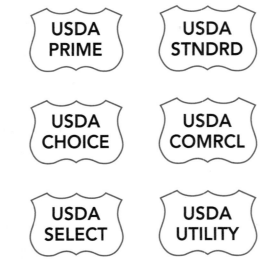

FIGURE 23.6 Federal grade stamps used for meat items. *Source:* United States Department of Agriculture.

government grades as one selection factor when they purchase meat. However, some cattle breeders and meat packers feel that grading is too capricious and inconsistent, and some people are not happy with the changes and proposed changes (usually done for health and nutrition concerns) in the grading systems that have occurred over the years. Nevertheless, approximately 50 percent of the meat sold in the United States is graded for quality. Despite the problems associated with federal grades, those mentioned above among others, buyers have not been deterred from using those systems. Buyers may not rely so heavily on the grades as they once did, but most meat specifications contain some reference to a U.S. grade.

Quality grades for slaughter cattle are based on an evaluation of factors related to the palatability of the meat. Federal graders primarily evaluate beef quality by the amount and distribution of "finish," that is, the degree of fatness; the firmness of muscling; and the physical characteristics of the animal that are associated with maturity. Other grading factors the federal grader evaluates include: the age of the animal at the time of slaughter; the sex of the animal; the color of the flesh; the amount of external finish; the shape and form of the carcass; and the number of defects and blemishes. Foodservice buyers consider the amount of "marbling," or the little streams of fat that run through meat, present in the flesh to be a primary factor.

U.S. quality grades for beef also are subject to several limiting rules. The USDA grading system strictly defines some, while others grant some discretion to the federal grader. The most severe limiting rule, and the one that normally causes a great deal of anxiety among meat producers, is the regulation associated with the beef animals' "maturity class." These animals are divided into five maturity classes:

Class A: Age at the time of slaughter is 9 to 30 months.

Class B: Age at the time of slaughter is 30 to 42 months.

Classes C, D, E: Age at the time of slaughter is greater than 42 months.

It is the grader's responsibility to determine an animal's physiological age at the time of slaughter. He or she does this by examining the color and texture of the lean meat, the condition of the bones, and the amount of hardening, or ossification, of the cartilage.

Beef animals' quality grades are affected by their maturity class. For instance, regardless of the quality present in Class C cattle, it cannot be graded Prime. In general, any beef animal older than 42 months at time of slaughter cannot receive the highest-quality grade regardless of the score it received on the other factors the grader considers (see Figure 23.7).

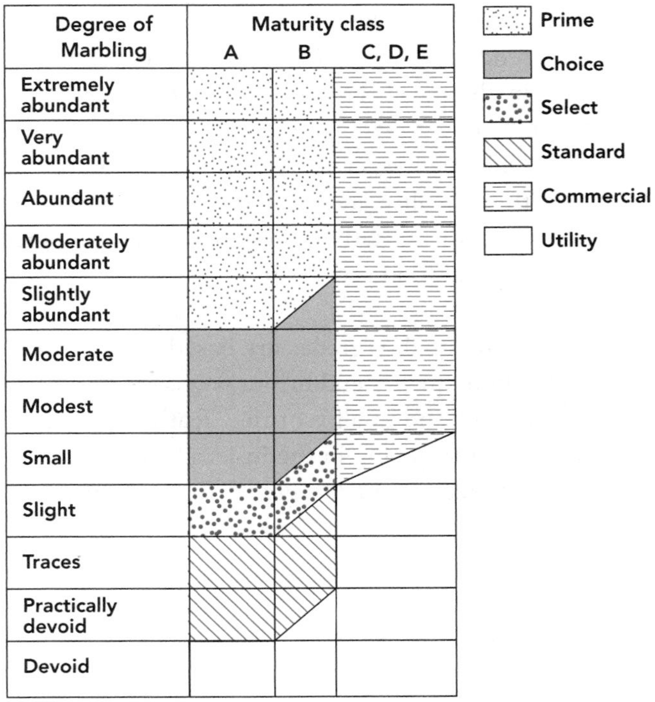

FIGURE 23.7 How beef quality grades are determined.

The federal quality grades for beef are:

1. **Prime.** This is the best product available. Tender and very juicy, Prime beef contains 8 to 10 percent fat. Usually, the animal has been grain-fed for at least 180 days in order to develop the exceptionally large amount of firm, white fat. The meat is extremely flavorful.

2. **Choice.** Choice grade beef contains at least 5 percent fat. Three levels exist: high, medium, and low. High Choice is similar to Prime, although the animal has been grain-fed for only about 150 days. Medium Choice indicates that the animal has been grain-fed about 120 days; Low Choice, for about 90 days. Foodservice operators normally purchase High and Medium Choice; Low Choice is typically sold through supermarkets and grocery stores.

3. **Select.** This beef is a very lean product, containing 4 percent fat and sometimes referred to as "grass-fed beef." The fat on this product usually is not very white, nor very firm. This grade is popular in supermarkets. It is a low-cost item and is more healthful than higher-quality grades, but it lacks flavor.

4. **Standard.** While similar to Select, Standard beef is even less juicy and tender. It has a very mild flavor. This product also tends to be referred to as "grass-fed beef."

5. **Commercial.** Beef from older cattle, Commercial grade is especially lacking in tenderness. Usually, dairy cows receive this quality grade. Because of the animals' age at the time of slaughter, some of this meat may be quite flavorful.

6, 7, 8. **Utility, Cutter, and Canner.** No age limitation exists for these quality grades. Old breeding stock (older cows and bulls) is usually classified into one of these three quality grade categories. Generally, these products are not available as fresh meat. Rather, these manufacturing grades are intended for use by commercial food processors.

Lamb quality grades are based primarily on the color, texture, and firmness of the flesh; quality and firmness of the finish; the proportion of meat to bone; and the amount and quality of the "feathering," which is the fat streaking in the ribs and the fat streaking in the inside flank muscles.

The federal quality grades for lamb are:

1. Prime

2. Choice

3. Good

4. Utility

If a foodservice operation offers fresh lamb on the menu, the Prime and Choice quality grades are normally used. Lower-graded products are not intended for use as fresh meat items. As is typically the case in the hospitality industry, commercial food processors primarily use manufacturing grades to prepare convenience food items.

Pork quality grades are based almost exclusively on yield. The most important consideration is the amount of finish, especially as it relates to color, firmness, and texture. Feathering is also an important consideration. Grain-fed pork make better-quality products, which are far superior to those animals that are given other types of feeds.

The federal quality grades for pork are:

1. No. 1
2. No. 2
3. No. 3
4. No. 4
5. Utility

Most pork is used by commercial food processors to fabricate a variety of convenience and processed items, such as ham and bacon. As a result of this and the fact that most pork is separated into small cuts before it leaves the meat-packing plant, very few pork carcasses are graded for quality. Meat packers and purchasing agents rely on the various packers' brands (i.e., packers' "grades") that are available.

If fresh pork is included on the menu, the typical foodservice operation necessarily must use the No. 1 or No. 2 quality grade, or equivalent packers' brands. Lower-quality items will shrink too much during the cooking process, resulting in an unacceptable finished menu item.

Veal quality grades are based on the color, texture, and firmness of the flesh; the proportion of meat to bone; the quality and firmness of the finish; and the amount and quality of the feathering. High-quality veal will have a pink color and smooth flesh.

The federal quality grades for veal are:

1. Prime
2. Choice
3. Good
4. Standard
5. Utility
6. Cull

The Prime and Choice quality grades are intended for use as fresh products. The lower-quality products tend to be tough and, therefore, are more commonly used to fabricate convenience items.

For more information on U.S. government inspection and grades, see www.ams.usda.gov/lsg/ls-mg.

Product Yield

The federal government provides a voluntary yield grading service for beef and lamb. Yield grades are numbered 1 through 5, with Yield Grade 1 representing the highest yield of cuts and Yield Grade 5, the lowest. Grading criteria are based on the following factors: (1) thickness of fat over ribeye; (2) area of ribeye; (3) percent of kidney, pelvic, and heart fat; and (4) carcass weight. Some limiting rules apply. For instance, USDA Prime beef cannot earn a Yield Grade of 1 or 2 because of its high percentage of fat, which reduces its edible yield.

Prime beef has a great deal of marbling—and, hence, flavor—and the amount of muscle is considerably reduced for this quality grade. For similar reasons, USDA Choice beef also cannot earn a Yield Grade 1. So, to a certain degree, quality and yield grades are interrelated.

Buyers who purchase beef sides, quarters, or wholesale cuts want to specify a desired yield grade. But with such large cuts of beef, an exact yield grade cannot always be specified. Instead, a yield range must be denoted. For example, a buyer may purchase a USDA Commercial beef brisket, with a U.S. Yield Grade 1–2, or its equivalent (see Figures 23.8 and 23.9).

FIGURE 23.8 A federal yield grade stamp used to indicate the yield of a carcass. *Source:* United States Department of Agriculture.

FIGURE 23.9 Federal inspector checking the quality of beef carcasses. *Source:* United States Department of Agriculture.

Buyers who purchase only retail cuts can use the federal-government standards to specify an exact yield grade. For example, a specification for sirloin strip steak can state that it must be cut from a beef carcass that carries U.S. Yield Grade 1, or its equivalent.

If buyers use the IMPS system and/or the USDA yield grades, they can be assured of standardized edible yields for the fresh products they purchase. If, however, they do not utilize these systems, they will need to indicate on the specification the minimum yield, or the maximum trim, they will accept.

No formal yield grading system is available for pork and veal. Recall, though, that the U.S. quality grades for pork are based primarily on yield. The pork grades are sometimes referred to as "yield standards." The U.S. No. 1 pork grade represents the leanest, meatiest product, whereas U.S. No. 4 product has about twice as much fat and one-third less muscle.

Packers' Brands (or Equivalent)

Many meat producers have developed their own grading procedures for branding their fresh meat. As mentioned earlier, this branding system is sometimes referred to as "packers' grades." For instance, Armour sells "Star Deluxe," "Star," "Quality," and "Banquet." A significant number of foodservice buyers find this procedure quite acceptable. Although packers' grades are similar to federal grades, they may not reflect an objective viewpoint.

Some meat producers sell "certified organic" products. A qualifying entity must have: (1) standards for what constitutes an agricultural product that is "organically" produced, and (2) a system for ensuring that the product meets those standards. Once the associated animal husbandry and production methods meet USDA standards, the meat items can be labeled as "certified organic by [the certifying entity]" (see www.fsis.usda.gov/OPPDE/larc/Certified_Organic and www.fsis.usda.gov/OPPDE/larc/Organic_Claims for more information on this topic).

Any type of processed meat, other than fresh-frozen or portion-cut, is often purchased on the strength of a brand name. Most pork products, particularly those that are cured, are purchased this way. In almost every instance, these brand names are the only indication of quality. We have seen few specifications for cold cuts that did not rely on a brand name or its equivalent. (It is possible to detail the material used in these items. For a product like breakfast sausage, it would be easy to specify the amount of pork, fat, seasonings, water, and type of grind. For most other types of products in this area, it would not be this simple.)

Packers' brands are sometimes used when purchasing portion-cut meats. Buyers should be concerned with uniformity. Although portion-cut items have a standardized weight, not all packers necessarily supply the same shape. Second, the packaging can differ drastically; steaks may be individually wrapped and neatly stacked, or tossed together in a box. In addition, equal weights are not necessarily an indicator of uniform appearance; some items may be sloppily cut, with excess nicks and tears.

Other forms of brand name identification exist in the meat channel of distribution. For instance, the SYSCO brand Supreme Angus Beef products include only young beef of predominantly Angus breed that fall within the upper two-thirds of the USDA Choice grade. Also, if a meat packer's products meet the quality standards that the popular Certified Angus Beef Program mandates, they are allowed to carry the certification seal. The program, developed by the American Angus Association, stipulates that a beef product must have at least modest marbling, be in the youngest maturity class, and qualify for U.S. Yield Grade 1, 2, or 3.

Product Size

Invariably, buyers must indicate the size of the particular piece of meat they order. This task is made easy because the *MBG* notes weight ranges for wholesale cuts of meat, as well as standardized portion sizes for retail cuts. For example, all large cuts are categorized into four weight ranges: A, B, C, and D. Small retail cuts can be purchased in several sizes. The IMPS regulations stipulate that portion cuts specified between 6 to 11 ounces must be accurate to within $1/2$ ounce; those specified between 12 to 17 ounces must have a tolerance of $3/4$ ounce; and those specified 18 ounces must be accurate to within 1 ounce.

If buyers purchase processed convenience items, such as frozen, preprepared, stuffed peppers, a size indication may also be required. Usually, a particular packer's brand carries only one size, so if buyers consistently indicate the same brand on their specification, they will not need to specify product size information.

Size of Container

Container sizes are standardized in the meat channel of distribution. Processed products come in package sizes that normally range from about 5 pounds to more than 50 pounds. For instance, frozen, preprepared beef stew may be packed in a 5-pound Cryovac® bag, packed six bags to a case. Alternately, the stew may be packed in a 5-pound, oven-ready, foil tray, which is sometimes referred to as a "steam-table" pack, packed six trays to a case.

Fresh, portion-cut meat products are usually packed in 10-pound cases. Some, such as ground beef, normally come in 5-pound and 10-pound Cryovac bags. Fresh, wholesale cuts of meat are typically packed in a container that is big enough to accommodate them. For example, if buyers order beef rib, IMPS number 109, weight range C (18 to 22 pounds each), the items will usually be packed three to a case. In such instances, buyers would not specify the size of the container if an accurate size could not be determined. Another option is to specify a "catch weight" (approximate weight) of 60 pounds per case.

If buyers purchase canned or bottled merchandise, they must specify the appropriate can number or volume designation. For instance, they can purchase canned chili in a No. 10 can and beef jerky in a 1-gallon jar.

Type of Packaging Material

Packaging materials play an integral role in maintaining product quality by minimizing the degree of product deterioration. As a result, meat buyers should specify materials that optimize product quality in accordance with intended use. The typical packaging used in the industry comprises moisture- and vapor-proof materials. Cryovac plastic, or its equivalent, is particularly popular because it is ideal when a meat packer wants to "shrink wrap" the product; this involves packing the meat in plastic and pulling a vacuum through the parcel so that air is removed and the wrapping collapses to fit snugly around the product.

Packaging quality has a significant effect on a meat product's AP price. Most suppliers adhere to standardized materials. However, a supplier who seeks to undercut his or her competitor could easily do so by using inferior packaging materials. This is false economy because buyers must be concerned with protecting meat properly, especially if it is or will be frozen.

Packaging Procedure

The packaging procedure for meat items parallels those procedures used in the poultry and fish channels of distribution. With the exception of the ice pack method, all other procedures are available from at least one supplier. The choice of packaging procedures varies. Large cuts of meat are necessarily slab-packed in containers that are big enough to hold them. Portion cuts are usually layered, but if buyers prefer, the packer will wrap each portion cut individually and then layer them in the case. Bacon comes in a "shingle pack," which is the way it normally appears in a supermarket; a "layout pack," in which several bacon strips are placed on oven paper and the cook can then conveniently place a layer of this bacon on a sheet pan and pop it into the oven; or a "bulk pack," which is a type of slab-packing procedure. Not every supplier offers a wide range of packaging options because this practice adds to the cost of doing business. However, most suppliers will accommodate buyers' needs if they are willing to pay for these services.

Product Form

Once again, we note the usefulness of the *MBG*. If buyers use the IMPS numbers when specifying meat cuts, and sellers follow them, the meat will be cut and trimmed according to the standards that exist for those items. If buyers are purchasing processed items, they can rely, to some extent, on the *MBG* because it contains IMPS numbers for several convenience items. However, many more items are available in the meat channel of distribution that are not noted in this reference book. Buyers must be very careful to indicate the exact product desired; usually, the best way for buyers to ensure that they obtain a suitable convenience product is to rely on a packer's brand name.

Preservation Method

Most meat products that foodservice buyers purchase are preserved in one of two ways: refrigerated or frozen. Canned, dehydrated, and pickled products are also available. For example, buyers can purchase canned soups and canned chili products; however, many operators tend to favor the frozen varieties.

Meat is also preserved by curing and/or smoking. Curing is accomplished when the meat is subjected to a combination of salt, sugar, sodium nitrite, and other ingredients. Smoking preserves the meat and, in most instances, cooks it as well. Many cured items are also smoked. Foodservice buyers purchase a good deal of these products. The primary factors used for the selection of cured and smoked meats are the unique flavor, texture, and aroma that these preservation methods create. Usually, these products are refrigerated when delivered to a hospitality operation, though many of them could be frozen. For instance, bacon, which is a cured and smoked product, may be refrigerated or frozen.

The hospitality industry has witnessed a great deal of controversy concerning the use of nitrites. Sodium nitrite combines with certain amino acids to form nitrosamine, a carcinogenic substance. Nitrites continue to be used, though in lesser amounts than before, because of their superior preservation qualities and because they can control the growth of *Clostridium botulinum*, the deadly bacterium that causes botulism food poisoning. Nitrites also are responsible for the characteristic color and flavor of cured meat products.

If operators use cured and/or smoked products, they must ensure consistent culinary quality by specifying very clearly the types of products they desire. Ordinarily, the only way to obtain consistency is to specify a particular packer's brand. The many combinations of curing and/or smoking procedures that can be used almost force buyers to select one desired packer's brand for each item purchased. Product substitutions are inadvisable because customers would notice them very quickly.

Tenderization Procedure

If buyers purchase meat to be used for steaks and chops—meat that will be broiled or fried—it has to have a certain degree of tenderness. High-quality meats come with a good measure of natural tenderness. In other cases, it may be necessary for someone in the channel of distribution to introduce a bit of "artificial" tenderization. And, usually, a primary source or an intermediary contributes this.

The natural tenderization process is referred to as "aging" the meat. Beef and lamb can be aged. Pork and veal usually are not. One of several aging methods may be employed. The first is called "dry aging." This method tenderizes the meat and adds flavor. Only high-quality grades of meat can be dry aged successfully. Although a very old animal would be flavorful, no amount of aging would tenderize it. Conversely, young meat that is aged goes through a rushed maturation process. In fact, a couple of weeks of dry aging may produce as much flavor as an extra year of life. USDA Prime beef and USDA Choice beef (High Choice and Medium Choice, not Low Choice) are good candidates for dry aging.

Dry aging is expensive. This method requires the meat to be held for about 14 days in carefully controlled temperature and humidity. As a result, the meat loses moisture. So it weighs less after aging, which forces up its AP price. Also, dry aging requires an additional investment in facilities and inventories, which forces up the AP price even more. Buyers should never assume that the meat they purchase has been dry aged. They must request this expensive procedure—and must be prepared to pay for it.

In the late 1970s, the Food and Drug Administration (FDA) approved a new aging process for beef that involves spraying meat with a mold. (Mold naturally forms during dry aging; this new process simply speeds it along.) This process claims to accomplish in 48 hours what used to take two weeks or more to accomplish under the conventional dry-aging method.

Another type of aging done in the trade is called "wet aging," also referred to as "Cryovac aging" (www.cryovac.com). This method is less expensive than the conventional dry-aging process and causes no weight loss. This method involves wrapping the meat cuts in heavy plastic vacuum packs, sealing them tightly, and keeping them refrigerated for about 10 to 14 days. The wrapped meat can be in transit, aging, while it is trucked to the restaurant. Unfortunately, wet aging causes very little flavor development. Also, wet-aged meat seems to be much drier than dry-aged meat if it is cooked past the medium state. The wet-aging process is the most common form of aging available. If buyers do not specify a tenderization procedure, they can expect that the fresh meat they purchase will undergo this wet-aging process.

The biggest disadvantage of using aged meat is that it quickly cooks to the well-done state. However, if hospitality operators are going to roast large wholesale cuts, they can do a bit of aging themselves. By cooking these items in a slow oven, say, at between 200°F and 225°F, they actually simulate aging. They do not add much flavor, but at these temperatures the meat tenderizes somewhat while it cooks. Whatever the method used, aging usually provides a good meat product.

Some people are under the impression that they can purchase unaged meat, which is sometimes referred to as "green" meat, and successfully age the product themselves in the refrigerator or freezer. Certainly, purchasing green meat is tempting because the AP price would be significantly lower than that of a properly aged product. Unfortunately, meat will not age in the typical refrigerator. Meat also will not age if it is frozen or once it is cooked. It will age properly only if its storage environment has the required temperature and humidity.

Another type of tenderization procedure that can be used on beef animals is a process called "beef electrification." This was introduced in 1978. It consists of subjecting a beef carcass to three 15-minute, 600-volt electric shocks. This process allows meat to be aged for only about two-thirds of the normal aging procedure. In addition, the electrification process not only reduces the aging time, but also increases tenderization by about 50 percent.

Meat can also be "chemically" or "mechanically" treated to tenderize it. Chemical tenderizing involves adding an enzyme to the meat that changes the protein structure. Meat packers can inject enzymes into live animals just before slaughter. They also can give postmortem injections. Alternately, after dressing the meat and, usually, cutting it into no more than $1/2$-inch-thick pieces, packers can dip the meat into an enzyme solution and allow it to remain there for about 30 minutes. This dipping method, however, prevents the enzyme from penetrating the muscles too deeply.

Restaurants may use the dipping tenderization procedure in their own kitchens when they offer a low-priced steak dinner. The steaks probably came from a low-quality animal. The operations want it tender, though, and chemical aging is a way of achieving this.

These chemical procedures are not as popular today as they once were in the hospitality industry. A major problem concerns the possibility that the enzymes used will continue to attack the muscles and connective tissues of the meat if the meat product is kept at a temperature range of approximately 120°F to 140°F. This could easily result in a product that is very mushy and, hence, unacceptable to customers.

Mechanical methods, such as grinding and cubing, alter the shape of the product, but not so much the taste. Tenderizing via physical techniques may be preferable to chemical means. However, if not applied properly, mechanical methods can ruin the product.

Mechanical tenderization can be accomplished using the "needling" method. This procedure involves submitting a wholesale cut to a machine with several tiny needles. The needles penetrate the meat, tenderizing it without altering its shape. Chefs have to look carefully to see the needle marks, and, once the meat is cooked, they are not visible. This method can be used on boneless or bone-in wholesale cuts. Most often, operators use it on wholesale cuts that will be served as steaks or roasts.

Inexpensive, tough pieces of meat can also be tenderized by the "comminuting," or flaking and re-forming, process. These pieces are flaked, not ground, and then pressed together to resemble, for example, a loin of beef. "Steaks" are then cut from this "loin."

Hospitality operators can accomplish mechanical tenderization themselves; they can even buy an expensive needling machine if they wish. For that matter, they can age their own meat and apply a dipping chemical bath. The question is: Who can provide these services less expensively—the buyer or the supplier?

Usually, the tenderization question arises only when buyers purchase fresh beef products. If veal is tenderized at all, the mechanical method is used. More typically, veal is roasted very slowly. Also, operators rarely experience a tenderness problem with pork. Lamb is aged, but only about half as long as beef.

Point of Origin

Occasionally, a foodservice operator notes on the menu the point of origin for a meat entrée. For example, guests may see "Iowa Corn-Fed Beef," "West Virginia Ham," "Wisconsin Veal," or "Belgian Blue Cattle" (a rare, costly, imported breed that is exceptionally low in fat and calories) listed on a menu. If hospitality operations want to use this form of advertising, they must purchase the appropriate product or else they will be violating any relevant truth-in-menu legislation.

Inspection?

Some buyers may be concerned with the various chemicals and additives that suppliers can use to enhance meat production. If buyers are worried, they should seek out meat producers who do not use these methods. Alternately, buyers can hire private inspectors, such as the USDA's Acceptance Service, to ensure that meat products meet their standards. The USDA also has an inspection program for which buyers can contract that guarantees that the meat they purchase is free of pesticides and pesticide residues.

As noted earlier, rabbit meat is not required to be federally inspected for wholesomeness. If inspection of this item is important to buyers, they need to indicate this on their specification.

If buyers purchase meat that comes from another country, its inspection for wholesomeness may not be as demanding as the one U.S. meat must undergo. For instance, many U.S. foodservice operations purchase large quantities of beef from other countries. The federal government must inspect these meat products before they are allowed to enter the United States, but the inspection is hampered some-what because some exporting countries use additives and chemicals that U.S. reg-ulations do not cover. As far as we can determine, this practice has not caused any health hazards. But, again, if buyers are very concerned with product safety, they should indicate on the specification that they want considerably more inspection than is normally provided.

Imitation Meat Products

Several imitation meat products are available. For instance, hospitality operators can use soybean and oat bran as meat extenders. Alternately, they can use these products to create such items as "bacon bits." Many meat producers sell "ham," "hot dogs," and other similar items that are made with chicken, fish, and/or turkey.

Imitation meat products seem to be very popular in the institutional segment of the foodservice industry. However, there is no reason why they cannot enjoy success in any type of foodservice operation. If operators introduce them as a new "alternative" menu item, they may sell briskly.

Some foodservice operators like imitation meat products because they can manipulate the fat content. This generally translates into a lower AP price; how-ever, a low-fat product may sometimes be more expensive than the traditional item. Imitation meats may even have positive health implications. Reducing the fat con-tent and/or substituting polyunsaturated oils can lead to an imitation meat prod-uct that is lower in calories and cholesterol compared to the real item.

One-Stop-Shopping Opportunity

Not every meat supplier carries all the meat products buyers need, especially if they occasionally purchase some unusual items or convenience entrées. In general, the more processing hospitality operations want, the more suppliers they need. One-stop-shopping opportunities are not the rule in meat buying unless the shopping list contains only the common items. Buyers must ask themselves a question: "Should I tailor my menu around one or two suppliers, or should I write the menu and take my chances with a lot of suppliers?" Buyers should not take this issue lightly. On one hand, buyers like to make deals and bid buy because of the potential savings. But, on the other hand, they do not enjoy taking risks with signature items.

AP Price

Since meat represents such a large part of the foodservice purchase dollar, buyers are mindful of AP prices. AP prices vary for meat items, types of packaging, and any other value-added feature in a rather predictable way. However, some buyers are concerned about how the meat industry sets contract prices. In some cases, large meat contracts are prepared in such a way that the eventual AP price is not known until the day the hospitality operation takes delivery. On that day, the price reported on the "Green Sheet," or in some comparable market pricing report, may be the one the buyer must pay the supplier.

The Green Sheet is the trade nickname for the *HRI Meat Price Report*. It is a weekly guide to current AP prices buyers are paying to U.S. meat producers for beef, lamb, pork, veal, and poultry, as well as for several types of processed-meat items. While it is true that with this type of pricing mechanism, the eventual AP price may be lower than expected, it is also true that it could be much higher. This is a risk some buyers do not want to take—or it may be a risk that some foodservice firms forbid their buyers to take.

One way to keep AP prices down is to bid buy among acceptable suppliers. The time involved, as well as the inconvenience, may be worthwhile. Good savings can accrue by this method. But switching suppliers indiscriminately, especially for signature items, can be risky. Different delivery times, supplier capabilities, and product form may be trivial concerns for other items, but they are usually crucial for meat.

If buyers have adequate cash reserves, they may do well with quantity buys once or twice a year for fresh meat and many processed-meat items. On the cash market, purchasing day to day, buyers take their chances. While a good deal represents potentially great savings, a miscalculation represents potentially serious losses. Several companies keep statistics on both AP prices and the availability of meat supplies. By tracking the supply and demand over time, buyers can develop models to predict the optimal times to purchase meat in large quantity. (Recall that not everyone agrees that large contracts, the futures market, and other such strategies are profitable ventures.)

PURCHASING MEAT

A buyer's first step in purchasing meat is obtaining a copy of the *MBG*. This unique publication is an indispensable reference source that every meat buyer should have. Other good meat reference books are available, but the *MBG* is the only source that addresses the purchasing function exclusively.

The buyer's next step is to determine precisely what meat his or her operation needs. As noted earlier, fresh meats are usually selected on the basis of U.S. grades and IMPS numbers, while processed convenience items are typically selected on the basis of packers' brands. Supplier selection may be based on numerous criteria, including availability, reliability, accountability, shipping, and price.

After the buyer determines the meat products the operation requires, it is always wise to prepare specifications for each item whether or not he or she uses them in bid buying (see Figure 23.10 for example meat specifications, and Figure 23.11 for an example of a product specification outline for meat products).

Once the buyer writes the specifications, he or she must evaluate potential suppliers, determine order sizes, fix order times, and so on. Many suppliers work in the fresh- and processed-meat areas. Most parts of the United States are a bid buyer's paradise. Purchasing meat, therefore, can be as easy or as difficult as the buyer wants to make it. In fact, as long as the buyer avoids obscure meat items, he or she can often find one-stop-shopping opportunities. Conversely, the buyer can shop around or practice trade relations.

New York strip steak Used for dinner entrée IMPS number 1180 USDA Choice (High Choice) Cut from USDA Yield Grade 2 carcass Dry aged 14 to 21 days 12-ounce portion cut Individually wrapped in plastic film Layered pack 10- to 12-pound case Refrigerated	Flank steak Used for London broil entrée IMPS number 193 Sipco® brand Weight range B (1 to 2 pounds) Packed 8 pieces per Cryovac® bag Packed 6 bags per case Case weight, approximately 70 pounds (catch weight) Refrigerated
Beef base Used to prepare soups and sauces LeGout® brand 16-ounce resealable plastic containers Packed 12 containers per case Refrigerated	Vegetable beef soup Used for lunch appetizer Campbell's® brand 51-ounce can Packed 12 cans per case Unrefrigerated

FIGURE 23.10 **Examples of meat product specifications.**

Intended use:

Exact name:

U.S. grade (or equivalent):

Product yield:

Packer's brand name (or equivalent):

Product size:

Size of container:

Type of packaging material:

Packaging procedure:

Product form:

Preservation method:

Tenderization procedure:

Point of origin:

FIGURE 23.11 An example of a product specification outline for meat products.

Even though meat buying is a bid buyer's dream, most buyers approach it cautiously. We may see some long-term contract bidding, perhaps three or six months, but we rarely see indiscriminate shopping around. Most meat buyers seem to be concerned with supplier services, especially dependability. A good reputation helps meat suppliers tremendously. After all, their customers must have their signature items. Stockouts are intolerable to buyers; they must have the right item at the right time.

Naturally, cautious buyer attitudes make it difficult for new meat suppliers to establish themselves. In theory, no difference in items should exist for the same grade and cut of meat. But suppliers' item handling, delivery service, and dependability tend to overshadow this fact. Consequently, new suppliers must resort either to offering low AP prices, at least on an introductory basis, or to offering exceptionally attractive supplier services.

The quality and style of processed-meat items are not easily decided. So packers' brands and suppliers' capabilities tend to weigh heavily in these decisions. The owner-manager, either alone or in consultation with others, determines the requirements. Of course, if the hospitality operation needs esoteric meats, it will have more trouble finding suppliers. Packers' brands are important guides, but the brand the owner-manager wants may not be available in the local community, or, more likely, only one supplier will stock that brand. We have often noticed such items available on a cost-plus basis only.

Of course, the independent farmer is ever-present. Some independent farmers sell fresh meat, but many sell products like homemade sausage. We suggest staying away from all uninspected meat.

Before purchasing any meat item, and usually before or during the writing of specifications, buyers should take the time to evaluate the multitude of substitution possibilities.

Meat buying does not have to be difficult, but it certainly is not easy, especially if the buyer is responsible for procuring a wide variety of meat products. In general, the minimum knowledge the buyer needs can be summarized as follows: the different types of meat, the U.S. grades, the appropriate brand names, the various cuts, and the intended uses for the meat items (see Figures 23.12 through 23.15).

RECEIVING MEAT

When meat products reach a hospitality operation, many owner-managers insist that all inspection be done in the walk-in refrigerator. This practice minimizes spoilage opportunities, but it may be too cautious for some. However, it drives home the fact that an operation cannot take chances with meat—it is too expensive to treat carelessly.

The chef, or someone else in the operation who is also knowledgeable about meat quality, should handle the quality check. This receiver must be able to determine that what the buyer ordered matches what is being received. For instance, suppose a purchase order is for top round, High Choice, but the item received is bottom round, High Choice. This mistake could lead to a stockout and potential disgruntled customers at the dinner hour.

The receiver should check the condition of the meat. For example, all meats have a characteristic color. Fresh beef is a bright, cherry red. If it is not, it could be old. Also, it could be vacuum packed, such as the Cryovac-packaged meat, so that it is not exposed to oxygen to give it the bright, cherry red color, or "bloom," as it is sometimes called. If the characteristic color does not appear to be correct, the receiver should double-check the meat.

Odor is another sign of bad meat. If meat has an unpleasant odor, refuse it. (Fresh pork is difficult to check for odor because it deteriorates from the inside out, not the outside in.)

If meat products have a slimy appearance and are slimy to the touch, the receiver should refuse them. This slime consists of spoilage bacteria.

The receiver should also check the packaging. It should be appropriate for the item purchased. Proper packaging is essential for reducing loss in quality, es-

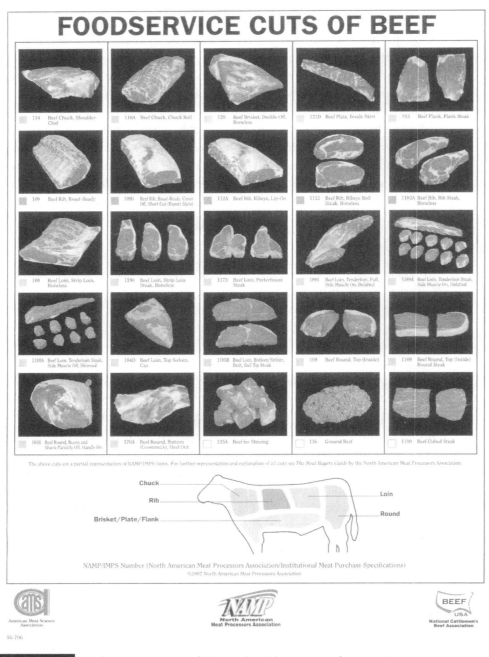

FIGURE 23.12 Beef chart. Courtesy of National Cattlemen's Beef Association.

LAMB CUTS AND HOW TO COOK THEM

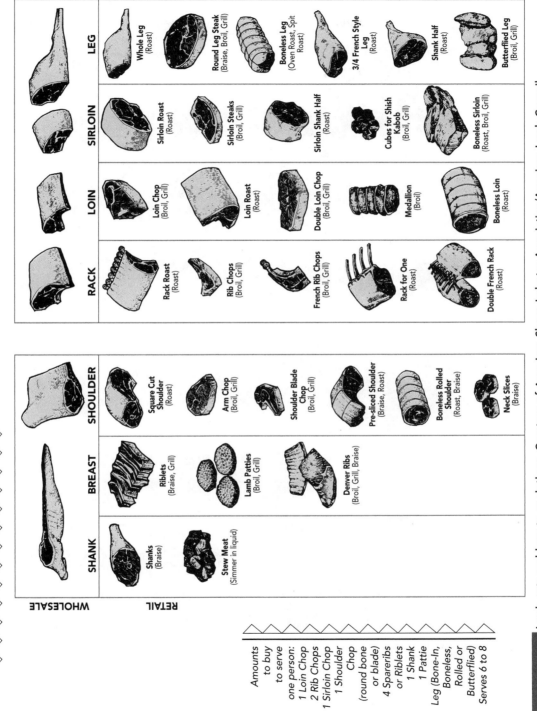

FIGURE 23.13 Lamb cuts and how to cook them. Courtesy of American Sheep Industry Association/American Lamb Council.

PURCHASING PORK

A Consumer Guide To Identifying Retail Pork Cuts.

Left: tenderloin
Right: Canadian-style bacon

TENDERLOIN & CANADIAN-STYLE BACON

CHOPS

RIBS

ROASTS

CHOPS
Upper row (l-r):
sirloin chop, rib chop, loin chop.
Lower row (l-r):
boneless rib end chop (Chef's Prime Filet™), boneless center loin chop (America's Cut™- 1 1/4-1 1/2" thickness), butterfly chop.

ROASTS
Upper row (l-r):
center rib roast (Rack of Pork), bone-in sirloin roast.
Middle: boneless center loin roast.
Lower row (l-r):
boneless rib end roast (Chef's Prime™), boneless sirloin roast.

SHOULDER BUTT
Upper row (l-r):
bone-in blade roast, boneless blade roast.
Lower row (l-r): ground pork (The Other Burger®), sausage, blade steak.

SHOULDER BUTT

RIBS
Left: country-style ribs.
Right: back ribs.

PICNIC SHOULDER
Upper row (l-r): smoked picnic, arm picnic roast.
Lower row: smoked hocks.

PICNIC SHOULDER

SIDE
Top: spareribs.
Bottom: slab bacon, sliced bacon.

SIDE

LEG

LEG
Upper row (l-r):
bone-in fresh ham, smoked ham. Lower row (l-r): leg cutlets, fresh boneless ham roast.

SHOULDER BUTT

LOIN

PICNIC SHOULDER

SIDE

LEG

pork

©1997 NATIONAL PORK PRODUCERS COUNCIL IN COOPERATION WITH THE NATIONAL PORK BOARD.

THE MANY SHAPES OF PORK CUT LOOSE!
When shopping for pork, consider cutting traditional roasts into a variety of different shapes.

ROASTS
No-fuss family dinner, holiday favorite.

CHOPS
Dinner, backyard barbecue or gourmet entrée.

CUBES
Great for kabobs, stew and chili.

STRIPS
Super stir fry, fajitas and salads.

CUTLETS
Delicious breakfast chops and sandwiches.

O3542 4-97

FIGURE 23.14 Retail cuts of pork. Courtesy of National Pork Producers Council.

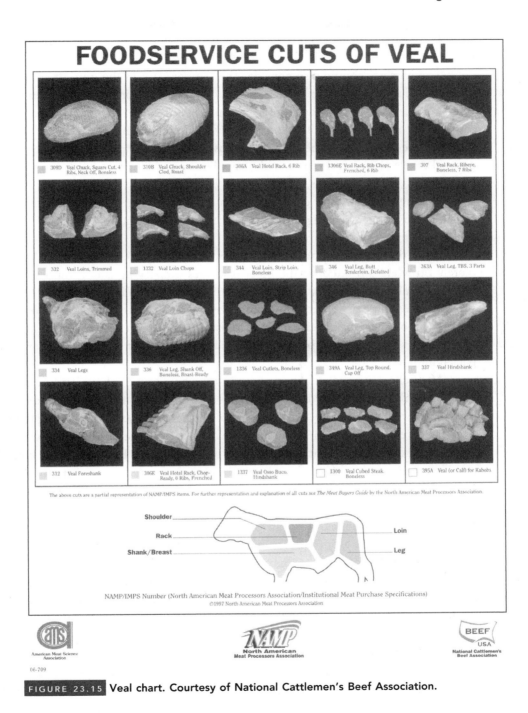

FOODSERVICE CUTS OF VEAL

309D Veal Chuck, Square Cut, 4 Ribs, Neck Off, Boneless	310B Veal Chuck, Shoulder Clod, Roast	306A Veal Hotel Rack, 6 Rib	1396E Veal Rack, Rib Chops, Frenched, 6 Rib	307 Veal Rack, Ribeye, Boneless, 7 Ribs
332 Veal Loins, Trimmed	1332 Veal Loin Chops	344 Veal Loin, Strip Loin, Boneless	346 Veal Leg, Butt Tenderloin, Defatted	363A Veal Leg, TBS, 3 Parts
334 Veal Legs	336 Veal Leg, Shank Off, Boneless, Roast-Ready	1336 Veal Cutlets, Boneless	349A Veal Leg, Top Round, Cap Off	337 Veal Hindshank
312 Veal Foreshank	306E Veal Hotel Rack, Chop-Ready, 6 Ribs, Frenched	1337 Veal Osso Buco, Hindshank	1300 Veal Cubed Steak, Boneless	395A Veal (or Calf) for Kabobs

The above cuts are a partial representation of NAMP/IMPS items. For further representation and explanation of all cuts see *The Meat Buyers Guide* by the North American Meat Processors Association.

Shoulder _____

Rack _____

Shank/Breast _____

_____ Loin

_____ Leg

NAMP/IMPS Number (North American Meat Processors Association/Institutional Meat Purchase Specifications)
©1997 North American Meat Processors Association

American Meat Science Association

NAMP North American Meat Processors Association

BEEF USA National Cattlemen's Beef Association

06-709

FIGURE 23.15 Veal chart. Courtesy of National Cattlemen's Beef Association.

pecially for frozen meats. For instance, frozen meats whose packaging is split should be refused.

The receiver should also consider the temperature of the item. It should be about 40°F, minimally, for refrigerated meat, and 0°F, minimally, for frozen meat. Other processed items—those that are preserved with chemicals, like some sausages—could be less chilled. But a receiver should not make a habit of accepting even these products when warm because this could imply a certain degree of general carelessness on the part of the supplier or a willingness on the part of the operation to relax standards.

Making these kinds of checks on fresh meat and some processed items is not difficult. However, checking frozen meat can be problematical because detecting spoilage in frozen items is more difficult.

Next, the receiver should check quantities. He or she should not rely completely on what is printed on the meat packages. Repacking is not impossible for an unscrupulous supplier or a larcenous employee. The receiver should look for such specifications as weight, count, and sizes. If all of the meat the buyer ordered is in one container, the receiver should separate and weigh the contents individually. He or she must also make sure to deduct the weight of the carton and the packaging.

After checking the quality and quantity, the receiver should move to the prices. As might be expected, meat requires a strong emphasis on record keeping. The receiver should devote a reasonable amount of attention to recording the deliveries. Receiving sheets, bin cards, and meat tags are all methods that can be used to protect expensive meat items. Before a purchase, most buyers express considerable concern with suppliers regarding the actions needed to correct any potential problems. And, if a supplier is out of stock on the buyers' regular orders, he or she often quickly adjusts any agreements in the policies regarding returns, credit terms, and substitute meat items to maintain the buyers' loyalty.

Hospitality operators can streamline the meat-receiving process by using the USDA's Acceptance Service. This practice is popular in meat purchasing, even though it is expensive. Using this service, a hospitality operator can pay a meat expert to write meat specifications and to ensure that the specified products are actually delivered. Acceptance buying is sometimes referred to in the meat trade as "certified buying" or "certification" (see Figure 23.16).

A related program the USDA offers that may also interest meat buyers is called the "Product Examination Service." With this service, a federal inspector examines the purchased meat while it is in transit. The primary purpose of this service is to ensure that product quality does not deteriorate during shipment.

FIGURE 23.16 Federal stamps used to indicate that a meat product meets the buyer's specification under USDA Acceptance purchasing. *Source:* United States Department of Agriculture.

STORING MEAT

Mandatory government inspection ensures that most meat is very clean when it is delivered. The onus is on the foodservice operation to receive and store meat in the correct environment. Whether fresh or frozen, meat must be kept clean and cold. In addition, the stock must be rotated properly.

Meat products are susceptible to bacterial contamination; keeping them clean and sanitary is a big challenge. A dirty storage refrigerator can contaminate good meat. Therefore, it is important for hospitality operations to perform the necessary housekeeping chores in order to minimize contamination.

Operators should store fresh meat in a meat refrigerator apart from cooked-meat items, at a temperature of 35°F to 40°F. If this is not possible, operators should designate a segregated area of the refrigerator for meat storage. To prevent contamination from raw-meat drippings, operators should place cooked items above the raw meats. Also, they should not wrap fresh meat too tightly or stack it too tightly. Both of these practices tend to cut down on the beneficial cold-air circulation around the pieces of meat.

Operators should store frozen products at −10°F or lower. If they must freeze some chilled meat, they must be careful to wrap it correctly and to store it in a freezer no longer than suggested. (It is not a good idea to freeze fresh meat because the typical hospitality operation's freezer is designed to hold frozen foods, not to freeze fresh products.)

ISSUING MEAT

Operators should properly rotate the stock so that the oldest items are issued first. Meat is rarely received and sent straight to production; an employee typically needs a stock requisition to get it. More control of meat items tends to exist at the requisition stage. In many cases, operators add to a perpetual inventory when the meat is delivered. Also, the stock requisition is commonplace. The requisitioner should return any unused meat at the end of his or her shift. The meat consumed should be consistent with the guest checks, that is, the number of meat items sold during that shift. Managing these controls may be somewhat time-consuming, but the practice is quite common in hospitality operations for meat and other expensive items.

By all means, operators must make sure that the requisitioner gets the right item and the right quantity, and must make sure that the in-process inventory does not get so large that it encourages waste or pilferage.

IN-PROCESS INVENTORIES

Surprisingly, in-process meats cause relatively little trouble. These items receive the bulk of the supervisory efforts; moreover, the penalties for pilferage and waste are normally quite severe.

Some employees will make "mistakes." For example, they may burn a steak, accidentally on purpose, and give it to a friend or eat it themselves. Operators can reduce the number of these "errors" by demanding that the mistake, along with the rest of the leftover meat, be turned in to the storeroom at the end of the shift so that it can be accounted for at that time.

Meat also provides some opportunity for shortchanging customers. For example, a server might slice the beef a little thin and keep the extra few ounces handy to trade for a few ounces of gin that the bartender saved in a similar fashion. As is usually the case, effective supervision is the best answer.

KEY WORDS AND CONCEPTS

Advantages and disadvantages of portion-cut meat

Agricultural Marketing Act

Agricultural Marketing Service Livestock Division (AMS Livestock Division)

American Angus Association

As-purchased price (AP price)

Beef electrification

Botulism

Bulk pack

Carcass

Catch weight

Certified Angus Beef Program

Certified buying

Chemical tenderization

Comminuting process

Cryovac aging

Curing

Dry aging

Edible by-product

Edible-portion cost (EP cost)

Exact name

Feathering

Federal Meat Inspection Act

Finish

Flaked and reformed meat products

Food Safety and Inspection Service (FSIS)

Grading factors

Grass-fed beef

Green meat

Green Sheet

Has meat been subjected to United States Department of Agriculture (USDA), or equivalent, inspection?

Hedging

Imitation meat products

In-process inventories

Institutional Meat Purchase Specifications/North American Association of Meat Processors numbers (IMPS/NAMP) numbers

Institutional Meat Purchase Specifications numbers (IMPS numbers)

Intended use

Layout pack

Limiting rule

Long-term contract

Management considerations when purchasing meat

Manufacturing grade

Marbling

Maturity class

Meat Buyers Guide (*MBG*)

Meat Buyers Guide numbers (*MBG* numbers)

Mechanical tenderization

National Live Stock and Meat Board

Needling procedure

North American Association of Meat Processors (NAMP)

One-stop shopping

Packaging procedure

Packers' brands

Point of origin

Popular types of meat products

Portion-cut meat

Preservation method

Primal cut

Product form

Product size

Product yield

Purchasing, receiving, storing, and issuing meat products

Reluctance to change meat suppliers

Retail cut

Sausage

Shingle pack

Shrink-wrap

Side

Signature item

Size of container

Smoking

Sodium nitrite

Standard of identity

Standardized cut

Steam-table pack

Substitution possibilities

SYSCO Brand Supreme Angus Beef

Tenderization procedure

Truth-in-menu legislation

Type of packaging material

United States Department of Agriculture (USDA)

United States Department of Agriculture Acceptance Service (USDA Acceptance Service)

United States Department of Agriculture Agricultural Marketing Service (USDA AMS)

United States Department of Agriculture Product Examination Service (USDA Product Examination Service)

U.S. quality grades

U.S. yield grades

Variety meat

Voluntary inspection for rabbit meat

Weight range

Wet aging

Wholesale cut

Wholesale Meat Act

QUESTIONS AND PROBLEMS

1. On what are the quality grades for beef primarily based?
2. All meat must be inspected during production in the United States except _____ meat.
3. What are the USDA quality grades for beef?
4. What are the USDA quality grades for pork?
5. What are the USDA quality grades for veal?
6. What are the USDA quality grades for lamb?
7. Assume that you manage a high-check-average, full-service club, with annual food and beverage sales of $1.8 million. Your normal purchase order size of T-bone steaks, per week, is approximately 1200 pounds. The current AP price is $7.80 per pound, which will probably hold

steady for the next six months. Your current supplier is a longtime good friend, and you are his biggest account. He has carried you during lean times in the past, and you have never had any problems with him. He is dependable and delivers twice a week, in the morning. Down the street is the ABC Corporation's central distribution center, whose management is after your T-bone steak business. Their deal comprises a six-month contract; an AP price of $7.55 per pound; the same quality, cut, yield, and packaging of the T-bones; and afternoon deliveries twice a week. What do you suggest?

8. What are lower-quality grades of meat typically used for?

9. What is the primary reason food buyers use the IMPS numbering system when preparing meat specifications?

10. You notice that your delivery of 500 portion-cut steaks is not up to your usual standard; each weighs 10 ounces instead of the normal 12. It is Friday at 4 P.M., and these steaks are for that weekend. Your meat supplier is usually closed on weekends. What would you do? If possible, ask the owner of a specialty restaurant to discuss this problem with you.

11. On what are USDA yield grades primarily based?

12. A product specification for fresh pork chops could include the following information:
    (a)
    (b)
    (c)
    (d)
    (e)

13. It is painfully evident to you that meat prices are continually rising, and no relief is in sight. But this inflationary spiral has not been enough to encourage you to purchase large quantities and invest in freezer storage facilities. Just recently, your meat supplier has indicated that he intends to go out of business. This supplier calls you and asks whether you wish to purchase his large inventory of meat products at distress prices. Obviously, you are overwhelmed at the possibility of tremendous cost savings.
    (a) What must you know before making an intelligent decision concerning the purchase of this huge inventory?
    (b) Assume that you wish to purchase this inventory. Must you also purchase a freezer? Why or why not?
    (c) Under what conditions would it be advisable to purchase a freezer in this situation?

14. Briefly describe the maturity classes for beef.

15. What is the primary purpose of using the USDA's Product Examination Service?

16. What critical information is missing from the following product specification for lamb loin chops?
    LAMB, LOIN CHOPS
    USED FOR DINNER ENTRÉE
    IMPS NUMBER 1232
    6-OUNCE PORTION CUT
    PACKED IN 10- TO 12-POUND CONTAINERS

17. Assume that you manage a full-service country club. Wesson Brothers, purveyors of fine meats, has been your main source of meat supply for a considerable period. Recently, Wesson proposed to its customers a rather interesting "trade-off." Wesson would like to get out of the transportation business and is seriously considering allowing all its customers to pick up their own orders; in return for their picking up their orders, Wesson will reduce their AP price by 8 percent. Wesson is asking its customers for their opinions. If at least 50 percent of Wesson's existing customers perform the transportation function for themselves, the company will expect all other customers to do likewise.

    (a)   Would you like to perform the transportation function? Why or why not?

    (b)   If Wesson introduces this proposed policy, how much would you want the AP price of your purchases to decrease? Is an 8 percent reduction enough? Do you think the EP cost of the proposed method would equal that of the current method? Why or why not?

    (c)   Assume that Wesson introduces the policy, that you do not wish to perform the transportation function, and that Wesson is an exclusive distributor for certain products you must have. What do you suggest? If possible, ask a country club manager to comment on your answer.

18. Assume that you manage a hospital food service. Currently, it costs about $52 per day to feed one patient. This figure includes food, labor, and direct operating supplies. You expect meat prices to increase by approximately 7 percent the following year, but the hospital administration will not increase your food budget. You must make do with the $52 amount all next year. Currently, you are serving meat at least two times a day on the average. You do not want to reduce this frequency, but you must cut meat costs somewhere. You ask the food buyer for some suggestions. What do you think he or she would propose? Why? If possible, ask a hospital foodservice director to comment on your answer.

19. List some differences between dry aging and wet aging.

20. Give an appropriate intended use for hamburger that has been extended with soybean.

21. Why are meat buyers reluctant to shop indiscriminately for their meat items?

22. The AP price of lean hamburger is $1.89 per pound. The AP price of regular hamburger is $1.09 per pound. The lean meat shrinks 10 percent when cooked; the regular meat shrinks 30 percent.

    (a)   At what AP price must the lean hamburger sell at to make it equal in value to the regular hamburger?

    (b)   Assume that the EP cost of both the lean and regular meat is equal. What other specific considerations should you examine before purchasing either the lean or the regular?

23. Prepare a product specification for the following meat products:

    (a)   Veal cutlet

    (b)   Skirt steak

    (c)   Prepared chili with beans

    (d)   Breakfast sausage

    (e)   Ham

24. When would a buyer purchase an imitation meat product?

25. When would a buyer purchase a flaked and re-formed meat product?

26. What benefit would a restaurant owner gain if he or she listed on the menu the point of origin for the meat offerings?

27. Briefly describe one type of meat product you might purchase that would be a good candidate for the needling tenderization procedure.

28. What are the quality grading factors for veal and lamb?

29. Define or explain briefly the following terms:

(a)	Variety meat	(i)	Certified buying
(b)	Wholesale cut	(j)	Layout pack
(c)	Retail cut	(k)	Bloom
(d)	Marbling	(l)	Beef electrification
(e)	Product Examination Service	(m)	Green Sheet
(f)	NAMP	(n)	Shrink wrap
(g)	Curing	(o)	Manufacturing grade
(h)	Feathering		

24

BEVERAGES

The Purpose of this Chapter

After reading this chapter, you should be able to:

- Identify management considerations surrounding the selection and procurement of beverage alcohols and nonalcoholic beverages.

- Explain the selection factors for beverage alcohols and nonalcoholic beverages.

- Describe the process of purchasing, receiving, storing, and issuing beverage alcohols and nonalcoholic beverages.

BEVERAGE ALCOHOLS

Beverage alcohols (also referred to as "liquor") include wines, beers, and spirits. Wines result from the fermentation of sugars in fruits or berries (most commonly grapes), various plants or their saps, honey, and even milk. Beers are produced by the fermentation of grains after the starch in them is converted to sugar. Spirits are distilled from wines or beers.

Beverage alcohol products are often the easiest items a buyer can purchase. These are standardized products that are manufactured under controlled conditions. Accordingly, the quality of beverage alcohol is very consistent. While most beverage alcohols will not spoil, some products, such as canned and bottled beer, and some wines, tend to lose their quality over a period of time. Beer and wine are sensitive to changes in temperature, humidity, light, and vibration. Exposing canned and bottled beer and wine to extreme temperature during shipping and storage can result in its degradation. Draft beer, with its limited shelf life, will spoil if it is not consumed within a short period of time. Bottled beer is especially susceptible to light, particularly in green or clear bottles that allow sunlight to react with hop compounds, which can produce a "skunky" character. Some beer manufacturers are now combatting this phenomenon by using chemicals to stabilize these hop compounds. Generally, however, when hospitality operators store beverage alcohols under controlled conditions, buyers do not have to worry about an oversupply spoiling before they can serve it to customers.

Another favorable factor relating to beverage alcohols is that many customers tend to order a preferred, or "call," brand. For instance, typical customers would not ask a restaurant operator for Heinz® catsup; they would take the one the establishment offers and, usually, not give it a second thought. However, these customers may specify an exact brand name when ordering a favorite beverage alcohol. This type of "pull" strategy in the beverage alcohol distribution channel can facilitate the buyers' job. Also, because of beverage alcohols' popularity, some bar owners can easily inventory these preferred brands.

In some instances, selected suppliers are exclusive distributors for one or more products in a given market area. Under such conditions, if bar operators want specific brands, they will have only one source of supply. Since several exclusive distributorships exist in the beverage alcohol trade, buyers do not need to shop around very much.

In extreme cases, state governments (and some counties, such as Montgomery county in Maryland; http://www.co.mo.md.us/services/liquor.html) regulate and control the manufacturing, possession, sales, transportation, and delivery of beverage alcohols (see Figure 24.1). Also in these "control" states, the buyers must follow the states' specific ordering and bill-paying procedures. This makes the buying job easier; however, the excessive regulation found in control states tends to increase the edible-portion (EP) costs of beverage alcohols.

Alternately, some states regulate beverage alcohol commerce through the issuance of "licenses." These license states also simplify the buyers' job. For instance, a certain amount of price control exists in some areas; the state or local government agency stipulates that beverage alcohols must be sold at minimum wholesale prices and minimum retail prices. While as-purchased (AP) price discount opportunities and other sorts of "deals" available in license states exist, buyers do not have that many to evaluate; fewer opportunities imply less work for buyers.

License states are slightly more liberal than control states in terms of liquor-ordering and bill-paying procedures. For example, licensed distributors are able to deliver products, whereas in control states, buyers usually must pick up the order

ALABAMA Beverage Alcohol Control Board:	http://www.abcboard.state.al.us/
IDAHO State Liquor Dispensary:	http://www2.state.id.us/isld
IOWA Alcoholic Beverages Division:	http://www.iowaabd.com/
MAINE Bureau of Alcoholic Beverages:	http://www.maineliquor.com/
Montgomery County Dept. of Liquor Control, Maryland:	http://www.mcdlc.com/
MICHIGAN Liquor Control Commission:	http://www.michigan.gov/cis
Mississippi State Tax Commission, ABCDivision:	http://www.mstc.state.ms.us/abc/main.htm
MONTANA Department of Revenue:	http://www.discoveringmontana.com/revenue/css/4forprofessionals/04liquorstore.asp
NEW HAMPSHIRE State Liquor Commission:	http://webster.state.nh.us/liquor/
NORTH CAROLINA Alcoholic Beverage Control Commission:	http://www.ncabc.com/
OHIO Department of Commerce Division of Liquor Control:	http://www.state.oh.us/com/liquor/liquor.htm
OREGON Liquor Control Commission:	http://www.olcc.state.or.us/
PENNSYLVANIA Liquor Control Board:	http://www.lcb.state.pa.us/
State of UTAH Department of Beverage Alcohol Control:	http://www.alcbev.state.ut.us/
VERMONT Department of Liquor Control:	http://www.state.vt.us/dlc/
VIRGINIA Beverage Alcohol Control Board:	http://www.abc.state.va.us/
WASHINGTON State Liquor Control Board:	http://www.liq.wa.gov/
WEST VIRGINIA Beverage Alcohol Control Administration:	http://www.wvabca.com/
WYOMING Department of Revenue Liquor Division:	http://revenue.state.wy.us

FIGURE 24.1 Control States Agencies and Links. Courtesy of National Alcohol Beverage Control Association, http://www.nabca.org/.

at a state liquor warehouse. License states are also allowed to offer credit terms, while in control states, buyers usually must pay cash when they pick up their order. The license states, though, do not grant carte blanche to their liquor distributors. These states tend to restrict the amount and types of supplier services that can be provided, much more than other types of suppliers. Consequently, even in a state where two or more suppliers carry some of the same brands, buyers may not be able to exploit the situation.

MANAGEMENT CONSIDERATIONS

The problems associated with beverage alcohols rarely center on purchasing procedures. The fundamental questions follow here.

Should We Offer Beverage Alcohol Service to Guests?

This is not an easy decision. On one hand, many foodservice operations rely on both food and beverage alcohol sales to achieve profit. When compared, food sales are generally less profitable than beverage alcohol sales. Not only are liquor sales more profitable, beverage alcohols are easier to produce and serve. Yet hospitality operators must be aware of the steady decline in United States liquor consumption. The basis for this decline may be attributed to increased health and nutrition concerns, laws prohibiting happy hours, and tougher driving while intoxicated (DWI) or driving under the influence (DUI) laws. Also, the social pressures created by such groups as Mothers Against Drunk Driving (MADD) have had an impact on the consumption rate. Furthermore, when hospitality operations want to cultivate a family image, serving beverage alcohols may compromise this perception.

Once operations decide to sell beverage alcohols, they must obtain a liquor license, or, sometimes, a permit. This can be an arduous process. The paperwork, legal proceedings, and hearings can quickly drain the operations' resources. Sometimes, even if operators want to serve liquor, they may not be able to secure a retail liquor license from the appropriate government agency. In most parts of the United States, liquor licenses are restricted in number. For instance, only one liquor license may be available for every 2000 to 3000 residents of an area. If the allotment of licenses that the government agency issues is depleted, operators must try to obtain one by purchasing it from an establishment that has one. This can be very expensive, particularly when the demand for these licenses far exceeds the restricted supply. However, if operations serve only beer and wine, the procedure usually will not be as difficult.

Other major expenses are associated with liquor service—expenses that alcohol-free establishments do not incur. These include increased liability insurance premiums and license renewal costs. Additionally, compliance with government-mandated record-keeping procedures, participation in a safe-driver program and/or a designated-driver program, and employment of floorpersons, or bouncers, to restrict minors may substantially increase operating expenses.

Some hospitality operations try to maintain their beverage profit margins by altering their marketing policies to capitalize on the consumer trend toward drinking more wine, beer, and nonalcoholic beverages. For instance, in states where the law allows, some bar operators have opened "brew pubs," which combine food service and a small, in-house mini-brewery. Other operators offer wine bars, while others may publish a wine list, a cocktail list, and a water list.

What Quality of Beverage Alcohol Should We Serve?

An age-old argument centers on the value of premium brands versus nonpremium brands. This decision is further complicated because operations usually serve "well brands;" "call brands," such as Absolut® vodka, Sauza® tequila, and Bombay® gin; and "premium brands," such as Belvedere® vodka, Hennessy XO® cognac, and Lagavulin® single malt Scotch whisky. Well liquor, sometimes called the "house brand," is served when a patron asks for a shot of Scotch without specifying a particular brand. The term *well* derives its name from where this type of liquor is located, typically being stored in a well located just below the bar top. Call liquor refers to specific brand names, as when a patron asks for a Seven and Seven (the cocktail that contains Seagram's 7 Crown® and 7-Up®) or a shot of Cutty Sark®. A premium brand would be an expensive call liquor that commands a high price, such as a glass of Richard Hennessy® cognac.

Generally, the AP price difference at wholesale between a call brand and a well brand is not too significant. But if operations sell a considerable quantity of liquor, the savings from even a modest difference can amount to a considerable sum. The question, then, becomes "Should we save a few pennies on each drink, or should we influence our customers by pouring only recognized brand names?" This question generates wildly differing opinions and should not be taken lightly.

Part of this controversy can be attributed to another difference between seemingly comparable liquor brands. This difference is the "proof." The proof number is an indication of alcoholic strength. It correlates to twice the percent alcohol present in the liquor. For example, "100 proof" bourbon contains 50 percent alcohol.

Some equally well-known brands have different proofs. Some have 80; some, 86; some, 90; and some 100 or more. If a hospitality operation serves a nonpremium brand with a low proof, the dilution factor in a mixed drink may need adjustment. Premium-brand advocates point out that the EP cost per serving, sometimes referred to in bars as the "pouring cost," for lower-proof brands may not be significantly less than that of a higher-proof brand.

Many foodservice and bar operations serve premium brands as their well brands. This is sometimes referred to as the "premium well," which may include items such as Original Baileys Irish Cream®, Cointreau® triple sec, Wild Turkey® bourbon, Absolut vodka, and Bombay Sapphire® gin. Apparently, these operators are willing to forgo the extra profit per drink to satisfy their customers. Through the creation of a positive image, this approach may have an overall favorable impact on the net profit of the entire hospitality operation.

Should We Serve Draft Beer, Bottled Beer, or Both?

Many guests prefer draft beer. It is something they cannot normally get at home. Unfortunately, draft beer is difficult to serve properly. In addition to sanitation concerns, new kegs must be tapped, tap pressure must be monitored, and the lines must be kept clean and flowing. Nevertheless, draft beer is a good merchandising tool, and it can attract considerable business (see Figure 24.2). Also, draft beer can yield a lower pouring cost than bottled beer, even when operators take into account the additional labor and other costs involved.

Even if operations want to serve draft beer, acquiring the preferred brand may not be possible. Beer distributors sometimes want to restrict the number of retail

FIGURE 24.2 Adam Carmer, proprietor of the Freakin' Frog, serving draft beer.

outlets for their product. This is especially true of small, regional breweries seeking exclusivity for their products.

Which Wines Should We Serve?

Which wine should hospitality operators use as their "house wine"? House wine, like well liquor, is served when someone orders a glass or carafe of wine without specifying any particular brand or vintage.

Buying wines is trickier than buying other beverage alcohols. Since restaurant patrons do not always have one or two preferred brands of wines in mind, as they often do for beer and distilled spirits, the buyer or the owner-manager is required to have considerable product knowledge. The sommelier, wine steward, or other service personnel may have to suggest wines, and it is important that they provide correct choices that will complement the customers' dining experience. This requires solid training and knowledgeable supervision.

Perhaps the major concerns are how many varieties and types of wines to carry. With increased complexities of the wine list come increased complexities of the operation. Some operational challenges are: (1) wine is difficult to store properly, (2) it requires considerable storage space, (3) it may be in storage a long time before it sells, (4) service personnel must be trained to sell and serve it correctly, and (5) a variety of wines may require several suppliers.

A substantial wine inventory can also mean tying up large amounts of capital. The capital costs—the interest on borrowed money or the loss of interest on alternate investments; that is, an opportunity cost—of a large wine cellar can be a major consideration in wine list design.

A well-stocked wine cellar can, however, offer many potential advantages. The main ones include: (1) prestige, (2) indulging and pleasing patrons, (3) a marketing edge, and (4) bigger profits. This is evident in such operations as Charlie Palmer's Aureole Restaurant inside Mandalay Bay Hotel and Casino (see Figure 24.3). The four-story "Cellar in the Sky" wine tower has 1800 wines from which the wine stewards, strapped in harnesses to hoist them up the tower, can make their selections.

On the other hand, an emphasis on wine can lead to a misallocation of dollars and effort in many operations. Furthermore, some operations are in between. For instance, a steak house could have a minimal or a broad wine list, depending on the clientele.

Some operators like to speculate in wine. They buy wine and wait for its value to significantly increase for the purpose of selling it at a high profit. For these operators, wine speculating is like playing the stock market. This sort of "investing" goes beyond the responsibility of ordinary buyers.

FIGURE 24.3 Aureole's wine cellar. Photo by Mark Ballog, Steinkamp/Ballog Chicago.

The Appropriate Number of Brands of Distilled Spirits and Beer to Carry

Unless a hospitality operation offers a number of brands as a promotion, few patrons expect a wide choice of beers. But guests can be annoyed when they cannot get their favorite brand of distilled spirit. However, if the operator decided to opt for a wide variety of brands, the same difficulties and potential advantages that we noted for wines may result.

Deciding what to carry is not easy. Management must determine what is optimal for the operation. It is not feasible to stock everything. But where does an owner-manager draw the line? Past experience indicates that the added investment between a restricted stock and more variety is not substantial, especially when the initial investment in the hospitality operation is taken into consideration. For example, it can cost more than $100,000 to erect one first-class hotel room. What, then, are a few more bottles of liquor and the space needed to store them? Nevertheless, in striking a balance, the owner-manager cannot ignore the costs and benefits of holding inventory discussed earlier in this text.

The Appropriate Menu Price for Beverage Alcohols

Customers are very sensitive to menu prices for beverage alcohols because they usually have a good idea of the retail price of these items in their local liquor store. As such, a bar operator must emphasize service and other value-added features. A pricing policy can be a reflection of the type of operation. For example, if a restaurant or bar is rather plain and does not offer guests a unique experience, the pricing system must take that into account. In contrast, a fine-dining or drinking establishment should have more flexibility in its menu-pricing procedures.

Today, many customers are switching from distilled spirits to wine, beer, and nonalcoholic beverages. So, operators must consider a pricing strategy that takes into account this shift in customer preference. Otherwise, a potential loss in net profit may result. This is why a bottle of Fiji® water is commonly priced as high as a Dewar's® and soda; an operation cannot survive unless it achieves a certain profit margin per drink, regardless of the type of drink a customer demands.

The issue of menu pricing, as with many other marketing decisions, is replete with opinions and gut feelings that seem to be more prolific with liquor than with other menu items, which, in turn, makes this aspect of the hospitality industry a bit more difficult to handle.

SELECTION FACTORS

For discussion purposes, we assume that the hospitality operation has a full liquor license and is allowed to serve wine, beer, and distilled spirits. As mentioned earlier, purchasing beverage alcohols is not as complicated as purchasing other food and nonfood items. But operators must consider a few selection factors, as discussed in the following sections.

Intended Use

As always, buyers want to determine exactly what the intended use of an item is so that they will be able to prepare the appropriate, relevant specification. For example, a house wine may be packaged differently than wines that will be sold by the bottle.

Exact Name

Numerous types and variations of beverage alcohols exist (see Figure 24.4 for some of the more popular products the beverage service industry uses). Therefore, to avoid the risk of receiving something that will not suit their needs, buyers must specify the exact name of the item they want. Usually, this selection factor presents no difficulty because over the years, a great deal of standardization has developed in this channel of distribution. Liquor-producing countries and states typically define several of the alcoholic products made within their borders, as well as part or all of the production processes. Also, standards of identity exist for many items. For example, bourbon must meet a certain formula, as must Tennessee whiskey. Furthermore, vintners who grow their own grapes typically must follow certain pruning processes on the vines; this is especially true in Europe.

Brand Name (or Equivalent)

The most fundamental selection factor is the brand name. For the vast majority of beverage alcohols, a brand name tends to be the only characteristic a patron considers. Substituting an "equivalent" brand may be difficult if patrons insist on being served a specific wine, beer, or spirit. Convincing customers to try a different brand of beer or wine instead of the preferred one may be possible. Also, guests may allow the usage of comparable brands under certain situations, such as a banquet. But generally, many guests have specific desires and are not eager to change.

Where the law allows, some hospitality operators can purchase beverage alcohols that carry customized brand labels. Private labeling of wines is common. For instance, hotel guests may find the hotel's name on a bottle of wine that is stocked in their room's minibar refrigerator. This tactic enhances the hotel's advertising and promotion program. It also makes it difficult for guests to compare the hotel's price with comparable wine prices at a local liquor store.

BEER	DISTILLED SPIRITS	WINE
Altbier	Bourbon whiskey	Aromatized wine (e.g., Vermouth)
American lager	Brandy	Fortified wine (e.g., Port and Sherry)
American pale ale	Canadian whiskey	Dessert wine (e.g., Eiswein and Sauternes)
Barleywine	Cordial	Sparkling wine (e.g., Champagne)
Belgian ale	Corn whiskey	Table wine (e.g., Chardonnay and
Bitter and English	Grappa	Cabernet Sauvignon)
pale ale	Gin	
Bock	Irish whiskey	
Brown ale	Liqueur	
English, Scottish, or	Rum	
Belgian strong ale	Rye whiskey	
European dark lager	Scotch whiskey	
European pale lager	Tequila	
French ale	Vodka	
Fruit beer		
German amber lager		
Imperial stout		
India pale ale		
Koelsch		
Lambic		
Light ale		
Porter		
Scottish ale		
Smoked beer		
Stout		
Wheat beer		

FIGURE 24.4 Popular types of beverage alcohols the beverage service industry uses.

Vintage

The vintage, or the year in which the wine is produced, is associated with most fine wines. As such, the vintage is an essential selection criterion. Also, the year or date of production is important when buyers purchase products that could lose quality. This is especially true of wines with low tannins (i.e., compounds that precipitate proteins), such as Chenin Blanc or Sauvignon Blanc; low-alcohol or lightly hopped beers, such as stouts; and other beverage alcohols that have a limited shelf life. Unfortunately, some wine and beer companies do not indicate production years.

In addition to the vintage, skilled buyers also consider the wine manufacturer. They must also check the production date for nonalcoholic beers. Alcohol acts as a preservative, so old nonalcoholic beers may not have a satisfying taste. Most brewers have realized this and typically date-code these products.

Alcohol Content

Beverage alcohols have varying levels of alcohol content. In general, the alcohol content in beer products ranges from approximately 3.2 percent to more than 6 percent. Wines contain approximately 12 percent to as much as 20 percent alcohol. Most distilled spirits rate about 70 proof, or 35 percent alcohol, up to 151 proof, or 75.5 percent alcohol.

Usually, the state or local government agency controls the alcohol content of these beverages. For instance, some areas prohibit the sale of any distilled spirit that exceeds 100 proof. Because of such restrictions, many breweries, wineries, and distilleries manufacture products with varying alcoholic strengths.

Since brands of liquor can have different alcoholic strengths, buyers must be very careful to avoid ordering and receiving products that they cannot use. For example, it is not uncommon for a distiller to sell an 80-proof bourbon and a 100-proof bourbon under the same brand name, such as Wild Turkey. In addition to a brand with different proofs, "light" distilled spirits are about 54 proof; that is, they contain approximately one-third less alcohol than a standard 80-proof spirit. Furthermore, nonalcoholic beers and wines are available.

Some buyers are concerned primarily with the alcohol content of a beverage. For instance, brandies used in flaming dishes should have a high alcohol content. Buyers may also consider alcohol content when they compare various brands of the same liquor. For example, having decided on a well Scotch, a buyer might opt for a higher-proof beverage even though its brand name may be unfamiliar. Some hospitality operators believe that brand names need not be a major consideration if guests are not likely to see them. Obscure brands of liquor with proofs equal to or greater than premium brands are attractive products that may not differ significantly in taste from the premium brands. So, if purchasing unfamiliar brands is more economical and does not compromise the operations' standard of quality, then operators should at least consider them.

Size of Container

Package sizes are standardized in this channel of distribution. As a result, buyers should have little difficulty with this selection factor (see Figure 24.5).

BEER

12-ounce bottle (available in plastic or glass)
12-ounce can
Keg (15.5 gallons)
Keg (13.2 gallons)
$1/2$ keg (7.75 gallons)
$1/4$ keg (3.88 gallons)

DISTILLED SPIRITS

750-ml bottle
1-liter bottle
1.75-liter bottle

WINE

$1/4$ bottle	175 ml	
$1/2$ bottle	375 ml	Demi-bottle (split)
1 bottle	750 ml	Bottle
2 bottles	1.5 l	Magnum
4 bottles	3.0 l	Jeroboam
6 bottles	4.5 l	Rehoboam
8 bottles	6.0 l	Methuselah
12 bottles	9.0 l	Salmanazar
16 bottles	12.0 l	Balthazar
20 bottles	16.0 l	Nebuchadnezzar

FIGURE 24.5 **Popular container sizes for beverage alcohols the beverage service industry uses.**

Of course, buyers must determine the size that best fits their needs. For example, generally, the larger the size, the less per milliliter or ounce buyers will pay for the product. However, they may not want to invest in a large package size if the item purchased is a slow mover or is subject to spoilage.

Type of Container

Packaging materials are also standardized in the beverage alcohol distribution channel. Generally, products come in cans, kegs, or glass or plastic bottles. Some products, such as a few wines, come in "bag-in-the-box" packages; these are bulk wines packed in a plastic liner and then placed into a cardboard box, similar to the bulk milk containers used in milk-dispensing machines.

It is possible that a company will manufacture a product, such as table wine, and package it in corked bottles and in bottles with screw-top lids. Usually, a distinction in the exact name indicates this type of packaging difference. However, buyers must ensure that they do not accidentally purchase a product that their hospitality operation cannot use.

Some opportunities are available for buyers to personalize their beverage containers. Recall that buyers might consider purchasing beverage alcohols from a supplier who is willing to include their hospitality operation's name and logo on the package label, thereby creating a more impressive merchandising effect and customer experience. Personalized packaging for liquor products is especially popular in hotels that use these products for room service and catered events. Personalized items also make excellent additions to complimentary fruit baskets in guest rooms.

Some suppliers also number, or code, the liquor containers. This provides a means of inventory control. For instance, it is sometimes easy for a bartender to bring his or her personal liquor bottle to work, sell the contents, and pocket the receipts. With coded containers, the supervisor can quickly notice any unauthorized bottle.

Point of Origin

The point of origin is a very important selection factor for wines. It implies taste variations. In some cases, as with imported wines, the point of origin denotes the type of government inspection to which the products were submitted.

Preservation Methods

Although operators normally serve red wines at about 60°F, and white, rosé, and sparkling wines at refrigerated temperatures, about 40°F, they and the distributors should maintain all wines at cool temperatures.

Distributors and operators should keep canned and bottled beers cool as well. In addition, they must keep draft beer, which has the shortest shelf life of all beverage alcohols, under constant refrigeration. Otherwise, this type of beer tends to lose its culinary quality very rapidly. To maintain the quality, distributors should ensure that canned, bottled, and draft beers are transported under optimal conditions.

Distributors should store wines and beers in a dark environment. Light has a negative impact on these products. In fact, even a brief exposure to natural light can adversely affect their flavor.

Distributors can, however, keep distilled spirits at any temperature, although excessive heat will tend to cause them to evaporate. Also, products with considerable sugar in them can sour under extreme heat conditions. Generally, though, since distilled spirits are inert products, their shelf lives are virtually unlimited.

Distributors usually do not find it too difficult to maintain proper temperatures, but this is not the case in the control states where buyers must pick up their orders from the state liquor store warehouses. Unless they have an appropriate vehicle, or can hire one, their liquor items will not have the best possible in-transit storage environment.

AP Price

Normally, buyers must pay the going price for the liquor items they stock. The price is controlled directly, as in a control state, or indirectly, as in a state that requires minimum wholesale prices. Today, price maintenance for beverage alcohols is not as restrictive as it once was. Liquor buyers and liquor retailers in some states have more flexibility in setting their prices. But since the largest part of the price can represent tax, we may never see a completely free market in beverage alcohols.

As with most products hospitality operators purchase, quantity buys for beverage alcohols are available. Because of this, buyers can expect to achieve a quantity discount. However, other ways to attain potential savings exist, so buyers are not required to invest in considerably more of a product than they might be able to use within a reasonable time.

One of these other ways buyers can save on liquor, typically about 10 percent, is by purchasing the largest possible containers, such as the 1.75-liter bottle of distilled spirits. These containers are clumsy, but they are acceptable or even preferable when a bar has automatic dispensers. When a bartender uses an automatic dispenser, a push of a button can automatically dispense a portion-controlled amount of beverage into a glass.

States sometimes permit distributors to offer price discounts. These discounts are sometimes referred to as "post-offs" in control states. Distributors can and usually do grant these discounts, which do not always take the form of money. Sometimes buyers receive, for example, a free bottle of liquor for every case or two that they purchase at the regular AP price. Post-offs normally do not require buyers to greatly alter their orders to obtain them. These discounts may, perhaps, require them to slightly increase their order size to achieve a substantial savings.

Buyers must also be concerned with import duty. Taxes and tariffs levied on imported products can have a major impact on the AP price. Some imported products have lower tariffs than others; consequently, a considerable price differential may exist among several similar items. For well items, buyers have an opportunity to at least consider the AP price differences when making a decision in this area.

Supplier Services

For well brands, management has a choice about which brands to use; hence, the AP price might be important for these items. But since differences in AP prices among the major brands is slight, supplier services may be more important.

One supplier service that distributors provide is the simplification of clerical routines; for example, they may be able to provide paperwork forms, such as blank purchase orders and bin cards, to their customers. These forms can save operators some money, and since they are required to maintain records of their purchases of beverage alcohols, the forms represent indeed a worthwhile supplier service. As we move toward a paperless environment, distributors may improve services by operating in a virtual marketplace. Distributors who are efficiently and seamlessly linked with buyers through online services can further streamline the purchasing process. For example, the automation of the entire request for quote/purchase order (RFQ/PO) process can result in substantial savings of both time and money.

Distributors extend their services by providing classes in understanding and complying with local liquor codes. Others offer personnel training in suggestive selling and merchandising. Some hold tastings of new recipes and conduct seminars on beer, wine, and spirits. While most hospitality operators are reluctant to let a supplier plan their food menus, they are usually willing to receive assistance in the preparation of a wine list. Operators who are not very familiar with wines find this service beneficial.

Some distributors allow for reasonable minimum-order requirements. This service is of particular importance when buyers need only one or two bottles of a slow-moving liquor. Conversely, buyers with extensive wine lists are eager to receive as much product as possible from the best wineries. When primary sources tend to "allocate" product, buyers consider a large allocation a much-prized supplier service.

Although liquor distributors do what they can to provide some supplier services, the law severely restricts them in what they can do for their customers. Federal, state, and local governments strictly limit the types of supplier services distributors can give because the governments worry about kickbacks and other diverse illegal temptations these supplier services invite.

PURCHASING BEVERAGE ALCOHOLS

To assist buyers in the purchase of beverage alcohols, the liquor industry generates a number of publications that note products, distributors, and AP prices.

For instance, in Nevada, a monthly publication titled the *Nevada Beverage Analyst* contains this information.

Once buyers select suppliers and determine the types of beverages they want, the purchasing procedure follows a fairly routine pattern. Ordering and delivery schedules become precise; buyers rarely have any control over them. In most cases, payment schedules are also predetermined. If buyers purchase product in a control state, the process follows strict regulations. Buyers usually order once a week and pay cash when they pick up their order. If they buy in a license state, limited credit terms may be available.

Probably the biggest decision buyers face is how much to order. The typical par stock is set for one week; slow-moving items may be ordered once a month or less often. Normally, buyers purchase in case lots with minimum-order requirements. This may present problems in situations where purchasing case quantity is not feasible. For example, if buyers' needs for a particular premium brand, which takes a year to sell, are less than the minimum-order size, they may be faced with the dilemma to carry it or drop it.

Many distributors may allow buyers to "break" the case. Buying a bottle from a "broken case" is usually more expensive than its case price. However, some distributors may permit buyers to combine different items to form a case lot. For instance, they may be able to buy two bottles each of six different brandies and receive a "mixed-case" price. This practice is regarded as an attractive supplier service because this price may be considerably lower than purchasing each bottle separately.

Buyers often face two other major decision points when purchasing beverage alcohols: (1) the post-off opportunity discussed earlier, and (2) the need, perhaps, to purchase a very large supply of one brand. For example, there is only so much Ferrari Carano® vintage Merlot to go around. If customers like this wine, buyers might consider purchasing as much as possible to ensure that they can offer it for as long as possible. But such a large purchase may require a stockless purchase, which would require buyers to pay now for the large order and have partial deliveries sent at specified times.

Once buyers know what they need, it is a good idea for them to prepare specifications for each liquor product (see Figure 24.6 for some examples of product specifications, and Figure 24.7 for an example of a product specification outline for beverage alcohol products).

The tendency in liquor purchasing exists to downplay the use of specifications, primarily because very few bid-buying opportunities are available. Also, buyers sometimes have the opportunity to evaluate products available only in their local area. This is especially true for fine wines and other specialty products.

Brandy Used for drink service at main bar E & J® brand (Original Extra Smooth) 80 proof 750-ml bottle	Alcohol-free White Zinfandel Used for wine list in main dining room Sutter Home Fre® brand Less than 0.5% alcohol by volume 750-ml bottle Delivered at cool temperature
London Dry Gin Used for drink service at main bar Gilbey's® brand 80 proof 750-ml bottle	Vodka Used for drink service at service bar Smirnoff® brand 80 proof 1.75-l bottle

FIGURE 24.6 **Examples of beverage alcohol product specifications.**

Today, it is possible for buyers to contract a winery, brewery, or distiller to prepare products according to their precise formulas. Some large hospitality operations may consider offering these house brands to customers. As with personalized packaging, the added prestige and merchandising value may more than compensate for the extra cost and effort that operations expend to secure these products.

Intended use:

Exact name:

Brand name (or equivalent):

Vintage:

Alcohol content:

Size of container:

Type of container:

Point of origin:

Preservation method:

FIGURE 24.7 **An example of a product specification outline for beverage alcohol products.**

RECEIVING BEVERAGE ALCOHOLS

Because alcohol has a high cost and involves extreme exposure to pilferage, hospitality operators spend much care and effort in the receiving area. Generally, the receiver is a supervisor, an owner-manager, or an assistant manager, and much less often a receiving clerk.

If a hospitality operation has an extensive wine list, and few staff members are sufficiently knowledgeable about wines, it is traditional, if not necessary, for a company to employ a sommelier, or wine steward. Contrary to the generally acceptable operating procedure of the separation of duties, the wine expert usually does it all. He or she buys, receives, stores, and sells the wine in the dining room.

Whoever receives the product typically follows the procedures noted in Chapter 14. This individual checks the quantity, sometimes by weighing unopened cases, and compares the invoices against the POs, as well as against the beverage labels. It is crucial for the receiver to check labels very carefully. For example, some liqueurs are made with a brandy base and some are made with a neutral-spirits base; the labels indicate this distinction, but these labels may be unclear to the uninitiated receiver. Also, he or she may mistake a 750-milliliter bottle for a liter bottle.

Beer kegs can present some receiving difficulty. Some delivery agents want to attach the kegs in the operation's refrigerator, or at least deliver them to the refrigerator, which may be against company policy. Another problem is that the kegs may be jostled too much at the receiving area, which can cause quality deterioration.

The receiver must also carefully compute the exact amount of the deposits that the company must put up for bottles and kegs. He or she must make certain that these deposits are correct and that the company receives the appropriate credit for those kegs and bottles it is returning to the distributor.

After examining the merchandise and being satisfied that everything is correct, the receiver completes any required paperwork. It is important to keep in mind that the federal government requires hospitality operations to maintain liquor invoices and bill-paying records. State and local government agencies may have similar requirements.

STORING BEVERAGE ALCOHOLS

Storing beverage alcohols is easier than storing many other food products. Typically, hospitality operations designate a separate storage facility exclusively for beverage alcohols. It is commonplace for operations to inventory all beverage alcohols within the same general area. However, some operations also maintain separate storage facilities for beer and wine.

Stolen liquor can be easily converted into cash. Therefore, operations should store beverage alcohols in a well-secured facility. In addition, they must keep the storage facility locked, with as few individuals as possible having access to the keys. For example, the keys to a well-stocked wine cellar might be restricted to the wine steward and, perhaps, one or two other service personnel.

As mentioned previously, many operators maintain a perpetual inventory of most beverage alcohols. It is common to add the amount of new product placed in the storeroom to a bin card or to enter this figure into a computerized inventory management system. With beverage alcohols, most operators take the bottles out of their shipping containers. This extra security precaution, although less popular for bottled beer, eliminates the possibility of operators later discovering an empty bottle, or no bottle, in the liquor case.

Distilled spirits, wine, and beer all have somewhat unique storage requirements. These are as follows:

Distilled Spirits

This liquor requires little care, and its storage life is usually long. Hospitality operators should place distilled spirits in a dry storage facility devoid of direct sunlight and excessive heat. Some people believe that these spirits improve in flavor when they age a while, but this is not true once they are put in a bottle. In addition, if staff members leave some bottles even slightly open, evaporation can occur. Furthermore, operators should not store spirits that contain sugar for long once they have been opened; not only do they evaporate, they also develop offensive odors and flavors.

Wine

Wines are harder to store than other beverage alcohols. They require specific temperature and humidity conditions. Generally, operators should store red wines in a cool area, while they usually should refrigerate white wines and sparkling wines because they are served cold.

Cork-bottled wines are stored on their side. This position enables the cork to remain moist, which facilitates its removal. When bottles are stored standing up for a protracted period, the cork may dry out. A dry cork permits more air to pass through it, and this air, in turn, causes wines to change gradually in flavor and eventually to become a type of vinegar. A final reason for storing wine bottles on their sides relates to old wines that contain sediment. If these wines are properly stored, the sediment will collect in the neck of the bottles, making it easier to remove it at the time of service.

Not all wines need to be stored in this manner. Wines that come in screw-top capped bottles and fortified wines can be stored upright. Fortified wines, such as Madeira, sherry, and port, are wines to which brandy has been added in order to increase the alcohol content.

Wine should not be exposed to excessive heat or to widely fluctuating temperatures. Both conditions can activate a chemical reaction that turns the wine into a form of vinegar. Consequently, operators should avoid displaying wines in the dining areas for long periods. Also, jostling wine bottles can cause the settled sediment to go back into the solution.

In contrast to distilled spirits, some wines improve in flavor as they age in the bottle. In fact, wine has a life cycle: birth, adolescence, maturation, adulthood, and death. Red wines have longer lives than white wines. At times, buyers may have to purchase wine that is immature and wait for it to mature before it can be served.

Most wine sold in large bag-in-the-box bulk containers is sometimes referred to as "jug wine." This kind of wine is often used for the house wine. Although this type of wine does not improve in flavor as it ages and has a relatively long shelf life, it can spoil if operators keep it too long after opening it.

If a hospitality operation wishes to serve leftover wine or to serve fine wines by the glass, it should consider purchasing a wine-dispensing unit specifically designed to store opened bottles of wine. An operator can open a wine bottle, serve one glass, and put the opened bottle in this unit where its quality will be maintained. The unit uses a nitrogen-flushing process to eliminate oxygen, which causes quality deterioration; it also maintains the proper storage environment. Such a unit is very expensive; however, if an operation wishes to offer a "wine bar," it is an essential piece of equipment.

If an operation does not have this type of wine-dispensing unit, it can still save the opened wine and serve it later. To do this, the operator must reseal the bottle tightly, refrigerate it, and try to serve it as soon as possible. A bottle seal device on the market enables an operator to reseal an opened bottle, attach a hand pump, and physically pump out as much air from the bottle as possible. By pumping out most of the air, the operator extends the leftover wine's shelf life.

If it is impossible, or undesirable, to save opened wine, operations can, perhaps, use it for cooking purposes. They can also use it to make vinegar; for instance, a vinegar-starter kit on the market lets an operator add wine and possibly one or more other ingredients. Eventually, the operator can use the wine vinegar for salad dressings and other vinegar-based food items.

Beer

Keg beer is not pasteurized; therefore, hospitality operations must refrigerate it at approximately 36°F to 38°F. Otherwise, the active yeasts continue to work, manufacturing more alcohol and carbon dioxide gas. If this process continues long enough, it can negatively affect the beer's flavor. It can also cause a keg to explode.

Operations should not keep kegs more than two weeks. By this time, the quality and fresh taste will have vanished, and patrons will be sure to complain if operators try to serve it. At the very least, companies should plan to properly rotate the kegs and, if possible, to arrange for weekly deliveries.

Usually, operators store beer kegs in a walk-in refrigerator that is very close to the bar. They are tapped in place, and the beer travels through the lines to the bar. If an operation has more than one bar, it might find it necessary to have a refrigerator for each one.

Operators must be careful when it comes to freezing beer. If it freezes and then thaws, they will find that a quantity of flakes will settle and refuse to go back into the solution. This will change the integrity of the beer and, therefore, it must be discarded.

Unlike keg beer, most canned and bottled beers are pasteurized. They have a longer life as a result of this process. When operators store canned beer in refrigerated conditions, it has a shelf life of approximately four months; bottled beer, on the other hand, has a shelf life that ranges from one to approximately six months. Without refrigeration, these shelf lives shrink to fewer than three months. By no means do canned and bottled beer retain their quality and fresh taste indefinitely.

Canned and bottled beers are often delivered in trucks that are not refrigerated. As a result, some quality deterioration will have already begun before the beer is received. However, operators may be able to retard the process if they immediately place these beers in a refrigerator. The life of canned and bottled beer is similar to that of fresh eggs: both time and warm and fluctuating temperatures are their greatest foes.

Once an operator opens a can or bottle and pours the beer, there is no way that he or she can save any leftovers for later. The operator can use the open beer in some recipes, such as fish batter and cheese soup, but even here, fresh beer is preferable. Consequently, if the beer is not consumed, the operator can do little to preserve it for later.

ISSUING BEVERAGE ALCOHOLS

Unlike most other food and nonfood items, beverage alcohols call for the strict scrutiny of owners and managers. In fact, some sort of perpetual inventory implemented in conjunction with tight security on the physical storage facilities is the rule rather than the exception.

Many operations may leave food and nonfood storage facilities unattended and unguarded, but not beverage alcohol storage areas. Even if no full- or part-time storeroom manager is on hand, the owner-manager, assistant manager, or head bartender will complete this task. Employees rarely have the authority to get their own beverage alcohols.

Typically, a receiver prepares a stock requisition. In addition, he or she also may be required to turn in an empty bottle for every full one requisitioned. Technically, however, this might be illegal in some states because those states require the empties to be broken as soon as they are drained.

Management also should set fairly strict par stocks for most, if not all, beverage alcohols. This makes it easier for bartenders to requisition only what they need. This practice also ensures that excess stock does not accumulate around the bar areas.

In operations that demand the strictest control, or in those that have several banquet bars or temporary bars, we might encounter a slightly different form of issuing. In these places, the head bartender or assistant manager might stock each bar; that is, he or she will bring it up to par. During the shift, if an employee needs additional product, he or she obtains it from the head bartender or assistant manager.

At the end of the shift, the employee either returns all the remaining stock to the storeroom or locks it up at his or her station. The head bartender or assistant manager counts what is left and determines the liquor usage. This quantity of liquor should be converted to theoretical sales, and should agree with the amount of sales recorded on the cash register and with the amount of cash and/or drink tickets collected from guests. This control procedure represents a little more work, but it is a worthwhile procedure. For places that can afford it, there are private companies, such as Bevinco (www.bevinco.com), that provide this service for a very modest fee.

Before issuing beverage alcohols, especially distilled spirits, management may want to code the bottles with a number or with some other mark that can be seen only with an infrared light. As noted earlier, coding is done so that dishonest employees cannot slip in their own bottles, sell their own beverage to the guest, take the money, and pocket it without ringing up a sale.

If an operation maintains an extensive wine list, it might consider giving the wine steward free access to the wine storage facilities while he or she is selling it in the dining room. This may sound like poor management, but it can work out well if operators keep track of what the wine steward buys and what he or she sells in the dining room. A physical inventory, performed regularly, can also help to uncover any inexplicable shortages or other problems attributable to the wine steward.

Operations that have an extensive automatic bar system can simplify the issuing process and, in some cases, eliminate it for many beverage items. For example, in a large hotel, several bar areas throughout the property may be connected to a central liquor-dispensing room. This room holds all the liquor, which is fed through lines that end at the dispensing heads located at each bar. Bartenders, therefore, do not have to requisition these beverage alcohols since someone, usually an employee of the food and beverage control office, loads the beverages on the system and is responsible for maintaining a constant supply.

IN-PROCESS INVENTORIES

Purchasing, receiving, storing, and issuing beverage alcohols are not difficult tasks, although selecting and procuring a list of fine wines can be. The real difficulties lie in the preparation and service of these products. The general feeling in the hospitality industry seems to be that when dealing with food, operators must be primarily concerned with quality and product control—for example, with meat shrinkage and excessive trimming losses. But since beverage alcohols do not involve such problems, the primary concern is personnel control.

Certainly, some problems can be associated with beverage alcohol product control, but they are minimal: basically, a bit of over- or under-pour, spillage, and an occasional mistake. These problems are easily controlled and generate much less alarm than can an overcooked prime rib or a salty clam chowder.

Security considerations are the real problem in bars. Bartenders may begin to pour free drinks for other employees or for their friends. They may take it upon themselves to pour drinks "on the house." In addition, they may over-pour for their friends and make up the difference by under-pouring for other patrons or by replenishing the liquor supply with water. This method is a form of inventory padding. Alternately, they may charge their friends for less than they actually consumed, making up the difference by overcharging a guest who is not fully aware of what he or she actually purchased. This is sometimes referred to as *check padding*; that is, an unsuspecting patron's guest check is padded with overcharges. Some bar operators employ a mystery shopping service to help prevent these problems.

So many opportunities for dishonesty exist in the bar business that it can be tiring just to enumerate them. But hospitality operators cannot ignore them. Operators must practice tight security procedures, and when they do, they need to take note of the most important security measure of all: supervision. Since our primary concern in bars is personnel control, it stands to reason that the most effective tool is employee supervision.

NONALCOHOLIC BEVERAGES

The growth in the nonalcoholic beverages industry is evident by the expanding number of both traditional and new beverages available in the marketplace. Café latte, green tea, specialty waters, sports drinks, and energy drinks are now commonplace in foodservice operations.

In many respects, the purchasing of nonalcoholic beverages parallels that of beverage alcohols. Of course, operators have more freedom here, mainly because patrons do not seem to have the same brand loyalties as they do for beverage alcohols. For instance, if an operation does not serve Coca-Cola®, only a few customers will balk at Pepsi®. On the other hand, some soft-drink companies are very active in enforcing their rights under copyright law, and so, in listing soft drinks, as on a menu or drink list, operators must take care to be accurate. The terms "Coca-Cola" and "Coke®" are proprietary brand names and can be used only when Coca-Cola is served.

Management Considerations

Management must make several decisions about nonalcoholic beverages, but the three most important are: (1) How many varieties should the operation carry? Operations could offer several types of soft drinks, juices, teas, and mixers. One brand of coffee and milk is sufficient, but soft drinks represent a major area of decision. (2) Should the operation have soft drinks available in bottles and cans, or should it use dispensing machines that mix concentrate, water, and carbon dioxide? Although canned and bottled products are more convenient, they are less profitable. Additionally, some customers prefer soft drinks in a glass or disposable container, with ice, because the beverage stays fresher and colder. (3) Who will supply the coffee? Because of the various types and qualities of products available, selecting the right coffee supplier is critical. Choosing the right coffee supplier is a lesson that most seasoned hospitality operators learn quite early in their careers. With the aid of the supplier, an operator very carefully selects coffees and teas that are appropriate for his or her type of hospitality operation. When compared with the impression coffees and teas leave with customers, the portion cost of coffees and teas is insignificant. A great deal of hand-wringing accompanies a hospitality operator's decision to take a chance with a product that will "save money." So, as in the selection of a meat supplier, it is unusual for operators to switch coffee suppliers capriciously.

SELECTION FACTORS

Despite the relative purchasing freedom nonalcoholic beverages permit, buyers must quite carefully consider the selection factors before deciding what to purchase. Once they know what they want, the buying is easy, especially since the same type of exclusive wholesale-distributorship system that exists for many beverage alcohols also exists for many nonalcoholic beverages. The major selection factors are as follows:

Intended Use

As always, buyers need to determine exactly the intended use of an item so that they will be able to prepare the appropriate, relevant specification. For instance, a soda used in an alcoholic punch recipe may be of lower quality than one that will be served straight.

Exact Name

Some nonalcoholic beverages have standards of identity that the federal government sets. For instance, the word "juice" on a label or package implies that the product is 100 percent derived from the fruit or vegetable—no water is added.

This is not true for all products, though. For instance, several types of "drinks" are on the market, and buyers need to examine these items very carefully for taste, color, and so forth before determining their suitability.

To some extent, certain types of nonalcoholic beverage producers follow and adhere to trade association standards. For instance, the New York Coffee, Sugar, and Cocoa Exchange sets minimum standards for coffee products.

U.S. Government Grades (or Equivalent)

Grades exist for fruit and vegetable juices, as noted in Chapter 18. Green tea also has a grade standard, as does milk. But other nonalcoholic beverages carry no grades, although some products, such as coffee and tea, can receive an endorsement from one or more institutes.

Brand Name (or Equivalent)

Brand names are important to buyers, who are accustomed, through habit and advertising, to relying on certain products. But many customers are indifferent to brands. One point buyers need to keep in mind about brand names is that they may be able to promote a certain brand, thereby enhancing their business. Some suppliers help buyers by providing some type of promotional discount, customized events, or point-of-sale materials.

Buyers are not tied to a brand. They can shop around, and if the quality and customer acceptance are similar, they will have a reasonable choice among brands. However, buyers must remain mindful of what we said earlier about copyright laws and proprietary rights of suppliers in regard to brand names.

Size of Container

A fairly wide array of package sizes is available to buyers of nonalcoholic beverages. Sizes normally range from 6-ounce, single-serve containers to 5-gallon kegs of syrup. In general, in the carbonated-soft-drink trade, the sizes are not as numerous as they are in, say, the fruit and vegetable juices line. Nevertheless, it is very important for buyers to select and procure the package size that suits their needs best.

Type of Container

Nonalcoholic beverages come in different sizes and types of containers made of various packaging materials. The quality of these materials is very standardized. Consequently, the buyers' major decision is determining which type of material suits their needs most effectively. For some products, such as soft-drink syrup, their choices usually are limited to bottles, kegs, and bag-in-the-box containers. But for other items, such as ready-to-serve drinks, additional options are available.

Some suppliers offer unique types of containers, though these ordinarily can be used only in the dispensing equipment that they provide. For instance, some Vitality® brand juices can be purchased in an Express Pak® that fits snugly into the Vitality dispenser. The dispenser releases a programmed portion size at the push of a button.

Buyers might be interested in personalized packaging for some of their non-alcoholic beverages. For instance, some dairies will use private labels on the single-serve containers of milk that operations purchase. A corollary might be the willingness of a soft-drink company to personalize the disposable drink cups sold to operations, along with the syrup.

As a convenient alternative, hospitality companies can purchase some nonalcoholic beverages that are not packaged. For instance, certain soft-drink suppliers can pump syrup from their trucks into the operations' reusable tanks, which are attached to the dispensing machine. This can reduce packaging needs and contribute to a cleaner environment.

Product Form

Buyers can purchase ready-to-serve, i.e. "premix," beverages. These beverages can be purchased in bottles, plastic cartons, waxed cartons, cans, kegs, and bag-in-the-box containers. Buyers can also purchase "postmix" beverages. Postmix products require someone on the staff of the hospitality operation to do some additional preparation. Buyers purchase these products in forms similar to the containers in which premix products are packed.

With postmix products, buyers anticipate saving a few dollars because they are purchasing concentrates—frozen, dried, or liquid—and are providing the reconstitution needed to make the item ready for service. For instance, most carbonated-soft-drink dispensing units are set up in such a way that a hospitality staff member must hook up a water supply line, a container of concentrate, and a cylinder of carbon dioxide gas. When a customer orders a soft drink, the ingredients are mixed as they flow through the lines into the glass or disposable drink cup. This procedure also provides a freshly mixed finished product, which is pleasing to the customer.

Buyers must consider other product characteristics when purchasing nonalcoholic beverages, such as whether the cola is diet or regular and whether the coffee is regular or decaffeinated. Other considerations may include the type of grind desired for brewed coffee and the size and type of crystals for instant coffee.

Buyers can purchase most nonalcoholic beverages with varying degrees of form value. In general, the more convenient the form, the more buyers pay for the item. But a high AP price means nothing if the EP cost and overall value are acceptable. If buyers are concerned about the AP price, though, they can, quite possibly, reduce it considerably by accepting less form value.

Preservation Method

Generally, suppliers deliver premix products at room temperature, although there is no reason not to insist that suppliers maintain refrigerated temperatures while the products are in transit. They should, for example, keep some specialty products, such as "natural" apple juice, under constant refrigeration in order to preserve their quality and extend their shelf lives.

Depending on the type of item, postmix products are held under refrigerated, freezer, or dry-storage temperatures. For instance, liquid coffee concentrates are normally kept at refrigerated temperatures, liquid juice concentrates are normally delivered at freezer temperatures, and powders are normally kept at dry-storage temperatures.

Some products, such as ground coffee and whole coffee beans, are normally kept at dry-storage temperatures, unless something different is specified. However, since refrigerated and freezer temperatures tend to extend these products' shelf lives, buyers may want to consider dealing only with those suppliers who provide that service.

AP Price

Quality and AP price appear to be positively correlated. A higher quality seems to imply, within reason, a higher AP price. This may not always be the case, especially when a certain soft-drink company tries to gain a foothold by reducing prices temporarily. But the straight-line relationship between AP price and quality holds up reasonably well. For example, a less expensive, premix soft drink implies that the flavorings are artificial; in addition, these products do not hold carbon dioxide gas very long once they are opened. Thus, their overall value is seriously undermined.

EP cost can also rise disproportionately for some nonalcoholic beverages. For instance, several coffees taste somewhat similar, but the type of grind and the type of bean involved can make a difference in how much coffee you need to use to brew a pot.

Many nonalcoholic beverages present opportunity buys, such as quantity and promotional discounts. For example, Coke may help defray a hospitality operation's menu-printing costs if it includes its brand name on the menu. Also, price wars can occasionally erupt between the major soft-drink companies.

Buyers can save money by continually switching from one soft-drink brand to another. Pepsi and Coke constantly strive for operators' business. So if a hospitality operation owns its own refrigeration and dispensing and ice-making machinery, the switch is easy. If the supplier owns this equipment, however, it is not convenient to change, even though it may be economical. Another problem: an operation cannot sell Pepsi if it advertises Coke on its menu.

Sometimes, the AP price is irrelevant. For instance, some states require wholesale price maintenance for milk; some even require retail price maintenance for milk. While suppliers or retailers can charge more than the minimum required under the law, the minimum requirement is the price that all buyers are usually charged.

Supplier Services

Supplier services are crucial when buyers purchase nonalcoholic beverages. If buyers have two relatively similar brands to choose from, they will tend to select the one that carries with it more supplier services. Some manufacturers give away or lend items—anything from menu decals to refrigerators—as long as buyers agree to purchase their products. In general, however, buyers are not interested in such trinkets as clocks. But their interest surely will be piqued when a "free" refrigerator awaits them. The fact that this refrigerator can be used for items other than those they purchase from that distributor (and that it will be maintained by the distributor free of charge) makes such a "gift" useful indeed.

Some suppliers also lend to buyers for free, or charge only a token amount for, the use of brewing equipment, dispensing equipment, coffee pots, and so forth when they purchase beverage products. These "equipment programs" are popular in the hospitality industry. Buyers tend to pay more for the beverage products when they participate in these programs, but the convenience may be worthwhile. Also, if they really want a particular beverage product, they might as well take the equipment program because, unless they work for a very large hospitality company with a great deal of purchasing power, it is unlikely that they will receive a discount if they do not agree to the program.

The types of delivery schedules, ordering procedures, and minimum-order requirements also are important. Moreover, if buyers are participating in an equipment program, they must ascertain how well the distributor will maintain the equipment.

PURCHASING NONALCOHOLIC BEVERAGES

Once buyers have decided on the types of beverages they want, their purchasing procedure follows a fairly routine pattern. Ordering and delivery schedules are pretty well set, although they are not as restrictive as those for beverage alcohols. In addition, buyers have more payment freedom; the credit terms are subject to more negotiation possibilities than are those for beverage alcohols.

As with beverage alcohols, the buyers' primary decision is how much to order. The par stock for these items usually varies quite a bit from one operation to the next. When buyers purchase soft drinks, a three-day stock is typical. The par stock for coffee and frozen beverages might run a week or more. Buyers should purchase perishable products, such as milk, on a day-to-day, standing-order basis when possible. Usually, buyers can arrange a standing-order agreement for some of these types of items. In such arrangements, it is normal for a route salesperson to call on buyers and "bring them up to par."

Some suppliers stipulate minimum-order requirements, but this rarely presents a difficulty. Unlike with beverage alcohols, buyers probably would not carry an exceptionally slow-moving nonalcoholic beverage.

Like beverage alcohols, nonalcoholic beverages encourage hospitality operators to follow the par stock approach entirely and to deal with several distributors to obtain the desired variety of beverages. Some distributors carry wide lines of beverages, but most carry only one or two varieties of nonalcoholic beverages.

With the exception of normal quantity and volume discounts, other opportunity buys are infrequent. Those available usually take the form of introductory offers or, more commonly, promotional discounts. Ordinarily, these discounts take the form of menu printing and the provision of other signs. Introductory offers and free samples occur sporadically, such as when soft-drink firms make a concerted effort to increase market share. Sometimes buyers can obtain a cash discount if they pay the route salesperson cash on delivery (COD).

As with beverage alcohols, though, detailed specifications usually are not prepared for these items because brand-name merchandise that can fit an operation's particular storage and dispensing machinery tends to be a major consideration. However, some large hospitality enterprises with the resources to shop around might prepare detailed specifications for such products as coffee, tea, and juices (see

Figure 24.8 for some examples of product specifications, and Figure 24.9 for an example of a product specification outline for nonalcoholic beverage products).

RECEIVING NONALCOHOLIC BEVERAGES

Hospitality operations should use the suggested receiving principles noted in Chapter 14. Unfortunately, though, the care operations exercise when receiving beverage alcohols often dissipates when it comes to nonalcoholic beverages.

Receivers normally check the quantity, AP prices, and condition of the delivered goods. Refrozen merchandise, split packages, and broken glass are the major quality checks, along with a careful examination of the labels to see whether the supplier has delivered the correct product. The best quality check is to note the effective age of the product, but this is difficult. For example, time is an enemy of coffee quality; unfortunately, it is hard to tell how old coffee is when it is received unless the package has some type of dating. Some companies, such as PepsiCo, put freshness dates on some of their products; for instance, Diet Pepsi package labels contain a "Best If Consumed By" date.

Receivers must also be careful to correctly account for any returned merchandise, especially empty returnable containers. Since bottle and keg deposits may

Coffee Used for drink service at main bar and at dining room side stands Yorkshire® brand Ground, decaffeinated 12-oz. packets, vacuum packed Packed 24 packets per case	Tomato juice Used for drink service at main bar Campbell's® brand (or equivalent) 46-oz. can Packed 12 cans per case
Cola Used for drink service at main bar and at dining room side stands Pepsi® brand 5-gal. bag-in-the-box Syrup Postmix	Orange juice Used for breakfast beverage Sunkist® brand (or equivalent) U.S. Grade A (or equivalent) Concentrate (3 to 1) 32-oz. can Packed 12 cans per case Frozen

FIGURE 24.8 **Examples of nonalcoholic beverage product specifications.**

Intended use:

Exact name:

U.S. grade (or equivalent):

Brand name (or equivalent):

Size of container:

Type of container:

Product form:

Preservation method:

FIGURE 24.9 **An example of a product specification outline for nonalcoholic beverage products.**

exist, receivers should ensure that the appropriate credit is received when the empties are returned. Once receivers examine and approve the merchandise, they must complete any necessary paperwork.

STORING NONALCOHOLIC BEVERAGES

Storing nonalcoholic beverages in the correct environment can retard quality deterioration. Coffee quality, for example, rapidly fades in heat. Many operators keep ground and whole-bean coffee under refrigeration or even in the freezer. Canned and bottled beverages do best in a refrigerator, although some products, like canned tomato juice, keep well in a dry storeroom.

Operators must store frozen items in a freezer and should not thaw them in advance. For instance, they should not thaw frozen juice concentrate prior to preparation; a hospitality staff member should mix it with water while it is frozen and allow it to thaw in this manner. Ideally, operations should have a dispensing unit that is programmed to mix one glass of juice at a time, using the frozen concentrate stored in the unit. This ensures a high-quality finished product—and satisfied guests.

With frozen beverages, operators should take the time to periodically check the condition of their containers because these tend to crack and split.

ISSUING NONALCOHOLIC BEVERAGES

Some operators do not exert a great deal of control over nonalcoholic beverages. The fact that many of these products go directly to a production department, or sometimes even to self-service dispensing units in the dining room, works against a strict accounting. Ideally, they should control nonalcoholic beverages as much as they do any other product. But because nonalcoholic beverages rarely represent a great portion of the total purchase dollar, they tend to be taken for granted.

Managers and owners slight nonalcoholic beverage control for three major reasons. First, the cost of controlling these items may be much higher than any potential savings. Second, many operators permit employees to drink soft drinks, milk, and coffee for free, or for a modest "drink fee" deducted from their paychecks. If so, why would employees steal them? However, employees may abuse the situation by giving these drinks away to their friends. And third, these beverages may get shifted back and forth between the bar, the kitchen, room service, and poolside service, which makes monitoring difficult. However, when bartenders are responsible for their mixers—the soft drinks, cream, and juices used in the preparation of cocktails—operators pay more attention to them, usually the same consideration that they give beverage alcohols. This is especially true of operations that generate high-volume bar business.

IN-PROCESS INVENTORIES

Many problems with nonalcoholic beverages center on the prepreparation, preparation, and service functions: (1) How much do operators let employees drink on the job? (2) Who makes the coffee: an idle warewasher? A server who is not busy at the time? (3) Who refills the milk dispenser? (4) Who retrieves the single-service cans of tomato juice? (5) How much coffee should operators make at one time? How much iced tea?

Once again, supervision is the key. Waste can be a problem in this area. Operators who carefully monitor and control the use of these items have the greatest potential to accrue reasonable savings.

KEY WORDS AND CONCEPTS

Alcohol content	Brand name	Drink fee
Allocation	Brew pub	Driving under the influence (DUI)
Appropriate menu price for alcohol	Call brand	
	Capital costs	Driving while intoxicated (DWI)
As-purchased price (AP price)	Case price	Edible-portion cost (EP cost)
	Check padding	Equipment program
Automatic dispenser	Control state	Exact name

Exclusive distributorship

Freshness dates

House brand

House wine

Importance of the coffee supplier

In-process inventories

Intended use

Inventory padding

Inventory sales control procedure

Jug wine

License state

Light liquor

Liquor industry publications

Liquor license

Management considerations when purchasing beverages

Mixed case

Mothers Against Drunk Driving (MADD)

Nitrogen flush

Perpetual inventory

Personalized packaging

Point of origin

Popular types of beverage alcohol products

Postmix

Post-off

Pouring cost

Premium well

Premix

Preservation method

Price maintenance

Product form

Proof

Pull strategy

Purchasing, receiving, storing, and issuing beverage products

Route salesperson

Size of container

Standard of identity

Stockless purchase

Supplier services

Type of container

U.S. grades

Vintage

Well brand

Wine-dispensing unit

Wine speculating

QUESTIONS AND PROBLEMS

1. Which type of hospitality operation is most inclined to use a premium well brand? Why?

2. What is the alcoholic content of a spirit of 100 proof?

3. What is the recommended storage procedure for white wines?

4. What is the recommended storage procedure for keg beer?

5. An owner-manager would be interested in a soft-drink company's equipment program because he or she could achieve several advantages from this program. What are some of these advantages?

6. Identify one major disadvantage of an equipment program.

7. Assume that you own a small neighborhood tavern. You employ one bartender and one bar-back, that is, someone who assists the bartender. You also tend bar. Who should order the items? Why? Who should receive and store them? Why?

8. What are the major advantages and disadvantages of providing your guests with a well-stocked wine cellar?

9. What is the major selection factor for beverage alcohols?

10. Why is the selection factor "point of origin" an important consideration for beverage alcohol products?

11. A product specification for fruit juice could include the following information:
    (a)
    (b)
    (c)
    (d)
    (e)

12. Assume you are a country club manager. You are choosing the well brand you want to use for Scotch. One brand is 86 proof. Its AP price is $12.40 per liter. Another brand, with the same proof, has an AP price of $11.50 per liter. The former brand is fairly well known and is thought to be a respectable product. The latter brand is rather obscure. Which brand would you select? Why? If possible, ask a country club manager to comment on your answer.

13. What is the primary difference between a premix beverage and a postmix beverage?

14. Why do buyers seldom prepare detailed specifications for beverage alcohol products?

15. Is it a good idea to let a wine steward purchase, receive, store, and sell the wines? Why or why not? Assume that as the owner-manager of the operation, you allow this practice. How would you exercise control over the wine steward? If possible, ask a hotel food and beverage director to comment on your answer.

16. What critical information is missing from the following product specification for beer?
    Beer
    Used for bar service
    Packaged in 12-ounce, nonreturnable bottles
    Packed 24 bottles per case

17. What are some of the differences between a license state and a control state?

18. The consumption of beverage alcohol in the United States has declined over the past few years. What are some of the reasons for this decline?

19. When would you specify personalized packaging for a beverage product?

20. Define or explain briefly the following terms:

(a)	Liquor license	(h)	Case price
(b)	Inventory padding	(i)	House brand
(c)	Pull strategy	(j)	Wine steward
(d)	Pouring cost	(k)	Check padding
(e)	House wine	(l)	Price maintenance
(f)	Jug wine	(m)	Wine speculation
(g)	Post-off	(n)	Perpetual inventory

25

NONFOOD EXPENSE ITEMS

After reading this chapter, you should be able to:

■ Identify management considerations surrounding the selection and procurement of nonfood expense items.

■ List the types of nonfood expense items that might be purchased by a hospitality operator.

■ Describe the major selection factors for nonfood expense items.

INTRODUCTION

Some operations devote a great amount of money to nonfood expense items, which are sometimes referred to as "operating supplies." (An expense item is one that hospitality operations can write off in the current year's income statement; that is, it is not a "capital" item that must be depreciated over a period of years.) But the attention that operations lavish on food and beverage items typically is greater than what they devote to these types of purchases.

Buying nonfood items is sometimes a highly routine activity. Buyers usually establish the major guidelines, and department heads are held responsible for ensuring an orderly flow of cleaning agents, stationery, glassware, and so forth. In these instances, operations pay at least some minimal attention to purchasing decisions.

Unfortunately, small operations tend to view these purchases as nuisances and may try to conclude them as speedily as possible. But this can be a serious mistake. Although these purchases often represent a comparatively small portion of the total purchasing dollar, a considerable number of managerial concerns surround them—concerns that can, upon closer examination, dramatize the need for careful nonfood procurement procedures.

MANAGEMENT CONSIDERATIONS

Buying nonfood expense items sometimes presents difficult decisions. The quality of mop buyers purchase probably will not influence their sales volume, but the quality of guest amenities—such items as individually wrapped or liquid soap, and paper or linen towels in rest rooms—definitely help to shape the operation's image. Consequently, buyers should not make purchasing decisions regarding these items lightly. Some of the considerations that can affect these decisions are discussed below.

Personalization of Nonfood Items

The degree of personalization that hospitality operations want in a nonfood item is related to the image they wish to create. How customized do they want their nonfood products to be? Will any old paper napkin do, or should it have their name or, perhaps, some other type of advertising or insignia on it? In some cases, nonfood items become advertisements in disguise, and operators should treat them accordingly. (This issue is discussed further in Chapter 26.) This fact makes it difficult for buyers to evaluate the price of nonfood items. Generally, the more personalized these items become, the higher their price.

When buyers consider the price of a matchbook, for example, they have to divide it into two components: the advertising component and the functional component. They can note the price for plain matchbooks, to which any increment in price would represent an advertising expenditure.

Sometimes buyers form the habit of staying with a certain style of nonfood guest supplies. Salespersons know this, so it is only natural for them to sell buyers one item, such as a personalized napkin, for a very reasonable price. The idea might be for buyers to work the item into their business, for their customers to become enamored of it, and then for the salesperson to urge the buyers to purchase similar, additional nonfood expense items for perhaps a slightly higher price.

The process may not work quite like this, but image is crucial to the sale of nonfood items, and salespersons know this. They continually remind buyers of this. By doing so, they can place buyers accustomed exclusively to food buying on the defensive. The image phenomenon does complicate some nonfood purchases. Moreover, once buyers have decided what they want, it may be hard to turn back, since they cannot necessarily go to another supplier and get exactly the same product.

This is not to say that buyers will be stuck for life with a certain type of napkin, but they may hesitate to change styles too abruptly. They do not make major changes without incurring some risk. For instance, customers really notice when a hotel moves from high-quality guest amenities to lesser-quality items. As such, buyers should make sure that several of their nonfood items will serve their needs for a long time.

Nonfood Product Variety

Another major concern involves the many nonfood items available on the market and the numerous suppliers who carry items of this type. This situation favors bid buyers. However, it can also cause confusion and anxiety for typical owner-managers, who may seek relief with a sympathetic one-stop supplier. They must be aware, though, that many of these selection and procurement decisions may affect their image for quite some time and that it may be wise to take more time and try bid buying.

Bid buying offers a bit more potential benefit in the nonfood area because when buyers purchase in large quantities, they can often get favorable bids from several competing suppliers. In addition, since they may not need to go through the time-consuming bidding procedures too often, the little bit they do endure can lead to impressive savings. Finally, because these items are not perishable, they do not spoil; hence, their as-used cost is quite predictable—unless, of course, operators fail to exert the proper supervision over in-process inventory use.

If buyers purchase a lot of standard nonfood items, such as plain napkins, ordinary flatware, and standard drinking glasses, bid buying may be less beneficial. These standard items typically have a small spread in price, quality, and supplier services among suppliers. Wider spreads normally occur when buyers purchase personalized items and have varying quality requirements.

Degree of Product Convenience

An interesting managerial issue is the degree of convenience to specify in certain nonfood items. For example, does the hospitality operation want one all-purpose cleaner, which, according to some people, does not exist, or does it want to spend time selecting individual cleaning agents for specific uses?

In this situation, form economic value comes into play once again. Obviously, the greater the convenience, the greater the form value; hence, buyers can expect a higher as-purchased (AP) price.

Perhaps the touchiest issue associated with nonfood convenience centers on disposable versus reusable items—for example, linen napkins and place mats versus their paper or plastic counterparts. The permanent-versus-disposable argument that surrounds permanent dish and silverware and disposables is especially acute. Several studies "prove" the economics of permanent ware. But, as you can imagine, a lot of people consider disposables the wiser choice. Complicating the issue further is the negative environmental impact associated with disposable ware, although some buyers overcome this by purchasing items made with recycled materials.

For some types of hospitality operations, permanent ware is necessary to maintain the appropriate image. But any operation can work with at least a few disposables, and most customers accept some, if only paper towels in the rest room. The convenience of using such items is certainly something we cannot argue with.

We think that permanent ware is the logical choice when operations are concerned with cost savings. With reusable items, they minimize the cost of solid-waste disposal. Moreover, not only is disposable ware expensive, it is a waste of natural resources unless operators take the time to send the disposable ware to a recycling plant after use.

Nonfood Impulse Purchasing

A subtle problem in buying nonfood expense items is the impulse purchase. At times, buyers might purchase a nonfood item on the spur of the moment. A lot of little items, such as coin-rolling devices and vegetable cutters, enter the operation and, perhaps, operators use them rarely, if at all. The lesson here is: buyers should not purchase any item unless they are absolutely certain it is needed.

Supervising Nonfood Items

Another problem associated with nonfood items is the hospitality operators' tendency to neglect the supervision of employees when they use them. Although few of these items represent a large portion of the purchase dollar, their continual disappearance and misuse can significantly increase overall operating costs. All too often, for instance, a cook who delimes the steam table pours in a half-gallon of delimer solution instead of the recommended half-quart. Similarly, he or she might toss out a dirty mop head instead of sending it to the laundry.

Examples of wasted nonfood items are numerous and small expenses add up. So supervisors should strictly monitor the usage of them. Large operations consider this need for supervision to be a given. But they, too, can become lax at times. For example, during a rush period, who stops to make sure that only one paper doily, instead of two or three, is under the shrimp cocktail boat?

Even large operations have a tendency to set flexible par stocks for nonfood items and then to allow the department head to monitor the usage rates and order replacement items he or she deems necessary. In these situations, frequent stockouts of these items can occur, since these purchases may not be monitored closely.

Quantity and Volume Discounts

Whenever possible, buyers should make every attempt to purchase large amounts of these products. Our experience suggests that significant savings are associated with this practice. The discounts available in the nonfood channel of distribution are quite attractive, and if buyers have the money and the storage space necessary to participate in this practice, their as-used costs for the supplies usually will be considerably less than those obtained with small order sizes.

Nonfood Packers' Brands

The use of packers' brands as a selection factor does not seem to be as prevalent for nonfood expense items as it is for food and beverages. Buyers might rely on a specific producer, especially for personalized items, but not for standard, everyday items. So many producers and varieties of standardized nonfood expense items exist that buyers are often encouraged to shop around.

Systems Sale

A systems sale occurs when buyers purchase a particular product, such as a specific type of point-of-sale (POS) system, that can accept only paper guest checks and/or paper cash register tapes that one company manufactures, usually the company that also manufactures the system.

An owner-manager must consider a type of trade-off whenever the opportunity arises to participate in a systems sale. On the one hand, the salesperson of the main item, such as a cash register, might be willing to sell the register for a very low price. But when buyers need the paper products, parts, and so forth, for their operation, they could be staring at expensive prices, with no alternatives.

Operating-Supplies Schemes

For one reason or another, hospitality operations are more vulnerable to ripoff artists in the nonfood expense items, capital equipment items, and services channels of distribution. The care and diligence buyers exercise in their food and beverage purchasing somehow appear to wane a bit when they buy nonfood products. For example, buyers tend to order nonfood expense items from a catalog or from some other type of advertising solicitation, such as one that shows up in a trade magazine. Buyers should keep in mind that it is possible that items ordered in such a way may not be satisfactory because the catalog description may be misleading.

Another problem many businesspersons encounter is the office supply telephone salesperson. These "WATS-line hustlers" (Wide Area Telecommunications Service) or "toner-phoners" offer what appear to be tremendous bargains, but, unfortunately, the merchandise delivered is often inadequate. The Better Business Bureau (BBB) offices throughout the United States probably have thick files listing all sorts of scams like this.

It is important for buyers to follow rigorous selection and procurement procedures for all products and services they must purchase. For instance, in the examples discussed above, buyers would not get hurt if they followed an approved-supplier list that restricted their purchasing authority.

Safety Considerations

Some nonfood expense items may present a safety hazard. For instance, hospitality operations must be concerned with toxic chemicals, cleaners that impart distasteful odors, and cleaners and similar products that, while safe in and of themselves, could, through mishandling, become dangerous.

Operations cannot always refuse to purchase an item because it represents a possible danger. But they should be well prepared to store and use such items properly. Local health districts normally require stringent storage procedures for toxic materials. Operations can also obtain safety regulations regarding such items from

the Occupational Safety & Health Administration (OSHA) Website at www.
osha.gov. Operations must, however, supplement these legal requirements with
stringent operating procedures of their own to ensure that no harm comes to their
guests or themselves.

Some operators would rather eliminate the need to store and to use toxic
products by purchasing a service to do the work for them. For example, instead of
purchasing, storing, and using pest control materials, operators might prefer to hire
a pest control company to perform this function.

New versus Used

Buyers can purchase some nonfood expense items in a used condition. Such products as china, glass, and silver often are available from secondhand dealers, at
auctions, or from other hospitality companies that are liquidating their assets.
Buyers can also obtain items by going to online auction sites, such as
www.ebay.com.

Our experience suggests that buyers can save a tremendous amount of
money if they are lucky enough to stumble onto a good deal. As with any type
of used item, though, they must be willing to take chances. Furthermore, they
must be willing to spend considerable time and effort to locate this type of merchandise.

Equipment Program

It is possible for buyers to purchase a nonfood expense item and concurrently obtain from the supplier the equipment needed to use it. For instance, if buyers purchase a certain amount of dishwashing machine chemicals, they might be able to
rent the machine from the chemical supplier at a very favorable rate. Buyers may
also be able to receive the use of a dishwashing machine and all the chemicals they
need while paying a certain amount for each rack of soiled tableware they run
through the machine.

These equipment programs are similar to the ones for nonalcoholic beverages we discussed in Chapter 24. The same advantages and disadvantages apply
here. Owner-managers, though, seem to prefer some sort of equipment program
because it eliminates the need to invest in equipment and because the equipment
generally is maintained free of charge. In the long run, it probably costs more to
operate in this fashion; however, in the short run, such a strategy can enhance a
hospitality operation's cash flow.

Lifetime Cost

Some nonfood expense items have a long life. They are not used once and discarded, but remain with an operation for a reasonable period of time. Consequently, when computing their as-used costs, buyers must consider additional factors. For long-life items they must be interested in the products' original AP price. They must also be aware of any operating costs that will be associated with the use of these items. For instance, a cleaning tool must be wielded by someone who receives a wage. Furthermore, if the cleaning tool is less expensive than another one, but requires more time to wield, buyers will do the operation a financial disservice in the long run if they purchase such an item.

Similarly, buyers must consider the potential salvage value of a long-life item. For example, somewhere down the line they might be able to trade in a cleaning tool for a new model and receive a very generous trade-in allowance. Buyers can probably best understand this concept via the "new car" example. A very expensive new car can easily cost less to operate and can retain its value much longer than an automobile with a much lower sticker price. Furthermore, a more expensive car may require less routine maintenance and may be more energy efficient.

Credit Terms

Sometimes, buyers must purchase a large amount of nonfood expense items. They should consider shopping around for the best credit terms if this option is available. They should be especially discerning about the amount, if any, of deposit they must put up before they are allowed to place an order for a customized item. Furthermore, they must consider what will happen if they change their minds about the item later on and they do not wish to purchase the product even though they ordered it. They need to find out ahead of time what will happen to their deposit: will they lose all of it or only part of it?

PURCHASING NONFOOD EXPENSE ITEMS

Buyers can purchase nonfood expense items several ways, although fewer ways exist to buy them than to buy food. However, perhaps because nonfood expense items are not perishable, the various alternatives available can be quite viable and represent a few cost-saving opportunities. Buyers can purchase many of these items on a day-to-day basis. Alternately, they can be purchased as far in advance as the foodservice operation's storage permits.

The major problems are identifying the proper par stock and the appropriate supplier. These are not easy questions because several quantity and volume discount variations exist among suppliers. Also, since nonfood expense items are not perishable, most suppliers will try to accommodate your needs.

Typically, par stocks are large. Furthermore, if buyers want any sort of personalization, usually they must purchase these items in huge quantities from one supplier. Also, it is common to find some sort of stockless purchase arrangement.

Multiunit operations save the most when they exercise their quantity buying power. Franchisees also tend to purchase from the company commissary because this usually represents the lowest possible price.

The principal step in purchasing nonfood expense items is for buyers to decide exactly what they require. This is not necessarily an easy task because many potential suppliers and many varieties of items are available. For some products, though, such as cleaning supplies, the quality and as-used cost differences among the suppliers may not be readily apparent.

Once buyers know what products will suit their needs, it is a good idea for them to prepare specifications (see Figure 25.1 for an example of specifications, and Figure 25.2 for a sample specification outline for nonfood expense items).

As when purchasing liquor, buyers tend to deemphasize the use of specifications when buying nonfood expense items. Many times when they need these prod-

Irish coffee mug Used for bar service Standard restaurant logo on white background Libbey® brand (or equivalent) $8^1/_2$-oz. mug Packed 24 per case	Disposable foam cup Used for hot drinks Plain white color CODE® brand (or equivalent) 6-oz. cup size 25 cups per plastic sleeve Packed 40 sleeves per case

Bar straw
Used for bar service
House brand (or least expensive brand)
Red color
$7^3/_4$-in. straw
500 straws per box
Packed 10 boxes per case
	Liquid chlorine bleach
	Used for general cleaning purposes
	House brand (or least expensive
	  product)
	1-gal. plastic container with screw-
	  top cap
	Packed 4 to 6 gallons per case

FIGURE 25.1 An example of nonfood expense item specifications.

Intended use:

Exact name:

Safety needs:

Convenience requirement:

Odor limitations:

New versus used options:

Promotional needs:

Maximum as-used cost:

Personalization requirement:

Effectiveness requirement:

Compatibility requirement:

Product form:

Product size:

Size of container:

Type of container:

Brand name (or equivalent):

Color:

Material used to make the item:

FIGURE 25.2 An example of a specification outline for nonfood expense items.

ucts, buyers go to the supplier and examine the items in person before placing an order. Alternately, it is common for salespersons to demonstrate and/or show these products to potential buyers before soliciting purchase orders.

Purchasing nonfood expense items can be as easy or as difficult as buyers want to make it. As we have already noted, it may be to the buyers' benefit to expend a lot of effort to select and procure these products because their work may be rewarded with lower AP prices and, it is hoped, lower as-used costs. Realistically, many hospitality operations use one-stop shopping; perhaps for these operations, the number of dollars saved do not compensate for the extra purchasing efforts.

TYPICAL NONFOOD ITEMS THAT HOSPITALITY OPERATORS USE

Hospitality operators typically purchase in the following nine nonfood expense categories: (1) cleaning supplies, (2) cleaning tools, (3) maintenance supplies, (4) permanent ware, (5) single-service disposable ware, (6) preparation and service utensils, (7) fabrics, (8) other paper products, and (9) miscellaneous items. We discuss each of them in the following sections.

Cleaning Supplies

Hospitality operations normally purchase several types of cleaning supplies: guest supplies, such as moisturizing cream; chemical cleaners; soaps; detergents; bleach; and polishes and waxes. The guest supplies usually represent as much advertising as they do guest convenience. For instance, the individually wrapped soap, shampoo, and shoe polish placed in guest rooms normally carry some type of advertising.

When purchasing guest amenities, buyers might be able to bargain for a promotional discount. For example, Procter & Gamble might offer a price reduction if a hotel uses its soap in the guest rooms, guest rest rooms, and poolside showers.

Cleaning supplies, other than those purchased for customer needs, are usually selected on the basis of the following factors:

- **As-Used Cost.** Buyers are concerned with a cleaning agent's efficiency. Efficiency is especially critical because in addition to the cost of the cleaner, buyers must consider the cost of the labor and energy needed to use it. For example, buyers are concerned with the cost of cleaning a square foot of floor or a square foot of wall tile. When examining various samples of these cleaners, then, buyers often must make several cost computations, but this is necessary if they are concerned with efficiency.

- **Product Effectiveness.** Can the product actually get the job done, or are one or more of the claims exaggerated?

- **Adaptability.** Can the cleaner be adapted to other cleaning needs? That is, can the operation use one cleaner instead of two or more? This is a controversial issue; many people do not believe that one all-purpose cleaner exists. Besides, they point out that even if buyers do find one, their total stock of cleaning agents may not be any smaller. Although this may be true, it is more convenient for buyers to purchase one variety instead of several. Also, it is possible that the AP price of all-purpose cleaners may be less than the combined AP prices of seldom-used, one-purpose cleaners.

- **Product Safety.** Will the product harm the item being cleaned? Can it harm the person using it? Does it have the potential to harm the environment? If so, buyers should consider hiring a professional service instead of having employees use it.

- **Ease of Use.** Is the product easy to use, or do employees have to undergo extensive training or briefing to master it?

- **Odor.** Does the cleaner have a strong, lingering odor sufficient to cause guest and employee discomfort?

- **Container Size.** Is the cleaner available only in very large containers? Although they are cheaper per unit than smaller containers, they are harder to handle and can cause waste due to spillage.

- **Supplier Services.** Carefully examine supplier services and the product information. For instance, do employees require personal instruction for items like dishwashing-machine chemicals and silver-polish usage? Also, at times, employees may encounter some difficulty when using the products, so it would be helpful to be able to call the supplier or salesperson and ask him or her to help at a moment's notice.

A very popular service is the 24-hour maintenance and troubleshooting service that such chemical companies as EcoLab provide. In some cases, this service can be more important to customers than the products themselves.

Purchasing cleaning supplies is not particularly difficult once buyers select the suppliers they wish to deal with. Similarly, receiving these products poses no more than run-of-the-mill problems.

Storage, though, can present some difficulty. Operators must store these cleaning supplies away from foods and beverages to avoid contamination. Most likely, operators will be in violation of the local health department's sanitation regulations if they do not segregate these products.

Cleaning Tools

Food services and lodging operations buy several types of cleaning tools, such as brooms, mops, buckets, vacuum cleaners, pot brushes, and squeegees. Several selection factors affect these purchasing decisions, including:

- **Cost.** Determining the long-term cost of a broom is not easy because buyers never know how long a broom will last. Nor do they always know who will be pushing the broom: someone paid specifically to push it or an idle employee whose salary remains the same regardless of his or her activity behind a broom. Consequently, most buyers consider a broom's purchase price to be a minor selection factor. The general feeling seems to be that it pays to purchase high-quality hand tools because: (1) they withstand the tough punishment that busy employees normally mete out, (2) the product cost pales in comparison to the cost of the labor needed to wield these tools—high-quality tools should be more efficient, and (3) since high-quality tools generally last longer, the as-used cost should be minimal.

■　**Employee Skill.** Buyers need to consider the skill of the people using the tools. Low-skill, or low-cost, employees usually need better products and, perhaps, more convenient products to work with.

■　**Material Used to Make the Item.** Brushes and brooms, for example, are manufactured from a variety of raw materials. Sponges and scouring pads also come in a range of materials. It is important for buyers to identify the type of material that best suits their needs and budget.

■　**Used Tools.** It is possible for buyers to purchase used tools at a salvage sale, going-out-of-business sale, auction, or used-products stores. The savings are usually considerable. Buyers agree to take the items on an as-is, where-is basis. Although the savings may be attractive, the quality of the tools may be quite low. In addition, buyers must take the time to shop around for these types of deals. Also, they must usually arrange for delivery themselves.

Cleaning-tool-procurement procedures are fairly routine. As usual, buyers first either bid buy or find suppliers who understand what they need and are willing to work with them. Buyers often make impulse purchases in this area. Moreover, many buyers are sometimes tempted to purchase some type of gadget that may carry an exaggerated claim.

Receiving and storing cleaning tools pose no more than the ordinary problems. Their in-process storage and use, however, can create problems. Keeping the tools maintained—that is, the mop heads clean, for example, or the mop buckets empty when not in use—can be difficult. High-quality tools should minimize these difficulties and make cleaning easier and more efficient.

Maintenance Supplies

Hospitality operations purchase several types of maintenance supplies: light bulbs, plumbing parts, and other similar items. The supplies that operations purchase usually depend on the type of service or maintenance contracts they have with a professional service. Generally, for most repair and maintenance needs, operations contact a professional service that provides the necessary parts and labor.

But all operations buy at least some maintenance supplies. Small operations may buy only light bulbs and a few other products. But larger operations, especially the big hotels, may stock everything from light bulbs to water pipes. Buyers use several factors for selecting these items, which follow:

- **Cost.** The price of maintenance supplies may or may not be relevant. When buyers purchase items like circuit breakers or water pipes, they must purchase good-quality merchandise. No inferior-quality products exist since many of these items must pass safety and other building-code standards that federal and local governmental agencies establish.

  If buyers have a choice among a variety of qualities, they need to consider the life of the replacement part. If they do not want to change light bulbs every other month, they should buy a high-quality, expensive bulb. A higher-quality item will also be more energy efficient.

  Buyers also need to consider the length of time their operation will continue to exist in its current form. If, for example, the owner-manager intends to sell the business next year, he or she may not want to splurge for the best maintenance part; perhaps a lower-quality, less expensive item will do.

- **Labor Availability.** Buyers should consider the labor time available to do the maintenance. If they have only a few labor hours for maintenance, they should consider purchasing easy-to-use replacement parts or long-life parts or engaging in a maintenance contract with a professional service. This trade-off is one that operators contemplate quite often. When buyers purchase replacement parts, they also have to think about providing the labor. Labor is quite expensive, and operations want to reduce it. As a result, many small operators learn how to "fix the ice machine" themselves.

- **Used Supplies.** Should buyers ever purchase used maintenance supplies? Similar to a car owner saving old spark plugs and using them in the power lawn mower, the possibilities exist if buyers care to trouble themselves.

- **Sizes.** Maintenance supplies come in various sizes, shapes, model numbers, and the like, so buyers must be very careful to purchase the exact product required or it will not serve their needs. For instance, an air-conditioning filter of the wrong size can be used in an air-conditioning system only at the risk of damaging the machinery.

- **Capitalizing Expenses.** If operators get tired of replacing parts and maintaining equipment, buyers can "capitalize" these expenses; that is, they can buy more expensive capital equipment that does not need much maintenance work. But this decision represents a major capital equipment decision that typically, only the owner-manager makes, not buyers.

The procurement procedure for these supplies is reasonably straightforward, and receiving and storing them present no more than the average problems. However, two unique issues can occur with these items. First, a hospitality operation can tend to carry a lot of these supplies in stock. This tendency is understandable because an owner-manager can get annoyed very quickly if there are no light bulbs to replace the burned out pool lights. If buyers work at it, they might be able to reduce the stock level, although only the owner-manager can decide how much of a stockout potential he or she is willing to accept.

Second, maintenance schedules can be a headache. For example, should operators replace light bulbs as they burn out, or should they estimate the average life of the bulbs and change all of them at once, thereby saving some labor cost?

Permanent Ware

A hospitality operation's initial investment in permanent ware may be a capital expenditure that has to be depreciated on the income statement. But once an operation buys its original stock, the replacements it buys every so often—or has delivered, if it is on a stockless purchase plan—are generally considered "costs of doing business," or expenses that will be written off on the operation's current year's income statement.

Several types of permanent ware enter the typical food service operation: plates, silver (or other flatware), glasses, ashtrays, vases, salt and pepper shakers, creamers, sugar bowls, and so forth (see Figure 25.3). Operators may, however, have the option of using disposables for some or all of these, depending on their operation.

Comparatively few selection factors exist for permanent ware, but they are very critical. Buyers should consider the following points:

- **Permanent Ware Needed.** Operators must decide exactly what type of permanent ware they want. If they want standardized items, their buyers could go to just about any supplier and buy them. For run-of-the-mill products, buy-

FIGURE 25.3 A typical permanent ware setup for a foodservice dining room. Courtesy of PhotoDisc/Getty Images.

ers will find very little spread between prices. Determining exactly what operators want depends on how much impact they think these items have on their image. The more personalization required, the more these products cost and, typically, the fewer suppliers buyers have to choose from. In addition, the greater the degree of personalization, usually the larger the quantity the buyer must purchase, or guarantee to purchase, in order to make the transaction economical for the operation and the supplier.

■   **AP Price.** The AP price for these items may be a marginal consideration if buyers purchase highly personalized products. But for standardized products, buyers can reduce the price by opting for lesser quality.

　　Buyers can also reduce the price of certain personalized items. For example, manufacturers produce standard shapes to which buyers can ask them to apply certain lettering or other pictorial designs. Typically, buyers receive only a few options, but these may be enough to satisfy their taste and budget.

- **The Need to Match.** How well does the plate the operators selected go with the salt and pepper shaker set, or with the general decor? Operators tend to select all of the permanent items together as one set to ensure compatibility and a standard design and image throughout. Operations that have mismatched permanent ware risk developing a poor image.

- **Source of Supply.** Should buyers purchase these items directly or from local suppliers? As with all direct purchases, operators must be able to provide the missing economic values, which, in many cases, is best left to professionals. If buyers purchase directly, they probably cannot obtain a stockless purchase plan, which is something of great value to most operations with limited storage facilities.

- **Material Used to Make the Item.** A seemingly endless variety of materials can be used to manufacture permanent ware. Vitrified china, cut crystal, plastic, and so forth are available. Prices vary with the type of material, as will the image operators create.

- **Sizes.** Operators must note the specific size of product they require. They must consider, for instance, the volume of glasses and the shape of plateware.

- **Length of Service.** To a certain extent, operators must make a trade-off between price and durability. But durability is not the same as the life of a product in this case because theft is a constant problem that all hospitality operators face; shoplifting, in particular, is a major concern. So when operators pay more for higher-quality and more durable products, ironically, they may make these items more attractive to thieves.

- **Used Permanent Ware.** Again, operators can purchase used items and incur the advantages and disadvantages noted earlier.

The major purchasing concern, of course, is deciding what products operators need and want. Once they determine this, buyers should shop around a little, at least initially. When buyers settle on a supplier—and they normally settle on one, especially if they purchase highly personalized items—the rest falls easily into place because they stay with this supplier for their replacements. Similarly, receiving and storing are not major problems with permanent-ware items.

But difficulties can occur with the in-process inventory. Waste, breakage, and pilferage take their toll. In a busy restaurant, the manager may go through a full set of glasses every 3 to 6 months. When they do, operators may be tempted to replace the original item with a cheaper imitation. This practice works for some operations, but it can potentially hurt the image of most companies. Operators must always consider very carefully the decision to reduce quality.

Single-Service Disposable Ware

As noted earlier in this chapter, the operators' major decision in this area is whether to use disposable ware exclusively, permanent ware exclusively, or some combination of the two. In some states and local municipalities, the disposables purchase decision is restricted considerably. For instance, some areas outlaw the use of any type of disposable product unless it is biodegradable. Some areas also mandate the use of paper goods made with unbleached materials; for instance, instead of purchasing white paper coffee filters, buyers may be restricted to the brown, unbleached alternative. It may also be necessary for buyers to purchase products made from recycled materials.

Several types of disposable ware are available from a multitude of suppliers. For instance, buyers can purchase single-service plates, platters, bowls, cups, glasses, knives, forks, spoons, and ashtrays. The selection factors for these items are similar to those for permanent ware, with the addition of the following:

■ **What Do You Need?** The operators' decision about precisely what they want and need is critical. A variety of items is available, as are numerous quality variations. Furthermore, operators can make several possible substitutions for permanent ware.

Operators can find just about any item they want, too. They can usually select from among several acceptable degrees of personalization and from among several price and quality combinations. They can choose exceptionally strong, attractive items, or they can opt for very inexpensive, standard items. Once operators figure out what they want, though, the number of potential suppliers diminishes in proportion to the amount of personalization they want.

■ **Packaging.** Buyers can purchase some disposable ware packaged together. For example, they can get a single-service package that includes a fork, knife, spoon, napkin, and individual salt and pepper packets. These are expensive, but they are very convenient for some applications, such as take-out meals.

To save money, and to help protect the environment, many operations try to minimize these packaging alternatives. For instance, they may purchase recyclable, single-service cups packed in cases without dividers. Paper saved this way not only helps the environment, it can also mean long-term AP price reductions.

Some operations, like fast-food restaurants with brisk carry-out business, use a good deal of disposable ware. Other operations, however, would never consider these products. The operations of the multitude of properties that fall between these two extremes must do some serious decision making. It is possible to include at least some disposable ware. But this can be costly since the price of these items, many of which are petroleum-based products, is high. Their convenience, however, cannot be denied. Operators must keep in mind, though, that the cost of dishwashing machines, their space requirements, and their operation, can be costly as well—not usually as expensive as disposable ware in the long run, but in the short term, disposable ware may be the logical alternative.

When operators decide what they want in the way of disposable ware, it is typical, as noted for some other nonfood expense items, for them to settle on one supplier. They must certainly do so if they want a high degree of personalization.

Once operators have selected their supplier(s), the procurement procedures, receiving, and storing then follow a fairly routine pattern. Issuing and the in-process inventory of disposable ware present few problems, primarily because places that use them can keep track of their usage as an extra control measure. For example, many fast-food operators keep track of the number of single-service cups used during a shift. If 100 are missing, management takes it to mean that 100 drinks were sold. So, the missing inventory of beverage and the cash taken in should be consistent with the missing 100 cups.

Finally, waste can become a problem if operators let customers help themselves to disposable ware or permit employees to use these items indiscriminately.

Preparation and Service Utensils

A hospitality operation's initial purchase of these items, say, when it first goes into business, may need to be treated as a capital investment. That is, the initial purchase is depreciated. But replacement items can be treated as a current expense. Normally, a hospitality operation must keep several preparation and service items on the premises, including pots, pans, service trays, dish racks, carts, and cutting boards.

Generally, the selection factors noted for permanent ware are the same as those for preparation and service utensils. Two additional concerns exist, though. First, operators must be alert to any safety hazards and any unusual sanitation difficulties with such objects as knives and other utensils. Second, the material used to make the item is an important consideration. For example, aluminum, copper, cast iron, and stainless steel can be used to make pots, but each material serves a different purpose and carries a different AP price.

In some situations, operators might consider replacing some of these products with their disposable counterparts. For instance, buyers can purchase single-use steam table pans, which are used for cooking or reheating food and then holding it on a hot steam table for service. Generally, buyers do not have to be especially concerned with the image aspect of these items. The procurement procedure for such products parallels that for permanent ware: in both situations, the owner-manager tends to settle on a particular supplier.

Some utensils lend themselves to only one or two choices of suppliers. Buyers may have to purchase such items as dish racks and refrigerator trays from the equipment dealer(s) who sold them the dishwasher and the refrigerator. Fortunately, a reasonable amount of standardization exists among most equipment, so buyers may be able to avoid this potential problem.

Operators must closely supervise the in-process usage of these items. Our experience suggests that these utensils will yield years of acceptable service if they are not abused; once abused, they tend to deteriorate rapidly.

Fabrics

Hospitality operations may purchase several types of fabrics, such as uniforms, bed and table linen, costumes, drapes, table skirting, and curtains. Three ways exist to procure fabrics: buy them, lease them, or use disposables. If operations buy or lease permanent fabrics, they must then decide whether they will clean and maintain the fabrics themselves or whether they will use some type of laundry service. (See the discussion of laundry and linen supply service in Chapter 26.) It is possible for operations to buy disposable fabrics, such as aprons and hats. Operations can even purchase completely disposable uniforms and costumes.

If operations care to, they can buy uniforms and let the employees clean and maintain these garments. Alternately, operations can even let employees buy their own uniforms and costumes, as well as clean and maintain them. When companies do this, they must be sure that they do not violate the federal and/or state Department of Labor's regulations governing employee compensation.

As with all nonfood expense items, operators must decide precisely what they want. With fabrics, they must be prepared to like what they select since they cannot easily change their minds without incurring some extraordinary added expense.

Many concerns related to permanent ware are also applicable to fabrics, especially the concern about image. However, a few additional considerations exist. These are as follows:

■ **Length of Service.** Operators must decide how long they want fabrics to last. In addition to being more costly, long-life fabrics may outlast an image and may have to be discarded if operators remodel their facilities, even though they may still be functional.

■ **Maintenance.** Operators must determine a maintenance schedule for the fabrics. Large hotels usually employ laundry and seamstress workers who keep these items in good repair. Smaller hospitality operations usually must decide whether they want to provide these services for themselves or to purchase a professional laundry and linen supply service that will take over these duties. Generally, smaller operations opt for the professional service.

■ **Who Chooses?** Who should choose the fabrics and fix their specifications? This might be an emotional issue. For example, an owner-manager may buy dust-catching draperies, leaving the housekeeper to clean and maintain them. Perhaps it might be best to have a group of employees involved in the selection process. This way, once the draperies are installed, those responsible for their maintenance will be aware of the reasons for their selection.

If operators expect employees to clean and maintain their uniforms, they should bear this in mind when selecting the clothes. A little advice from the users will go a long way toward promoting harmonious relations in the future.

■ **Fabric Types.** Should operators consider easy-care, wash-and-wear types of fabrics? At one time, these items looked poor, but their appearance has improved significantly. The good ones are very expensive, though, and they have shorter life spans than alternative fabrics. Operators must weigh these disadvantages against the convenience and savings associated with less care and maintenance, as well as, if applicable, the savings operators realize by not investing in ironing equipment.

Once operators determine the fabrics they want, as well as how they want to have them cleaned and maintained, their purchase is not particularly difficult. In general, they will not have a large number of suppliers from which to choose, especially if they decide to purchase a laundry and linen supply service. When selecting this type of supplier, operators must keep in mind that some of them will help select uniform styles and give related advice regarding other types of fabrics needed.

Fabric receiving and storage are not particularly difficult, although operations might have some receiving problems if they use a professional laundry and linen supply service. Some difficulty with services of this type exists because when they deliver, they also pick up soiled items; sometimes items that should be in the soiled batch are missing and this can cause some confusion and delay. It is also costly because many laundry and linen service suppliers require operations to pay for lost items.

In-process care and maintenance can cause some difficulties, too. Large hotels usually do a good job when taking care of these items; these operations have linen rooms, which are analogous to food storerooms with all the proper controls. But smaller operations cannot afford this luxury. Furthermore, they are less likely to clean and maintain fabrics on schedule, which, if not done, will shorten their useful life.

Other Paper Products

Several types of paper, other than paper cups, plates, and napkins, appear in hospitality operations. These include: guest checks, cash register tape, tissues, doilies, scratch pads, take-out containers, stationery, purchase order forms, and other accounting documents. These items are usually selected according to the following factors:

- **Image.** Once again, operators must consider the operation's image. Patrons, suppliers, and the general public will see most of these paper products.

- **Special Requirements.** An operation's product needs might inadvertently restrict the number of potential suppliers from whom buyers can choose. For instance, operations may require a special type of guest check to fit the cash register they have; the tissue must fit the tissue dispenser; and the purchase order records must fit the filing system.

- **Personalization.** Operations may choose to personalize some paper products. Such personalization requirements may reduce the number of suppliers from whom operations can choose. They can, of course, always get what they want, but if they resist a standardized format, they might have to turn to specialized suppliers.

- **AP Price.** The price of many of these items is important because operators often encounter considerable waste in usage. Effective supervision can minimize this problem. This problem can be expensive, especially if employees misuse the expensive multipart forms. Some suppliers, as a service, might provide complimentary forms of one type or another. Even though operators may pay for these forms in the long run, chances are that the supplier can get these much more cheaply because of his or her quantity purchasing power.

Operators may be able to get a promotional discount for some items. For instance, paper towels or tissues may carry a brand name, which may justify a lower purchase price for operators.

- **Minimum-Order Requirements.** Generally, a large order size requirement is common for some of these items. This saves operators quite a bit of money, but they might encounter unforeseeable storage costs. They also might get a stockless purchase plan for such items as personalized stationery or business cards. Alternately, if operators accept a standard type of product that differs only in that it has their name on it instead of someone else's, perhaps they will not have to buy as much at one time.

Once operators decide what they want, the purchasing, receiving, and storing of these products rarely present any particularly troublesome problems. Typically, management sets par stocks, and the users order up to par level as needed or as management dictates.

The in-process inventory may, however, generate some waste. It is probably impossible for operations to avoid it entirely, although good supervision can keep it down to acceptable levels. However, some waste is inevitable with paper products, if only because it is not cost-effective to continually monitor the paper tablets customers take. Also, operators cannot eliminate completely employee mistakes.

Miscellaneous Items

Such products as pest control supplies and plant food fall into this category. Operators should avoid purchasing many of these items, especially insecticides, and should avoid storing them on their premises as well. Kept on the premises, these materials could contaminate food and injure guests and employees. It is best for operators to hire a professional service to handle these dangerous products.

As with all nonfood expense items, the same selection factors and managerial concerns apply: image is a major factor for many of them. Also, depending on the miscellaneous product that hospitality operations are evaluating, most of the other criteria discussed in this chapter will dictate the selection and procurement process.

KEY WORDS AND CONCEPTS

As-purchased price (AP price)

As-used cost

Bid buying

Capital item

Capitalizing expenses

Credit terms

Depreciation

Disposable versus reusable

Employee skill

Equipment program

Exact name

Expense item

Image

Impulse purchase

In-process inventories

Intended use

Labor availability

Labor skill

Length of service

Lifetime cost

Management considerations when purchasing nonfood expense items

Material used to make the item

Minimum-order requirement

New versus used

Online auction sites

Operating supplies

Operating-supplies schemes

Packers' brands

Personalization

Product color

Product compatibility

Product convenience

Product effectiveness

Product form

Product odor

Product safety

Product size

Promotional discount

Promotional needs

Purchasing, receiving, storing, and issuing nonfood expense items

Quantity discount

Size of container

Stockless purchase

Supplier services

Systems sale

Toner-phoners

Type of container

Typical nonfood expense items

Volume discount

Wide Area Telecommunications Service–line hustlers (WATS-line hustlers)

QUESTIONS AND PROBLEMS

1. Five typical nonfood expense items that hospitality operators might purchase are:
   (a)
   (b)
   (c)
   (d)
   (e)

2. A product specification for permanent ware could include the following information:
   (a)
   (b)
   (c)
   (d)
   (e)

3. To fully stock your restaurant with new preparation and service utensils, you will have to pay about $6000. After scanning the newspaper classifieds and calling equipment dealers, you esti-

mate that you could get everything you need in a used, as-is condition for about $2000. What do you suggest? If possible, ask a restaurant manager to comment on your answer.

4. What is the primary difference between a nonfood expense item and a nonfood capital item?

5. When considering the lifetime cost of some nonfood expense items, operators should compute the:
    (a)
    (b)
    (c)

6. What are the primary advantages and disadvantages of purchasing used nonfood expense items?

7. What critical information is missing from the following product specification for dinner plates?
    Dinner plates
    Used for entrées and some desserts
    Permanent, vitrified china
    House brand (or least expensive items)
    Bulk packed

8. Assume the following facts: Cleaning agent A costs $1 per quart, cleaning agent B costs $1 per pint, and both agents will do the same cleaning job. What other information would you like to have before deciding which cleaning agent to buy?

9. Outline the specific procedures catering operators would use to purchase, receive, store, and issue disposable ware. If possible, ask a caterer to comment on your answer.

10. Assume that you operate the food service in a 500-bed hospital. You currently use permanent ware, own a dishwashing machine and dishes, and employ seven full-time (40 hours per week) dishwashers with an average wage, including fringe benefits, of $12.65 per hour. You are exploring the possibility of converting to disposable ware. Preliminary estimates suggest an $18,500 per-month expense for the type and amount of disposable ware you need. What do you suggest? If possible, ask a registered dietitian (RD) to comment on your answer.

11. The concept of image is central to the selection of many nonfood expense items. Why is this true? What types of operations do you think must be most concerned with this issue? Which do you think must be the least concerned? Why?

12. The "color" selection factor would be an important consideration for the following nonfood expense items:
    (a)
    (b)
    (c)

13. Briefly describe the concept of "capitalizing" an expense.

14. Briefly describe the "systems sale" concept.

15. Safety is an important consideration when preparing a product specification for the following nonfood expense items:
    (a)
    (b)
    (c)

16. Prepare a specification for the following nonfood expense items:
    (a)   Water glass
    (b)   Silver polish
    (c)   Plastic fork
    (d)   Mop
    (e)   Ounce scale

17. Determine which type(s) of disposable products, if any, are outlawed in your local market area. If one or more items are banned, what does the typical foodservice operation use instead?

18. Why is the selection factor "employee skill" an important consideration when operators purchase cleaning supplies and cleaning tools?

19. Given the following data, determine the most economical product.

	CLEANER A	CLEANER B
AP price	$3.25/qt	$4.15/liter
Amount of cleaning solution yield per container	4 qt	4$^1/_2$ liters
Amount of area cleaned per container	100 ft^2	125 ft^2

20. What are some of the advantages of an operation hiring a professional pest control provider instead of handling its own pest control work? What are some of the disadvantages?

26

SERVICES

The Purpose of this Chapter

After reading this chapter, you should be able to:

- Identify management considerations surrounding the selection and procurement of services.
- List the types of services that might be purchased by a hospitality operator.
- Outline the general procedures used when purchasing services.
- Describe the major selection factors for services.

INTRODUCTION

In most hospitality operations, managers purchase the services needed. The purchasing directors of large corporations may contract for some services or department heads might purchase one service specifically for their department. But, as a general rule, since local suppliers primarily provide many services, the unit manager, whether employed by an independent operation or part of a chain, tends to have a great deal of input in the selection and procurement process.

MANAGEMENT CONSIDERATIONS

When managers buy services, many of them assume that service costs are fixed costs. That is, they believe that they must spend a certain number of dollars per year for services and that they cannot get along without these services.

It is true that some services are unavoidable costs of doing business. Expenditures for such items as legal, accounting, bookkeeping, and insurance services are necessary, although the range in cost and quality can vary considerably. Some other services, though, are more or less discretionary. For example, managers do not necessarily have to purchase menu-design services or cleaning services; in many cases, operators are perfectly capable of completing these tasks themselves.

Thus, one of the main points that managers must remember about services is that not all of these are fixed costs. Managers do have some discretion. Consequently, they should consider spending as much purchasing time and effort on these services as they would on food, beverages, and supplies.

Perhaps managers should even spend a little extra time. If they receive a load of bad tomatoes, they can correct the mistake or change suppliers without too much difficulty, but if they purchase a service that turns out to be poor, they may well find the first problem creates additional problems. First, managers may not know that a service is being poorly done until the job is completed. Moreover, if they buy a poor service, it is poor—period. No such thing as an in-between service exists. Managers may be able to salvage a few good tomatoes from the bad load delivered to them. But such partial value is usually not the case with services.

Obviously, it may be difficult for managers to judge the quality of a service in advance. For instance, it is difficult to judge a carpenter's ability unless managers have samples of his or her work: even then, however, managers have no guarantee that he or she will replicate past performance. Only when the work is finished will managers really know, but at that point it may be difficult to do much about it if major alterations are needed.

Faced with this problem of evaluating service performance, managers or department heads may find it is easy to neglect inspecting a service provider's performance. Managers who never think of receiving a food item without inspecting it assume that the maintenance crew that comes around once a month performs its assigned tasks.

We once purchased a chimney-cleaning service. The crew came in one night every six weeks to clean the chimney directly over the open-pit charcoal broiler. None of us ever checked to see what the crew members were accomplishing because we assumed the crew to be conscientious. One night, however, we had a good-sized fire in this chimney. Sure enough, the fire marshal quickly discovered that the chimney had not been cleaned for months and was coated on the inside with several inches of grease.

Thus another concern with services is whether they are hard to monitor and inspect. Managers' or department heads' inability or unwillingness to inspect can easily lead to completely overlooking poor performance.

Another major service concern for managers and department heads is whether they should buy a service or provide the service themselves. In many cases, the same considerations that determine whether hospitality operations cut their own steaks or purchase portion-cut steaks enter the picture here. Moreover, the same emotional arguments usually surface. One of the major differences, though, is that some services do, in fact, require experts. For example, it is unlikely that managers can provide their own legal and insurance services.

A cost-benefit analysis of managers doing their own service work will probably indicate which pattern is best. Their decision to provide their own economic values and supplier services when they purchase products can be based on previous experience, but there is no clear-cut historical pattern to guide their decision in this situation. In some instances, it is cheaper for managers to wash their own windows; in some cases, it is not. Contrast this to the readily compiled evidence that shows, for example, that cutting their own steaks from a side of beef may be too expensive for most hospitality operators.

Thus managers and department heads normally have a little more flexibility when pondering the question of whether to provide some of their own services. A great deal of tradition, however, suggests that operators should buy some services while providing others on their own. Traditionally, hospitality operators purchase a service when one (or more) of the following apply: the service is impossible for them to do, that is, it might require a complicated expertise; it is too expensive, that is, it might require costly equipment; or it is very inconvenient to provide it themselves.

Lately, managers more commonly practice what is referred to as "outsourcing." This involves identifying work that is not central to their hospitality operation's primary mission and contracting with a service provider to do it. For instance, payroll processing is necessary, but it is something guests will never encounter. As such, it may be a good candidate for outsourcing.

The number and types of outsourcing opportunities in the hospitality industry have exploded over the past few years. Managers have become more focused on their core businesses and do not wish to be distracted by noncore activities. A considerable majority of all companies in the United States are thought to outsource one or more functions.

If hospitality operators are leasing their real estate facilities, the landlord may provide certain services as part of the lease contract. For instance, tenants in a shopping center normally pay a monthly rental fee plus a common area maintenance (CAM) fee. The landlord uses this CAM fee to defray the costs of parking lot maintenance, window cleaning, waste removal, rest room maintenance, and other expenses related to the general upkeep of the shopping center's common areas. Usually, the CAM fee is not as negotiable as the monthly rental payment. In this situation, the landlord shoulders the burden of selecting and procuring the necessary services. On one hand, this relieves tenants of this time-consuming activity; on the other hand, however, they relinquish the opportunity to do the work themselves or to shop for the best possible prices.

Examining a service provider's background and abilities is another major management consideration. It is necessary, at times, to contact current and/or previous customers and solicit their advice. It is a good idea for managers to ask the business license bureau about such particulars as the service provider's status, whether he or she carries the proper insurance coverage, and whether customer complaints have been lodged against that service provider. It is also a good idea to contact the local Better Business Bureau (BBB) and ask to examine the file that might exist on the service provider.

Avoid unlicensed, uninsured service providers. Their mistakes can cost operators a great deal of money. These providers have no insurance to handle any claims for damages operators may sustain. Also, if they install, for example, some electrical wiring incorrectly, and this leads to a fire, the operation's insurance company may not honor any claims the operation makes for damages.

Some unlicensed and uninsured service providers are moonlighters, but not all moonlighters are uninsured and/or unlicensed. Unfortunately, moonlighters cannot always provide service exactly when operations need it. Consequently, even though a moonlighter may be a less expensive choice, whether or not operations can tolerate such delays in service is a major management concern. In some situations, delays are no problem, but they can be devastating at other times.

To recap, at least five major concerns come into play when managers or department heads purchase services: (1) they must recognize that services are not fixed costs; (2) they must realize that evaluating a service provider's performance can be difficult; (3) they must decide whether to provide their own service or buy it; (4) they must examine a service provider's background and abilities; and (5) they must consider the advantages and disadvantages of using moonlighters.

Other less worrisome concerns can also plague managers, and even though they're usually minor problems, they may become very important under certain circumstances: (1) managers may have to permit strangers on the premises; (2) managers may have to give strangers access to personal and confidential information; and (3) managers may have to let a third party have direct control over some aspect of their businesses.

GENERAL PROCEDURES IN SERVICE PURCHASING

Once managers or department heads decide which services they intend to purchase, they should prepare a specification for each one, detailing as much as possible the desired criteria (see Figure 26.1 for a sample specification outline for services).

Preparing some parts of the specification is not particularly difficult. Managers usually can include what they want accomplished and when they want the work completed. Their inspection procedures, however, are not as easy to detail. Nev-

---

Intended use:
Exact name of service required:
Quality of materials that must be used:
Quality of the finished work:
Completion time:
Required work schedule:
Amount and type of experience required:
Business license:
Other licenses required:
References:
  BBB:
  Licensing division(s):
  Current customers:
  Former customers:
  Other:
Insurance coverage (bonded) for:
  Security:
  Property damage:
  Liability:
  Incomplete work:
  Deposits:
  Other:
Moonlighting restrictions:
Priority restrictions:
Guarantee(s):
Desired bill-paying procedure:
Inspection procedure(s):

FIGURE 26.1 **An example of a specification outline for services.**

ertheless, complete specifications are absolutely essential if managers intend to use a bid-buying strategy.

Bid buying services is just as risky as bid buying products. But bid buying services can produce a potentially greater monetary reward, because prices for services tend to vary considerably from one provider to another. Also, in many cases, the lowest-price service will still provide acceptable quality. This is true because service providers are more eager to reduce their prices when business is slow. Most service providers are small firms, and if they do not work at that particular service, they do not have sales of other services or product lines to support them until business picks up. A less acceptable standard of quality may accompany a lower price. But, assuming managers can inspect and monitor the service provider's performance, they should be able to extract maximum value.

Bid buying, negotiating with service providers, and monitoring the actual work—all of these tasks can be time-consuming. Although it is commendable for hospitality operators to get the most for their purchase dollar, they must get the results they need. Thus, their service-purchasing strategy has to be constructed with this in mind; it is worthless to save a dollar only to find out that the chimney is still dirty. Although we do not condone careless spending, operators must keep in mind that if they pay too much for products, all they really lose is money. But if they fail to get the service results they want, they will lose whatever they paid and will receive very little in return. If the canned goods are unsatisfactory, they can quickly rectify the error. If a service is unsatisfactory, however, they are less likely to be as forgiving—and are more apt to dismiss the offending service provider and contact someone else. The delays associated with an inadequate service can be bothersome.

We do not intend to suggest that bid buying is ineffective. But bid buying always carries inherent dangers, particularly if operators do not have the time to do it correctly. They must do what they feel is best, but, really, the most important aspect of service purchasing is for operations to get what they want. Perhaps the best way for operators to accomplish this is to settle on one service provider and, together, determine what they need, when they need it, how much it costs to do the job correctly, and what payment arrangements will ensure that they receive the quality of service necessary. While discussing their needs, operators should also evaluate the service provider's past performance by asking for and calling his or her references, who are former or current clients.

These are general guidelines about service purchasing. Emphases change a little as operators go from one particular service to another. For instance, it seems more appropriate to bid buy a contract cleaning service than to bid buy a lawyer's service. Operators can probably make an intelligent decision about the buying strategy best for them after considering the services they are most likely to purchase.

TYPICAL SERVICES THAT HOSPITALITY OPERATORS PURCHASE

Hospitality operators typically use the following services: (1) waste removal, (2) financial, (3) groundskeeping, (4) pest control, (5) advertising, (6) consulting, (7) decorating and remodeling, (8) maintenance, (9) vending machine, (10) insurance, (11) laundry and linen supply, and (12) cleaning. These are considered in turn in the following sections.

Waste Removal

Operators will probably need to purchase their own disposal service since few cities and towns provide a tax-supported service for hospitality operations. If they are located in a shopping center or office park, part of their CAM fee may cover the cost of waste removal.

Many small operators exist in this area; the person who buys a truck and goes into business is typical. Sometimes these small operators are efficient; sometimes they are not.

Whomever operators hire, they should make sure that the disposal service: (1) provides on-time collection; (2) does not mangle and destroy containers; (3) does not mangle the containers' enclosed housing area, if any; (4) removes all refuse piled on the ground; (5) replaces containers in the proper locations; (6) provides suitably large and strong containers for their type of business; (7) provides containers with locks, if necessary, in order to prevent others from dumping on the hospitality operation's premises; and (8) charges a competitive price.

The primary purpose of waste disposal is to maintain a neat and sanitary garbage area. Operators must find a company that will maintain this area in the way that is appropriate for their type of business.

Another detail is the pickup schedule. Operators do not want a refuse service driving through their parking lot in the middle of the lunch or dinner hour. Also, if the refuse company's truck looks unkempt, the hospitality operator probably should shy away from that service, although, realistically, they may not have a large selection of potential suppliers in their vicinity from which to choose.

If operators have a grease trap that must be cleaned periodically, they will find it convenient to use a waste removal firm that can provide this additional service. They may be willing to pay a bit more for this one-stop-shopping opportunity.

In a few parts of the United States, the local government may be the only waste removal service available. Alternately, it might mandate that all businesses use a specific waste removal company. In this situation, hospitality operators cannot shop around for the best deal; they must agree to the legislated terms and conditions.

Some waste removal companies may pay companies for their waste. For example, some recycling firms, such as grease salvers and metal salvers, may pay a modest amount for recyclable waste. However, to take advantage of this other-income opportunity, businesses generally need to take the time to segregate their wastes. Furthermore, in some instances, they may even need to deliver their wastes to the recycling plant.

Financial

Hospitality operators usually have flexibility when they shop for loan capital, checking services, or other types of financial services. Banks, for example, do not all charge the same rates and provide equal services. Even though financial institutions are regulated by law, it is incorrect to assume that one institution is as good as another. These institutions do have some discretion within the law, and the intangible "supplier services" they provide more than likely vary considerably.

Hospitality operators need bankers who will provide them with checking accounts, petty-cash accounts, payroll accounts, loans, cash management techniques, computer services, and, perhaps, monitor benefit packages for their employees. In most cases, the accountant, bookkeeper, or owner-manager negotiates for a banker's services, either with banks or, for some other services, with other types of financial institutions. In too many instances, operators hesitate to negotiate. In these situations, they often become a house account, particularly in those areas of the United States where few financial institutions exist.

Financial institutions are like any other supplier: they want a hospitality operation's business, and they want it to become a house account. They strive to make it very inconvenient for a company to purchase one service from them and other services from their competitors. Some banks, for instance, might offer a better rate of interest on a loan if operators keep a savings or payroll account with them or permit them to make a bit of income by processing the firms' payroll checks. Also, some banks' credit and debit card services may be more timely and convenient.

Typical hospitality operations usually have little time available to evaluate several financial institutions when purchasing these services. Often, an operator will tend to "grow up" with a local banker, the banker who was there to encourage and nurse the operator along during the company's early days. As long as this banker can consistently provide a wide range of services, the grateful operator will tend to remain a house account. In some situations, such an arrangement is mutually beneficial.

A large hospitality operation using one-stop shopping for financial services would be very unusual, however. These big firms usually have more time and skill for determining the combination of services and service providers most favorable to them. Moreover, the amount of cash turnover a large company deals with gives it a strong bargaining position. Like corporate purchasing directors who have the time, ability, and responsibility to seek out better deals, corporate accountants and treasurers have the same capabilities. For smaller operators who use one-stop shopping for other items, it is probably best to use the same purchasing procedure when buying financial services.

Groundskeeping

Few operators are able to provide their own landscaping, snow removal, or parking lot maintenance services. Typically, companies purchase these services from reputable service providers. In addition, a landlord commonly provides these services as part of the CAM-fee arrangement.

Probably the most difficult groundskeeping service to purchase is a landscaping service. Small firms are particularly prominent in the landscaping business. Anyone with a rake or a shovel can easily enter the business. Operators should avoid anyone who does not have a demonstrated knowledge of this trade.

Landscapers usually undertake snow removal in the winter months to supplement their income and to keep busy all year long. As a result, operators can contract with one firm to handle all of their grounds maintenance.

The operators' objective is clear: they want an attractive exterior. Rather than negotiate a low price, they might economize by minimizing the number of plants, trees, and lawns they nurture—assuming that they are more interested in a price they can afford than in an extravagant outdoor display. (Some landscape service providers also maintain inside plants, although operators often must go to another source when they want to purchase or rent house plants.)

When operators purchase a landscaping service, they must be specific about what they want done and when they want it done. They should resist the temptation to say, "Cut the grass when necessary." Ambivalent instructions like these can lead to conflicts later on. Operators should, instead, say something like, "Cut and edge the lawn, and clean up afterward, every Thursday afternoon after 4 o'clock."

Landscaping services often have a firm rate schedule, unless operators happen to find one whose business is slow. Operators need to keep in mind, though, that a landscaper with few customers may be a poor choice. The good ones often have more business than they can handle.

Another possible difficulty is that neighborhood children, and other similar groups, may pester operators to let them perform these tasks so that they can earn a little spending money. As with all amateur work, usually something could have been done better. On the other hand, though, assuming no potential liability problems exist, operators might build some good community relations by agreeing to this.

Pest Control

Pest control is one of the trickiest control areas in the entire hospitality industry. It is easy for some hospitality operators to feel that they are pest control experts since spraying chemicals appears to be the only necessary action. But pest control is a difficult service to perform, and some chemicals are so dangerous that only licensed pest control operators (PCOs) can legally handle them (see Figure 26.2).

FIGURE 26.2 **A national pest control company.** *Source:* **United States Department of Agriculture.**

Probably the best strategy is for hospitality operators to contract for a weekly or monthly visit, as well as a price to be charged for emergencies, such as an unanticipated infestation. Calling a pest control service only when an obvious problem arises is bad business. A great deal of damage to the operators' building, as well as to their reputation, may have already occurred.

Operators will learn that purchasing this service is, generally, preferable to providing it themselves. When they purchase a service, they need not store poisonous chemicals on their premises, which is always a risky practice.

The operators' purchasing objective here is obvious: no pests. They must determine what pest control services charge, and they should check various companies' performances by conferring with their customers. Normally, prices among these firms are very competitive. The pest control company that can provide the best service schedule, solid advice on how to correct any building problems that invite infestation, and direction regarding the appropriate sanitation procedures employees should follow probably will be an operator's first choice.

A few national pest control companies exist. Large chain operations might consider negotiating one contract at a lower price that includes every unit in the chain.

The cost of pest control service is small indeed compared with the problems it can solve and the expenses it can save. This is no area for operators to be sticklers over a few cents difference among service providers.

Advertising

Most hospitality operations use some sort of advertising—newspaper, magazine, radio, television, Web, or some combination thereof. Printed or online brochures, flyers, and menus all serve as advertising media. In addition, several in-house promotion kits are available on the market.

When operators evaluate advertising purchases, an important element they need to keep in mind is the audience they intend to reach with their message. They must select the advertising medium, or media, that will reach this audience. They should not, for example, buy a newspaper ad strictly on the basis of its low price. When purchasing advertising, operators will find that it is usually best to opt for quality over quantity.

In most instances, the amount operators must pay is directly related to the size of the intended audience. They will need to ensure that the advertising medium consistently delivers the guaranteed audience size by periodically checking independent rating services' reports detailing these statistics. Reputable on-air, print, or online advertising media will issue "make-goods," which are blocks of free advertising time or space granted to buyers when the actual intended audience size was smaller than the guaranteed one.

When operators choose advertising, one of their major concerns is the cost per potential customer reached by or influenced by the ad. The cost is difficult to compute, but the media buyer, or the medium itself, usually can come up with a reasonably accurate figure.

Another important consideration is the ability for operators to trade their products or services for advertising. One problem with this kind of advertising is that, if the ads are not to the operators' liking, they may have less influence than cash-paying customers. By the same token, a radio station manager can complain about an operator's products or services, although he or she can hardly complain if the operator pays cash.

Another question for operators to ponder is the use of soft-drink-company signs and printing. Coke®, for instance, often shares the cost of menu printing and sign preparation as long as its logo is prominently displayed. Operators must decide, then, as with all promotional discounts, whether they want to be closely identified with a particular supplier.

Still another consideration for operators involves both sponsoring local athletic teams and advertising in local high school and college newspapers. As far as we can determine, no studies have been done to evaluate the efficacy of these types of advertising. Many companies, though, feel that these methods contribute to good—and profitable—public relations.

Operators can go through an advertising agency or other media-buying service rather than deal with the various advertising media in person. When they select an agency, they normally discuss what they want and how much they can afford. The agency develops an overall advertising strategy and selects the various media to use. Operators pay the cost of the advertisements, and the agency often takes a percentage, or commission, of these expenditures as its fee. Usually, the agency is paid on a sliding-percentage scale. However, it could receive a flat rate. Alternately, it might be paid on "merits"; that is, its income could be directly related to the sales success the advertised product or service generates.

Many experienced hospitality operators prefer using an intermediary when purchasing advertising services. They consider it more convenient and efficient, as well as less costly in the long run. Some buyers think that, as in purchasing food, it may be cheaper to purchase directly from the primary source. However, this usually is not true in the advertising channel of distribution. Furthermore, a qualified media-buying service will see to it that operators' advertisements are located and displayed correctly, and at the right time.

Newspaper Ads Typically, commercial restaurants purchase newspaper ads. In addition, they normally purchase an ad on a run-of-the-press basis, which means that the ad will be put any place in the paper at the discretion of the advertising editor, though operators can specify in a very general way what they do and do not want (see Figure 26.3).

A trick of the newspaper advertising business is for the salesperson to offer to do a story on an operator's business. Operators must be careful in this situation, because the salesperson can deliver on this promise only if he or she controls the paper's editorial department. An article, though, often has much more influence on consumers than one ad.

If operators decide to purchase a newspaper ad, they will probably see it featured in the local restaurant section. Indeed, it may cost them more to put the ad somewhere else in the newspaper. Operators can usually save money by contracting for an ad space over a period of time, such as an ad that is printed once a week for 25 weeks. Over the long run, the cost of each of these ads should be less than the cost of individual ads purchased once in a while. As with all purchases, quantity discounts are available.

The cost and benefits of newspaper advertising are hard to calculate accurately. Computing them is especially hard when, for example, operators buy an ad in the local high school newspaper. If they use newspaper ads to recruit employees, they probably can assess the ads' value a little more easily. Also, operators can count the number of coupons that customers tear out of their ad in response to, for instance, a special-price promotion. Newspaper ads do serve as good reminders to customers. They keep the operations' name in the public eye.

Radio Ads Radio ads are charged on a different basis than newspaper ads. They are sold on a space-available basis, sometimes referred to as run-of-the-station. Depending on the station, the length of the ad, and the time of day desired, the price varies considerably.

Radio stations can usually tell operators who is listening with reasonable accuracy. Newspapers and magazines cannot be as accurate because these pieces may be read by more than just the original buyer before eventually being discarded.

Unlike other advertising media, radio tends to build business slowly over the long run. Consequently, operators must be patient. They will usually have to run radio spots for quite some time before they experience significant results. How-

FIGURE 26.3 A newspaper advertisement for a restaurant. Courtesy of *Las Vegas Life* magazine.

ever, although it takes time for a radio campaign to generate results, radio is an efficient medium because specific audiences are fairly easy to target.

Television Ads Network television is usually too expensive for hospitality operations except at the regional or national-chain level. Most operations, though, can afford it if they agree to run commercial messages during nonprime time, or on local independent stations. If they opt for television advertising, they usually need the help of a professional advertising agency or another media-buying service.

It is not a good idea for operators to begin television advertising unless they can sustain it. The costs are prohibitive for a one-shot ad. For the production of a few commercials, they might pay, for example, excluding the cost of airing the commercials, several thousand dollars.

It is common for radio, newspaper publishers, publishers of playbills and other types of programs, and outdoor billboard companies to trade their services for food, beverage, and rooms. This type of exchange bartering, usually referred to as "trade outs" or "due bills," can save hospitality operators a great deal of money by reducing their out-of-pocket expenses. Many television stations, though, are reluctant to trade air time.

Web Ads Web advertising has recently become a common practice among hospitality operators. They can advertise in this manner two ways: (1) by developing their own Website (or outsourcing the development) and marketing it on online Yellow Pages, and (2) by placing ads on other related Websites (sometimes referred to as banner ads) that their intended target market might frequent, such as a local online directory (see Figures 26.4 and 26.5). The costs associated with using this medium are, typically, comparable to traditional forms of advertising.

Magazine Ads Hospitality operators must use magazine advertising selectively. Some magazines of the gourmet, airline, and tourist variety may reach the operators' intended market, especially if the operations tend to attract people from a wide geographical area. Other magazines are published in order to meet the tourism needs of a single city, and many hospitality operators find advertising in these periodicals profitable. Some trade magazines and travel indexes can be useful, especially to lodging operations that want to advertise to and solicit business from business travelers, travel agents, and companies seeking convention and meeting facilities.

FIGURE 26.4 An example of a hotel banner ad. Courtesy of Hotel Discount.com.

FIGURE 26.5 An example of a restaurant Website. Homepage for Mary Sue Milliken and Susan Feniger—chefs, restaurateurs, cookbook authors, radio and TV personalities—and for their restaurants, Border Grill and Ciudad.

Magazine ads are excellent sources for operators to use when recruiting management employees. Trade papers are particularly helpful in this situation.

Telephone Directories The prices of most directory advertising are fixed. The main decision hospitality operators must make is whether to buy an illustrated ad or to accept the one- or two-line notations most operations choose. Some operators like the bigger, illustrated ads that enable them to depict a map, prices, services available, hours of operation, and so on—additional information that is useful to out-of-town visitors. These larger ads, though, are fairly expensive.

The most common directory that hospitality operators use is the Yellow Pages directory. However, many others are available. Approximately 6000 directories are published in the United States each year.

When selecting a directory, operators should consider the cost, the number of years it has been published, the target audience, and the way it is distributed to readers.

Some computer online services provide directory services that operators can purchase or otherwise acquire. These are especially popular and helpful in tourist destination locations.

Printed Brochures, Matchbooks, and Menus Brochures and flyers are quite useful in some circumstances and for some operations. Their publication rates are usually fairly standard; they vary according to, for example, the number of colors, the quality of the paper or other materials, and the printing style. In addition, printers often offer generous break points, that is, very attractive quantity discounts; this may be a curse, though, if operators cannot use all that they buy, which might be the case with printed menus.

Operators may wish to hire a graphic artist to design a logo or pictorial layout, and an editor to develop the wording style. Naturally, this adds to the expense, but it is often worthwhile in the long run to have a professionally completed document.

Most operations purchase such items as matchbooks, swizzle sticks, and napkins emblazoned with their logo. These items, too, keep their name before the public. In fact, bars usually must rely on this form of advertising and internal promotion since they usually cannot advertise on radio or television.

Outdoor Ads Billboards are especially useful when hospitality operators have continuing messages to display. For example, if operators book entertainment and the entertainers change weekly, they can use a billboard to convey this message to several thousand people effectively and cheaply. Billboards are also a good choice when operators want to build awareness.

Hospitality operations along the side of or near a highway often use billboards and signs to guide travelers. However, the law strictly regulates the use of these media along highways.

The main disadvantage to outdoor ads is the community's concern about visual pollution. Billboards and signs have come under heavy attack in some areas of the United States. These sections severely restrict the amount and type of outdoor advertising a company can display. In some states, such as Hawaii, billboard advertising is prohibited.

The rates for outdoor advertising are fairly well established and, to a certain extent, are influenced by the type the company wants, how much time it is willing to contract for, and other similar considerations. Numerous options are available. For instance, hospitality operators can spend a minimal amount by arranging for a joint promotion with some related firm, such as a soft-drink company. Alternately, they might splurge on an expensive sign linked to a computer that can change messages quickly and easily. The range between these two extremes is considerable.

Direct-Mail Advertising Many hospitality operations use periodic mailings to current and/or prospective customers promoting some sort of special price, event, or other form of offering. If operators have a reasonably updated mailing list or can purchase a useful one, all they have to do is to arrange for the design of an appropriate flyer, stamp it, and mail it.

Purchasing a mailing list can be expensive. Most lodging operations maintain a guest history, whereas foodservice operations usually do not. However, operators must compare the cost of the list, the printing, the postage, and so forth to the expected increase in net income that the direct-mail campaign will produce.

The best part about direct mail is that operators usually can develop a promotional piece whose effectiveness can be tested very easily. If, for instance, they include a response option for the customer, such as a coupon, they can determine very quickly the success rate of the direct-mail campaign. If the campaign is deemed unsuccessful, it is very easy for operators to alter the direct-mail literature and schedule another mailing.

Another dimension of the direct-mail campaign is the telephone solicitation effort. Generally, instead of mailing the information, operators would solicit prospective business via telephone. This option can be very effective, say, for banquet business, in which an effort is made to arrange for an appointment for operators to meet with prospective catering, meeting, or convention customers.

Consulting

Consultants abound in the hospitality industry. Some of the most typical consultants include: (1) designers, (2) feasibility researchers, (3) attorneys, (4) accountants and bookkeepers, (5) operations planners and counselors, (6) energy advisers, (7) employee trainers, (8) architects, (9) building contractors, (10) property appraisers, (11) engineers, (12) real estate advisers, (13) business brokers, (14) fire and safety inspectors, (15) data processors, (16) printers, (17) equipment rental firms, and (18) computer specialists.

Some trade publications publish lists of consultants in some of their issues. These lists typically include national consultants, those who work in more than one part of the United States. But, as a rule, local firms provide most consulting work.

Generally, operators tend to purchase a consultant's service whenever the task to be performed is relatively complicated, highly technical, and not part of the owner-manager's daily routine. For instance, accounting and bookkeeping, design, legal, and computer consulting services are the types of tasks operators may not be able to do very well for themselves.

A company staff member can perform some other types of consulting in-house. Many operators can easily complete such tasks as menu design and certain feasibility studies. An operator may not do as well with menu design as a professional menu designer, but he or she can probably do reasonably well.

Large organizations often hire in-house consultants as permanent staff members to handle these functions. Usually, these specialists are required to travel from one unit operation to another, solving problems, doing research, and performing several other related activities.

A user somewhere in the organization or the owner-manager normally determines the need for a consulting service. Purchasing this service can be tricky. In some cases, the user or owner-manager can map out exactly what he or she wants, thereby occupying a relatively good position for evaluating various consultants. But for the most part, the operator will be dealing with professionals, some of whose work he or she may not completely understand.

Operators can use a certain type of bid buying when purchasing this kind of service. Essentially, this would require them to describe the problem they have and the results they would like. Then they might ask two or more consultants to prepare a proposal for them. The proposal would typically include such considerations as the objectives of the job, what will be done to achieve them, what the final results will be, which approach the consultant will take, the time constraints, and the fee for the consulting service. The operators' job, then, would be to evaluate the proposals and select one.

A beneficial aspect of these proposals is that they rarely cost operators anything. In addition, during proposal preparation, the consultant may help operators define more clearly just what it is they need. Some consultants assume the buyers' role by engaging in what is sometimes referred to as "negative selling." They tell operators how severe the problem is and how busy their schedule is, but that they have to see what they can do since the operators definitely need help quickly. Operators may find themselves begging the consultants to save them; that is, operators try to sell the consultants on taking the job—and their money.

If operators use the proposal approach, they should try to negotiate a firm contract; unfortunately, some consultants have a strong incentive for milking the job. A fixed-fee contract will protect operators from this tendency.

Operators should examine a consultant's references and be watchful of negative selling. If they can, they should ask the consultant to perform a "trial job," an inexpensive job that the operators need done, which can be an excellent test of the consultant's future work habits and overall competence.

Operators should try to negotiate on price but should be careful not to rush the work. They might want to make a bonus offer for early completion or some other incentive for good, quick work. They should also make sure that how much money they can potentially save does not completely determine the fee, because, as per the recommendation, operators might have to invest too much in order to save this money.

The objective is, in short, to complete the job satisfactorily. As a result, cost considerations might sometimes be a secondary concern.

Operators must sometimes use trust as their sole criterion in selecting consultants because the consultants often direct some of their money to other people. For instance, when discussing a consulting job possibility with a professional consulting firm, operators will probably talk to one of the partners, usually a seasoned veteran in his or her field. Although this partner will retain limited supervision of the job, one or more junior members of the consulting firm might do the work or it might be subcontracted to another party. This is sometimes done in feasibility studies and real estate appraisals.

The key to operators' developing an excellent working relationship with a consultant is to be very clear about what they need. They must be willing to spend as much time as necessary with the consultant so that he or she can obtain the information needed to do the job properly. Also, while operators certainly must maintain their privacy, they cannot expect positive results if they treat the consultant as an outsider.

Before purchasing a consulting service, operators might try to get it free. For instance, if the problem relates to energy, the public utilities companies might do a free energy audit and recommend ways of conserving precious fuel. The operators' trade association might have a staff member who can help them design a menu. Suppliers and salespeople are often ready to offer valuable advice. In addition, the federal government's Small Business Administration (SBA) sponsors consulting, and other similar programs, for qualified small businesses.

Decorating and Remodeling

These services are almost always purchased, and small contractors dominate these fields. Hospitality operators must be wary of them and be careful if the contractors they hire are moonlighters. The smaller the contractor, the less likely he or she is to be able to afford the equipment necessary to do an excellent job. Also, a moonlighter, although perhaps good, may have trouble meeting a deadline. Operators should take the time to solicit competitive bids from established contractors who can provide several references and are licensed, insured, and familiar with their needs.

When evaluating these services, operators may be concerned more with time than with money. That is, they certainly do not want to pay outrageous prices, but they must first make sure that they are not unduly inconvenienced or closed down too long. Since time is money, they may be willing to pay a bit more to get the work completed earlier.

It is probably a good idea for operators to see, in person, examples of the contractors' work before they contract for it. They should go to a place where the workers have hung wallpaper and see whether or not they like the job. This is the best part about purchasing these types of services: operators can always see what the contractors have done, and this past work serves as a continuing standard of quality for contractors to maintain in their future work. Operators must watch, though, not to see only the best work, while the contractors' skeletons remain safely in the closet.

When buyers purchase this type of service, they appear to be very concerned and quite fearful about the possibility of incomplete work or work that is shoddy and cannot, or will not, be repaired by the service provider. It would be well worth the operators' extra expense in terms of forcing the service provider to purchase a performance bond, which is an insurance policy guaranteeing satisfactory completion of all work.

A related problem with this type of work is the lien-sale type of contract that these service providers normally want clients to sign. This contract stipulates that the service provider can attach a lien to the entire property if clients fail to pay him or her for the work performed. The logic in this contract suggests that the service provider can hardly "take back" an improvement to a customer's property and that this improvement by itself is worthless. Hence, the service provider must be able to take over the entire property to gain satisfaction. To counteract this problem, operators must insist that they will make installment payments that correspond with the major stages of the project, and that they will pay only when a stage is completed satisfactorily. Once operators pay for the entire project, the service provider must agree to sign an unconditional lien release, verifying that he or she has been paid in full. This can be a difficult and inconvenient process if several persons are working on your place, but it is necessary to avoid any possible loss of your entire property. If operators do not have the time to do this, they can hire a specialized service, such as a construction management firm, to oversee these details.

Maintenance

An almost endless variety of repair and maintenance services appear to exist in the hospitality industry. Some of the more typical ones are: (1) security; (2) fire and intrusion alarm; (3) locksmith; (4) dishwashing machine; (5) knife sharpening; (6) plumbing; (7) electrical; (8) refrigeration; (9) heating, ventilation, and air conditioning (HVAC); (10) beverage-dispensing equipment; (11) elevator; (12) sign; (13) water systems; (14) office machines; (15) cooking equipment; (16) computers; and (17) transportation services.

Typical hospitality operators tend to purchase one or more maintenance contracts in order to supplement the service agreements that normally accompany new equipment purchases. Although operators often use the terms "maintenance contract" and "service agreement" interchangeably—along with the more generic term, "service contract"—the actual meanings are different. While a service agreement covers equipment defects and malfunctions during the warranty period, a maintenance contract is much more detailed. Usually, for a consistent monthly fee, the maintenance contractor provides routine maintenance, such as periodically changing filters and lubing mechanical parts. Most contracts also cover emergency service when you need it, such as when a freezer suddenly breaks down.

Most new mechanical equipment operators purchase generally comes with some sort of warranty or service agreement. During the guarantee period, usually only major repair problems are covered; operators are responsible for routine maintenance. Many equipment dealers, though, sell "extended" warranty coverage in the form of a maintenance contract, which is designed to relieve operators of all repair and maintenance responsibilities. Also, after this period expires, the dealers usually are willing, for a price, to extend the buyers' coverage once again.

Some operators do not wish to purchase maintenance contracts. They would rather wait until they need service, and then pay only for what they need. This may be a good idea because maintenance contracts, especially those that equipment dealers and manufacturers sell, tend to be very lucrative for these primary sources and intermediaries. However, many operators like the "insurance" that maintenance contracts provide and are willing to pay for peace of mind.

Buying a contract is not an easy decision. First, operators are generally asked to pay up front for the following year's service. Also, the price usually is not negotiable. Another major difficulty is the possibility that the servicepersons will take care of cash customers before taking care of any of the operators' emergency needs. Now that the maintenance company has the operators' money, it may not be eager to be as punctual as it might be for cash customers, though it should be equally as concerned about the operators' future business once the initial contract expires.

One item that must always be done before signing a maintenance contract: be certain that the service is available as advertised. For example, if the service is supposedly available 24 hours a day, 7 days a week, operators should make sure that this is always the case. They might, for instance, call the serviceperson at 3 A.M. If no one answers the telephone, operators should forget that maintenance contractor.

Vending Machine

Some operations use coin-operated vending machines for both customer and employee convenience. The machines dispense cigarettes, candy, soft drinks, food, video games, telephone access, Web access, music, and many other items.

In many cases, these machines come with established agreements: the company puts them in the operators' property, the operators agree to provide adequate space and necessary utilities to power the machines, the company takes full responsibility for the maintenance and restocking of the machines, and the operators get to keep some percentage of the gross sales of the machines.

A major purchasing consideration for operators is whether or not they want such machines on their property.

Another major concern is the potential quality differences among competing companies' machines and the products in these machines. Also, one company may service its machines much better than the others, as well as restock them more regularly.

Of course, operators must be concerned with the commission split to which the company agrees. They are also interested in the "user" discounts provided; that is, the hospitality operator would like to use these machines personally at no cost or at a reduced cost. These financial considerations, along with the services provided, are normally the deciding factors when operators shop for vending-machine service.

Another major consideration is whether or not operators want to buy their own machines and do all the work themselves. Operators can make a good profit with these machines, but the initial cost and the ongoing maintenance costs can be exorbitant. But if the sales revenue is large, operators might do very well with their own machines. However, they may not want to add more requirements to their already long list: the work can be tedious, especially the maintenance aspects, which require operators to have a highly trained repair person, someone large vending-machine companies have.

A large hospitality operation can contract with an intermediary who will oversee the vending-machine program in effect for all of the company's individual locations across the United States. For instance, some intermediaries will take on the responsibility of ensuring that all locations have the latest, state-of-the-art equipment; receive the appropriate service; and earn the maximum commission split. Usually these intermediaries develop national contracts with the hospitality operations. This is quite convenient because it means that the hospitality operation will receive one report and one commission check each period. This practice also eliminates the need for unit managers to deal with several local vending-machine companies on a day-to-day basis.

Insurance

Unfortunately, no single, all-inclusive insurance policy that hospitality operators can buy exists. They must purchase more than one. The typical policies, often dictated by state and local laws and codes, by lenders, and by landlords, include: (1) fire and extended property damage; (2) storekeeper's liability; (3) business interruption insurance; (4) crime coverage for burglary and robbery; (5) personal injury insurance, with protection for libel, slander, defamation, or false arrest; (6) glass insurance; (7) product liability; (8) vehicle insurance; (9) fidelity bonds for those employees who handle money; (10) third-party liability insurance for bars; (11) workers' compensation; and (12) comprehensive insurance to protect against an employee's dishonesty toward customers.

Operators can purchase several additional insurance policies at their discretion. These include: (1) health or life insurance for company personnel; (2) other types of policies to be used as employee benefits, such as disability insurance; and (3) extra insurance on expensive antiques, works of art, and furnishings.

Generally, when evaluating insurance coverage, operators should consider three major factors: (1) the extent of the coverage, or the amount of deductible they must pay; (2) reimbursable losses, or the types of exclusions for which they cannot collect damages; and (3) the conditions they must satisfy before they can collect.

Before contracting with an insurance company, operators should also determine the skill of the persons handling the claims. Some discreet conversations with other customers of the insurer(s) with whom an operator is thinking of dealing can give the operator a sense of the promptness and fairness of claims adjustments.

Another major consideration involved with selecting an insurer is the number of policies operators can obtain from one source. The more they can receive under one roof, so to speak, the smaller the number of insurers they need to deal with. Thus, it is common for operators to go to one independent insurance broker and secure all of their insurance needs through one person. Brokers work for the buyer. They deal with insurance agents and insurance companies when putting together an insurance package that will meet their clients' needs.

If operators prefer, they can buy insurance directly. That is, they can buy from a company that sells directly to the insured. This is cheaper because operators save the agent/middleman's fee; however, they do not get the advice and counsel of this agent/middleman. Companies that sell directly are sometimes referred to as direct writers. Automobile and life insurance can easily be purchased directly.

Operators can also purchase insurance from an exclusive insurance agent. However, this type of agent represents only one insurance company. Consequently, if operators need some unique insurance coverage, they may have to deal with several exclusive agents.

If available, operators should consider joining a risk-purchasing group. This is a type of co-op purchasing arrangement that, essentially, enables individuals to become part of a larger group and, thereby, reduce insurance costs for all of the group members. Hospitality chain organizations can easily qualify for these plans. Independent operators might consider joining a group that buys insurance for its members, such as groups that most restaurant and hotel associations maintain. Group plans are always less expensive than individual plans.

Operators can evaluate an insurance company's performance reasonably easily because most states keep records of their dealings with the various companies. Also, operators can check an insurance company's rating in one of several rating agency publications, such as *Best's Insurance Reports*. This publication notes each insurance company's history, financial performance, and other related data. Sound companies are rated A or A1.

Insurance is often highly technical, and it is appropriate for operators to consult legal counsel before making a decision. Some busy managers leave much of the dealing with insurance companies to their attorneys, but this is an expensive move since attorneys charge by the hour and happily interview anyone operators send them. As with so many other complex decisions, it may be best for operators to determine what coverage they want and then negotiate the price with a limited number of reliable bidders, and in this case have their judgment backed up by their attorney. Furthermore, it is usually to the operators' advantage to shop and compare insurance policies every year or so. Our experience shows that a wide spread in prices exists for essentially equal coverage.

Laundry and Linen Supply

No service generates as much disagreement as laundry and linen supply. Some hospitality operators seem to have a good experience with these suppliers, while others simply are not satisfied.

If operators use linens and uniforms, they may: (1) buy their own and purchase a laundry service, (2) purchase the laundry service and rent the fabrics, or (3) purchase their own fabrics and laundry machines and do their own work.

The first two options require less work on the operators' part than the third, in that they order just what they need, receive it, store it, and use it. Also, they expend only a minor amount of effort to shop around since, normally, they have only two or three laundry and linen supply services in their area to choose from.

Large operations are more interested in the third option. They often own an in-house laundry system. Smaller operations might experiment with their own laundry machinery. However, the cost of the space needed to house the machinery, the labor cost, the cost of cleaning chemicals, and other overhead costs usually seem to be too expensive for these properties.

Some operations have gone so far as to eliminate linens and uniforms altogether; these companies use disposable linens and give employees a uniform allowance so that they can provide their own uniforms.

Renting a laundry and linen supply service is more convenient, and operators receive professional service. If operators erect their own laundry, they must be prepared for more responsibility to accompany the savings they may realize. If they eliminate permanent fabrics, they need to be prepared for the high cost of disposables and, possibly, customer resistance to disposable napkins, tablecloths, and bed linens.

If operators decide to rent linen and laundry service, they should evaluate each potential supplier based on the following factors: (1) length of contract; (2) service schedule; (3) how seasonal fluctuations are handled; (4) variety and quality of products offered; (5) overall cost of the service; and (6) cost of lost, damaged, or stolen products for which operators are responsible.

It is possible for operators to have an outside management contractor manage their own laundry and their own dish- and pot-washing system in their establishment. Some independent contractors supply laundry and steward services. In some cases, they might provide the least expensive alternative.

Cleaning

Several specialized contract cleaning services are available. Some of the more typical ones include: (1) exhaust hood, (2) degreasing, (3) window, (4) carpet and upholstery, and (5) concrete cleaning.

Unlike many services, cleaning is one that typical hospitality operations conceivably could perform on their own. Consequently, using contract cleaners tends to generate a good deal of discussion, which usually centers on the crucial question: Should I purchase this service, or should I do it myself?

It is probably better for operators to do some cleaning tasks themselves, particularly ones that must be done every day. Weekly or monthly cleaning tasks that require a great deal of specialized equipment should probably become the responsibility of a contract cleaner. Unfortunately, the distinction between these two types of tasks is not always clear.

Many operations contract for an outside firm to take care of almost all the cleaning. Hospitals often use these services, and some housekeeping contractors try to sell complete services to hotel properties.

For heavy cleaning, such as carpet shampooing, it seems best for operators to purchase this service. This eliminates the need for expensive equipment, for storing expensive shampoo, and for expensive labor.

Of course, operators must also consider the disadvantages of contract cleaners. One drawback is the lack of complete control over the workers. Another disadvantage is the cost, which may be quite expensive—although it is unlikely that operators could provide some of these services more cheaply.

Contract cleaners are numerous. But, like decorators, they are relatively easy to evaluate. Operators can contact references and ask to examine the cleaners' work.

If contractors do a poor job, usually several others can take their place. The number of competitors in the field helps keep their prices within reasonable limits and their service timely.

Another problem with contract cleaners is the laxity with which hospitality operators examine and inspect the work done in their establishments. (Recall the chimney story earlier in this chapter.)

Yet another problem is that operators may sometimes want to use friends, neighbors, or high school students. Letting these amateurs earn a few dollars may be convenient and neighborly, but the quality of their work probably is not very professional or competent. Furthermore, it is not wise for operators to expose themselves to potential liability.

A final concern is that some contract cleaners have trouble maintaining a complete staff themselves. They are frequently shorthanded and may, as a result, provide operators with poor service. In addition, when operators inspect work that they have done for someone else, the operators do not know whether the same people working for the contract cleaners today were the ones responsible for the job they are checking.

ANOTHER WORD ABOUT SECURITY WHEN BUYING SERVICES

Shady characters are always ready to sell hospitality operators a nonexistent product or service or to pretend that they have a real bargain to offer—a bargain that never materializes. Hospitality operators do not usually buy questionable advertised bargains. However, services invite all sorts of ingenious tricks. For instance, purchasing an ad in a soon-to-be-published directory can be costly: the directory may never be printed. Also, donating money to buy ad space in a charitable association's publication may be costly and wasteful unless operators have verified that the charity is a bona fide operation.

Invoices for services usually go directly to the bookkeeper, who might pay them routinely. Therefore, operators should check these bills and initial them because a dishonest company may send an invoice that resembles the ones their bookkeeper always pays.

Dishonest service providers may also try to slip in extra invoices for the service that operators pay for on a regular, periodic basis. Again, if the bookkeeper does not check the bills carefully, operators might pay for the same service twice. In fact, one local restaurant in Las Vegas regularly paid its alarm company twice a month instead of once, for more than a year.

Another insidious problem, to which small operators are particularly vulnerable, is the contractor who demands a deposit before beginning work but then never returns. For example, suppose an operator wants someone to install new cabinets in the room service area of a hotel. A contractor tells the operator that he needs $400 to procure the materials required to complete the job. The operator gives him the money—then never sees this contractor again.

Admittedly, this problem occurs more with homemakers than with commercial businesses. But this can happen to hospitality operators if they deal with moonlighters and other contractors who are not licensed by the state or city. If operators have any doubts about a contractor, they can contact the Better Business Bureau (BBB). Alternately, they might put their deposit money in an escrow account, which the materials supplier will receive only after delivery of the materials. Another option is for operators to pay the materials supplier directly without giving any money to the contractor. Finally, operators might consider working strictly with their friends, with those with whom they have had positive business dealings, or with members of the local chamber of commerce or other similar civic groups.

In Chapter 16, we discussed the major security problems associated with purchasing, receiving, storing, and issuing. The problems we noted there seem to multiply when operators buy several services, especially services that are difficult to monitor and are paid for on a regularly scheduled basis.

Small businesses, rather than large firms, are usually targets for dishonest persons who realize that small operators have less time to examine every detail. But, as we noted in Chapter 16, all hospitality operators must force themselves to be careful. Dishonest acts are just too common and too easily perpetrated.

KEY WORDS AND CONCEPTS

Advertising service

Banner ads

Best's Insurance Reports

Better Business Bureau (BBB)

Bid buying

Bonding

Business license

Cleaning service

Common area maintenance fee (CAM fee)

Completion time

Construction management firm

Consulting proposal

Consulting service

Decorating and remodeling service

Direct writer

Due bill

Either a service is good or bad—no in-between exists

Exact name

Exclusive insurance agent

Experience requirement

Extended warranty coverage

Financial service

Groundskeeping service

Guarantee

Inspection procedures

Insurance broker

Insurance service

Intended use

Laundry and linen supply service

Lien-sale contract

Maintenance contract

Maintenance service

Make-goods

Management considerations when purchasing services

Media-buying service

Merits

Moonlighter

Negative selling

Outsourcing

Performance bond

Pest control operator (PCO)	Security problems	Types of cleaning services
Promotional discount	Service agreement	Types of consultants
Purchasing services	Should operators perform	Types of insurance coverage
Quality of the finished work	the work themselves or hire	Types of maintenance
Quality of the materials	a service?	services
used	Small Business	Unconditional lien release
References	Administration (SBA)	User discount
Required work schedule	Some services must be	Vending-machine service
Risk-purchasing group	purchased	Warranty
Run-of-the-press	Trade out	Waste removal service
Run-of-the-station	Types of advertising services	Web ads

QUESTIONS AND PROBLEMS

1. A specification for pest control service could include the following information:
    (a)
    (b)
    (c)
    (d)
    (e)

2. What is a disadvantage of hiring a moonlighter to provide a service to a hospitality operation?

3. List some disadvantages of hiring an unlicensed service provider.

4. Assume you manage a full-service restaurant. You are paying $48,000 a year for linen service, which is mediocre. Setting up an in-house laundry would cost $20,000. Operating the in-house laundry would cost $22,000 per year. What do you suggest? Also, what does the $22,000 include? If possible, ask an owner-manager of a full-service restaurant to comment on your answer.

5. Why is completion time a very important selection factor when operators evaluate potential repair and maintenance service providers?

6. What is the difference between run-of-the-press and run-of-the-station?

7. Should operators trade their products for advertising services, or should they pay cash? Why?

8. Assume you are the owner-operator of a quick-service hamburger operation with annual sales revenue of $850,000. What services would you consider purchasing? Why? If possible, ask an owner-operator of such an operation to comment on your answer.

9. A specification for vending-machine service could include the following information:
    (a)
    (b)
    (c)
    (d)
    (e)

10. List some advantages and disadvantages of purchasing a cleaning service.

11. Assume that you run a school food service serving 500 elementary students, lunch only, five days a week. Currently, you use no pest control service, having opted to let the school custodian spray the necessary chemicals. Lately, though, you feel that an outside service could handle the insect problem much better. Prepare a specification for this service. If possible, ask a school foodservice manager to comment on your answer.

12. What is the major disadvantage, for operators, of a lien-sale type of contract?

13. What is the major disadvantage of operators' purchasing their insurance from a direct writer?

14. Assume that you own a small, 30-room motel. You have no food service. You wish to expand to 50 rooms, but you need to research the market to determine whether a demand for more rooms exists. Should you do the research yourself, or should you hire a consultant? If possible, ask an owner-manager of such an operation to comment on your answer. Assume that you want to hire a consultant to do this work. How would you go about selecting one?

15. Briefly describe the concept of "negative selling."

16. What are some of the costs and benefits of operators managing their own laundry machinery and purchasing their own linens?

17. What is the primary purpose of purchasing a fidelity bond?

18. List some advantages and disadvantages of purchasing a maintenance contract.

19. What is the difference between a service agreement and a maintenance contract?

20. A specification for financial services could include the following information:
    (a)
    (b)
    (c)
    (d)
    (e)

21. Assume that an operator's real estate lease contract requires it to pay a monthly CAM fee. What is the purpose of this fee?

22. A recycling operator contacts you and offers the following deal: if you save your aluminum and cardboard and bring it to her plant, she will give you $0.45 per pound for the metal and $0.08 per pound for the cardboard. How much money would you want to earn each month before you would be interested in this deal? If possible, ask a restaurant manager to comment on your answer.

23. When would operators expect an advertising medium to issue "make-goods" to its customers?

24. Briefly describe how a buyer could use an escrow account as part of a bill-paying schedule set up to pay a remodeling contractor.

27

FURNITURE, FIXTURES, AND EQUIPMENT

The Purpose of this Chapter

After reading this chapter, you should be able to:

■ Identify management considerations surrounding the selection and procurement of furniture, fixtures, and equipment.

■ Outline the general procedures used when purchasing furniture, fixtures, and equipment.

■ Describe the major selection factors for furniture, fixtures, and equipment.

■ Explain methods to finance the purchase of furniture, fixtures, and equipment.

INTRODUCTION

Furniture, fixtures, and equipment (FFE) are sometimes referred to as "capital items." Most capital items are depreciable assets. Unlike the cost of the nonfood expense items discussed in Chapter 25, under some circumstances, the cost of FFE items cannot be used as tax deductions in the year in which they were purchased. Instead, hospitality operators must depreciate the value of these items over a period of years; operators can take only a part of the purchase price as a tax deduction in one year.

A capital item is a long-life item. Managers anticipate that it will last in service for more than a year, and perhaps as long as 20 years, if properly repaired and maintained. While its value may be depreciated over, say, a 3-year period, it can, conceivably, remain useful and productive for a much longer period of time under normal operating conditions.

The selection and procurement procedure for these items generally involves the typical principles enumerated in this text. Of course, FFE items have an added dimension: they stay around a long time. Consequently, operators are very conscious of even the smallest potential for error. If they receive a poor batch of tomatoes, they can rectify this problem relatively easily. But if they select and procure an inappropriate personal computer (PC), they may have to live with this white elephant longer than they care to.

MANAGEMENT CONSIDERATIONS

On the surface, determining the types of FFE they need appears to be a relatively easy task for managers. Basically, the kinds of products hospitality operators sell—menu items, quality of rooms, guest transportation to the airport, and so forth—usually dictate the types and qualities of FFE they must have in order to run their business sufficiently. Unfortunately, this is only the first step in determining FFE requirements.

A major concern is the effect that any future plans might have on the operators' need for FFE. For instance, they might want to alter their menu. Alternately, they might wish to add more banquet rooms. Should operators select FFE today in anticipation of tomorrow's needs, or should they take care of today only and worry about tomorrow when it comes?

All operators have growth aspirations, and they all should be concerned about tomorrow because these days, FFE can become obsolete quickly. If operators do not have some foresight, their hospitality company could, conceivably, become dated almost overnight. They must balance today's budget demands with tomorrow's requirements if they expect to withstand the ebb and flow of the competitive pressure in the hospitality industry.

Another major FFE concern operators must face is the issue of capitalizing an operating expense. This means reducing a current expense, such as the energy expense, by investing today in machinery that is expensive yet will reduce energy consumption. The added investment in higher-quality equipment will lead to operational savings later on. But at what point is this trade-off economically advisable?

In the hospitality industry, most operators seem willing to invest a dollar today if they can recoup that dollar in two to three years. That is, if the operational savings are such that the original investment is paid back in two or three years, generally most hospitality owner-managers will consider capitalizing an expense.

The prediction of savings is, however, difficult. The credibility of operators' estimates must be acceptable before they trade dollars today for perceived savings tomorrow. They can never be 100 percent certain of their predictions. Also, they can never tell when operational costs will level off, drop, or suddenly rise dramatically. For example, in some properties, the initial investment in computerization is much more than the amount of labor savings that can be experienced over a two- to three-year period. Labor may be the least expensive alternative for today. But what about tomorrow?

Several other related problems arise whenever operators contemplate the capitalization of expenses. These problems almost always involve future considerations and the operators' inability to predict them adequately. Not being able to foresee the future completely puts operators in something of a ticklish position.

Deciding on the person or persons who should select and procure the FFE items is another major managerial concern. When hospitality operations plan FFE choices, four categories of persons are typically involved: (1) user(s), (2) owner-manager(s), (3) buyer(s), and (4) consultant(s).

The user sometimes is involved in the process because his or her performance on the job may be directly related to the equipment used. In addition, since the user's job performance evaluation is critical to his or her success in the company, it generally is a good idea to invite user input. The user sometimes is also involved as the instigator of an FFE purchase. For instance, he or she may suggest to a supervisor that a dated meat slicer should be replaced with a more modern piece of equipment.

The owner-manager makes the final decision regarding any FFE purchase. He or she must take the ultimate responsibility for any FFE purchase, so it is logical that he or she makes this decision. The owner-manager will probably set the quality standards, note the preferred supplier, and oversee the receiving and installation of the items. Normally, he or she will be more actively involved in the purchase of FFE than in the purchase of other products. Since these items are expensive and remain a part of a hospitality operation for quite some time, the owner-manager is motivated to be very careful.

If a hospitality firm employs a full-time buyer, he or she typically would be involved as a technical resource person, answering such questions as: Is the desired quality available? What type of payment plans are available? How long will it take to receive the merchandise? What options or alternatives are available?

Depending on the magnitude of the FFE purchase, owner-managers may seek the assistance of one or more consultants. For instance, they may ask an accountant to prepare various installment payment options for their review. Alternately, if they are considering firing someone and replacing him or her with a machine, they might hire an accountant to prepare an estimate of future savings.

If operators are contemplating a major remodeling job, they might consider using a designer or architect to assist them in their efforts. These types of individuals normally are employed when a company is building a new facility. Multiunit hospitality companies also typically employ them full-time.

Consultants often are worth the added cost operators must pay to procure their services. They can detail the FFE needed, as well as determine the most effective and efficient layout and design for the specific type of operation. Furthermore, they will see to it that the FFE are installed according to existing fire, health and safety, and building codes. Since these consultants normally deal in a highly technical area, operators probably cannot get too far without their help. They do not come cheap, but the efficiency they may be able to build into the operators' design can take care of their fee and leave a bit of savings besides.

Operators can often obtain some consultants or consulting advice through FFE dealers. That is, operators can do business with a "design/build" dealer who is prepared to provide, free of charge, all the advice and assistance operators need, as long as they purchase all of their FFE from that dealer. This is a one-stop arrangement, and the operators become house accounts. There are disadvantages to this arrangement; however, these disadvantages can often be offset by better supplier services, as well as by a decrease in the amount of "downtime" operators might need to incur. This is the length of time during which operators cannot profitably conduct business because they are still waiting for some FFE to be delivered and installed.

Another choice is selecting a foodservice design consultant who works for the general architect or operator and who is not a part of the FFE sale. These design consultants provide an unbiased evaluation of FFE that are available and that fit into the overall design and purpose of the operation. Foodservice design consultants typically charge an overall project fee or base their fees on a time and expense structure.

Determining from whom to buy is another major managerial concern. For most operators, the decision is simple: they usually satisfy their needs by selecting a reputable FFE dealer or dealers. This is especially true when they are considering a reasonably large purchase and supplier services represent a major requirement.

Other FFE supply sources exist, though. For example, operators may be able to procure FFE through contract supply houses, a sort of co-op arrangement available in the lodging trade; from food and beverage suppliers who deal in FFE as a sideline; from mail-order or online catalogs; from primary sources; through other types of local co-ops; through chain headquarters that may offer their affiliates the opportunity to purchase FFE; through consultants, such as designers and contractors, who may sell FFE; through leasing companies that can provide some items; from firms that deal in used merchandise, repossessed merchandise, and the like that may be available in the local area; through warehouse clubs; and from auctioneers, who sometimes are instrumental in liquidating FFE. Usually, operators must balance convenience, the suppliers' reputation, and so forth with the purchase price, installation costs, and other related costs when making their decisions.

With so many choices and options available, operators may find it difficult to locate those suppliers who are knowledgeable and prepared to offer the necessary level of service. The optimal supplier is critical for FFE, and to drop that person in favor of someone else can cause tremendous problems, especially time-delay problems. In our experience, the amount of supplier service the supplier will provide and its quality are major considerations for operators in most instances.

Another major managerial concern with FFE is the question of reconditioning versus replacing these items, when such a choice is possible. In some cases, it might be economically attractive for operators to recondition, remodel, and/or rebuild some items instead of purchasing new ones. The cost of making do with an existing item may be much less than the purchase price for a new replacement.

But while the reconditioning cost may be quite attractive initially, other problems may result. For instance, reconditioned machinery does not appear to have the anticipated long life that a new replacement has, so the long-term cost of reconditioning may not be beneficial at all. Another problem might be the downtime experienced during the rebuilding stage for, say, a walk-in refrigerator. Typically, it takes longer to recondition, rebuild, and/or remodel than it does to provide a new installation.

In the short run, rebuilding can be the best answer, but in the long run, it may not satisfy operators' needs. They should, however, at least consider the potential of reconditioning because they do not want to spend any more money than necessary to accomplish their goals.

A final concern to management that we have experienced is the impulsive purchase of certain types of FFE items, such as furnishings. An owner-manager may return from a vacation trip with an antique clock in tow that will "be perfect for the lobby." Alternately, he or she may visit another restaurant and fall in love with the wall coverings in that establishment, prompting him or her to do a bit of remodeling. Not all impulsive purchases are bad, but it's unlikely that something purchased on the spur of the moment will turn out to have a positive effect on the operation.

GENERAL PROCEDURES IN FFE PURCHASING

Preparing some type of specification for FFE is not particularly difficult for operators. Often, operators do not prepare formal specifications for replacement FFE because most of them will "look around," for instance, at trade shows, in competitors' operations, in catalogs, and in trade papers, before forming an opinion. These operators usually have a very good idea of the type of FFE they require before they actually sit down to negotiate with one or more FFE suppliers.

Usually, operators have past experience to guide them as they formulate the appropriate purchasing strategy for replacement FFE. Generally, if operators have had a good experience with the current items, they are likely to replace them with the same brand, or an equivalent. This dependence on yesterday makes it difficult for new manufacturers to gain a foothold unless they offer something unique.

Operators normally examine replacement FFE very closely before making their purchase decisions. For instance, many of them like to attend trade shows that cater to our industry because, usually, several FFE dealers will be in attendance with demonstration models available for inspection. Attending a trade show seems preferable to visiting a dealer's showroom or viewing an online video presentation. It offers the opportunity to compare and contrast several alternatives.

Visitors to trade shows typically preplan their activities in order to maximize their time. Since time is limited, operators are able to evaluate only a few FFE selection factors; otherwise they will get bogged down at one dealer's booth display. Trade show visitors want to view many alternatives. To do this, they should generally evaluate only a few major factors, such as the item's functionality, quality of construction, warranties, total cost (the as-purchased [AP] price plus delivery and installation charges), and the supplier's depth of knowledge and amount of service that can be provided.

When a major FFE purchase is contemplated, specifications are normally necessary. Chances are, operators will need to finance part of this purchase through a lender, who usually requires them to obtain competitive bids for the FFE that will be used as collateral for the loan.

The FFE specification will include many of the selection factors we note later in this chapter. For all intents and purposes, these specifications are similar in scope to those operators prepare for food and beverage items. These requirements do tend, though, to be purchase specifications rather than product specifications. This is because the required supplier services, which are not a part of the product specification, are very important when operators plan a major FFE purchase.

In addition to the major types of supplier services operators will require, the FFE purchase specification will ordinarily include further information:

1. **Instructions to Bidders.** This is the where, when, and how of submitting a competitive bid. Included in the specification is all of the pertinent information of which bidders should be cognizant, information that will, in turn, indicate how operators will award the project and what criteria, such as lowest cost, fastest completion time, and so forth, operators will use to make the award decision.

2. **General Conditions.** Operators must note several contingencies in this section of the specification. For instance, they could detail: (a) code requirements; (b) access rights, such as whether the community will permit the transportation of heavy equipment on the roadways, or if the equipment must be delivered in pieces; (c) royalties that must be paid; (d) other local ordinances; (e) provisions for modifications; (f) the treatment of cost overruns; (g) the treatment of delays; and (h) liability coverage the supplier needs.

3. **Specific Conditions.** In addition to the list of FFE needed and their desired characteristics, operators also must note delivery dates and procedures, installation dates and procedures, and other related details.

4. **Detailed Drawings.** This probably is the most important distinction of FFE specifications. For a major purchase, operators typically include architectural drawings of all of the custom equipment, as well as any pertinent layout and design plans. These drawings aid bidders. They also help to prevent ambiguity.

Once operators have prepared specifications, they should make a list of potential suppliers and, from that list, develop an approved-supplier list. After selecting the best supplier, operators may need to modify the specifications, monitor FFE orders and delivery, monitor any subcontracting that may be necessary, and obtain the training and other start-up help needed.

SELECTION FACTORS

Several selection factors exist for FFE items. This is expected because the purchase of FFE is a major decision, one that operators cannot perform hastily. Fortunately, they do not need to purchase these items very often. But when they do, they must plan procedures very carefully. The major selection factors are discussed in the following sections.

Intended Use

As with all purchased items, operators must identify the intended use of an item so that they can detail the appropriate, relevant specifications. This is a bit more difficult to do in the FFE area, primarily since so many items must be used to satisfy several production and service requirements. But difficult or not, operators cannot proceed very far until they isolate the intended use of the FFE needed.

Exact Name

At times, this selection factor can cause a bit of confusion. For instance, operators cannot simply note the term "oven" on their specification. Rather, they must be careful to detail the specific type of oven they need. For instance, a great deal of difference exists between a standard convection oven and a convection-steam oven.

Another dimension of the exact name is the model numbers that manufacturers use to distinguish similar types of equipment items. When operators compare different brands of the same type of item, it is important for them to determine the comparable model numbers.

Lifetime Cost

The FFE purchase decision is a long-term investment. Sometimes, operators must plan one or more years in advance of their actual purchase. Also, the items operators are buying are expected to have a reasonably long operating life. Consequently, it is impractical for operators to consider only the initial AP price of the FFE since there are so many other expenses incurred with them over their normal life span.

Besides the AP price, it is imperative that operators consider:

1. The trade-in value of the operators' old FFE
2. Delivery costs
3. Installation and testing costs
4. Relevant operating costs
5. Potential operating savings

6. The trade-in value of the new FFE when operators decide to replace it or liquidate it

The related costs can add up very quickly. Inexperienced buyers may not realize this. For instance, delivery, installation, and testing costs can easily be 10 percent, or more, of a walk-in refrigerator's AP price. When soliciting competitive bids, wise buyers always ask suppliers to quote the "installed, ready-to-operate" purchase price.

If the initial AP price exceeds the buyers' budget, they generally tend to forgo the purchase or to settle for lesser-quality, hence less expensive, FFE. This may or may not be an appropriate strategy. On one hand, a new piece of equipment might improve worker productivity significantly. But if buyers are struggling under a heavy debt load, it may be unwise for them to risk bankruptcy.

Sometimes, operators can save money by setting up a personal "equipment rental" firm and purchasing all of the FFE through this firm. For instance, an operator can call this firm "XYZ Rentals," send a purchase order (PO) directly to a manufacturer and, usually, obtain the lowest AP prices possible. Manufacturers ordinarily quote their lowest prices to customers who will lease or resell the merchandise because those customers do not need the extra supplier services that typical hospitality buyers require.

In some cases, operators might be swayed by a low AP price only to get stung later with high operating costs. For instance, an equipment dealer might quote a low AP price, knowing full well that operators will need to purchase expensive parts, supplies, and so forth because no other alternatives exist.

Operators should be skeptical of any unusually low AP price quotations. If a quotation sounds too good to be true, they might be getting hit with a lowball bid.

Lowball bids can take many forms. For example, some salespersons might justify their equipment by pointing out its labor-saving potential. Labor saving in the hospitality industry is very difficult to achieve, and quite often it is illusory. For example, operators might save two work hours per shift if they purchase a floor-washing machine, but if they must fire a full-time employee to save these two hours, chances are they will find this impractical because they will have a hard time replacing the remaining six work hours of other necessary duties that employee performed per shift. Similarly, even if operators do fire a full-time person, before they know it, they have hired a part-time employee, and, eventually, that person becomes a full-time employee. The result: operators realize smaller labor savings than originally anticipated.

Other lowball possibilities operators need to consider include the following:

1. Equipment loans or sample test periods that allow operators to try equipment in actual use may spoil the persons using the equipment. Sometimes, once operators order an item and accept a loan or test period, the salesperson sees this as an excuse to stop by a lot, thereby allowing him or her to convince the users that they should have some expensive attachments. As a result, what seems economical to start with may become quite expensive in the long run.

2. The new equipment may not be compatible with what operators currently have; therefore, they may need to purchase expensive adapters to make it work.

3. If operators get a stripped-down model, the users may persuade their employer to obtain expensive options.

4. The supplier might be offering a low price because he or she is discontinuing that particular line of equipment; where will operators get replacement parts?

5. The supplier may put in several exceptions on any warranty or guarantee; for example, operators may have to pay the first $500 of any service calls during the first year.

6. Operators may find out too late that they are required to purchase a large inventory of spare parts right now. (This could be an illegal tying agreement, however.)

Generally, the issue with any capital expenditure is not what it costs initially, but what it is worth over its lifetime. Judging FFE on the AP price alone is usually a mistake. Operators must force themselves to consider the FFE's lifetime cost. However, if operators plan to be out of business one or two years from now, then an overreliance on AP price might be appropriate.

Potential Operating Savings

Quite often, operators purchase a piece of equipment primarily to effect a savings in operating expenses. That is, they make their decision in order to capitalize an operating expense by investing in something today that will cause some of their expenses to decrease in the future (see Figures 27.1 and 27.2).

Management can control several operating expenses that are good candidates for possible future reductions. For example, the cost of merchandise, labor, energy, taxes, water, waste removal, and so forth might all decrease if managers proceed

FIGURE 27.1 Operators sometimes purchase equipment because of its product-saving potential. Courtesy of Winston Industries.

FIGURE 27.2 Operators sometimes purchase equipment because of its labor-saving potential. Courtesy of Server Products, Inc.

to invest in something today. Operators can use several mathematical models to test the feasibility of buying equipment based on its potential operating savings. A typical formula that operators use to make a capital investment decision is the "payback period formula." The payback period refers to the amount of time it takes operators to recoup the original investment. For instance, if they must invest $5500 in an energy-saving oven today, how long will it take—how many years, perhaps, will it take—for them to save $5500 of energy costs? If it takes them more than three years to recoup the initial investment, operators typically will not purchase the oven.

Probably, operators will find it most helpful to use the "net present value procedure," which takes into account the time value of money: a dollar saved next year is worth considerably less than a dollar saved today. The net present value procedure requires operators to first compute the present value of the future savings. To do this, operators estimate the future savings and then discount them to take into account the fact that the longer they must wait to receive these savings, the less the savings are worth today. Furthermore, the longer operators must wait, the greater the risk of losing the savings becomes; this implies that the future savings are worth even less today.

Second, the net present value procedure requires operators to subtract the amount of the initial investment they must make today from the present value of predicted savings. If the answer is greater than zero—if the present value of the predicted savings is greater than the amount of money they must invest today—the current investment is economically attractive.

Several other types of formulas have been developed for specialized applications. For instance, some formulas tell operators in what year a piece of equipment should be replaced, and others indicate when operators need to perform maintenance. These formulas are useful, but they do require numbers; the answers are only as good as the numbers operators provide. Consequently, the use of the formulas is anticlimactic. The real challenge is for operators to come up with the proper number estimates. Knowing the formula is useful only if they can come up with reasonably accurate numbers. Herein lies management's challenge.

In many cases, predicting future operating savings is very difficult. Operators should, for example, consider the potential to save time and to increase the overall productivity of their hospitality firm. If they own a buffet, they might consider purchasing a more modern point-of-sale (POS) system because this might get customers through the line faster. However, some salespersons might comment, "If we get the customers through faster, we can serve more customers." Hence, a new

POS system causes an increase in customers. But wait. How does this all connect? Do patrons eat in a particular place because of this speed? This is hard to say.

Operators might also hear the same argument with a faster dishwashing machine. For instance, if they wash dishes faster, they can serve more meals since they get the dishes back faster. Again, this is an illusory argument because operators can always increase their stock of dishes. Similarly, it is unlikely that customers visit a hospitality operation because it has a fast dishwasher.

Operators must also be careful of other productivity arguments. For example, it is not advantageous for them to own a 400-slices-per-hour toaster if they sell considerably less toast.

Potential product savings may also be illusory. For example, someone selling automatic bars may tell operators that free pouring of liquor wastes 2 to 3 ounces per bottle. We agree with this figure. However, we do not agree when a salesperson tells operators that if they save those ounces, they can sell them at $3.50 each and, as a result, save $7.00 to $9.50 per bottle, all because they have the automatic bar. Simply not wasting the ounces is no guarantee that customers will come in and buy them. Operators have only a certain number of customers. If they are wasteful, it costs them more product to serve them. Consequently, operators save the cost of the liquor with the automatic bar. But having an automated bar does not enable operators to save an amount equivalent to the sales price of each drink. If that were the case, operators should buy two or three automatic bars.

Energy efficiency is another noteworthy concern. One of the potential advantages of new equipment over old is a more efficient energy usage pattern. Unfortunately, many bogus "energy-misers" are on the market. Operators must be aware of the potential for exaggerated claims.

Sometimes, operators purchase energy-saving equipment that they really do not need. For example, it may be futile for them to purchase an expensive cook-and-hold oven that guarantees both less energy use and less meat shrinkage. By cooking roast beef in a regular oven at 250°F instead of 375°F, operators can accomplish almost the same savings. In addition, existing equipment can sometimes be modified to produce similar savings, and this modification might be a much cheaper alternative.

However, cook-and-hold ovens do have their place. They are excellent at low-temperature cooking and they are mobile, allowing for extra oven capacity that usually does not require expensive ventilation systems. These types of ovens also allow for overnight cooking with very little trouble, thereby saving money by using off-peak energy rates.

Some potential problems exist with labor savings. To reiterate, hospitality operators usually need a certain number of employees just to open the doors. They cannot very easily replace workers with machines. Usually, only the largest operations might save a bit of labor over the long run.

If operators are purchasing a capital item primarily to effect a reduction in future operating expenses, they must do their homework very, very carefully. Speculation about future costs is a hazardous undertaking; the pitfalls are many. However, the potential to save a considerable amount of money in the long run makes some operators eager to take their chances.

Direct Purchase

Should hospitality operators go straight to the manufacturer and purchase their FFE items, or should they go through the local dealer? The choice is not always clear. Most of the time, it is a matter of personal taste. If operators buy direct, the AP price, obviously, will be lower. But since they usually must put up the cash and provide their own transportation and installation, the costs can quickly increase. If they bypass the local dealer, chances are good that they will need to provide their own maintenance and other supplier services.

In our experience, too many operators have been duped into the "bypass the local dealer" routine. When their equipment breaks down, who will help them? This is not a problem if they have their own maintenance crew. However, if they do not, a middleman might be worth the added markup.

It is also becoming more common that equipment manufacturers will not sell directly to the end user because they do not want to maintain credit or provide local support that the dealer or distributor can supply. In essence, they would rather focus on manufacturing and utilize the channel of distribution for selling their products. This is not to say that equipment manufacturers do not want to provide customer support. In fact, many times labels on equipment request that opeators contact the mannufacturer directly when serious problems occur.

Demonstration Models

Many manufacturers and dealers use FFE models—items in their showrooms, items at industry trade shows, or items a traveling salesperson uses—for demonstration purposes. In many cases, operators might be able to purchase these items and save a considerable amount of money. If they buy this type of FFE, normally they must: (1) put up the total amount of the AP price in cash, (2) take the item as-is, and (3) provide their own transportation and/or installation. Typically, these items are inexpensive primarily because they are used products, that is, they are somewhat depreciated already in value.

Generally, a very good savings opportunity is associated with this type of purchase. If operators can live with the absence of supplier services, have the cash in their pocket, and can handle all necessary installation chores, they should be able to save quite a bit of money.

Operators must, however, consider the downside. For example, they may not be able to obtain state-of-the-art items. Most FFE available may not fit their needs exactly; they may have to compromise too much to take advantage of the savings. In addition, they may not be able to obtain adequate maintenance contracts, or, if they can, these may be shorter than they would like.

Equipment Programs

In the discussion of nonalcoholic beverages in Chapter 24, we introduced the concept of an equipment program. Recall that under this program, operators can use a company's machinery as long as they are using the food, beverage, or cleaning product that this machinery dispenses. For example, operators might be able to receive "free" use of a laundry system if they agree to purchase all laundry chemicals from a specific firm. Of course, the machinery is not "free" since the chemicals are usually priced to take into account the value of the equipment.

In some instances, operators cannot buy, for example, the juice, soap, or soda that they want without taking the machine. Since this might represent a tying agreement, some companies will sell the product without the machine, but they usually keep the surcharge on the product. As such, operators might just as well take the "free" machine since they will be paying for it anyway.

Some operators resent an equipment program arrangement because they believe that the supplier will get rich by extracting a surcharge every time they purchase the products used in the machinery. In other words, they might pay the initial cost of the machinery over and over again.

However, in some situations, the supplier may not extract a surcharge. The equipment itself might represent only a form of discount to operators. The supplier may be willing to toss in the equipment if an operator buys a large supply of products over a long period of time. Alternately, the supplier might merely be motivated to ensure that the products are dispensed properly and not be interested in earning a markup. Furthermore, most suppliers maintain the equipment, freeing operators from a costly headache.

In our experience, equipment programs have generally been advantageous to hospitality operators. We periodically compare the cost of coffee with and without machinery, and the coffee with machinery usually turns out to be only a few pennies more per pound than the cost without the machinery. So, purchasing, installing, and maintaining coffee-brewing equipment is not necessary.

Custom FFE

Generally, operators are motivated to purchase standardized FFE. That is, usually they do not want to purchase anything that violates height, width, veneer, and other standards.

Customized FFE are very expensive. It may not be worth the extra cost and inconvenience to procure such items. Aside from the normally high AP price, other major costs of purchasing customized FFE exist: (1) the company producing the desired item(s) may go out of business, which can be troublesome if it is the only firm capable of maintaining and servicing that item; (2) if it is a very odd piece of custom work, it is unlikely that operators can borrow against its value; (3) the item may have several bugs, which can increase both operating costs and aggravation in the long run; (4) probably no future trade-in value exists; (5) the manufacturer may be forced to pass on cost overruns to operators; and (6) the item(s) may not be ready on time because of a production and/or installation delay.

Operators might be able to save some of the expense of customized FFE if they can locate a supplier that has merchandise that is part standard and part customized. For example, some kitchen equipment manufacturers produce standard stainless steel tables that allow operators to customize them in a limited way.

Several potential advantages of customized FFE exist. These include: (1) operating savings may be available; (2) the items may be easier to operate, maintain, and clean; (3) the items may be more attractive; (4) operators can customize their image; (5) usually, operators can get exactly what they want; and (6) in the long run, the lifetime cost of these items can be more attractive than that associated with their standard counterparts. In fact, a custom installation may be economical in a hospitality operation because it will fit exactly the space and need for which it was designed. The idea of operators buying stock material is not a good one if it means getting something that is less than exactly what they want.

New versus Used FFE

Occasionally, operators may come across merchandise that, while technically classified as used, could actually have suffered little or no use. We have already considered the possibility of buying demonstration models. Similar opportunities might involve kitchen equipment that trade show exhibitors offer at "show-special" prices; this equipment may be just as good as new. Also, FFE manufacturers and dealers sometimes have "freight-damaged" items that they are willing to sell for a fraction of the original AP prices. Some of these damaged products may need a lot of work before operators can put them into service. However, many of these products may have only cosmetic damage; a couple of bumps and bruises may be inconsequential when operators are purchasing, for example, work tables.

Of course, most used items available for purchase have been in use for some time. In most cases, operators can purchase these items for a small fraction of their original selling prices; our experience shows that they can save as much as 70 percent of new AP prices. Again, as with most bargains of this type, operators are normally required to put up the cash and take the items as-is. Often, there are secondhand dealers in the area who specialize in this type of merchandise. These persons, though, are not usually prepared to service what they sell.

Operators can sometimes purchase used merchandise from a new products dealer who makes a market in trade-in items. Quite often, a local new products dealer will have available like-new merchandise that recently was exchanged for more modern models. If operators are on good terms with the dealer, he or she may even call them to let them know about something recently available that might be useful to them.

Trade papers often carry ads soliciting purchasers of used FFE. In our experience, most hospitality operators are leery of these arrangements. They have no qualms about dealing with someone local or someone with whom they are familiar, but it is unusual for operators to answer ads or online solicitations placed by unknown, individual businesspersons.

At times, operators hire an auctioneer to liquidate the FFE. More than likely, a tax collector, or lender, forecloses on a hospitality operation and hires an auctioneer to liquidate the property to satisfy past debts. In our experience, if operators know what they are doing, they can get an extremely attractive bargain at these auctions (see Figure 27.3).

Some operators seek out auctioneers and other individuals and businesses involved in liquidation procedures, such as attorneys, trustees, escrow companies, and title companies. These operators want to be on any mailing lists that are used to advertise liquidation sales. The obvious advantage of being on such a mailing list is learning about potentially attractive opportunities. The drawback, though, is the possibility of making an impulse purchase that will not suit the operators' needs.

FIGURE 27.3 Operators sometimes purchase FFE at an auction. Normally, these items are sold as-is, where-is, but despite these disadvantages, a huge savings is possible. Courtesy of Joe Presswood Co., Inc.

The major potential advantage of used merchandise, of course, is the huge reduction in the purchase price. Also, if operators are lucky, they can obtain an item that still has a long, useful life ahead. Unfortunately, operators may encounter several disadvantages associated with procuring used FFE. They might acquire: (1) obsolete merchandise, (2) an energy guzzler, (3) an item that inefficiently uses floor space, (4) merchandise that is expensive to maintain, or (5) an item that does not meet current fire, health and safety, and building codes. Operators must also consider: (6) the time needed to seek out these bargains, (7) the time needed to examine the items before purchasing them, (8) the fact that the item lacks a guarantee, (9) the possibility that replacement parts are no longer available, (10) the possible damage to their image, and (11) the inability to predict exactly the amount of money needed to recondition the item if necessary.

Buying used FFE is a gamble; operators must take a risk in order to reap the savings. They can minimize their risk, though, if they limit their purchases to nonmechanical pieces, as well as to small wares, such as pots and pans. Risk-averse operators should shy away from mechanical items, especially those with complex, computerized control systems.

Versatility

Whenever possible, hospitality operators should try to purchase versatile equipment, that is, equipment that can do more than one job. For example, tilt kettles are popular in many kitchens because they can be used to satisfy so many different production requirements. This type of kettle can be used as a grill, a steam kettle, and a braising pan.

Today, versatility is increasingly important because the cost of space in hospitality operations is very expensive. Places of business are located in prime retail areas. As a result, the cost of the real estate is high, which means that operators are motivated to reduce the size of their production facilities and increase the size of their income-producing facilities, such as the dining room and lounge. But operators cannot do this unless they are willing to pay a little more for versatility.

Compactness

Expensive real estate makes it necessary for hospitality operators to purchase several FFE items that are compact. For instance, kitchen and laundry equipment that require minimal space can be very valuable in the long run. Similarly, foldaway types of furniture are valuable. These items certainly will cost more initially, but operators cannot ignore their convenience and space-saving capabilities.

In a related issue, operators must be concerned with the overall weight of the FFE items they are considering buying. Their business may be housed, for instance, in a building structure that cannot support very heavy pieces of production equipment. Alternately, their facility may not have a sufficiently large opening to permit delivery of the equipment to its exact location.

Compatibility

Hospitality operators should attempt to ensure that new purchases will intermingle easily with their current stock of FFE. New FFE items should be compatible with the existing stock in many ways, such as aesthetically and functionally. Otherwise, operators might experience some production problems and/or some damage to their overall image in the eyes of their customers. In some cases, such as with a systems sale, operators have no choice; they must purchase compatible merchandise that will meet their specific needs.

Appearance

Image is a precious commodity in the hospitality industry. As such, hospitality operators must do whatever is feasible to protect and enhance it. One way they can do this is to select FFE items that have a high-quality appearance.

Manufacturers of similar FFE items often compete strictly on superficial appearance differences. For instance, counter fixtures may vary somewhat: for example, veneers, widths, and heights may differ a bit from one manufacturer to another. These differences are not substantial, but they could be very important. If customers will see the FFE items, operators may want to spend a few extra dollars to ensure that what customers see pleases them.

Brand Name

In our experience, most hospitality operators use this selection factor almost exclusively to purchase replacement FFE. Some operators are not necessarily concerned with brand names when they buy an item for the first time. But once they have had some experience with an item, either good or bad, the memory of it remains very strong. Consequently, brand name recognition will probably always be a major selection factor.

Something can be said for the effect that some brand names might have on the operators' image. For instance, some customers may recognize high-quality brand names for refrigeration. So, if it is important for operators to display one of these brand name fixtures on their premises, their purchasing decision becomes an easy task.

Another dimension to the brand name selection factor is the "halo effect" that operators can develop as they gain experience with a certain brand of merchandise. The halo effect suggests that if operators have a positive experience with a particular brand, not only will they be predisposed to purchase the same brand name merchandise when it is time to replace some worn-out FFE, but they will also tend to feel more positive about that particular manufacturer's entire product line. Consequently, the brand name selection factor grows more important as their experience with the items increases.

If operators invite input from employees when they are developing an FFE purchasing strategy, they almost always can expect them to think in terms of brand names. Most are familiar with certain brands that some other place of employment used. Alternately, employees who attended, for example, a culinary school, learned their craft on particular brands of kitchen equipment and are apt to favor these.

Portability

This could be a very important selection factor for kitchen equipment. For instance, hospitality operations that have a good deal of banquet trade will enjoy the convenience of portability. Being able to quickly disconnect and rearrange the equipment to suit the specific needs of a party is a major advantage.

Mobile FFE also create another advantage: the ability to move the items so that the maintenance staff can do deep cleaning easily and effectively. Also, service staff will be able to perform their tasks more quickly if the items are not stationary.

Mobility also means that if a piece of machinery breaks down, operators may not need to have it repaired in place. Service staff can remove the item easily, replace it with a loaner item, and proceed to take the broken item to the shop where it can receive the proper attention. Other employees, then, do not need to sidestep a service staff member while trying to perform their duties.

Portable equipment also tends to retain its value over the long run. Since it is easy to move, it can be removed from service and sold easily.

Of course, portable items are not inexpensive. They cost more because of their convenience and their ability to accommodate several needs. In some hospitality operations, their initial cost will generate significant savings, as well as a higher trade-in value, over the years.

Ease of Cleaning

All FFE items must be cleaned periodically. The amount of time needed to clean these items varies with the quality of items purchased. For example, hospitality operators will pay a bit more for an item that is very easy to clean. They gain an advantage, though, when their employees are more motivated to clean it than another similar item. Furthermore, clean FFE, especially clean equipment, should last longer under normal operating conditions. The operators' lifetime cost for an easy-to-clean item, therefore, can shrink appreciably.

Further, equipment that is not properly designed could harbor bacteria, pests, and dirt in creases and corners and transfer unwanted flavors and aromas to other products. Operators should select only equipment that has an approval label (such as International NSF that indicates that the product has been designed with cleaning and sanitation in mind.

To save labor, operators might consider purchasing self-cleaning devices. For instance, self-cleaning ovens, dispensing equipment, ventilation ducts, and exhaust fans are very convenient items to own. Operators are assured of clean equipment when they purchase these types of items, but they must be willing to pay a higher AP price, as well as being willing to incur additional energy costs over the equipment's lifetime; this is because self-cleaning items normally require a good deal of expensive energy in their operation. The convenience and labor savings, though, can easily exceed these costs.

Ease of Maintenance

Most equipment requires some sort of repair and maintenance. The amount required directly affects the total operating costs hospitality operators will incur over the useful life of the items. The ease of providing a service also affects the total operating cost, primarily because the labor cost involved can increase dramatically if the operators' equipment items require considerable effort to maintain.

Operators make a major mistake when they overlook the maintenance requirements of any type of FFE. Ignoring this potential problem is very tempting if they are blinded temporarily by an attractive AP price. This usually turns out to be false economy. Labor costs will continue to rise. Operators should strive to build a hedge against this inflationary expense by ensuring, as much as possible, that they minimize future labor requirements whenever they can.

Degree of Automation

Hospitality operators can earn some savings when they purchase equipment that provides some labor-saving opportunity. For instance, they may be able to save a bit of labor cost by using automated broilers. The related labor costs, such as payroll taxes and other employee benefits, represent additional savings. Furthermore, if operators can reduce the number of required work hours, they may be able to reduce the number of employees needed, which implies that they can economize on space needed.

As we have noted before, however, in our experience labor saving is very difficult to attain. Unless operators run a very large facility, it is quite difficult to trim even a little bit of their payroll budget without risking alienating their guests through poor service. Consequently, it is difficult to justify automated equipments' higher AP price strictly on the basis of the potential amount of labor savings.

Instead, operators should judge automated equipment on its ability to provide standardized products and to assist their control efforts. For example, fully automated espresso machines enable operators to serve consistent coffee products quickly and easily. Furthermore, machines with enhanced diagnostic capabilities, advanced computer controls, and several digital readouts can be operated by less skilled employees who will not require extensive training. This streamlines both quality control and cost control efforts.

Some automated equipment also enables operators to control the cost of sales and the cash they collect from guests. For instance, fully automated bar dispensing systems can pour an accurate, preplanned portion of liquor, record the liquor usage, and ring up the sale on the cash register.

Availability of Replacement Parts

Hospitality operators must ensure that an inventory of spare parts will be available for the FFE they want to purchase. If they have any doubt about this, they may want to either reconsider the purchase or immediately buy a spare-parts inventory to protect themselves. Maintaining their own inventory exposes them to normal storage costs, costs they would rather leave to their supplier. But an additional cost of this type can pale in comparison to dealing with a broken machine that might need to be scrapped because of the lack of one or two parts.

In addition to the availability of parts, operators should also consider the time lag that might exist between the ordering and the delivery of a part. The lead time can be very short or, as in the case of foreign-made FFE, quite lengthy. A short lead time implies that the supplier maintains an inventory of parts locally, thereby increasing his or her cost of doing business. The supplier will eventually pass this cost on to operators, but that might be far less burdensome than having a broken item hampering an operation's production needs.

Operators should assume that they may not be able to obtain replacement parts if they purchase a used piece of equipment. While this is not always the case, they should always be prepared for this possibility when buying used items. For instance, only electronic cash registers are manufactured today. Old, gear-driven models may be attractive additions to the operators' lounge, but they will pay the price for this luxury when the old registers need service and parts.

In addition, operators also may find obtaining parts and service difficult when they purchase technologically unique equipment that is just being introduced to the marketplace. These items may have bugs that have yet to be remedied. Even worse, the manufacturer of a new item may drop the line due to lack of interest from other hospitality operators, which could leave the operators who purchased the item begging for parts and service. Furthermore, service staff may be unfamiliar with a new item.

A similar situation can develop when operators purchase customized FFE. The probability is high that they will not be able to procure parts and service without expending a great deal of effort.

Supplier Services

The main supplier service hospitality operators are concerned with is the proverbial "service after the sale." FFE items will, undoubtedly, need repair and maintenance service, as well as replacement parts, during the warranty period. Also, operators must have the appropriate information economic value, such as installation and operating instructions, where applicable.

Service appears to be one of the most, if not the most, important of the selection factors. Operators must have a trustworthy supplier if they do not have the capacity to handle this type of service themselves. Not only will inadequately installed or serviced FFE increase their operating costs, it will also affect the quality of service they can provide their guests. The specter of customer dissatisfaction is fearful, and operators, generally, are not eager to suffer its consequences.

After the warranty period and the break-in period expire, operators may wish to engage other service providers to maintain their FFE. But at the outset, they will find that several things can—and will—go wrong. This is when they will need help the most. The ability to assist operators might ensure an FFE supplier's place on their approved-supplier lists. Many suppliers sell FFE, but not too many of them sell FFE and service. Operators cannot afford to discover that they have chosen the wrong type of supplier after submitting their purchase orders.

When operators purchase FFE directly, they must be willing to forgo any type of service after the sale. While some manufacturers of highly specialized equipment give operators an 800 or 900 number to call for technical support, operators should always assume that they will be on their own when they buy direct. Operators may consider this to be acceptable for some items, such as certain types of furniture. But for mechanical devices, if operators have any doubt about their ability to help themselves, it may be a good idea for them to seek the services of a reputable equipment dealer.

Employee Attitude and Skill Level

Before purchasing any equipment that is complicated to use in production or service, hospitality operators must ensure that the staff is able to comprehend the operating procedures. At the very least, employees must possess the aptitude to learn the operating procedures within a reasonable period of time.

Operators must also be certain that everyone in their company will accept the new equipment, which represents change to the employees. Resistance to change has caused many good ideas to fall by the wayside. For instance, employees may resent an automatic bar installation. This does not mean that operators should not invest in one of these machines, but it does mean that they should be prepared to smooth the way for its implementation within the operation.

Energy Source

Hospitality operators can run machinery using various energy sources. For example, they may be able to utilize natural gas, electricity, steam, oil, or solar power to operate some of their equipment. In some instances, they have no choice; for example, they may be stuck with an all-electric kitchen, with no possibility of converting to an alternate energy source. If, however, operators have a choice, they should consider equipment that can be powered by a less expensive source of energy. Alternately, operators might be interested in using only energy that is least damaging to the environment.

Generally, in order to acquire equipment that can utilize less energy, an inexpensive energy source, and/or an energy source that is most favorable to the environment, operators must be willing to pay a significantly greater AP price for it.

As with the potential savings of any type of operating cost in the future, usually, operators must be willing to invest today to reap the benefit tomorrow. For instance, a natural gas–powered machine may cost more initially than a standard electric one. Furthermore, installing it may cost more. Operators hope, though, that they will save enough money down the road to make such an investment economically attractive (see Figure 27.4).

Excess Capacity

In some cases, hospitality operators may need to decide whether they should consider the potential growth of their business when they are about to make an FFE purchase. When buying equipment, especially kitchen equipment, operators might think about the possibility that two or three years from now, they will need equipment that can handle twice the number of customers they currently serve. The question, then, is "Should operators buy kitchen equipment that handles the current customer load only, or should they purchase excess capacity equipment now?"

If the larger equipment is available today at an attractive AP price, operators might consider purchasing it. If not, they probably should avoid these items for several reasons: (1) they often can buy equipment that has add-on capability; (2) they will waste money maintaining a larger-than-necessary piece of equipment; (3) they will have capital tied up in the larger equipment that might be best used in some other income-generating activity; and (4) they have no guarantee that their business eventually will increase according to their expectations.

Adding on to the physical space when operators' customer count increases is more difficult. Also, the costs of construction tend to increase considerably in just a short period of time. Consequently, it may be advisable for operators to erect a physical structure that can service their future needs. But they should probably purchase the FFE as the need arises.

Add-On Capabilities

If hospitality operators anticipate an increase in business in the near future, they might want to consider purchasing FFE items that can be modified and adapted easily to service the additional business. Operators should expect to pay a bit more today for this feature.

Operators might discuss their needs with their supplier and agree to purchase the added capacity later on if the supplier will take this into consideration when setting the AP price of the items that the operators currently wish to purchase.

FIGURE 27.4 Operators sometimes purchase equipment because of its energy-saving potential. © 2001 Hatco Corporation.

Warranty

It is unusual for suppliers to sell any FFE item without a manufacturer's warranty. The typical warranty covers parts and repair for 12 to 24 months from date of shipment. It is strongly suggested that the operator contact the manufacturer or dealer after purchiung FFE to make sure that the warranty only starts when he or she places the product into service. Failure to do this could result in the warranty starting after a prodct has been on a dealer floor or in inventory for 6 months and the warranty might only be for the remaing time. It is also a good idea to keep records on equipment, including purchase date, serial numbers, and maintenance/use history, in a safe place should problems arise.

The main issue with a warranty is not the warranty itself, since just about every item has one, but the convenience, or lack thereof, with which hospitality operators can receive satisfaction if they must have an item serviced. For instance, they may need to ship an item to the factory for repairs. Alternately, they may need to wait too long for the work to be performed, which can cause customer dissatisfaction when their operation has considerable downtime.

Warranties are only as good as the manufacturer's, and/or the dealer's, intention and ability to honor them. In our experience, the best warranty is the supplier's reputation for ensuring customer satisfaction.

If operators purchase FFE items directly, the warranty provision might be very limited. Furthermore, suppliers may not even offer a warranty for items shipped directly. So when operators buy direct, they may have to surrender this benefit.

Code Compliance

Local governments normally enforce several laws governing fire, health and safety, and building procedures to which all businesspersons must adhere. The FFE that hospitality operators purchase must meet the existing legal codes, including health district codes, safety codes, electrical codes, and noise pollution codes. If operators buy new equipment, they would expect it to satisfy the current legal requirements. Used equipment may not, so they need to be a bit cautious to ensure that they do not purchase FFE only to find out later on that the government will not permit the FFE to be used in their establishment.

Several organizations endorse certain types of FFE. Buyers normally look for their seals of approval when purchasing these items. The most common endorsements are made by NSF International—sanitation certification; Underwriters Laboratories (UL)—electrical safety certification; American Gas Association (AGA)—gas safety certification; National Fire Protection Association (NFPA)—fire safety certification; and American Society of Mechanical Engineers (ASME)—steam safety certification.

In some parts of the United States, operators may need to purchase items that carry these or other appropriate seals of approval. In Clark County, Nevada, for example, all food-contact equipment used in food services must carry the NSF International seal.

FINANCING THE FFE PURCHASE

When hospitality operators purchase capital items, almost invariably the subject of financing the transaction arises. In most cases, operators must devote as much thought to the financing of the purchase as they do to the various selection factors discussed in this chapter.

Purchasing FFE is not an everyday occurrence. Operators do not expect to pay for many of these items by writing a check on their current bank account. Rather, they often must determine the various alternative financing arrangements available and decide which one, or ones, they can use to their best advantage.

Of course, operators may indeed be able to finance some FFE purchases with money that currently sits in the property's bank account. So, one financing alternative is financing an FFE purchase through the normal cash flow of the hospitality operation. Quite often, though, operators might use a bit of cash and supplement it with some sort of installment credit. For example, operators might be able to make a down payment to a dealer and convince him or her to carry a personal promissory note for the remainder of the balance. Operators expect to pay the current market interest rate to the dealer since he or she is acting as their lender in this transaction, as well as their FFE dealer.

Working a credit arrangement with the dealer may be advantageous for operators for several reasons. For instance, he or she may know the operators very well and dispense with the normal credit checks and other costly loan application fees, thereby saving the operators a bit of money. Furthermore, operators might be able to combine some sort of discount with their purchase, such as a cash discount, if they pay the final installment before the due date.

In our experience, FFE dealers are a bit more inclined to grant favorable credit terms than food and beverage suppliers. While not all of these FFE dealers may be willing to grant large amounts of credit, operators might consider dealing only with those suppliers willing to finance their purchases regardless of the dollar amount.

If operators arrange an installment payment plan with a dealer, normally he or she will expect them to make a down payment equal to one-third of the purchase price, make monthly payments (that include interest and principal), and sign a "security agreement," which grants the dealer the right to foreclose and take back the FFE item if the operators fail to make their installment payments. Usually, the loan term will not exceed 36 months.

Some dealers and manufacturers are willing to accept credit cards for payment. However, this is an expensive option for both buyers and suppliers. Credit card interest rates are usually much higher than the rates the suppliers would charge if they extended credit themselves. Furthermore, suppliers accepting credit card payments must pay a fee to the credit card company; suppliers may add this extra cost to the AP prices operators must pay for their FFE items.

Operators can use FFE as collateral for a loan from a commercial lender. This is also an expensive alternative. For instance, lenders normally require a relatively large down payment because they are unwilling to finance more than 40 to 50 percent of the value of these items. They also assess a variety of credit expenses, such as loan origination fees, and require operators to sign a security agreement. Also, if operators are dealing with a commercial bank, it might require them to maintain a non-interest-bearing checking account with a reasonably large balance; this increases the effective interest charges on the loan since operators now have the use of less money than they originally borrowed.

Finally, operators could opt for some sort of a lease arrangement for FFE items. While not all FFE are available for lease, operators can lease a great number of items. For instance, leasing computers, ice machines, and refrigeration machinery is somewhat common in the foodservice industry, whereas leasing television sets and laundry equipment is common in the lodging industry.

Leasing is a very expensive form of financing. For example, with some leases, operators pay and pay, but they never own the leased item. With others, such as "rent-to-own" plans, operators have an opportunity, and sometimes are required, to buy the item at the end of the lease period for a specific stated amount. Lessors normally require lessees to purchase full insurance coverage for the leased items, which might be more than they would be willing to do if they owned these items. Also, unless maintenance comes with the leased item, operators may be required to spend more money for maintenance than they would consider spending if they owned the item. Furthermore, lease payments are usually based on the FFE item's list price; as a result, operators do not have the opportunity to negotiate the underlying purchase price.

Leasing does have advantages, though. Operators do not need to put up a large amount of money as a down payment; this helps preserve their working capital. Also, operators can experiment with new technology without making a long-term purchase commitment. And, generally, it is relatively easy for operators to set up a lease arrangement: less paperwork and fewer other related problems are involved with a lease than with a loan from a commercial lender. Unfortunately, these advantages aside, leasing is almost always more expensive in the long run than buying.

KEY WORDS AND CONCEPTS

Add-on capabilities

American Gas Association (AGA)

American Society of Mechanical Engineers (ASME)

Appearance

Availability of replacement parts

Brand name

Capital item

Capitalizing an expense

Code compliance

Compactness

Contract supply house

Customized FFE

Degree of automation

Delivery cost

Demonstration model

Depreciable asset

Design/build dealer

Detailed drawings

Direct purchase

Downtime

Ease of cleaning

Ease of maintenance

Employee skill level

Energy source

Equipment dealer

Equipment program

Exact name

Excess capacity

Financing the FFE purchase

Foodservice design consultant

Freight-damaged

General and specific conditions

Impulse purchase

Installation and testing costs

Instructions to bidders

Intended use

Lifetime cost

Liquidation

Lowball bid

Management considerations when purchasing FFE

National Fire Protection Association (NFPA)

Net present value

New versus used FFE

NSF International

Operating costs

Operating savings

Payback period

Portability

Purchasing FFE

Reconditioning versus replacement of FFE

Rent-to-own plan

Security agreement

Service after the sale

Show-special price

Supplier services

Systems sale

Trade-in value

Trade show

Types of FFE suppliers

Underwriters Laboratories (UL)

Versatility

Warranty

QUESTIONS AND PROBLEMS

1. What are some advantages and disadvantages of leasing FFE?

2. A specification for a dining room table could include the following information:

   (a)

   (b)

    (c)

    (d)

    (e)

3. Briefly describe the concept of "capitalizing" an expense.

4. What are some advantages of hiring a consultant to assist in the development of FFE purchase specifications?

5. What are some possible disadvantages of purchasing reconditioned equipment?

6. When should an equipment purchase specification include detailed drawings?

7. The lifetime cost of an FFE item could include the following information:

    (a)

    (b)

    (c)

    (d)

    (e)

8. Briefly describe the concept of "net present value."

9. What are some advantages and disadvantages of purchasing a personal computer direct from the manufacturer?

10. A specification for a microwave oven could include the following information:

    (a)

    (b)

    (c)

    (d)

    (e)

11. What are some advantages and disadvantages of purchasing customized kitchen equipment?

12. Why would an equipment dealer be willing to sell a demonstration model for much less than the normal purchase price?

13. When would "compactness of FFE" be an important selection factor?

14. When would "availability of replacement parts" be an important selection factor?

15. Briefly describe the concept of "payback period."

16. Why would a commercial lender require a borrower to sign a security agreement?

17. If an operator purchases a natural gas-powered clothes dryer, it will usually be more expensive than a similar electrically powered one. However, what would entice a buyer to consider spending more money for the gas-powered appliance?

18. What are some advantages of purchasing portable kitchen equipment?

19. What are some advantages and disadvantages of purchasing used FFE?

20. A specification for a walk-in refrigerator could include the following information:

    (a)

    (b)

(c)

(d)

(e)

21. What are some disadvantages of using a credit card to finance an equipment purchase?

22. What type of FFE items would operators usually be willing to purchase from a local warehouse club? Why?

23. What are some advantages and disadvantages of equipment programs?

24. When would operators select FFE strictly on the basis of brand name?

Equipment Purchasing in 2035?

George E. Baggott *Former Chairman of the Board of CresCor,*
an international manufacturer of mobile foodservice equipment

The equipment world of the future: What is in store? What will change? Of course we cannot predict the future, but by looking at the trends of today we can catch a glimpse of what is to come.

Globalization. Foods of many lands. Foods from different cultures; equipment manufacturers will need to customize some of their products in order to accommodate specialized foods.

Kitchens. Space will be tight and rent will be at premium pricing; therefore equipment will need to perform multiple tasks. For example, a steaming unit will also act as a skillet and a combo-oven will have several new features.

Training. Because equipment will be multifunctional, training of chefs and employees will be crucial.

Technology. The Internet will be a key source of an equipment manufacturer's operation. Training, tracking of orders, usage, application, and communication between all parties will happen via the Web. We also must include Auto CAD, which will be able to take customers on a virtual tour of a new kitchen layout or give them an inside look of how the unit is assembled. Directions for installation will be made easy due to this technological breakthrough, as well as servicing of equipment.

Safety. All equipment will have to pass rigorous safety tests before being distributed. Stock pots will have to have a cool down and dispensing feature. Holding ovens and refrigerators will be extremely sensitive in order to prevent food-borne illness. And hand-held tools, such as knives, will have a new design in order to protect the end user.

Trade Shows. Networking and developing new relationships will continue to be extremely important. Shows will be done via the Internet, where new product designs can be shown and new deals made.

Customer Service. Where would the world of purchasing be without the people who buy the equipment? Keeping these people happy now and in the future will make or break a business. Training, follow-up, servicing, and availability of parts will be crucial for success, as well as for gaining repeat business.

INDEX